BEYOND THE EPIC

BEYOND THE EPIC

THE LIFE & FILMS OF
DAVID LEAN

GENE D. PHILLIPS

THE UNIVERSITY PRESS OF KENTUCKY

Publication of this volume was made possible in part by a grant from the National Endowment for the Humanities.

Scholarly publisher for the Commonwealth,
serving Bellarmine University, Berea College, Centre
College of Kentucky, Eastern Kentucky University,
The Filson Historical Society, Georgetown College,
Kentucky Historical Society, Kentucky State University,
Morehead State University, Murray State University,
Northern Kentucky University, Transylvania University,
University of Kentucky, University of Louisville,
and Western Kentucky University.
All rights reserved.

Editorial and Sales Offices: The University Press of Kentucky
663 South Limestone Street, Lexington, Kentucky 40508-4008
www.kentuckypress.com

10 09 08 07 06   5 4 3 2 1

Library of Congress Cataloging-in-Publication Data

Phillips, Gene D.
  Beyond the epic : the life and films of David Lean / Gene D. Phillips.
    p.   cm.
  Includes bibliographical references and index.
  ISBN-13: 978-0-8131-2415-5 (hardcover : alk. paper)
  ISBN-10: 0-8131-2415-8 (hardcover : alk. paper)
  1. Lean, David, 1908–1991. 2. Motion picture producers and
directors—Great Britain—Biography. I. Title.
  PN1998.3.L43P45 2006
  791.4302'33092—dc22
  [B]
                              2006028044

This book is printed on acid-free recycled paper meeting
the requirements of the American National Standard
for Permanence in Paper for Printed Library Materials.

Manufactured in the United States of America.

 Member of the Association of
American University Presses

To Sir Alec Guinness

David Lean regarded the making of films as a deadly serious business. He had caught the spirit of those pioneers who thought what they were doing was of great significance. He thought about film as a Jesuit thinks about his vocation.

—*Anthony Havelock-Allan, producer*

CONTENTS

Illustrations follow page 262

FOREWORD

ALEC GUINNESS SPEAKING

The people whom Guinness plays best of all are iceberg characters, nine-tenths concealed, whose fascination lies not in how they look but in how their minds work; people with secrets to hide from their fellow men, people like poets and killers and saints. Guinness can convey, by his voice and bearing, the existence of little fixed ideas frisking about behind the deferential mask of normality. His territory is the man within.

—Kenneth Tynan

I left school at eighteen and took acting lessons from Martita Hunt, who dismissed me after two lessons with the advice that I would never be an actor, though later she continued the lessons. (We were subsequently to appear together in my first film, David Lean's *Great Expectations*.) Undaunted, I managed to obtain a two-year scholarship to a dramatic academy in 1934. Later I joined the Old Vic, and in 1939 I played Michael Ransom in a revival of Auden and Isherwood's *The Ascent of F6*. I was drawn to the latter role because Ransom reminded me of T. E. Lawrence and I admired explorers, leaders, heroes, and other men who aspire and achieve dangerously. I was later to play the title role in *Ross,* the play modeled on Lawrence's life, as well as to appear as Lawrence's Bedouin ally, Prince Feisal, in David Lean's film *Lawrence of Arabia* (1962).

In 1941 I joined the navy; after the war I returned to the Old Vic to resume my stage career. Since I had portrayed Herbert Pocket, the hero's friend, in my own stage adaptation of Dickens's *Great Expectations* in 1940, it was natural that I should be asked to re-create the role in David Lean's 1946 film of the novel. With this film began a professional association between Lean and myself that has proved mutually fruitful.

When David Lean formed his own independent film unit after the war, he firmly believed that British films should be made to appeal primarily to the home market, rather than to the elusive American market, which other producers, like J. Arthur Rank, were trying to conquer. Ironically, it was Lean films like *Brief Encounter* (1945) and *Great Expectations* (1946), which were wholly English in character and situation, that were the first British films to win wide popularity in America. And I still maintain that we should aim at making films that will be truly British in character. After all, we go to French and Italian films because they *are* French and Italian. A country's films should reflect that country's history and temperament.

Two years after *Great Expectations,* Lean gave me my second film assignment in another Dickens adaptation, *Oliver Twist* (1948). Because of the touchy temper of the times, my portrayal of Fagin was criticized as being anti-Semitic, and the release of the film was delayed for a time in the United States. If one views the film now, however, one can, perhaps, see that I attempted to invest the character of the old rogue with human qualities.

After all, it was ridiculous to denounce the film since we all fell over backward to ensure that even the word *Jew* wasn't mentioned in the film. I really don't think the film did any harm. Be that as it may, I owe my film career to David Lean, and I shall always be grateful for his letting me play Fagin.

Some years later David offered me the role of Colonel Nicholson in *The Bridge on the River Kwai* (1957). I rejected the first version of the script because it was rubbish—filled with elephant charges and that sort of thing. For a while they were thinking of getting Charles Laughton to do the part, but it was offered to me again after the script was revised. I turned it down a second time because I found Nicholson to be a blinkered character. I wondered how we could get the audience to take him seriously. Then Sam Spiegel, the producer of the film, took me to dinner. He is a very persuasive character. I started out maintaining that I wouldn't play the role, and by the end of the evening we were discussing what kind of wig I would wear.

The film deals with a British battalion captured by the Japanese in 1943. Nicholson has his men contribute to the building of a bridge to accommodate the Thailand-Burma railway. Nicholson ultimately becomes obsessed with the idea of making the bridge a tribute to British know-how and resourcefulness.

I attempt to submerge my personality in every part that I play; so, with Nicholson, I aimed to make him understandable and even sympathetic. I try to get inside a character and project him—one of my own private rules is that I have not got a character until I have mastered exactly how he walks. In short, I endeavor to inhabit any role that I play.

After *Kwai,* David offered me the part of Prince Feisal, a Bedouin chief, in *Lawrence of Arabia.* I again sought to submerge myself in this character. In my years of apprenticeship before the war, the minor roles that fell to me had often required me to play a variety of older men. I was very happy to disguise myself. I was always rather embarrassed with myself personally, and I was glad to go into a disguise. In effect, the wide range of parts that I had played on the stage prepared me to play character parts like Prince Feisal.

Though I have created a gallery of film portrayals, I still have mixed emotions about film acting: you have no control over the final performance as it is seen by the public. That's in the hands of the director and the editor. I have sometimes found that something has disappeared from a performance of mine, something that I was relying on, so that I would have played the whole thing differently had I known that that particular thing was going to go. I prefer rehearsing a film beforehand as long as possible since the scenes are not shot in sequence. I also prefer working in the controlled conditions of the studio to going on location. So often you have to rush things through on location because of weather conditions. When we made *Dr. Zhivago* for David Lean back in 1965, we were all in Madrid in a temperature of 116 degrees, muffled up to the ears in Russian furs. We just wanted to say our lines and get out of that heat!

Despite my reservations about film acting, I still find it challenging. Every day provides some little scene—even if it is only a minute or so—in which you have the opportunity for a little moment of genuinely creative work. That helps make it all worthwhile.

ACKNOWLEDGMENTS

First of all, I am grateful to Sir David Lean for reading the précis from which this book was developed and for examining an early draft of the chapters on *Lawrence of Arabia*. In addition, I wish to single out the following among those who have given me their assistance in the course of the long period during which I was engaged in remote preparation for this study: I interviewed Sir Alec Guinness in London about the Lean films in which he appeared. I also spoke in London with Deborah Kerr and Eric Portman, who appeared in films that Lean edited early in his career; with Rita Tushingham, who was in *Dr. Zhivago;* with the filmmaker Thorold Dickinson, who coedited a film with Lean; with Sir Carol Reed, Fred Zinnemann, George Cukor, Stanley Kubrick, Roy Boulting, Ken Russell, John Schlesinger, and Bryan Forbes, Lean's friends and fellow directors; and with the British filmmaker Karel Reisz, who discussed Lean's expertise as a film editor. I also corresponded with the cinematographer Guy Green, who photographed four Lean films. I met with the actress Ann Todd at the Cannes International Film Festival about her Lean films. In Hollywood, the filmmaker William Wyler shared his thoughts about adapting stage plays for film, and Katharine Hepburn went over an early version of my treatment of *Summertime*. The film archivist Robert Harris discussed with me his restoration of *Lawrence of Arabia* to its original length for its rerelease.

Many institutions and individuals provided me with research materials. I would like specifically to mention the following: the staff of the Film Study Center of the Museum of Modern Art in New York; the staff of the National Film Archive of the Library of the British Film Institute in London; and the staff of the Motion Picture Section of the Library of Congress. Research materials were also provided by the Margaret Herrick Library of the Academy of Motion Picture Arts and Sciences; the Theater Arts Library as well as the Michael Wilson Collection in the Department of Special Collections of the Research Library at the University of California, Los Angeles; the Script

Acknowledgments

Repositories of Columbia Pictures and Metro-Goldwyn-Mayer; the David Lean Archive of the Netherlands; the T. E. Lawrence Collection at the Harry Ransom Humanities Research Center of the University of Texas, Austin; Kevin Brownlow, David Lean's biographer; the Lean scholar Paul Rowan; and Vincent LoBrutto, a research professor at the School of Visual Arts, New York. Also, Stephen Foster, a distinguished research professor in the Department of History, Northern Illinois University, advised me about modern British history in Lean's films, particularly *This Happy Breed,* and Major D. K. Farmer, USAF-Ret., who served at Wright Air Force Base, discussed aircraft experiments relevant to Lean's film *The Sound Barrier* with me.

Alec Guinness's account of working with David Lean, which appears as the foreword to this book, is adapted from the interview with him that I conducted in London. Some material in this book appeared in a completely different form in the following publications: *The Movie Makers: Artists in an Industry* (Chicago: Nelson Hall, 1973), copyright 1973 by Gene D. Phillips, used with permission; and *Columbia Pictures: Portrait of a Studio,* edited by Bernard Dick (Lexington: University Press of Kentucky, 1992), copyright 1992 by the University Press of Kentucky, used with permission.

CHRONOLOGY

1908   David Lean born in Croydon, England, March 25, the son of
              Francis William and Helena Tangye Lean.
1920–1926   Educated at Leighton Park School, a Quaker institution in
              Reading.
1927   Employed by Gaumont-British Studios in Lime Grove as an
              apprentice and all-around factotum.
1928–1930   Works as a cutting room assistant, camera assistant, and assis-
              tant director.
1930   Becomes chief editor for Gaumont-British News.
1931–1932   Becomes editor for British Movietone News and assists in edit-
              ing feature films.
1934   Edits "quota quickies" at Elstree Studios.
1935   Edits his first important feature film, Paul Czinner's *Escape Me
              Never.*
1936   Edits Czinner's *As You Like It.*
1938   Edits and assists in the direction of *Pygmalion* for Anthony
              Asquith and Leslie Howard.
1939   Edits *French without Tears* for Asquith.
1941   Edits and assists in the direction of *Major Barbara* for Gabriel
              Pascal. Edits *The 49th Parallel* (U.S. title: *The Invaders*) for
              Michael Powell.
1942   Edits *One of Our Aircraft Is Missing* for Michael Powell.
1943   Forms, in association with J. Arthur Rank, an independent
              production company, Cineguild, with Ronald Neame and
              Anthony Havelock-Allan.
1944   Directs *The Happy Breed,* his first venture as a solo director.
1945   Directs *Blithe Spirit* and *Brief Encounter;* becomes first British
              director to be nominated for an American Academy Award for
              Brief Encounter.
1946   Directs *Great Expectations,* which wins three Academy
              Awards.

1948   Directs *Oliver Twist;* the release of this film in the United States is postponed because of charges of anti-Semitism.

1949   Directs *The Passionate Friends* (U.S. title: *One Woman's Story*).

1950   Directs *Madeleine;* Cineguild dissolved; joins Alexander · Korda's London Films.

1952   Directs *The Sound Barrier* (U.S. title: *Breaking the Sound Barrier*).

1953   Named a commander of the British Empire (CBE) by Queen Elizabeth II for his contribution to British cinema.

1954   Directs *Hobson's Choice.*

1955   Directs *Summertime* (British title: *Summer Madness*).

1957   Directs *The Bridge on the River Kwai,* which wins seven Academy Awards, including best director.

1962   Directs *Lawrence of Arabia,* which wins seven Oscars, including best director.

1965   Directs *Dr. Zhivago; The Greatest Story Ever Told,* for which Lean assisted George Stevens by filming the prologue, released.

1970   Directs *Ryan's Daughter;* a retrospective of Lean's films held at the Museum of Modern Art, October 29–November 3.

1973   Presented with the Lifetime Achievement Award from the Directors Guild of America.

1981   After considering a series of possible film projects, including *Captain Bligh and Mr. Christian* (a new version of *Mutiny on the Bounty*), finally opts to make *A Passage to India,* from the E. M. Forster novel.

1983   Receives British Film Institute Fellowship for Lifetime Achievement.

1984   Directs *A Passage to India;* knighted by Queen Elizabeth II.

1988   Honored with a special tribute at the Cannes International Film Festival.

1989   Restored version of *Lawrence of Arabia* given a successful theatrical rerelease.

1990   Receives the American Film Institute Life Achievement Award.

1991   David Lean dies on April 16; posthumously honored by the dedication of the David Lean Building at Shepperton Studios, outside London, to his memory as an enduring monument to his incalculable contribution to British cinema.

1997   The National Film Registry of the Library of Congress, which preserves films of enduring quality, includes *Bridge on the River Kwai* and *Lawrence of Arabia* in its collection.

1998   The American Film Institute chooses the hundred best films in the first century of cinema in a television special broadcast on

July 16, including *Bridge on the River Kwai, Lawrence of Arabia,* and *Dr. Zhivago.*

1999   The British Film Institute honors the hundred outstanding British films of the first hundred years of cinema; *Brief Encounter* and *Great Expectations* are in the top ten.

2002   The *Sight and Sound* international poll of film directors and film critics chooses Lean as one of the top ten directors of all time and *Lawrence of Arabia* among the top ten films of all time. The American Film Institute chooses the hundred outstanding love stories in movie history in a television special on June 11, naming *Dr. Zhivago* among the first ten selections.

2003   In a nationwide poll conducted by *Premiere* magazine, *Lawrence of Arabia* is voted one of the hundred greatest films of all time. The American Film Institute names T. E. Lawrence of *Lawrence of Arabia* one of the top ten heroes of all time in a television special aired June 3.

2004   Release on DVD in the United States of the David Lean Collection: seven of Lean's British films, including the original, uncensored British version of *Oliver Twist,* which had not been available on home video in the United States before.

BEYOND THE EPIC

PROLOGUE

A WORLD ON FILM

Hollywood is the Roman Circus—and damned near the end of civilization.
—*Raymond Chandler*

The French filmmaker Jean Renoir once said that, if all the films of a good director are laid end to end, what results is not a group of separate films but a series of chapters of the same film. This is another way of saying that, more than anyone else involved in the production of a film, it is the director who leaves his personal stamp on a motion picture. Filmmaking, it is true, is a corporate effort to which a whole host of individuals, from actors to technicians, must make their contribution. But it is the director who must create a unified work of art from all these varied contributions.

Even though David Lean adapted for the screen several literary works by worthy authors ranging from Charles Dickens to E. M. Forster, there is little question that, despite the films' distinguished literary antecedents, he is really the creative genius behind the films that bear his name. In discussing the degree of personal involvement in his motion pictures, Lean pointed out that his work on a film began at the script stage and continued throughout the filmmaking process.

"In the early stages I suppose the director is, as it were, a shaper of the film. And then, of course, as the shooting gets nearer, he takes more and more responsibility," Lean said. "One tends to put one's own point of view over through the actors. And so, a kind of personal taste or touch will come out. Above all, the director chooses what the audience sees, and when. He decides whether you shall see it in a close-up or long shot. . . . So that in itself

3

has quite an effect, of course."[1] Once a film was finished shooting, Lean said, he was particularly interested in supervising the editing. Since he had been an editor, he found it hard to keep his hands off the celluloid. Furthermore, he always tried to shoot with a plan for editing the film in mind, in order to be sure to get the shots he knew would be needed.

Andrew Sarris, one of the most articulate champions of the film director's vital role in the filmmaking process, has written: "Only the director can provide a unity of style out of all the diverse ingredients at his disposal. The script writer will find his words chopped up into shots. The actor who performs continuously on the stage is recorded intermittently on the set, where his part is slowly eroded out of sequence into little bits and pieces."[2] Consequently, it is the director and the director alone who can and must confer artistic unity on a motion picture. Accordingly, the key role that the director plays in the creation of a motion picture has been compared to that of a company commander, a quarterback, an orchestra conductor, a trail boss, even a lion tamer.

The auteur theory maintains that the director is at the center of the filmmaking process. When the role of the director is viewed in this fashion, it is clear that he is the true author of a film in much the same way that a writer is the author of a novel. A film director who merely puts together a motion picture as if he were a foreman on an assembly line would not, of course, be considered the author of a film that he has directed, and there are many such directors in the history of cinema. But a film director who uses cinematic techniques to express his personal vision of reality in film after film will build up a coherent body of work like that which the novelist produces.

This is not to say that a given film cannot be analyzed and enjoyed apart from the other films made by the same director, but one's appreciation of a given film can be greatly enhanced when it is examined in the context of the director's total body of work. "The fact that most directors do not write their own scripts," says Sarris, "is enough to discredit the role of the director in the eyes of the literary establishment. Such discredit is often unjustified even on literary grounds simply because many directors decline to take credit for collaborating on the writing of their films."[3] Alfred Hitchcock implicitly supported Sarris's view when he wrote, "Under ideal conditions the screenplay is prepared by the writer in collaboration with the director."[4]

As Lean himself testified, he collaborated on the screenplay of every film he directed, whether he was credited as a screenwriter or not. It was his custom to hold script conferences with his writers prior to filming, in order to trade ideas about plot and dialogue with them—even when one of the screenwriters was an estimable author like Noël Coward, who was involved in coauthoring four films that Lean made early in his career. Lean was confident that he knew how to aid screenwriters in improving what they had written. "Working on a script is important and very necessary," he said, "but I'm not a word man; I'm a picture man. I love getting behind a camera and getting images on a screen."[5]

Furthermore, whether or not a director has taken a hand in script preparation, he can still be considered the author of his succession of films if he has consistently chosen material that is in keeping with his own personal vision and directorial style. Lean saw in his own style an attraction to characters who refuse to accept defeat, even when their most cherished hopes go unfulfilled. His protagonists seek to transform their lives, but often fail to do so. Pip in *Great Expectations,* Colonel Nicholson in *The Bridge on the River Kwai,* and T. E. Lawrence in *Lawrence of Arabia,* among others, struggle against the limitations of their own personalities to achieve a level of existence that they deem higher or nobler. And so a director like David Lean created in his films "a world of his own, a world no less unique for having been filtered through the varying verbalizations of scores of screenwriters."[6]

"Hollywood's like Egypt," the producer David O. Selznick remarked late in his career, "full of crumbled pyramids. It will just keep crumbling until finally the wind blows the last studio prop across the sands. . . . There might have been good movies if there had been no movie industry. Hollywood might have become the center of the new human expression if it hadn't been grabbed by a little group of bookkeepers and turned into a junk industry."[7] These are bitter words indeed to come from the man responsible for producing films like *Gone with the Wind* (Victor Fleming, 1939). Nonetheless, Selznick accurately expressed the problem that has vexed filmmakers since the movies developed from their humble beginnings into a full-scale industry: How does a creative artist make a film that is a personal, unified work of art when the production process is a huge financial undertaking involving the contributions of a large group of people ranging from the cast to the technical crew?

The auteur theory can be readily applied to European directors working in relatively small industries such as that in England, where David Lean got his start making movies. Indeed, Lean was one of the top directors of postwar British cinema. In the relatively small British film industry, he could control every aspect of the production of his films from beginning to end. But it seemed at first that the auteur theory could not be applied so easily to Lean when he became associated with Hollywood because directors working in a larger industry have found it so much more difficult to gain artistic control over their films.

On closer examination, however, it is clear that, just as he had done while working for British studios, Lean was able to impose his personal stamp on his films while working for American studios. Moreover, it was relatively easy for him to move from the British film industry to the American. This is because "the British film industry has maintained a symbiotic relationship with Hollywood since the end of World War I, a relationship intensified by the sharing of a common language after the conversion to sound."[8] This relationship has been further intensified because American financing largely controls the British movie industry. Almost three-quarters of the major films made in Britain are backed by American capital. Moreover, Lean had an affinity for Hollywood pictures from his youth because he grew up with them. "I had a tremendous love of American films," he told a television interviewer; "they influenced me enormously."[9]

Once Lean began working for American production companies in the mid-1950s, he officially became a Hollywood director, even though his films continued to be largely concerned with British subject matter, from *The Bridge on the River Kwai* (1957) onward. Moreover, the far-flung locations in which his Hollywood films were made were an indication of the global nature of the film industry. Like Alfred Hitchcock, he was British born and worked in the British film industry for roughly the first half of his career, but he became part of the American film industry for the balance of his career, making movies for major Hollywood studios.

Still, whether Lean was making pictures for British or American film corporations, he insisted on maintaining his independence; as such, he was bent on making one film at a time, not on machine-tooling several at once, as the executives at the big studios had always done. As a result, his films were more personal in style and point of view than had been customary for Hollywood films of the past. "People tell me I'm not a personal filmmaker," Lean observed. "I don't know what they mean by this. Everything goes through me from script to final print, and nothing is done which I am not a part of."[10] In this way, he was implicitly endorsing the auteur theory by declaring himself the author of his films.

Significantly, Lean was able to make his films his own, notwithstanding the diversity of genres in which he worked—from war pictures to high comedy and domestic drama. Indeed, one suspects that the studio system presented him with a challenge to his artistic creativity, a challenge that sharpened his determination to turn out films that he could in some true sense call his own. Hence, he helped make possible the individualism and independence that are the hallmarks of today's new breed of directors. We have come a long way from the days when motion picture companies sought to make films that were essentially anonymous studio products. The following pages pay tribute to a filmmaker who was able through his resourcefulness to place on his films not the stamp of the studio but the stamp of his own creative and personal vision. Consequently, it is evident that Lean's work warrants and repays further critical examination along the lines of the auteur theory.

The present study is designed to provide a complete critical study of Lean's career. Therefore, it does not focus only on his most celebrated achievements, like *Lawrence of Arabia,* a supreme cinematic epic, and *The Bridge on the River Kwai,* a great war film. Rather, it also gives equal time to his other pictures, some huge box office successes, movies that have not received sufficient critical attention in previous studies of his work: *Blithe Spirit,* a charming comedy-fantasy with Rex Harrison, and *Summertime,* a bittersweet May-December romance with Katharine Hepburn. In addition, I have made an effort to reassess those Lean films that have been neglected, like *Madeleine,* a murder mystery, and *The Sound Barrier,* a film about test pilots. Surely these underappreciated movies deserve reappraisal since they all reflect the genius of the director who made them.

That several important works on Lean have been published indicates the continued interest in his films over the years. Kevin Brownlow's *David Lean* (1997) is the authorized biography, done with Lean's cooperation; Stephen Silverman's *David Lean* (1989) is a survey of the films; Sandra Lean's *David Lean: An Intimate Portrait* (2001) is an anecdotal reminiscence by his widow; and Howard Maxford's *David Lean* (2000) is a superficial pictorial history of the films with plot summaries.[11] None of these works are really critical studies. The same can be said of Morris and Raskin's *Lawrence of Arabia* (1992) and Adrian Turner's *The Making of Lawrence of Arabia* (1994), which are production histories of one particular film.[12] Among the true critical studies of the films, Gerald Pratley's *The Cinema of David Lean* (1974) and Michael Anderegg's *David Lean* (1984) are out-of-date and incomplete (they do not include Lean's final masterpiece, *A Passage to India*), and Silver and Ursini's *David Lean and His Films* is also out-of-date since it was originally published in 1974 and only one chapter has been added to the 1992 edition.[13] Silver and Ursini, like Pratley and Anderegg, could not draw on recent scholarship on Lean and his movies.

My procedure has been to interview individuals connected with Lean's films and to read the screenplays and other documentation in film archives and studio files. All this gives the book a firsthand dimension lacking in some other books on directors and increases its merit as a work of original scholarship. I have weighed the evaluations of other commentators on Lean's work against my own, in order to arrive at a balanced consensus. Consequently,

7

this is not "instant criticism" but an in-depth examination of all Lean's motion pictures.

The present volume endeavors to prove that a director like David Lean could be not only a genuine artist but a popular entertainer as well. Lean made several enduring works that still appeal to filmgoers today, as attested to by their ready availability, whether through reruns on television or for purchase or rental in DVD and other formats. Even his early British films were released in the United States and are, therefore, known here. What's more, Robert Murphy's *British Cinema Book* demonstrates that scholarly and popular interest in British cinema has never been stronger than it is now.[14] Lean's mature works were made for Hollywood studios and are acknowledged as world-class motion pictures. Indeed, when it came to staging epic scenes in a historical spectacle, Lean was without a peer.

The successful films that Lean made more than justify the artistic independence that producers extended to him. "This question of freedom, it's a question of one's record, I suppose; and I suppose that I've had a fairly good record," he noted. "The financing of movies is a big gamble, and, considering the high stakes involved, I feel that I have been treated well. On the whole my own final cut of a picture has been allowed to stand. This may be partly due to the fact that I was an editor for many years and am generally more ruthless than the producer."[15]

As a matter of fact, the very popularity of his movies is reason enough for some critics to write Lean off as a mere crowd-pleaser, rather than recognize him as an authentic artist of the cinema. That a director can be both is suggested by the fact that his finest films, for example, *Great Expectations* and *A Passage to India,* are also among his most popular.

This book might be called an informal essay in cinema history since Lean's work covers a wide time span, ranging from the silent period, when he served his apprenticeship in the film industry, to the advent of sound, and through the era of color and wide-screen motion pictures. The present study is intended not for cinema specialists but for those filmgoers who have enjoyed the movies made by David Lean, in order to provide them with a context in which they can appreciate his work more fully.

Part One

GETTING STARTED

Chapter One

FROM SILENTS TO SOUND

THE EARLY YEARS AS A FILM EDITOR

The last draft of a screenplay is in the editing room.

—*Ted Tally, screenwriter*

In my opinion, film editors make great movie directors.

—*Martin Scorsese*

The American Film Institute bestowed on David Lean its Life Achievement Award for his contribution to the art of the cinema in a television special that aired on March 8, 1990. Among those who paid tribute to Lean on that occasion was Billy Wilder, a former recipient of the AFI award. He concluded his remarks with the succinct "Who more than David Lean deserves this award?" After all, when one considers the positive critical and public response to many of Lean's films, it is evident that few directors have commanded such a large portion of the mass audience.

In his acceptance speech, Lean noted that previous winners of the AFI award, like Billy Wilder and Orson Welles, were innovators and that "this business lives on creative pathfinders." Press reports of the event referred to Lean as the prototype of the ideal Hollywood director, for he managed over the years to weather changes in public taste and the pressures of the studio system without compromising his style, his taste, or his ethical standards.

Lean also admitted in his acceptance speech that the scenes from his films that were screened during the course of the evening "were better than I thought they were." They reminded him of what he had learned in his early days as an apprentice in the film industry.

The Early Years

David Lean was born in Croydon, a suburb south of London, on March 25, 1908, the son of Francis and Helena Tangye Lean. The Leans lived at 38 Blenheim Crescent. Frank Lean was a chartered accountant in the firm of Viney, Price, and Goodyear in the City of London (i.e., the financial district). Lean's parents were Quakers, a religious influence most noticeable in his father's side of the family. Lean confessed to being slightly intimidated by the Leans, a very austere set of relatives. By contrast, his mother's people, the Tangyes, were more pleasant types with an artistic flair, and, consequently, they appealed to young David more than his father's relatives did. By the same token, David never had the personal relationship with his father—a remote, cold type—that he experienced with his more affectionate mother.

David had little affinity to the Quaker sect to which his family belonged; the strain of Puritanism in the Quakers was the basis of their rejection of the arts, especially the movies, which were considered to be a corrupting influence on the young. Nevertheless, Lean always acknowledged the influence of his Quaker upbringing on his moral attitudes; he firmly believed, for example, that one should never lie or cheat, and he acknowledged the existence of God. "I don't think that it's a Godless universe," he added, "but I wouldn't know what God is."[1]

When it came time for David to start school, the nearby elementary school would not accept him. "It was Church of England, and wouldn't have me," he explained.[2] So he attended the local Quaker school. David did not make much of a mark as a student; more than one of his teachers wrote him off as an underachiever. The headmistress sent home a report to his parents, stating that she feared that he was incorrigibly lazy and might never learn to read and write. She stated flatly, "David daydreams."[3] His younger brother, Edward (who was known by his middle name, Tangye), was a better student, and David felt, with some reason, that Tangye was his father's favorite.

Because David believed that his father did not appreciate him, he grew sullen and silent. Indeed, throughout his life Lean would lapse into prolonged silence when pondering a problem, and his silences became legendary in the film colony. As one friend put it later on, he felt comfortable with silences others might feel compelled to fill.

Good Quakers that they were, Lean's blinkered parents would not permit him to go to the pictures. Films, especially the lurid vehicles for vamps like Pola Negri and Theda Bara, were condemned as wicked. Moreover, movies were despised by many cultured, middle-class people like the Leans as pretty common, cheap entertainment for the uneducated.

Since David was barred from going to the movies, the Leans' house-keeper, Mrs. Egerton, who was a fan of Charlie Chaplin, acted out Chaplin's raucous antics for the boy. She would twirl a cane and even run around the kitchen table, skidding around corners just like the Tramp, keeping David in stitches. Lean later felt that it was at this time that he got bitten by the bug that made him a confirmed movie fan. In fact, he later hung a photo of Chaplin in *The Gold Rush* (1925) on his bedroom wall.

In 1920, when he was thirteen, David was enrolled in the Leighton Park School, a Quaker boarding school in Reading; Tangye joined him three years later and continued to outshine him academically. Sandra Lean, Lean's widow, would later remark: "David was not good at school, but his brother was; and he felt his father worshipped his brother and neglected him. He channeled his frustration into the one thing that fascinated him—photography."[4]

David showed genuine enthusiasm for his hobby, still photography. His uncle Clement Tangye had given him a Kodak Brownie camera when he was fourteen, and from then on David harbored a passion for photography. He became an avid shutterbug around school and spent his spare time in the darkroom, developing his own pictures. Lean admitted that he was "mad keen" for taking snapshots while he was on vacation, as when he attended the Empire Exhibition at Wembley in 1924, with its colorful sideshows and elaborate exhibits, celebrating a time when the sun never set on the British Empire. David's attention was particularly drawn to the exhibition's Palace of Engineering, where Phonofilms were shown; these short talking pictures, developed by the American inventor Lee de Forest, presaged the advent of sound feature films, only three years away.

By this time the Leans had moved to 97 Park Lane in East Croydon. David was painfully aware that his parents were growing apart, as he could sense a palpable chill in the house. Hilary Tangye, one of Helena's nieces, confirms that the Tangyes had quick tempers, and Helena Lean was no exception. So Frank Lean finally decided to leave her. Frank and Helena then officially resigned from the Quaker sect because they did not want their Quaker friends to witness the disintegration of their marriage, the Quakers taking a dim view of divorce.

Frank moved out of the house in 1923 and subsequently moved in with a war widow named Margaret Merton. Still a Quaker at heart, Helena would not hear of a divorce, so Frank and Margaret lived together at Margaret's place in Hove. David, who was fifteen when his parents parted, never quite got over what he considered his father's abandonment of the family. Still, he could muster some sympathy for Frank Lean: "My father, poor man, plagued by guilt." The failure of a marriage is a difficult thing in the best of times, "but," as Lean later remarked, "in those days, and being a Quaker, you can imagine." Later on, David came to know Margaret and found her a nice woman.[5] Helena suffered from melancholy after the break with her husband and cried a lot—with the result that David became even more isolated and took refuge in daydreaming more than ever.

Since Leighton Park was a boarding school, David could sneak out to a cinema in Reading in a way that he could never do while at home with his mother in Croydon. At age thirteen, he saw his very first silent film, *The Hound of the Baskervilles* (1920), directed by Maurice Elvey and featuring Eille Norwood as Sherlock Holmes. Norwood was one of the first movie actors to play the celebrated detective and one of the best Holmeses in the silent period. According to the film historians Chris Steinbrunner and Norman Michaels: "Norwood was able to bring color and dash even to the medium without a voice." He was a "towering Sherlock Holmes, and his rendering of Holmes is very much on target."[6] David was fascinated by the horrific tale of Holmes tracking down the spectral hound threatening the life of an English baron. Little did he realize that he would one day work as a camera assistant for the prolific Maurice Elvey. "That beam of light, travelling through the dark [from the movie projector to the screen]," Lean later recalled, "it had an immediate magic for me. I never thought that I would have the luck to go into films."[7]

In 1926, David graduated from Leighton Park at age eighteen. That meant returning home to live with Helena. According to Lean, his mother never recovered from the failure of her marriage, and it left a heavy cloud over her household for the rest of her days. To make matters worse, in the wake of the loss of her husband, she doted on her older son in a manner that made David uncomfortable. He later referred dourly to the tyranny of her tears, implying that she was too emotionally dependent on him.

Not surprisingly, David sought escape from the home situation by means of his hobby of photography and by making home movies. He acquired a Pathescope silent motion picture camera and set up a photo lab in his bedroom, in order to continue his practice of processing his own work, as he had done when he was taking still photographs. He would show his amateur films to his mother on the living room wall, using the Pathescope projector that he had also acquired. Since Helena thought little of movies, she wondered whether her son was going slightly mad. Nevertheless, the knowledge of camerawork that David gained by taking still pictures and by making home movies helped account for the perfection of the cinematography in the features that he later directed.

Once he had graduated from school, David was a young adult, and his mother could no longer prohibit him from going to the pictures. Consequently, he regularly took the commuter train from Croydon to London in order to see the latest releases in the West End cinemas. He particularly loved the sweeping, swashbuckling adventure movies from America, with their larger-than-life heroes. "They hit me right in the eyeball," he said. "If you knew what the London suburbs were like, you would understand—they were dreary, very grey; and the movies were a journey into another world."[8]

After the movies were over, David dreaded the thought of returning home to his melancholy mother, so he sat in the refreshment room in Victoria Station, sipping coffee and chain-smoking. Then he took the last train to Croydon, "hoping when I reached home my mother would be asleep." When he tiptoed into "the wretched little house," however, Helena would inevitably call out, "Is that you, Dave?" He invariably answered, "Who else would it be?"[9] Lean would make use of those late evenings spent in the buffet bar at Victoria Station when he made *Brief Encounter* in a similar setting two decades later.

On one of his excursions to the West End he saw *The Four Horsemen of the Apocalypse* (1921), directed by Rex Ingram and starring Rudolph Valentino. The story ranged from the pampas of South America to Paris during World War I. In short, the movie had all the ingredients for a successful cinematic epic—impressive battle scenes, a handsome gigolo (Valentino), and a tale of illicit love. Furthermore, David Lean, the fledgling filmmaker, would have been struck by the manner in which Ingram "infused the film with great visual beauty, a sensitivity to light and shade, and an unusual feeling for composition."[10]

There is little doubt that Lean's taste for directing cinematic epics like *Great Expectations* and *Dr. Zhivago* began with Ingram's *Four Horsemen,* his favorite silent movie. Rex Ingram—a very imaginative director with a particularly rapturous visual style—expanded Lean's horizons by exhibiting the breathtaking scope that a motion picture could encompass. Indeed, he made the young David Lean realize for the first time that there was a director behind the camera, "guiding everything and choosing the camera angles." Lean later pointed out that, like Ingram, he too was often described as a "great pictorialist," and he appreciated the comparison very much.[11]

David occasionally ventured into a screening of the London Film Society, which showed foreign films like *Potemkin,* Sergei Eisenstein's 1925 spectacle of revolutionary Russia. Years later, Lean paid homage to Eisenstein by staging the massacre of peaceful demonstrators by Russian Cossacks in *Dr. Zhivago* in a manner that recalled a similar scene, the massacre on the Odessa Steps, in *Potemkin.*

David had another hobby besides the movies, and that was radio. He had a crystal set that he tinkered with, in order to get shortwave broadcasts from as far away as the Continent. Yet another way of escaping the dull atmosphere of his home life was to visit the Croydon Aerodrome, which in those days served as the airport of London. It was there that David witnessed Charles Lindbergh's landing on the grass runway in the *Spirit of St. Louis* after his triumphant flight across the Atlantic in 1927. He never forgot the thrill of that event, and it was one motivating factor in his making an aviation picture, *Breaking the Sound Barrier,* a quarter of a century later.

But becoming a filmmaker was still far in the nineteen-year-old Lean's future; in the present it was time for him to consider finding gainful employment. Because of his poor scholastic record, his father had no intention of sending him to Oxford, which is where his brother, Tangye, was headed. Accordingly, Frank Lean decided that David should take an entry-level job with the accounting firm in which he was a senior partner. Even as a junior accountant in a firm in the financial district of London, David had to don formal attire, complete with a black coat, pin-striped trousers, a bowler hat, and a rolled-up umbrella that served as a walking stick. Thirty years later, Lean had an officer in *The Bridge on the River Kwai* voice his own experience as an accountant: "I checked columns of figures that three people had checked before me, and which would be checked again by two more people after I had checked them." For someone like David Lean, who all his life counted on his fingers, such a job was unbearable.

David gained some relief from "the damned office that I hated so much" by reading film magazines on the trip home on the suburban train to Croydon. One afternoon, Helena Lean was having tea with her sister-in-law Edith Tangye, whose husband Clement had presented David with a Brownie camera when he was a boy. Edith sagely observed that David seemed to be totally uninterested in accounting. At least there were no accounting books around his room. But she did notice movie magazines. "Why doesn't he go in for films?" she inquired. When Helena put the question to David, he responded that the thought of entering the film industry had never occurred to him. He was overawed by motion pictures. "I never thought that I would personally go into that box of magic," he later recalled, because he considered himself to lack the aptitude for making feature films.[12]

When David subsequently approached his father about pursuing a career in the film industry, Frank initially reacted as if his son were planning to run away with the circus. Nonetheless, realizing that David was committed to a film career, he relented and acknowledged that he knew one of the accountants at Gaumont-British Studios at Lime Grove in Shepherd's Bush on the outskirts of London. Frank got in touch with a Gaumont executive, Harold Boxall, who offered David a temporary job without pay for a two-week probationary period; David jumped at the chance to see how a movie studio operated. In due course, Gareth Gundrey, the studio chief, put David to work at menial tasks, such as serving tea to the cast and crew during breaks in shooting. After two weeks, Lean remembered, Gundrey hired him as an apprentice for a meager ten shillings a week.

David was eternally grateful to his father for this opportunity, and he deeply regretted that Frank, who drifted further and further away from his son as the years went by, never grasped how successful David eventually became as a filmmaker. Lean wistfully remembered sending his father a ticket years later to the premiere of *Lawrence of Arabia*, only to have him decline to attend.

The Apprentice in the Film Studio

The nineteen-year-old Lean was anxious to learn all about filmmaking, so one day, during his lunch break, he stole into the storeroom where the cameras were kept. When he gingerly examined a Bell and Howell camera, one of the technicians told him that it was the very camera that was used for Maurice Elvey's pictures. Lean was entranced to be touching the camera that might well have photographed *The Hound of the Baskervilles*. "I couldn't believe that this was the source of all the magic," he mused.[13]

In those preunion days, a single individual could fulfill a variety of functions around the studio. At various times, Lean worked as an assistant director, rounding up the actors and extras for a scene, and as a camera assistant, loading film in the camera and at the beginning of each shot holding up in front of it the slate board with the shot number. By the time Lean went to work for Gaumont in 1927, a film studio had become a factory, and the motion pictures turned out there were simply referred to as the product to be merchandised. He was surprised to see that, while shooting a scene for a silent film, some directors bellowed at everyone through a megaphone like a foreman on an assembly line; that was not his idea of how a director should behave.

The first film production that Lean worked on as a camera assistant was *The Quinneys* (1927), directed by none other than Maurice Elvey. The story dealt with Joe Quinney (John Longden), who buys some Chippendale chairs from an American furniture salesman and retails them for £200 apiece—only to find that he has been hoodwinked by the sly Yank because the chairs are fakes.

Since Elvey was the first director that Lean ever worked for, he was very impressed by him. Around the studio, however, Elvey was thought of as a perfunctory filmmaker who directed any script that was handed to him. He was little more than an average hack; indeed, the actress Rosamund John, working on an Elvey picture as late as 1943, found him to be a pedestrian director. She described him as a pompous little man with a pince-nez whose manner belied the fact that he was basically indecisive. Sometimes he could not decide which take to print after filming a scene: "The technicians would shout, 'Print number three, Maurice!' It was appalling."[14] Withal, Lean countered: "He was very effective and did some excellent pictures."[15] One such was *The Hound of the Baskervilles*. Elvey also made *The Passionate Friends* (1922) two years after *The Hound of the Baskervilles*; it was based on a novel by H. G. Wells and would be remade by Lean himself in 1949.

In any case, Lean was always the first to admit how much he learned about the picture business under the tutelage of the professional craftsmen and technicians at Gaumont. He worked with a more experienced camera assistant, Henry Hasslacher, who wrote film criticism for the highbrow film journal *Close-Up* in his spare time under the pseudonym Oswell Blakeston. Hasslacher was homosexual, and Lean dreaded accompanying him to the darkroom to turn in the footage that had been shot each day. But in between their darkroom skirmishes, Lean said, he learned a lot from Hasslacher about the film medium. Twenty years down the road, Hasslacher, as Oswell Blakeston, would edit a book, *Working for the Films*, to which Lean would contribute the essay "The Film Director."[16]

Lean became friendly with a studio projectionist named Matthews who allowed him to watch the day's rushes (the footage shot on the previous day) when they were run for the director. In those early days of picturemaking, a director would often edit a film himself, aided by an editorial assistant. One day, Matthews was screening the preliminary edit of a scene that Elvey had shot for *The Quinneys*. Lean was fascinated to see how Elvey and his assistant had assembled a group of shots into a seamless whole; to him this seemed like a magician's trick. From that day forward, David Lean wanted to be a film editor. He asked Elvey if he could help him out in the editing room. Since there were no unions, Elvey had no problem with a camera assistant working with him in cutting his film. Lean was assigned the task of keeping track of the footage that was shot, putting it in film cans, and marking it for future reference.

Most of the films that Lean was assigned to at this juncture were not remarkable, but then few British films before World War II were. In the silent period, British film distributors depended so heavily on films from abroad, especially the United States, that in 1927 the British government established a quota system whereby British studios regularly had to produce a specified number of domestic motion pictures if they were to be permitted to continue importing movies for distribution from America and elsewhere.

The Cinematographic Act (or Quota Act) of 1927 led to the production each year of several "quota quickies," films that were, with rare exceptions, bargain-basement imitations of Hollywood movies, slipshod affairs turned out just to meet this need. As a result, movies of artistic quality became something of a rarity among British productions and were, of course, the work of directors like Hitchcock in his pre-Hollywood days.

In short, the Quota Act regulated the quantity—but not the quality—of British movies, as the British film historian Rachael Low points out;[17] and most American films were far superior to the low-budget programmers that came off the assembly line at Gaumont and other British studios. One Hollywood wag tagged the quickies *cuff operas* (as in off-the-cuff) to describe how some of the dialogue was improvised by the actors.

The cinematographer Ronald Neame, who worked on several films with David Lean later on, remembers that most London cinemas slotted quota quickies as second features on double bills. But some cinemas in London's West End merely honored the letter of the law by screening quickies in the mornings, when only the janitors were in the auditorium! "That would leave the rest of the day free for the more popular product from Hollywood."[18]

Be that as it may, the quota system provided employment in the British film industry since quickies were being churned out by the studios with great regularity. One of the studios that took advantage of the Quota Act in this way was Gaumont, which took on additional employees because of increased production: "The rapid expansion of the film companies that supplied quota films gave many prominent movie figures their start in the industry."[19] David Lean was one of the aspiring British filmmakers for whom quota quickies provided a training ground, not unlike the education that students receive in film schools today.

In point of fact, some British films of the period were above average and achieved some degree of popularity. For one thing, "Some of the quota quickies were perceived to be reasonably well-made at the time of their release." And these films could be described as slick, fast-moving melodramas. "To suggest that all of the quota films were worthless denigrates an entire decade of British cinema."[20] Thus, Maurice Elvey managed to make a few films of quality, such as *Balaclava* (1928), on which Lean served as a production assistant. It was a costume drama with the British fighting the Russians during the Crimean War, highlighted by the gallant Charge of the Light Brigade, inspired by Tennyson's immortal poem.

Meanwhile, sound pictures had taken Hollywood by storm. For the record, the sound era was officially inaugurated in Hollywood on October 6, 1927, with the premiere of Alan Crosland's *The Jazz Singer*, starring Al Jolson. The film had a musical score and four musical numbers but only one dialogue sequence. It was followed in July 1928 by Bryan Foy's *The Lights of New York*, a gangster movie that was the first all-talking picture. And by 1929 the sound era was in full swing in America.

The coming of sound pictures in Hollywood, of course, cued a frantic rush to convert studios to sound in Britain. Alfred Hitchcock made *Blackmail*, the first major British talking picture, starring John Longden (*The Quinneys*), at Elstree, one of the first British studios to be wired for sound. When the movie was premiered in June 1929, its huge success made it clear that talking pictures were there to stay in Britain. Admittedly, spoken dialogue made for more character development, individual characters now being able to reveal themselves more effectively through the nuances of speech.

By 1930, nearly every film was a talkie, and "movies haven't shut up since." *The Jazz Singer* uttered "a shout that was heard round the world."[21] For his part, Lean was not enthusiastic about the advent of sound. He observed that directors were being hired by the studios from the London stage; they were familiar with spoken dialogue but not with cinematic techniques. It was not surprising, he explained, that, combined with the tyranny of the new sound equipment, the influence of these theater-oriented directors produced movies that differed little from stage plays. Alfred Hitchcock, who was working at Elstree Studios at the time, complained, "With the appearance of sound, directors forgot that *talking* pictures should still be *moving* pictures." Too many films were, he felt, just "photographs of people talking."[22] It was at this point that Lean got his first lesson in the craft of editing sound films.

Lean's first opportunity to edit a talkie came when Sewell Collins, an American director at Gaumont, frankly admitted that he was at a loss when it came to editing his first sound picture, *The Night Porter* (1930). It was a twenty-minute music hall sketch about a hotel employee who mistakes one of the guests for a burglar. Collins, who came from the stage, had no idea how to synchronize the sound track with the picture. John Seabourne, who edited the Gaumont sound newsreels, was the only technician on the lot who knew how to combine sound and image effectively. When Lean, who had been assisting Collins in the cutting room, got to hear that Seabourne was going to attempt to teach Collins to edit sound movies, he was on hand to observe. Lean watched as Seabourne demonstrated how to run the sound track and the optical track simultaneously on the editing machine, called a Moviola, in order to synchronize sound and picture; Lean caught on immediately, while Collins confessed that he still did not have a clue about how to edit sound footage. Collins was very relieved, then, when his assistant cutter volunteered to edit *The Night Porter* for him, while Collins looked on.

Lean quickly mastered the craft of editing sound movies and continued to assist other directors in cutting talkies. He developed his own approach to assembling the footage for a sound picture, virtually ignoring the sound track, and cutting the film primarily by focusing on the images. Michael Powell, who would one day commission Lean to edit a couple of his films, approved of Lean's method. The tendency of a film editor, Powell pointed out, is to "follow the bloody words": "But cinema is all about images." Lean cut the footage in terms of what he wanted to see on the screen—"and to hell with the sound," which is, according to Powell, primarily just "actors yakking." If the editor concentrates on the images, Powell concluded, "the words take care of themselves."[23]

Lean remained fascinated by the art of film editing to the end of his days. He saw it as a kind of "conjuring trick" (he often described films in terms of magic), and he loved to watch the flow of images.[24] John Seabourne, the chief editor of Gaumont-British News, left Gaumont for another studio, and, in 1930, his place was filled by David Lean, who had developed the reputation of a promising young editor in film circles.

On June 28, 1930, Lean married his cousin Isabel Lean, the first of his six wives, and his only child, Peter, was born a few months later. Lean was the first to admit that he was not a good husband or father since, for him, family life always took a backseat to work. The marriage lasted only until 1935. Lean rationalized the matter by saying that he had barely started his career when his son was born and that he simply could not cope with the worries of caring for a family at that point. He felt trapped, so he walked out. Commenting on the number of Lean's marriages (not to mention the affairs), Ronald Neame, a close friend of Lean's, opined that his Quaker roots created a conflict between his sense of morality and his more bohemian spirit. It was a conflict he never adequately resolved, though he did try. Looking back on his multiple marriages, Sandra Lean, his sixth wife and widow, remarked, "When he had lived with a woman for quite a long time, somehow guilt caught up with him and he decided to do the moral thing and marry her."[25] But he had difficulty staying married.

Editing Gaumont-British News was nerve-racking and backbreaking. Gaumont released newsreels twice weekly, and often Lean was editing the news footage around the clock to meet the release deadlines. He regularly used a Moviola to cut the film footage; it was a standard editing machine that reproduced in miniature the images of the film being edited. Sometimes, however, when he was running behind schedule, he would edit the footage by simply running it through his fingers and cutting it with a pair of ordinary scissors. Often, because of time constraints, he not only wrote the voice-over commentary but also spoke the narration himself on the sound track.

In 1931, Lean was lured away from Gaumont to become an editor of British Movietone News. Movietone could afford to offer him a bigger paycheck than Gaumont because it was backed by Twentieth Century–Fox in Hollywood. Keith Ayling, who supervised Movietone News, was also associated with Herbert Wilcox's British and Dominions Productions (B&D) at Elstree Studios. Ayling was instrumental in arranging for Lean to gain further experience as a film editor by assisting an editor at Elstree in cutting feature pictures. Elstree Studios, which housed not just B&D but other production companies, was backed by Hollywood's Paramount Pictures, and Lean believed it to be the best studio complex then in operation in England (Hitchcock made *Blackmail* there).

A number of American technicians were employed by British studios. This was because the Hollywood craftsmen who helped staff a studio like Elstree were acknowledged to be among the best in the industry. Lean appreciated how much he learned about film editing from Merrill White. Herbert Wilcox had imported White from Hollywood to run the editing department for B&D when sound came in. White had cut two landmark Hollywood musicals, Ernst Lubitsch's *The Love Parade* (1929) and Rouben Mamoulian's *Love Me Tonight* (1932), both starring Maurice Chevalier, before settling in at Elstree. Lean recalled that he and White would work together on editing a quality picture during the day; then, at 6:00 P.M., they would switch to a quota quickie. White would take the first three reels, Lean the second three.

Lean found the experience that he accrued by working with White invaluable; White encouraged Lean to concentrate primarily on the visuals, rather than on the sound track, when editing a motion picture. "I think dialogue is nearly always secondary in a movie," Lean maintained. Whereas it was, in his opinion, "awfully hard" to remember a single line of dialogue from a film, "you will not forget the pictures."[26]

Keith Ayling was associated with Paramount's studio in France, on the outskirts of Paris. He arranged to have Lean edit a British film being shot there, Louis Mercanton's *These Charming People* (1931), a frothy comedy about high society. It featured a teenage Ann Todd, who would one day become Lean's wife and star. Lean was overenthusiastic about editing a feature film and overcut the first reel of the picture in a jerky fashion; the action seemed to jump all over the place. One of the executives at the studio was Alexander Korda, a Hungarian-born producer, who would soon inaugurate his own independent production company in England, London Films. Lean would direct some pictures for Korda two decades later. At this moment, however, Korda thought Lean's work on the first reel of *These Charming People* less than adequate, and he demoted Lean to assistant editor. Korda ultimately decided that he was not ready to move up to editing feature films on his own, so it was back to Movietone News in London for Lean, where his work as a film editor continued to be admired.

At long last Lean got the chance to edit a feature film on his own, *Insult* (1932), which was directed by Harry Lachman, an American director and a protégé of Rex Ingram's. Lachman had made *Insult* at Elstree for B&D; it was a turgid thriller set in North Africa, about intrigue in the French Foreign Legion. It starred John Gielgud in a role that hardly did him justice. Still, the film was momentous for Lean since it was the first feature film for which he received an official screen credit as a full-fledged film editor. Granted, the film was a routine programmer with shallow characterizations; nevertheless, Lean proved himself a promising young editor by cutting the picture so that the action moved along at a brisk pace.

Insult made a decent showing at the box office, and Lean was accordingly asked to edit two more quota movies in quick succession. Lachman and other directors were impressed with how speedily he could cut together a low-budget picture. After all, when a director was making a movie on a shoestring, an efficient editor was a definite plus. Lean would sometimes work all night in the editing room so that he could spend time on the set during the day and watch the director at work, with a view to eventually becoming a filmmaker himself.

Lean's reputation as an accomplished editor spread throughout the film colony in Britain; he was often called on to act as a "film doctor," to reedit or shorten a film that was in trouble during postproduction. Thorold Dickinson told me in conversation that, when he was editing J. Walter Ruben's *Java Head* (1934)—a steamy melodrama about an ill-fated expedition to the Far East—Lean was called in to help him try to save the picture in the cutting room. Ralph Richardson (who would later star in Lean's *The Sound Barrier*) was wasted in a thankless role; indeed, Dickinson said that Ruben's stilted direction of the actors all but sank the movie. "Some of the actors," he told me, "seemed to be behaving in front of the camera, rather than acting."

Dickinson, who was later to become a director of films like *The Queen of*

Spades (1949), was already a prominent director at Elstree when Lean collaborated with him. He contended that editing taught one the art of filmmaking, a dictum with which Lean heartily agreed. Martin Scorsese has said, "Dickinson had a great editor's instinct for . . . cutting right at the moment when the emotion registers [with the viewer]."[27] With Dickinson's guidance, Lean skillfully padded out the narrative material by the inventive use of stock footage and by prolonging certain key close-ups. Dickinson remembers Lean as a taciturn individual, but he much admired him as a talented cutter.

Lean was invited to direct some quota quickies, but he declined, firmly believing that directing quickies could be a filmmaker's graveyard. He feared that, if he made a film of this sort and it flopped, people would say that he had done a poor job, not that he had not had enough time to make it right. So he stuck to film editing for the foreseeable future. Meanwhile, back at Elstree, Merrill White was editing *Nell Gwyn* (1934), a B&D picture produced and directed by Herbert Wilcox. Lean agreed to assist his mentor in the cutting room without receiving a screen credit, in order to profit further by White's experience.

Nell Gwyn (1934)

Nell Gwyn was the first important picture that Lean worked on, either as an editor or as an assistant editor; it told the story of one of history's most famous courtesans. Set in seventeenth-century England, it was a historical epic—a genre with which Lean's name would be inextricably linked later on. Nell Gwyn (Anna Neagle) is a two-bit entertainer and good-time girl in a smoky café who eventually catches the eye of King Charles II (Cedric Hardwicke). "It was quite racy for its day," writes the English filmmaker Ken Russell in his book on British cinema. "I know what you want," Nell says with a saucy wink to a customer in the seedy tavern where she works, pulling up her skirt and adding, "The price of a drink." Whereupon she takes a coin from the purse attached to her garter. According to Russell, there was "for once" no pretense that a girl like Nell was anything but an earthy trollop, "in pursuit of the monarch she eventually seduces in the aptly named King's Arms."[28] Nell then becomes the king's favorite.

The movie was frank, even ribald, and Neagle's costumes were revealing for the time. *Nell Gwyn* was a big hit in England, but Joseph Ignatius Breen, the film industry censor in America, was not amused. Breen required thirty-five cuts, including several shots of Neagle's "cleavage." Herbert Wilcox attested to the fact that this was the first time that the censor had employed that term to refer to the female anatomy. Lean recalled that the movie ended with the death of King Charles, and the final shot was of Nell walking out of the king's castle. As Lean later remembered, however, before the film could be released in the United States, an epilogue "had to be shot and tacked on to the English version," in order to round off the scandalous doings with an obvious moral lesson. Actually, the Hollywood censor demanded both a prologue and an epilogue to frame the bawdy story. The prologue shows Nell shivering in the gutter; this short scene dissolves to the opening of the original film—thereby making the entire British movie a flashback. In the epilogue, Nell is once more penniless and in the gutter, but this time a hag. "It showed Nell in abject poverty," Lean concluded with no little irony, "as an object lesson to all American ladies not to be the mistress of a king."[29]

Given the censor's snipping away at the film, not to mention the addition of the moralistic framing story, the film historian Ivan Butler simply assumes that *Nell Gwyn* failed in America.[30] In actual fact, the expurgated version did "reasonably well."[31] Indeed, *Nell Gwyn* and *The Private Life of Henry VIII* (1933), which was produced and directed by Alexander Korda, were among the first British pictures to successfully break into the American market. Such films helped infuse the British film industry with a new spirit of energy and optimism.

The cinematographer on *Nell Gwyn*, Freddie Young (who would later photograph some of Lean's films), said of Wilcox that he didn't think him a "great director," in the sense of being a brilliant stylist. "What he had," according to Young, "was the popular artist's sure sense of his public . . . the flair for a good subject—seeing the appeal in stories like that of Nell Gwyn. . . . He got many of his films distributed in the U.S., when that was far from easy."[32] In an essay on British films in the United States that mentions British movies that achieved an unexpected American box office breakthrough, Philip Kemp includes "Herbert Wilcox's silent *Nell Gwyn*."[33] This is the silent version of *Nell Gwyn*, which Wilcox made in 1926 with Dorothy Gish.

Besides producing the movies that he himself directed, Wilcox also produced films for other directors working for B&D. He wanted to ensure that B&D turned out some pictures that would earn critical respectability for his production company. "One spot of prestige in a spate of popular box-office successes was *Escape Me Never*, which helped to introduce the Austrian actress Elizabeth Bergner to British films"—and which was edited by David Lean.[34]

Escape Me Never (1935)

Elizabeth Bergner, a leading actress in Germany, fled to England in the wake of the rise of Hitler; she was accompanied by her husband-to-be, Dr. Paul Czinner, a filmmaker with a doctorate in literature. Czinner and Bergner had made some popular movies together in Germany, so Wilcox wooed them to Elstree to make a major movie for B&D.

Wilcox assembled a first-class production team for the film, led by Georges Périnal, a French cinematographer who had come to England to shoot Korda's *Private Life of Henry VIII* and stayed on there to become an influential director of photography. Moreover, the film's score was composed by William Walton, a distinguished British composer. Last, but certainly not least, David Lean was chosen to edit the picture, at the suggestion of Richard Norton, a studio executive who was familiar with Lean's work (Norton would hire Lean again to edit *Pygmalion*). Lean was gratified to be a part of this venture, for *Escape Me Never* was no quota quickie. In fact, one sequence was scheduled to be shot on location in Venice, at a time when taking a British film unit on location to another country was not common. In sum, the picture was the first big-scale, prestige film that Lean would edit solo.

Since Czinner was still a newcomer to the British film industry, Lean was regularly present on the set to offer the director suggestions. Lean did not make the trip to the Continent with the film unit. When he looked through the lens of his Moviola at the sun-drenched scenes shot in Venice for an early sequence in the movie, he was thrilled to discover the fabulous city. Venice would figure in his own film *Summertime* two decades later.

The plot of *Escape Me Never* revolves around Gemma Jones (Elizabeth Bergner), the mother of an illegitimate baby. Gemma marries Sebastian Sanger (Hugh Sinclair), a struggling young composer who is willing to provide for her and her infant son. But Sebastian becomes more and more absorbed in the ballet score that he is composing, and he neglects Gemma and the child, even when the infant becomes seriously ill.

Lean learned much from watching Périnal, one of the world's best lighting cameramen, photograph the film. The movie is lighthearted at the beginning—in the Venice sequence, before Gemma immigrates to England—and Périnal gave the early scenes a bright, sunny look. Lean noticed that, as the picture moved toward melodrama in the later scenes, Périnal used sharp, hard lights in the night exteriors, making the streets slick and misty, and bathed the interiors in deep shadows, as befits a serious drama.

On the night that Sebastian's ballet is premiered, the infant dies in the hospital. When Gemma learns of her little boy's death, she walks out of the hospital in a daze and collapses on the front steps. Lean deftly intercut the scenes in the hospital with those of the performance of the ballet, ironically juxtaposing Sebastian's professional triumph with Gemma's personal tragedy. Lean demonstrated a flair for synchronizing music and image in an imaginative manner throughout this sequence. The short but elegant ballet that Walton wrote for the movie became a standard concert piece and has often been recorded. Its centerpiece is a shimmering waltz that rises to a lyrical peak for a stunning finale. But even beyond the ballet, Walton's sumptuous score unquestionably enhances the movie as a whole.

Escape Me Never was a favorite with critics, who applauded its well-knit, arresting story as well as the consistent craftsmanship of the production team. One review singled out Lean's editing, mentioning that he instinctively knew how to cut before a grimace congealed or an action went over the top. The story provided potent fuel for the star, who earned an Academy Award nomination as best actress.[35]

Escape Me Never proved to be Bergner's most memorable and likable performance in a British film. Lean, by now the highest-paid editor in the British film industry, found that he had priced himself out of the market. Producers considered him a luxury they could not afford, so he found himself out of work and flat broke—for the time being, at least. Since calls for his services were few and far between, he took whatever editing jobs came down the pike. As luck would have it, he would soon be invited to collaborate on a screen adaptation of George Bernard Shaw's *Pygmalion,* which would turn out to be a box office bonanza and put him on the road to financial recovery. Moreover, working on *Pygmalion* would be the first time that he took a hand in directing a film—albeit unofficially—and that would, in turn, bring him one step closer to becoming a full-fledged motion picture director.

Lean had learned his craft the hard way—few major directors had ever started on such a low rung of the ladder. By the late 1930s, however, he had gained a marked interest in making quality pictures, and, with films like *Pygmalion,* his craftsmanship would become finely honed.

Chapter Two

A TOUCH OF CLASS

PYGMALION, MAJOR BARBARA, AND OTHER FILMS

These films of my plays are a revolution in the presentation of drama on film. They should be advertised as "all-British films made by British methods, without interference by American screenwriters." . . . Producers must understand that the art of telling a story is a knack very few people have. I am one of them.
—*George Bernard Shaw*

In 1938, the Quota Act was revised with a view to discouraging the production of quota quickies. The new version stipulated that British producers must allocate sufficient funds for the making of domestic films to allow an adequate amount of time for preproduction preparation, shooting, and the final shaping of each picture. At this point, Hitchcock was soon to depart for America, but directors like Anthony Asquith and Michael Powell took advantage of this increased support to produce films that, though still modestly made by Hollywood standards, demonstrated incontestably the artistry of which British filmmakers were capable.

"Naturally we were delighted," says Ronald Neame, a cinematographer who later worked on Lean's pictures. "Even if our films were on a smaller scale than those from Hollywood with an assured market, we would be able to spend more and improve quality."[1] British directors began making movies that frankly showed life in Britain, including social problems like unemployment and class barriers. An outstanding example of this new trend was *Pygmalion,* which consciously dealt with one of the underlying themes of the decade: class distinctions and class standards. Asked to edit *Pygmalion,* Lean was determined to prove once and for all that he was a highly skilled film editor—and so he did. Furthermore, *Pygmalion* was the first film on which David Lean acted unofficially as a codirector.

Pygmalion (1938)

Gabriel Pascal, a Hungarian-born film producer, arrived in Britain in the mid-1930s without a penny to his name. Yet he was determined to convince the playwright George Bernard Shaw to permit him to make films of his plays. Pascal had set himself a real challenge, since as early as 1924 Shaw had expressed his disdain for the silent cinema. Many motion pictures, he wrote, were "boresome blunders," marred by actors photographed in hideous makeup, shown in close-ups "that an angel's face could not bear. . . . Good sense is about non-existent among your filmmakers."[2]

Not to be deterred, the irrepressible Pascal managed to wangle an interview with Shaw. Pascal could be beguiling and charming, and Shaw was entranced by the enthusiastic Hungarian. Pascal was able to get the elderly playwright to grant him the screen rights to his 1913 play *Pygmalion*—though Pascal did not leave their first meeting with the *Pygmalion* contract in his pocket, as legend has it. It was only after further conferences that Pascal managed to convince Shaw that he was a conscientious filmmaker and that the film version of *Pygmalion* would not mutilate the play. Finally, Shaw ceded the film rights to Pascal—and even agreed to write the screenplay himself.

After beating the bushes unsuccessfully in search of financial backers for the project, Pascal eventually went straight to the top and got Richard Norton, the production chief at Pinewood Studios in Buckinghamshire, to help him secure backers for the movie. Norton wisely pointed out to Pascal that financiers had not been willing to put money into a Shaw film before because Shaw's plays were considered too highbrow; besides, they did not have enough sex to appeal to film audiences. Accordingly, Pascal cleverly coaxed Shaw into altering his "sacred text." A film, Pascal emphasized to Shaw, cannot be merely a photographed stage play. Shaw's secretary, Blanche Patch, commented, "It was the biggest concession Shaw ever made to anyone. Pascal now had [Shaw] well under control."[3]

The charm that Pascal exerted on Shaw is evident in Shaw's later description of the producer. "Gabriel Pascal is one of those extravagant men who turn up occasionally, say once in a century, and may be called godsends in the arts to which they are devoted," wrote Shaw. "The man is a genius."[4] Though hardly a genius, Pascal had an uncanny way of ingratiating himself with influential and powerful people, like Shaw and Norton. A wag at Pinewood quipped that Gabriel's last name should have been Rascal, not

Pascal. With Shaw in their corner, Pascal and Norton then formed Pascal Film Productions, an independent film company, and Norton employed his considerable influence with the moneymen to raise the capital needed to produce the film.

Moreover, Norton arranged to have the movie distributed by J. Arthur Rank's General Film Distributors. Rank had made a fortune with his flour mills before entering the film industry in 1933. By 1937, he had acquired Pinewood Studios. So *Pygmalion* was to be made at a studio where one of Rank's own executives was in charge of production; consequently, Rank obviously thought *Pygmalion* a promising project. Rank's ultimate goal as a film mogul was to get good British films into the American market, and he shrewdly guessed that *Pygmalion* would attract audiences in the United States as well as in Britain.

Pascal had an unerring eye for choosing the right personnel to collaborate on a project. He engaged David Lean to edit the film, with the warm approval of Norton, who remembered Lean from *Escape Me Never.* Lean willingly took a cut in pay in order to be part of this prestige production. In addition, Pascal secured the services of Anthony Asquith to codirect the film with Leslie Howard, who was also to play the male lead. Asquith was a prominent British director who came from an upper-class milieu and was noted for his screen adaptations of stage plays, particularly those about people of status and breeding. Therefore, *Pygmalion* was right up his alley, dealing as it does with the class distinctions in British society. The story is about an imperious speech teacher named Henry Higgins who on a bet transforms Eliza Doolittle, a cockney flower girl, into the belle of a society ball.

Pascal gave the production team an international flavor by importing the leading American cinematographer, Harry Stradling (who would photograph *My Fair Lady,* George Cukor's 1964 musical remake of *Pygmalion,* a quarter of a century later). He also enlisted the gifted French composer Arthur Honegger to compose the score. Shaw, who took a hand in choosing the cast, balked at Pascal's choice of Leslie Howard to play Higgins, an egotistical, stuffy pedagogue. Shaw cavalierly dismissed Howard, who had appeared in romantic films like *Berkeley Square* (Frank Lloyd, 1933), as a matinee idol who was too urbane and charming to fit the part. But, once again, Shaw gave in to Pascal, conceding that the public would like him.

Shaw consoled himself with having picked Wendy Hiller to play Eliza. He had remembered her playing Eliza at the Malvern Festival in 1936 and correctly guessed that she would be perfect in the role. According to the film critic Stanley Kauffmann, Shaw had been captivated by her Malvern performance and told her: "If a film gets made of this, you are Eliza."[5]

Though Shaw was to be given a screen credit as the author of the screen-play, Cecil Lewis, W. P. Lipscomb, and Ian Dalrymple worked on his draft of the script at various stages, in order to make it more screenworthy. Pascal held story conferences with these screenwriters, conferences that Lean was also asked to attend since he was known to have a good sense of narrative structure. Shaw had condensed some of the play's dialogue in his draft; nevertheless, his screenplay hewed very close to the stage version. In fact, in his exhaustive study of the films made from Shaw's plays, Donald Costello affirms that the published version of Shaw's draft "is closer to the text of the play than it is to what is presented in the actual movie."[6] Hence the need of Pascal's team of writers to revise the draft.

Departures from Shaw's version of the script had to be approved by the Maestro (as Pascal called Shaw) through Pascal's intercession. In all, four-teen new scenes were either written by Shaw or approved by him. These scenes incorporated events that, for practical reasons, had to take place off-stage in the play but could be effectively depicted in a film. The ones that Shaw wrote himself are, of course, included in the published version of his draft of the screenplay.[7]

The title of Shaw's play is a reference to an ancient king of Cyprus who fell in love with the statue of a beautiful maiden that he had carved out of ivory and that Aphrodite then brought to life in answer to his prayer. Shaw viewed the play as centering on two headstrong characters who clash when Higgins tries to change Eliza into a proper lady; only later does the romance emerge. Eliza is very much the daughter of her father, Alfred P. Doolittle, a dustman (Wilfrid Lawson)—wild and untrammeled. Her intelligence manifests itself slowly under Higgins's tutoring, and, as she realizes that in the professor she is up against an extremely complicated individual, one very much like herself, she gradually comes to respect him.

Shaw allowed the ending of his play, in which the estranged couple do not kiss and make up at the final curtain, to be altered so that in the film Eliza and Henry are clearly reconciled before the final fade-out. This happy resolution to the plot does not do violence to Shaw's play, as some critics have charged, since the original ending of *Pygmalion* was really ambiguous and did not close off entirely the possibility of an eventual reunion between Henry and Eliza.

Even though, in the epilogue that he appended as an afterthought when the text of the play was published, Shaw suggested that there was a good chance that Eliza might opt for marrying Freddy Eynsford-Hill, a well-bred young gentleman who adores her, the dramatic thrust of the play itself indicates that she would be much more likely to select a mate who possessed a strength of character akin to her own, such as Henry Higgins, rather than a vapid, immature fop like Freddy. As for the corresponding likelihood of Higgins's eventual willingness to wed Eliza, the very title Shaw chose for his play in the first place forecasts that Higgins, like his counterpart, Pygmalion, before him, will finally fall in love with his own creation. Consequently, it seems dramatically right that the film version should end with Higgins and Eliza getting back together again, and the film's ending is well suited to the audience's expectations.

In the final scene of the movie, Higgins finds himself alone, bemoaning the fact that, in spite of himself, he has undeniably become attached to Eliza. The guarded sentiments that he expresses are as close to a declaration of love as the reserved professor would ever permit himself to utter. Eliza steals into the room and finds that there is something deeply touching about a man who had fancied himself a confirmed bachelor having to admit his need and love for another human being. Not wishing to give Eliza the satisfaction of knowing that he is overjoyed to see her, Higgins shrugs cavalierly: "Eliza, where the devil are my slippers?" It was David Lean who came up with that closing line during a story conference.

Shaw accepted the revised ending of the film, which he did not actually see until he attended a preview of the finished film. Observing that he did not explicitly indicate in the play that Eliza and Higgins would marry, he added that the film's ending "is too ambiguous to make a fuss about."[8] On the contrary, Pascal's biographer confirms that the ending of the movie was clearly designed to anticipate the marriage of Higgins and Eliza: "The movie ended, leaving the public assured that Eliza would be running for those slippers to the end of her days."[9]

Leslie Howard was given a codirector screen credit with Asquith on *Pygmalion,* but Lean declared that Howard was not especially interested in directing at the time. After principal photography commenced on March 11, 1938, Howard limited his role as codirector to occasionally offering Asquith a suggestion or two during the rehearsal of a scene—but he was usually on the set only for the scenes in which he appeared.

Wendy Hiller stated, "I can say with confidence that I wouldn't have known Leslie was co-directing until the day we were shooting a tea party scene." In this scene, which occurs early in the movie, Eliza makes some hilarious social blunders. Howard strongly disagreed with the way in which Hiller was playing it—employing, in his opinion, too much broad humor—and she rushed to her dressing room in a flood of tears. Afterward, she explained to Asquith that she was playing the scene the same way she had done it at Malvern, where it had brought down the house. "Poor

Leslie must have been warned to leave me alone," she recalled, as he gave her no more direction.[10]

During the shooting period, Lean spent his nights preparing a preliminary edit of each scene and his days, as usual, on the studio floor observing filming. Asquith frequently consulted with him about composing the shots and selecting the camera angles; in effect, Lean was often "directing the director." In addition, Asquith asked him to shoot a couple of montage sequences for the movie. So it seems that Lean, more than Howard, was Asquith's real codirector, though Lean was officially credited only as the picture's editor. "It's a damned shame," Asquith told Lean. "You should be up there as co-director." Lean characterized Asquith as a "bloody good director" who could have been great had he not taken so mild mannered and diffident an approach to the actors.[11]

Among the scenes added to the film at the script stage is one in which Eliza visits Higgins for the first time. He has his housekeeper and maid strong-arm the scruffy, unkempt girl upstairs for a long-overdue bath. As Lean adroitly edited the scene, the steam from the hot tub billows up and blots her from view, as if the old Eliza has vanished, to be replaced by the clean-cut young woman who shortly emerges from the bathroom in crisp new clothes, ready to be remodeled into the fair lady that Higgins plans to make of her.

Asquith firmly believed that the montage sequences, which he had given Lean to direct as well as edit, were absolutely crucial to the movie. This is because they show Higgins bringing about Eliza's transformation into a refined lady.

The first montage is an extended sequence of Higgins coaching Eliza in her speech lessons. It begins with Higgins recording Eliza's voice on a phonograph record. He then takes her through a phonetic exercise, whereby she recites, with marbles in her mouth, the vocal ritual: "The rain in Spain stays mainly in the plain." When Eliza swallows one of the marbles, Higgins says, "Don't worry, I have plenty more!" Howard ad-libbed this line on the set, and Lean thought it worked well enough to leave it in. The montage ends with a shot of the stack of records that Higgins has made of Eliza's exercises, indicating how arduously he and his pupil are applying themselves.

The second montage is occasioned by Higgins receiving an invitation to a ball at the Transylvanian embassy. He plans to escort Eliza and pass "the guttersnipe" off as a duchess. That precipitates an elaborate montage, with Higgins instructing Eliza how to curtsey and waltz. When he feels that she has mastered these lessons, Higgins bellows, "Send for the dressmakers, hairdressers, makeup artists, manicurists, and all of the rest of those parasites!" There follows a series of shots of Eliza, her face encased in a mud pack, being worked over by an army of beauticians.

In these two montages, Lean employs the editor's shears to skillfully telescope time so that the two sequences take much less time on the screen than they would on the stage. "Everyone was stunned by the marvelous editing he did on *Pygmalion*," Michael Powell noted. "Those scenes of Wendy Hiller learning phonetic were created by brilliant editing."[12] What Lean remembered most about shooting the montage sequences was that Howard consistently came late to the set. "I used to wait two hours for him at Pinewood; and I thought I would kill him," Lean recalled. "But he had the charm of the devil"; it was impossible to stay angry at him.[13]

In his draft of the screenplay, Shaw had added a short scene in which Higgins shows off Eliza at a garden party. During a story conference, Lean and the other script doctors involved in revising the screenplay expanded Shaw's brief scene into the splendid embassy ball sequence. Higgins squires the elegant, poised Eliza to the embassy, where the guests gaze at her admiringly. The scene reaches a crescendo with Eliza as Cinderella incarnate dancing with a handsome prince. The camera pulls back, "giving a spectacular panoramic view of the whole glittering ballroom, with Eliza in triumph at the center."[14] Honnegar's lush, lyrical waltz surges to a peak as the scene ends.

Pascal was an enterprising producer, but he also fancied himself as knowing quite a bit about the filmmaker's art, which was not the case. While Lean was editing the rough cut of *Pygmalion,* Pascal suggested to Asquith that Lean reedit one scene in a way that neither Lean nor Asquith thought an improvement. They told him that they would make the change he had asked for within half an hour. After taking a coffee break, said Asquith, "we showed him the same reel again," and Pascal was delighted that the scene was much improved.[15]

Pygmalion was a tremendous success, both in England and in America, with Shaw winning an Academy Award for best screenplay. Reviewers noticed how large sections of the plot, like Eliza's faltering progress with her speech exercises, were whipped through in Lean's snappy montages. *Pygmalion* was characterized as a polished, captivating entertainment. Shaw, of course, ascribed the film's favorable reviews and popularity largely to his screenplay, but he also gave a lion's share of the credit to Pascal's abilities as a producer. He clearly underestimated the contributions made to the film by others, including Asquith. The latter, after all, was an experienced director with a respectable track record stretching back to the silent days. Yet Shaw described him condescendingly as "a talented and inventive youth who doesn't know the difference between the end of a play and the beginning";

he was not even impressed by Howard's winning a best actor award at the Venice Film Festival for his performance as Higgins.[16]

On the other hand, Pascal does deserve credit for being a prime mover in turning *Pygmalion* into the Broadway musical *My Fair Lady*, which debuted in 1956 and was filmed in 1964 by George Cukor. The musical version, both on the stage and on the screen, retained the ending of the 1938 film, whereby Eliza and Higgins get back together again.

Cukor, who directed such classic films as *The Philadelphia Story* (1940), told me in conversation that he had always been intrigued by Shaw's original play. As Shaw conceived the story, said Cukor, Higgins's attempt to fashion Eliza into a refined lady starts out as a battle of wits and only later turns into a romance. "It's the classic relationship of a bullying male and a girl who seems on the surface childlike and malleable but who possesses a fairly inflexible personality underneath."

Even in the wake of *My Fair Lady*, the 1938 *Pygmalion* continues to have its champions. In reassessing the film, Ivan Butler contends that it is "consistently more entertaining, amusing, and satisfying than *My Fair Lady*," despite the latter film's singable tunes.[17] What's more, Rex Harrison's Higgins has not eclipsed Leslie Howard's, and Audrey Hepburn's Eliza is by no means in the same league as Wendy Hiller's.

In any event, after *Pygmalion*, Lean edited *French without Tears* (1939) for Anthony Asquith. It was derived from the Terence Rattigan stage farce about young Britons studying in France who pursue the same French girl and was very well received. Lean then accepted Pascal's invitation to collaborate on another Shaw film, this time *Major Barbara*.

Major Barbara (1941)

Pascal had originally appointed Charles Frend, who had edited four pictures for Alfred Hitchcock, to edit *Major Barbara*. Remembering the montage sequences that Lean had shot and edited for *Pygmalion*, Pascal wanted him to handle the montage sequences in *Major Barbara* and to supervise Frend's editing of the picture as well. Having apparently been spoiled by the triumph of *Pygmalion*, Pascal decided to personally direct as well as produce his next Shaw venture. Many industry insiders thought he was biting off more than he could chew. So he was fortunate to have Lean on hand once more, officially as the editor of the film, and unofficially as a codirector.

Shaw's 1905 play tells the story of Barbara Undershaft, an officer in the Salvation Army who deplores capitalism—despite the fact that her father is a wealthy munitions manufacturer. The international success of *Pygmalion* made it relatively easy for Pascal to find financing for another Shaw film. J. Arthur Rank's General Film Distributors once again agreed to distribute the film. Donald Costello mistakenly states that Pascal operated the distribution company,[18] but Pascal Film Productions happened to be only one independent film unit functioning under the umbrella of the Rank organization's distribution system.

Wendy Hiller was a shoo-in to play Barbara, after her incandescent performance as Eliza. Her costar was Rex Harrison as Adolphus Cusins, a Salvation Army recruit who falls in love with Barbara. (It is interesting to see Hiller, a former Eliza Doolittle, matched with Harrison, who would one day play Henry Higgins.) The character actor Robert Morley took the role of Barbara's father, Andrew Undershaft; even though he was thirty-two and Hiller was twenty-eight, Morley managed to be credible as her father. Robert Newton played Bill Walker, a vagrant and a street tough; and Jenny, a devoted evangelist in the Salvation Army, was portrayed by Deborah Kerr in her maiden voyage as a film actress.

Pascal also brought in Harold French to help him direct the film; French had earned his spurs on the stage, directing Rex Harrison in the 1937–38 production of *French without Tears*. He was designated as dialogue director so that someone with theatrical experience could help Pascal coach the actors in speaking their lines. "Pascal knew nothing about directing," said French. "Sometimes he would look through the wrong end of the viewfinder! But he had the money and he had the ear of [Shaw]."[19] Pascal wanted both Lean and French to be on the studio floor during shooting; Lean would tell Pascal where to put the camera and what lens to use. "I was there for the camera set-ups and did a fair amount of the direction," Lean said afterward, "but I never got a screen credit for it." Neither did French.[20] Instead, Pascal paid both Lean and French a bonus for their willingness to be credited not as codirectors of the film but as assistants to the director. Nevertheless, French testified that Pascal left most of the direction to Lean.

Withal, Pascal had not lost his knack for assembling top talent. Besides Lean and a stellar cast, he got William Walton (*Escape Me Never*) to compose the underscore. And Ronald Neame was made director of photography. Freddie Young was originally scheduled to photograph the film, but, after sizing up Pascal as a tyro film director, he arranged to be called away to another picture. With Lean's support, Young recommended Neame to Pascal, and that was the beginning of Neame's long professional association with Lean. Finally, John Bryan was named production designer. Neame maintained that, the moment Bryan began sketching the sets, a movie started to come to life. Like Neame, Bryan would collaborate with Lean on a number of Lean's own films.

The first order of business in preparing to film *Major Barbara,* however, was the screenplay; Shaw once again opted to write the script himself. After Shaw turned in his draft, Pascal again held script conferences to rework Shaw's version. In attendance were Anatole de Grunwald, Harold French, and David Lean, as well as German screenwriter Carl Mayer (*The Cabinet of Dr. Caligari* [Robert Wiene, 1920]). They all discussed cuts and revisions in Shaw's draft, but only Shaw and de Grunwald received a screen credit for the script.

Shaw's version of the screenplay began with a printed prologue that was to appear on the screen in his own handwriting: "Friend, what you are about to see is not an idle tale of people who never existed or things which could never have happened. It is a parable. Do not be alarmed. You will not be bored by it. It is, I hope, both true and inspired. . . . Well, friend, have I ever disappointed you? I hope that I have not."

Pascal suggested that Shaw also add an introductory scene to depict how Barbara and Cusins met. "I believe a prologue of this kind is needed badly," he urged, "to introduce the relationship between Barbara and Cusins."[21] Shaw obliged with a ten-minute scene in which the two meet for the first time at a Salvation Army street gathering in London's East End. It is love at first sight for Cusins, but not for Barbara; she will only gradually come to return Cusins's affection. This touching scene in the film takes place before the rise of the curtain in the play.

In all, Shaw added nineteen new scenes to the screenplay, some of them quite brief. The reason for the additional material, he believed, was simple: "The greater resources of the film, both financial and artistic, make it possible to take the spectators through the great Undershaft factory." They also make it possible to take them to a Salvation Army rally in Royal Albert Hall, "instead of putting them off with a spoken description" of events that must take place offstage in the original play.[22]

Shaw retained only six of the nineteen new scenes in the published version of his draft of the script—not surprisingly, they were the ones that were most heavily freighted with dialogue. As was the case with Shaw's script for *Pygmalion,* the published screenplay of *Major Barbara* "was actually much closer to the text of the original play than what is seen and heard in the film."[23]

Shaw had jettisoned some of the dialogue from the play while writing his draft of the script. But he stubbornly refused to make the additional cuts that Pascal asked for at the behest of the script doctors. As usual, Pascal pleaded abjectly with the Maestro and ultimately prevailed: "I promise to keep my faithfulness to you as an artist." He beseeched Shaw to "have faith in my judgment where to cut. . . . I only do it in extreme necessity."[24]

Principal photography began on May 26, 1940, at Denham Studios outside London. As it happened, Charles Frend found the pressure of editing the film too much for him, and he suffered a nervous breakdown one day in the editing room; Lean found him beating his head against the wall. Lean blamed Frend's collapse to some extent on Pascal, who was known to bully both cast and crew while making a film. Frend became frazzled while trying to cope with Pascal, who badgered him to edit the footage more quickly than was humanly possible. So Lean took over as sole editor of the film midway through the shooting period; Lean insisted, however, that both he and Frend be listed as editors in the credits.

Since Pascal could be a real martinet while shooting a picture, he had many squabbles with the actors on the set. Though Lean was usually on the studio floor, he did not play referee when Pascal clashed with an actor. Shaw, who occasionally visited the set, did, however, sometimes intervene, by writing out rehearsal notes for Pascal as he watched from the sidelines.

Shaw observed Pascal wrangling with Wendy Hiller, who had little confidence in Pascal as a director. Pascal chided her for being ungrateful because she apparently did not appreciate that he had provided her with her first major film role. Shaw privately expressed to Hiller his concern that Pascal was "driving her mad"; then he dashed off a note to Pascal: "It would be the height of folly to quarrel with her after we have made her a star of the first magnitude." After all, she was going to be a box office draw for the movie.

Pascal did not get along any better with Robert Morley. When Pascal was dissatisfied with the way Morley was playing a particular scene, Morley moaned, "Gabby, dear, I'm doing exactly what you asked me to do." Shaw scribbled another note to Pascal: "Don't waste time trying to coach him. You will only worry him and drive yourself mad." Shaw added sardonically, "You might as well try to teach differential calculus to an umbrella stand."[25] From then on Pascal passed on his instructions to Morley through Lean.

Robert Newton's drinking habits presented a special problem to Pascal; Newton was accustomed to drink his lunch and would, accordingly, have trouble remembering his lines in the afternoon. Pascal became so exasperated with Newton that he bellowed, "You are ruining my picture. You are crucifying me!"[26] To be fair to Pascal, Lean would experience similar difficulties with Newton later on, when he directed him in two films and found him equally hard to handle.

Pascal was displeased with Deborah Kerr's performance as Jenny in the scene in which Bill Walker (Newton) throws a tantrum at Jenny for encouraging his girlfriend to break off her liaison with him. Deborah Kerr told me in conversation that Pascal scolded her while rehearsing this scene, saying that she came across as a "constipated virgin." Lean took her aside afterward and consoled her by assuring her: "You are going to be a star someday."

Wendy Hiller sized up the direction of the film this way: Pascal was supposedly the director, "but he was just an old bumbler with a certain appreciation of good acting and of Shaw." Harold French, she continued, was really a stage director, and David Lean, "who was very clever," edited the film "and directed most of it."[27] Rex Harrison viewed things similarly, writing in his autobiography, "David Lean was known to us as the 'whispering cutter.' It was part of his job to give Pascal advice even on the set. So that it would not be too obvious, he insisted on whispering his advice into Gabby's ear—which, of course, made it far more obvious than if he had shouted his head off."[28]

When Pascal called for a complicated lighting setup that would require Neame to spend an exorbitant amount of time relighting the set, Lean had him photograph the shot without taking the time to relight the set—but with no film in the camera—just to mollify Pascal. This was referred to by the camera crew as a *Gabby take*.

Shaw, who was monitoring the progress of the production, became alarmed when Pascal fell behind schedule and started to go over budget. He wrote Pascal a letter expressing his concern, and Pascal replied that a major obstacle to finishing the film was that the war had gotten under way in earnest. Air raids regularly interrupted filming because Denham Studios was near the Royal Air Force's Denham Airfield, which was a target for the Luftwaffe. "Every time we get the camera and players set up and ready to shoot," Pascal explained, "we must race to the air raid shelters," which were concrete bunkers under the floor of the sound studio.[29]

Lean grew impatient with "the bloody air raids" and delayed calling a halt to filming until the last possible moment. Then he would call "Cut," and everyone would run for cover.[30] *Major Barbara* finally fell so far behind schedule that J. Arthur Rank himself made a personal visit to Denham and asked Pascal and his staff for an explanation. At the ensuing meeting, Pascal predictably blamed the air raids; he added that Neame, the director of photography, was "a young man, very good but very slow." Neame recalls, "Gabby needed a scapegoat; I knew I wasn't slow." Having filmed "God knows how many quota quickies," Neame knew how to work at a brisk pace. Nevertheless, Pascal threatened to replace him; Lean rescued him by taking Pascal aside and indicating that, if Neame were fired, he would personally walk off the picture. Since Lean was playing a pivotal role in the making of the film, Pascal backed down.

Harold French then spoke up and volunteered that Pascal was "shooting far too many takes" and "generally interfering with everyone."[31] Lean privately warned French that his candor might just cost him his job. As a matter of fact, after Rank read the riot act to Pascal and departed, Pascal did fire French for openly criticizing him in front of Rank. So Lean more and more filled the role of codirector during the last weeks of shooting. It was becoming common knowledge in the British film colony that Pascal was an inept director. Michael Powell, never one to mince words, once described him as a showman of some magnitude, but not a director. He knew as much about directing as a cow does about playing the piano.

Principal photography was completed on November 16, 1940. The production, which was initially scheduled for a ten-week shoot, finally took twenty-four weeks—more than double the original schedule.

Two sequences that Lean masterminded especially stand out in the finished film. The first is the Salvation Army revival meeting at the Royal Albert Hall in London, in which the General (Sybil Thorndyke) announces a generous donation from Undershaft. Lean's camera pulls back for a sweeping, panoramic view of the cheering congregation that fills the hall, while the rousing march that Walton composed for the Salvation Army band resounds through the mammoth auditorium.

But Barbara does not share in the euphoria; she is disillusioned to learn that the Army can be "bought" by a capitalist like her father—and an armaments manufacturer at that. As the cynical Bill Walker puts it, "What price salvation?"

In editing the scene that immediately follows the rally, Lean recalled a discussion he had had with the scenarist Carl Mayer. Mayer had told him that an editor can tell how good an actor is by how long he can allow a close-up of the actor to remain on the screen when the actor is not speaking. Lean tested the theory in this scene: Barbara is sitting alone on a wharf, and Lean holds a close-up of her gazing silently into the water with a disheartened expression on her face. She then throws her Salvation Army bonnet into the water, symbolizing her desire to resign. Needless to say, this searching close-up of Hiller proved her mettle as a screen actress.

Lean's outstanding contribution to the film is the climactic scene in Undershaft's munitions factory. Though Barbara disapproves of his manufacturing munitions, Undershaft manages to cajole her into permitting him to conduct a guided tour of his plant for her and Cusins. Lean shot and edited a marvelous montage sequence portraying the assembly line at Undershaft's factory. He asked Neame to go with him to photograph the sequence on location at a steel factory in Sheffield. Neame notes that, from the first moment he and Lean worked together as director and lighting cameraman, they found a rapport.

The sequence amounts to a minidocumentary: the camera pans through the plant, focusing on white-hot molten steel in cauldrons and a workman in a leather apron using huge tongs to lift an enormous ingot of glowing metal out of a fiery furnace. This awesome montage, in which Lean unleashes all the power of the cinema, is accompanied by Walton's fierce, hammering musical theme, all blaring brass and thundering percussion.

Then Lean cuts to Cusins, who shouts amid the flying sparks that Undershaft is churning out "the raw material for destruction." The unflappable industrialist replies, "Or *construction*. How about railway lines?" Overhearing her father's remark, Barbara's expression gradually melts into a smile. This is another example of Lean holding a close-up even though the actor is not speaking because the close-up speaks for itself.

After visiting the model village where Undershaft's employees and their families live in contentment, Barbara is reconciled with her father. She decides to continue her work as an evangelist among the worker inhabitants of the company village. What is more, she endorses Cusins's plan to accept Undershaft's offer to take over as plant manager so that, as Cusins asserts, he can "help the working classes help themselves." Inspired by Jenny's forbearance toward him, the shiftless Bill Walker turns over a new leaf and takes a job in Undershaft's plant. At the fade-out, Bill joins Barbara and Cusins in a march through the village, to the tune of Walton's spirited "March of Progress."

Pascal did not take the same pains to transform *Major Barbara* into a truly cinematic version of the play that he had expended on the screen adaptation of *Pygmalion,* possibly because he was spoiled by the triumph of the earlier film. As a result, the stage version of *Major Barbara* was transferred to the screen with only moderate modifications; all too often the characters are conversing in front of a static camera. As Lean often said, an editor can do a great deal in the cutting room to improve a film, but he cannot provide what he does not have on film. The critical consensus was that neither Shaw nor Pascal had rethought the play in cinematic terms and that, at 131 minutes, the film was too long.

Nonetheless, the critics singled out Wendy Hiller's accomplished performance, especially her capturing of Barbara's idealism. They likewise praised Lean's inventive handling of the montage sequence in the factory. But the film did not fare well at the box office when it opened in April 1941—even after the general release prints in both England and America were cut from

131 to 121 minutes, in an effort to make the film move along at a brisker pace. Some reviewers found *Major Barbara* a handsome and stylish picture, but the majority viewed it as a ponderous, lackluster production that nevertheless contained some admirable performances.

For the record, the home video version of the film has restored the movie to its original running time, and the picture has achieved a more positive reputation in recent years, even at its restored length. Critics reassessing *Major Barbara* when it was released to television and on videocassette in the early 1980s deemed it an intelligent comedy, with impeccable acting on the part of the entire cast. When Hiller died in 2003, several obituaries focused on her two Shaw films. The film historian Brian McFarlane called her performance in *Major Barbara* a worthy successor to that in the earlier *Pygmalion:* "Almost everything she did was choice. Think of her true-hearted, muddle-headed Major Barbara."[32]

On November 23, 1940, one week after the completion of principal photography on *Major Barbara*, David Lean married the actress Kay Walsh, who had starred in a quota quickie entitled *The Last Adventurers* (Roy Kellino, 1937), a romantic drama set in the frozen North, which Lean edited. They had lived together for several months, but, ultimately, Lean's Quaker upbringing asserted itself, and he decided to do the proper, moral thing and marry Walsh. She would later appear in some of the British films that Lean directed.

In the course of Lean's career as an editor, he worked with only two major British directors; the first was Anthony Asquith (pace Bernard Shaw), and the second was Michael Powell. The two war films that Lean edited for Powell deserve some attention, particularly *The 49th Parallel*, one of the most popular British films to come out of the war. The filmmaker Michael Powell and the screenwriter Emeric Pressburger were a dynamic duo who produced their own films. It has been said that they were like two bookends, so closely did they work together. Powell and Pressburger were becoming a major force in British cinema with thrillers like *The Spy in Black* (1939). "As soon as war was declared, we dropped everything," said Powell, and started to make war pictures.[33] In good time, they presented the scenario for *The 49th Parallel* to the Ministry of Information and petitioned for support to make the film.

The 49th Parallel (1941)

The Film Division of the Ministry of Information agreed to back *The 49th Parallel* because the film met its standards as a propaganda picture designed to boost morale in wartime. But the propaganda was wrapped in an interesting adventure story; as such, it was to be filmed on location in Canada, where the story was set, with the full cooperation of the Canadian government. The plot concerns the Nazi U-boat (or submarine) known as U-37, sunk by patrol planes of the Royal Canadian Air Force in the Gulf of St. Lawrence. The shipwrecked sailors are stranded on the Canadian coast, and they endeavor to make a trek from Hudson Bay clear across Canada, until they reach the border between Canada and the United States—the only undefended frontier in the world (the Forty-ninth Parallel on the map). America was still neutral at the time and had not yet entered the war, so the Nazi sailors hoped for sanctuary there.

The 49th Parallel was to be distributed by Rank's ubiquitous General Film Distributors. It was around this time that Powell and Pressburger formed their own independent production unit, the Archers, through which they initiated projects, arranging to finance, shoot, and release them in cooperation with various major studios. The logo of the Archers was an arrow hitting a bull's-eye. The Rank organization had by this time bought Denham Studios, Gaumont-British, and Pinewood. It was becoming a canopy under which independent filmmakers like Powell and Pressburger, as well as Gabriel Pascal, operated. Indeed, Lean would join the Rank group of independents when he became a director.

The Ministry of Information envisioned *The 49th Parallel* as a large-scale production, so Powell was able to assemble some first-class talent, like the cinematographer Freddie Young (*Nell Gwyn*) and the editor David Lean, and the acclaimed British composer Ralph Vaughan Williams would provide the background music (his first film score). In addition, major stars like Leslie Howard, Laurence Olivier, and Raymond Massey agreed to do cameos in the picture for minimum wages.

Powell shot the exteriors in Canada's great outdoors in the fall of 1940, and Pressburger was on hand to revise the script when needed. The interiors were shot at Denham Studios from February 6 through April 18, 1941.

Initially, Powell had chosen John Seabourne to edit the picture, and Seabourne undertook the task. But, apparently, once he started working on the miles of location footage that Powell had brought back from Canada, he pushed himself too hard and soon collapsed from nervous exhaustion. When Charles Frend suffered a similar fate while editing *Major Barbara*, Lean observed that, because editing is a highly complicated process, an editor can easily get stressed out while cutting a picture. Powell remembered Lean's editing of the two Shaw films and requested that Harold Boxall, a studio executive, ask Lean to take over for Seabourne. Boxall, we remember, had given Lean his very first job in the film industry at Gaumont in 1927; he had followed his career and was gratified to obtain him for this movie. He even boosted Lean's salary to £75 a week as a reward for substituting for Seabourne in an emergency. Lean had replaced Seabourne as chief editor of Gaumont-British News a decade earlier, when Seabourne had moved on to edit features; now history was repeating itself, and Lean was filling on for Seabourne again.

"Somehow it had never occurred to me that I could command the services of a craftsman like David Lean," Powell reflected. "A load dropped from my shoulders. I realized what it would mean for the film to have an editor like Lean to review . . . those thousands of feet of film." He was confident that the edit of *The 49th Parallel* was in good hands.[34]

When Lean took over as editor, he read Pressburger's script. "I settled down with it after dinner," he said, "and I couldn't stop. I was still reading it at seven the next morning."[35] Then Powell showed him all the location footage, which amounted to five hours of film. When the lights went up in the screening room, Lean said laconically, "Well, you need an editor."[36] Lean spent six weeks trimming the location footage alone from five hours to a preliminary cut of two hours.

When Powell conferred with Lean from time to time about his edit, he discovered that Lean aimed to do more than just condense the rough cut to a manageable length. He would sometimes improve a scene while he was cutting it, for example, by adroitly inserting some stock footage: Lean thought that the opening sequence needed an introductory shot of the German submarine surfacing in Canadian waters before it was sunk by Canadian bombers. With Powell's approval, he obtained some captured German newsreel of a U-boat surfacing from the depths of the Atlantic Ocean and interpolated it into the film, accompanied by Vaughan Williams's bold, mighty music.

Lean was a miraculous storyteller, Powell explained; he had a knack for shooting additional footage in order to smooth out the narrative continuity of a scene. There is, for example, the scene that occurs shortly after the Nazi fugitives land their lifeboat on the Canadian shore. Lieutenant Ernst Hirth (Eric Portman) and his men ransack a Hudson Bay trading post to steal supplies for their cross-country hike. They shoot a French Canadian trapper named Johnnie (Laurence Olivier) when he attempts to stop them. Powell remembered Lean asking him while editing the scene, "Michael, do you mind if I take a camera and shoot some close shots of hands snatching guns and knives, that kind of thing?" Powell replied, "Go ahead." So Lean filmed these shots and then inserted them into the scene in order to punch it up a bit. Powell reflected, "I gave Lean carte blanche. I had been saved by some good editors, but never on this scale. . . . I recognized that Lean is the best editor I ever worked with—or should I say worked *for?*"[37]

Hirth and his men escape from the trading post in a fighter plane that they have commandeered, but the fighter plane runs out of gas, forcing them to crash-land in a lake and swim to shore. Still they press on. In the course of the full-scale manhunt conducted by the Royal Canadian Mounted Police, the fugitives are either killed or arrested, until only Hirth and one of his men are left. During their journey through the wilderness, the two surviving Nazis encounter Philip Armstrong Scott (Leslie Howard), a professor who has set up a camp in a clearing in the woods. He lives there with some woodsmen while he is researching a book on the Indian tribes of the area. The Nazis masquerade as huntsmen, but Scott suspects that they are Nazi fugitives and valiantly confronts them. The two sailors beat a hasty retreat, in an effort to avoid capture by Scott and his men. But only Hirth gets away and remains at large.

Hirth stows away on a freight train heading for Niagara Falls, with a view to finding sanctuary in the United States. He hides in the baggage car, where he meets Andy Brock (Raymond Massey), a Canadian soldier who has gone AWOL. When the train crosses the border into the United States, a customs inspector checks the baggage car. Hirth demands that he be taken to the German consul, but Brock gets a fresh surge of patriotism and persuades the inspector to send the train back across the border so that Hirth can be arrested by the Canadian authorities. *The 49th Parallel* ends with the train steaming across the screen, returning to Canada with Hirth under arrest.

Looking back on the film, Lean said that he respected Powell but conceded that, because he was so uncommunicative, he was the most difficult director he ever worked with. According to Lean, anyone who disagreed with Powell was squelched by a stony stare. By the same token, Eric Portman told me in conversation that he crossed swords with Powell during filming because he thought Powell sometimes behaved like a dictator rather than a director.

For example, when the unit was filming the aftermath of the crash landing of the fighter plane in the lake, the actors were to extricate themselves from the wreckage and swim to shore. Portman feared that Powell had not taken sufficient precautions to see that none of the actors were hurt while they were flailing about, attempting to climb out of the wrecked plane. "Michael, are you completely mad?" Portman shouted in a fit of panic. "You're going to drown us all for your damned movie!" Powell ignored Portman and simply ordered the cameraman, Freddie Young, to "keep rolling."[38]

Moreover, said Portman, Powell was prone to fits of anger when a scene was not developing the way he wanted during rehearsals, and Portman found that disturbing. Yet, he added, he never lost sight of the fact that Powell was a first-class filmmaker, and he returned to work for Powell in his very next film, the 1942 *One of Our Aircraft Is Missing,* which Lean also edited.

Googie Withers, who also appeared in Powell's next film, affirmed that she got along well with Powell. He could be very rude with members of the cast and crew, she conceded, in order to try and get the best out of them: "He was very meticulous about what he wanted, from actors as well as everyone else." In this regard, near the end of his career Powell himself noted that, when he started out directing pictures, he was "slim, arrogant, intelligent, cocksure, and irritating," and continued, "I'm no longer slim."[39]

It might seem arrogant for Powell to maintain in interviews that *The 49th Parallel* was a "great film," but he explained that what made it great were the electrifying performances of Laurence Olivier, Leslie Howard, and Raymond Massey, as well as Lean's expert editing.[40] Certainly, the reviewers hailed the movie as outstanding when it premiered on October 8, 1941, in London. The critical encomiums mentioned the awesome footage of the vast Canadian Rockies, Powell's taut direction, the uniformly fine cast, Lean's expert editing, and the deeply patriotic, stirring score by Vaughan Williams.

The 49th Parallel is really an extended chase sequence, with spectacular vistas and bravura action, all cut to the bone by Lean's editing. The band of Nazi sailors gradually diminishes throughout the film as they are tracked down in the Mounties' manhunt, until the final showdown between Portman and Massey. The villainy has bite, the acting has conviction, and the storytelling conveys the emotional power of Pressburger's scenario. In short, *The 49th Parallel* is one of the better British propaganda films of World War II.

The film was retitled *The Invaders* in America, and 16 minutes were shorn from the original running time of 123 minutes. (Both the film's British title and its original running time were restored when the movie was released on home video in America in 1984.) Nash and Ross surmise that the scenes that were trimmed were "mostly of a travelogue nature."[41] On the contrary, the excisions were made mainly for reasons of censorship.

Thus, Hirth's ferverino to his men was mostly jettisoned; in it, he speaks of the racial superiority of the Aryan race to the Jews and the blacks. The Hollywood censor cut these lines in order not to offend minorities in America; only Hirth's remarks about Germany bringing a new order to the world remained in *The Invaders,* ending with: "Today Europe, tomorrow the world!" Some of the more violent images were also excised; for example, the shot of Johnnie the trapper bleeding to death on the floor of the trading post, after he has been gunned down by a Nazi sailor, was deleted.

By the time *The Invaders* was premiered in New York City on March 5, 1942, the United States was at war with Germany; the movie thus went over very well indeed. In fact, *The Invaders* turned out to be the top-grossing British film in America up to that date. In addition, Pressburger won an Academy Award for best original screenplay, while the film itself was nominated for best picture.

Lean had served as uncredited codirector on two films that he also edited, *Pygmalion* and *Major Barbara;* he was much interested at the time in being recognized as a film director in his own right. He took another step in that direction when he was introduced to Noël Coward, the playwright and actor. Coward was about to embark on his first film as a movie director, the 1942 *In Which We Serve,* and was looking for someone who was technically skilled enough to codirect with him. He had a hunch that David Lean was the individual he was looking for.

Looking back on his career as a film editor in the 1930s, Lean had to admit: "I am really still an editor at heart. . . . It's a wonderful feeling, handling film." For one thing, when the film is cut, one begins to see how all the work done on the set is paying off. After "the great circus" that is shooting a film, "it's wonderful to sit quietly in an editing room with the film."[42]

Chapter Three

HOPE AND GLORY

IN WHICH WE SERVE AND *THIS HAPPY BREED*

You steer the ship the best way you know how. Sometimes it's a smooth voyage; sometimes you hit the rocks. But you do the best you can in life.
—*Corrado, an aging immigrant in* The Sopranos

Carol Reed, David Lean's fellow filmmaker, told me in conversation that British documentary filmmakers were put to good advantage in the production of propaganda films during the war. Under the banner of the Ministry of Information (MOI), Humphrey Jennings and Harry Watt filmed *London Can Take It* (1940); David Lean made *Failure of a Strategy* (1944), about preparations for the Allies' D-day invasion of occupied Europe; and Reed himself jointly directed *The True Glory* (1945) with Garson Kanin, also about D-day. "The documentary impulse was noticeable in many of the wartime fiction films as well," said Reed, many of which were explicitly propagandistic, like Reed's own *The Way Ahead* (1944) and Coward and Lean's *In Which We Serve.*

In Which We Serve was among the films made during the Second World War that, like *The 49th Parallel*, gave the British cinema a fresh impetus, as strong feelings of national pride and urgency percolated in topical fiction films about the war. Noël Coward was the writer and star of *In Which We Serve,* and from the get-go David Lean was gratified to be considered as a creative associate of Coward's on this momentous film.

Just as Bernard Shaw held the cinema in disdain until he became involved with Gabriel Pascal, so too Noël Coward was wary of getting involved with the movies. For one thing, he had been generally disappointed with the early talkies made from his sophisticated plays; thus, *Private Lives* (Sidney Franklin, 1931), which starred Robert Montgomery and Norma Shearer, seemed little more than a photographed stage play (even the exteriors were painted backdrops).

Coward's first brush with the cinema was a walk-on in D. W. Griffith's World War I propaganda film *Hearts of the World* (1918), starring Lillian Gish and Erich von Stroheim. He decidedly did not have a supporting role, as some film historians, who apparently have not seen the movie, have reported. His only other appearance on the screen before *In Which We Serve* was in *The Scoundrel* (Ben Hecht and Charles MacArthur, 1935), in which a famous writer is drowned at sea and comes back as a ghost to search for the meaning of life.

In Which We Serve originated with the independent producer Filippo Del Guidice, who was the moving spirit of Two Cities Films (a company named after London and New York). The career of the Italian-born Del Guidice paralleled that of Gabriel Pascal in many ways. Like Pascal, Del Guidice came to England in the 1930s as a destitute immigrant determined to produce motion pictures. He made his mark in the British film industry with the 1939 *French without Tears* (see chapter 2).

Del Guidice asked his partner, Anthony Havelock-Allan, who knew Noël Coward socially, to arrange a meeting in which they could persuade Coward to make a major film to serve the British war effort. Coward was intrigued with their proposal. "The actual proposition they put to me," Coward records in his autobiography, was that he was to codirect and produce a film for them—as well as write the script, compose the score, and play the lead. If he agreed, he would have complete artistic control over the production. "The very next evening Fate intervened," Coward continues. He was dining with Lord Louis Mountbatten, a commander in the Royal Navy, who had just come home after the sinking of his ship, HMS *Kelly,* in the Mediterranean off the island of Crete on May 21, 1941. "He told me the whole story; I was profoundly moved . . . by this odyssey of one destroyer. I knew this was a story to tell, if only I could tell it without sentimentality, but with simplicity and truth."[1]

Once Coward had made a definite commitment, Del Guidice obtained British Lion to distribute the movie. When Coward informed Havelock-Allan that he intended to take the role of the captain of the destroyer in the film, Havelock-Allan reflected that, though the debonair Coward was nobody's idea of a sea dog, he would do a credible job. Indeed, the press, particularly Lord Beaverbrook's *Daily Express,* raised a hue and cry when the project was announced. Beaverbrook's broadside, published on August 29,

1941, sneered at the very notion that Coward was to play a part modeled on the stalwart Mountbatten since Coward's public image was that of a matinee idol belonging to the cigarette holder and smoking jacket set. The yellow press also implied that the effete Coward, whose homosexuality was an open secret in theater circles, was not an appropriate choice for the role of a naval commander. Coward replied that he was not playing the real Mountbatten; rather, he was to enact the role of Captain Edward Kinross, a fictional character who was conceived as "an average naval officer," the skipper of the *Torrin*, not the *Kelly*. Admittedly, Coward writes, the film's scenario was inspired by the story of the *Kelly*. He was able to get "first-hand information and accurate technical details" from Mountbatten and those of his shipmates who survived the disaster. "The story told in *In Which We Serve*, however, could have applied to any other destroyer sunk in action during the war."[2]

In Which We Serve (1942)

Del Guidice and Havelock-Allan petitioned the Film Division of the MOI to cooperate with the making of the film, as it had given cooperation to Powell and Pressburger for the making of *The 49th Parallel* and *One of Our Aircraft Is Missing* (see chapter 2). Coward submitted a preliminary prose treatment to Jack Beddington, the director of the Film Division; it was a fictionalized account of the captain and crew of a destroyer from commissioning to sinking. Beddington responded in writing that the MOI could not endorse a film that portrayed an English ship being sunk by enemy action; that was bad for British morale, particularly in wartime. (Ironically, *One of Our Aircraft Is Missing*—a project that was heartily endorsed by the MOI—begins with the crash of a Royal Air Force bomber, shot down over enemy territory.) Beddington ended his report to Coward by questioning whether such a film should be made at all.

The contents of Beddington's memo, Coward recalled, "left me speechless with rage." He said to himself, "When else do ships sink so frequently," if not in wartime? Coward immediately contacted Mountbatten, who happened to be in London at the time, and the latter personally sent a copy of the scenario not only to Sir Thomas Phillips at the Admiralty but to King George VI as well. Sir Thomas took the view that the story was a patriotic tribute to the *Torrin*, a British destroyer fighting gallantly in defense of the realm.

King George responded, "Although the ship is lost, the spirit which animates the Royal Navy is clearly brought out in the men."[3] The king also accepted Coward's invitation for himself and Queen Elizabeth to visit the set during filming. Armed with an endorsement from the Admiralty—not to mention one from the king—Coward and Mountbatten paid a visit to the MOI. Mountbatten confronted Beddington, and the hapless official wilted before his tirade. As a result, the MOI did not again interfere with the production. Still, it extended to Coward for his war film none of the technical and logistic cooperation given Powell and Pressburger for theirs. Nevertheless, Coward obviously would have the support of the Royal Navy in the making of the movie because of Mountbatten's involvement in the project.

When Coward visited the set of *One of Our Aircraft Is Missing,* looking for technicians to be part of the production crew of *In Which We Serve,* he made a beeline for Lean, whom the director Carol Reed had already recommended to him. That recommendation was, as Sir Carol put it to me in conversation many years later, "the biggest goddamned mistake I ever made"—since, once Lean became established as a major director with *In Which We Serve,* a long-lasting debate arose in British film circles as to whether Lean or Reed was the top British director. Guy Green, who at various times had served as director of photography for both Lean and Reed, commented that the two filmmakers remained best friends over the years, despite the implicit rivalry that resulted from their both being considered Britain's two best directors.

At any rate, at the time Coward chose Lean, he was aware that Lean was not only a renowned film editor but also the putative codirector of *Pygmalion* and *Major Barbara* (see chapter 2). Hence, he realized that Lean's technical acumen would serve him well. Lean would handle the camera setups and tell him which lens to use; meanwhile, Coward would be free to concentrate on directing the actors.

There was only one hitch in Lean's negotiations with Coward, conducted in the sitting room of Coward's lush apartment in Gerald Road just off Eaton Square: Lean's screen credit. Sandra Lean recounts that Coward offered to list Lean in the film's credits as assistant to the director, which was the title that Pascal imposed on him for codirecting *Major Barbara.* Kay Walsh, then Lean's wife, had urged him to hold out for a full codirector screen credit. Consequently, Sandra Lean continues, Lean responded to Coward during their conference: "I want to be designated as codirector." Also present at the meeting was Gladys Calthrop, who had designed the sets for Coward's stage plays and was involved in the present film. A staunch member of the Coward camp, she interposed, "Everyone knows Noel Coward; who has ever heard of David Lean [outside the film industry]?" Lean replied, "One day I hope they will hear of me." Coward paused for a moment, mulling over Lean's demand, then snapped, "Agreed!"[4]

Coward chose Ronald Neame as director of photography; he had been introduced to both Neame and Lean on the set of *One of Our Aircraft Is Missing*. And he had heard good reports about Neame's work on that film and on *Major Barbara*. Thelma Meyers was to serve as Lean's assistant editor. Once it was settled that Lean was to be listed as the movie's codirector, union rules precluded his receiving an additional screen credit as film editor. So Meyers was officially designated as film editor, with the understanding that Lean would oversee her work.

"The people who worked with me on the film were hand-picked," Coward comments in his autobiography. "It would have been difficult to have gone astray with David Lean and Ronald Neame, from whom I had whole-hearted, intelligent, and affectionate cooperation." Besides Lean and Neame, Coward was to work with two producers: as executive producer, "the over-exuberant and loveable Filippo Del Giudice, who never allowed his faith in me and the picture to be shaken for a moment"; and as associate producer, the dependable Anthony Havelock-Allan.[5] Though Coward was the official producer of the picture, he himself admitted that, for all practical purposes, Havelock-Allan was in charge of production.

Lean very much wanted Havelock-Allan to engage Muir Mathieson to conduct Coward's background music for the film. Mathieson often selected the composers of the film scores he conducted, securing distinguished composers like William Walton, who scored *Major Barbara*, and Ralph Vaughan Williams, who composed the underscore for *The 49th Parallel*. Later on, Lean had Mathieson supervise the background music for all the British films he directed right up to the mid-1950s. He stated in a television interview that he was in agreement with Mathieson that the music should be an integral part of a film's creative process.[6] Like Mathieson, Lean believed that it must be not mere decoration or a filler of gaps, but accepted as part of the architecture of a film.

Coward's principal task during the weeks before production began was, of course, to fashion the first draft of the screenplay, which had the tentative working title *White Ensign*. After three months of work, Coward invited Lean, Neame, and Havelock-Allan to his flat in Gerald Road to hear him read the rough draft. Lean remembered that it took Coward two and a half hours to read all that he had written: "It was very rambling and contained a lot of dialogue." At the end of the reading, Coward asked Lean, "What do you think of that, my dear?" "Well, it was wonderful," Lean answered, "but what you've read would run for five hours on the screen."[7] To Coward's consternation, Neame and Havelock-Allan backed Lean's reaction.

The scenario started in 1922 in the Caribbean—long before the war—

and then went on to Paris. In this manner, Coward gave detailed background material on the principal characters, only gradually moving on to World War II and the saga of the *Torrin*. What is more, he had borrowed lengthy passages from Mountbatten's speeches to his sailors, passages that would slow the action down. Lean sought to mollify Coward by suggesting that he needed a method of choosing the best of the material he had already written. Perhaps he should structure the story around a series of flashbacks; this device would enable the telescoping of time by jumping from one flashback to another. Coward agreed to try this approach. A few days later, he advised Lean that the script would revolve around a group of survivors as they cling to a rubber raft floating in the sea. Each recalls in flashback how his life has been inseparably involved with the fortunes of the *Torrin* since joining her crew. Several incidents in the first draft constituted self-contained units, so Coward was able simply to pick the episodes that he judged suitable for the flashbacks and scuttle the rest. Coward told Lean that it would take him about two weeks to do the second draft of the script along these lines.

Though Coward's preliminary draft clearly needed work, Lean was hooked on doing the picture. Michael Powell phoned him around this time with another offer. Silverman says it was to edit a picture scripted by Emeric Pressburger. But it was, in fact, an offer to direct the film, which was entitled *Battle for Music,* about the trials and tribulations of the London Philharmonic bravely attempting to give concerts during the Blitz.

Lean informed Powell that he was committed to the Coward film. The volatile Powell exploded, calling Lean a cheap tart, window-shopping on Bond Street: "You see an expensive, glittering jewel in a window and you just can't resist it."[8] Lean correctly chose the more promising project; in the end, *Battle for Music* (1943) was directed by Donald Taylor and turned out to be a mediocre movie at best, while the Coward project went on to be a great success.

A couple of weeks after Coward began revising the script, he turned over to Lean his second draft, now definitely titled *In Which We Serve.* The title was derived from the morning prayer recited aboard all Royal Navy vessels: "Almighty God, receive under your protection this ship in which we serve. . . ." Coward then said to Lean, "Now, my dear, I don't know a damned thing about how to shoot things."[9] It was up to Lean to prepare the final shooting script. But Coward's second draft was still overly long, so Lean worked with Neame and Havelock-Allan on an abridged version, excising extraneous subplots and sticking to the story of the *Torrin,* from the time it was launched to the time it sank off Crete. Coward approved the suggested deletions.

Apart from the problem of length, the screenplay was a fine piece of work. Lean was impressed with the manner in which Coward delineated the personalities of the individual characters. Each one had been given a specific background, indicating where he grew up, whom he married, and who his friends were, thus suggesting what made him tick. Lean commented, "As Noel Coward said, 'You ought to know what they would eat for breakfast, though you never have a scene in which they eat breakfast.'"

Before developing the shooting script from Coward's second draft, Lean interviewed Mountbatten about the sinking of the *Kelly*. The two spent an evening in an office at Denham Studios, where *In Which We Serve* was to be shot, and where Lean had worked on *Major Barbara* and other films. Lean remembered Mountbatten describing how Messerschmitt fighter planes dive-bombed the *Kelly*. When the destroyer began to capsize, Mountbatten gave the order to abandon ship, but he stayed on the bridge, in accordance with the venerable navy principle that the captain should be the last to leave his vessel. "Before I knew it, I was underwater," said Mountbatten. "I was actually under the ship as it was turning over. I came up to the surface on the other side and got my first breath of air; and that saved my life." Lean added that this was the sort of invaluable background material that Mountbatten provided him with behind the scenes.[10]

Lean set about composing the final shooting script, aided by both Neame and Terry Lawlor, who had been Mountbatten's cabin hand. Lawlor was assigned by Mountbatten to serve as a technical adviser to Lean; he was an ordinary seaman who had survived the sinking of the *Kelly*. Lean would work out an action sequence, and then Lawlor would provide him with additional data. For example, he explained how, after the Nazi dive-bombers sank the ship, he and some of the other survivors clung to an inflated rubber raft (technically termed a Carley float) that was not big enough to hold all twelve of them. Lean would then write this material into the final shooting script.

In general, Lean saw the shooting script as the blueprint for filming the picture. Starting with *In Which We Serve*, he formed the habit of mapping out the action of every scene in a shooting script in great detail, in terms of camera angles, sound effects, and so on. This method was especially important, he stated in correspondence, for the big action sequences. All the important imaginative thinking, he maintained, had to be done before shooting commenced; there was no time for lengthy improvisations on the set when a director was working with numerous actors and technicians. Lean would alter the shooting script only slightly as filming proceeded; it was, after all, the handbook guiding the making of the film. He noted laconically that neither he nor Neame or Havelock-Allan, who assisted him in revising Coward's screenplay at various stages, received a screen credit for their efforts.

Neame recalls in his autobiography that, while he was helping Lean with the shooting script, Coward made a timely suggestion. Not forgetting the scathing campaign against the project waged by Beaverbrook, Coward thought they might get their own back by inserting a short scene into the shooting script as a jibe at the *Daily Express*. He said that Havelock-Allan had reminded him of a headline published in the *Express* in January 1939—"No War This Year"—when, in actual fact, war was declared just eight months later. He then said to Lean and Neame, "Get out your pencils, my little darlings!"[11]

Havelock-Allan states in his unpublished memoirs that Coward gave them the layout of a brief scene incorporating the headline and that he, following Coward's instructions, interpolated it into the final screenplay: "Long shot: the London docks filled with warships. Cut to a shot of the *Daily Express* headline, 'No War This Year.' Bits of excrement cling to the newspaper's edges as it floats slowly downstream in the filthy waters of the Thames." Suffice it to say, Beaverbrook was apoplectic when this scene appeared in the finished film. He blamed Coward alone for it, "never knowing," as Havelock-Allan says, "that it was me [who actually wrote it]; and Noel never disabused him of the idea."[12]

With the start of production nearing, Del Guidice rented two soundstages at Denham, one of which was among the largest in any British studio. On this gargantuan stage, the production designer, David Rawnsley, built a replica of a destroyer, working from the original blueprints of the *Kelly*. Rawnsley also chose the location sites for the exteriors. He was assisted in his work on the film by the art director, Gladys Calthrop, who was responsible for the interior settings.

Still actively supporting the production behind the scenes, Mountbatten saw to it that the *Torrin* was manned not only by film extras but by some authentic sailors as well. In fact, the latter were convalescents from a nearby naval hospital. Moreover, Mountbatten arranged for Havelock-Allan and Neame to take a camera crew to the Newcastle shipyards to shoot footage for the documentary-like opening sequence of the building of the *Torrin*. Havelock-Allan says in his memoirs that he was the director of the second unit and that Neame was the cinematographer. There were, according to Havelock-Allen, several vessels being built simultaneously, so he and Neame were able to film shots of ships at various stages of construction. Later on, Lean employed his editing expertise to interweave this compilation of shots "so that it looks like the building of a single ship."[13]

In the shipyard sequence, there are close-ups of hot rivets being driven into steel plates, girders being lowered into place, and the laying of the keel—all leading up to a champagne bottle being smashed across the ship's hull at the launching ceremony. The *Torrin* then steams grandly into the sea as the Union Jack is hoisted above the stern. Just before the principal photography began, as a final gesture Mountbatten loaned Coward his braided officer's cap to wear in the film.

Lean, Neame, and Havelock-Allan assembled a top-notch cast; indeed, they spent long hours interviewing candidates for each role. John Mills was recruited to play Ordinary Seaman Shorty Blake. "David Lean had the reputation for not getting on with actors," Mills commented, "but I can't join that club." As Mills noted, he and Lean "started together in *In Which We Serve*" and then went on to make four pictures together, a record topped only by Alec Guinness, with six Lean films.[14]

Bernard Miles was to play Chief Petty Officer Walter Hardy and Joyce Carey his wife, Kath Hardy. The stage actress Celia Johnson was cast as Captain Kinross's wife, Alix, after buttonholing Coward at a party and saying she would like to get into pictures. Coward gave her a screen test and found her right for the part, but Neame had doubts about her because he thought her unphotogenic. Coward overruled him, saying that the middle-aged wife of a sea captain did not have to be especially attractive, just a good actress. Johnson, Miles, and Carey would, like Mills, appear in subsequent Lean films.

Kay Walsh was up for the role of Freda Lewis, who marries Shorty Blake. Lean vetoed having his wife in the film because he feared the appearance of nepotism. But Coward tested her and wisely overrode Lean's decision. She would appear not only in this film but in other Lean pictures as well. In addition, James Donald took the part of the ship's doctor and would again play a medical officer for Lean in *The Bridge on the River Kwai*.

Care was taken even in casting the smallest roles; Lean rang an actor's agent in search of a youngster to play a cowardly sailor. "He's just a frightened rabbit," said Lean, "and one's heart should go out to him. . . . I think people will remember him afterwards."[15] The agent recommended seventeen-year-old Richard Attenborough. In retrospect, Attenborough is ambivalent about the role; it led, he says, to his being typecast for some time as a spiv or "the coward below decks." On the contrary, what leaps out today is "a nervous quality that barely masks an underlying vulnerability." Despite the fact that Attenborough was not listed in the cast credits, his part in *In Which We Serve* jump-started his film career.[16]

It is interesting to note how the cast of characters represents a cross section of British society. Captain Kinross is upper-class, Chief Petty Officer Hardy is middle-class, and Ordinary Seaman Blake (complete with a Cockney accent) is working-class. The implication for the audience is that "we are all in this together," war binding people together in solidarity and loyalty to a common cause in a manner that transcends class barriers.

Principal photography commenced on February 5, 1942. Coward recalled that he, Lean, and Neame were quivering with nerves at the prospect of the monumental production that they were undertaking: "But as the day went on [those nerves] evaporated, as they usually do under the stress of intense work."[17]

When Lean was assisting Gabriel Pascal in shooting *Major Barbara,* his responsibilities expanded to the point where his importance on the set grew to rival that of the director he was supposed to be assisting—until he virtually took over from Pascal. Something similar happened during the filming of *In Which We Serve.* "Noel very soon got terribly bored photographing the picture," said Lean. It often took an hour or more to light the set for each camera setup, and Coward got restless waiting around between shots. He finally told Lean, "Look, my dear, you know what you are doing. I'll leave it to you." He added that he would come to the set only whenever he was to be photographed in a scene. Still, Lean observed that Coward had a natural instinct for directing actors and that he often made worthwhile suggestions to the actors when they were rehearsing a scene that he was in. But he always left it to Lean to film each scene. "So," Lean concluded, "I virtually directed the film myself."[18]

Lean was at first nervous about coaching the actors when Coward was not around since his primary expertise was on the technical side of moviemaking, especially film editing. But he gained self-confidence as time went on, as the actors listened to his advice and followed it. He found that, the better and more experienced the actors were, like Celia Johnson and Bernard Miles, the easier they were to work with.

Lean particularly remembered Johnson's rendering of the toast that she proposes as the captain's wife at the ship's Christmas party while the *Torrin* is in port: "Ladies and gentlemen, I give you my rival—because to a sailor the ship always comes first. It is extraordinary that anyone should be so proud and so fond of an always permanent and undisputed rival. God bless this ship and all who sail on her." Lean said her speech brought tears to his eyes as she delivered it on the set.

Lean really showed his mettle as a director in his handling of one of the movie's big set pieces in its entirety. The scene dealt with the return of the British Expeditionary Force from Dunkirk, the beleaguered French beachhead where the Allied forces were defeated by the Nazis after suffering heavy German artillery fire. In June 1940, the *Torrin* and an armada of English vessels evacuated the survivors from Dunkirk and transported their human cargo to the safety of British piers. In the film, the wounded soldiers present a grim tableau as they stand on the Dover dock, tattered and tired. Lean's camera pans laterally across their weary, forlorn faces as they stare blankly ahead. But the troops snap to attention at the word of command, ready to proceed to inland relocation camps. Then they march away to the tune of a jaunty march, prefiguring the British prisoners of war marching to "The Colonel Bogey March" in Lean's *Bridge over the River Kwai*. The survivors of Dunkirk are played by the Fifth Battalion of the Coldstream Guards, and Lean executed the scene with the assured sense of a very promising young director.

Some commentators assume that this sequence was Lean's first complete scene as a solo director. They are apparently overlooking the two Higgins-Eliza montage scenes in *Pygmalion* and the factory montage in *Major Barbara* (see chapter 2).

During shooting, Mountbatten supplied two technical advisers, and both Coward and Lean were grateful. As Coward put it, "I realized from the outset that it was essential to the accuracy of the picture [to have experienced seamen on hand as consultants]."[19] One adviser was Commander L. T. Clarke, a former destroyer captain, and the other was Terry Lawlor, the ordinary seaman who had helped Lean at the script stage.

Filming proceeded slowly but steadily, Coward writes in his autobiography, but he found filming the scenes of the survivors of the *Torrin* floating in the sea very trying. The surface of the water was supposed to be covered with fuel oil that had escaped from the sinking ship, but a synthetic substance was, of course, utilized in place of real crude oil. Coward recalled "nine very uncomfortable days" when he, John Mills, Bernard Miles, and ten others spent from 8:30 A.M. to nearly 6:30 P.M. clinging to a rubber raft in the studio tank on the back lot at Denham Studios. The tank was filled with "warm but increasingly filthy water," and the actors were "smeared with synthetic fuel oil," which was hard to scrape off at the end of the day.[20]

But Coward's greatest ordeal came in late June, when he had to film some inserts of the sinking of the *Torrin*. A replica of the bridge of the destroyer had been erected on the back lot, Coward writes; above it, "three enormous tanks filled with thousands of gallons of water . . . were perched on a scaffolding," aimed at the set. "On a given signal, a lever would be pulled, whereupon the tanks would disgorge their load down a chute and overturn the bridge with me on it"—sweeping the captain overboard.[21]

Lean had assumed that a stunt double would stand in for Coward in this shot, but Coward would not hear of it. He wanted Lean and Neame to be able to get close shots of the captain. Still, when Coward got a look at the setup, he refused to shoot the take until the apparatus was tested, in order to ascertain what exactly the impact of that vast amount of water would be on the flimsy wooden bridge on which he was to stand. According to Coward's autobiography, Lean and Neame grumbled about the waste of time involved in the test. But Neame respectfully disputes this in his own autobiography; he writes that he and Lean agreed with Coward that they should do a test run of the shot before filming it.[22]

Lean accordingly gave the signal for the water to be released while he, Coward, and Neame watched. The torrent came hurtling down the chute with such force that it totally demolished the set. Lean and Neame, "pale and trembling," writes Coward, acknowledged that, had Coward been standing on the bridge, he could have been drowned.[23]

The set was rebuilt of stronger materials, and the shot was at last taken on June 27, 1942, the last day of filming. "The water struck me in the back," Coward records; "the structure slowly capsized as planned." Coward himself landed in the studio tank.[24] Perhaps because Lean felt that Coward had suffered enough while shooting this take, he told Coward it would not be necessary to get a shot of him flailing about underwater. Instead, he borrowed a shot from *The Scoundrel,* showing Coward floundering underwater, attempting to save himself from drowning. Then, in the editing room, Lean adroitly inserted the borrowed shot, and no one seeing the film was the wiser.

Lean spent the summer of 1942 editing *In Which We Serve* with his assistant, Thelma Meyers. He skillfully intercut shots of Kinross on the captain's bridge, binoculars hanging round his neck, with newsreel footage of aircraft overhead and a destroyer plowing through the waves. Indeed, Lean brought to bear the realistic techniques being used in wartime documentaries to give the film an urgent sense of authenticity, to which his experience as a newsreel editor contributed enormously.

The film's preface, spoken by the narrator, Leslie Howard (uncredited), states, "This is the story of a ship." But it is also the story of her crew, whose loyalty to one another is grounded in devotion to their ship.

The film proper begins with Lean's documentary-like sequence of the building of the ship, described already. The film that follows does not have a conventional linear plot. It consists, instead, of "a mosaic of episodes," developing in a series of vignettes encompassing the recollections of a handful of the *Torrin's* men.[25]

There are, for example, Captain Kinross's memories of his short holiday with his loyal wife, Alix, and their two children while he is on leave and of the time that the *Torrin* helped rescue the army at Dunkirk. Ordinary Seaman Shorty Blake remembers how he met and married Freda Lewis, who, coincidentally, is a niece of Chief Petty Officer Walter Hardy. In correlated flash-backs dealing with the memories of Blake and Hardy, the viewer learns of the attack by Nazi bombers on Plymouth, where Freda, who is pregnant, is living with Hardy's wife, Kath. When an enemy shell hits the house, Freda survives, but Kath is killed. Then, in a genuinely poignant moment, Shorty must break the news to Walter that he has lost his home and his wife to the Blitz. The "newly widowed sea salt" stoically mutters that he is glad that at least his shipmate's wife and her unborn child were miraculously saved. Then he walks out on deck and "mutely pitches overboard his last, unfinished letter to his wife."[26]

Not all the crew of the *Torrin* are heroes. "A coward was featured in the Coward epic, *In Which We Serve,* and it wasn't dear Noel," writes Ken Russell. The craven coward let his side down by deserting his post at the height of a battle. "Even when he goes on shore leave—alone, of course—he is not allowed to forget his shame. The pianola in the pub where he goes to drown his sorrows is playing 'Run, Rabbit, Run.' The same tune is later played on a harmonica by one of the other survivors, as he hangs on to the Carley float with one hand and holds his harmonica in the other."[27] Moments later, the cowardly lad is machine-gunned by a low-flying enemy plane, but he dies with a smile on his lips as Captain Kinross's consoling words ring in his ears: "I'll write your parents and tell them they can be proud of you."

At long last the survivors are rescued by another British vessel and taken to Alexandria to recuperate. In the closing scene, Kinross bids a dockside farewell to the remaining members of his crew in a dusty cargo shed, before their dispersal to new assignments. He gives a short speech, which Coward cribbed from a similar one given by Lord Mountbatten to the crew of the *Kelly.* He says in part: "The *Torrin* is gone; now she lies in fifteen hundred fathoms and with more than half our shipmates. They all lie together with the ship we loved, and they're in very good company." He concludes with a lump in his throat: "The next time you're in action, remember the *Torrin!*"

James Agee commented that, while Coward is "exceedingly good" in the film, his delivery of Kinross's farewell to his crew "is a really remarkable and moving tour de force."[28] So much for the press's complaining early on that Coward was miscast in the leading part. Accompanied by the rousing martial strains of Coward's underscore, the narrator declares, "Here ends the story of a ship. But there will be other ships and other men to sail them, for we are an island race. They give to us and to all their countrymen eternal pride."

Coward was on hand for the film's London premiere on September 27, 1942. The picture got an ecstatic reception, and, as Coward noted, in the notices in the press, "David Lean, Ronnie Neame, and I received most of the superlatives in the English language." Coward described Lean, Neame, and Havelock-Allan as his exceedingly staunch native bearers, who had guided him through the perilous terrain of the film business.[29] He went on to win a Special Academy Award for outstanding production achievement.

In Which We Serve was immensely popular on both sides of the Atlantic and proved to be the most successful British movie to come out of the war. Filippo Del Guidice, who was at first excoriated around Denham Studios for pouring £1 million into a motion picture production during wartime, won the day since the movie grossed twice its original investment in its initial release in England.

Prior to the movie's release in America the following December, the Hollywood censor, Joseph Ignatius Breen, required that the *hells* and *damns* that peppered the salty dialogue of the sailors be removed from the sound track. His action prompted a spirited debate in the House of Commons, whereby the American censor was himself censured for tampering with the dialogue of an important English film. The uncensored British version of the movie was released on home video in the United States in 1995. The DVD release in the United States in 2005 is likewise the original version. (The DVD lists David Lean as the director, not the codirector with Coward.)

The tempest in a teacup over censorship did not obscure the merits of the picture in America or anywhere else. To begin with, this wartime movie was helped along by the best efforts of the ensemble cast. Clearly affected by the grittiness of their surroundings, Coward, Mills, Miles, and the other players came together as a band of brothers coping with disaster. The flashbacks formed a succession of more or less self-contained segments, flawlessly melded together by David Lean's editing. What is more, Neame's crisp, clever cinematography transformed the studio tank into a cruel sea. Seen today, *In Which We Serve* holds up with nary a sag; it remains a hard-edged, unsqueamish war picture that is British to its back teeth. It keeps the screen packed with action and excitement in the war sequences; it also tells a thumping good personal story of the seafarers' families on the home front.

In Which We Serve was thought of by both the press and the public as largely a Noël Coward production since he wrote the script, codirected the film, and starred in it. But industry insiders were fully cognizant of the fact that Lean did most of the direction and was primarily responsible for editing the picture. For his part, Lean was gratified to have gained experience in directing actors. In an essay on film directing, he stressed the director's need not only "for technical knowledge about cameras and editing" but also for the ability of "working with actors."[30] All in all, the artistic and popular success of the film was something of a feather in Lean's cap. No one was more aware of Lean's contributions to the movie than Noël Coward, who made Lean an offer he could not refuse: "Well, dear boy, you can take anything I've written and make a film of it."[31]

Lean proceeded to form an independent production company with Ronald Neame and Anthony Havelock-Allan and set about arranging to film some of Coward's stage plays. The name of the company was suggested to Havelock-Allan by the most prestigious theater company in New York at the time, the Theater Guild. He thought they should call their production unit Cineguild because they wanted to produce significant films for British cinema in much the same way that the Theater Guild produced significant plays for the Broadway stage.

The team would eventually produce seven of Lean's films, but they decided to launch Cineguild with film adaptations of two Coward plays, *This Happy Breed* and *Blithe Spirit*. "Noel didn't really enjoy film direction," Lean explained. "He liked writing and acting best." So, by the time *In Which We Serve* was completed, he did not want to be actively involved in the next venture of Lean and company.[32] It was decided that Lean and Neame would compose the film script for *This Happy Breed*, while Coward was away entertaining British troops in South Africa and Asia, and that Coward would consult on the screenplay when he returned. "It was pleasant to be concerned with the picture, but not trapped by it," Coward writes in his autobiography. "With David and Ronnie doing all the actual work, I could say what I had to say and get out."[33]

Lean's triumvirate joined the cluster of independent film units operating under the financial umbrella of the Rank organization. This coalition of independent production units, already mentioned, was now known collectively as Independent Producers. J. Arthur Rank, who was nicknamed "King Arthur," offered unprecedented artistic freedom to Powell and Pressburger's Archers, Del Guidice's Two Cities Films, and Pascal Film Productions, as well as to Cineguild.

Rank firmly believed that the best way to deal with these independent moviemakers was to sign the checks and allow them to accomplish their creative work as they saw fit. He encouraged independent producers because he was now more convinced than ever that such enterprising individuals would help him penetrate the jealously guarded American market. He was "a man of vision who was committed to contesting the global stranglehold of the American film industry." After all, he emphasized, the continued existence of British film production depended on "overseas trade"—meaning mostly American distribution for British pictures.[34] Powell and Pressburger's *The*

49th Parallel, Pascal's *Pygmalion,* and Del Guidice's *In Which We Serve* had done just that—and David Lean was involved in all these films.

In sum, under Rank's leadership, some remarkable filmmaking talents "were allowed to flourish," and their films helped develop the American art house circuit during the postwar years. Whenever Rank's managing director and chief accountant, John Davis, complained that one of the independents was spending too much money on a film, Rank would reply, "Don't discourage the boys, John. It's their job to make the films and our job to sell them."[35]

Though the first feature on the Cineguild docket was a film adaptation of Coward's play *This Happy Breed,* Cineguild was also responsible for a short documentary, which Lean directed. *Failure of a Strategy* (1944) was made by Cineguild for the Film Division of the MOI, which had apparently forgotten about the controversy it had generated over the making of *In Which We Serve,* probably because Beddington was no longer in charge of the MOI.

Lean was asked to direct a twenty-minute documentary principally for distribution in countries liberated from Nazi occupation. Lean made the documentary in his spare time while working on *This Happy Breed.* He and the editor, Peter Tanner, screened miles of footage from British, American, and captured German newsreels in order to put together a survey of the war in Europe, from the fall of France to the Allies' preparations for the invasion of occupied Europe on D-day.

Lean edited much of the documentary himself. "You couldn't keep him away from the Moviola," says Tanner.[36] Once again, his training as a newsreel editor stood him in good stead. The documentary short was first shown in liberated French towns under the title *L'echec d'une strategie,* beginning on June 9, 1944, just three days after D-day. The film carried no screen credits except for "Written and Produced by Cineguild," but the movie had the mark of Lean's craftsmanship and was a flag-waver of some merit.

This Happy Breed (1944)

Most of Lean's efforts during this period were expended on *This Happy Breed,* his debut as a solo director, starting with cowriting the screenplay with Neame. The play dramatizes the lives of Frank and Ethel Gibbons and their working-class family between the wars. Though Coward was given a screen credit as the author of the screenplay, he served mostly in a consultative capacity. He did, however, contribute additional dialogue when it was required for a new scene, and he composed the film's score, as he had done for *In Which We Serve.*

In April 1943, Coward was appearing as the male lead in a limited engagement of the play in London. He would drive to Denham occasionally for story conferences with Lean and Neame, in which Havelock-Allan also participated. Coward was again billed as the producer of the film, as he was on *In Which We Serve,* and once again he left most of the producer's chores to Havelock-Allan, who was listed as associate producer. During these script conferences, Lean would submit to Coward the excisions in the play's dialogue that he, Neame, and Havelock-Allan thought necessary. Coward usually approved their decisions in these matters.

Lean did remember, however, that he and Havelock-Allan had a dreadful quarrel with Coward over an additional cut in the dialogue that they wanted to make at the eleventh hour, after the movie was already in production. At the end of the play, Frank addresses little Frankie, his first grandchild, in his baby carriage. This monologue ran more than an entire page in the play, a long, static speech with Frank mouthing patriotic platitudes to a small child. Lean, with Havelock-Allan's support, asked Coward if he could condense this speech. Like Bernard Shaw in the case of the film of *Major Barbara,* Coward had reached the point where he was not prepared to make any further concessions to the moviemakers. But, after much debate, he reluctantly agreed.

The oration that all the fuss was about says in part: "Ordinary people like you and me know what we belong to, where we come from, and where we're going. . . . We haven't lived and died and struggled all these hundreds of years to get decency and justice and freedom for ourselves without being prepared to fight fifty wars if need be to keep them."[37] As a matter of fact, Lean ended up deleting the entire speech. But Coward was sufficiently pleased with the finished film that he thought it would be captious to quibble about the missing monologue.

When *This Happy Breed* opened in London, Coward remembered, some critics implied that he had set the play "in a milieu far removed from the cocktail and caviar stratum to which I so obviously belonged." As a result, they detected "an attitude on my part of amused condescension" toward the common people. Orson Welles, reviewing the play for a New York daily, went so far as to pontificate that Coward was a "Mayfair playboy" and that his play was "perpetuating a British public school snobbery."[38] In point of fact, Coward was born in a lower-middle-class neighborhood in Teddington and grew up in similar neighborhoods in Battersea Park and Clapham Common. As he later wrote, "I can confidently assert that I know a great deal more about the hearts and minds of ordinary South Londoners than the critics gave me credit for."[39]

The play, as does the film derived from it, portrays how an average English family endured what befell them during a twenty-year period, led on by their common sense and natural resilience. The title alludes to John of Gaunt's speech in Shakespeare's *Richard II,* wherein the English people are described as "this happy breed of men." The emerging realism of British cinema in the early 1940s continued to grow during the war years because of morale-boosting movies like *This Happy Breed,* with its story about ordinary people coping with their daily lives as Europe moves ever closer to the brink of chaos.

In writing the screenplay for *This Happy Breed,* Lean realized that the play, which took place in the single setting of the Gibbonses' dining room, had to be opened out for the screen. That is, the film could and should present more incidents, spread out over more settings, than was possible within the confines of the proscenium arch of a theater stage. Accordingly, Lean decided to portray in a series of montages various national events that in the play took place offstage and were only referred to in the dialogue. In this fashion, he extended the action of the film and kept it from becoming static. These incidents included the parades of veterans returning home at the end of World War I in 1919, the Empire Exhibition at Wembley in 1924, and the outbreak of World War II in 1939. By the early winter of 1943, Lean and Neame had scouted locations in and around London where these episodes would be filmed.

The story begins with Frank and Ethel Gibbons and their three children, Reg, Vi, and Queenie, moving into 17 Sycamore Road, Clapham Common. The youngsters in due course grow up, with Reg marrying his childhood sweetheart, Phyllis, Vi wedding Reg's mate Sam, and Queenie being courted by Billy Mitchell, the sailor boy next door.

Lean and Neame believed that this tale of ordinary British folk maintaining a stiff upper lip in the face of domestic trials should be shot in Technicolor to make its somber story more attractive to the mass audience. Not many British films had been shot in Technicolor in those days; in fact, there were only four Technicolor cameras available in England. "Color was considered vulgar," Lean explained. That is, the colors in Technicolor movies were all too often too bright and garish. Neame assured Lean that he could keep the colors subdued, in keeping with the austere nature of the plot. In order to help make the Technicolor less vibrant in the movie, Lean had the production designer primarily employ shades of gray and brown to "dirty down" the sets. In addition, Neame was able to light the interiors so that everything looked fairly drab. As Coward put it, "The Technicolor was reduced to a minimum . . . and for once did not sear the eyeballs with oleographic oranges, reds, and yellows."[40]

When Lean was casting the picture, he invited back Celia Johnson, John Mills, and Kay Walsh from *In Which We Serve*. Noël Coward himself, who had played Frank Gibbons on the London stage, gave Lean a broad hint that he would like to repeat his performance in the film. Lean, however, believed that Coward's screen image was too much identified with the cocktail-and-dressing-gown set. Kay Walsh quipped that she could not imagine Coward as a working-class type with his sleeves rolled up and wearing suspenders. Admittedly, Coward had played Captain Kinross convincingly in *In Which We Serve*, but Kinross was, after all, upper-class. Lean suggested Robert Newton for the role of Frank, and Coward graciously acquiesced.

Newton, as we have seen, had a drinking problem. Lean, who frowned on anyone having even a light ale at lunch during the shooting period, was still something of a Quaker at heart. So he had written into Newton's contract that, if he was caught tippling during filming, he would be out of the picture. John Mills and his wife, Mary, were living in Denham Village near the studio; Mills writes in his autobiography that one night he and his wife encountered Newton weaving down the street roaring drunk. They steered him toward their bungalow before Lean, who was the Millses' neighbor, could see him. They let Newton sleep off his binge in their guest room before returning to work in the morning.

Mills was again playing a sailor for Lean, as he had done in *In Which We Serve;* this time it was Billy Mitchell, who falls in love with Queenie Gibbons (Kay Walsh). Celia Johnson took the role of Ethel Gibbons. Maxford and other Lean commentators state that Celia Johnson played Ethel opposite Coward on the London stage; for the record, Ethel was, in fact, played by Judy Campbell in the London production.[41]

This Happy Breed was filmed at Denham Studios from February to April 1943. "Celia Johnson was the only actress I ever knew who thought acting was of secondary importance to a private life," says Neame. "She was first and foremost a wife and mother."[42] Since the unit filmed six days a week, Johnson arranged with Lean to leave the studio every Saturday by 12:30 P.M., in order to catch the afternoon train to her home in Nettlebed; otherwise, she would have to take the evening train much later.

Throughout filming, Lean, with his eye for detail, made sure that both Johnson and Newton were made to age gradually as the years rolled by, with the help of wrinkles on the brow and streaks of gray in the hair. "The gradual stoop of Ethel's shoulders under the weight of the passing years is as noticeable as the changing style of her dresses, which always retain the dowdiness befitting her station."[43]

Because of his preoccupation with the technical side of filmmaking, Lean sometimes slighted the actors while rehearsing a scene, in favor of consulting with the camera crew. In planning one complicated shot, Lean polled the technicians about how it should be done. Though John Mills essentially admired Lean as a filmmaker, he was irritated by this procedure and blurted out, "Well, what about the fucking actors? Aren't you going to ask us what we think about it?"[44] Be that as it may, Celia Johnson testified that, in the last analysis, Lean did care about performance and tried his level best to guide the actors.

As for Robert Newton, he managed by and large to stay off the sauce for most of the ten-week shoot. But, near the end of principal photography, he did not show up for work one morning. He had to be bailed out of jail at the Bow Street police station, having gone on a spree the night before. It seems that he noticed Anthony Asquith, the codirector of *Pygmalion,* in a swanky restaurant. Like Coward, Asquith was known in film circles to be homosexual; Newton therefore addressed him with mock solemnity as "the First Lady of the English screen"—and was promptly hustled out of the eatery and onto the street.[45] Things went from bad to worse; Newton subsequently had a drunken scuffle with some London bobbies and sustained a nasty cut on his face from a policeman's nightstick.

But Lean did not make good his threat to fire Newton for excessive drinking; it was too late in the shoot to replace him in the picture. Lean did have to photograph Newton exclusively on one side of his face for a couple of days thereafter, as the other side had a small bandage on it, covering the still-healing cut.

Guy Green served as camera operator on both *In Which We Serve* and *This Happy Breed.* Carol Reed told me in conversation that one day he saw Lean and Neame lunching with Green in the Denham commissary during the *Happy Breed* shoot. Reed, who was himself preparing a war picture, said to Lean, "I can't find a cameraman for *The Way Ahead.*" Lean answered, "Why not use Guy?" Reed commented, "So I made Green director of photography for my picture on David's recommendation." Green returned Lean's favor by subsequently acting as lighting cameraman on no less than four of Lean's pictures later on. By the same token, Jack Harris, the film editor who cut *This Happy Breed,* stayed on with Lean for five more films.

In opening out the play for the screen, Lean decided to begin the movie with a panoramic shot of the London skyline; then the camera pans across the rooftops, zeroes in on terraced houses on one particular street, and pauses at a window of the Gibbons house, the film's principal setting. The camera then glides through the window and continues down a hallway to the front door. The Gibbons family is just entering the house for the first time in 1919.

After a twenty-year tenure in the house, Frank and Ethel, the only two members of the family left there at film's end, take their leave in 1939 to move into a flat. The opening shot is reversed at the end of the picture, as the camera retreats through the hallway and out the window and returns to the general view of South London once more.

Andrew Higson, in his very close reading of the film, shows that the opening and closing shots, which center on the Gibbons domicile, "enable the film to symbolically establish the family" as the stable and secure corner-stone of the nation.[46] This concept is reinforced in the opening narration by Laurence Olivier (uncredited). A printed title states, "This is the story of a London family from 1919–1939." Then Olivier says, "After four long years of war the men are coming home; hundreds of houses are becoming homes once more."

Since Frank is a veteran of World War I, he attends the Armistice Day parade, celebrating the return of the fighting men to hearth and home. Lean's camera dollies alongside the marching men, who are buoyed up by the brass band and cheering crowds. This is the first of the montages, already mentioned, that Lean interpolated into the screenplay.

An experienced editor, Lean employed these historical events to reflect the passage of time in the course of the picture. Thus, we first see the window of the travel agency where Frank works in 1919, displaying a poster advertising tours of the World War I battlefields. The scene then dissolves to the same shop window in 1924, advertising the Empire Exhibition at Wembley. Lean thus utilizes this transition to smoothly bridge a gap in time. Lean—who had himself attended the exhibition as a lad—portrays it just as he remembered it, as a lavish pageant showcasing the wonders of British initiative and achievements.

Billy Mitchell, who is home on leave from the navy, attends the exhibition with Queenie, whom he has been dating. As they walk arm in arm past a gaudy carousel and some opulent exhibits, Coward's musical score provides a jazzy Charleston on the sound track. Billy is deeply disappointed when, shortly afterward, Queenie declines his marriage proposal. She explains that she wants "too much," more things than Billy can give her; put simply, she does not see herself leading the dull, domesticated existence of a common housewife in suburbia.

When Frank confronts his headstrong daughter about her rejection of Billy, Queenie insists that she is really rebelling against what she views as the stifling conformity of Clapham Common. "I hate living in a house like a hundred other houses," she says to Frank, "because it's all so common." Frank, in turn, berates her for putting on airs: "We're as we are, and that's how we're going to stay. One of these days you'll find out that there are worse things than being just ordinary and respectable and living the way you've been brought up to live." Queenie is one of the first of Lean's characters to reflect the ongoing theme of his films: she is someone who yearns for a better life and finds it difficult to accept second best when that is all that can realistically be hoped for in life.

Queenie resents her father's moralizing and eventually takes up with a married man. He is higher on the social ladder than Billy Mitchell, and she runs off to Marseilles with him. She leaves a note for her parents on the mantel; after reading it, Frank laments that he and Ethel spoiled Queenie, always letting her have her own way. Ethel's reaction is harsher; she sternly disowns her wayward daughter. The scene concludes with a shot of Frank and Ethel seen through the dining room window; then the camera falls back from the house to reveal a dark and rainy night, which is an emblem of the gloom that Queenie's departure has cast over the Gibbons household.

Frank and Ethel are consoled by the marriage of their daughter Vi to Sam in 1928 and of their son, Reg, to Phyllis in 1933. But tragedy strikes when Reg and Phyllis are both killed in a traffic accident. Vi comes to the house to break the news to her parents. Lean thought that, instead of having an interchange of dialogue between Vi and her parents at this point, it would be more effective to handle the scene visually.

Vi pauses in the dining room, preparing to go out to the garden where her parents are chatting and tell them what has happened. The camera follows her as she moves toward the French doors that lead to the garden, which can be glimpsed through the windows of the doors. But the camera does not follow her outside; instead, it glides around the empty dining room, taking in the entire set with its panoramic gaze, while Vi tells her parents offscreen of the deaths. After a prolonged, excruciating moment, the grief-stricken father and mother silently enter the dining room, holding hands. The camera pulls back from them as the screen fades to black. The only sound during the scene is the jazzy music issuing from the radio that Reg had given his mother; the music provides a poignant counterpoint to the sad scene.

Lean, in consultation with Neame, opted to shoot the scene in a single, unbroken take, in order to allow the camera to move around the set and, thus, keep the film from looking static or stagey. In the course of this extended take, Lean works the camera around the actors, taking in first Vi, then her parents, so that the pace never falters. Nash and Ross single out this sequence as "one of the most memorable scenes in British cinema."[47]

The Gibbonses experience national events as well as personal crises, but they manage to carry on their daily routine, making tea, washing up, tending the garden. Queenie in particular has to learn life's lessons the hard way. She is deserted by her inamorato in a boardinghouse in Brussels and finds herself alone in a foreign country. She decides to swallow her pride and return to the fold—and, hence, comes back to England, where she finally elopes with Billy. Billy then brings her back to Sycamore Road in Clapham Common. When Billy inquires whether Ethel is glad to have him for a son-in-law, she replies stoically, "Better late than never." With that, she embraces her prodigal daughter.

Neame remembers the Saturday morning that Celia Johnson rehearsed this reconciliation scene on the set. She reminded Lean that she was permitted to leave at 12:30 P.M. in order to catch the train to her suburban home. Lean asked her to stay on a little longer and rehearse the scene again. Johnson bristled: "You promised I would be away on time, and promises are meant to be kept!" She finally agreed to go through the scene one last time. When the rehearsal was finished, she departed for the station posthaste. Lean said in correspondence that she was completely unaware that her playing of this moving scene, in which Ethel takes her daughter back, had left everyone, including the camera crew, electricians, and carpenters, in tears. He was amazed that she could so abruptly switch off the emotions of the scene and come back to reality. "She was not remotely aware," Neame concludes, "that she had created a piece of magic!"[48]

At film's end, Queenie has gone off to join Billy on active service in Singapore, leaving Frankie, her baby, in the care of his grandparents. With Frank's long-winded ferverino to his grandson removed from the script, the film concludes with Frank and Ethel taking leave of the house on Sycamore Road on the eve of World War II. It is the same house that in the opening scene they had moved into at the end of World War I, thereby bringing the action full circle. An instrumental version of Coward's morale-boosting song "London Pride" swells on the sound track at the final fade-out.

When it opened in London in June 1944, *This Happy Breed* was a smash hit, in the tradition of *In Which We Serve,* and it went on to become the top moneymaker in Britain for 1944. For a director who claimed to lack experience in coaching actors, Lean extracted some fine performances from the cast.

Kay Walsh was commendable for the compassion and understanding that she brought to the role of Queenie, the discontented young woman who kicks over the traces. Robert Newton gave a remarkably controlled performance as Frank, especially when one considers his penchant for scene-stealing in other movies, including Lean's later *Oliver Twist*. Celia Johnson brought conviction to the part of Ethel as a tight-lipped, stoic wife and mother, endeavoring to cope with domestic upheavals. As a matter of fact, Johnson was only six years older than Walsh when she played Walsh's character's mother, but she brought off the role very convincingly.

This Happy Breed was not received with much enthusiasm in the United States, where it was not released until April 1947, in a version running 101 minutes, 9 minutes short of the original 110-minute British version. (The film as released on DVD in America in 2004 is still the 101-minute American-release version.) According to the British film historian Tony Williams, one American reviewer reacted: "It's too English for me—too much niddy-nodding over a glass of port." Some American reviewers complained that Lean hammered away at his patriotic theme with the dedication of a doctoral candidate laboring over a thesis. Others felt that the film was too plot heavy, without enough character delineation; as a result, it seemed to lack a sufficient complexity and wrenching human content. Still, *This Happy Breed* is not the "relic" of Britain's wartime spirit that Williams calls it.[49] A colossal amount of effort was poured into the production; the craftsmanship was neat, the performances nicely understated. In the last analysis, the movie is a warm, tearful picture of life on the home front between the wars.

Since *This Happy Breed* was the first film that Lean directed solo, it is ironic that the promotional material on the box containing the videocassette, which was released in the United States in the mid-1980s, inadvertently listed David Lean and Anthony Havelock-Allan as codirectors—despite the screen credit in the film itself, which patently identifies Lean alone as the director. Stating that the associate producer was also the codirector is a blunder of considerable proportions.

In any event, since Cineguild was committed to filming both Coward's *This Happy Breed* and his *Blithe Spirit,* it was a foregone conclusion that Lean's next picture would be the latter. This comedy-fantasy would provide a marked change of pace for Lean, in the wake of the sober war pictures that he had edited for Michael Powell and made from two Coward works.

Part Two

THE PEAK YEARS IN BRITAIN

Chapter Four

ENCHANTMENT

BLITHE SPIRIT AND *BRIEF ENCOUNTER*

Tomorrow is promised to no one.
> —*Frankie, a cabaret manager in the film* Assassination Tango

Alas, I missed the Beaux Art Ball
And what is twice as sad,
I was never at a party
Where they honored Noel Coward.
> —*Lorenz Hart and Richard Rodgers, "The Lady Is a Tramp"*

The budding realism that had been initiated in British cinema in the early 1940s by films like Powell and Pressberger's *The 49th Parallel* continued to grow during the war years because of stark patriotic films like *In Which We Serve* and *This Happy Breed*. Nevertheless, escapism dominated most of the output of British studios during the war.[1]

Light-minded farces, as well as historical spectacles, were also part of this trend in escapist entertainment, and to the former genre Lean contributed *Blithe Spirit*. The film was derived from a Noël Coward play that the playwright had described as an improbable farce about ghosts. In this ectoplasmic comedy, Charles Condomine, a harried husband, discovers that his first wife, Elvira, has come back to haunt him after he has married for a second time. The title is a reference to Shelley's poem "To a Sky-Lark," which begins: "Hail to thee, blithe Spirit!"[2] When Coward replaced Cecil Parker in the lead in the London production for two weeks, he invited Lean and Neame to a performance, with a view to their carrying through on their plans to film it. They both liked the play's nonchalant approach to the supernatural.

Blithe Spirit (1945)

Coward's play had proved a gold mine both in London's West End, where it premiered in July 1941, and on Broadway, where it opened the following November. It ran for eighteen months in New York, but the London production topped that with an unprecedented four-year run. Coward had steadfastly refused to sell the film rights to Hollywood. He declared—with some degree of hyperbole—that the American screen versions of his plays had been "vulgarized, distorted, and ruined" by the Hollywood studios.[3] He pointed to the disappointing film of *Private Lives,* mentioned earlier, to prove his point; granted, it was a lackluster film, but hardly the disaster that Coward suggests.

Coward would consider turning the screen rights over only to Cineguild, which had recently served him well in the film version of *This Happy Breed.* Anthony Havelock-Allan thought that, in *Blithe Spirit,* Coward had offered Cineguild a tremendous plum of a property. Nevertheless, Lean was having second thoughts about directing it. Lean, who still bore traces of his Quaker upbringing, was prejudiced against the frivolity of the upper class and found the play merely a featherweight, surface farce. When Coward discussed the project with him, Lean stated flatly, "Noel, I know nothing about high comedy." But Coward insisted, "I'm sure you can do it."[4]

Furthermore, Ronald Neame, who would photograph the movie in Technicolor, managed to convince Lean that "the public had been saturated with propaganda films, and was longing for lighter fare."[5] Lean conceded his point. He now came to see that "the time was right for a comedy": "People had endured the darkness of war; we had done two films, which, while not without humor, were about the trials and tribulations of wartime and daily life." Besides, as Coward had earlier advised Lean, "Always come out of another hole." By that, Lean explained, Coward meant: "If you do a story like *This Happy Breed,* follow it with something completely different."[6]

So plans for the production got under way, and Rex Harrison was brought in to play Charles Condomine, with Margaret Rutherford as a medium and Constance Cummings as Ruth, Charles's second wife. Besides Lean regulars like Ronald Neame as director of photography and Anthony Havelock-Allan as producer, Jack Harris was again pressed into service to edit another Lean film. J. Arthur Rank was delighted to agree to distribute such a promising film; after all, Cineguild was one of the independent film units that Rank was committed to supporting as part of his Independent Producers combine. *Blithe Spirit* would represent one of Rank's first serious attempts to break into the elusive American market. Indeed, in 1945, the future of British films seemed bright, with films like Lean's *Blithe Spirit* in the works.

Though Coward was once again given an official screen credit as producer, the producer's chores were actually handled by Havelock-Allan, as had been the case on *This Happy Breed*. Similarly, Coward was listed as the author of the screenplay, but he really served in the same consultative capacity on this film as he had on *This Happy Breed*. Coward pored over a preliminary draft with his editing pencil and condensed some of the dialogue, but the screenplay was really the work of Lean, Neame, and Havelock-Allan. When Coward attended story conferences, he would jot down some additional dialogue to provide transitions between scenes, for example, to take the action from the sitting room to the bedroom.

Because of the play's enormous success, Coward was "more possessive of this play than any of his others" and instructed Lean not to tamper with it.[7] Before Coward left for another Far Eastern tour to entertain the British troops, he wagged his finger at Lean and admonished him, "Just photograph it, dear boy."[8]

It is true that, in some ways, Coward's plays seemed to be ready-made for filming; after all, his somewhat fevered world, with its violent clashes of temperament, could be transposed easily to the film medium. But Lean was wary of "just photographing it"—for he feared creating a film of *Blithe Spirit* that was merely a photographed stage play. Consequently, he would not consider having the film take place entirely in the sitting room of Charles's country home, which was where the play was set.

The filmmaker William Wyler, who adapted Lillian Hellman's *Little Foxes* and other plays for film, told me in conversation that, whereas "the playwright had to discipline himself to concentrate his action in a circumscribed area," the film director should take advantage of the fact that he can open up the play for the screen. Wyler continued, "My approach to filming a play, consequently, has been to retain the basic construction of the original, while at the same time lending the story the illusion of more movement than took place on the stage. For example, *The Little Foxes*, which I filmed in 1941, was originally staged in one room in an old Southern mansion. I extended the action by playing it throughout the two-story house, from the basement to the roof, as it were. The constant movement back and forth among these various playing areas kept the film from being static."

Lean, who knew William Wyler through his brother, the producer Robert Wyler, followed William Wyler's lead in approaching the screenplay of *Blithe Spirit*. The action of the play was limited to a single room, but he decided to open out the play for the screen by having a composite set of

Charles's country home constructed. In this manner, he could move the action throughout the house. In addition, he decided to play some scenes outdoors on the sunporch and the terrace. What is more, in transposing *Blithe Spirit* from stage to screen, he decided to write into the action events that took place offstage and were merely related in dialogue passages in the original play. For example, the scene in which Charles drives Elvira, his ghostly wife, into nearby Folkestone is portrayed in the movie.

Still, Havelock-Allan was worried about the scene in the script in which Charles has Madame Arcati, a spiritualist, hold a séance in his living room; as written, it would run nearly a half an hour of screen time. Lean solved the problem of having a lengthy scene played in the same setting by never allowing the pace of the action to slacken. He gave variety to the scene by covering all aspects of the action from various camera angles. Consequently, Harrison's comment to a television interviewer some years later seems unfair: "David set up a stage set for the séance sequence and just photographed it. We sit around a table watching [Margaret Rutherford] pulling faces."[9]

On the contrary, in shooting and editing the séance sequence, Lean kept the action moving at a lively pace. After all, as Wyler maintained, a filmmaker does not add variety to a scene simply by breaking up the dialogue from the play with shots of the Seagram Building and three or four other backgrounds. The variety must come from within the scene by photographing the action from different points of view. Thus, a director like Lean "carefully lets us see the faces, catches each subtlety of expression in a way that places us with the characters as we can never quite be with them in the theater."[10] In mapping out the shots in the shooting script, Lean showed that he knew when to cut from one face to another and when to hold a close-up of an individual as well as when to keep the camera still.

Gladys Calthrop, who had designed some of the sets for *In Which We Serve* and *This Happy Breed,* designed the lush interiors of the Condomine home in Kent. The composer Richard Addinsell, best known for "The Warsaw Concerto" from *Dangerous Moonlight* (Brian Desmond Hurst, 1941), did the score—instead of Coward, who had composed the background music for both *In Which We Serve* and *This Happy Breed.*

Coward had played Charles on tour for several weeks in the winter of 1943, and Cecil Parker had originated the role in London. But Lean decided on Rex Harrison to play the part in the film. Lean had worked with Harrison on *Major Barbara,* for which Harrison got good notices. But Lean did recruit two of the cast of the London production, who had road tested their parts on the stage: Kay Hammond, who had played the ghostly Elvira, and

Margaret Rutherford, who played Madame Arcati. The cast was rounded out by Constance Cummings as Charles's second wife, Ruth.

Blithe Spirit was shot in the spring of 1944, at Denham Studios; given the comic subject matter, Lean had Neame employ a much brighter Technicolor palette than he had used for *This Happy Breed*. During the first couple of days of shooting, Lean could not shake the uneasy feeling that high comedy was alien to him. He was so dissatisfied with one scene when he viewed it in the rushes that he wanted to reshoot it, but he feared that such a decision might make him look like an indecisive amateur. He therefore went to his erstwhile mentor Michael Powell, for whom he had edited two films, for advice about the scene. "Scrap it; go back and reshoot it. You are the boss," Powell promptly told him. "We are all fallible." The cast and crew "will respect you for having the cheek to say you're going to retake it. You've got a ten percent contingency fund in the budget that will take care of that."[11] Lean took Powell's advice, and it paid off with a better scene.

Lean had a lot less trouble coping with the special effects in this ghost story than he had anticipated. He commented, "Considering the wartime shortages and problems which plagued the studios at that time, I think the special effects worked rather well."[12] The movie's stringent budget allocated only a minimal sum of money for special effects. So Lean compensated by having Neame and the special effects technician Tom Howard achieve most of the visual tricks without the benefit of expensive technical wizardry.

Photographing Kay Hammond's Elvira presented Neame with a difficult problem. Coward stipulated that he did not want Elvira's figure to be transparent, as ghosts frequently are in movies. "He wanted Elvira to be solid, as she had been on the stage," says Neame. In the theater, suggesting that Elvira was a spirit was accomplished by having the actress dressed in gray chiffon with a gray wig and gray makeup. "She was followed by a green spotlight, which created a ghostly gray-green aura," according to Neame, and Coward insisted that this technique be employed in the film. Neame had to ensure that, as Elvira moved around the set, "the green light never spilled onto other characters."[13] Neame and Howard employed such quaint cinematic techniques as double exposures, slow fades, and dissolves to achieve spectral effects. They also borrowed gimmicks that were used to produce magical effects in a stage play, as with the green light focused on Elvira, just described.

Lean decided that additional comic implications would arise from having Elvira visible from Charles's point of view only: when anyone else looked in her direction, she was simply not there. Thus, when Elvira enters a room where someone other than Charles is present, the door seems to magically open by itself. This effect was accomplished by a stagehand pulling a hidden wire. Similarly, when the mischievous Elvira raises a chair in the air to bop Ruth on the noggin with it, Ruth can see only the chair mysteriously floating in thin air. This effect merely involved a stagehand hoisting the chair in the air on unseen wires. Consequently, these effects were of more a theatrical than a cinematic nature—just stage hocus-pocus.

Not only were these artfully composed visual effects economical, but they also proved very effective. Indeed, the film later won an Academy Award for its special effects; but Neame was not pleased that it went only to Tom Howard, who was listed in the credits as in charge of special effects for the movie, and not to him as well. After all, he pointed out, the principal effect "was the ghost Elvira, whom I created on film" with the green spotlight.[14]

The fact that only Charles can see Elvira makes for some witty dialogue interchanges. At one point, Elvira is making crude remarks to Charles about Ruth in Ruth's presence, but Ruth cannot hear them. Therefore, when Charles says to Elvira, "You're behaving like a guttersnipe," Ruth of course thinks he means her. Charles assures Ruth that he was addressing Elvira. "In that case," Ruth retorts, "that gives me quite a picture of your first marriage!"

During the shooting period, Lean found Margaret Rutherford very easy to work with. He became convinced that she was not conscious of just how funny she could be; in this view Neame concurred. Rutherford appeared in Neame's office four days before principal photography began, to show him the idiosyncratic outfits she planned to wear in the film, all tweed capes, beads, and long woolen scarves. Neame pronounced her costumes wonderful: "Where on earth did you get them?" "What do you mean?" she replied indignantly. "These are my own clothes."[15]

As the wacky medium, Rutherford rides a bicycle as if it were a broomstick. During the séance, she strides around the room with a skating motion, her double chin wobbling and her eyes darting about as she utters the most bizarre incantations with solemnity. *Blithe Spirit* was clearly Rutherford's breakout film; she became so identified with this movie that Dawn Simmons entitled her biography of the actress *Margaret Rutherford: A Blithe Spirit*.[16] (I happened to see a revival of the play on Broadway in 1987, with Geraldine Page playing Madame Arcati. Page gave a scaled-down performance that made one appreciate all the more Rutherford's outlandish reading of the role.)

If Rutherford was well cast, there were some doubts about Kay Hammond as Elvira, once shooting had commenced. Hammond had played the role satisfactorily on the stage, but she was not particularly photogenic. When seen up close by the camera, Hammond appeared to be older than her thirty-five years. Actually, she and Constance Cummings, who played Ruth, were the same age.

After Lean filmed a scene in which Elvira and Charles were frolicking on the couch, Havelock-Allan heard one electrician whisper to another, "What the hell is he wasting his time with *her* for, when he's got that dish waiting for him upstairs?" Obviously, concluded Havelock-Allan, Constance Cummings looked more attractive to the average male than Kay Hammond did.[17]

Lean found that Harrison was no picnic to work with. Neame thought Harrison insecure because he was never certain whether he was really coming across as funny. Lean was likewise insecure at times, wondering whether a comedy scene was working. Harrison writes, "David was ill at ease with comedy, and his tension communicated itself to me. I remember one occasion when I had struggled through a scene in rehearsal; and Lean turned to Neame and said, 'I don't think that's very funny, do you?' Neame echoed, 'No, I don't think it's very funny.' They could hardly have thought of a better way to hamstring an actor."[18] Havelock-Allan maintained that Harrison had misinterpreted Lean's observation: that Lean meant that the scene was supposed to be amusing but that, since high comedy was not his cup of tea, he was not certain that he had directed it properly.[19]

Lean himself did not remember the incident, but he did recall having a pitched battle with Harrison throughout the shooting period. In the course of the film, Charles becomes increasingly exasperated with Elvira for hanging around, jealously interfering in his relationship with Ruth. In directing one scene in particular, between Charles and Elvira, Lean instructed Harrison that Charles must snap at Elvira. But Harrison instead behaved nicely toward her. He did this because he wanted the audience to like him; he did not want them to think him rude. When he adamantly refused to modify his approach to the scene, Lean finally said, "Look, Rex, I know you think I'm no good as a director; . . . but I'm a bloody good cutter." He then suggested that Harrison cooperate, warning him that otherwise, "I'm going to leave you in shreds on the cutting room floor."[20] That made Harrison try to do things Lean's way.

Harrison never forgave Lean for hectoring him about the way he was playing his part. He remarked laconically in the same television interview mentioned above: "When you're on a comedy like *Blithe Spirit,* it is awfully hard working for a director who has no sense of humor. David doesn't understand comedy at all." Harrison contended that Lean all too often wanted him to stress Charles's coldness at the expense of his wit. Nonetheless, in

Lean's favor, it is only fair to say that, at times, the brusque manner that Lean sought to instill in Harrison's performance helped toughen the edges of the witty lines. Moreover, Lean's timing and pacing were seldom off.

Hence, for Harrison to say that Lean lacked an appreciation for comedy is a gross exaggeration. As a youth, we know, Lean idolized Charlie Chaplin and even had a photo of Chaplin in *The Gold Rush* on his bedroom wall. Later on, Lean acknowledged that it was Chaplin who had raised knockabout farce to the level of art.[21] When all is said and done, Harrison, under Lean's direction, gave an amusing, urbane performance in *Blithe Spirit*, one marked by a good sense of comic timing—prompting Noël Coward himself to observe that "Rex Harrison is the best light comedian in the business—after me."[22]

If Coward does not appear in the film of *Blithe Spirit*, his shadow broods over it from the very beginning. He provided a printed prologue that states, "When we are young, we read and believe the most fantastic things. When we grow older and wiser, we learn, with perhaps a little regret, that these things can never be." Coward then adds, in voice-over on the sound track, "We are quite, quite wrong!" He continues, "Once upon a time there was a charming country house, in which lived a happily married couple."

In the opening scene, Charles Condomine, a British novelist, and Ruth, his second wife, are well into their marriage; Charles has long since put away the follies of his younger days, spent with his first wife, Elvira, who died of a heart attack five years before. At present, he is working on a novel about a spiritualist entitled *The Unseen*. (By coincidence, Paramount released Lewis Allen's ghost movie *The Unseen* in 1945, the same year that the film of *Blithe Spirit* opened.) In order to gather material for his novel, Charles invites Madame Arcati, a medium, to conduct a séance in his home; he also invites Dr. and Mrs. Bradman (Hugh Wakefield and Joyce Carey), who are old friends, to the experiment.

Charles assumes quite gratuitously that Madame Arcati is an imposter and a charlatan, but he could not be more wrong. Indeed, Madame Arcati conjures up the spirit of Elvira—just inadvertently, by playing a recording of "Always," which just happens to be Elvira's favorite song. As at one point the medium gazes intently into her crystal ball, the husky-voiced Elvira whispers to Charles, "Merlin does this sort of thing at parties and bores us all stiff."

Elvira simply refuses to return to the otherworld. Instead, she "ensconces herself in the home Charles now shares with his second wife and flits about, making salacious comments," as Pauline Kael puts it. To his dismay, Charles finds himself in an involuntary state of "astral bigamy."[23]

Always vigilant to keep the film from turning into a photographed stage play, Lean definitely did not want the extended quarrel between Charles and Ruth over Elvira to turn into a static dialogue scene. So he staged it as taking place throughout the day, in various locations around the house. Lean bridges space and time, beginning the quarrel in one place, and continuing it through a series of locations and situations. To be specific, the quarrel begins at breakfast on the sunporch in the morning, continues at lunch in the dining room at noon, and ends in the evening with coffee after dinner on the terrace. Ruth begins the argument by snidely suggesting that, if Charles thinks his deceased wife materialized for him alone during the séance, it is because he was drunk! She ends the quarrel hours later by conceding that Elvira is, indeed, present in the house—but then accuses Charles of preferring the company of his departed wife to that of his second wife in the flesh.

Lean utilizes a series of dissolves to link together the short segments that constitute the quarrel sequence, implying that at this point in time Charles and Ruth's marriage is one endless quarrel. He reinforces this notion in a most inventive way. Each succeeding scene shows the distance between them growing, as the table between them literally gets longer, from the small breakfast table to the much longer dining room table. As the quarrel ends on the terrace, Charles and Ruth are sitting apart, and Charles has turned his back on Ruth. This is a subtle way of symbolizing their increasing estrangement. Lean may have been influenced by a similar sequence in Orson Welles's *Citizen Kane* (1941), which was, in fact, a favorite film of his.

Only when Lean borrows gimmicks from other films about ghosts does the movie become unconvincing, opines Anderegg. Thus, the "invisible" Elvira driving Charles's convertible, says Anderegg, is "too hoary a cliché to be very funny." To set the record straight, Anderegg's memory has played him false. The scene, as it appears in the film, has Charles driving Elvira into Folkestone to see an old friend. As the car passes an intersection, the policeman stationed there overhears Charles addressing Elvira, who is invisible to the bewildered policeman, but visible to Charles.[24]

Elvira eventually grows tired of competing with Ruth for Charles's affections, so she tampers with the brakes on Charles's car, in order that he will die in a car crash and join her in the great beyond. But, as luck would have it, Ruth takes the car out for a spin before Charles does, so it is Ruth, not Charles, who joins Elvira in the hereafter. As a result of this neat plot twist, Charles now has not one but two deceased wives to haunt him.

Fed up with the two ghosts jealously squabbling over him, Charles decides to go away for a restful vacation. Lean, with Coward's permission, altered the ending of the play at this juncture. In the play, as Charles goes out the front door, the unseen hands of Elvira and Ruth smash some of the living room furniture, implying that his two ghostly wives will continue their mad mischief when he returns. In the movie, however, as Charles drives off, Elvira and Ruth sit together on a stone wall by the side of the road and watch his car pass by. A crash is heard offscreen, and Charles's ghost materializes between them. Obviously, Elvira and Ruth sabotaged his car so that he would join them in the echoing corridors of eternity, where they can vie for his affections forever. And thus the film ends.

Coward returned from abroad in time to view the rough cut. After the screening, he turned to Lean and barked, "You've just fucked up the best thing I've ever written."[25] He believed that *Blithe Spirit* had stretched what he now considered to be Lean's meager comic sense to the limit and that Lean had approached with a straight face what the playwright had designed as tongue-in-cheek farce, punctuated with sardonic repartee. Coward was more tactful about his response to the film in his autobiography: "I will draw a light, spangled curtain over the film of *Blithe Spirit*. It was a great deal less good than it should have been."[26] The fact remains that the film did well at the box office when it opened in Britain in the spring of 1945 and when it opened in the U.S. in the fall of the same year.

Fate proved to be ultimately on Lean's side when, twelve years later, on January 15, 1957, Coward played Charles opposite Lauren Bacall's Elvira on American television. Lean thought the television version was appalling, compared to his film, and he told Coward so: "You've just fucked up the best thing you ever wrote!"[27] Coward good naturedly allowed Lean to have the last laugh.

In retrospect, it does appear that Coward was too harsh in his assessment of Lean's film. Lean served up a delightful comic fantasy, much appreciated in both England and America, where it prospered on the art house circuit. Lean's film remains a high-style British comedy, marked by subtle wit and impudent grace, in which lives are sent spinning in unlikely directions by a ghost. It is a well-crafted and well-acted movie. It is fitting that the often-underrated Margaret Rutherford should steal the few deft scenes she is in. Wry and reckless, she proves herself an actor who can manage farcical material when many actors would struggle to hit the right note of lunacy.

Furthermore, when examining the movie, we cannot overlook the background music supplied by Richard Addinsell. Addinsell came up with a delicious, effervescent score, highlighted by the beguiling theme that he wrote to accompany Elvira's apparitions. The score was skillfully conducted by Muir Mathieson, as was always the case with Lean's British films.

In summary, *Blithe Spirit* is one of the British films of the 1940s that looks better as the years go by (it was released on DVD in 2003). Though it is quite untypical of the bulk of Lean's work, it gives us a version of Coward's frothy ghost story that is handled with fine technical assurance. Nevertheless, even though Lean did not feel at home in the world of lightweight romantic comedy, *Blithe Spirit* is not his only film in the genre, as some commentators on his work persist in saying. But it is significant that he did not return to comedy until *Hobson's Choice* nearly a decade later.

After *Blithe Spirit*, Lean wanted to get back to more familiar territory and make a more serious psychological drama. Fortunately, Coward had a property made to order, a one-act play entitled *Still Life* about a sad, middle-aged romance.

As realism gained the ascendancy in postwar British cinema, Lean thought Coward's bittersweet drama an ideal choice for his next picture. After all, wartime movies like *In Which We Serve* and *This Happy Breed* had conditioned moviegoers to expect a greater degree of realism. So audiences were ready to respond to the "new realism" that Lean brought to *Brief Encounter*. In this film, Lean conjured up the suffocating world into which he had been born—the drab refreshment rooms in railway stations, the oppressively dreary streets and alleyways of provincial towns. As a matter of fact, according to Sheridan Morley, Coward's biographer, "Lean's technique set a pattern of postwar realism in the English cinema which was to be followed for some years to come."[28]

Though *Blithe Spirit* and *Brief Encounter* were both released in 1945, they were not made back-to-back, as some critics have assumed. They were, in fact, shot several months apart: *Blithe Spirit* February–May 1944, premiering April 5, 1945; *Brief Encounter* January–April 1945, premiering November 26, 1945.

Brief Encounter (1945)

In the mid-1930s, Noël Coward wrote a cycle of nine one-act plays (not twelve, as Brownlow mistakenly asserts) under the collective title *Tonight at 8:30*.[29] Coward later admitted, "I wrote the *Tonight at 8:30* plays as vehicles for Gertrude Lawrence and myself." They were presented in repertory on three successive nights in groups of three. The third bill included *Still Life*, "the most mature play of the whole series," according to Coward. "Later it was made into an excellent film and retitled *Brief Encounter*. I am fond of both the play and the film." Still, he retained a slight bias in favor of the play: "It is well-written, economical, and well-constructed. The characters, I think are true; and I can say . . . that I am proud to have written it."[30] The cycle of plays premiered at London's Phoenix Theater in May 1936, and the production moved successfully to Broadway, with Lawrence and Coward still playing the leads.

Coward offered to write a preliminary screen treatment of *Still Life* for Lean when they discussed using it to follow *Blithe Spirit*. "I will do it very quickly," Coward promised, "because I know the play backwards and forwards."[31] True to his word, two weeks later Coward handed Lean a prose treatment of the script, to be entitled *Brief Encounter*. He "then persuaded David Lean, Ronnie Neame, and Tony Havelock-Allan to put it into production": "This they agreed to do." So A. R. Fulton is mistaken when he baldly declares that Coward alone wrote the screen adaptation.[32]

The Rank organization had purchased the screen rights to the entire cycle of nine plays but had not yet filmed any of them. When Cineguild sought to purchase the screen rights to *Still Life,* Rank, having lost interest in the project, insisted that Cineguild buy the rights to all nine plays. Later on, when Lean showed Rank a draft of the script for the film that he, Neame, and Havelock-Allan had prepared, Rank's interest was renewed, and he agreed to a distribution deal. A budget of £270,000 was agreed on—not a substantial one for a British film of the period.

Still Life, a short play that runs just under an hour, sketches out a tragic love story in five brief scenes. Dr. Alec Harvey and Laura Jesson meet by chance in a railway station and subsequently fall in love. But they mutually agree to part and return to their separate families for good.

In a 1947 essay on *Brief Encounter,* Lean writes that the plot remained essentially faithful to the stage play: "There was an unhappy ending to the main love story. The film was played in unglamorous settings; and the leading characters were approaching middle-age." In sum: "A few years ago this would have been a recipe for box office disaster, but this wasn't the case with *Brief Encounter*."[33]

Brief Encounter succeeded because of the "new realism," mentioned above, that flourished in postwar British cinema.[34] During the war, audiences had gotten used to the documentary realism employed in making even fiction films about the war, and afterward they continued to demand this kind of naturalism. More and more, films were shot on location, actors abandoned theatrical for more natural mannerisms, and a newsreel-like style was employed to photograph the action. There was no doubt, according to Lean, that *Brief Encounter* was in the vanguard of films representing the new postwar realism.[35]

Ronald Neame writes that he, Lean, and Havelock-Allan "transformed

Noel's somewhat static one-act play into an effective shooting script." Lean decided that the story should be told in a complex pattern of flashbacks, even though in the play the events unfold in chronological order. After all, the flashback structure had worked very well in *In Which We Serve*. "Because of David's choice of telling the story through flashback, we decided to have a narration spoken by Laura," adds Neame.[36]

Accordingly, the events are seen through the eyes and mind of Laura, whose voice is the source of what we see and hear. Putting it another way, the voice-over narration comes out of the narrator's conscious recall. In short, the camera shows us what happened while the narrator comments on the action. In this fashion, the film foregrounds Laura not only as the principal character but also as a presence—someone whose comments presented in voice-over color the viewer's perception of events.

Having Laura narrate the whole story from her point of view was a felicitous decision. This is because "what Laura tells us about what is going on inside her . . . as a rule complements the visuals." Indeed, we now have a strong point of view with which to identify.[37] Bruce Eder remarks, "Because Laura *relives* each incident that she recalls, she brings the viewer inside her psyche. Hence, she brings us closer to the central character than anyone might have expected" (emphasis added).[38]

The screenplay introduces into the framing narrative the figure of Laura's husband, Fred, who is only referred to in the play's dialogue. Laura sits near her husband in the library of their home as they listen to Rachmaninoff's Piano Concerto no. 2 on the radio. As she recounts the story of her recent involvement with Alec in voice-over, she imagines that she is telling it all to Fred, but, in reality, she is talking to herself. For she would not want to hurt her husband by revealing her affair to him.

Since *Still Life* is a short play, the screenwriters could retain nearly all Coward's original dialogue. One thing that particularly appealed to them about the play was the manner in which Coward could write dialogue that played against the action; that is, the characters say one thing but actually mean something quite different. As Coward himself put it, there is a love scene between Alec and Laura in which they are both bashful about pursuing their amorous intentions toward one another: "He's a doctor and talks about preventive medicine and the different diseases one gets; and all the time he is looking at her. And then she says, 'You suddenly look much younger, almost like a little boy'—which cuts right through the barriers and forces them to talk about themselves at last."[39] This is an example of Coward's tight-lipped, understated dialogue.

Additional dialogue would be required to expand the play into a feature-length movie. Consequently, adapting the one-act play to the screen represented for the screenwriters a form of artistic creation, the process involving the addition of new material. Thus, Lean and his collaborators could fill in the backgrounds of the characters, to a degree that was simply not possible within the limits of the one-act-play format.

To be more precise, the scriptwriters faced the task of turning the one-act play into a feature film running nearly an hour and a half. They therefore opened out the play for the screen with additional scenes set in locations that ventured well beyond the railway station refreshment room, where the entire play takes place. Location work in Lean's previous films had been minimal. "He began introducing location work in *Brief Encounter*," says Eder; "he brought his cameras out-of-doors, making the picture seem more real than any studio scenes could have."[40]

Coward at the time was entertaining British troops in India, and Havelock-Allan remembers cabling him for some additional dialogue whenever they got stuck. "Look, we've decided to send them rowing," Havelock-Allan said in one cable, "and Alec accidentally falls into the water." He requested that Coward supply a minute's worth of dialogue for the scene. Coward cabled back on that occasion, "I'm sending you a minute and forty seconds. If you really mean a minute, take out the following words."[41]

Sometimes, one of the triumvirate of writers would try his hand at creating the dialogue for a new scene not in the original play, always subject to Coward's approval. Neame wrote the scene between Alec and Laura that takes place in the boathouse, where Alec is drying off by the fire after having fallen in the lake. After Neame submitted the scene to Coward, the latter congratulated "the little darling who wrote the brilliant Coward dialogue."[42]

Besides adding new scenes and locations to the original play, the scriptwriters also created a couple of new characters for the film. As already noted, Laura makes allusions to her husband, Fred, in the film's literary source, but he never appears in the play. In the film, Fred is presented directly, as Laura and her husband are shown together at home. By the same token, both of Laura's children appear in the film and not in the play.

When it came to sorting out the screen credits, Coward agreed to be listed only as the author of the original play on which the screenplay was based, but Lean, Neame, and Havelock-Allan were credited as coauthors of the screenplay. In fact, the Academy of Motion Picture Arts and Sciences recognized their joint authorship of the screenplay by nominating Lean, Neame, and Havelock-Allan for Academy Awards for the script, but not Coward. Coward was again listed as the producer of the film, and again the producer's responsibilities actually fell to Havelock-Allan, along with Neame, both of whom were officially tagged as associate producers.

Neame told Lean that he would like to become a full-fledged producer and that coproducing *Brief Encounter* with Havelock-Allan would enable him to learn the ropes. He recalls that Lean "wondered if it was such a good idea for me to drop the camera, although he accepted that I'd be a supportive partner." Still, Neame knew that his new role in Cineguild would alter his relationship with Lean: "David got on tremendously well with his cameramen, but as a rule he had a more problematic relationship with the producers."[43]

Robert Krasker, who had just come off photographing Laurence Olivier's *Henry V* (1944), was chosen to succeed Neame as Lean's cinematographer. Jack Harris continued as Lean's film editor, and Gladys Calthrop likewise returned as a set designer.

Coward decided that there was no need to engage a composer for the film's score since he was convinced that the grand passion of Rachmaninoff's Piano Concerto no. 2 would provide highly charged, emotional music for this tragic romantic tale. Muir Mathieson was again on hand, this time to conduct the National Symphony Orchestra in the concerto, with Eileen Joyce as soloist. Billy Wilder, incidentally, paid homage to *Brief Encounter* by employing the same concerto on the sound track of his *The Seven Year Itch* (1955) in a romantic scene in which a middle-aged man (Tom Ewell) attempts to seduce his neighbor (Marilyn Monroe).

It was a foregone conclusion that Celia Johnson would play Laura Jesson, considering her fine work in *In Which We Serve* and *This Happy Breed*. Kate Fleming, Celia Johnson's daughter, states in her biography of her mother that Johnson played the role with "a lack of sentimentality, an absence of technical trickiness, but with intelligence and sensitivity."[44] Indeed, Johnson agreed to play the part without makeup because Laura lacks conventional good looks.

As for the casting of the role of Alec Harvey, Carol Reed told me in conversation that Lean was much interested in Trevor Howard, who enacted the role of the commanding officer in Reed's *The Way Ahead* (1944), a drama about the ordinary fighting man's view of the war. Reed heartily recommended Howard to Lean for *Brief Encounter,* and Coward endorsed the choice since he had seen Howard in another war picture, Anthony Asquith's *The Way to the Stars* (1945), in a private screening that Asquith had arranged for him in advance of the film's release.

The other major roles were taken by actors with whose work Lean was familiar. Joyce Carey, who had appeared in both *In Which We Serve* and

Blithe Spirit, reprised her role from the London production of *Still Life*—that of Myrtle Bagot, the buxom proprietress of the station buffet. (Maxford insists on calling the character Bagshot.)[45] Everley Gregg, who had appeared in *Pygmalion,* was also brought over from the stage production to play the part of Dolly Messiter, Laura's gossipy friend. Cyril Raymond, who was in Paul Czinner's 1937 *Dreaming Lips,* which Lean had edited, took the role of Laura's husband, Fred. Finally, Stanley Holloway, who had a role in *Major Barbara,* was cast as the stationmaster, Albert Godby.

Joyce Carey and Stanley Holloway furnish some much-needed comic relief in the melancholy movie. Albert makes some crude attempts to win Myrtle's affections, but Myrtle, who likes to put on airs, rebuffs him in a genteel accent that is obviously phony. The comic casualness of their relationship is, of course, a caricature of Laura and Alec's relationship.

The film was shot on a ten-week schedule, from January through April 1945. The interiors for the movie were shot as usual at Denham Studios; Lean opted to film the railway station exteriors at the suburban station at Carnforth in Lancashire, on the edge of the Lake District. For two weeks of the film's ten-week schedule, the cast and crew worked from 10:30 P.M. to 6:00 A.M. in the Carnforth Station, in order to avoid the daytime crowds of commuters. In the opening sequence, a tall individual wearing a trench coat can be seen in profile on the station platform; it is David Lean making a rare cameo appearance in one of his films.

Lean still suffered from stage fright at the beginning of principal photography on a film, and *Brief Encounter* was no exception. "I know I'm over-meticulous and I worry too much," he confessed. But after a few days things would get better: "I know where to put the camera and how to talk to the actors. . . . I suppose directors are like actors. I suppose that we all pretend that we are more confident than we are."[46] As the shooting progressed, Lean began to feel more at home on the set, especially in the railroad station refreshment room, which reminded him of the buffet bar at Victoria Station, where as a teenager he used to wait for the suburban train home (see chapter 1).

Lean got along splendidly with Celia Johnson from the start. In one scene, Alec invites Laura to an apartment that belongs to a friend of his for an assignation. She initially declines and goes straight to the railway station. Instead of taking the train home, however, she impulsively heads for the exit and runs down the sloped platform that will take her out of the station and onto the street leading to the flat where Alec is temporarily staying. Laura struggles to maintain her outward calm and dignity while at the same time endeavoring to convince herself that consummating her passion for Alec is the right thing to do.[47]

Lean observed how Johnson's somewhat halting gait conveyed Laura's indecisiveness. After he called "Cut," he asked Johnson how she worked out the way that Laura should walk out of the station. "I didn't work it out," she replied. "She would just do that, wouldn't she?"[48] Apparently, good acting needs no explanation.

The director's interactions with Howard were not always so pleasant. Occasionally, Lean had strong disagreements with Howard on the set, recalling his clashes with Rex Harrison while shooting *Blithe Spirit*. The scene in which Laura arrives at the apartment Alec has borrowed for the occasion is a case in point. It has been raining, and the couple chat about whether they should light a fire in the hearth. Alec opines that "the wood is probably damp" and succeeds only in creating a cloud of smoke in the fireplace. "I hope the fire will pick up," he mutters, perhaps subconsciously thinking of the fire that he hopes he and Laura can enkindle between them.

While rehearsing the scene, Howard took Lean aside and told him that it was just not working. He could not comprehend why Alec delayed making advances to Laura by attempting to build a fire in the grate. He thought the small talk was a waste of time, adding bluntly, "Why doesn't he just fuck her?" Lean responded that Laura and Alec are both embarrassed about having a tryst in a bleak, borrowed flat; hence, they are hesitant to carry out their plan to make love. Lean insisted that that was the way the scene was going to be played, even though his explanation did not satisfy Howard. "He just thought I was mad," Lean concluded.[49] Yet Howard gave a sensitive performance in this poignant scene, as he did in the love scene, described earlier, in which Laura and Alec again beat around the bush before expressing their feelings for each other.

Shooting was interrupted on May 4, 1945, when the BBC announced that Germany had surrendered to the Allies and that the war in Europe was, thus, at an end. The cast and crew had an impromptu celebration at lunch and then dutifully went back to work.

Lean was very satisfied with Krasker's camerawork; he had known Krasker since he had been a camera operator on Michael Powell's *One of Our Aircraft Is Missing*, which Lean edited. Krasker sets the proper mood for the film by making the most of the rain-washed streets and the dingy railway station. The movie reflects a somber world, one in which buildings loom over Laura and Alec, who seem "isolated and vulnerable," as they attempt to pursue their doomed relationship.[50]

The film begins with the opening bars of the Rachmaninoff concerto accompanying the credits, "which are superimposed on night shots of an express train roaring through a suburban station illuminated by cameraman

Bob Krasker's cunningly placed backlights."[51] One might say that the film begins at the end, in the same sense that Lean first portrays the final parting of Alec and Laura. Laura Jesson, as we know, is a housewife who goes to town every Thursday to shop and see a matinee at the pictures. She meets Dr. Alec Harvey on one of her excursions, and their casual relationship slowly develops into a romance. Both agree that they should part, in order not to jeopardize the happiness of their respective families.

Laura and Alec are first seen at a table in the refreshment room of the Milford Junction Station, saying good-bye, when Laura's flighty friend Dolly Messiter intrudes on their private conversation with a barrage of chatter. At this point, filmgoers are not aware of the deep significance of Laura and Alec's parting, but they will be by the time the scene is repeated at film's end. Consequently, the opening and closing scenes bookend the picture as a whole.

After Laura takes leave of Alec at the beginning of the movie, she rides the commuter train to suburban Ketchworth. That evening, she is sewing in the library at home while her husband, Fred, works a crossword puzzle. Fred is a dull, humdrum individual who takes his wife for granted. Laura is listening intently to the Rachmaninoff concerto on the radio; the wistful music prods her memories and accompanies her narration. Laura can be heard, in voice-over on the sound track, narrating her memories of her love affair, as if she were verbalizing her thoughts out loud to Fred. "I am a happily married woman—or at least I was until a few weeks ago," she begins pensively. "But, oh, Fred, I've been so foolish; I've fallen in love." The shot of Laura in her easy chair at home slowly dissolves to a shot of Laura in the railway station waiting for her train. For an instant, Laura at home is watching herself in the station, indicating how she is reliving her experiences of the recent past.

While waiting on the platform for her train, Laura gets a cinder in her eye. Alec Harvey removes it for her, and they go their separate ways. "That's how it began," Laura muses. "I completely forgot the whole incident. It didn't mean anything to me at all; at least I didn't think it did." Actually, Laura was quite taken with Alec, who—compared to Fred—is a raffish, passionate Romeo. "From that moment on Laura is putty in the handsome doctor's hands."[52]

That Laura and Alec's relationship centers on a railway station symbolizes the transitory nature of their affair. People's lives temporarily intersect in a station, but they inevitably go off in different directions. On a subsequent Thursday, Alec explains that he comes to Milford every week to cover for another doctor, Stephen Lynn, at the local hospital. On this particular day, Alec decides to play hooky from the hospital and go with Laura to a movie;

they choose *Flames of Passion*. Eder comments, "There never was a movie called *Flames of Passion*, but there were films like it, the kind of empty, studio-bound films that David Lean didn't make."[53] Actually, Lean had in mind a film of that name, a 1922 silent picture directed by Graham Cutts and, more important, produced by Herbert Wilcox, for whom Lean worked as a neophyte film editor in the 1930s (see chapter 1). It was an overheated melodrama about a woman with a guilty secret, and, to that extent, the heroine's conflict had an implicit parallel with Laura's secret romance with Alec.[54]

At any rate, the version of *Flames of Passion* that Alec and Laura view turns out to be appallingly bad, and they walk out on it. The fact that they dislike it implies that the title reminds them of their own romantic attachment, which will ultimately burn itself out. Afterward, they go boating on the lake in the Milford Botanical Gardens, but Alec is not an experienced rower, and he literally rocks the boat and falls into the water while attempting to avoid ramming into a low bridge.

They retreat to the boathouse, where Alec dries off; over a cup of tea, they confess to each other that they have fallen in love. Then they return to the station, where they kiss for the first time in an underpass at the station. They are pictured in the shadows as a passing express train reflects the rush and power of their passion. This is as close as their affair ever comes to igniting into flames of passion.

Laura looks out of the train window as she rides home; the window becomes a movie screen, whereon she imagines that she sees Alec and herself in Venice, floating in a gondola on the Grand Canal—a shot that prefigures Lean's later *Summertime*, which features a May-December love affair in Venice.

The following Thursday, Alec tells Laura that he has borrowed his friend Stephen Lynn's apartment for the evening and asks her to join him there. Laura at first declines but abruptly changes her mind just before her train leaves the station. She then goes to the flat for an illicit rendezvous with Alec.

Stephen returns unexpectedly, however, and Laura is forced to escape through the kitchen and down the back stairs before he sees her. But Stephen does hear her scuffling out the back door and senses what is going on. In a voice dripping with suspicion and disapproval, he pointedly requests that Alec return his latchkey.

Meanwhile, Laura heads back to the station in the rain, walking briskly through puddles but in a daze. After the rain stops, she sits for a while on a bench near the station, feeling remorseful. An ominous figure approaches her in silhouette; it is a policeman. He is an authority figure and, thus, an emblem of the social order and its conventional morality. The policeman looks down at her momentarily and then moves on, but Laura nevertheless feels judged, as if she has committed a crime. She proceeds to the station.

Alec soon catches up with her in the refreshment room. "We know we really love each other," he says soothingly. "That is all that matters." "It isn't all that really matters," she replies. Laura, who has always been the personification of middle-class propriety, continues, "Other things matter too—self-respect matters, and decency. I can't go on any longer." Having experienced the shame of lies and subterfuge, which they both find degrading, they agree to give each other up. Alec then informs her that he has been offered a post in Johannesburg. He had initially decided to turn the job down, but now he sees that taking it is the best way to short-circuit their relationship.

The plot of *Brief Encounter* is reminiscent of the kind of romantic tale that fills the pages of the "true confessions" type of magazine, but Lean treated his material with a degree of taste that this type of story rarely receives. The scene in which Laura and Alec see each other for the last time is an index of the skill with which he keeps the tender moments of the film from slipping into sentimentality.

The story develops to the point where it leads up to the final parting, which we see again; but this time we have "a full realization of its pain and tension" since we now perceive it "with new eyes."[55]

Alec and Laura sit in the grubby refreshment room waiting for Alec's train, which will arrive before Laura's. Suddenly, their quiet intimacy is interrupted by Laura's gossipy friend Dolly, who joins them and begins chattering in her usual inane fashion. Alec and Laura can say nothing to each other, realizing that this unfortunate happenstance has robbed them of the opportunity of even saying good-bye. Over Dolly's prattle, Alec's train can be heard pulling into the station. Alec slowly rises, and we see in close-up his hand gently come to rest on Laura's shoulder before he goes out into the night. Laura is left staring blankly at Dolly, who does not even notice that no one is listening to her.

Suddenly, at the sound of an oncoming train speeding toward the station, Laura rushes out onto the platform. As the lights from the windows of the passing train flash across her face, we know that she has conquered her impulse to commit suicide, in favor of her resolution to return to her husband and two children. This is a moment of triumph for Laura, whose sense of devotion to her family has overcome her despair at losing Alec. In essence, *Brief Encounter* implies that "Laura has not married the man of her dreams" and that "when she finds him she cannot keep him": "So she returns home to the kitchen sink."[56]

The film concludes back in the Jessons' library, where Fred intrudes on Laura's reverie just as the concerto is reaching its conclusion. He kneels beside her armchair and says that she seems to have been far away, as if she were dreaming. He adds, "Whatever your dream was, it wasn't a very happy one, was it?" He concludes, "Thank you for coming back to me." They embrace at the final fade-out. Some critics have inferred that Fred's last line suggests that he has intuited the now terminated affair. On the contrary, there is no indication anywhere in the film that Fred is suspicious of Laura's behavior. Rather, the film ends on an ambiguous note. To Fred, his own words merely mean that Laura has come back to him from her reverie; but, to Laura, they mean much more, that is, that she has come back to him. Laura has, in fact, returned to the safe, solid, everyday world. Ken Russell writes that the concerto and the film reach their conclusions simultaneously: "And both are masterpieces of their kind."[57]

"This ending is happier than the one in *Still Life*, which ends with the emotionally unresolved parting of the lovers," remarks Eder. "This scene is modeled on the ending of another play in the *Tonight at 8:30* portmanteau, *Shadow Play*."[58] In *Shadow Play*, a husband and wife renew their love for each other before the final curtain.

In his monograph on *Brief Encounter*, Richard Dyer hazards that, though the plot of the film deals on the surface with a heterosexual relationship, beneath that surface there is a veiled narrative that relates to Noël Coward's homosexuality.[59] As a matter of fact, Coward had a brief encounter with a sailor in the Royal Navy while he was filming *In Which We Serve*, before the young seaman went on active service.[60] The furtiveness and fear of discovery that brought to an end Laura and Alec's heterosexual affair perhaps reminded Coward of his own homosexual relationships. The film explores the anguish and frustration caused by having one's desires thwarted by the pressures of social conventions, something that Coward had experienced. But this does not mean that Coward consciously implanted a homosexual subtext in the present story.

Yet Stephen Bourne goes so far as to describe Alec's smarmy friend Stephen Lynn as the "queeny bachelor." Stephen seems, to Bourne at least, to be jealous that Alec has chosen Laura instead of him.[61] On the contrary, Stephen's disapproval of Alec's behavior represents the judgment of the bulk of Alec's friends and colleagues, were they to learn of his behavior.

Bourne further points to an allusion to *Brief Encounter* in a homosexual context in Billy Wilder's movie *The Private Life of Sherlock Holmes* (1970).[62] Dr. Watson informs Holmes that some people are beginning to suspect that they have a homosexual relationship because they share a bachelor flat. When Watson suggests that they live apart, Holmes replies, "Of course, we can continue to meet clandestinely, in the waiting rooms of suburban railway stations." Granted that this is an implicit reference to *Brief Encounter*, Holmes in point of fact is merely suggesting a parallel between the secretive liaisons that occur between a heterosexual couple and those that occur between a homosexual couple—which some think he and Watson are. In any event, in the balance of the film, Wilder establishes that Holmes and Watson's relationship is platonic.

When all is said and done, one must take Coward's play and Lean's film at face value; Coward declared explicitly that *Still Life* was an examination of an extramarital fling on the part of a middle-aged man and woman.[63] Both Bourne and Dyer seem to be drifting into an overinterpretation of the film when they bring in Coward's personal life to explain the implications of the story. *Brief Encounter* remains a straightforward narrative about a thwarted extramarital affair. For Lean, the whole point of the movie was the cost of maintaining a marriage: "One chooses either erotic love and romance or domestic stability, respectability, and the happiness of children; it was far better to chose the latter of the two options if one had to."[64]

Had Coward wanted to write a play about a homosexual relationship, he could have done so without beating around the bush. Indeed, he did so—in the 1943 *Present Laughter*, in which a middle-aged man pursues a younger chap. In the last analysis, to see how Lean dealt with homosexuality on the screen, one need look no further than *Lawrence of Arabia*, as we shall see. But it is not valid to superimpose a homosexual subtext on *Brief Encounter*, whereby the film is ultimately said to be about veiled gay yearnings. That, says Laura Miller, is to ensnare the film "in the elastic web of gay revisionism."[65]

Implicit in *Brief Encounter* is the theme that would become prominent in Lean's work. "I am drawn to the person who refuses to face defeat," he said, "even when they realize that their most cherished expectations may go unfulfilled."[66] In retrospect, one sees that this theme was already beginning to take shape in the story of the survivors of the *Torrin* in *In Which We Serve* and in the family facing wartime privations in *This Happy Breed*.

Raymond Durgnat calls *Brief Encounter* "the *locus classicus* of the renunciation drama" and declares that it still rings true "as a domestic drama about the commitment to a defined set of values."[67] As a matter of fact, *Brief Encounter* was the first British film to deal with middle-aged love outside the confines of marriage. So Lean worried that, if Laura and Alec were to consummate their sexual desire for each other in the film as they do in the play, it might not be approved by the British film industry's censor. Therefore, he forestalled complaint by having the love affair take the form of unfulfilled yearnings. As with earlier film adaptations of Coward's works, the film escaped censorship because of its moral resolution; it was passed uncut in September 1945.

By the time *Brief Encounter* was ready for a test screening, Lean was shooting his next film, *Great Expectations,* on location near Rochester. He decided to have a sneak preview of *Brief Encounter* at a cinema in Rochester, only to learn too late that the theater was near the Chatham dockyards. Hence, the audience was made up predominantly of dockworkers and their womenfolk. This tough working-class crowd was totally out of sympathy with the sensitive, subtle film.

"A woman in the front started laughing at the first love scene," Lean recalled. "Pretty soon the laughter spread right through the cinema." The hysterics grew worse, with one boisterous individual calling out in a Cockney accent, "When is he going to have it off with her?" Lean concluded, "I fled, convinced that I had a total disaster."[68] In a moment of panic, he even considered breaking into Denham Studios and destroying the negative of the film so that prints could not be manufactured for the movie's release. Neame writes that Havelock-Allan reassured Lean of the film's commercial potential by arranging for another screening: "When the film reached a more appropriate public, the accolades were resounding."[69]

Brief Encounter is really a simple story about a transient relationship between people who cannot hold on to each other. Haunting close-ups catch the undertones of hope and worry. At first, Alec begins to sense something wistful and possibly yearning in Laura—something that contrasts seductively with her brisk, bourgeois manner. For her part, Laura's tender emotions toward Alec gradually give way to distress and lurking dread, not satisfaction. Fundamentally, the film is about great passions in ordinary lives. *Brief Encounter* is a chamber piece, marked by understated performances on the part of the principals. As such, it does not have lavish production values; there are neither car chases nor explosions, as in formula commercial films. Yet the dialogue is so strong that viewers cannot tear their eyes away from the screen, and the film continues to attract even today.

Brief Encounter eventually brought a great deal of prestige to the British film industry; its mature adult realism was heralded by the critics as a breakthrough. It won the Critic's Prize at the Cannes International Film Festival, and Celia Johnson received the New York Film Critics Award as best actress.

Johnson was also nominated for an Academy Award, as were Lean, Neame, and Havelock-Allan for their screenplay. In addition, Lean himself became the first British director ever to receive an Academy Award nomination for directing a British production.[70]

In retrospect, one wonders why Trevor Howard was not also nominated, as best actor. Perhaps it was because Celia Johnson had more opportunities to display passion and pain throughout the film than he did. Howard played the self-effacing doctor in such a nuanced fashion "that you half-suspect it's Leslie, not Trevor, Howard in the role."[71] Trevor Howard was surprised at the film's international success: "We realized at the time that it was a good film. It was honest, and it certainly had its heart in the right place. But great? That's not for us to say."[72]

Brief Encounter was, indeed, an instant commercial success when it opened in London on November 26, 1945, as well as later when it played overseas, "even though there were no big star names," as Lean later wrote. "As films go it was inexpensive to make." Consequently, it quickly turned a profit. "But *Brief Encounter* was not a huge box office success." The problem? "The greater proportion of filmgoers are under twenty-one mentally or physically; they go to the movies to escape reality [not to be confronted with it]." As Lean noted, however, "The film did very well in this country in what are known as 'the better class halls.'" And it had a similar success in America, where it opened in August 1946. It went far in helping develop the postwar art house circuit. (I first saw it in 1946 at the World, an art theater near the campus of Ohio State University, where it fared very well with the college clientele, as it did elsewhere in the country.) What is more, writes Lean, *Brief Encounter* "broke the box office record" for the theater it played in New York City, becoming "a sort of cult film," and it has been regularly revived on television and released successfully on home video.[73]

In the late 1990s, Will Salas of Criterion Video found in London a print of the film made from the camera negative. He and the technical staff at Criterion restored the print to its original condition—as it was when it was released in 1945—removing dirt and scratches inevitably found in a print of that age. As a result, they restored the overall image with its visual details and rich blacks and whites in a way that yielded a perfect transfer. It was this restored version that was released on DVD in 2000.

So the picture has maintained its place as a classic love story in the years since it was made. When in 1999 the British Film Institute drew up a list of the hundred best English pictures of the twentieth century, *Brief Encounter* ranked second, right after Carol Reed's *Third Man* (1949). Since, as we have seen, over the years Lean and Reed maintained a friendly rivalry about which one was the better British director, they would both have been gratified to know that they were paired by the membership of the BFI as making the two top British films of the twentieth century.

Some film historians have dismissed *Brief Encounter* as belonging to the category *women's pictures,* also known as *three-handkerchief movies.* There were many such films being released in the 1940s, all of them about hapless females buffeted by failed relationships or unfulfilling marriages. When Laura returned to her life of conformity at the end of *Brief Encounter,* it appeared to one sardonic critic that the movie's theme was: "Make tea, not love."[74] However, in reassessing *Brief Encounter,* Ronald Bowers describes it as "the complete opposite of Hollywood's glossy women's pictures" because it is directed sparingly, with insight and detachment. The picture is "a convincing account of basic human nature." It was made, Bowers explains, with the kind of touching restraint that was not often found in Hollywood's women's pictures of the period, like the Bette Davis vehicle *In This Our Life* (John Huston, 1942) or the Joan Crawford vehicle *Daisy Kenyon* (Otto Preminger, 1947). Thus, *Brief Encounter* "remains one of the screen's most durable romantic films."[75]

In 2003, *Premiere* magazine included *Brief Encounter* in its list of the hundred greatest movies of cinema's first hundred years, calling it "a perfect gem" of a film.[76] After all, the film is an enduring classic; in fact, in Carnforth, where some of the film was shot, there are *Brief Encounter* tours to this day.

In light of the praise heaped on *Brief Encounter* when it was first released in 1945, Noël Coward felt obliged to assure Lean that he was in no way disappointed with the film, as he had been with *Blithe Spirit:* "My dear, I must tell you, you are the most resilient young man I have ever met."[77] Truth to tell, Coward would have liked Lean to continue adapting his plays for film. But Lean had grown restless doing one Coward play after another on the screen and longed to strike out in a new direction. Ronald Neame, we know, had already moved on to producing, and he was planning to mount a production of Dickens's *Great Expectations* for Cineguild, a project Lean was interested in directing. Though Neame did not have the same camaraderie with Lean as a coproducer on *Brief Encounter* that he had enjoyed as his cameraman on earlier films, he and Lean had gotten along reasonably well, and he wanted to continue to work with Lean.

When Lean broke the news to Coward that *Brief Encounter* marked the end of Cineguild's association with him, Neame remembers: "Noel responded . . . with sarcasm and objections about our ambitions." But Coward subsequently reversed himself and became "tremendously gracious."[78] He acknowledged that Lean needed to go off on his own.

For the record, Coward had good reason to lament the departure of Lean from his camp. The next adaptation of a Coward play was *The Astonished Heart* (1949), based on another of the one-acters from *Tonight at 8:30*. Coward costarred with Celia Johnson, but they could not rescue the film. Leslie Halliwell terms the movie the nadir of Coward's association with the cinema. It was "inelegantly directed" by Terence Fisher and Anthony Darnborough from a slight play "about boring and effete people."[79] Coward's own judgment about *The Astonished Heart* was that its theme, "the decay of a psychiatrist's mind through a personal sexual obsession," was "too esoteric to appeal to a large public."[80] Michael Redgrave, who was cast as the psychiatrist, may have sensed disaster in the offing when he walked off the picture and left Coward to play the lead role himself. Then again, they had never really gotten on after their affair ended a few years earlier (see above and n. 60) and found it difficult to work together.

On the other hand, there was no doubt that the Coward plays that Lean had brought to the screen, especially *Blithe Spirit* and *Brief Encounter*, had gained international prestige for British cinema. It was not just that they were derived from the work of a writer of considerable cultural status. These faithful adaptations "exhibited a strong respect for the precursor text," and there was about them "a degree of sophistication in the writing and filming that marked them out as fare for discriminating audiences."[81] This was particularly true of *Brief Encounter*, and Lean planned to be as faithful to Dickens's fiction in making *Great Expectations* as he had been to Coward's plays when he filmed them.

Chapter Five

LONG DAY'S JOURNEY

GREAT EXPECTATIONS

Search deep inside yourself, and when you find out who you are, don't look away.

　　　　　　　　　　　　　—*Theo, a student in the film* Perfect Son

British films during the war years and after were characterized largely by escapism. As already stated, highly romantic historical pictures were much in evidence. These movies gloried in "endless permutations of the same star équipe, as James Mason and Stewart Granger, Margaret Lockwood and Phyllis Calvert flung themselves into Regency disguise, took to the roads as highwaymen, poisoned off old retainers (with, if memory can be trusted, doses from large bottles obligingly labelled 'poison'), and cheated each other out of inheritances." To keep the audience's interest from flagging, the director could always have the villain unhook the heroine's bodice. "One way or another, this was a cinema for a society weary of restrictions and ration-books; and it seems more than mere coincidence that it barely survived the end of rationing." In fact, after a steady diet of historical epics of this sort, one small-town exhibitor is said to have written his distributor, "Don't send me no more pictures about people who write with feathers!"[1]

In early 1945, Ronald Neame approached David Lean about the possibility of producing Lean's next film for Cineguild, and Lean reached back to the nineteenth century for *Great Expectations,* a Victorian novel by Charles Dickens that he much admired. But Lean hastened to make clear that he had in mind a serious sort of costume drama that would depart drastically from the romantic presentation of adventurous heroes so common in the British cinema of the time. In *Great Expectations*, Dickens wanted to expose the underside of corruption beneath the elegant surface of that bygone era. Dickens's characters may write with feathers, but they inhabit a world populated by scoundrels, frauds, criminals, and lunatics.

Lean's interest in Dickens as a literary source for a motion picture is not surprising. Filmmakers had turned to Dickens for story material for movies from the dawn of cinema history. As early as 1909, D. W. Griffith, often called the Father of Film, had made a short film version of Dickens's *Cricket on the Hearth*. The Russian filmmaker Sergei Eisenstein (*Potemkin*) enshrined Dickens as the forefather of cinematic narrative in a celebrated essay in which he analyzes Dickens's influence on Griffith: "Let Dickens . . . be a reminder that both Griffith and our cinema prove our origins to be not solely of Edison and his fellow inventors, but based on an enormous cultural past, i.e., on literature."[2]

Dickens had more than once declared that his task as a novelist was to make the reader "see." Similarly, Griffith stated, "The task I am trying to achieve is to make you see."[3] At first glance, it seems that both artists were saying virtually the same thing. Yet the written image, that is, a metaphor on the printed page that the reader "sees" with the eye of the imagination, is not the same thing as the visual image that the filmgoer sees on the movie screen. In sum, the different methods of seeing, to which Dickens and Griffith are referring, are a vivid reminder that fiction and film are essentially different media, one primarily verbal, the other primarily visual.

Nevertheless, Eisenstein reminds us that Griffith learned certain aspects of his craft by examining Dickens's fiction. According to Rick Altman, Griffith was influenced by Dickens in his use of episodic plots, boldly drawn characters, and the parallel structuring of narrative strands, called *crosscutting* by filmmakers.[4]

In short, Lean turned to Dickens because, as Eisenstein maintained, the novelist appeared to have a definite affinity for film. Furthermore, *Great Expectations* is among the most perennially popular of Dickens's novels: "That made for one of the most valuable of screen assets: the proverbial proven property."[5] As a matter of fact, when, in 1860, *Great Expectations* was first serialized in *All the Year Round,* its popularity bolstered the sagging circulation of the periodical. What is more, it became an immediate best seller when, the next year, Chapman and Hall brought out the three-decker set.

The novel first depicts Pip as a poor orphan who lives with his sister and her husband, Joe Gargery, the village blacksmith. Pip aids Abel Magwitch, an escaped convict, by giving him food before he is recaptured and deported to Australia. The lad goes on to become involved with the eccentric Miss

Havisham, a neurotic recluse who lives in her crumbling mansion with her haughty ward, Estella. As a young adult, Pip is handsomely supported by an unknown benefactor, who employs the lawyer Jaggers as a go-between. Pip courts Estella, but instead she marries Bentley Drummle, an aristocrat, who seems to her a much better catch. Magwitch comes back into Pip's life when he returns to England illegally; Pip again seeks to help him escape recapture but is unsuccessful in doing so.

Dickens clearly had problems with the ending of the novel, because he wrote two versions. The original ending has Pip and Estella meeting accidentally in London, after not seeing each other for years. Pip infers that the ill-treatment that Estella endured at the hands of Drummle has softened her. She was widowed when Drummle was trampled by a horse he had cruelly mistreated. But she has since remarried, this time to a Shropshire doctor who had attended Drummle in his last illness. Hence, she is still not available to Pip, and Pip and Estella part forever. In retrospect, Pip realizes that his obsessive love for Estella is at long last a thing of the past. Then he reflects, "I was glad afterwards to have had the interview; for in her face, and in her voice, and in her touch, she gave me the assurance that suffering had . . . given her a heart to understand what my heart used to be."[6]

Dickens's fellow novelist Edward Bulwer-Lytton (*The Last Days of Pompei*), who read the novel in galleys, convinced Dickens that Pip should not be left a solitary man. He argued that the readers of their day had grown to expect that a romantic novel would end with the marriage of the hero and the heroine and that Dickens's public would, thus, be very disappointed if Pip and Estella were not reunited on the book's last page. Dickens acceded to Bulwer-Lytton's entreaties and substituted an alternate ending before publication. "I have no doubt the story will be more acceptable through the alteration," he wrote at the time.[7]

This ending has Pip, who had pined for Estella ever since they were separated, meeting Estella on the grounds of the late Miss Havisham's decayed estate. Estella is still the widow of Bentley Drummle, but she has not remarried. Pip has been a success in business, and Estella has an inheritance from Miss Havisham, so the couple will not be impoverished. The last paragraph of the novel as published reads, "I took her hand in mine and we went out of the ruined place. . . . The evening mists were rising now, and in all the broad expanse of tranquil light they showed to me, I saw the shadow of no parting from her."[8]

If this is a happy ending, it is a muted one since Dickens does no more than imply that a happy marriage lies ahead. Be that as it may, George Bernard Shaw argued that Dickens's original ending fit the tone of the searching, tough-minded novel better than the revised ending.[9] Since Shaw, we recall, had implied that Henry Higgins and Eliza Doolittle would not be reunited at the end of *Pygmalion,* it is not surprising that he did not think that Pip and Estella would marry at the end of *Great Expectations* (see chapter 2).

In any event, all the screen adaptations of the novel have drawn on Dickens's alternate ending.[10]

Great Expectations (1946)

David Lean became aware of *Great Expectations* when he saw Alec Guinness's stage adaptation of the novel, which opened in December 1939 in the tiny Rudolf Steiner Hall in Baker Street, just off London's West End. Guinness narrated the play and also played Herbert Pocket, Pip's sidekick; Martita Hunt enacted the role of Miss Havisham. Guinness writes in his autobiography that Lean came to the performance with Ronald Neame, but Kay Walsh, Lean's wife at the time, told Kevin Brownlow that she accompanied Lean at the invitation of Martita Hunt, whom Walsh knew. In any event, Guinness goes on to say that Lean was fascinated by the production and stated that he hoped to make a film of the book one day, "with Martita Hunt as Miss Havisham and me in my old role of Herbert Pocket."[11]

In fact, Lean remembered Guinness's stage adaptation when he was discussing Cineguild's next production after *Brief Encounter* with Ronald Neame. It was then that Lean suggested *Great Expectations* to Neame; he and Neame read the novel twice before definitely committing themselves to the project. Since Cineguild still belonged to the combine of independent production units that operated under the umbrella of the Rank organization, Neame accordingly asked Rank whether he was willing to back Cineguild's production.

Rank was canny enough to realize that a handsome film of a beloved Dickens novel would appeal to a mass audience. He also knew that American distributors would be willing to help finance a prestige production at a modest price. So he told Neame, "Let me have an approximate cost and bring me a good film." Neame soon came up with a budget of £375,000—a quite reasonable price tag for a costume picture. Rank "immediately green-lighted the project," officially appointing Neame producer and Havelock-Allan executive producer.[12] As it happened, Universal-International agreed to distribute the movie in the United States. Lean himself later wrote that Rank was aware that only British films of quality could penetrate the world market and that the best English movies were made by independent filmmakers, who were not subservient to the front office of any major studio. For Lean, the chief benefit conferred by Rank on filmmakers was that "directors were enabled to please themselves"—and, thereby, please the public.[13]

Though the trio of Lean, Neame, and Havelock-Allan proved quite capable of adapting Noël Coward's plays for film, they felt daunted by the prospect of tackling Dickens's huge novel. So they engaged the playwright Clemence Dane (*A Bill of Divorcement*) to draft a screenplay for them. Clemence Dane (the pen name of Winifred Ashton) was a proficient playwright whom Lean knew through Noël Coward, a close friend of hers, and she was known to be a Dickens expert.

When Lean and Neame read Dane's draft of the script, however, they realized that it had been a mistake to entrust the screenplay to her. "It was no bloody good," Lean recalled with his usual frankness. Dane had attempted to present a superficial survey of nearly all the events in the novel "so that one never came to grips with any one scene."[14] In brief, she did her job as a screenwriter not wisely but too well, for she overloaded the script with too many incidents and too many characters.

"I think the thing is, not to try to do a little snippet of every scene in the book, because the script is going to wind up a mess," Lean continued. "Choose what you want to do from the novel and do it proud. If necessary, cut characters; don't keep every character and just take a sniff of each one."[15]

Lean and Neame closeted themselves in a country inn for three weeks and hammered out a preliminary prose treatment of the scenario. The serialization of Dickens's novels in magazines prior to their book publication encouraged his use of an episodic narrative structure. This made his novels easily adapted for film. Many of the episodes constituted virtually self-contained units. Lean was, therefore, able to pick the episodes he judged screenworthy and drop the rest. Accordingly, before getting down to work on the screenplay itself, Lean went through a preliminary procedure that would ensure that all the key events of the novel would find their way into the script. He went through a copy of the novel and chose which episodes would be in the film and which bypassed. He ruthlessly jettisoned any episode that did not clearly advance the plot. Then, Lean explained, Neame helped him sketch out the action for each scene selected and "join them by creating links between them."[16] In other words, they devised transitional material to bridge the episodes that had been scuttled, thereby providing overall narrative continuity.

One way of providing these transitional bridges was to have Pip narrate the film, a strategy that allowed him to summarize in his voice-overs events not dramatized. In having Pip narrate the film Lean was actually following Dickens's lead; moreover, his decision to have the main character narrate *Brief Encounter* had added depth and complexity to that film.

As in *Brief Encounter,* in *Great Expectations* events are seen through the eyes of the central character. Accordingly, the narrator comments on the action for the viewer and is an abiding presence in the film. He is kept firmly before us throughout the movie, recounting the past as it later appears to a reminiscing participant. Specifically, the mature Pip who narrates *Great Expectations* comments on the behavior of his younger self—a self that we watch grow from childhood to adult status. As Brian McFarlane notes, "As we observe Pip's behavior even at its least attractive, we are always aware, comfortingly, of the man he will grow into." That is, the older Pip contemplates his younger self with "an adult, superior understanding."[17]

With this road map for the screenplay in hand, Lean worked with Neame and Havelock-Allan back in London to expand the treatment into a full-length script, complete with dialogue. They used Dickens's dialogue verbatim whenever possible. Many dialogue passages were carefully selected from the book and judiciously trimmed, in order to serve as acceptable screen dialogue. Kay Walsh and Cecil McGivern, who worked on television dramas for the BBC, supplied additional dialogue where it was needed, because they both possessed the knack of devising dialogue passages that had a genuine Dickensian ring to them.

When this preliminary draft of the screenplay was finished, Lean wrote the final shooting script, which he based on the draft that he and the others had composed. Garry O'Connor mistakenly writes, "Ronald Neame wrote the script for Lean to film." But Lean and Havelock-Allan, as well as Neame, were all jointly nominated by the Academy of Motion Picture Arts and Sciences for Oscars for the screenplay, not Neame alone.[18]

One thing that became increasingly clear to Lean while he worked on the script was that "film is very good at conveying considerable information and detail in a short space."[19] For example, it would take Dickens several phrases to build up on the printed page a description of a given object or incident, whereas Lean could show the same thing on the screen in a single image.

Consider Dickens's description of Miss Havishamn's cluttered, decaying dining room when young Pip visits her. Miss Havisham was jilted on her wedding day some years before, and the ruined wedding banquet has been lying on the table ever since. Dickens has Pip describe the room in part this way: "It was spacious, and I dare say had once been handsome, but every discernible thing in it was covered with dust and mold, and dropping to pieces. The most prominent object was a long table with a tablecloth spread on it, as if for a feast. . . . A centerpiece of some kind was in the middle of the cloth; it was so heavily overhung with cobwebs that its form was quite indistinguishable." The indistinguishable centerpiece was, in fact, the spoiled wedding cake.[20]

In the book, it takes Pip several sentences to describe Miss Havisham's lair even though his eyes took in the entire scene in a single flash of vision. In the film, however, as Neame points out, Lean is able to show the same scene in a single image, just as Pip himself saw it. When Pip timidly opens the door to Miss Havisham's inner sanctum, the room is immediately revealed to the viewer: "Mice nibbling at the moldy wedding cake, the cobwebs, the candlesticks, the rotting fabric."[21]

In the end, Lean was confident that he and his cowriters had been faithful to the spirit of Dickens's novel, despite the fact that they had to condense the plot and drop some minor characters in an effort to construct a compact scenario of manageable length for filming: "By drastic and intelligent pruning of the novel, Lean proves once and for all that the essence of a sprawling masterpiece can be distilled for the screen."[22]

Lean declared his intention to be faithful to the spirit of Dickens's novel by writing into the screenplay on the very first page an opening shot of a hand turning to the first page of the book and the voice of the adult Pip actually reading the first paragraph of the novel, in voice-over on the sound track: "My father's family name being Pirrip, and my Christian name Philip, . . . I called myself Pip." With that, the adult Pip begins to narrate the film, just as he narrates the book.

With the onset of the preproduction period, Lean began assembling a production crew. He chose as production designer John Bryan, who had helped design the sets for both *Pygmalion* and *Major Barbara*. Jack Harris, the editor of Lean's previous three films, was again engaged, as was the cinematographer Robert Krasker, who shot *Brief Encounter*. Since Noël Coward was no longer around to take charge of the musical score, Lean obtained the services of the German composer Walter Goehr, who had been composing music for movies in Britain since the mid-1930s.

Goehr was used to symphonic scoring, especially for period pictures like the Douglas Fairbanks Jr. adventure film *The Amateur Gentleman* (Thornton Freeland, 1936), and Lean thought this the right kind of music for *Great Expectations*. Nevertheless, he ultimately found Goehr's underscore too heavy and turgid, so he got Kenneth Pakeman and G. Linley to modify some of the more fulsome passages. Their work was uncredited, however, since Goehr was very protective of his screen credit as sole author of the score.

Lean made good his promise that, if ever he filmed *Great Expectations,* Alec Guinness would be his first choice to play Herbert Pocket, Pip's guileless, genial friend. (Lean also made good on his promise that Martita Hunt would be brought into the film from Guinness's theatrical production to re-create her role as Miss Havisham.) "I was still in uniform, but about to be demobbed, when David Lean asked me to do a screen test for his film of *Great Expectations,*" Guinness told me in conversation. Of course, he got the part.

Apart from accepting a bit part as a British soldier in Victor Saville's *Evensong* (1934), Guinness had made no effort to appear before the cameras until Lean commandeered him for *Great Expectations.* "The theater was my prime interest in those days," Guinness told me. "I had little ambition to be a movie star." He owned that he thought himself "very fortunate" to be doing as his first important film role a part he had played on the stage. But he was still "somewhat nervous at the prospect of appearing on the screen."

He need not have worried: "Guinness's performance in his first movie role is a breath of fresh air—rarely if ever again would he be so boyish and charming."[23] In his Victorian top hat and long scarf, Guinness is an authentic Dickens character; in fact, he seems to have modeled his character on the drawings of George Cruikshank, one of the chief illustrators of Dickens's novels.

As for the role of Pip, the actor John Mills was cast. Mills assumed that this was because he had appeared in both *In Which We Serve* and *This Happy Breed,* but Lean told him in a phone conversation that he simply could not see any other actor filling the role as well as Mills. Lean also cautioned him that the part was not an easy one, that the character of Pip was "a sort of coat hanger" on which Dickens had draped a lot of wonderful garments, that is, a number of marvelous characters.[24] Lean's point was that Pip is surrounded by a gallery of colorful characters who influence his life in a variety of ways.

But whom to get to play those colorful characters? "In England then (as today) we had some of the best character actors in the world," says Neame, who, as the producer, had a say in casting. Vivid characterizations were contributed to the film by Finlay Currie (Abel Magwitch), who had appeared in *The 49th Parallel;* by Bernard Miles (Joe Gargery), who had appeared in *In Which We Serve;* by Francis L. Sullivan (Jaggers), who was repeating his role from the 1934 Hollywood version of the novel; and, of course, by Alec Guinness and Martita Hunt.

Valerie Hobson, who had done a bit part in the 1934 film, was asked to play Estella this time around. Hobson was then the wife of Anthony Havelock-Allan, but he had not requested that she be cast. He left the decision to cast her to others, just as Lean had done with the decision to cast his wife, Kay Walsh, in *In Which We Serve* and *This Happy Breed*. Hobson also made a brief, uncredited appearance as Molly, Jaggers's cleaning woman. The film historian Kenneth Von Gunden mistakenly asserts that, at the time, Hobson was married to Lean, not Havelock-Allan.[25]

Sixteen-year-old Jean Simmons was quickly chosen for the young Estella, but Lean had problems finding a boy suitable for the role of the young Pip. He sent out a general casting call and screen-tested the six finalists; he finally picked thirteen-year-old Anthony Wager, who proved to be a scene-stealer.

Principal photography commenced at Denham in September 1945 and wrapped in April 1946. Most of the picture was shot there, where John Bryan had created some atmospheric sets modeled on the drawings done for various Dickens novels by Dickens's principal illustrators, George Cruikshank and Phiz (Halbot Browne). There is, for example, the storm-threatened churchyard where young Pip visits the graves of his parents on Christmas Eve. When Pip puts flowers on his mother's grave at dusk, John Bryan's huge, gnarled trees in the graveyard look like giant, hovering figures reaching out with their claw-like branches to grasp the boy. Bryan even had a grotesque face carved in the trunk of one of the trees to make it all the more frightening to the lad. The old church in the background was actually a model only six feet tall; Bryan was a master at making models that looked real when seen at a distance, thereby keeping production costs down.

Bryan also did a marvelous job of designing the interiors of Miss Havisham's mansion. He did, however, overlook one detail. A cartoon about wartime rationing had been posted on the wall of the set of Miss Havisham's dining room by a technician as a gag. He assumed that it was out of camera range, but it was actually visible in one shot, when it was reflected in a mirror. No one noticed it until the film was in release, when it was too late to remove it from the shot, but no one has adverted to it since.

Robert Krasker's cinematography had been just right for the realistic drama *Brief Encounter*. But his naturalistic lighting was not appropriate for a Gothic tale like *Great Expectations*. In keeping with Dickens's story of doom-ridden characters involved in perilous plights, Bryan had designed dark, gloomy sets. Consequently, Lean wanted Krasker to provide chiaroscuro cinematography that would infuse the settings with forbidding shadows looming on walls and ceilings. Lean admonished Krasker, "Bobby, be much more daring; use huge, great black shadows, because that's Dickens." But Krasker apparently could not achieve this effect, said Lean; so the footage he shot looked "flat and uninteresting."[26]

When Lean finally requested that Krasker be replaced, Neame suggested Guy Green, who had been a camera operator on *In Which We Serve* and *This Happy Breed* and had since been the director of photography on *The Way Ahead* for Carol Reed. Krasker was understandably upset when he was terminated, but Neame assured him that he was too talented for this temporary setback to affect his career. That was absolutely true, for Reed told me that he assigned Krasker to photograph his *Odd Man Out* (1947)—the prestigious film about the troubles in Ulster—as soon as he heard that he was available. "He was my cinematographer on *The Third Man* [1949] as well," said Reed, "and he won an Oscar for that one."

Guy Green shot the picture according to Lean's specifications; he summoned up a threatening atmosphere with night-shrouded streets, ominous corridors, and dark archways—quite appropriate to a tale of psychological obsession and derangement. I once asked Green in correspondence to compare Lean to Reed since he had shot films for both. He replied that, whereas Lean "was inclined to view the actors as part of the overall design of the film," Reed was more friendly with them. Lean seemed to relate better to the technical people.

Green said that he always endeavored to light a set in terms of "the light source from which the light would ordinarily come in real life"—for example, a window in the daytime, a lamp at night. This makes the settings look more like rooms in real buildings and not just movie sets. There is, for example, the scene in which Estella takes young Pip to Miss Havisham's room for the first time, snapping at him peremptorily, "Don't loiter, boy!" Green used dim lighting as Estella leads Pip through the murky corridors of Miss Havisham's ramshackle house and up the stairs to her room. He thus helped give the scene a spooky, cave-like atmosphere.

Source lighting was particularly difficult in this scene, according to Green, "because the only apparent light source was the candle held by Estella as she and Pip moved across the screen." Consequently, he had to throw a dim light on the children—so that they would be visible on the screen—yet make the illumination seem to be coming solely from the candle. This was a long, complicated tracking shot, and Green had to work with a battery of technicians for a whole day in order to light the path that the children would follow through the uncharted darkness of the old house with a minimum of illumination.

Green also arranged some lights off-camera in this scene to throw great shadows on the walls in the background in order to emphasize the sinister atmosphere of Miss Havisham's dingy domain. Though Green understandably did not care to comment on Krasker, one can say that it was precisely this kind of somber scene that Lean felt Krasker had overlit and, by so doing, dissipated some of the spooky atmosphere.

When all the interiors had been shot in the studio, the production unit went on location for six weeks. The production office was established in Rochester, where Dickens himself had lived, and Lean filmed at various sites in the area. For example, it was in the Thames marshes that Lean filmed the sequence early in the movie in which Magwitch is captured by a squad of soldiers. Location shooting also took place on the River Medway near the Thames. Lean and Bryan found a small, muddy island in midriver and arranged to borrow a navy landing craft to transport the cast and crew there every day during shooting. There was an abandoned building on the island, in which the cast and crew took shelter while shooting on the river surrounding the island.

Lean used the River Medway to stage much of the sequence late in the film in which Pip, Herbert, and Magwitch are in a rowboat, attempting to intercept the paddle steamer that can carry the fugitive Magwitch away from England for good. Bryan found a vintage packet boat that had seen service in the English Channel in the mid-nineteenth century to use in this scene. Much of the footage for the scene was shot on the River Medway, utilizing the paddle steamer. Maxford notes, however, that close shots of the actors in the scene were filmed in the studio tank at Pinewood, a fact that has led John Tibbetts and some other commentators to gratuitously assume that the bulk of the movie was filmed at Pinewood, instead of at Denham, Lean's old stamping grounds.[27]

After principal photography wrapped, Lean turned his attention to postproduction. The veteran cutter Jack Harris was editing his fourth Lean film in a row; nevertheless, Lean, as always, supervised the editing process closely. The British filmmaker Karel Reisz (*Saturday Night and Sunday Morning* [1960]) included a detailed study of the opening sequence of *Great Expectations* in his *The Technique of Film Editing*.[28] He did so, he told me in conversation, because he "was aware that Lean had been a premier film editor before he became a director and had strongly influenced the editing of his pictures": "Everywhere in the film, there is evidence that the experience that Lean had gained in his years as a cutter had taught him how to build a scene with perfect timing." The opening scene of *Great Expectations* is justly famous in this regard.

Lean had intended to make the opening scene of *Great Expectations* a riveting one. "The film director has the same problem that any storyteller has," said Lean, "and that is to capture the attention of his audience. . . . I know that if I can get the interest of the audience in those first three minutes, I am halfway there to holding them [for the rest of the movie]."[29]

The opening scene, as already noted, begins with Pip placing flowers on his mother's grave. Pip is terrified by the eerie atmosphere, which is heightened by the ominous sound of the wind moaning through the creaking tree limbs. The final shooting script describes the scene this way: "Pip kneels at the foot of a tombstone. The wind is blowing the leafless branches of a tree, and to Pip they look like long hands clutching at him. . . . Pip jumps up from the grave and runs away."[30] Harris comments, "The boy is running away from this ghost-like, frightening atmosphere." In this manner, Harris continues, Lean has effectively aroused filmgoers' apprehension for Pip, and their worst fears are confirmed when he suddenly runs into a horrifying object.[31]

Neame points out that there are two ways to play this moment: with suspense or with surprise. Viewers might be made aware in advance that Magwitch is hiding behind some gravestones, about to pounce on Pip. That would create *suspense* because they know about a danger of which the character is unaware. Or viewers might be left in the dark about Magwitch's presence. That would create *surprise* because they as well as the character are caught off guard.[32]

Lean chose surprise rather than suspense. As Pip turns away from the grave to depart, Lean's camera moves slightly ahead of him to reveal a ferocious figure moving into the frame; just at that moment Lean cuts to a close-up of the brutish Magwitch, who grabs Pip and claps his hand over his mouth. Lean allows the audience to see Magwitch a split second before Pip does, thus creating a sense of shock that is immediately reinforced by Pip's own terrified reaction.

Lean wanted the spectator to recoil at the sight of the threatening figure of Magwitch at the same moment that Pip did. "The best thing was to frighten the audience, as the convict frightened the boy," he commented.[33] Lean set out to grab the audience's attention right from the beginning, and he succeeded in creating one of the most stunning opening scenes in the history of cinema.

Magwitch barks at Pip, "Keep still, you little devil, or I'll cut your throat!" This line of dialogue comes right from the novel, as does much of what Magwitch says in this scene. Magwitch orders Pip to bring him food and threatens him with dire consequences should he give him away to the police.

What he was trying to do in the scenes of Pip's childhood, Lean explained, was to make everything larger than life, as it is in a boy's imagination. The scenes of "the boy Pip lying terrified in his bedroom after a night of fear, then creeping downstairs at dawn" and stealing food at the behest of the convict hiding out on the moors, were "something Dickens wrote as if he were right inside the boy himself": "We tried in the film to make the audience share Pip's fears."[34]

Lean makes skillful use of the sound track when Pip is creeping out to the marshes to meet Magwitch again. Pip imagines that the cows he passes in a pasture are accusing him of thievery; he hears one cow say, "Stop him!" while an ox adds, "You thief!" Pip answers the ox, "I couldn't help it, sir."

The soldiers searching for Magwitch soon catch up with him in the marshes, and Pip, silhouetted against a darkening sky, watches as they take Magwitch into custody. Pip shakes his head "no" to Magwitch, to indicate that he did not turn him in. Before he is taken away, Magwitch declares to the arresting officer, loud enough for Pip to hear, that he stole some "wittles" (victuals) from the blacksmith's pantry. He says this so that Pip will not be accused of helping him in any way during his attempted escape.

"It was a year later," the adult Pip says over the sound track, when he was invited by Miss Havisham to Satis House, her enormous, hermetic home, to play cards with Estella, her ward. The reclusive Miss Havisham still wears her tattered wedding dress and sits next to the table where the wedding banquet rots away under a canopy of spiderwebs, even as the spiders themselves scurry in and out of the cake. All the clocks in the house are stopped at 8:40 A.M., the precise moment when she learned that she had been jilted twenty years before. Both the wretched condition of the house and the wilderness of weeds in the yard outside "bespeak her psychological deterioration over the years of her willful self-confinement."[35] The fearsome Miss Havisham is Lady Macbeth in a wilted wedding gown. She snaps at Pip, "You are not afraid of a woman who has not seen the sun since before you were born?" Pip responds, without much conviction, that he is not.

Billy Wilder paid homage to Lean's movie in his own *Sunset Boulevard* (1950), when he has the narrator describe the old mansion that is occupied by a has-been silent movie star: "A neglected house gets an unhappy look— this one had it in spades. It was like that old woman in *Great Expectations*, that Miss Havisham, with her rotting wedding dress and her torn veil, taking it out on the world because she had been given the go-by." As Noel Sinyard notes, Lean's film had been popular in America, "so Wilder would expect an audience to pick up the reference."[36]

Pip continues to come to Satis House to play cards with Estella, visits that Miss Havisham allows because watching their game helps her while away her empty hours. She encourages Pip to develop a schoolboy's crush on the supercilious Estella. When she notes later on that he has done so, the man-hating spinster whispers in Estella's ear, "You can break his heart."

The day finally comes when Pip must tell the old lady that he cannot come any more, that he has been apprenticed to Joe as a blacksmith. A shot of the young Pip dissolves to a shot of the shadow cast on the wall of Joe Gargery's forge by the older Pip, who can be heard talking with Jaggers, the solicitor. Then Pip is shown in conversation with the lawyer. The shadow and the voice thus precede the adult Pip himself and make for a smooth transition from Pip as a boy to Pip as a man.

The formidable Mr. Jaggers informs Pip that he represents an anonymous benefactor who has provided Pip with income enough to enable him to lead the life of a gentleman in London. Pip, he states emphatically, is now a young man of great expectations. Pip assumes that Miss Havisham is his benefactor, and she allows him to think that she is. Once in London, Pip shares a flat with Herbert Pocket, who undertakes to give him a crash course in the social graces.

At first Pip is so anxious to look like a gentleman that he behaves like a chucklehead. Herbert is appalled when he observes Pip dressing ostentatiously, even to the point of vulgarity, and he schools him in choosing more proper attire. When he notices Pip's dreadful table manners, he suggests tactfully, "It's not usually considered necessary to fill the mouth to its utmost capacity."

When Pip learns that Joe is coming to visit him in London, he admits in a voice-over, "If I could have kept him away by paying money, I would have done so." This line is taken directly from the novel, where Pip adds, "Even though I was bound to him by so many ties . . . I looked forward to his coming with considerable disturbance and some mortification."[37] In the film, when Pip observes Joe's arrival from his window, he looks down at Joe both literally and figuratively, ashamed of associating with such a country bumpkin in London.

Pip is condescending to Joe, treating him like an uncouth hayseed. After Joe departs, Pip gazes in a mirror at himself in his fashionable dressing gown; in retrospect, he recalls Joe's simple dignity and feels some remorse at the way he treated him. He comments in a voice-over, "In my effort to become a gentleman, I had succeeded in becoming a snob." This is an excellent scene, well dramatized from the novel.

Pip encounters Estella in London and falls in love with the beautiful but cruel young woman—clearly the protégée of Miss Havisham. She disdains Pip as a social climber and chooses Bentley Drummle (Torin Thatcher)—an upper-class gentleman, something that Pip assuredly is not—as her favored suitor. Pip is heartbroken.

One stormy night, Pip sits alone in his lodgings while rain pelts his windows. There is a knock at the door, and he opens it. As the door swings open, the muffled figure standing in the shadowy corridor is gradually revealed to be Magwitch. Magwitch explains that, after his capture, he was transported to a convict colony in Australia, where he became a prosperous sheep farmer. Pip now understands that it was Magwitch—and not Miss Havisham—who financed his affluent life in London. He did so in order that Pip could enjoy all the privileges that Magwitch himself had been denied in life. The fastidious Pip is devastated to learn that this coarse, crude convict is his benefactor because this means that his livelihood comes from a creature of the underworld.

Magwitch has returned surreptitiously to England in order to see the young man he thinks of as his foster son. In due course, he reveals that he once had a daughter but that he lost touch with her while he was in prison and does not know what became of her. In Magwitch's mind, Pip has taken the place of his daughter, and that is why he has taken the risk of coming back to England to see him. If the London police find out that Magwitch has fled from the convict colony, he will be hanged as a felon.

Magwitch adds that Arthur Compeyson, an ex-convict, is also in London and that he and Compeyson are sworn enemies. In the novel, Magwitch explains to Pip that Compeyson got him involved in a good deal of skullduggery, including swindles, fraud, and forgery. When they eventually got caught, each blamed the other—the old story of thieves falling out. But, in the movie, Magwitch never discloses to Pip the source of the enmity between him and Compeyson. He merely mentions ruefully that their involvement was an episode from the dark part of his life and lets it go at that.

In this manner, Lean wisely avoids developing a complicated subplot that would slow down the progress of the main plot. In the novel, Pip also learns that Compeyson was the very man who left Miss Havisham at the altar on her wedding day, but Lean likewise bypasses this story element in the film, again in order to simplify the plot of the movie.

At any rate, Magwitch warns Pip that he should be on the lookout for Compeyson, who is easily identifiable by the ugly scar on his left cheek. For Compeyson will certainly turn the fugitive Magwitch over to the authorities if he discovers his presence in London. Though Pip is repulsed by the brutalized convict, he grants him temporary asylum in the apartment, with Herbert's agreement, since he believes that he owes him a debt of gratitude.

Pip subsequently goes to visit Miss Havisham in her domain, to chide her for allowing him to think that she was responsible for his great expectations. He is distraught when she informs him that Estella is now engaged to Bentley Drummle. The desiccated old woman explains that, after she was betrayed by a faithless man, she vowed to take vengeance on all men; in encouraging Estella to abandon the lovelorn Pip, she has satisfied her vow. Pip says to her laconically, "Was that kind?" She replies pointedly, "Who am I, that I should be kind?" As she converses with Pip, "she is pictured beside a roaring, smoking fire" in the hearth, "with her face lit by the hellish flames."[38] This image implies that the heartless, bitter old woman is a fiend from hell, bent on inflicting misery on hapless individuals like Pip who have never done her any harm.

Nevertheless, when she sees Pip's anguish over the loss of Estella, Miss Havisham murmurs, "What have I done?" She is apparently appalled by her own duplicity. Pip gives her a reproachful look and stalks out of the room. He angrily slams the door, thereby inadvertently dislodging a smoldering log from the fireplace. It rolls onto Miss Havisham's gown and ignites it; the dress catches fire like a tinderbox. Pip is halfway down the stairs when he hears her screams, and he rushes back into the room. In a futile effort to smother the blaze, he drags the rotted tablecloth from the dining room table, and the wedding cake and all the porcelain dishes on the table come crashing to the floor. The tablecloth comes apart in Pip's hands, symbolizing the disintegration of Miss Havisham herself. For Pip is too late; Miss Havisham is consumed by the flames, and her corpse lies smoking on the floor.

Concerning this scene, John Mills recalls, "It took five hours to set the table, laden with the cake, the dishes, the cobwebs, and the mice." Just before they started to shoot, Neame came on the set. He said to Lean and Mills, "If you can get this in one take, it would be great." They asked why, and he replied, "Because it will take another five hours to set the bloody table up again." "And we did it in one take; it was sheer luck!"[39] Neame adds that Lean did not welcome a producer's appearance on the set to make practical suggestions of this kind. Though he and Lean were chums off the set, Neame says, Lean did not like anyone exercising authority over him—even though it was the producer's job to monitor the shoot in order to keep the film on schedule and on budget.

After the demise of Miss Havisham, Pip turns his attention to arranging—with Herbert's assistance—to smuggle Magwitch aboard a paddle steamer that is crossing the English Channel to France. In the course of a discussion with Pip just before Magwitch's departure, Herbert reminds Pip that they must be wary of running into Compeyson, who will certainly try to block Magwitch's flight. As a matter of fact, Compeyson has been following Magwitch all along. He can be seen standing furtively in the shadows on the pier, watching as Pip, Herbert, and Magwitch prepare to leave the dock, to row out to intercept the packet boat.

As Pip and Herbert are rowing Magwitch toward the channel steamer, Compeyson, a phantom in a black cloak, suddenly appears in another rowboat, leading a party of soldiers to overtake them. The packet boat collides with both rowboats, and Magwitch and Compeyson are hurled into the sea. They remain locked in a death struggle until Compeyson drowns. Magwitch is returned to prison and shortly thereafter is convicted of being responsible for Compeyson's death.

Meanwhile, Pip pays a visit to Jaggers and inquires about Magwitch's daughter; Jaggers informs him that Magwitch is Estella's father and that Molly, an ex-convict, is Estella's mother. Jaggers hired Molly as a charwoman in his office after he got her a parole. While she and Magwitch were both in prison, Jaggers arranged on his own to have their child adopted by Miss Havisham. So Estella is Magwitch's long-lost daughter.

Pip gets to hear that Magwitch is languishing in the prison infirmary, close to death, and visits him just before he expires. He is deeply moved when, with his last breath, Magwitch says that he is consoled to know that he has helped Pip get on in life.

Dickens, we remember, framed the story with first-person narration, in order to involve the reader in the book more immediately. Lean, in turn, followed Dickens's lead, not only by having first-person narration in the movie, but also by using the subjective camera deftly at crucial moments. Lean thus reminds us that the story is being told from Pip's point of view. For example, he employs the subjective camera in the sequence immediately following Magwitch's death scene. The fundamental concept of the subjective camera is that virtually everything in the sequence is seen through the eyes of the narrator. The technique accordingly provides a visual corollary to Pip's first-person narration in the book and to his running commentary voice-over on the sound track of the movie.

In the scene in question, Pip becomes distraught in the wake of Magwitch's demise and succumbs to a fever. As he wanders the streets in a disoriented state, his delirium is conveyed to the viewer by a series of images photographed by the subjective camera: "Pip is disoriented in the London street by a heaving sea of glinting satin top hats." These top hats represent that "gentlemanly order into which Pip has never successfully inserted himself."[40] Blades of light appear before his eyes and distort the images of passersby until the screen fades to black, signaling his loss of consciousness. Then the image of Joe gradually comes into focus. He is looking down on Pip, who lies in bed in his old room in Joe's cottage, where Joe has nursed him back to health. "I brought you home, old chap," Joe tells him.

Though this scene represents Lean's most ingenious use of the subjective camera in the movie, he used it in earlier sequences as well, in order to permit the filmgoer to share Pip's point of view. For example, there is Pip's first visit to Satis House, described above. When Pip enters Miss Havisham's room, the camera peers over his shoulder so that "Pip and the spectator take in the decaying room as a whole, before getting a clear view of its extraordinary occupant."[41] The technique allows the viewer to experience what Pip is experiencing at this moment in the movie.

Though Lean and his coscriptwriters agreed that they would employ the ending of the story that Dickens published in the novel, they were not satisfied with the manner in which they had dramatized it in the screenplay. Kay Walsh offered to give it a try. Walsh thought that, when Pip returned to Satis House, he would hear voices from the past. She also was convinced that, since Miss Havisham had had such a pervasive influence on her, Estella would repeat the pattern of Miss Havisham by proposing to live a life of neurotic withdrawal. She therefore came up with the following ending, which Lean used in the film.

Pip, now a successful businessman in partnership with Herbert Pocket, makes a final nostalgic visit to Satis House, which has survived the fire that killed Miss Havisham. As he goes through the gate and enters the mansion, he hears ghostly voices from the past, lines of dialogue from earlier scenes reproduced on the sound track: Estella's "Don't loiter, boy!" and Miss Havisham's "You can break his heart." In this fashion, we learn that Pip is reliving earlier visits.

The voices cease when Pip enters Miss Havisham's apparently deserted room; he is startled to find Estella there. In the novel as published, Bentley Drummle is deceased, but Estella has not remarried. In the film, Estella is not Drummle's widow; as she explains to Pip stoically, "When Mr. Jaggers disclosed to Bentley Drummle my true parentage, he no longer wished me to be his wife." So Estella has been jilted just as Miss Havisham was before her, and she accordingly intends to take over the old woman's role as a lonely and embittered spinster.

What is more, she believes that "Miss Havisham is still here with me." In short, "Estella has been bewitched by Miss Havisham."[42] Pip is determined to break Miss Havisham's evil spell, however. He shouts to the rafters, "I have come back, Miss Havisham, to let in the light!" He defiantly tears down the ancient curtains from the windows, and sunlight floods the room. "Come with me out into the sunlight," he exhorts Estella, and together they run hand in hand from the crumbling mausoleum where Miss Havisham had imprisoned herself. As the screenplay puts it, "Pip takes her hand and they run from the house; they pause in the garden and look back towards the decaying building, then continue through the gate into the sunshine. *Great Expectations* is superimposed over the shot."[43]

Lean was pleased with this ending, particularly because the sunlight imagery implicitly recalls Miss Havisham's remark to Pip the first time they met: "You are not afraid of a woman who has not seen the sun since before you were born?" Therefore, Pip's letting in the sunshine "is a final exorcism of the dead hand of Miss Havisham on his life."[44] Furthermore, the ending as filmed harks back to Pip's reflection in the novel—which may well have inspired Walsh—that it is up to him "to restore the desolate house, admit the sunshine into the rooms, set the clocks going and the cold hearths blazing, tear down the cobwebs, destroy the vermin—in short do all the shining deeds of the young Knight of romance and marry the Princess."[45] In keeping with this passage, Lean indicates explicitly that Pip will marry Estella, his "Princess." Consequently, the final scene as Walsh wrote it and Lean shot it is totally in keeping with the spirit of the film's literary source. Therefore, Regina Barreca is wide of the mark in referring to Lean's "infamous 'hand-in-hand toward the sunset' finish [as] unconvincing."[46]

In the novel, Magwitch wants to leave his fortune to Pip because he has lost touch with his daughter. But his worldly goods are forfeited to the crown because of his criminal status. In the film, Jaggers informs Pip that Magwitch's property can go to a blood relative, if not to Pip; that means that Estella is in the chips when she and Pip plan to marry at the film's fade-out. Julian Moynahan opines that this factor renders the ending "strictly movieland."[47] On the contrary, Pip is a success in business on his own; as Von Gunden maintains, Estella's inheritance from her father simply helps Lean meet the viewer's expectations that Pip and Estella will live happily ever after. As a result, the movie's ending "leaves the viewer satisfied and enriched."[48] In point of fact, Lean underscores the happy ending by superimposing the movie's title over the final shot. In other words, Pip's great expectations have finally been fulfilled.

Great Expectations is very much in tune with the theme that repeatedly crops up in Lean's movies: that one should not give up hope even when one's fondest expectations seem doomed to go unfulfilled. Pip articulates these sentiments when he says to Estella in the final scene, "I never ceased to love you, even when there seemed to be no hope for my love." This is the sort of determination that often marks Lean's heroes and heroines, as we have already seen.

In turning Dickens's novel into a serious work of cinematic art, Lean sagely eliminated some subplots and minor characters from the book's swarming canvas without leaving any visible scars on the finished film. Moreover, Lean's textual surgery excised Dickens's more implausible coincidences, such as having Compeyson turn out to be the heartless groom who left Miss Havisham at the altar. Compeyson is evil enough as it is, without laying that particular act at his door. Withal, the film still bursts at the seams with memorable incidents and characters.

Lean's last chore on the film was to submit it to the British Board of Censors—at the time headed by Brook Wilkinson—which rates films according to their suitability for general patronage, for children accompanied by an adult, or for adults only. Theater owners throughout Great Britain are bound by law to adhere to the censor's ratings. Brief encounter had been passed without cuts, and Lean expected the same verdict on *Great Expectations.*

Instead, Wilkinson did ask for cuts. Lean recalled that he objected to the brutality of Magwitch's attack on Pip in the graveyard scene and to the vivid portrayal of Miss Havisham's being burned to death. "Films are shown in darkened theaters," Wilkinson declared to Lean; hence, scenes of violence can prove upsetting for younger members of the audience. Wilkinson then proceeded to explain that he looked on himself "as a shield for the more sensitive members of the public."[49]

Lean thought it curious that Wilkinson deemed *Great Expectations* too violent for children since during the war they had been exposed to newsreels featuring graphic images of battles and bombings. Furthermore, the movie was certainly no more frightening than the book, which is regularly taught in schools. Lean steadfastly declined to excise any footage, and the censor responded by refusing to label the picture for general patronage, instead limiting the audience to adults and children accompanied by an adult.

Wilkinson was simply not prepared for Lean's grim film because it went a step beyond the kind of turgid costume pictures churned out by British studios in those days: for example, the James Mason vehicle *The Man in Grey* (Leslie Arliss, 1943), an empty historical melodrama featuring the usual dashing hero, gushy heroine, and black-browed villain. This was the sort of picture that one British critic dubbed "kitchen maid escapism."[50] Lean's *Great Expectations,* on the other hand, depicts a stark, tough Victorian world with characters blighted by bitterness and disillusionment.

Dickens's world was realized deftly and with uncommon insight by Lean and his firecracker cast. Mills and Hobson play the romantic leads with thoughtful control; they capture the Victorian ethos of outward formality masking seething emotions. Furthermore, they are supported by a full complement of England's best character actors, all of whom give performances to relish.

Though Lean was not much taken with Goehr's score, it makes a suitable contribution to the movie. There are, for example, the eerie strings and dissonant brass that accompany the scenes in Satis House, as well as the lush love theme, which is played to good advantage during both the opening and the closing credits.

Furthermore, Green's camerawork and Bryan's sets capture the smoke and ashes of infernal London, thereby giving the film power and resonance. The sun rarely shines; it is all winter light, driving rain, dimly lit rooms. Lean, a showman as well as an artist, transformed Dickens's splendid melodrama into topflight entertainment on the screen, with all concerned in cracking form. Both Green and Bryan won Academy Awards for their work on *Great Expectations*. Furthermore, Lean was for a second time nominated as best director; Lean, Neame, and Havelock-Allan were nominated for their screenplay; and the movie was nominated for best picture.

It was a great pity that Martita Hunt was not nominated for her extraordinary portrayal of Miss Havisham. Perhaps because Hunt was so eccentric in real life, it was assumed that she was playing herself when she enacted the role of the eccentric dowager. Guinness told me that she was given to wearing leopard-skin coats, ostentatious hats, and extravagant hairdos. She was known to fly into a rage at the least provocation, said Guinness. One night after *Great Expectations* had been released, Hunt invited Guinness and his wife to dinner. When the chicken she had roasted did not turn out properly, she hurled it on the kitchen floor, tore off her apron, and threw herself prostrate on the living room divan. Still, Guinness concluded, he never questioned her talent as a character actress of great accomplishment, and she did herself proud in *Great Expectations*.

The film itself was hailed by the critics as a model screen adaptation of a beloved classic and as a milestone in British cinema when it opened in London in December 1946. *Great Expectations* got a similar reception when it premiered in New York in April 1947. James Agee, the dean of American film critics at the time, deemed it "never less than graceful, tasteful, and intelligent; and some of it is better than that," especially when Lean lays hold of the crueler aspects of the story.[51]

Many commentators assume that, like Lean's previous films, *Great Expectations* played the art house circuit in the United States. As a matter of fact, it was booked into movie theaters in certain large cities that usually showed commercial Hollywood films. For example, I first saw the film in 1947 at the Loew's Theater, the biggest movie house in downtown Dayton, Ohio, which normally showed Hollywood products.

"No other film or television adaptation of *Great Expectations*," writes Robert Murphy, "has managed to achieve anything like the dramatic intensity and visual richness of Lean's film."[52] A 1989 made-for-cable version produced by Disney was noteworthy solely because Jean Simmons, who played young Estella in Lean's movie, took the role of Miss Havisham. "In 1989," Simmons recalled, "I had the guts to come back and play Miss Havisham. It was crazy, but I thought, 'Why not?'"[53] Predictably, Simmons was not nearly as good as Martita Hunt, though she did a credible job.

In adapting Dickens's novel to the screen, Lean managed to evoke the past as a vivid present. His characters inhabit a motion picture that came closer than any costume film before it had to showing us a historical era not as part of a dead past but as a living present.

If *Great Expectations* was a happy professional experience for Lean, his personal life at the time was not happy at all. "By the end of *Great Expectations*, David's marriage to Kay Walsh was over," Neame states. "There had been foreshadows; many fights and separations." Lean told Walsh that he was convinced that his career made too many demands on him and that he had decided that "it was best to live alone."[54] More to the point was the fact that he had apparently developed the habit of having an affair with a young woman involved in the making of every picture he directed. On *Great Expectations*, it was Margaret Furse, the wardrobe assistant, who was his inamorata. These affairs were passing fancies and never lasted longer than the duration of the production period of the film in question.

Neame, we recall, was aware that Lean had an inner conflict about his promiscuity because of his strict Quaker upbringing. Similarly, Havelock-Allan observed, "I've never seen a man who was in more of a subconscious dilemma between his sensuality and his strict sense of morality."[55]

In any event, by the end of the *Great Expectations* production period, Lean had broken off personal relations with Walsh, who would eventually divorce him. They both moved out of the house they had occupied near Denham Studios, and each took a flat in London. Lean's relationship with Furse also came to a close soon after.

Nevertheless, Lean respected both women as professionals, so he gave a major role in *Oliver Twist*, his next film, to Walsh and appointed Furse the film's costume designer. After Lean had dropped both of them, Walsh and Furse became good friends and worked together well on *Oliver Twist*.

Chapter Six

CHILD'S PLAY

OLIVER TWIST

Our heroes are simple. They are brave, they tell the truth, and they are never in the long run really defeated.

—*Graham Greene*

With *Great Expectations,* Lean had taken "a glorious plunge into the surging emotions and melodramatic fiction of Dickens." The film had taken the period movie well beyond the "historical escapism" of many of the British costume dramas made in the 1940s; unlike them, it had "a feeling for the daily life of the times."[1]

Lean was initially hesitant about adapting a second Dickens novel for the screen. For one thing, he feared repeating himself. For another, he had no wish to pigeonhole himself as a mere illustrator of classic novels and plays. Still, he reasoned, he had adapted three Noël Coward plays successfully, so it did not seem to him to be a "serious crime" to return to Dickens.

Moreover, Lean conceived of *Oliver Twist* as a darker, gloomier film than even *Great Expectations.* Dickens's *Oliver Twist* was "a grimly realistic study of what poverty was like in that time," he explained. So Lean's film would be a sordid tale of social evils, involving underprivileged urchins, squalid workhouses, and rampant crime.[2] Harsh, and characterized by brutish violence and a host of rapacious characters, it would be light years away from the kind of starchy costume pageants that other directors had often made of Dickens's works.

The novel covers young Oliver's life as a pauper in the parish workhouse and continues on to his apprenticeship to Mr. Sowerberry, an undertaker, and to his eventual flight to London, where he comes under the tutelage of the old scoundrel Fagin and his gang of young thieves. Oliver is temporarily rescued from a life of crime by the kindly Mr. Brownlow, but he is soon kidnapped by Fagin's cohorts, Bill Sikes and Nancy, Bill's mistress, and returned to the gang.

As the novel goes on, Nancy is killed by Sikes when he thinks she has betrayed him and the gang to the authorities. Sikes himself dies while trying to escape from a police manhunt, and Fagin ends up on the gallows. Oliver, however, is ultimately restored to Mr. Brownlow.

Dickens, who was only twenty-five when he wrote *Oliver Twist*, indicated in the preface to the novel that, when it was serialized in the London magazine *Bentley's Miscellany* in 1837–38, many readers found it "coarse and shocking." This was because some of the characters had been chosen, as he said, "from the most criminal and degraded of the London population": "Sikes is a thug, Fagin a receiver of stolen goods, and the girl Nancy is a prostitute." He continued: "It appeared to me that to draw a knot of such associates in crime as really do exist; to paint them in all their wretchedness, . . . forever skulking uneasily through the dirtiest paths of life, with the great, black, ghastly gallows closing up their prospects, turn where they may—it appeared to me that to do this would be a service to society."[3]

The readers of *Bentley's* were startled to find Fagin schooling innocent boys as pickpockets and rewarding them for their efforts with swigs of gin. Some commentators reacted in a similar fashion after the novel was published in volume form in 1838, finding it a depressing work; others, however, thought that the sordidness of the tale conferred a touch of honesty on it.

Oliver Twist went on to become one of Dickens's most perennially popular works. In fact, in later life, when he gave public readings from his fiction, audiences were mesmerized by his rendition of the horrible murder of Nancy. After one performance he wrote, "We had a contagion of fainting. I should think we had a dozen to twenty ladies taken out stiff and rigid at various times!"[4]

As he did with *Great Expectations*, Lean read *Oliver Twist* twice over, in order to come to grips with the plot, before attempting a screenplay. He was more convinced than ever that Eisenstein was correct in maintaining that Dickens had an affinity for the screen (see chapter 5). Recall that, as Anderegg puts it, Eisenstein analyzed the influence of Dickens's narrative technique "on D. W. Griffith and on the development of film narrative in general."[5] As a matter of fact, he pointed out that Griffith developed the concept of cross-cutting from Dickens's novels.

Eisenstein found Dickens a master of crosscutting, that is, depicting "*the progression of parallel scenes, intercut with each other.*"[6] To be specific, Dickens switches back and forth from one area of action to another in order to portray parallel incidents. By the same token, Griffith employed crosscutting by interweaving shots of scenes taking place simultaneously in two different locations, in order to keep the audience abreast of what was transpiring in both places.

To exemplify crosscutting in *Oliver Twist,* Eisenstein uses the episode that shows in alternating blocks of narration how Mr. Brownlow waits for Oliver to return while Oliver is captured and taken back to Fagin. Eisenstein writes, "Mr. Brownlow shows his faith in Oliver, in spite of the lad's reputation as a pickpocket, by sending him to return books to the bookseller." He also gives him £5 to pay his bill. "Oliver again falls into the clutches of the thief Bill Sikes, his sweetheart Nancy, and old Fagin."[7] Eisenstein emphasizes how Dickens shifts back and forth between Brownlow waiting for Oliver and Oliver being snatched by Bill Sikes and Nancy and taken back to Fagin's lair.[8] It goes without saying that, in the script, Lean followed Dickens's lead in crosscutting between the same two scenes.

Filmmakers before Lean had been attracted to *Oliver Twist* because of its larger-than-life characters and its visual potential. But the only sound version had been William J. Cowen's low-budget 1933 Monogram version. Cowen's *Oliver Twist* is a "laundered" reading of the novel (e.g., Nancy is Bill's wife, not his mistress), a superficial retelling of a few key episodes. And the performances are never more than adequate. Still, even though the picture received scathing notices, particularly in England, George Minter, who had distributed it in Britain in 1933 through his Renown Pictures, decided to steal Lean's thunder by rereleasing it in 1947, before Lean's film came out. The film historian William K. Everson, who was working for Minter at the time, told me in conversation that "Lean asked for a private screening of the 1933 movie at Minter's office." Everson thought "Lean seemed miffed that Minter was cashing in on the advance publicity for his version, but he didn't let on." Lean remarked afterward—but not to Minter—that Cowen's movie suffered from a clumsy screenplay and inert direction and could have used another coat of varnish. He then got on with the Cineguild production.

Oliver Twist (1948)

When Lean began to mount his own production of *Oliver Twist,* as usual he asked Arthur Rank to distribute the movie in England. After the phenomenal success of *Great Expectations,* Rank was enthusiastic about the project. The film would be distributed in the United States by Eagle-Lion, Rank's American distributor.

After *Great Expectations* was finished, Ronald Neame decided to try his hand at directing a film, so made an unpretentious thriller entitled *Take My Life* (1947), which was produced by Anthony Havelock-Allan. "Since I had been a cameraman," Neame writes, "I knew how to plan the shooting of the various sequences." And Lean advised him on the final edit.[9] Still, Lean was not pleased that his two partners in Cineguild were going their own ways. So Neame agreed to produce *Oliver Twist,* with Havelock-Allan acting as (an uncredited) associate producer.

Since Neame and Havelock-Allan were both still involved with *Take My Life,* however, they could not help Lean with the script for *Oliver Twist.* So Lean brought in Stanley Haynes to coauthor the screenplay with him. Lean remembered Haynes from *Major Barbara,* for which he had served as the production manager, impressing Lean as an intelligent and cooperative young man.

Lean estimated that it would take ten hours to make a scene-by-scene film adaptation of Dickens's book. So he utilized a procedure for mapping out the screenplay for *Oliver Twist* similar to that which had worked so well on *Great Expectations.* He first went through the novel chapter by chapter and pinpointed the key episodes that he wanted to include in the screenplay, briefly summarizing each and identifying its core. Then he and Haynes used these summaries to build the scenes in the screenplay. Consequently, even before beginning to write, Lean had already trimmed away superfluous episodes and banished some minor characters.

Later on, he was amazed that, when people saw the picture, "they thought they were seeing the whole book." The art of adaptation, Lean commented, means that the director includes all the main events in the film so that the spectator feels nothing important is missing.[10] In composing the script, Lean once again endeavored to incorporate snatches of Dickens's dialogue whenever possible. Nevertheless, he wisely employed Dickens's words sparingly since the novelist tended to be verbose and even florid at times.

Lean and Haynes completed the screenplay in only a month's time, on April 12, 1947. They were satisfied with their efforts, except for the opening scene. Dickens begins the novel simply with Oliver's birth in the workhouse, describing in prosaic fashion how the infant was ushered into a world of sorrow and trouble. Kay Walsh, who was being considered for a part in the picture, offered to try her hand at fashioning a more interesting opening for the movie. Lean remembered how she had come to his rescue when he was stalled for an ending for *Great Expectations* and encouraged her to try.

Walsh scribbled a couple of pages in an exercise book and turned them over to Lean. She suggested that the movie should open with a pregnant woman trudging through a storm on her way to the workhouse, where her son, Oliver, is soon born. Lean was confident that Walsh's material would make for a vivid and dramatic opening for the movie.

Lean once again constructed from a meandering Dickens novel "a flowing, filmic narration that would satisfy the literary purists and the mass audience," just as his *Great Expectations* had done.[11] In *Oliver Twist,* Lean told the whole story from the point of view of a small boy, as he had done in the early sequences of *Great Expectations.* "The whole film was outsized," Lean remembered, "from the stylized sets to the stylized performances of the villains of the piece."[12]

That Lean had settled on stylized sets for the movie is already evident in the screenplay. For example, the script indicates that the establishing shots of the workhouse where Oliver and the other orphans are interned "should give the idea of the boys passing through a human rabbit warren."[13] And their cramped quarters look precisely like that.

For *Oliver Twist,* Lean brought back major production artists who had done yeoman service on *Great Expectations,* notably the editor Jack Harris, the costumer Margaret Furse, the cinematographer Guy Green, and the production designer John Bryan. Together they helped Lean faultlessly re-create the stark period ambience of Dickens's novel. The camera operator, by the way, was Oswald Morris, who would go on to be the director of photography on *Oliver!* (1968), Carol Reed's musical remake of *Oliver Twist.*

Bryan turned to the etchings executed by Dickens's illustrator George Cruikshank to help him conjure up the moody and threatening atmosphere that surrounds Fagin and his gang in their underworld haunts. With Cruikshank's vision in mind, he designed dark and forbidding sets for the East London slum neighborhood where Fagin's hideout is located in a run-down tenement. A bridge with the London skyline in the background leads to the ramshackle tenement building. Bryan created "a masterly design of chimney pots, rooftops, menacing shadows, smoke, and spires." Even the interior set for Fagin's attic quarters is marked by grimy brick walls and "rotting timbers" overhead.[14]

Green helped Bryan evoke London's teeming slums, a cesspool of poverty and degradation, as a nightmare world with dimly lit tenements and crooked streets cloaked in dense shadows. He reinforced the gloomy atmosphere by using diffused lighting, giving the impression of weak sunlight coming through dirty windows.

Lean was gratified to obtain the composer Sir Arnold Bax, honored with the title "master of the queen's musick," to write the underscore for the film. By the mid-1940s, Bax's musical output had declined as he sank into alcoholism, so his score for *Oliver Twist* was one of his last great works, and it was eventually turned into a concert suite that has been recorded repeatedly over the years.

Years before, Bax had left his wife for the concert pianist Harriet Cohen, and he had from time to time written piano works for her; one of them was the score for the present film. He designed the musical score for piano and orchestra explicitly for Cohen to play on the sound track, and she is featured in the credits as performing with the London Philharmonic. Bax lifted the film's splendid closing theme from his little-known 1916 concert piece *In Memoriam,* which he had dedicated to his Irish friends who had perished in the Easter Rebellion of 1916. He apparently assumed that he was free to steal from himself when, in fact, composers rarely incorporate passages from their concert music into their film scores, a practice frowned on by producers and directors.

Neame states that *Oliver Twist* marked Bax's "first time composing for a movie."[15] Actually, his first film score was for *Malta GC* (Eugeniusz Cekalski and Derrick De Marney, 1943); Bax was among a number of British composers who wrote background music for propaganda films during the war. Ralph Vaughan Williams, we remember, scored Powell and Pressburger's *The 49th Parallel* (see chapter 2).

Lean engaged several actors he had worked with before to appear in *Oliver Twist:* Robert Newton (*This Happy Breed*) as the cruel Bill Sikes, Francis L. Sullivan (*Great Expectations*) as the bumbling beadle of the workhouse, Kay Walsh (*In Which We Serve* and *This Happy Breed*) as the pathetic Nancy, and Alec Guinness (*Great Expectations*) as the wizened old Fagin.

Guinness had to campaign for the role of Fagin. He took Lean to lunch at the Savoy to ask for an audition. "David was not keen on my playing the part," Guinness recalled in conversation with me. "He wanted an older, more experienced actor." After all, Guinness's only previous film work was a small part in *Great Expectations,* so Lean waffled about the screen test. "He's going to be covered with crepe hair and he'll look awful," he later confided to Neame.[16] But Guinness persisted and got his screen test.

Guinness arranged to have Stuart Freeborn, whom Lean had engaged as a makeup artist on the film, help him devise a full makeup job for the test. They were guided by the way in which Cruikshank had pictured Fagin.

Guinness was fitted with a putty nose that "in profile looked like a Toucan's beak."[17] He looked and acted during the screen test as the very image of malignity. "Of course, I was bowled over by it," said Lean. "Alec got the part without another word."[18]

The Rank organization had dispatched a copy of the screenplay to Joseph Ignatius Breen, the American film industry's censor. Breen replied that the screenplay was acceptable, but he warned that the portrayal of Fagin should not in any way prove offensive to a specific racial group. This was obviously an allusion to Fagin as Dickens's Jewish villain. Freeborn accordingly asked Lean whether he should tone down the "Jewish" hooked nose he had designed for Guinness. "To hell with them!" Lean responded, referring to Breen and his board. "We're not going to change a thing."[19] He pointed out that the British censor had no reservations about the portrayal of Fagin and that he had already seen to it that Fagin was not once identified in the screenplay as a Jew. So he let it go at that. (He would live to regret his stance.)

Casting the title role was easy. Lean and Neame were both friends of the *Daily Express* film critic Jack Davies, who had an eight-year-old son, John Howard, who suited the part, "a pale, angelic-looking lad, with large, expressive eyes." As a matter of fact, Lean did not give the lad much to say in the screenplay and "allowed the boy's expressive face to do his talking for him."[20] Kay Walsh found fourteen-year-old Anthony Newley for the role of the Artful Dodger, one of Fagin's chief rapscallions. She was at the time acting with Newley in *Vice Versa* (1947), a film directed by Peter Ustinov, and rightly guessed that the spirited Newley would be a good Artful Dodger. (Though Davies had no interest in an acting career, Newley went on to a successful career on both stage and screen.)

John Davis, Rank's business manager and chief accountant, persuaded him that they should close down Denham Studios and concentrate production at Pinewood, a much larger facility. Principal photography on *Oliver Twist* commenced there. During shooting, Lean continued to have misgivings about his casting of Newton because he was concerned about the actor's drinking problem, which had surfaced during the filming of *This Happy Breed* (see chapter 3). Though Lean's Quaker upbringing inclined him to have little patience with heavy drinkers, he had admired Newton's work in *This Happy Breed* and said so to the insurance company, which was wary of approving his acting in the picture. Lean favored casting Newton because he had played a ruffian convincingly in *Major Barbara*. Lean finally promised the insurance company that he would keep an eye on Newton. And, as shooting progressed, Newton behaved himself.

Still, Lean remembered that, on *This Happy Breed*, Newton took to drink during the later stages of filming; hence, he began to worry as Newton's final scene on the production schedule approached. That scene involved a police raid on Fagin's hideout during which Sikes endeavors to escape capture by climbing out on the roof. When Lean was preparing to shoot the scene, he could not tell whether Newton was drunk or sober—he seemed to be in a daze. "I'm afraid he's going to fall," Lean whispered to Green. So Green attached a safety wire to Newton's belt and "fed it through the tiles of the roof." If he stumbled, the wire would hold him firmly. While Newton was, in fact, a bit tipsy, he somehow got through the scene.[21] Lean was finally fed up with Newton's shenanigans, however, and never hired him again.

In any event, having chosen his cast and crew, Lean was ready to begin filming. As the film opens, "A pregnant woman, who is in the throes of labor, struggles at night across a storm-whipped heath." She desperately trudges on until she reaches a gate. She rings the bell and collapses "just as a flash of lightning illuminates the words on the gate above her: Parish Workhouse."[22] Inside, she gives birth and soon thereafter expires: "Her birthbed thus becomes her deathbed; and the flickering candle by her cot symbolizes how her own life is being snuffed out."[23] No dialogue accompanies this three-and-a-half-minute sequence, until the workhouse physician comments laconically to a nurse, "It's all over; the old story—no wedding ring, I see." This short speech is plucked from half a page of dialogue in the first chapter of the book and, therefore, represents the economy with which Lean and Haynes pruned Dickens's dialogue for the film.

At the close of the sequence, the last paragraph of the first chapter of the book appears on the screen as a printed prologue: "Oliver cried lustily. If he could have known that he was an orphan, left to the tender mercies of the beadle and the matron, perhaps he would have cried the louder." (Anderegg notes that "a voice intones" this passage on the sound track, but that is not the case.)[24] Mr. Bumble, the beadle, eventually marries the matron, Mrs. Corney, and together they ruthlessly rule the orphans in the workhouse.

Guy Green was pleased with the opening scene, which was shot in the studio, making full use of Pinewood's technical facilities, which were far more elaborate than Lean and his crew had been used to at Denham. Green had made a complex arrangement of lights to throw shadows on the pregnant woman as she crossed the desolate marshlands. Moreover, John Bryan had supplied a cloud-streaked sky on a cyclorama overhead, along with torrents of rain. When Lean viewed the rushes the following day, however, he turned to Green with a scowl and said, "We're going to have to redo all of this." He wanted it "rougher and harsher," with more storm. Green says that Lean's purpose was to establish at the very outset that this was going to be a darker, more despairing movie than *Great Expectations*.[25]

Normally Lean supervised the recording of the musical score, but he was off in America at that point in postproduction, conferring with the American distributor. Neame had to preside over the recording session, with Muir Mathieson conducting the London Philharmonic and Arnold Bax observing from the sidelines. As Oliver's mother makes her painful way to the workhouse, there is "a cutaway to briars, with their spikes bending in the howling wind": "This visually emphasized her torturous pains, and the music had to underscore her agony as well."[26] But that bit of music was missing from the score.

Neame turned to Bax and inquired, "What about the briar sound?" A morose, touchy man, Bax replied in a huff that this passage of music had completely slipped his mind. "You must do it now," Neame insisted. "We can't afford to call an orchestra of seventy-five again tomorrow." Bax jotted down some dots and squiggles on a scrap of paper and handed it to a copyist. Shortly thereafter, a new page of music was distributed to six members of the orchestra. Mathieson cued the musicians, "and out came this incredible musical pain," a burst of high-pitched string music.[27] Bax had composed these extraordinary bars of music on the spot, proving that he was still a master composer.

The entire sequence that follows, in which we see Oliver as a boy of nine, is very faithful to the spirit of Dickens's novel. Oliver and the other starving boys watch through a skylight as officials of the workhouse dine ravenously on succulent joints of meat. The boys later draw straws to see who will ask for more of the watery gruel that is their meager sustenance. Oliver gets the short straw, and he is soon seen giving a little shudder of alarm as he prepares to confront the master of the dining hall.

Lean films the master from below so that he appears to be towering over Oliver. "Please, sir," Oliver says timidly, extending his empty bowl, "I want some more." Lean expertly edits together three rapid shots of the master, the matron, and beadle, each bellowing in astonishment at the boy's cheek. "With the economy of an experienced editor," Lean employs three terse cuts to suggest the consternation that Oliver's request for more food inspires in the workhouse staff. By contrast, it took Dickens several sentences to describe their reaction.

Oliver's "rebellion" precipitates a near riot among the boys in the grubby dining hall. Hence, Oliver is expelled as incorrigible, and he is apprenticed to Mr. Sowerberry, a mortician. Forced to sleep among the coffins in the cellar of the funeral home and to feed on scraps of meat left for the dog, Oliver finally does really rebel against his cruel taskmaster, and he is given a whipping. The sight of Oliver being thrown down on the top of a barrel and whipped anticipates a similar shot in *Lawrence of Arabia*, when Lawrence is spread-eagle on a table as he is lashed by the Turks.

When Sowerberry complains of Oliver's recalcitrant behavior to Mr. Bumble, the beadle sanctions Sowerberry's brutal treatment of the boy. He is convinced that the undertaker erred in giving Oliver scraps of meat: "Too much meat made the boy strong; and he turned vicious." Since Dickens customarily sees to it that his evil characters get punished, Mr. Bumble and his strong-willed wife are eventually removed from their positions at the workhouse. In Francis Sullivan's finest moment in the film, Bumble tells an official that he only treated the boys the way his domineering wife told him to. The official responds, "The Law supposes that a wife acts under her husband's direction." Bumble bellows in reply, "If the Law supposes that, then the Law is a bachelor; and I wish that the eyes of the Law may be opened by experience!"

Finding his life at the funeral parlor intolerable, Oliver sneaks away one night and heads for London. In the crowded streets of the city, the lonely boy encounters the Artful Dodger, a young ruffian who lures him to the lair of Fagin and his youthful gang of pickpockets. Fagin runs the gang in cahoots with Bill Sikes and Nancy.

Lean follows Dickens in introducing Fagin as a despicable old man, frying sausages while wielding a toasting fork like a scepter. Fagin trains Oliver as a cutpurse by having some of the other boys demonstrate the craft of picking pockets. In a delightful comic scene, Fagin places snuffboxes, jewelry, and silk handkerchiefs in the pockets of his greasy flannel gown and pretends to be looking in a shop window. One of the boys steps on Fagin's foot to distract him while another snatches his watch. Within a few moments, all Fagin's treasures are artfully lifted from his pockets by the boys. Bax's musical accompaniment for the scene, which he entitled "Fagin's Romp" in the score, is a sprightly passage of music, all chortling trombones, snare drums, and tambourines.

The next morning, Oliver awakes to see Fagin rummaging through the sparkling trinkets in his casket of jewelry. When Fagin notices him, he winks and says, "They call me a miser, but these things are to support me in my old age." This is another example of Fagin's humorous side.

But the game turns serious when Fagin sends Oliver out on the streets to observe the Dodger lifting a gentleman's purse for real. Mr. Brownlow, the victim (Henry Stephenson), erroneously identifies Oliver as the thief, and the boy makes a mad dash through the crowd. At one point, Lean stations his camera in a narrow street and watches Oliver run from the opposite end toward the camera, thereby giving the filmgoer the feel of Oliver's exhausting run without ever moving his stationary camera. At another point, Lean has the camera operator, Oswald Morris, pushed down the street in a baby carriage, in order to film a tracking shot of the running boy. Then the camera shifts to Oliver's point of view, as a man on the street throws a punch right at the camera (i.e., at Oliver). Oliver is flattened, and the screen goes black to indicate that he has been knocked out. This shot exemplifies another interesting use of the subjective camera, whereby the camera represents Oliver's perspective (see also chapter 5).

Oliver is taken to court by the police, and an eyewitness testifies that another boy, not Oliver, was the real culprit. Still dizzy from the blow he received, Oliver faints, and the humane Mr. Brownlow takes him to his home to recuperate. Nancy, who has observed the whole incident, informs Fagin what happened, and Fagin plots to get Oliver back before he can give the gang away to the authorities.

In an effort to display his confidence in Oliver, Mr. Brownlow sends him to return some books to a lending library and gives him some money to pay the bill. While on this errand, Oliver is kidnapped by Bill Sikes and Nancy and returned to Fagin's den. As we have seen, Lean switches back and forth between Brownlow disconsolately waiting for Oliver's return and Bill and Nancy spiriting Oliver away to East London.

Nancy comes to consider Oliver as the kind of innocent soul that she was before she fell in with Fagin. "I thieved for you when I was a child not half the boy Oliver's age; and I've thieved for you ever since," Nancy snaps at Fagin. "And the cold, wet, dirty streets are my home; and you're the wretch that drove me to them long ago." These bitter words make Fagin wonder whether she will continue to be a faithful member of his gang. Nancy develops something like maternal affection for Oliver and decides to return him to Brownlow, who has in the meantime established that he is Oliver's grandfather (in the novel Brownlow turns out to be the best friend of Oliver's deceased father). Lean portrays this revelation visually by dissolving from a close-up of a picture of Brownlow's long-lost daughter in a locket that he cherishes to a close-up of Oliver, who bears a strong resemblance to his mother—Brownlow's daughter in the film.

Nancy meets Mr. Brownlow clandestinely on London Bridge, in order to arrange to return Oliver. "*Oliver Twist* is a film of shadows," Maxford writes, and Lean makes clever use of shadows here, as "the entire conversation between Nancy and Brownlow takes place in silhouette."[28] Fagin, who has grown increasingly suspicious of Nancy, sends the Dodger to shadow her and report on her activities. Nancy has refused to divulge the location of Fagin's hideout to Brownlow. But, when Sikes hears of her meeting with Brownlow, Fagin convinces him that she did rat on the gang. Fagin encourages Sikes to liquidate Nancy, adding with hypocritical compassion for the hapless woman, "You won't be too violent, Bill."

In a fit of fury, Sikes accuses Nancy of betraying him and the mob. Robert Newton really shows his mettle as an actor in this scene. His Bill Sikes is a snarling, bug-eyed creature with a sandpaper voice and a menacing growl. Sikes ruthlessly bludgeons Nancy to death with a cudgel. Lean employs artistic indirection to imply Sikes's brutality. Instead of focusing on the savage act itself, he shows the reaction of Sikes's dog, as it yelps and claws furiously at the door, in an effort to escape the terrible scene. A slaying that could cause even Sikes's ferocious dog to recoil must be brutal indeed.

When Lean was filming this scene, the tough-looking but really gentle bull terrier could not be coaxed into appearing desperate. Finally, a property man volunteered to handle the situation. He opened the door on the set and showed the dog a stuffed cat; then he shut the door. When Lean called for action, the trainer released the dog, which made a beeline for the door, attempting to get at the cat on the other side. Lean was convinced that portraying Nancy's murder by way of the dog's reaction to it was worth the trouble it took to get the shot: "I think violence is much more frightening when you leave it to the viewer to imagine."[29] As a matter of fact, this scene is one of the outstanding examples of horror induced by artistic indirection in all cinema.

Lean implies the first stirrings of guilt creeping over Sikes by showing him on the following morning, sitting in a daze next to the corpse. The camera pans from the dog, still cringing in the corner, to reminders of Nancy, such as her hairbrush and comb, on a table. The sun is by now streaming through the window, and Sikes shuts the curtains, in a subconscious effort to hide his crime. He also drags a blanket from the bed and throws it over the body, symbolically covering up the vicious murder.

Sikes then fantasizes that he sees Nancy's ghost telling him that she did not betray him and the others, as Fagin said. "Yes she did," says Fagin, as he materializes as well. Sikes raises his cudgel and strikes the image of Fagin with it, indicating that—too late—he now believes Nancy, not Fagin.

Nancy's corpse is soon discovered, and the police, accompanied by an angry mob, mount a manhunt for Sikes in the precincts of East London. They are also after Fagin. In the course of the search, Lean evokes a London of dark alleys and festering slums. The searchers come on Sikes's dog frantically looking for its master in the dark cobblestone streets. The flaming torches carried by the mob reflect how the rage of the common people has been ignited. The dog leads both the police and the crowd to Fagin's hideout, where they find Sikes and Fagin.

The police immediately capture a terrified Fagin, but Sikes climbs out on the roof. In the novel, Sikes is alone on the roof, but Lean increases the suspense of the scene by having him take Oliver with him as a hostage. A police marksman fires at Sikes and wounds him. Sikes has slipped a rope around his body and tied it to a chimney stack, in order to keep from losing his balance, but he falls from the roof when he is shot. He is brought up short by the rope, which winds around his neck, and he accidentally hangs himself from the chimney: "He ends like an animal, cornered and lashing out in terror; . . . his ugly death at the end of a rope is cheered by the mob milling around below."[30] Lean was already demonstrating his ability to cope with crowd scenes, an ability that would come in handy later on when making his epic movies.

Oliver is reunited with Mr. Brownlow, and together they enter Brownlow's mansion, Oliver's permanent home. Bryan designed Brownlow's house with a dazzling white facade to serve as a contrast to the grubby workhouse and Fagin's filthy den. Brownlow's home, after all, is a bright sanctuary for Oliver from the grim world he has left behind.

When *Oliver Twist* was released in Britain in June 1948, reviews were generally favorable. As with *Great Expectations,* Lean had once more marshaled an exceptional roster of British character actors. Moreover, Kay Walsh's compelling performance as Nancy avoids the tart-with-a-heart clichés, and truth shines through John Howard Davies's unaffected performance as Oliver. Furthermore, the film was selected for the royal command performance of 1948, at which the royal family was present.

In February 1949, the film opened at the Kurbel Theater in Berlin. The Jewish community was so offended by the characterization of Fagin that a riot ensued; the demonstrations ended only when the cinema manager withdrew the movie. This episode was the harbinger of more troubles to come.

"In England we had no trouble at all," Lean writes, with reference to censorship. He accepted the British censor's classifying the film for adults and children accompanied by adults, which was the same rating that *Great Expectations* had received. "But when it reached the States the balloon went up," he continues, "and to our surprise it was accused of being anti-Semitic." "We made Fagin an outsize and, we hoped, an amusing Jewish villain," Lean concludes.[31] However, because of the touchy temper of the times, in which the memory of the Holocaust was so fresh, Guinness's portrayal of Fagin was criticized as racist, and the release of the film in America was delayed for a time.

In his production notes for the movie, Lean had written that he wanted Fagin to start off in Oliver's eyes "as an amusing old gentleman; gradually this guise falls away and we see him in all his villainy."[32] Guinness accomplished this change perfectly. He projects Fagin as a grotesque individual who is, nevertheless, not entirely devoid of human qualities, even possessing a sense of humor. Indeed, the conception of Fagin as played by Ron Moody in Carol Reed's *Oliver!* (1968) owes more than a little to Guinness's portrayal. In fact, Guinness's Fagin, cavorting with his tribe of boys, makes Oliver laugh. Consequently, the seeds of Ron Moody's Fagin are already present in Guinness's.

Representatives of the Anti-Defamation League and the American Board of Rabbis, who had attended a private screening of *Oliver Twist*, condemned the presentation of Fagin as a stereotypical Jewish caricature, prompted very likely by the beaked nose that Guinness wore as Fagin. Still, Guinness's Fagin was true to Dickens, who described the character as "a very old, shriveled Jew, whose villainous-looking and repulsive face was obscured by a quantity of matted red hair."[33] Red hair was one of the standard accoutrements of Jewish characters on the London stage in Dickens's time, and he picked up on that detail when describing Fagin.

Nevertheless, Eagle-Lion—a small studio that had been put on the map by crime films like *T-Men* (Anthony Mann, 1947)—was anxious to release a prestige picture like *Oliver Twist*, which had been favorably compared to *Great Expectations*, Lean's instant classic, in the British reviews. It therefore opened negotiations with Joseph Breen. Eagle-Lion was aware that, without Breen's approval, few American exhibitors would book the movie. In fact, the censorship code contained a section stating, "The just rights, history, and feelings of any nation are entitled to consideration and respectful treatment."[34] Breen declared that, unless *Oliver Twist* met the code's stipulation in this regard, it would be denied the industry's seal of approval.

When Rank learned that the Jewish opposition was intransigent, he postponed the U.S. release of *Oliver Twist* indefinitely. That meant the cancellation of the film's premiere engagement at Radio City Music Hall, the largest movie theater in New York. John Davis, Rank's general manager, wanted to make "clean box office hits" that would make "world-wide profits."[35] So he was furious when the picture lost the booking. He personally kept an eye on Eagle-Lion's negotiations with Breen.

Eagle-Lion resubmitted *Oliver Twist* to Breen in 1950, and two special interest groups quite unexpectedly came to the defense of the film. First, the American Council for Judaism openly opposed any efforts to boycott the film because they saw film censorship as a greater threat. The filmmaker Otto Preminger (*Laura* [1944]), himself of Jewish origin, told me in conversation that the council's point was that "the right of free speech will be lost in this country if it is not defended" and that that applied to any attempt to suppress Lean's *Oliver Twist*. Second, the National Conference of Christians and Jews went to bat for the picture. In January 1951, Eagle-Lion had approached the conference, asking it to evaluate the film. The conference agreed and, in a letter of January 5, 1951, declared unequivocally that Lean's *Oliver Twist* would not stoke the fires of anti-Semitism, that Guinness's Fagin was "so far removed from twentieth-century American Jews in appearance and occupation that we see no likelihood of a widespread transfer in the minds of American audiences to their Jewish neighbors."[36]

Breen wrote Eagle-Lion on January 18, 1951, that he had carefully examined *Oliver Twist*. He stipulated that, in order to get the industry seal of approval, sixty-nine cuts, many of them minor (amounting to eight minutes, twenty seconds of footage), would have to be made. These excisions, including several close-ups, were meant to "eliminate whenever possible photography of the character of Fagin," without impairing "the clarity of the plot or the dramatic continuity."[37] Eagle-Lion, at Davis's prompting, made the cuts, which amounted to eleven minutes of screen time. Breen accordingly approved the film in February 1951. So Silverman errs in asserting that the film "never did receive the seal."[38]

Since Cineguild, Lean's independent production unit, had no control over the American release of the movie, Lean was not consulted by Eagle-Lion about the negotiations with Breen. He found out about the censored version of the movie only from reading the trade press, not from the distributor. "I often wonder if these people realize that we read the papers," he said laconically.[39]

Lean also found out that Davis had endorsed the shortened version of the film sight unseen. So he knew that he would get nowhere attempting to negotiate with Davis, Rank's hatchet man. He did, however, think that he might be able to negotiate further with Eagle-Lion in New York. So, on April 2, he fired off a cable to Eagle-Lion that he was distressed by the reports that a full eleven minutes of footage had been scuttled. He warned that, if the general public learned that the movie had been cut, they would imagine "that what has been deleted is unspeakable anti-Semitic propaganda; and the thought of such an unfounded assumption gravely disturbs me." He earnestly requested that the distributor inform Breen that he stood ready to shoot an additional scene, wherein a respectable Jewish leader offers the services of his community to the police when the hunt for Fagin is on. "The object would be to demonstrate the indignation of the Jewish community that one disreputable member endangers the reputation of many."[40]

This may have seemed a panicked gesture on Lean's part, yet there was a precedent for what he was requesting. The American director Howard Hawks added a scene to *Scarface* (1932) to satisfy the censor. In it, a group of concerned citizens express their consternation that an Italian American criminal like Tony "Scarface" Carmonte (based on Al "Scarface" Capone) was receiving too much coverage in the press, implying that this was unfair to the Italian immigrant population.[41] Nevertheless, there is little doubt that Lean's willingness to supply the new scene represented a last-ditch effort to keep the shortened version of the film from being released. But Breen was adamant that the cut version of the film be distributed.

Eagle-Lion finally shipped an American release print of the movie to Lean, and he was appalled. "They had cut the character down to the bare bones, and in so doing had removed all the comedy—thus leaving Fagin as a straight Jewish villain. In my opinion, this version *was* anti-Semitic."[42] Lean's point was well-taken. Two comic scenes were jettisoned: Fagin catching Oliver observing him greedily going through his jewel box and Fagin dexterously demonstrating the art of pocket picking for Oliver's benefit. In the latter, Guinness gracefully spins and prances about in a way that was quite rare for him to do onscreen. Yet even that lively scene hit the cutting room floor. By contrast, the scenes that showed Fagin in all his villainy were retained, most notably his stirring up Sikes's wrath to kill Nancy for allegedly betraying them.

Ronald Neame, for his part, could not imagine what the Jewish community was going on about. Dickens, he pointed out, provided two villains for the story: the shrewd, witty Jew Fagin and the bullying, sadistic gentile Bill Sikes, who was most certainly far worse than Fagin. So, Neame added somewhat facetiously, the picture "might just as well be accused of being anti-gentile as well!"[43] By the same token, Arthur Rank reflected, "If every race, profession, and sect objected to the unflattering portrait of its members, there could be no fiction at all."[44]

When I mentioned the controversy to Alec Guinness, he replied, "I was not aware that the American distribution of the movie was held up for so long." He further noted that Fagin was never once called a Jew in the picture, whereas Dickens referred to him as a Jew three hundred times in the book. As a matter of fact, Fagin is even called a "Jewish devil" in the novel, though that term does not appear in the serialized version.[45]

By the summer of 1951, Eagle-Lion had become a subsidiary of United Artists, which green-lighted the release of the American version of the picture on July 31. Even in this truncated version, *Oliver Twist* received some excellent notices. *Time* acknowledged, "The movie treats Fagin consistently as an individual (as Dickens did), never as a group symbol or scapegoat." Noting that the film had been trimmed, the reviewer nevertheless asserted, "*Oliver Twist* is long enough and rich enough to spare the cuts. . . . It is a brilliant, fascinating movie, no less a classic than the Dickens novel which it brings to life."[46]

One of the most ringing endorsements came from Bosley Crowther in the *New York Times:* "The character of Fagin and the fact that he is a Jew are mere part and parcel of the whole canvas of social injustice and degradation, which is so brilliantly filled out in Charles Dickens's great work. And it is an extraordinary canvas, this vast picture of poverty and greed which oppressed nineteenth-century England, that has been reproduced here."[47]

The movie, perhaps helped by Crowther's review, did remarkable business when it premiered in New York City at the Park Avenue Theater. (Under the circumstances, it was not to play Radio City Music Hall, as previously arranged.) It also fared well in some other key cities. But, elsewhere, the negative press that had dogged the movie in the months prior to its American release overshadowed its genuine merits, with the result that it was not shown widely in the United States.

For the record, the original running time of *Oliver Twist* was 116 minutes, while the American theatrical release prints ran 104 minutes. The film was released in America on DVD in 2004 in a restored version. This version clocks at 116 minutes; it is prefaced by the seal of approval of the British Board of Censors, which indicates that the restored version is the original British version.

The controversy long since having died down, the film can be assessed in a more clear-eyed fashion. Lean brilliantly projects a consistently dark vision throughout; the city's criminal subculture reflects a pervasive sense of corruption and blighted lives—a rogue's gallery of shifty, evil types. Furthermore, the film focuses on fallen women and waif-like children, thereby forcing us to look at the menace and unfairness faced by those who lack the reserves to protect themselves from the larger society. Lean gave credit to Guy Green for helping him achieve the grim look of the movie. He called Green "the Prince of Darkness" because of his ability to photograph the depths and densities of black in this dark and shadowy world.

In addition, Lean's *Oliver Twist* is a faithful rendition of Dickens's work. Indeed, it is astonishing how many of the marginal incidents of Oliver's life found their way into the film. Some of the episodes have, admittedly, been telescoped for the sake of brevity. Thus, Dickens's depiction of Fagin's trial and last night in jail, where he bemoans his fate before going to the gallows, are distilled into a single cry to the bloodthirsty mob that descends on him when he is apprehended: "What right have you to butcher me?" Only die-hard Dickens fans would cavil about how Lean has compressed the action. The movie nonetheless encompasses the vast canvas of the original story, as Crowther maintained.

Looking back on Lean's two Dickens films, it is evident that he took on two rather unwieldy novels, with their crude, melodramatic plot contrivances and craggy, awkward situations, and transformed them into screen masterpieces in their own right. Roger Ebert notes that, because of the way Lean brings the story to life with such unforgettable characters as Miss Havisham, his "*Great Expectations* has been called the greatest of all Dickens films."[48] In that regard, Lean's *Oliver Twist* runs a close second, with such memorable characters as Fagin. Lean himself was proud of both films: "With the two Dickens films I did—they are, oh, pencil sketches of those great novels that he wrote; but I think they are faithful. I wouldn't have been ashamed to show [Dickens] the films."[49]

Because the problems of children abandoned, kidnapped, and sold into crime are perennially with us, Roman Polanski (*Chinatown* [1974]) released a remake of *Oliver Twist* in the fall of 2005. Ben Kingsley, who enacts Fagin in Polanski's version, said that he had not seen Lean's film adaptation since he was a child. He stated that his portrayal of Fagin was in no way a response to Guinness's interpretation and that he was not aware of the controversy surrounding Guinness's performance. Instead, Kingsley declared, his portrayal was inspired by "Fagin's warped but empathetic stance toward Oliver," whom he both protects and uses.[50]

Though Kay Walsh had turned in an affecting performance in the picture, her on-again, off-again professional relationship with Lean was petering out. When Lean broke his promise to go on holiday with her as soon as *Oliver Twist* wrapped, it was evident that she no longer played a significant part in his life. As for Neame, with *Take My Life* under his belt, he was penciled in to direct *The Passionate Friends,* Cineguild's next production—until he was replaced by David Lean. And thereby hangs a tale.

Part Three

FROM RANK TO KORDA

Chapter Seven

THE BEAUTIFUL AND THE DAMNED

THE PASSIONATE FRIENDS AND *MADELEINE*

Life is a chain of losses; and we must confront these losses.
> —*Alijandro Iñárritu, filmmaker*

Many women haven't the courage to face themselves; they look for escape in one excitement after another.
> —*Richard Caleb, a psychiatrist in the film* Dishonored Lady

After *Oliver Twist*, David Lean made two melodramas, both vehicles for Anne Todd, who would become his third wife. *The Passionate Friends* was the first; it began its artistic life as a novel by H. G. Wells. No commentator on Lean's films examines the novel from which this film was derived in any detail. Yet, because the book is the work of a major English novelist, it deserves attention. Wells is mostly known as the author of science-fiction tales like *The Shape of Things to Come* (1933). This novel was filmed as *Things to Come* (1936) by William Cameron Menzies, who was known primarily as a production designer, from a screenplay by Wells himself (revised by Lajo Biro). Menzies's skill as a production designer was evident throughout, and audiences were dazzled by the film's imaginative vision of the city of tomorrow.

Wells also wrote several domestic dramas punctuated with Dickensian humor and keen social observations. In fact, these works recall novels by Henry James like *The Ambassadors* (1903) that examine the social mores of polite upper-class society. One such is *The Passionate Friends* (1913), which takes the form of a series of letters written by a father, Steven Stratton, to his son about his adulterous love affair with a younger woman, Mary Justin.

They are the passionate friends of the title. The concept of framing the novel as a series of letters was probably inspired by Samuel Richardson's *Pamela* (1741), another epistolary novel and one of the first novels in English.

The Passionate Friends is something of a roman à clef since Wells, a married man, made a habit of having extramarital relationships with younger women. Though the heroine of this novel is modeled on more than one of his mistresses, she was primarily inspired by Rebecca West. West would herself become a novelist during the period she remained Wells's mistress, making her literary debut with *The Return of the Soldier* (1918). After the publication of *The Passionate Friends,* Wells and West had a child who was named Anthony West. Yet Wells makes only one reticent reference to West in his autobiography, wherein he writes that he had a relationship with Rebecca West that was "in much the same spirit" as the one described in *The Passionate Friends*.[1] More to the point, as the Wells biographer Michael Foot writes, is that, "without Rebecca West, Mary Justin could never have happened."[2] As a matter of fact, during a rocky period in their relationship (which lasted ten years), West threatened suicide in one of her letters to Wells; similarly, Mary Justin contemplates suicide in the novel.[3]

The story is told almost entirely from Steven's point of view. However, in an effort to give Mary's perspective on their relationship, Wells devoted a chapter to her letters to Steven. "I am entirely wretched," Mary writes after they have severed their relationship. She adds that she no longer finds "life worth living," a remark that implies her intention at that point to take her own life.[4]

Rebecca West reviewed *The Passionate Friends* in the *New Freewoman* when it was published in September 1913. She praised it as a noble effort but criticized the solemnity with which Wells discussed marital infidelity, which she found all too depressing. Still wishing to remain on good terms with his inamorata, he wrote her on October 4 that her review was "first-class criticism."[5]

A silent movie of *The Passionate Friends* was made in 1922 by Maurice Elvey, the first director Lean had ever worked for as an apprentice at Gaumont (see chapter 1). As noted before, Elvey was no more than a journeyman director, but he managed to turn out a movie that was essentially faithful to Wells's book. Mary Justin (Valia), who is involved in a loveless marriage, carries the torch for Steven Stratton (Milton Rosmer) until her husband, Harrison (Fred Rayham), learns of her affair and threatens to divorce her, naming Steven as a co-respondent. To avoid scandal, Mary kills herself, as in the novel. Elvey did his usual routine job in directing the picture, which turned out to be nothing special.

Lean's producer, Ronald Neame, we recall, had enjoyed some success with his first directorial effort. So he was anxious to tackle another picture. Consequently, it was Neame, not Lean, who decided to do a remake of *The Passionate Friends*. He had come across Wells's novel when casting about for a suitable subject for filming. He was intrigued by it because a love triangle is a powerful engine, something that can keep a melodrama thrumming along. Specifically, Mary and Harrison's relationship represents the kind of repressed marriage that haunts British cinema: one in which a wife harbors secret yearnings that her conventional husband cannot satisfy. So perhaps it was inevitable that some twenty-five years later the novel should be filmed again.

Neame interested the novelist Eric Ambler (*Journey into Fear*), who was also a screenwriter, in writing the script. Ambler had cowritten the screenplay for Carol Reed's successful war film *The Way Ahead* (1944). *The Passionate Friends* was a period piece, but Neame and Ambler both were confident that it could be done in modern dress. After all, they reasoned, love stories can happen at any time; it was not a time-dependent story.

Neame proposed the project to Arthur Rank as a Cineguild production. As it happened, Rank and John Davis, his general manager, were interested in making more love stories that appealed to women, as *Brief Encounter* certainly had, so they green-lighted the project. Ambler then went ahead and turned out a screenplay—at which point David Lean and his protegé Stanley Haynes entered the picture.

The Passionate Friends (1949)

David Lean and Stanley Haynes, who had coscripted *Oliver Twist*, were still looking for their next project for Cineguild. Haynes phoned Neame about three weeks before shooting was to begin on *The Passionate Friends*, and, with studied casualness, Haynes asked if he and Lean could read the screenplay. Neame sensed that Haynes, a rambunctious eager beaver, betrayed some irritation that Neame and Ambler had a picture about to go before the cameras and that he and Lean did not. Still, Neame did not hesitate to send Haynes the script since, as Haynes reminded him, they were all working for Cineguild.

Neame's firsthand testimony in his autobiography of the chain of events from this point on is invaluable because accounts of how Lean came to direct the picture, instead of Neame, differ from one Lean biography to another. As Neame tells it, two days after Haynes received the screenplay, he phoned Neame again. With his customary tactlessness, he declared that he and Lean had both read the script: "And we both think that you and Eric are in trouble."[6]

Haynes went on to say that he and Lean had arranged for a conference with Neame and Ambler for that same evening in the private dining room of a London restaurant, and both Neame and Ambler agreed to come. Neame remembers the meeting as a nightmare. For openers, Haynes repeated his judgment of the screenplay as inadequate and in need of a major overhaul. "I agree with Stanley," Lean chimed in. "It won't work as it is."[7] Neame and Ambler felt that, when a canny filmmaker like David Lean tells you that you are sick, maybe you should lie down. Therefore, when Lean and Haynes asked that they push back the start of the principal photography for three weeks while they reworked the screenplay in tandem with Ambler, Neame and Ambler both acquiesced. Neame reflected afterward that at no time during the conference—or at any time afterward—did Lean and Haynes specify precisely what was wrong with Ambler's draft. But he and Ambler were knocked sideways by the united front that Lean and Haynes presented to them and, thus, simply concurred with what the pair proposed.

Neame phoned Rank the next day to request a postponement of the shooting date; since Rank was to distribute the film, his permission was required. When "King Arthur" heard that David Lean was involved in the rewrites, he readily agreed. Meanwhile, Neame continued with preproduction.

Ambler, who was never awed by Lean, was not happy to be collaborating with him on the revised script. "David didn't want a writer to work with him," he groused. "He wanted an amanuensis like Stanley Haynes."[8] He viewed Haynes as Lean's sycophant: "He made a damned nuisance of himself; he was trying to latch on to David, so that he had a job."[9] To put it even more frankly, Haynes appeared to Ambler to be an opportunist who sought his own advantage in any situation. Moreover, he was a driven individual who never seemed to settle down; he was involved in an unhappy marriage, had been divorced twice, and had had a number of affairs. Anthony Havelock-Allan, who was still a partner in Cineguild, shared Ambler's assessment of Haynes and steered clear of him.

Neame was dismayed when he read the pages of the revised screenplay that Haynes forwarded to him in dribs and drabs. For one thing, some of the sets that had been constructed for the movie by John Bryan, the production designer, were no longer needed for the revised draft. In fact, new sets had to be constructed, and the studio had to absorb the costs involved. Rank and Davis understandably were miffed by this turn of events.

Lean observes that, since this particular Wells novel was not nearly so well-known as the two Dickens novels that he had filmed, he felt freer to depart from the text while still maintaining the spirit of the literary source. One major departure from Wells was that Mary does not commit suicide, as she also does in Elvey's silent movie version. (This was a change from the novel with which Neame agreed.) Furthermore, whereas the novel is narrated by Steven, the script is narrated by Mary (thereby providing a notable similarity to *Brief Encounter*). Moreover, Lean and his collaborators did not utilize very much of Wells's turgid and wordy dialogue; only a few scattered sentences reminiscent of it found their way into the screenplay. For example, the independently minded Mary insists that she wants to belong only to herself, not to any one man. Hence, she tries to hold on to both her husband and her lover.

Even in his autobiography Neame gives no specifics on precisely how Lean and Haynes's version of the script differed from Ambler's first draft. And Lean's own remarks about the revised screenplay are likewise unenlightening. He merely declares that he and Haynes (no mention of Ambler) "worked day and night": "We redid the script and kind of sharpened it a bit."[10]

Clearly, however, one of Lean's revisions was the introduction of a scene at the Chelsea Arts Club Ball, a dazzling masquerade ball usually held in the Royal Albert Hall. Part of the impetus behind this scene was the fact that, back when he was still a film editor, Lean had gate-crashed the ball and never forgotten the experience.[11] But he was also concerned that, owing to similarities in story lines, the critics would consider *The Passionate Friends* a mere remake of *Brief Encounter* even if the main protagonists were younger and more affluent. So he was bent on incorporating more glamorous settings in the screenplay. A replica of the Royal Albert Hall had, accordingly, to be constructed on the soundstage.

By the time filming finally commenced, Neame still had only an unfinished screenplay to work with, as Lean and his cohorts were still making their revisions. Ann Todd, one of Britain's top stars, who was to play Mary, had just returned from Hollywood, where she had appeared in Alfred Hitchcock's *The Paradine Case* (1947). Neame recalls that she was upset that the final script was not in her hands and was insecure because she did not know where her character was headed. When she heard that David Lean was working on the screenplay, moreover, she wondered why an experienced director like Lean was not directing the picture. She began bickering with Neame about every scene, thereby undermining his self-confidence still more—it had already been shaken by Lean and Haynes rejecting Ambler's original script, which he had approved. With an unfinished script and a temperamental leading lady to cope with, says Neame, "I was a lost soul. There was no way that I could have succeeded, and by the end of the fourth day I was contemplating suicide."[12]

At this point, Haynes rang Neame again, this time requesting that

Neame ship the rushes of what he had shot so far from Pinewood to London so that he, Lean, and Ambler could view them, and Neame once again complied. The following day, Haynes phoned Neame to arrange another conference with him and the others. At this meeting, Neame was advised that the rushes fell considerably short of expectations. Haynes then spoke up and announced that he and Lean had decided that Neame must be replaced as director. They further proposed, Haynes continued, that production be shut down for two weeks, until the script was finally ready, and that filming would then resume with David Lean at the helm. As an accommodation, Neame was to be officially named the film's producer, a task he had been carrying out unofficially during preproduction anyway. Finally, Haynes and Lean proposed that Ambler be listed in the screen credits as principal author of the screenplay, with the collaboration of David Lean and Stanley Haynes. A totally demoralized Neame gave in and accepted the inevitable.

For his part, Ambler was convinced that Lean had sold Neame down the river, but had gone along with Lean and Haynes because he was convinced that, were there any more delays in production, Davis might well persuade Rank to cancel the picture. As a matter of fact, Ambler believed that Lean had never wanted Neame to direct a picture for Cineguild in the first place. According to Ambler, Lean assumed that Cineguild existed to make pictures directed by David Lean alone: "He didn't want Ronnie going off and deserting the ship—*his* ship."[13] Ambler resolved never to make another picture with David Lean, and he never did.

Even John Mills, who to this point had a good working relationship with Lean, was keenly disappointed in his treatment of Neame. When Lean took *The Passionate Friends* away from Neame, "people rallied round Neame," Mills remembered, realizing that "Lean had done a bad thing."[14]

Ambler's belief that Lean wanted no one but himself to direct a Cineguild picture might seem to suggest that, from the beginning, Lean planned on taking over *The Passionate Friends*. There is, however, no evidence that this was, in fact, the case. Lean himself always contended that he did so only reluctantly—because "I wanted to help Ronnie." It was not, he insisted, a project in which he was personally interested. "I don't think I did wrong."[15]

Still, Lean tended to fob off specific questions about how he came to direct *The Passionate Friends*. He did, however, tell Kevin Brownlow that, when he learned that the picture was in trouble, he looked at the footage that Neame had already shot: "I realized that it was no good. Then I took over. I stopped for two weeks, got the script and rewrote it with Stanley Haynes. We wrote like hell."[16] Interestingly, Lean's recollections are inaccurate. For one thing, he makes no mention of Ambler's role in the rewrite.

Furthermore, as Neame's autobiography makes clear, Lean intervened at the script stage, three weeks before there were any rushes to see.

Lean had, in fact, never expressed much confidence in Neame's abilities as a director. Neame was, after all, a cinematographer, and Lean was convinced that, because they lack experience directing actors, cameramen never make good directors. Seeing the rushes for *The Passionate Friends* can only have confirmed his initial misgivings, convincing him to risk such a major change so far into the production process.

The upshot was that Neame went to see Rank at his home in Reigate one Saturday and broke the news that he was stepping down in favor of Lean. Rank agreed to abide by the Cineguild partners' decision. The following Monday, Neame assembled the cast and crew in the boardroom in Pinewood and made a formal announcement: "I've spoken to my friend David Lean, and he's going to take over the picture. I will be producing. It's going to be a bloody marvelous production."[17]

As it turned out, Lean had no difficulty relating to the production crew when he took over as director. Neame had already brought together several individuals whom Lean had worked with before: the director of photography, Guy Green; the camera operator, Oswald Morris; the production designer, John Bryan; the costumer, Margaret Furse; and the supervising editor, Jack Harris. By this time they had all developed into a finely honed team. In addition, Richard Addinsell, who scored *Blithe Spirit*, was composing the background music.

Besides casting Ann Todd as Mary Justin, Neame had tagged Claude Rains (*Casablanca* [Michael Curtiz, 1942]) as Mary's husband, now renamed Howard, and Marius Goring (*The Red Shoes* [Michael Powell and Emeric Pressburger, 1948]) as her lover, Steven Stratton. Lean went along with Neame's casting choices, except for Goring, whom he replaced with Trevor Howard. This was a curious decision since all along Lean had wanted to avoid having *The Passionate Friends* considered a mere reworking of *Brief Encounter*. Yet putting Howard in the role of the adulterous lover would clearly invite comparisons.

The one member of the cast Lean was concerned about was Ann Todd. Though he respected her as a talented actress, word had reached him about how she had badgered Neame. Lean told Neame that he had no intention of rolling out the red carpet for her because she was an international star just back from Hollywood, where she had made a Hitchcock movie—which is precisely what Neame had done.

Todd was not aware of the tough stance that Lean planned to take toward her; indeed, she looked forward to working with him. She told me in conversation that she met Lean on the first day of shooting the Chelsea Arts Club Ball sequence. (She mistakenly recalled that they were shooting on location, in the real Royal Albert Hall, not in the studio.) Lean was stationed on the camera crane above the set, doing first long shots of the dance floor below, then a close shot of her dancing. "David swooped into my life on a camera crane," she said, "and I was very impressed since he was a very imposing figure." But she never imagined at that moment that she would make more pictures for him, much less that she would become his third wife.

Lean kept his resolution to remind Todd who was boss from the get-go. She told me that, when she was tardy in arriving on the set for a take later on, he remonstrated with her about having kept the cast and crew, not to mention the crowds of extras in fancy dress, waiting. She explained that the call boy had failed to alert her, but Lean replied sternly, "An actress should be on time, whether she is summoned or not." Todd added that Lean apparently assumed she fancied herself "a conceited grande dame" and thought she should be taken down a notch or two.

Todd was furious at Lean's abrasive manner toward her and let off steam to Claude Rains, who was a gracious gentleman offscreen. He reminded her that movies are made in a factory atmosphere. She remembered him saying, "You do your job, earn your paycheck, and don't fuss." "I never forgot Claude's advice," she concluded. And she got on better with Lean as time went on.

The camera operator Oswald Morris saw Lean as an inveterate perfectionist, and perfectionists can be difficult to deal with at times. Morris recalled Lean often quizzing him after he had finished a take, asking, for example, whether he was absolutely certain he had kept the camera steady when doing a panning shot. Guy Green had noticed Lean behaving in this fashion while he was a camera operator on one of Lean's early movies. Both Morris and Green felt that they had learned from working with Lean, however, because he demanded the best they had to offer.

Lean always maintained that Claude Rains was one of his favorite actors and worked with him again. Rains, he found, was always instrumental in settling the disagreements that inevitably crop up during filming. One such disagreement occurred on Rains's first day on the picture. Rains had just arrived from Hollywood, where he had finished the thriller *The Unsuspected* (Michael Curtiz, 1947). Lean went straight into the scene in which Howard—who has just discovered Mary and Steven's affair, though they are not immediately aware of this—is making drinks for them with feigned nonchalance. Lean thought that Rains was coming across as too polite.

Lean called a halt; he explained to Rains that Howard is playing a cat-

and-mouse game with the straying pair and that his voice should, therefore, have "a cutting edge to it." Howard looks on them with veiled condescension and scorn, Lean continued. "You are in a way being very cruel. The wife gets it, the lover doesn't."[18] Lean's point was that Howard exemplifies how a civilized gentleman can be vicious underneath his courteous exterior. Rains, who had studied this scene while crossing the Atlantic by ship, was chagrined that he had misinterpreted it. He said that he would take a new approach to the scene after he studied it again overnight and promised to be ready to film it in the morning. The next day, said Lean, Rains did the scene properly—the injured husband indulging in small talk, biding his time before he finally confronts his wife and her lover. "This turned out to be the best scene he did in the picture."[19]

The Passionate Friends afforded Lean the chance to shoot on location on the Continent. He had gone on location to Carnforth in northern England to shoot exteriors for *Brief Encounter* and had filmed on the Thames for *Great Expectations*. But this was the first time he had done location work abroad. He first took the film unit to Lake Annecy in central France (standing in for Switzerland) to film the scene in which Mary and Steven meet by chance at a Swiss resort after a long separation.

Lean had chosen what turned out to be one of the area's rainiest summers in living memory, and stormy weather held up shooting because the script called for a sunny atmosphere, as Mary and Steven fall in love all over again. When the sun finally did come out, Lean shot the scene in which the couple go for a speedboat ride on the lake. Since the front seat of the boat could not accommodate both the driver (who had a few lines of dialogue) and the director as well as the camera, Lean decided to play the driver—and, thus, drive the boat—himself, donning a beret for the role. His only other cameo appearance in one of his films up to this point had been as a passenger on the station platform in *Brief Encounter.*

Shooting was delayed not only by bad weather but also by Lean's taking Todd for boat rides on the lake. The antagonism that Lean had displayed toward Todd early on had faded away, and they were becoming emotionally involved. The director and his star would sometimes disappear for forty-five minutes or so while Lean piloted Todd in a Chris-Craft speedboat across Lake Annecy and back. Meanwhile, the rest of the cast and crew were waiting around to shoot a scene. Neame would phone the associate producer, Norman Spencer, from the production office at Pinewood and complain that Lean was falling behind schedule. He had received reports from the location about how Lean, usually so conscientious about not wasting time while shooting, was now playing hooky with his leading lady.

From France, the unit went on to the Swiss Alps, near Chamonix, for some mountain sequences. While Steven and Mary were flirting on-camera as they picnicked on a mountain slope, Lean and Todd were flirting off-camera. The Lean-Todd affair was an open secret—at least to the location crew since Todd was spending most of her off-hours in Lean's hotel suite. She told me in conversation that the crew suspected that "David had a number of lingering close-ups of me in the picture because he was so preoccupied with me at the time." Lean was still married to Kay Walsh, but they were estranged, and she was conveniently too far away to find out that Lean and Todd were an item, at least for the time being.

The sequences shot in the Alpine locations were among the principal reasons that *The Passionate Friends* has often been called a glamorized *Brief Encounter.* "We were playing love scenes against cumulus clouds and beautiful mountains," said Lean.[20] The Alpine vistas provided a lustrous scenic backdrop for Mary and Steven's outings. Furthermore, the extensive location shooting in foreign climes that Lean did on this picture took him one step closer to the epic-scale films of his later career, when he would be shooting movies literally all over the globe, from the jungles of Ceylon for *The Bridge on the River Kwai* to the Arabian Desert for *Lawrence of Arabia.*

When *The Passionate Friends* went into postproduction, Richard Addinsell's score was recorded with Muir Mathieson conducting the orchestra as usual. When Mary and Steven's love affair blossoms in the flashbacks in the early part of the picture, Addinsell proved himself more than equal to providing the called-for lyrical efflorescence for the romantic music.

Jack Harris, who had edited several of Lean's previous pictures, supervised the editing of the movie by a young editor named Geoffrey Foot. Foot had started his apprenticeship as an editor working under Thorold Dickinson, with whom Lean had himself collaborated in editing *Java Head* in 1934. Foot had edited Ronald Neame's *Take My Life,* and Lean had given him a helping hand in the cutting room on that picture as a favor to Neame. Foot well knew Lean's reputation as one of the foremost film editors in Britain—and was also well aware that Lean personally monitored the editing of his films—and, thus, was diffident about working on a Lean picture on only his second outing as an editor. During postproduction, however, Foot found Lean supportive and encouraging. He still remembers carefully cutting the first sequence of the film on his own and showing it to Lean; he was relieved to hear Lean say, "Jolly good!"[21]

The first sequence of the film, to which Foot refers, begins with Mary arriving by plane at a resort hotel in Switzerland for a holiday with Howard, who has not yet returned from a business trip in Germany. It is there that she runs into Steven, who quite by chance is staying at the same resort. This situation occasions a flashback to 1939, when Mary and Howard encountered Steven at the sumptuous Chelsea Arts Club Ball, a festive New Year's Eve celebration complete with balloons, streamers, and confetti. Leaving the ball with her husband in their chauffeured limousine, Mary recalls in flashback her relationship with Steven back in 1935.

In this flashback within a flashback, we see Mary and Steven, a professor of biology, involved in an ardent love affair. In one scene, they pause on the shore of a lake, and Lean shows their images reflected on the surface of the water: "When Steven throws a stone into the shimmering water, the lovers disappear beneath the ripples." This signifies the fragility of their love.[22] This visual image is linked to another, in which the leaves of a nearby tree shadow the lovers' faces, as if the leaves are throwing shadows over the relationship, thereby prefiguring that the romantic idyll will not last.

As a matter of fact, when Steven proposes to Mary, she rejects him, preferring to accept the proposal of Howard Justin, a wealthy stockbroker at least twenty years her senior. She explains to Steven that she finds him too possessive. In one of the few snatches of dialogue taken directly from the novel, she exclaims, "Why can't there be love without this clutching, this grasping?" Hence her decision to enter a comfortable marriage of convenience.

Steven is crestfallen and leaves Mary with this bitter recrimination: "Then your life will be a failure." With that, the flashback within a flashback ends. Howard's frigid personality is the underlying cause of his rejection of a genuine love relationship and explains why he prefers a companionate marriage with Mary. For her part, Mary can hardly be sexually attracted to the much older man. Thus, Lean shows Howard and Mary sleeping in separate beds, not because the censor required it, but to make a point about their loveless marriage.

The flashback to 1939 continues. Sometime after their meeting at the Chelsea Arts Club Ball, Mary and Steven resume their affair. While Howard is in Germany, they see each other regularly. Howard returns sooner than expected, and Mary informs him that she and Steven have tickets for a play that same night. Later that evening, Howard notices that Mary has left the theater tickets behind. He accordingly suspects that they were merely cover for a tryst. He goes to the theater and is ushered to the two empty seats that Mary and Steven had booked; before returning home, he purchases a program, with which he plans to lay a trap for them. Ironically, the play is entitled *First Love,* for Steven was Mary's first love.

If a screenplay is to keep the audience's interest, there must be in it crucial scenes that move the action forward decisively. There is in an extended

1939 flashback sequence one such scene. Karel Reisz included a detailed study of this very sequence in his book on film editing,[23] just as, as we have seen, he included one of a sequence from *Great Expectations* (see chapter 5). Reisz told me in conversation that in both cases, "David's supervision of the editing of his films proved time and again that, as a skilled film editor, he was without a peer."

The scene in question is the one in which Howard confronts his wife and her lover after Steven escorts Mary home from their evening together, pretending to have been to the theater. Claude Rains may have had trouble rehearsing this scene, as noted above, but he gives an impeccable performance in the scene as filmed.

The scene begins with Howard setting about mixing drinks for Steven and Mary. He behaves in a calm, cool fashion because he wants to avoid an ugly quarrel. He prefers, instead, to stage-manage a carefully orchestrated showdown. So he begins by asking Mary some apparently casual and innocent questions about the play. As Reisz writes, "Actually, as the audience knows, [the questions] are carefully and precisely calculated to drive Mary into a corner where she must confess her lies."[24] Howard continues his game of cat and mouse with her. His smooth, controlled behavior and his persistent questions about the play finally lead Mary to suspect that he is on to her deception. Consequently, she responds with short, evasive answers.

During this interchange, Lean intercuts shots of Howard looking down at Mary with shots of her looking up at him. That Howard is looking *down* at her implies that he is in the superior position, that he is in complete control of the situation. (There is something of the disapproving father in his manner.) That Mary must look *up* at him implies that she is in the inferior position, that she is on the defensive.

Before Howard began fixing the drinks, he placed the theater program on the coffee table in the center of the room where it would be conspicuous. For good measure, he sets Mary's drink down on top of the program, where she cannot help noticing it. Lean cuts from a close-up of the program to a huge close-up of Mary as she suddenly spots the program, then to a medium shot of Mary and Steven as she endeavors to catch Steven's eye and get him too to notice the program and realize that the game is up. Lean follows this series of shots with an extreme close-up of Howard as he asks Mary with a sneer, "Ice?" There is an iciness in his voice that puts a chill in the air. This whole series of shots is carefully mapped out in the final shooting script.[25] It exemplifies Lean's careful planning.

Up to this point, Latin music has been playing softly on the radio; the bouncy music provides an ironic counterpoint to the tension in the room.

When Howard is quite ready to have it out with Steven, he snaps off the radio. After a moment of tense silence, Mary says ruefully to Steven, "Howard knows we weren't at the theater." Steven, attempting to muster some degree of composure, declares to Howard, "I'm sorry you had to find out this way, but I think you had better know the truth. Mary and I still love each other." Howard counters that Mary still belongs to him, and Steven scoffs at the notion. Seeing that his confrontation with Steven has degenerated into the vulgar row that he had sought to avoid, Howard at last explodes and exclaims, "Get out!" Instead of having a close-up of Howard shouting these words, Lean has a close-up of Steven looking startled as he hears Howard yelling off-camera. Lean, always the clever editor, thought it was interesting for the viewer to see Steven being taken aback by Howard's bellowing at him since, up to this point, Howard has not raised his voice at all.

A few days later, Steven comes back to the Justin mansion, endeavoring to see Mary, but runs into Howard instead. Howard again affirms quite sternly that Mary prefers to stay married to him. Steven storms at Howard, "You have a cold, bloodless point of view, and I don't believe a word of it." But Mary subsequently informs Steven herself of her decision not to leave Howard, adding that she still finds Steven too possessive, the judgment she first rendered when she turned down his marriage proposal four years earlier.

Mary obviously wants love on her own terms; she is determined not to belong completely to any one man. She chose to marry the frigid Howard Justin because he makes no sexual demands of her. But she has preferred to have sex with Steven so long as there are no strings attached to their relationship. Therefore, when Steven insists that she leave Howard for him, she refuses, staying with Howard for the wealth and security he offers her. With that, the flashback to 1939 is at an end.

The story returns to the present, and we are once more in the hotel resort where the film began. Mary and Steven spend a day picnicking on the slopes of the Swiss Alps, which are breathtakingly photographed by Guy Green. To her regret, Mary finds that Steven has found happiness by marrying someone else and is not the least bit interested in having a secret fling with her while they are at the hotel. On reflection, she realizes that her passion for Steven has likewise been eroded by time and disappointment. So Mary and Steven are no longer passionate friends.

Still, for old times' sake, they take a ride in a speedboat across the lake and decide to part for good. They come ashore on the hotel pier; Howard, who has been waiting on the hotel terrace for Mary, observes her with Steven at the dock. He totally misconstrues the whole situation and immediately assumes that they have had a rendezvous. He is outraged, and, when he and Mary get back to London, he instigates divorce proceedings against her, naming Steven Stratton as correspondent. He demands that she move out of his house into a hotel.

When she later comes to the house and pleads with Howard to take her back once more, he replies with rancor, "I knew you liked me when you married me, and the money and position which came with me. I didn't expect love from you, or even great affection. I'd have been well satisfied with kindness and loyalty. You gave me love and kindness and loyalty. But it was the love you'd give a dog and the kindness you'd give a beggar and the loyalty of a bad servant!"

After that dressing-down, Mary walks out of the house in a daze. She aims to take her life, in order to forestall a scandal that would ruin her life as well as Steven's career. She goes straight to the nearest underground station, and Lean employs visual metaphors to indicate her distraught state. There is a close-up of an exit in the station that reads "WAY OUT," implying that Mary sees suicide as the only solution. Then she descends an escalator to the platform below, which suggests her downward spiral toward despair and death. She is just about to hurl herself under a speeding train when Howard pulls her back to safety. He had followed her there only because she had left her purse behind when she rushed from the house. When he sees how wretched she is, Howard's cold personality melts, and he realizes that he genuinely loves his wife after all. By the same token, Mary sees Howard in a new light, in the wake of his saving her life. The film ends with their mutual agreement to give their marriage another chance.

As mentioned, there are similarities between *Brief Encounter* and *The Passionate Friends*, but there are differences as well. Laura and Alec's relationship is straightforward; they have both been married for some years before meeting and pursuing an abortive affair. But Mary and Steven's relationship is more complicated; they had an affair, then parted, then had a second affair after Mary's marriage. Furthermore, while Laura and Mary both consider suicide, their near deaths are only superficially similar. "Laura's flirtation with suicide is a momentary impulse," and she changes her mind.[26] Conversely, Mary is snatched from the jaws of death by her husband—she certainly would have jumped had Howard not intervened.

Silver and Ursini consider the final scene of *The Passionate Friends* "Lean's most ambiguous ending."[27] Mary renews her commitment to her marriage, but she remains married to an older man who at times behaves toward her more like a father than a husband. So her promise to be faithful may not be kept. That is as far as the picture goes.

Mary exemplifies Lean's ongoing theme, that of people who go on with their lives despite the fact that their fondest hopes will not be realized—in Mary's case the unrealistic hope that she and Steven could somehow remain together as lovers. In a larger sense, *The Passionate Friends* is about a kind of moral bankruptcy in modern society, among people who have every resource of our civilization yet cannot cope with life. It is about conspiracy and betrayal despite declared loyalties. As such, it is thought provoking, just as was Wells's novel.

When it opened in London in January 1949, *The Passionate Friends* received lackluster reviews. A number of critics dismissed the film as merely a gussied-up version of *Brief Encounter*, tricked out with the scenic grandeur of sunlit lakes and snowcapped mountains, along with handsomely tailored wardrobes for the characters. In addition, some complained that the film's narrative structure was confusing.

When the film was released in the United States in June 1949, American reviewers for the most part did not mind the flashbacks and in general were kinder. *Variety* rhapsodized, "Polished acting, masterly direction, and an excellent script put the film in the top rank of class British productions. The Cineguild team of David Lean and Ronald Neame has produced a worthy successor of *Brief Encounter*. . . . The three stars carry the picture with quiet dignity and restraint."[28]

The Passionate Friends was retitled *One Woman's Story* when it played in the United States. "Don't know why they do this rechristening," Lean mused; he believed that *The Passionate Friends* was a strong title and showed the link with the Wells novel and that *One Woman's Story* was commonplace.[29] The reason for the title change was that the Hollywood censor would not allow the word *passionate* to be featured on theater marquees, a fact of which Lean was, apparently, not aware. In any event, when the picture was released on home video in 1992, the original title was restored, so I have used the original title throughout.

As things turned out, the picture had only modest box office returns in both England and America. Lean had a hunch that the mass audience found the characters too cold and remote and could not identify with them; in fact, no one in the film was particularly sympathetic. Still, there is much to be said for *The Passionate Friends* as an intricate study of midlife urban angst. Lean gets down to the hidden undergrowth of a group of interconnected lives, into the thickets and self-lacerating spikes of their emotions. On the other hand, the movie takes a fairly acidic view of human relations. This makes the stressful soul-searching of the principal characters seem at times less like heartfelt confession than indulgent fits of petulance.

Nevertheless, most of the time the film comes across as a tense, intelligent drama about a love affair that goes wrong, issuing in hurt feelings, unfulfilled desires, and loss. In addition, the heart-stopping beauty and the luminous naturalness of the Continental locations are a joy to behold. (The light and composition of these sequences are particularly shown off to good advantage in the thirty-five-millimeter print available in the National Film Archive in London.)

Moreover, as *Variety* noted, Lean extracted strong performances from his trio of principal players, though it is Claude Rains who steals several scenes. He stands out at times like a crisp martini at a soda fountain.

After the release of *The Passionate Friends*, Ronald Neame and Anthony Havelock-Allan decided not to work with Lean on his next project for Cineguild. Lean's taking over the direction of the movie from Neame had been traumatizing for Neame, and that made it awkward for him to continue producing Lean's films. Besides, Neame still had his sights set on becoming a film director. Lean accordingly made Stanley Haynes the producer of his next picture. As a result, Havelock-Allan declined to help out with the producing chores. "I didn't like Haynes," Havelock-Allan stated flatly. "His principal idea was always to insinuate himself into a situation." (This was just what Haynes had done—with Lean's approval—on *The Passionate Friends*.) Havelock-Allan concluded sardonically, "As far as I know, he didn't create anything but havoc."[30]

So it looked like the partnership of Lean, Neame, and Havelock-Allan was beginning to become unglued. Neame and Havelock-Allan agreed to continue managing Cineguild with Lean since the company produced films by other directors besides Lean. But they would not become personally involved in another Lean project. Havelock-Allan, for example, produced Marc Allégret's *Blanche Fury* (1948), a colorful swashbuckler starring Stewart Granger, for Cineguild.

As for Neame, Michael Powell and Emeric Pressburger, for whom he had served as director of photography on *One of Our Aircraft Is Missing*, encouraged him to direct another film. The producer Sasha Gulperson in due course offered him *The Golden Salamander* (1950), an action picture about gun smuggling in Tunisia, starring none other than Trevor Howard. Despite Lean's prediction that he would never be a competent director, Neame continued directing movies for the next four decades.

The gossip about Lean's affair with Ann Todd had begun to spread when the unit returned to England and eventually reached Lean's wife, Kay Walsh, and Todd's husband, Nigel Tangye, an aviator. Tangye was, in fact, a second cousin of Lean, whose mother was a Tangye. Tangye sued Todd for divorce, naming Lean as correspondent. Here was life imitating art, the situation recalling *The Passionate Friends,* with Tangye as the cuckolded Howard Justin and Ann Todd and David Lean as Mary Justin and Steven Stratton.

Todd notes in her autobiography that, at the time, evidence of adultery had to be established by having the couple in question check into a hotel for the benefit of a private detective, who would then testify to their presence there for the purpose of "misconduct." Lean and Todd were obviously not going to return to Switzerland, where their adultery actually occurred, so they went to a hotel at Aldwych.[31]

Nigel Tangye was granted a divorce decree nisi. The decree was to take effect after thirty days, unless the petitioner changed his mind. Suffice it to say that he did not.[32] Walsh had been hoping for yet another reconciliation with Lean, but Lean's affair with Todd, which by now had reached the tabloids, made her see the handwriting on the wall. She sued Lean for divorce and was likewise granted a divorce decree nisi, and her marriage to Lean was soon dissolved.

Ann Todd became David Lean's third wife on May 21, 1949, in a ceremony at a registry office in Slough, on the outskirts of London. Lean's brother, Edward, and the whole Tangye side of the family boycotted the nuptials, scandalized by Lean's involvement with his cousin's wife. By this time, Noël Coward had taken up residence in Blue Harbor, Port Maria, Jamaica, and he invited Lean to honeymoon with his new wife in his tropical paradise. When the newlyweds returned to England, they took up residence in Ilchester Place, next door to Michael Powell.

There is a footnote to the breakup of Todd's marriage to Nigel Tangye. While Lean was filming a beach scene for *Madeleine,* as the movie was to be called, a small plane interrupted a shot by swooping down on the terrified cast and crew and flying very low along the shore. Lean angrily shook his fist and shouted imprecations at the pilot, whom he did not recognize. But Todd did; it was Tangye, whom Lean had never met. She never told Lean since he had said that he was going to report the pilot to the local flying club if he learned his identity. This nasty prank was, presumably, Tangye's parting shot. But Todd told me that she did not hold it against him. "Nigel was an absolute saint," she said, "and he just was not himself for some time after the ordeal of the divorce."

As for Lean's ex-wife, Kay Walsh, she continued appearing in movies like Hitchcock's *Stage Fright* (1950). In 1960, she was reunited with Alec Guinness, with whom she had costarred in *Oliver Twist,* in *Tunes of Glory,* a film about the military directed by none other than Ronald Neame. Walsh and Neame joked at the time about being seasoned veterans of the David Lean wars.

The Passionate Friends and his divorce now behind him, Lean began looking for a project that would serve as an appropriate vehicle for Todd. She herself suggested the real-life story of Madeleine Smith, the young woman who had been tried for and acquitted of the 1857 murder of her lover. In 1944, Todd had appeared on the London stage in Harold Purcell's *The Rest Is Silence,* a dramatization of Smith's trial. Lean took on the project, though he opted to base the movie on the records of the actual case, not on Purcell's play.

Madeleine was something of a companion piece to *The Passionate Friends,* in that it examines another illicit love affair that leads to tragic consequences. "Ann was terribly stuck on this idea," Lean remembered; she was "mad keen" about the infamous murder case. She personally owned some of Smith's love letters to Emile L'Angelier, her French inamorato, as well as the ivory-handled sunshade that Smith had held in court. She even carried the sunshade in the courtroom scenes of *The Rest Is Silence.* Lean wasn't keen on the project—as he put it, *Madeleine* "really wasn't my cup of tea."[33] But he took it on for Todd's sake.

When Lean began preparing *Madeleine,* he discovered that there had been an American play inspired by the murder case—*Dishonored Lady,* by Edward Sheldon and Margaret Ayer Barnes, which opened on Broadway in 1928 with Katharine Cornell as the star—and that Robert Stevenson (best known for his film version of *Jane Eyre* [1944]) filmed an adaptation of the play in 1947 as a vehicle for Hedy Lamarr (*Algiers* [John Cromwell, 1938]). *Dishonored Lady,* both play and film, was a fictionalized version of Smith's story updated to the present—unlike *The Rest Is Silence,* which stuck closer to the facts and set the story in the proper period. Lean, as we have seen, would stick even closer to the facts, going back to the documentary evidence. Rank—who had already considered backing a film adaptation of *The Rest Is Silence*—approved the project as a Cineguild production and agreed to distribute the movie in England. Universal, the American distributor of *The Passionate Friends,* would release *Madeleine* in the United States.

Madeleine (1950)

Purcell's play implies that, even though Smith was not found guilty, she got away with murder. But, in the news stories and court records of the period on which Lean based *Madeleine,* her guilt was never officially established. The documentation does make it evident that her love letters to Emile L'Angelier, some of which were read in open court, shocked the public as much as the murder charge. They found it hard to believe that the twenty-one-year-old daughter of an affluent Glasgow architect, fresh from a London finishing school, could have penned such passionate epistles to a rake. Her lover, after all, was a penniless Frenchman whose noble family back in France had fallen on evil days and who was, therefore, reduced to earning meager wages as a clerk in a Glasgow office. He was hardly a suitable mate for the likes of Madeleine Smith.

There was ample documentation available, including two volumes in the Notable British Trials series.[34] In one of the letters cited during the trial, Smith sought to justify her sexual relationship with Emile by writing him on May 6, 1856: "Am I not your wife? Yes I am, and you may rest assured that, after what has passed, I cannot be the wife of any other but dear Emile; though we should, I suppose have waited till we were married."[35] The prosecuting attorney commented that the excerpts from Smith's letters that were read into the record reflected passion the like of which had never before been heard in a court of law.

The *Madeleine* screenplay is credited to Stanley Haynes, who was also producing, and to Nicholas Phipps, who had done some screenplays for Herbert Wilcox. Their script hews close to the actual events throughout. For example, in the courtroom sequences that make up the last third of the movie, Haynes and Phipps followed the court transcripts assiduously. Thus, the defense attorney's eloquent final plea on Madeleine's behalf, which is derived directly from the court records, represents a fine example of screenwriting.

To costar with Ann Todd as Emile D'Angelier, Lean selected Ivan Desny, a French actor who was appearing in his first British picture. Lean became aware of Desny when he dubbed Trevor Howard's dialogue for the French-language version of *Brief Encounter*. Leslie Banks, a veteran character actor who had appeared in Hitchcock's 1934 version of *The Man Who Knew Too Much*, was to be Madeleine's domineering father; and Norman Wooland, who stood out as Horatio in Laurence Olivier's *Hamlet* (1948), was cast as William Minnoch, Madeleine's fiancé.

Lean's "stock company" of production artists was once again on hand—the cinematographer Guy Green, the production designer John Bryan, the costume designer Margaret Furse, and the film editor Geoffrey Foot (with Lean supervising the editing).

In harmony with his custom of commissioning important British composers to score his films, Lean called on William Alwyn to compose the background music for *Madeleine*. Alwyn had won plaudits for his underscore for Carol Reed's *Odd Man Out* (1947). Alwyn was, in fact, the most prolific of the major British composers who wrote for the cinema. "I am passionately fond of films," he said. "You must believe in pictures, have faith in your artistic medium, and you can produce good scores."[36] He produced a fine score for *Madeleine,* ranging from luscious waltzes and spirited Scottish reels to momentous dramatic themes. Muir Mathieson, the head of Rank's music department, always conducted the orchestra at the recording sessions, in this case the Royal Philharmonic.

Madeleine was shot at Pinewood in the summer of 1949, with a location stint in Cornwall for Madeleine's seaside holiday with William Minnoch. While the picture was in production, the director and the female lead did not get on nearly so well as they had on their previous picture together. Todd fell into the same pattern of behavior with Lean that had driven Ronald Neame to distraction when he was briefly directing *The Passionate Friends.* That is, she incessantly attempted to second-guess the director about how each scene should be played. She engaged Lean in lengthy discussions during rehearsals in which she endeavored to psychoanalyze her character, and these endless squabbles put the movie behind schedule. To make matters worse, there was an electricians' strike at the studio in August, which caused further delays.

In her own defense, Todd later complained that Lean did not understand actors: "He never had much consideration for what actors had to go through—just a relentless drive for what he wanted from a scene."[37] For his part, Lean always contended that he had an enormous respect for an actor's insecurity: "A lot of my job is to give actors confidence."[38]

Todd did eventually get around to paying Lean a grudging compliment, noting the great effort that he put into making a film. She was impressed with the manner in which he would oversee every aspect of production. (She thereby anticipated Lean's recognition later on as an auteur film director.) "David liked to have every detail right under his thumb," she observed. When people asked her whether it was difficult for her as his wife to be working with him, she replied, "Of course it is; having a genius around the house *is* difficult."[39] Todd remembered Lean regularly having John Bryan and Guy Green come to the house for breakfast during filming, to plan the day's shoot.

John Bryan's settings for this movie were just as evocative of Victorian Glasgow as his sets for Lean's two Dickens films were of Victorian London. He reproduced the exterior of the Smith family homestead at 7 Blythswood Square in authentic detail.

"Guy Green's attempt to light Ann Todd in a lush and elaborate way," writes Robert Murphy, "was dismissed as a vulgar manifestation of Lean's affection for his new wife." That was hardly the case; given Todd's bickering with Lean on the set, it was evident that the honeymoon was over. "As so much rests on Madeleine's character, though," Murphy continues, "[Green's flattering manner of photographing her] was entirely justified; and Ann Todd, with her sad, fragile face, responds with a performance full of nuance and subtlety."[40]

"In this great city of Glasgow," says a narrator voice-over on the sound track as the camera moves along the streets of the city, "there is a square which has nothing remarkable about its appearance; but there is one house that is exceptional: number seven. This house, which still remains, was the home of Madeleine Smith; perhaps her spirit still remains there, to listen for the tap of Emile L'Angelier's cane at her window." With this spoken introduction, the setting shifts from present-day Glasgow to the day when Madeleine's father bought the house for his family.

This prologue recalls that of *This Happy Breed,* which begins with a panoramic shot of London that gradually hones in on the house of the Gibbons family on the day they move into it (see chapter 3). In both films, the family domicile plays a symbolic role.

In the present movie, Madeleine, while exploring the house, comes on a basement room that she promptly decides will be her bedroom. It is here that she has clandestine rendezvous with Emile. As one critic has written, "Madeleine's immediate fascination with the dark, isolated basement symbolically expresses the subterranean emotions of this apparently well-bred Scottish young woman."[41]

The Smith family lives a very proper but stodgy existence, which bores Madeleine. One night, sometime later, while she is playing and singing listlessly for her family, the shadow of a man cavalierly twirling a cane appears on the sidewalk before the house. Madeleine knows that it is time for her rendezvous with her lover Emile and begs off continuing her concert. Her rush through the corridors of the mansion toward her tryst is accompanied by a lush waltz on the sound track, symbolizing the romance that Emile has brought into her dull life. Emile's cane becomes a phallic symbol as the film unreels; we notice Madeleine fondling it during their evenings together within the dark confines of her cellar bedroom.

Yet Madeleine consistently keeps up the appearances of being a respectable young lady who is submissive to her authoritarian father. When Mr. Smith commands her to remove his boots, a task normally carried out by a domestic servant, Madeleine complies. As she kneels at his feet, she seems to be the picture of a pliant daughter. Little does Mr. Smith suspect that Madeleine is secretly defying him by taking up with a down-at-the-heels Don Juan, of whom he would thoroughly disapprove. She is, in fact, sinning beneath her station, as the saying goes.

Lean uses several visual images to indicate that the love of the wealthy

Madeleine and the impecunious Emile is outside the conventions of the society in which she moves and, therefore, must be kept a secret. In one scene, she and Emile are walking in the woods and hear the sound of bagpipes accompanying a dance in a nearby dance hall. Madeleine begins dancing a reel to the music issuing from a party of happy dancers that she and Emile can never join.

Lean, the master film editor, cuts back and forth between Madeleine and Emile dancing in the forest glade and a couple in the dance hall, adroitly forging a network of parallel shots. When Alwyn's fevered Scottish reel reaches its climax, Madeleine drops to the ground and lures Emile down toward her to make love. The couple at the dance meanwhile rush out of the hall with similar amorous intentions.

Somewhat later in the film, Lean offers a contrast to the spirited folk dance with Emile, the preferred suitor, when he shows Madeleine executing a sedate Caledonian dance with William Minnoch, her fiancé and a man of her own class, in a lavish ballroom. Emile watches them jealously as he furtively lurks in the shadows of a balcony above the dance floor.

When Emile subsequently insists that Madeleine break off her engagement to Minnoch and marry him, she refuses, finally realizing that there is little but lust keeping them together. Emile abandons his courtly manners and warns her that he can blackmail her into marrying him on the strength of her love letters. He reminds her that in them she referred to herself as his own darling wife. Madeleine is dismayed to realize that Emile can be as overbearing as her father. Indeed, if she elopes with him, "she will merely pass from one form of paternalistic oppression to another."[42] Madeleine at last sees through the superficial gloss of Emile's charm to the very flawed character of a fortune hunter underneath. She perceives that she has sold William short, and she now values him as a genuinely worthy suitor.

Lean builds a dandy visual metaphor around the social barriers that separate Madeleine from Emile. He visualizes the obstruction that class distinction places between them by photographing them on different sides of symbolic barriers. Thus, Madeleine asks Emile to return her letters as she converses with him through the barred window of her basement bedroom. Emile finds stooping to talk to her demeaning and demands that she meet him at the front gate. They continue to quarrel while standing on opposite sides of the fence enclosing the Smith mansion. These images suggest how Emile is barred from entering the world that Madeleine still shares with William. Since Emile views her letters as his meal ticket, he absolutely refuses to give them back. Madeleine is, of course, painfully aware that the letters are a ready-made instrument of blackmail.

True to form for an English costume drama (see chapter 5), at one point in the film Madeleine is shown grasping a bottle with a label bearing a skull and crossbones, which patently identifies it as poison! Earlier, when she purchased what turns out to be arsenic, she told the pharmacist that the cook had spotted a rat in the kitchen. (One wonders whether she has in mind the "rat" in her basement bedroom.) When she later serves Emile a cup of cocoa in the living room of the Smith mansion, where she has invited him ostensibly to coax him into relinquishing her letters, a close-up of his cup as he is about to sip from it arouses filmgoers' suspicions. Madeleine serves Emile cocoa on other occasions as well. Then he becomes deathly ill and, eventually, succumbs to arsenic poisoning.

Lean introduces a scene not in the screenplay at this point, one that Ann Todd told me he devised one evening during the shooting period. Madeleine is cheerfully trying on her wedding gown, preparing for her marriage to William, who of course knows nothing of how she has been cheating on him with Emile. The immaculate wedding gown symbolizes purity; the white apparel belies the way in which she has stained her character. At this point, according to Todd, "The audience sees that she doesn't give a damn about how she has cavalierly two-timed her fiancé; she's really a bitch."

The police inevitably discover Madeleine's purchase of arsenic in the druggist's records, and she is charged with murder. When she arrives in court for the first day of the trial, she wears a veil. This signifies that she seeks to hide her true feelings from everyone in the courtroom behind a sphinx-like composure, much as she hides her face behind the veil. Interestingly, the drawing of Madeleine executed by a newspaper sketch artist during her trial shows her wearing no veil; she is simply staring impassively into space. The detail must have been Lean's idea.

The ensuing trial is the high point of the film, which has built steadily in suspense from the beginning. Lean gives the court proceedings the air of spare, unvarnished realism, typified by the stark, authentic, documentary-like quality of Green's cinematography. The viewer listens intently as the lawyers for the prosecution and for the defense match wits, spinning intricate arguments punctuated by briskly paced bits of testimony from the witnesses for both sides. Lean adamantly refused, as he put it, "to show anything which was not in accord with what was brought out in the trial."[43]

The final verdict is one that could be given only in Scotland: Madeleine's guilt, says the jury, was "not proven." That verdict, the narrator explains, "means that Madeleine Smith left the court neither guilty nor not guilty because the charge was 'not proven.'" According to one film historian, the predominantly male jury "finds it impossible to believe that a woman who in appearance conforms to the norms of Victorian respectability could be capable of the flagrant violations of which she is accused."[44] In other words, though they could not bring themselves to clear her name, they were not prepared to see her hang. As Madeleine leaves the courthouse, the narrator addresses her directly: "Madeleine Smith, you have heard the indictment: were you guilty or not guilty?" Madeleine looks into the camera as she drives off in a carriage, and a wry smile crosses her face. With that, the film ends.

The prevailing critical opinion of the film, when it was released and ever since, is that Lean's steadfast objectivity, which had led him to give no hint whether Madeleine's guilt or innocence is the more probable, succeeds in leaving the audience with the feeling of frustration that comes from witnessing a stalemate. Lean is, however, in perfect accordance with the known facts in leaving the viewer with a question mark rather than a solution to the case of Madeleine Smith. The filmgoer is never shown any concrete evidence that Madeleine did, in fact, lace Emile's cocoa with arsenic.

Yet, even in the movie as it stands, there is evidence sufficient to offer a credible solution to the murder mystery. In point of fact, the possibility is suggested more than once that Emile took his own life.

There is, for example, the scene in which Monsieur Thuau, a fellow Frenchman and close friend of Emile's, goes to visit Emile in his shabby flat, only to find him dead. The doctor who attended Emile in his fatal illness is still present and informs Thuau that Emile succumbed to arsenic poisoning. Thuau states that he strongly suspects that Emile, who had recently seemed very despondent over his breakup with Madeleine, killed himself. He immediately hastens to the Smith residence for an interview with Madeleine but is intercepted by her father. Thuau frankly declares to Mr. Smith his conviction that Emile committed suicide: "He hoped he was going to marry your daughter. Her letters to him support that suggestion." Mr. Smith is absolutely devastated to hear of his daughter's illicit love affair. He summons Madeleine, and Thuau repeats to her his belief that Emile took his own life.

Furthermore, Thuau testifies in court that Emile had considered suicide once before—"because a lady jilted him." And the physician who examined Emile's corpse testifies in court that the substantial amount of poison found in Emile's system could well have been self-administered. Certainly, suicide seems the most plausible explanation, especially as it was the theory advanced by the man who knew the deceased best.

But, for reasons best known to himself, in building his case the defense attorney, who was the dean of the faculty at a Glasgow law school, never pursued the possibility that Emile ended his own life. He preferred to emphasize that the charges were based on circumstantial evidence and that the prosecutor never proved beyond the shadow of a doubt that the arsenic that Madeleine bought was the arsenic that killed Emile.

In any event, when *Madeleine* premiered in London in February 1950 and subsequently opened in New York the following September, it was not a success. Many in the audience felt cheated that no conclusive explanation of the facts of the case was offered. Moviegoers were apparently expecting a routine whodunit.

This was undoubtedly the reaction of Noël Coward, who was filming *The Astonished Heart* (Antony Darnborough and Terence Fisher, 1949) at Pinewood when Lean completed *Madeleine*. After Lean screened the movie for him, Lean recalled, Coward commented: "I don't think you can end the film not knowing whether she did or didn't kill him. Somehow you've got to tip the scales one way or the other."[45]

In retrospect, it seems that Lean's prime purpose was not to settle the question of Madeleine's guilt or innocence once and for all. Rather, he aimed to portray a forbidden love and its tragic consequences. "Madeleine must have been a passionate woman by all accounts, also somewhat enigmatic," Lean noted. "I think we got a good romantic structure out of her story; and I think it was very original, very romantic, and not a little sad."[46]

Lean conceived a movie that is more complex and demanding than a mere whodunit. It is a meticulous psychological drama that explores the dark corners of human behavior; it is dense with emotions, especially jealousy and hatred. Ann Todd, as Madeleine, with her patrician beauty and inner fire, illuminates the dark center of the movie. Once she is accused of murder, the film's protagonist exists in stark isolation, as she stoically endures the increasingly dread-filled trial with glacial reserve.

Madeleine is not available on home video in the United States. It is an underappreciated picture that deserves wider viewing. After all, even a lesser Lean film runs circles around the competition in terms of character delineation. And the cast is uniformly superb—especially Ivan Desny, whose Emile adapts his slick behavior to suit Madeleine's myriad moods, and Leslie Banks, who turns in a memorable performance as Madeleine's unrelenting father.

In one of the more favorable notices that the movie received in America, *Variety* praised the performances and the production values of the film. The review ended with the observation: "*Madeleine* bears the known Cineguild stamp of quality and polish."[47] The reviewer could not have known that *Madeleine* was the last of the Cineguild productions.

Throughout the 1940s, as we know, J. Arthur Rank had been revered as a major force in offering financial support to independent film units like Cineguild and the Archers. But, by 1950, Rank's empire was crumbling.

Though Rank had backed some successful British films (e.g., *Brief Encounter* and *Great Expectations*), he had also backed some commercial failures (e.g., *The Passionate Friends* and *Madeleine*). His most disastrous financial flops were expensive historical epics like Gabriel Pascal's 1945 film of Shaw's *Caesar and Cleopatra*—Lean had wisely ended his association with the recklessly extravagant Pascal after working on the 1941 *Major Barbara* (see chapter 2).

Another factor that contributed to the decline and fall of Rank's empire was that, in spite of his strenuous efforts, he never really penetrated the American market beyond the art house circuit. As a result of his huge financial losses in the late 1940s, the board of directors of the Rank organization mandated that he step down as chief executive officer and that John Davis, his astute business manager and chief accountant, take control. Rank was kicked upstairs and stayed on mostly to manifest support for his successor's policies.

Davis was now in charge and implemented his decision to close Denham Studios, where Lean's early films were made. He concentrated all production at Pinewood. In addition, he instituted "a new production regime, by which he could exercise tighter control" over every aspect of the production of the films made for the Rank organization.[48] Davis made it clear to independent production units like Cineguild that the era of Rank's benevolent paternalism was over. He would require that the independents work on tighter budgets and not exceed them. As Ronald Neame exclaimed, "The Golden Years were over!"[49]

The temper of the times could be measured by the experience of Lean's friend and colleague Carol Reed, who made the prestigious *Odd Man Out* (1947) for Fillipo Del Guidice's Two Cities Films, another independent film unit functioning under the banner of Rank's Independent Producers. Reed told me in conversation that, though *Odd Man Out* was a popular and critical success, the picture had gone considerably over budget: "So dear Fillipo Del Guidice was the first independent to be swept away by John Davis's broom." Anthony Del Guidice told me that, after that, his father could not find financing for his projects. He ultimately entered a monastery, where he hoped to make religious films, but nothing came of it. Reed complained with some bitterness, "Rank had encouraged us to make high-quality films, and then Davis criticized us for being extravagant!"

Davis's standard reply to such allegations was to point out that the independents lacked the business acumen to set up a realistic budget and keep to it, which meant that the studio could not expect a reasonable return on its investment. In short, they failed to reckon with the fact that the movie business is just that: a business. A new broom sweeps clean: "And by the end of 1950 Davis was beginning to achieve results." He was able to announce to the Rank shareholders that the company's bank loans and overdrafts had been reduced from £8 million to £5 million.[50]

Since the Rank organization was now functioning in a conservative financial environment, Neame and Havelock-Allan broached to Lean the idea of disbanding Cineguild. Lean had, of course, seen the handwriting on the wall when they had declined to collaborate with him on *Madeleine*—or any other project, for that matter. They did agree, however, to continue for the time being their involvement in Cineguild's other productions.

Neame wanted to continue directing films on his own, not to serve as Lean's producer. He later reflected that, had he continued to be associated with Lean, he would have been "overshadowed by David": "So it was better that we part."[51] As a matter of fact, while Lean was directing *Madeleine* at Pinewood, Neame was already directing *The Golden Salamander* on a neighboring soundstage.

Meanwhile, Havelock-Allan had formed a small independent production company of his own, Constellation Films, refusing to work with Lean while Haynes, whom he saw as an upstart, was Lean's right-hand man. So it was inevitable that the former Cineguild partners were going to go their separate ways. Lean was disconsolate to see the demise not just of Cineguild but of the entire Independent Producers combine. "We had a wonderful time at the Rank studios as independent producers," he remarked with some nostalgia, "and I think we really had made some good pictures between the lot of us."[52]

Lean and some of the other filmmakers who had been involved in Independent Producers, like Powell and Pressburger, defected to Shepperton Studios, where Rank's chief rival, Alexander Korda, held sway at London Films. Korda seemed to promise them the kind of creative freedom that they could no longer hope for under the reign of John Davis at Pinewood.

Lean was interested in making *The Sound Barrier,* an epic picture about aviation, for Korda. He hoped that, after two flops in a row, the project would restore his standing in the industry as a major filmmaker. Stanley Haynes assumed that he would continue as Lean's producer. But Korda curtly informed him that his services were not required—that Korda himself would be the executive producer of *The Sound Barrier* and that Lean could act as his own producer. Haynes, who fancied himself Lean's partner, was distraught; he told Lean that he should refuse to make *The Sound Barrier* under Korda's conditions.

"David didn't see it that way," says Neame laconically. After Independent Producers collapsed, Lean felt stranded and could not afford to pass up a chance to direct a movie for a major player in the British film industry like

Alexander Korda. Besides, Lean had never made a long-term commitment of any kind to Haynes. That he had was merely wishful thinking on Haynes's part; as Havelock-Allan had warned Lean early on, Haynes saw Lean as his ticket to a career in the film industry. For the next five years, Haynes tried to put together production packages of his own but all too often failed to find funding. He grew increasingly despondent, Neame recalled. "Finally he committed suicide." He mailed a suicide note to Kay Walsh, with whom he had gotten on amicably while *Oliver Twist* was in production. "He blamed his imminent death on David Lean."[53]

Chapter Eight

THE WILD BLUE YONDER

THE SOUND BARRIER

How many lives have been lost on the cutting edge of discovery? It's the price we pay for a place in history.
> —*Robert Doniger, a research scientist in the film* Timeline

The failure is the man who stays down after he falls.
> —*David Buick, auto manufacturer*

It was inevitable that, having made films under the banner of J. Arthur Rank, David Lean would eventually become allied with Alexander Korda, the British film industry's other major movie mogul. Korda had established his own production company in his native Hungary in 1917, for which he also directed some films. After an interlude as a director in Hollywood in the late 1920s, he returned to Europe in 1930. Korda worked as a producer briefly at Paramount Pictures' European studio in France, where he first encountered David Lean (see chapter 1).

Like his fellow Hungarian Gabriel Pascal, Korda settled eventually in England and started his own independent production company there in 1932. As the founder and production chief of London Film Productions, he produced, and occasionally directed, some fine films. Yet the novelist-screenwriter Graham Greene, who was a film reviewer in those days, was appalled that a native Hungarian had set up shop in the British film industry. "In what can with technical accuracy be termed an English company you have a Hungarian producer, assisted by a Hungarian art director [Vincent Korda, Alexander Korda's brother]," he complained, not to mention some

Hungarian technicians. Greene commented wryly that it was "only natural" that Alexander Korda would find jobs for his compatriots at his studio.[1]

Greene's condescending attitude toward Korda was really not fair since Korda's films boasted a number of English directors, actors, and writers. As a matter of fact, in due time London Films became synonymous with prestige British movies. Korda himself, we recall, produced and directed *The Private Life of Henry VIII* (1933), the first English movie to achieve widespread distribution in America. He was an entrepreneur who infused the British film industry with "much-needed creative energy" and business enterprise, along with "vitality and imagination."[2]

Once Cineguild had disbanded and its parent company, Independent Producers, had shut down, working for Korda looked like a promising proposition to Lean. Indeed, according to Harper and Porter, "Most of [Independent Producers'] privileged incumbents went to work for Korda." Among them were Carol Reed, who, like Lean, had become "disillusioned with John Davis's draconian control at Rank" (see chapter 7),[3] and Michael Powell and Emeric Pressburger, Powell finding Korda an astute, audacious producer who was willing to gamble on making "classy pictures" for the world market.[4] In fact, Graham Greene himself wrote screenplays for two Carol Reed films made under Korda's aegis.

Korda's productions were released in Great Britain by British Lion, a distribution company in which Korda had a controlling interest; hence, he acted as the managing director of British Lion. (It was British Lion, in the pre-Korda days under Sam Smith, that was the only English distributor willing to release *In Which We Serve*.) Korda's American distributor was Lopert Films, which was run by Ilya Lopert.

Carol Reed directed his finest achievement, *The Third Man* (1949), for Korda's London Films, whose logo, Big Ben chiming the hour, was becoming familiar to moviegoers. Reed told me that Korda was proud that he could get major English writers like Graham Greene, who scripted *The Third Man,* and H. G. Wells, who scripted *Things to Come,* to write for the screen. Wells said at the time, "The cinema provided a more effective way of reaching a large audience than any other form of communication."[5] (A pity he did not live to see Lean's film adaptation of *The Passionate Friends.*)

The film historian Paul Tabori states, "Korda pressed a button and the greatest storytellers of the world went to work in turning out plots and scenarios." One hard-nosed executive at another company who had dealt with Korda said that he was adept at manipulating talented people into working on his films because of "his engaging personality and charm of manner." He was difficult to resist, "owing to his powers of persuasion."[6] In fact, several of England's most illustrious moviemakers worked for London Films, including Britain's two top directors, Lean and Reed. Lean observed that Korda was "something of a father figure" to his directors, actors, and technicians and that he often called them "my children."[7]

Lean was much impressed by Korda, whom he saw as a lion of a man, a highly intelligent and charismatic producer. Because Korda had directed some pictures himself, he understood the craft of filmmaking better than most film executives ever could. As a matter of fact, Lean's tenure at Korda's Shepperton Studios ushered in a new period of achievement for him. Korda gravitated toward epic movies with grand themes and was willing to gamble on large-scale British films. So he was very receptive to Lean's proposal of *The Sound Barrier,* a spectacular tale of the conquest of space.

But teamwork was never Korda's strong suit. "You can work *for* Korda," one of his colleagues observed, "but not *with* him." He could be paternalistic as well as paternal.[8] He was a hands-on executive who preferred to deal directly with a filmmaker and not use a producer as an intermediary. This was why he told Lean in no uncertain terms that there was no need for Stanley Haynes to act as producer on *The Sound Barrier.* Lean endeavored to mollify Haynes by offering to keep him on as his personal assistant, with the title of associate producer. But Haynes, deeply offended by what he considered a brush-off, would not hear of it. So Norman Spencer, who had been Lean's production manager at Cineguild, became associate producer on the film.

Years later, Lean reflected that, had Haynes been willing to accept a subordinate position, "Alex would have taken him on board." As it was, said Lean, Kay Walsh "to this day thinks I was responsible" for Haynes's suicide. It was all "a bloody shame."[9]

The Sound Barrier would be a film of epic scope about courage and heroism, a subject that always interested Lean: "I'd always wanted to make an adventure film about man's explorations into the unknown."[10] He thought of Robert Scott's expeditions to the South Pole and of Henry Stanley and David Livingstone's explorations of the African jungle, for example. "They were great stories of human courage," he explained, but they had already been filmed: *Stanley and Livingstone* by Henry King and Otto Brower in 1939 and *Scott of the Antarctic* by Charles Frend in 1948.[11] So Lean set his sights on the onset of the space age with the invention of jet-propelled airplanes that would fly into the stratosphere, where no man had ever flown before. Consequently, he envisioned *The Sound Barrier* as a spectacle; as such, it would foreshadow his colossal Hollywood films to come about heroic endeavors, like *Lawrence of Arabia* and *Dr. Zhivago.*

Another reason that Lean wanted to work on an aviation picture was that he had been fascinated by air power from his youth, when he lived near the Croydon Airdrome. He never forgot Lindbergh's landing there on his way home from Paris, after his history-making solo flight across the Atlantic. "Lucky Lindy" remained a hero of Lean's.

The Sound Barrier (1952)

Lean decided that his next film would be about heroic aviators when he noticed a headline in the February 16, 1950, edition of the *Evening News* (London). Squadron Leader J. S. R. Muller-Rowland had been killed when his test plane crashed. He had apparently not been aware that he had been flying faster than the speed of sound when his aircraft disintegrated in midair. The newspaper article recalled the death of Geoffrey de Havilland, whose test plane had likewise fallen to pieces in the air on September 24, 1946, under similar circumstances.

Lean thought that the death of de Havilland, the son of the aircraft industrialist Sir Geoffrey de Havilland, could serve as the spine of his film. The actress Olivia de Havilland (*Gone with the Wind*) told me in conversation that she was related on her father's side to Sir Geoffrey de Havilland. She remembered, "We were all proud of the headway that Sir Geoffrey was making in the manufacture of state-of-the-art planes. But when his son Geoffrey was killed in a test flight, we realized the price of progress."

After Lean himself had made a flight in a jet plane, he was absolutely certain that there was a dramatic story in a tale about the breaking of the sound barrier. Man's endeavors to fly faster than the speed of sound had resulted in planes disintegrating in midflight. So, Lean said, breaking the sound barrier to achieve supersonic flight seemed to be "the great modern adventure story," one to rival the daring exploits of Scott and of Stanley and Livingstone.[12]

Lean pitched the idea to Korda, who said that he would consider it after Lean had thoroughly researched the test flying of jet planes. Lean spent several months talking with aircraft manufacturers and test pilots; he made field trips to the de Havilland and Rolls-Royce aircraft factories. He spent quite a bit of time in the aeroengine division at Rolls-Royce. The chairman of Rolls-Royce, Lord Hives, regaled him with anecdotes about Henry Royce, the founder of the industrial firm. Royce was a perfectionist who demanded the best that his staff of experts had to offer in designing topflight Rolls-Royce planes. Lean eventually modeled Sir John Ridgefield, the aircraft manufacturer in the film, on Henry Royce as well as on Sir Geoffrey de Havilland.

The test pilots whom Lean interviewed, like John Derry, were initially put off by Lean's questions. They were concerned that Lean was going to make an overblown melodrama about flight experiments and romanticize their accomplishments. Then, after a short time, they saw that he was serious about the subject, and they were more responsive to his inquiries.

When I discussed flying at the speed of sound with Major D. K. Farmer, USAF-Ret., who served at Wright Air Force Base, not far from Dayton, Ohio, the home of the Wright brothers, he explained, "When an aircraft was going more than 750 miles per hour, the air could no longer get out of the way of the oncoming plane. So waves of air would build up into a massive wall—the sound barrier—which the plane could not penetrate." As Lean put it, "The sound barrier was invisible, yet able to tear an airplane to pieces." So man must make an assault "on this treacherous mass of air" and break the sound barrier.[13]

Lean said that he gathered all the information that he had gleaned from his interviews into a notebook, "a diary of about forty pages, I suppose" (and not three hundred pages, as Sandra Lean asserts).[14] When he discussed the diary with Korda, he realized that he had accrued a mass of salient background material but that he still had no dramatic story line. At this point, Korda suggested that playwright-screenwriter Terence Rattigan could employ Lean's research to fashion a screenplay that would flesh out a scenario with solid characters. Lean was familiar with Rattigan from the time when he edited *French without Tears,* which was based on Rattigan's screenplay from his own stage play. He was aware that Rattigan was one of the rare screenwriters capable of writing an original screen story from the ground up. (The novelist-screenwriter Raymond Chandler once said, "Good original screenplays were almost as rare in Hollywood as virgins.")[15] So he seconded Korda's motion to employ Rattigan.

Korda phoned Rattigan during the course of a story conference with Lean, only to have Rattigan decline the offer. Rattigan had been a pilot during World War II and had written the screenplay for Anthony Asquith's *The Way to the Stars,* which was about fighter pilots during the war, but he maintained that he knew nothing about jet-propelled planes. Undaunted, Korda pressed on and persuaded Rattigan at least to accompany him and Lean to the Farnborough Air Exhibition, where they met some fascinating test pilots. Furthermore, Rattigan became intrigued with Lean's diary, so he finally relented and agreed to write the screenplay for *The Sound Barrier.* He saw it as the dramatic story of men obsessed with technological progress who bravely sacrificed their lives to push back the frontiers of aviation. This would make for a tragic tale with a heroic uplift.

In his diary, Lean had scribbled some ideas for plot points that he now discussed with Rattigan at great length. For example, he had discovered that Sir Geoffrey de Havilland had lost not one son but two as the result of failed test flights. His son John had perished when his Mosquito aircraft crashed in 1943, three years before Geoffrey was killed. Rattigan accordingly suggested that, in the movie, both John Ridgefield's sons lose their lives.

Both Lean and Korda were disappointed with the first draft of Rattigan's script. Not only was it substantially overlength, but the scenes taking place on the ground were also too stagy and theatrical—Rattigan was, after all, primarily a playwright. In a script conference with Rattigan and Lean, Korda suggested that Ridgefield's second son be changed to a daughter, Susan Ridgefield. She, in turn, would be married to a test pilot, Tony Garthwaite, who succeeds her brother, Christopher, as Ridgefield's chief test pilot after Christopher is killed. Then she would question whether technical progress is worth the loss of life and try to dissuade Tony from participating in further test flights. Rattigan recognized the dramatic possibilities in Korda's concept and revised his screenplay accordingly.

Korda wanted one son changed to a daughter because he wanted a female lead that could be played by Ann Todd. He saw the publicity value of having Lean direct his wife in another picture. He knew that Herbert Wilcox had mined publicity from directing his wife, Anna Neagle, in pictures like *Spring in Park Lane* (1948). Given the clashes that Lean and Todd had while filming *Madeleine,* however, Lean was not thrilled with the prospect of directing Todd again. Nor did he want to have Korda play up Lean and Todd as a husband-and-wife team. "Do we have to have the Herbert and Anna lark?" he asked Korda, but he acquiesced.[16]

All things considered, Lean enjoyed hashing out the script with Rattigan; he particularly helped out with the domestic scenes between Susan and Tony. Since Rattigan was a bachelor, he claimed to be inexperienced in such matters and welcomed Lean's assistance. In the end, Lean found the experience of working with Rattigan "bloody good." Indeed, as Sylvia Paskin writes, "Rattigan managed to craft a film of great emotional depth and power."[17]

For the crucial role of Sir John Ridgefield, Susan and Christopher's father, Korda nominated Ralph Richardson, who had distinguished himself as a murder suspect in Carol Reed's *The Fallen Idol* (1948). But Lean had his doubts about Richardson; he thought the actor had played too many poker-faced character parts (in Korda movies!) and was better on the stage than on the screen. Moreover, Lean had edited *Java Head* (1934), a quota quickie in which Richardson had given an over-the-top performance. Undaunted, Korda had Richardson dressed up like a business tycoon in a proper three-piece suit and, for good measure, had a studio makeup artist accentuate

Richardson's bushy eyebrows to make him look more like an industrialist. Then he presented him to Lean. The director accordingly agreed to cast Richardson, who gave a marvelous performance. Nigel Patrick (*Spring in Park Lane*) was tagged to play Tony Garthwaite, and John Justin (*The Thief of Bagdad* [Ludwig Berger and Michael Powell, 1940]) took the part of Philip Peel, another test pilot.

Lean and Korda put together an impressive production staff, despite the fact that Lean had parted company with John Bryan and Guy Green after the demise of Cineguild. Vincent Korda replaced John Bryan as Lean's production designer. Despite Graham Greene's insinuations (see above), Vincent Korda was a talented artist. In fact, he had already won an Academy Award for designing the sets for *The Thief of Bagdad*. Jack Hildyard replaced Guy Green as Lean's cinematographer; Lean remembered Hildyard as a camera operator on *Pygmalion*. The film editor Geoffrey Foot, working on his third Lean film, rounded out the principal production artists.

Malcolm Arnold followed Arnold Bax and William Alwyn in the ranks of British composers who scored Lean's films. "Arnold was outstanding for the range of his musical styles, which made him ideally adaptable as a composer for film, since he readily adjusted himself with infectious enthusiasm to each individual film's dramatic needs."[18] This was borne out in his close collaboration with Lean on the score of *The Sound Barrier*.

The production experience was not a pleasant one for Lean insofar as he had to deal with Ann Todd. As she had when working on *Madeleine*, Todd insisted on carrying on lengthy debates with Lean on the set about how each scene should be played. Their professional relationship became increasingly strained as time went on.

To make matters worse, Todd was disgruntled because Lean had clearly not intended *The Sound Barrier* to be a vehicle for her, in the way that both *The Passionate Friends* and *Madeleine* obviously had been. The film was solidly built around the character of Sir John Ridgefield, not that of his daughter, Susan. Unfortunately, as Anthony Havelock-Allan remarks, Todd thought "that she would be the leading lady in all Lean's films from then on." In fact, she gave Lean the impression that she planned to use him as a "stepping-stone" for her movie career. Lean, of course, declined to be a stepping-stone for anyone's career, except his own.[19]

The deterioration of the Lean-Todd working relationship was apparent when they shot a night scene that takes place after Tony is killed. Susan visits the site where her husband's plane crashed. Lean planned to film the scene in one night, but Todd disputed his handling of every shot, with the result that shooting took two nights instead of one. Jack Hildyard overheard Lean bemoaning the fact that he had to cope with his intractable wife on the set throughout filming. He cautioned Lean about making such remarks in front of the cast and crew. For her part, Todd told me in Cannes that she usually gave in to Lean when she had a row with him on the set. "You're the director," she would say. "Have it your way."

Still, Lean got along with the rest of the cast. John Justin remembers rehearsing a scene with Nigel Patrick. Lean sat in on the rehearsal for a while and then told them that he was going to let the two of them work it out for themselves. "Let me know when you are ready," he said, and walked off the set. They sent him a message when they were prepared to show him the scene. After watching a run-through, Lean said, "Shoot it." Justin was pleased because, as he later reported, "I don't like too much direction."[20]

Harold Boxall, who gave Lean his first job in the film industry, was now an executive at London Films. When Lean told Boxall that he intended to shoot the aerial sequences himself, Boxall turned thumbs down on the idea. That, he said, would send the production over schedule and over budget. A second-unit director, working while Lean was filming the bulk of the movie, could do the aerial cinematography.

Lean disliked having to cede even a small part of the direction of a film to a second-unit director, and he had never done so before. But he had no choice. Actually, Boxall had done him a favor. Because in the years ahead Lean would regularly have to employ second units on mammoth productions like *The Bridge on the River Kwai* and *Ryan's Daughter*, it proved important that he learn how to collaborate with a second-unit director. On *The Sound Barrier*, it was Anthony Squire who filled that role.

Lean—who wanted the aerial photography to give a sense of the immensity of space by frequently showing the test planes in long shot against a vast expanse of sky—often conferred during the shooting period with Squire. Squire had been a fighter pilot in World War II, as had John Derry, the ace airman who flew the jet plane for most of the aerial sequences photographed by the second unit. Derry had earned a Distinguished Flying Cross, and after the war he was employed by De Havilland Aircraft as a test pilot.

The close shots of a pilot in the cockpit of a test plane were, of course, filmed in the studio. Lean shared Hildyard's dissatisfaction with the common method of rear-screen projection, whereby an actor would perform in front of a screen on which images of exterior locations (in this case, panoramic shots of cloudscapes) were projected from behind. Rear-screen projection yielded images that were not in sharp focus, and that was not good enough for Lean.

So Lean and Hildyard decided to employ matte work, rather than rear-screen projection. Employing matte work meant that the cockpit scenes would be filmed against a blank screen and then the cloudscapes added in the laboratory by optical printing in the background of each shot ("matted in"). For example, Nigel Patrick played the scene where Tony Garthwaite attempts to fly faster than the speed of sound while seated in the cockpit set, which was attached to a rostrum. A technician would jostle the rostrum, which in turn would shake the cockpit, thereby making it appear that the plane was being buffeted by powerful winds. The effect achieved was wondrously realistic.

After the shoot wrapped, Lean joined Geoffrey Foot in the editing room. One of Foot's assistants was Teddy Darvas, a native Hungarian hired by Korda. Darvas recalled that Lean ignored him at first, assuming that he was one of the "refugees" that Korda had imported to work at Shepperton Studios and not a particularly competent film editor. But, when Lean realized that Darvas was serious about the craft of film editing, he often gave him advice on how to improve his editing skills.

Lean remembered Carol Reed saying that a cardinal principle of editing was never to let a scene run on so long that it bored the audience. A scene that is good at four minutes, Lean explained, can be weakened if overwritten into five.[21] One example of this principle is the scene portraying the building of a destroyer in *In Which We Serve*. Another is the montage in *The Sound Barrier* depicting a plane at various stages of construction, which Lean put together with documentary-like realism, and which climaxes in a shot of the finished product. When shown the final cut of *The Sound Barrier*, Korda pronounced this montage overlength. So Lean went back to the editing room and cut the sequence to less than four minutes. Lean trusted Korda's instincts in these matters because Korda had a sense of what an audience would sit through without becoming restless.

Lean remained close to the documentary impulse of *In Which We Serve* while shooting *The Sound Barrier*. This is evident in the film's prologue, which precedes the opening credits. Some members of the production staff had expressed to Lean early on their doubts that an ordinary filmgoer would understand what flying at supersonic speed meant. "So we thought we'd open the film on an incident that actually took place during the war," said Lean.[22]

The prologue is described in the program notes for a special London screening of the film held in 1990: "The scene is the chalk-cliff coast of Sussex in wartime; on the coast are anti-aircraft gunners, and, in the sky above them, the pilot of a single Spitfire in sheer exuberance is indulging in aerobatics which culminate in an all-but-fatal dive." As the plane plunges, it begins to vibrate, and the pilot pulls out of the dive just before he crashes. As a matter of fact, the airman "had inadvertently touched the edge, as it were, of the sound barrier": "The beauty and tenseness in this often beautiful and tense film is foreshadowed and synthesized in these opening shots."[23]

Lean the meticulous film editor collaborated closely with Malcolm Arnold when the composer scored this opening scene. The result: "As the Spitfire lifts and soars, so do the strings of Arnold's composition." Then, with the shot of the battering of the diving aircraft, "the music shifts into an ominous, chattering sound, which ceases when the pilot pulls the craft out of the dangerous dive." Arnold comments that, when he took on the scoring of a Lean film, his fellow English composers told him that Lean would be sure to want a "big tune" à la Rachmaninoff (recalling *Brief Encounter*).[24] But there is more than the flavor of Rachmaninoff in Arnold's rhapsodic background music for the film, as evidenced by his serviceable music for the sequence just described. It is marked by strains of atonal music and an eerie piccolo theme; together, these themes give this and other aerial scenes a touch of wonder.

Arnold insisted on conducting his own score at the recording sessions, as Walter Goehr had done for his score for *Great Expectations*, rather than have a studio conductor do the honors. Indeed, he arranged to work with the Royal Philharmonic—and at the Royal Festival Hall, rather than at the recording studio on the Shepperton lot. He later carved out a concert suite from the music for *The Sound Barrier*, just as he would do with his scores for *Hobson's Choice* and *The Bridge on the River Kwai*. All three suites are available on CD.

After the prologue, the film proper gets under way. Sir John Ridgefield's dreams that his son Christopher (Denholm Elliott) will be the pilot who will break the sound barrier are dashed when Christopher's plane crashes and burns in his first flight. Ridgefield then places his high hopes in son-in-law Tony Garthwaite; in effect, Tony becomes Ridgefield's protégé and surrogate son as well as his chief test pilot.

One evening, Susan ruefully confesses to her father that she cannot help wondering whether Tony will one day meet the same fate as Christopher. She goes on to question the value of her father's efforts to develop a supersonic plane. "Is the ability to travel at two thousand miles per hour going to be a blessing to the human race?" she inquires pointedly. Ridgefield answers: "Well, I'd say that is up to the human race. The real point is, it's just got to be done. What purpose did Scott have in going to the South Pole?" Ridgefield is, perhaps, thinking of Robert Browning: "Ah, but a man's reach should exceed his grasp, / Or what's a heaven for?"[25]

Tony's day of reckoning comes during a crucial test flight, when he experiences severe turbulence as he tries to force his jet plane through the sound barrier; his aircraft goes into a crash dive. He attempts to bail out, but it is already too late; the plane cracks up, and he is blown to bits. "Tony is the Icarus who flies too near the sun and is thrown back to earth. His ship, upon impact, is buried in the ground." Lean cuts to a farmer running past the charred pieces of wreckage strewn all over his field. Then "a panning shot reveals the crash site," and a high-angle shot "looks down on the black, smoldering crater."[26] The smoke from the burning fragments of the plane symbolizes how Ridgefield's hopes that Tony would break the sound barrier have gone up in smoke.

A personal crisis develops after Tony is killed, when Ridgefield must face his daughter. In the wake of the deaths of both her brother and her husband, Susan confronts her father in an emotionally wrenching scene. Aware that Tony's comrade Philip Peel will replace Tony as chief test pilot, Susan asks her father pointedly, "Wasn't Tony enough for you?" He replies stoically, "We learned a lot from Tony's crash." Then Susan launches into a tirade: "You want me to think of you as a man of vision; but there are evil visions as well as good ones, you know, Father." Ridgefield replies, "Can a vision be evil, Sue? It's a terrible thing to make a man doubt everything he's ever lived for."

Ridgefield's statement recalls his earlier declaration of his vision: "I believe we can force our way through the barrier; and, once through, there is a whole new world within the grasp of man." His credo may seem to brand him as a hopeless visionary, but we must remember that this film was made "when the world was on the threshold of jet-propelled aircraft," at a time when breaking the sound barrier with supersonic planes was thought to be "as remote as reaching the moon."[27] Time has vindicated Ridgefield's chimerical vision.

Yet Ridgefield does have an abiding sense of concern for his pilots. Consequently, he must reexamine in this moment of defeat whether he has a right to realize his dream if the price must be paid in human lives. After much soul-searching, he decides that the experiments must continue.

Recall that Lean once said, "I am drawn to the person who refuses to face defeat." Clearly, his sympathies—and, thus, ours—are with Ridgefield as he sits tense and anxious in his office listening over a loudspeaker as Peel describes what is happening to him and his plane as he tries to succeed where Tony has failed. Lean suggests how Ridgefield is living through the test pilot's experience with him by photographing Ridgefield for a moment at a tilted angle, as if he were in the cockpit with Peel, hurtling through space, plunging into a dive, then leveling off again.

As Ridgefield "sweats out" Peel's perilous flight, Susan is in his office with him. She becomes convinced that, "beneath his hard exterior," her father "has doubt, fear, and compassion," as Anderegg puts it. In the face of his anguish, "all is excused; all is forgiven."[28] She says to him afterward, when Peel has completed a successful test flight: "I never realized how lonely you were."

John Justin remembers shooting the scene in which Peel breaks the sound barrier. Peel says, "Here we go, full throttle!" As he goes into a tail-spin, he experiences the same turbulence that Tony faced. While rehearsing the scene, says Justin, a technical expert suggested that, if Peel pushed his steering stick forward when he went into a power dive, it would give the idea that he had "reversed the controls" and that the plane could pull out of the dive and level off. "So that's what I did. I said the words, 'I'm now going to push the stick forward.' That was a great moment."[29] In this nail-biting flying sequence, Justin plays Peel as the strong, silent type, thus resembling Lean's hero Lindbergh.

Chuck Yeager, a U.S. Air Force pilot, was the first American test pilot to fly at supersonic speed. After seeing the film, he commented that a Spitfire—the World War II fighter plane that Squire and his second-unit crew had used when filming this sequence—was not equipped for "an aerial stunt" like this. Any pilot who would have attempted to fly faster than sound in a Spitfire would have gone into a power dive and never come out of it; he would have simply "drilled himself into the ground." But, Yeager added, "it worked as a dramatic moment in the picture."[30]

In photographing the aerial footage for the scene, Squire had the Spitfire fly as fast as it possibly could, to suggest that it was Peel's plane in super-sonic flight. But, in the editing room, Lean thought that the plane did not look like it was going fast enough. So he obtained some sixteen-millimeter footage of a missile in flight from an army missile range and cut it into the scene. Therefore, the long shot of Peel's aircraft streaking across the sky is really a shot of a missile at full speed. Lean had developed the habit of inter-polating stock footage into scenes back in his days as a film editor. As we have seen, for *The 49th Parallel* he cut in some newsreel footage of a German U-boat surfacing in the Atlantic Ocean. So his insertion of the missile footage into *The Sound Barrier* was nothing new.

The epilogue of the film portrays the awkward reconciliation of father and daughter as Susan visits Ridgefield in his private observatory, where he is looking at the stars through his telescope. Susan acknowledges that ob-serving him during Peel's test run proved to her that he is a decent and car-ing man. After the ordeal is over and Peel has accomplished his mission, Ridgefield philosophizes to Susan that man ultimately has the advantage in his fight to conquer the universe. This is because he has the weapons of courage and imagination with which to carry on the struggle—virtues with which her late husband was certainly imbued.

At the fade-out, the camera closes in on Ridgefield's telescope and a model jet plane pointing skyward; this image implies that mankind will continue to have more creative encounters with the universe. At this moment, Arnold's principal theme, played by a piccolo and shimmering strings, returns for the last time; this unearthly music spirals upward. In tandem with the imagery it suggests the aspiration to scale the heights of human endeavor.

For the record, John Derry, one of the aviators whose flying feats were captured by Antony Squire's second unit, was the first British pilot to break the sound barrier. He did so on September 6, 1948. What neither Derry nor Lean nor anyone else involved in *The Sound Barrier* knew while they were shooting the picture was that the American Chuck Yeager had broken the sound barrier on October 14, 1947. But the American government had kept his aerial triumph classified. These were the cold war years, and the Pentagon did not want the Russians to know that America was getting ahead of them in the space race. So Lean's film portrays the British as being the first to fly faster than the speed of sound.

Lean got to hear about Yeager's accomplishment while the film was in postproduction and slipped a reference to it into the film. But the studio was not prepared to have a British picture admit that an American test pilot had stolen the thunder of an English pilot. "I'm afraid," Lean confessed, "that the line was cut."[31]

Yeager recalled attending the British premiere of *The Sound Barrier* on July 24, 1952. "When the lights came up," he writes in his autobiography, "I realized that people seated around me thought they had watched a true story." He turned to an American who happened to be sitting near him and exclaimed, "Hey, *we* broke the sound barrier, not the damned British! And I'm the guy who did it!!" But, he goes on, "I might have saved my breath. The movie was a hit, and many people who saw it believed it was a true story."[32]

The Sound Barrier was a popular film, both in England and in America, where it opened the following November. Ilya Lopert, Korda's American distributor, insisted on calling the movie *Breaking the Sound Barrier* for its premiere bookings in the United States. He claimed that, in America, no one had heard of the sound barrier and that the movie needed a more descriptive title, one referring to the challenge involved. Since the American title was dropped after the film's initial run in the United States, I have used the original title throughout.

Though a few negative notices pronounced Lean's picture "earthbound," the vast majority found it a mixture of exhilaration and adventure in the air and domestic drama on the ground. Lean had given "flesh and blood reality to the characters"; he was not content "to put dummies, as it were, into the aircraft."[33] Indeed, the dedicated test pilots played by Nigel Patrick and John Justin manage to maintain distinct personalities. Huzzahs were in order for the consummate acting of Ralph Richardson as Ridgefield in particular. Moreover, under Lean's direction, the entire cast creates a memorable collection of characters hewn from life on the edge, and they deliver as ensemble players.

With rare dexterity, Lean "succeeds," as Ivan Butler has written, "in involving the viewer in some of the stress and excitement of flying" as he celebrates human endeavor. He avoids the clichés of previous aviation pictures, which endlessly portrayed the strained expressions "on the goggled faces" of the pilots during their perilous flights.[34]

The British Film Academy voted *The Sound Barrier* the best picture of the year and Ralph Richardson best actor; the New York Film Critics followed suit. These awards were deserved. *The Sound Barrier* is disturbing and enthralling; the drama is taut, the aerial sequences electrifying. The picture has some ponderous stretches, but, in the end, it attains a certain grandeur. It is a trip that gives the passengers a great ride.

The Sound Barrier continues to have a following in England. Ann Todd said, "I was so proud and excited to see it shown at a National Film Theater special screening [in the spring of 1990]."[35] That screening likewise afforded me the opportunity to view a mint-condition, uncut thirty-five-millimeter print of the movie, which presented the aerial sequences to awesome effect on the big screen.

The Sound Barrier spelled the end of Ann Todd and David Lean's relationship, both professional and personal. Their marriage was obviously headed toward the rocks during the making of the film, and afterward they became increasingly estranged from one another. It goes without saying that they never worked together again. After *The Sound Barrier* wrapped, word got around in the British film colony that Todd's constant squabbling with Lean on the set of both *Madeleine* and *The Sound Barrier* had caused both films to fall behind schedule and to go over budget. Furthermore, the critics were not especially impressed with her work as the "obligatory" female lead in *The Sound Barrier*. As a result, producers were not prone to cast her in other pictures. So her films were few and far between for the balance of the 1950s.

Todd became very bitter about her breakup with Lean. In November 1954, Lean, who always avoided confrontation whenever possible, slipped his belongings out of the house in the dead of night when Todd was not at home and moved into rented rooms. He sent her a letter around this time, explaining that he was not cut out for marriage—though they did not actually divorce until July 1957. Referring to his letter at the time of their divorce, she stated, "David was not the sort of man that husbands are made from; too tense, too mercurial."[36] Elsewhere she added, "I don't think you can be married to a genius. David would go way into himself every now and then; he went dead on me." He was "never there" for her, she contended.[37] When Frank Lean heard about the breakup, he expressed disapproval that his son's third marriage had failed.

Lean learned that, after their split, Todd spread rumors that he was homosexual and, therefore, impotent with her. To bolster her claim, she further asserted that he had invited her son by a former marriage, David Malcolm, to go on vacation with him and Todd so that he could seduce the lad. When she repeated these gratuitous allegations during the divorce proceedings, Lean said he refused to answer them. "Like a fool, I resisted pressures to make her the guilty party," as his lawyers entreated him to do. "I had no resistance and very little self-respect," he explained, "and I ran." That is, he left the country for a time to escape the harassment of the yellow press in England. Moreover, Todd received a huge divorce settlement. Lean concluded: "I had to pay this woman for the harm I was supposed to have done her."[38] Todd was granted a divorce decree in an uncontested suit because of desertion by David Lean since 1954.

In the 1960s, Todd turned to writing and directing travel documentaries. David Lean's widow, Sandra, writes that she and Lean encountered Todd at a London film premiere in 1987, three decades after the divorce. Todd rushed up to Lean in the lobby of the cinema and embraced him; after they chatted briefly, Todd took her leave. At that point, Lean turned to Sandra and inquired, "Who the hell was that?" She responded that that was his third wife, Ann Todd. "But she was so old!" he exclaimed.[39] It seems that Lean tended to remember people from his past as they were when he knew them. Todd looked every bit of her seventy-eight years, so he did not recognize her. By contrast, Lean, who was seventy-nine, still looked younger than his years.

If Ann Todd's career was on the downswing after *The Sound Barrier,* David Lean's was on the upswing, given the international success of the picture when it was first released. Korda had taken a risk in allotting the film a budget more substantial than the average British film would receive, and the payoff was handsome. Lean's first collaboration with Korda had borne significant fruit.

Prior to the release of *The Sound Barrier,* however, Lean's reputation as a major British filmmaker had been eclipsed by that of Carol Reed, his friendly rival. "I had two recent international successes with *The Fallen Idol* and *The Third Man,*" Reed told me, "while David had lost ground with *The Passionate Friends* and *Madeleine.*" In fact, on the occasion of the Festival of Britain in 1951, the British Film Institute published *Films of 1951: The Festival of Britain,* an overview of the British film industry at the time; the book devoted much more space to Reed than to Lean.

Still *Films of 1951* also featured the article "Ten Years of British Films," by Sir Michael Balcon, who had been an executive at Gaumont-British when Lean was editing newsreels there. In it, Balcon expressed complete confidence in Lean: "He has had recent setbacks, but his extraordinary single-mindedness and tenacity make me certain that he will survive these and again take his proper place as a director of international calibre."[40]

Balcon's remarks were prophetic. As the British film historian Roy Armes notes, Lean's next two films after *The Sound Barrier* "can be seen as a farewell to the limitations of his British productions, and as a further step towards the later epics, particularly in their use of powerful Hollywood star personalities."[41] Lean's next film, *Hobson's Choice,* would star Charles Laughton, and the one after that, *Summertime,* would be a vehicle for Katharine Hepburn. So his projects were now attracting major Hollywood stars.

Chapter Nine

THE STAG AT EVE

HOBSON'S CHOICE

The stag at Eve had drunk his fill.

—*Sir Walter Scott,* The Lady of the Lake

Sometimes we are forced into directions that we ought to have found for ourselves.

—*Lionid, the concierge in the film* Maid in Manhattan

Alexander Korda casually inquired one day whether David Lean had heard of a stage comedy called *Hobson's Choice* by Harold Brighouse. Lean was vaguely familiar with the play, set in the north of England, which had been popular in repertory and in summer stock since it was first staged in 1915. Brighouse set the play in 1880, in the late Victorian era—though several commentators assume that, because it was written in 1915, it takes place in 1915. Brighouse chose to set the play in 1880 because that was when the first stirrings of the women's rights movement were being felt in England. Indeed, Maggie, the play's heroine, would be portrayed as an early feminist.

Henry Horatio Hobson, Maggie's father, is the main character in the play. He is the proprietor of a well-established boot shop (shoe store in American parlance) in Salford, in industrial Lancashire. Hobson, a widower, has three daughters. He depends on them to run the shoemaking shop and to take care of the domestic duties around the house, which is attached to the shoe store. Hobson is, thus, free to spend a good deal of his time in the local pub, the Moonraker, with his fellow tradesmen.

Hobson's oldest daughter, Maggie, unlike her two flighty younger sisters, is a self-possessed, assertive young woman. She decides to rebel against her penny-pinching father, who pays his daughters only meager wages and rules them like an absolute monarch. Maggie is determined to find herself a husband with whom she can open a shoemaking shop that can rival her father's. In due course, she marries her father's timid but talented shoemaker, Willie Mossop, and lures him away from Hobson's shop to start an establishment of their own. A highly efficient saleswoman, Maggie, with Willie's help, makes a go of their new business.

Hobson's ailing business and his alcoholism finally force him to come to terms with Maggie and Willie. They insist on a merger, whereby they will take over and run his business. Their ultimatum to Hobson brings the play's title into relief. The expression *Hobson's choice* means no choice at all. It is a reference to Thomas Hobson, a seventeenth-century stable owner who rented horse-drawn carriages. He offered each customer the horse standing nearest the stable door or no horse at all. So, at play's end, Maggie and Willie tell Henry Hobson that he must go into business with them as his full partners, not his employees, or go bankrupt. In short, they leave him no alternative.

Hobson's Choice is a domestic comedy that, nevertheless, explores some substantial social issues. Brighouse employed the plot to examine aspects of feminism and to provide a rueful critique of patriarchy. By the time Brighouse penned *Hobson's Choice* in 1915, the movement for women's rights had gotten rolling in earnest in Britain. The movement was championed by eloquent feminists like Rebecca West, who contributed to the *New Freewoman*.[1] West, we know, was the model for the stubborn, independent heroine of *The Passionate Friends* (see chapter 7).

In Brighouse's play, Maggie, a strong-minded woman who defies her overbearing father, certainly reflects feminist attitudes. In the end, the old order, epitomized by the truculent, pompous Henry Hobson, must perforce give way to new, the upward mobility of his accomplished daughter and her pliable husband. In fact, Maggie inspires Willie with the optimistic motto: "There is always room at the top."

Lean was interested to learn that the play had already been filmed twice, by Percy Nash in 1920 as a silent movie and by Thomas Bentley in 1931 as a talkie. Korda had a hunch that another remake was in order. There is no record that Lean watched either of the previous two film versions (he did, e.g., see William Cowen's *Oliver Twist*, the first sound version, before he made his own). Nash's film starred Arthur Pitt as Hobson and Joan Ritz as Maggie. By all accounts, it was a mediocre flick, made somewhat gloomy by its drab, working-class settings. Nash appears to have fumbled Hobson's comic drunk scenes, which at times border on slapstick, and which had helped make the play a success in its day. Bentley's film starred James Harcourt as Hobson and Viola Lyel as Maggie. It was made not long after the birth of sound pictures, when, as Alfred Hitchcock observed, directors often "filmed stage plays straight," forgetting that talking pictures should also be moving pictures, not mere photographs of "talking heads."[2] Bentley's film, unfortunately, falls into this category. *Variety* was particularly acerbic in dismissing it as a stagy talk fest: "The only thing in its favor is its short footage" (sixty-five minutes).[3]

Korda assured Lean that the first two film adaptations offered little competition. Hence, Lean was greatly interested in doing a fresh film version—especially after he saw a spirited revival at the Arts Theater Club in the summer of 1952. Lean had not made a comedy since *Blithe Spirit*, and *Hobson's Choice* would be his second, and last, effort in that genre.

Korda firmly believed that, because it addresses some thought-provoking issues, *Hobson's Choice* was not out-of-date. It deals not only with feminism but also with alcoholism, failure, greed, and human beings' inability to communicate with one another. It is also a very entertaining, comic portrayal of a seedy, self-deluded petty tyrant who gets a long-overdue comeuppance. Korda had already purchased the screen rights to Brighouse's play. He commissioned Frank Launder and Sidney Gilliat to come up with a screenplay.

Launder and Gilliat were the writing team who had scripted Carol Reed's comedy-thriller *Night Train to Munich* (1940), and they sometimes directed their own scripts. And Launder had, in fact, written the script for Bentley's *Hobson's Choice*. Nevertheless, Korda was greatly disappointed by their draft. They specialized in a wry, breezy, clever type of comedy, and *Hobson's Choice* called for broad, unsophisticated, quirky humor. Accordingly, Korda asked Lean to try his hand at a new screenplay, urging him to ignore the Launder-Gilliat draft and rethink the movie adaptation for himself.

Hobson's Choice (1954)

Lean's commentators have frequently questioned his decision to lavish his filmmaking abilities on an aged Victorian vehicle like *Hobson's Choice*. For starters, he was again reaching back to the period of his two Dickens movies, making another costume picture. Furthermore, he chose *Hobson's Choice* for much the same reason he chose *Great Expectations* and *Oliver Twist*—they were proven properties. One of Britain's favorite plays, *Hobson's Choice* had been regularly revived in the theater for four decades. Moreover, Hobson, the blustery domestic tyrant, was almost a parody of Madeleine Smith's domineering paterfamilias in *Madeleine;* so *Hobson's Choice* did have another, implicit connection with one of Lean's previous movies.

Still, Lean was inclined to look on the project benignly because it represented a complete departure from *The Sound Barrier.* That picture had been a critical and popular success, and he wondered whether he could produce two blockbusters in quick succession. Consequently, he wanted to do something quite different, something not easily compared to *The Sound Barrier.* *Hobson's Choice* filled the bill. Whereas *The Sound Barrier* called for a vast canvas, *Hobson's Choice* would be a miniature.

Even at this preliminary stage in the filmmaking process, Lean tried to think of ways to ward off negative notices. Bad reviews inevitably called to mind his father's disapproval. They would also confirm Frank Lean's long-standing belief that his son would never be a credit to him.

All in all, *Hobson's Choice* looked like a safe and simple project. Besides, Lean had no other project in development when Korda offered him the play.

Norman Spencer, who had been the associate producer on *The Sound Barrier,* was continuing in that capacity on the present film. Lean asked Spencer to help him with the screenplay because Spencer had made some valuable observations about Rattigan's script for *The Sound Barrier.*

In January 1953, Lean and Spencer took up residence in Korda's office complex in downtown London, where they labored on the scenario for a month. Korda told them that he would bring in the screenwriter Wynyard Browne to assist them. "Wynyard Browne" turned out to be the pen name for a husband-and-wife writing team. Though Wynyard Browne eventually shared the official writing credit on the film with Lean and Spencer, Lean sent the pair packing early on. He and Spencer soldiered on without them.

Lean invited Brighouse, now a septuagenarian, to come down from Lancashire for a couple of story conferences. Brighouse did not have much to say, but he did make one significant suggestion. He singled out one of the highlights of the play, one that on the stage always brought down the house: when the mousey Willie Mossop employs delaying tactics on his wedding night, Maggie finally has to take him by the ear and drag him into the bedroom. Brighouse told the screenwriters to play up that scene for all it was worth and the script would be marvelous. With that, he departed for home.

Lean was too inventive and skillful a filmmaker to allow his version of Brighouse's quaint provincial stage play to turn into a dated, dull movie, which was the fate of the two previous film adaptations. So he made some substantial alterations for the screen. Most important, he kept in mind that the play, which took place in the single setting of Hobson's shop, must be opened out for the screen in much the same way as *This Happy Breed* (see chapter 3). His adaptation of *Hobson's Choice* adds several scenes that take place in other locations, providing "glimpses of Hobson's blustering behavior in the Moonraker, the local pub, and of Maggie's drive and determination."[4] For example, Maggie transforms an abandoned cellar into a shipshape shoe store fit to rival her father's.

Lean saw *Hobson's Choice* as a refreshing challenge because it enabled him to cut loose from the documentary-based realism of films like *In Which We Serve* and *The Sound Barrier*. He could treat the story as a fable full of characters who are deliberately drawn with the broad strokes of caricature, recalling some of the grotesques in the Dickens films. Henry Hobson, for example, is cut from the same cloth as the pompous, self-important Mr. Bumble in *Oliver Twist*.

With the script finished, Lean naturally turned to assembling his cast and crew. The composer Malcolm Arnold and the cinematographer Jack Hildyard, with whom Lean had worked on *The Sound Barrier*, were back in action. Hildyard would be photographing Lean's last black-and-white film. New to Lean's production team were the film editor Peter Taylor, who would be editing the first of three Lean films, and the production designer Wilfred Shingleton, who had assisted John Bryan on *Great Expectations*.

Everyone at Shepperton Studios marveled at the elaborate outdoor set that Lean built on the back lot: a replica of Chapel Street, a cobblestoned thoroughfare in the northern mill town of Salford, in which Hobson's shop is located. The set matched perfectly with the location sites that Lean and Shingleton chose in Salford itself, with its skyline of black smokestacks.

For the plum role of Henry Hobson, Lean believed that Charles Laughton was ideal. Laughton had actually played Hobson on the stage in his native Yorkshire when he was a precocious young actor. He married the actress Elsa Lanchester just before he made his debut in pictures; because he was homosexual, theirs was a companionate marriage. Lean remembered watching Laughton acting in the 1930 Albert de Courville film *Wolves* at Gaumont-British. Laughton's biographer Simon Callow is right in saying that, at the time, "the pains to which Laughton went for verisimilitude in a fight scene impressed Lean deeply." But Callow is wrong in saying that *Wolves* was Laughton's first film; it was his fourth.[5]

Laughton went on to make films in both England and America. In Hollywood, Cecil B. DeMille cast him as the emperor Nero in *The Sign of the Cross* (1932), one of Laughton's best early screen roles. Laughton dared to play Nero as effeminate, with his favorite slave boy always sitting next to his throne. He returned to England to take the title role in Korda's *The Private Life of Henry VIII* (1933), winning an Academy Award for his portrayal of the king. So, by the time he made *Hobson's Choice*, Laughton had, like Alec Guinness, achieved international stardom by playing character parts.

In February 1953, Lean, with Korda's approval, decided to cable Laughton in Hollywood and offer him the lead in *Hobson's Choice*. Given his prior experience working on film adaptations of Shaw (see chapter 2), Lean was interested to learn that Laughton had been touring America in a Bernard Shaw play, playing the Devil in the seriocomic *Don Juan in Hell*. (It just so happened that I saw that particular production. Laughton was a commanding presence onstage and stole the show from his costar, Charles Boyer as Don Juan.)

In his wire, Lean indicated that he would dispatch a copy of the just-completed screenplay to Laughton. He added the flattering observation that the script had been written with Laughton in mind. Laughton responded enthusiastically and positively to Lean—but sent his personal demands to Korda. He wanted to live in a house near the studio for the duration of the shoot since he detested hotels; he also demanded expenses for his young male companion. Korda replied, much to Laughton's displeasure, that he would provide living accommodations for Laughton and the lad in the hotel on the grounds of Shepperton Studios.

Laughton was pleased, however, that one of his friends and favorite actors, Robert Donat, was signed to play Willie Mossop. Donat had costarred with Laughton in *The Private Life of Henry VIII* and had gone on to win acclaim in Hitchcock's *The 39 Steps* (1934). But Donat fell grievously ill with a severe case of asthma, a chronic ailment, shortly before filming began, and the insurance company refused to take the risk of insuring the film if Donat was in the cast. Laughton was deeply disappointed.

Laughton had a reputation for being a troublesome and temperamental actor, one who was all too eager to take offense at slights and insults, real or imagined. Running true to form, he was already in high dudgeon by the time principal photography was scheduled to begin. He failed to come to the set on the first day of shooting. Korda was advised by an intermediary that Laughton was unhappy with the way in which Korda was handling the production. Laughton maintained that he had accepted the part of Hobson on the condition that Robert Donat played Willie and contended, quite illogically, that Donat's ouster constituted a breach of contract. Furthermore, he loathed the hotel accommodations that Korda had forced him to accept. Callow adds that Laughton was also depressed because he was having boyfriend trouble, though this factor was not disclosed to Korda.[6]

Laughton's homosexuality was an open secret in acting circles, as was the case with Noël Coward's (see chapter 3), but, again as with Coward's, it was not known to the general public. Lean was inclined to coax Laughton tactfully to come to the set, but Korda opted for a frontal attack because he saw Laughton's making trouble at the outset of filming as thoroughly unprofessional. He phoned Laughton's agent and issued the following threat: "You tell Charlie that, if he wants me to go to the scandal sheets, I will."[7] Korda's clear implication was that practicing homosexuals were still liable to arrest in England, and Laughton got the point. Soon after, he reported for work. Lean reflected afterward that he found it hard to believe that Laughton was homosexual; he was, after all, playing the father of three daughters quite convincingly. In any event, he said, Laughton's sexual preference never affected his relationship with the actor in any way.

John Mills, who had already appeared in three Lean films, was summoned as Donat's last-minute replacement. Mills accepted the part of Willie even before he read the script because his faltering career needed the boost that a David Lean film could give it. He was now too old to play romantic leads, as he had in his other Lean films, yet he was still too young for the character parts that he would take later on. "I had not been in a really successful picture since [Roy Ward Baker's 1950] *Operation Disaster* [known as *Morning Departure* in its British release]," in which he costarred with another Lean alumnus, Richard Attenborough.[8]

Mills, who was short of stature, writes in his autobiography that Lean frankly admitted to him that he had pictured Willie as awkwardly tall and shambling: "But he trusted me to come up with a performance. . . . The key to Willie was that he was a simple soul, utterly truthful."[9] His face is as innocent as an empty bowl. Willie was "an unglamorous chap": "But he was a hero, you see."[10] At film's end, he stands up to his ferocious father-in-law.

Brenda de Banzie was picked to play Maggie, who is thirty years old. Actually, de Banzie was forty-two, but she did not look a day over thirty. She had made only a few minor films but had had an impressive career in the West End.

The ten-week shoot commenced in July 1953 at Shepperton. Though Laughton was a difficult actor, he felt at home with Lean. When they discussed Laughton's role, Lean told him that he wanted Hobson, the eccentric shopkeeper, to be a grotesque character straight out of Dickens. Laughton went along with that but said, in addition, that his own conception of Hobson, with his three troublesome daughters, was that of a Lear figure. (Indeed, Laughton would play King Lear in 1959 during the summer Shakespeare festival at Stratford-on-Avon.)

Asked why he got along with Laughton better than most directors did,

Lean answered that most of the time directing actors is simply a matter of "gentle encouragement" and that that was certainly true of directing Laughton. A filmmaker must remember, Lean explained, that it is the actor's face up there on the screen, not the director's, and he can be worried and need reassurance. Lean said that he had been criticized for keeping his distance from actors when they were off the set. He responded that, as a rule, if the director gets too chummy with actors, it is hard to instruct them during rehearsal "and expect to be obeyed."[11]

Lean suspended his rule about not socializing with actors off the set while working with Laughton. Near Shepperton Studios, which was beside the Thames, there was a tavern. And Lean and Laughton sometimes repaired there after the day's shoot. Lean had noticed that Laughton intensely disliked Brenda de Banzie, that he was sometimes discourteous and sarcastic to her. So Lean took the occasion to sound Laughton out about his antipathy for de Banzie in the convivial atmosphere of the pub. Laughton replied that Maggie was a marvelous part but that de Banzie had not nailed it down: "Maggie is a real bitch, only Brenda doesn't understand that."[12] More to the point was the fact that de Banzie was giving a strong performance and at times threatened to upstage Laughton, who was a consummate scene-stealer.

Throughout filming Laughton continued to feud with de Banzie—and occasionally with some of the other actors as well. Mills thought that Laughton lorded it over the other players during rehearsals. "He was a weird one," Mills says, "talking in a rather high-falutin way when we were rehearsing."[13] One is reminded of Alfred Hitchcock's remark about working with Laughton on *The Paradine Case* (1947): "It isn't possible to direct Charles Laughton in a film; the best you can hope for is to act as referee."[14]

Withal, Laughton is in top form in *Hobson's Choice*. Since he hailed from Yorkshire, he had no trouble rejuvenating his northern accent. He gives a no-holds-barred characterization of Hobson, indulging in mugging, snarling, leering, and other bits of business from his actor's bag of tricks. "Lean clearly showcases and abets Laughton's interpretation," judges Anderegg, even though Laughton sometimes is outsized and mannered. Lean felt in retrospect that he might have restrained "dear old Charlie" at times.[15] Still, he had decided at the outset to give Laughton the minimum of direction. Mills and others observed on the set that Lean was really in awe of Laughton's reputation as an international star and, hence, left him pretty much alone.

The film unit spent a week on location in Salford in September 1953, toward the end of principal photography. Noël Coward once told Lean that a love scene should be played in a glum, grubby setting, as a counterpoint to the romantic action. One thinks of the love scenes played out in dirty back streets of the village in *Brief Encounter.* Following Coward's advice, Lean chose the banks of the polluted River Irwell in Salford's Peel Park for the scene in which Willie is courted by Maggie. This scene, of course, is not in the play and exemplifies Lean's opening the play out for the screen.

A reporter from the *Manchester Guardian* visited the location site. Maggie and Willie sat together on a bench under a lamppost, facing a grimy factory on the opposite shore, the journalist reported. "The script called for murk and gloom," but the riverbanks "were bathed in warm September sunshine." Therefore, Lean thought that the scene looked too bright and clear. So he had the cinder path near the bench splashed with black paint, "lest it appear too bright in the sunshine," and the lamppost smeared quickly with grime, to add to the characteristic Salford gloom. In keeping with the bleak atmosphere, he called for "smoke and sulfurous fumes from piles of burning auto tires" to drift over the scene.[16] For good measure, he ordered the property man to collect orange crates, tin cans, and other types of rubbish and hurl it all into the scummy river. At last Lean called for a take, and filming proceeded.

After filming wrapped late in September, Lean sequestered himself in the cutting room to supervise Peter Taylor's assembling and shaping of the footage. Two months later, on November 14, 1953, he was ready to screen a refined version of the editor's rough cut for Malcolm Arnold. Arnold had been sketching out his score in advance of the screening, so he had his music ready to be recorded by November 23. This time around, he did not insist on personally conducting his underscore in a concert hall, as he had done on *The Sound Barrier.* He was satisfied simply to preside over the recording sessions at the studio. Muir Mathieson, who had led the orchestra in recording the background music for most of the movies that Lean had made for Rank, conducted the Royal Philharmonic in Shepperton's recording studio. It was customary for Arnold to compose a movie score for a huge orchestra only if a particular picture warranted large orchestral effects, as was the case with *The Sound Barrier.* By contrast, *Hobson's Choice* was a small-scale movie, so Arnold limited the orchestral forces to twenty-five.

The opening scene is a prologue that "shows the inventive integration of Arnold's work" with the images on the screen.[17] Once again, Lean provides a superbly edited, virtuoso prologue for one of his films, just as he had done most notably for the two Dickens films and for *The Sound Barrier.* And, once again, the prologue is wholly visual. The camera begins outside Hobson's plush shop on a windswept, rainy night and focuses on a huge, boot-shaped sign swaying on its rusty hinges in the wind. Inside the deserted shop, the camera sweeps along a row of finely crafted shoes in the half-light of a flickering lamp. A creaking branch slaps the windowpane, a clock strikes one, and the camera pans to the door as it flies open. A giant shadow fills the doorway, and the drunken Henry Hobson lurches in with a resounding belch.

For the prologue, Arnold provides "a vigorous and tuneful music-hall style pastiche," which in the score he entitled "The Shoe Ballet." As the camera pans by a display of men's boots, ladies' shoes, and children's clogs, each group is accompanied by an appropriate burst of music. When Hobson enters, Arnold brings on a raucous theme featuring a chortling bassoon and a burbling tuba. The big finish is a precipitous drumroll, as Hobson shambles up the stairs to bed. In sum, Arnold's underscore for this scene is an "inventive component" of the scene as shot and edited by Lean.[18]

Lean seems to have patterned the beginning of this film after the celebrated opening of *Great Expectations* (the wind shaking the creaking tree branch etc.). He still maintained that a filmmaker must engage the viewer's attention with a striking opening for a movie, in order to stimulate interest in what is to come.

When Hobson sobers up the next morning, Maggie confronts him by announcing that, at thirty, she is tired of being on the shelf; she plans to forsake her father's domain and set her cap for an eligible bachelor. The crusty old curmudgeon responds that her two younger sisters may marry but that Maggie is "an old maid," too "overripe" for wedlock. She is therefore to continue managing the shop and running the house for him indefinitely. Though Hobson will not admit it, he sees his underpaid daughter as cheap labor. In order to make sure that she does not leave the nest, he denies her a dowry to offer a prospective suitor.

Maggie turns the tables on her father, however, by deciding to marry Willie Mossop, Hobson's meek but gifted shoemaker, and setting up a rival shoemaking store to boot. She subsequently launches her campaign to win Willie, believing that "where there's a will, there's a way," as the saying goes. She summons Willie from his workbench in the dingy basement of Hobson's shop and shares her plans with him. "Willie's first appearance is when he pops up through the cellar trap and squints at the world like a myopic mole."[19] When Maggie proposes that they wed and open their own shoe store, she declares gleefully, "My brains and your hands will make a working partnership!" Maggie has all the earmarks of a protofeminist. She breaks with Victorian tradition by not waiting for a man to propose to her, instead taking the initiative to snag the man of her choice. In addition, she marries beneath herself: Maggie is middle-class, Willie working-class.

In opening the play out for the screen, Lean devised a tour de force episode that, like the picture's prologue, is purely visual. Hobson leaves the Moonraker after hoisting several pints with his cronies, in an effort to drown his sorrows over Maggie's "desertion." He staggers drunkenly home; Jack Hildyard's camera sways slightly to approximate Hobson's unsteady gait as he gropes his way along the street.

En route he spies the moon reflected in a puddle on the wet cobblestones. Transfixed, Hobson gazes at it and leans on a lamppost for support—the drunkard's typical stance. Hobson "mistakes the full moon for a golden sovereign," and he tries to pluck it out of the rippling puddle. But the moon evaporates as soon as he comes near it, so he chases it from one puddle to the next.[20] He finally thinks he has it cornered in a shop window, but it again eludes his grasp.

This bizarre scene is accompanied by the tremulous chords of Malcolm Arnold's "Dance of the Puddles." To supply the sort of haunting background music required for Hobson's pursuit of the mysterious heavenly body, Arnold made extensive use of a musical saw played by a musician who was brought over from Belgium expressly for that purpose. The unusual instrument produces a high-pitched, quavering sound that perfectly augments the weird atmosphere of the scene.

Callow deems this sequence "a technical achievement of the greatest virtuosity."[21] Since the film was made long before the days of CGI (computer-generated imaging), the image of the "racing moon" was actually achieved by an elementary visual trick. Lean had an artist draw the moon on a piece of transparent paper and mount it on a stand. Then Hildyard placed a high-intensity spotlight behind the paper, and the lunar image was then reflected in the puddles and on the windowpane.

As the inebriated Hobson continues on his way, disaster strikes when he tumbles down an open hatchway into the cellar of the store run by Beenstock, a grain merchant. Hobson flounders about among the grain sacks like a beached whale. Arnold obliges with woozy trumpets and rumbling trombones. As Hobson sinks into oblivion, he looks up through the open hatchway at the sky above, where the moon still stares down at him impassively. Hobson's dark night of the soul ends the next morning with a shaft of sunlight illuminating his face. He then sheepishly makes his way home. The rotund and boisterous Laughton played this scene with evident relish.

The entire sequence, from Hobson's leaving the pub to his toppling into Beenstock's basement, has not a single word of dialogue. Because Lean joined the film industry before the movies learned to talk, he developed at the outset of his career a respect for the primacy of the visual over the verbal that served him well the rest of his life. The episode just described, with its emphasis on visual storytelling, could have been transplanted from a silent movie. The same can be said of the film's prologue.

Freddy Beenstock (Derek Blomfield), who happens to be engaged to Maggie's sister Vicky (Prunella Scales), manages the granary of Beenstock and Son for his father (Raymond Huntley). He informs Maggie that his father insists that he sue her father for drunken trespassing on their property. But Maggie says she is eloping with Willie that afternoon and that the lawsuit will just have to wait.

The same afternoon that Willie and Maggie marry, the couple move into an apartment attached to their shoemaking shop. The wedding night looms large in Willie's mind since he is diffident about his prospects for satisfying his bride. As we've seen, this scene in the play always gets a big laugh.

In the film, Lean shows Maggie preceding the groom into the bedroom; then Willie has to summon up the courage to follow her. In yet another wholly visual scene, "Willie does everything in his power to delay the moment, taking off his starched collar and dickey, and arranging them on the mantelpiece."[22] He awkwardly fumbles out of his trousers and bashfully changes into his nightgown. He stirs the fire in the grate with a poker—an obvious phallic symbol. His preparations to enter the boudoir drew from Arnold an "expansive splendor," recalling some of the more fulsome melodies in Richard Strauss's *Domestic Symphony*. It is turgid music, of a type that "Arnold never allows himself to write in his concert music," observes Hugo Cole in his book on Arnold. As Willie gallantly marches into the nuptial bedchamber, "the music changes to a brisk, semi-military march."[23] The camera stops at the doorway and does not venture to follow Willie inside. Instead, as the music reaches a climax, it slowly retreats.

After Maggie's wedding, Freddy Beenstock presses his court case against Hobson for drunken trespassing. Hobson rightly fears that, if Freddy takes him to court, his drunken escapade will make its way into the tabloids and his professional career will be ruined. Maggie intervenes by shrewdly arranging to have the complaint settled out of court. Freddy's lawyer is Albert Prosser (Richard Wattis), who is engaged to Maggie's sister Alice (Daphne Anderson). (Maxford erroneously states, "Freddy, who is training to be a solicitor, is also courting Alice. . . .")[24] Since the plaintiff is Vicky's fiancé and his solicitor is Alice's, Maggie has little trouble getting them to accept minimal sums for damages and legal fees. She consoles her father about how much the case is costing him by pointing out that, since Freddy and Albert are both engaged to his daughters, "the money will stay in the family."

Hobson's fortunes go from bad to worse when Maggie and Willie's rival shoemaking shop begins to syphon off his customers, and he sinks further into alcoholism. He asks Maggie and Willie to come back to work for him. His proposition enables Maggie to bring off her coup de grâce and give the belligerent old sloven a well-deserved comeuppance. She sets up a meeting with Hobson, Willie, and herself on New Year's Day. By this time, Willie has metamorphosed from a painfully shy shoemaker into a self-confident retail merchant, and his marriage, which began as a business deal, has become a loving partnership. Maggie cleverly puts Willie up to offering to merge the two businesses into one; he and Maggie will take Hobson into partnership with them, not vice versa. In exchange, Maggie will manage the store, and Willie will make the shoes. Hobson must agree not to interfere—he will be a silent partner.

The confrontation ends with Hobson capitulating and accepting "Hobson's choice," a take-it-or-leave-it proposition. It is significant that this takes place on New Year's Day, a detail that most critics of the film overlook: the beginning of the new year implies a fresh start in life for Maggie and Willie, presiding over Mossop and Hobson's shoe emporium.

By besting his formidable father-in-law, Willie has surfaced from the dungeon where he started out as Hobson's apprentice and taken his rightful place as Hobson's partner and equal. It is Maggie who brought him to see his true worth, as she herself is the first to acknowledge: "You're the man I made you, and I'm proud." It is clearly Maggie who wins the day, for she is a strong-willed woman who has vanquished a male bully, her own father. *Hobson's Choice* is now seen as an early feminist film, portraying a young woman seeking to find liberation from a stifling spinsterhood.

The movie opened in London in February 1954 and New York in June. Brenda de Banzie got the best notices of her career for her sensitive and savvy portrayal of Maggie. She was the perfect match for Charles Laughton, who gave a bravura performance—one of Falstaffian proportions—as Hobson. De Banzie provides the ballast that the film needs. John Mills's characterization of the self-effacing Willie was not overlooked by the reviewers; like de Banzie, Mills proved himself a match for Laughton's pyrotechnics. Many critics were pleasantly surprised that Lean displayed a knack for comedy, besides demonstrating once again his flair for period pictures.

Understandably, *Hobson's Choice* was more enthusiastically embraced in England than in America, based as it is on a thoroughly British comedy, peopled with stock English characters and marked by stock situations from traditional British farce. Still, *Variety* correctly predicted that the film would have "great box office appeal to class audiences, who appreciate the better type of productions."[25] Indeed, Lean's *Hobson's Choice* still stands as an intelligent adaptation of a stage play to the screen. It is "a fully developed comedy of human foibles and follies" that draws an acutely observed, consistently witty and heartfelt portrait of British lives.[26] All the characters are treated evenhandedly, with their shortcomings simply shown. A combination of believable dialogue and a well-chosen cast leads to exemplary ensemble acting throughout. (Asked by Lean whether he minded playing the small part of Freddy Beenstock's father, Raymond Huntley replied that there are no small parts in a David Lean picture.)

Some reviewers, as noted, wondered why Lean devoted his time and talents to an old-fashioned comedy. It seemed that a major director had decided to package and toss a bone to the groundlings. Perhaps Lean was being daring after all. He chose a story in which there are really no bad guys: Hobson is not a villain; Maggie is not a shrew. The characters by and large make their own troubles, so fate does not bother to conspire against them; that is particularly true of Hobson. Lean gives us a view of working-class life that is warm and spontaneous, observing his characters with wry humor. But he also exposes their weaknesses, examining their lives without sentimentality. He has nothing of nostalgia for the past, as in Wilcox's *Spring in Park Lane*, with its gossamer world of Victorian mansions.

Lean was rewarded for his efforts. *Hobson's Choice* did excellent box office business in England and good business in the United States. It remains available today on home video in a digitally remastered version in both countries. In addition, Lean's small-scale comedy collected some prestigious awards: the 1954 Berlin Film Festival Golden Bear (first prize) and the British Academy of Film and Television Arts best picture. Moreover, on July 21, 1953, while he was making *Hobson's Choice*, Lean was named a commander of the British Empire (CBE) by Queen Elizabeth II for his contributions to British cinema. He found it heartening to have his efforts recognized, but he ruefully wondered whether the critics might not expect too much of his next film as the result of an establishment accolade.

Lean was, in fact, set to direct *Summertime,* another stage adaptation, which Korda conceived as a vehicle for Katharine Hepburn. But there was a problem confronting Lean in terms of making another film for Korda's London Films. Korda was experiencing acute financial difficulties. So history was repeating itself, and Korda was suffering the same decline in the early 1950s that had overtaken J. Arthur Rank in the late 1940s (see chapter 7).

Korda's productions were released in England by British Lion, which provided some of the financial backing for his pictures; and Korda, as we know, was managing director of British Lion. It is true that Korda's support of Lean had been very productive. *The Sound Barrier* and *Hobson's Choice*, both Korda productions released in England by British Lion, had been commercially successful in their first-run engagements. In England alone, *The Sound Barrier* grossed £228,000 and *Hobson's Choice* £205,500—at a time when few British movies grossed more than £200,000 domestically. But some of Korda's other productions, also distributed by British Lion, had not fared well, for example, Powell and Pressburger's *The Tales of Hoffman* (1951), an expensive screen adaptation of Offenbach's fantasy opera, and Carol Reed's *The Man Between* (1953), a moody, torpid spy movie. These and other flops put both London Films and British Lion in the red.

The board of directors of British Lion pointed out to Korda that "very large profits are being made on a small number of films, but the losses on unsuccessful films are very high." They accordingly declared that the managing director of British Lion must be a man of imagination, someone who had not only the flair for assessing promising film projects but also "a stern regard for balance sheets."[27] They frankly declared that they were no longer convinced that Korda fit that profile.

"British Lion was in deep trouble," says Roy Boulting; he and his twin brother John were a producer-director team (they took turns producing and directing). The Boultings succeeded Korda as executives of British Lion. Roy Boulting, who had directed pictures like *High Treason* (1951), told me in conversation that, "despite the success of the two recent Lean films, Korda was in full retreat," his credit exhausted. As a matter of fact, Korda "smelled a rat" and sensed that his days as managing director of British Lion were numbered. He replied to the board of directors that he would relinquish control of British Lion, "rather than wait to be kicked out," especially since "the failure of British Lion" might be blamed on him.[28]

Korda's point was that some of the commercial failures released by British Lion were made not by Korda's London Films but by other independent producers. For example, Herbert Wilcox's production of *The Beggar's Opera* (Peter Brook, 1953), a raggedy stagebound presentation of John Gay's venerable opera, and Ivan Foxwell's production of *The Intruder* (Guy Hamilton, 1953), a dreary psychological study of a maladjusted World War II veteran, were financial failures.

Before his departure from British Lion, Korda was asked by one of the board who would be a likely successor for him as managing director. "I don't know," he answered with a Cheshire Cat smile. "I don't grow on trees."[29] Roy Boulting comments, "Korda was right in suggesting that, though his career had been punctuated with financial crises, enterprising producers of his stamp would always be in short supply." At any rate, the Boulting brothers became directors of British Lion, along with Michael Balcon, Frank Launder, and Sidney Gilliat.

Korda would continue to be in charge of London Films, the independent production company that he still personally owned and operated, despite the fact that he increasingly suffered from ill health. He was determined to get his production of *Summertime* off the ground. By now, he had both David Lean and Katharine Hepburn committed to the project, which indicated that he was still a major player in the movie game.

Alexander Korda made a deal with Ilya Lopert, his New York partner, to coproduce *Summertime* with him. Lopert's distribution company, Lopert Films, a subsidiary of United Artists, had released *The Sound Barrier* and *Hobson's Choice* in the United States. Korda would, as usual, be the executive producer of the picture, and Lopert would act as the producer. So Lean was no longer allowed to function as his own producer, as he had on his two previous films for Korda. Still Lean was now moving into the international arena of filmmaking, *Summertime* being the first British-American coproduction he had ever been associated with.

Chapter Ten

LOVE IN THE AFTERNOON

SUMMERTIME

Do I hear a waltz? It's what I've been waiting for all my life: to hear a waltz.
Magical, mystical miracle: Can it be? Is it true?
Everything suddenly lyrical: Can't be me. Must be you.

> —*Stephen Sondheim and Richard Rodgers, "Do I Hear a Waltz"*

If you are still a spinster by the time you are thirty, you realize that the gentleman you've been waiting for has lost his way. So you might as well enjoy life.

> —*Lily Moffat, a spinster in the film* The Corn Is Green

David Lean was bent on filming *Summertime* entirely on location in Venice, where the story takes place. Alexander Korda, the executive producer, and Ilya Lopert, the producer, agreed with him. Furthermore, United Artists, with which Lopert's American distribution company, Lopert Films, was affiliated, had provided major funding for the production, and it too went along with the decision to film in Italy.

Lopert's own judgment about Lean was that he would need the supervision of a vigilant producer while he was filming on the Continent. Lopert had, apparently, heard that Ronald Neame had complained about Lean's falling behind schedule while filming some sequences for *The Passionate Friends* abroad.

With British Lion now out of the picture, Korda had to find another company to distribute *Summertime* in Britain. He entered into an arrangement with the British film executive John Woolf, head of Independent Film

Distributors; Woolf was "the most successful film distributor and film financier of the decade."[1]

The Rank organization had abandoned its ambitious attempt to crack the American market and was making parochial British movies, concentrating its reserves on "safe, conventional, innocuous films at Pinewood."[2] By contrast, Woolf was prepared to risk investing in Anglo-American coproductions that could penetrate the American market in a way that Rank films seldom had. For example, *The African Queen* (John Huston, 1951), which starred Katharine Hepburn, was a coproduction of Woolf and the American producer Sam Spiegel. *Summertime*, in which Hepburn would also star, was likewise an Anglo-American coproduction, a joint venture of Korda's London Films and Lopert Films. Woolf was willing to help bail out Korda, who was financially strapped, by cofinancing *Summertime* and by distributing it in Great Britain.

When Woolf discussed his involvement in *Summertime* with Korda, he inquired why Korda had wanted to set the budget for the film at nearly £1 million. Korda replied that the budget was hardly a king's ransom (though it was more than Lean had had for his previous films). Besides, Korda favored big-budget, risk-taking movies. "I am not afraid of spending big money on big pictures," he declared.[3] *Summertime* would be one of the last films on which the ailing Korda would act as executive producer. In fact, "*Summertime* showed little evidence of input by Korda"—beyond his setting up the production and discussing casting choices.[4] Be that as it may, Korda had packaged a prestige project, with a major Hollywood star and a major British director.

Summertime (1955)

Summertime was derived from *The Time of the Cuckoo*, a play by Arthur Laurents, whose World War II drama *The Home of the Brave* had been adapted for film by Mark Robson in 1949. Unlike Brighouse's *Hobson's Choice*, which Lean had just filmed, *The Time of the Cuckoo* was a recent play; it had opened on Broadway at the Empire Theater on October 15, 1952, for a successful run of 263 performances. In the play, Leona Samish (Shirley Booth), a dowdy American spinster from the Midwest, vacations in Venice in the hope of finding a little romance. She becomes enamored of a down-at-the-heels Italian, a full-time antiques dealer and part-time gigolo named Renato de Rossi.

When Leona finds him to be somewhat less than the dreamboat she had fantasized about, Renato says sardonically that she wants beefsteak but that, because she is like a hungry child, she should be content to settle for ravioli instead. Before they can consummate their brief affair, Leona discovers that Renato is married with children. In addition, she learns that he is somehow involved in a counterfeiting racket. She tells him bitterly that she has swallowed all the ravioli she is going to and goes back home, sadder but wiser.

Though the play garnered some good notices, the theater critic Louis Kronenberger was right on the money when he wrote that *The Time of the Cuckoo* was a "slender drama" and something of a soap opera.[5] Still, the play was a commercial success, and Ilya Lopert, who saw it on the New York stage, brought it to the attention of Alexander Korda, who in turn asked David Lean to consider filming it. Lean was quite taken by the idea of an American spinster, pining for love, coming together with a middle-aged Italian roué in scenic, decadent Venice.

It shortly became known in the British film industry that Lean was slated to direct *Summertime* in Venice. The film was to be made entirely outside England; in addition, its source material, Laurents's play, and star, Katharine Hepburn, were not English. Lean was, accordingly, criticized in some quarters for abandoning the making of small-scale, unglamorous British movies like *Hobson's Choice* for the richer pastures of a cosmopolitan international coproduction with a Hollywood star.

For his part, Lean answered that a lot of the production crew was made up of individuals who had worked for him before in Britain: the cinematographer Jack Hildyard, the production designer Vincent Korda, and the film editor Peter Taylor. Moreover, *Hobson's Choice* had also had a Hollywood star: Charles Laughton. Consequently, Lean did not feel that he was making a huge leap in scale by making *Summertime*. In addition, the movie was still tied to the British industry since it was being coproduced by London Films and cofinanced by Independent Film Distributors.

What is more, *Summertime* had a definite affinity to Lean's greatest success so far, the definitely British *Brief Encounter*. Once again the subject was the awakening of passion in a lonely, middle-aged woman who is reluctant to defy convention for love. Then too, *Summertime* begins and ends in a train station. Indeed, Venice, the very locale of *Summertime*, is anticipated in *Brief Encounter* "by Laura Jesson's dream image of riding with Alec Harvey in a gondola on the Grand Canal."[6] In *Summertime* Laura's absurd fantasy actually comes to life.

When it came to adapting *The Time of the Cuckoo* for film, the title was the first thing to go. The epigraph on the title page of the play explains: "The cuckoo is a summer visitant to the whole of Europe. It proclaims its arrival by a cry heralding the season of love."[7] Jane—Lean had turned Leona Samish into Jane Hudson—may be a summer visitor to Europe like the cuckoo, but

Lean and Korda agreed that the title would be meaningless to the average moviegoer. So they chose the more attractive *Summertime*.

But John Woolf disagreed. He thought that, if the film was called *Summertime*, filmgoers would assume that it was a movie version of George Gershwin's folk opera *Porgy and Bess*, which features a song titled "Summertime." Lean countered: "Can you imagine Kate Hepburn in a Gershwin opera?"[8] But Lean was overruled, and the film was called *Summer Madness* in England. So Steven Caton is incorrect when he assumes that *Summer Madness* was Lean's chosen title and that "it was inexplicably changed for its American release."[9] In actual fact, Lean referred to the film forever after as *Summertime*. In any event, after the movie's initial release in Britain, it was the American title that stuck, and the movie has been called *Summertime* in England and America ever since. Hence I have used that title throughout.

Arthur Laurents had adapted Patrick Hamilton's play *Rope* for the screen for Hitchcock in 1948, so Lean asked him to have a go at the screenplay for *Summertime*. Laurents came to London on November 22, 1953, for story conferences with Lean, before beginning work on the script. When he submitted his draft of the script to Lean a few months later, Lean disapproved of the way in which he had adhered to the original play so rigidly. But Laurents was too close to his own material and so wedded to the play's text that he would not budge. Laurents did not like working with Lean, whom he termed "a cold fish." He was miffed that Lean had one of his minions tell him that his draft of the script would not be used, instead of informing him personally. Laurents therefore left London in a huff.[10]

Lean began to rework the play for the screen on his own in the spring of 1954 but made little headway. In due course, he engaged the services of the novelist H. E. Bates, on whose 1947 World War II novel Robert Parrish's 1954 *The Purple Plain*—starring Gregory Peck—had been based. Bates could not begin work immediately, however, because of other commitments. He and Lean finally decamped for Venice on June 22, 1954; Lean had decided that they should write the script there, in order to soak up the atmosphere of the city.

Lean was delighted to be in Venice since he had been intrigued by Venice's local color and cityscape ever since he edited *Escape Me Never* (1935), which had some scenes that were shot there. He and Bates holed up in the Grand Hotel to write the script while Charles Chaplin happened to be staying there. As we saw in chapter 1, Lean had loved Chaplin's work ever since he was a boy. He revered Chaplin as a true auteur, someone who wrote, directed, and starred in his own pictures, and he told Chaplin so.

As a filmmaker, Lean liked to tell a story in as clear and straightforward a fashion as possible. Consequently, he scrapped the incident in the play in which Renato reveals himself to be an opportunist: he obtains Italian currency for Jane at a very favorable rate of exchange, and it turns out to be counterfeit. In addition, Lean altered the play by making Renato less of the unscrupulous roué he is in the play and more of a suave, romantic leading man. Hence, in the movie, Jane sees Renato as a storybook prince, even though he is just an antiques dealer.

Laurents took one look at the Lean-Bates script and complained, "They jettisoned most of the play; it [i.e., their version] was an homage to Kate Hepburn." After the film had gone into production, Hepburn told Laurents, "You won't like it; but I'm brilliant." As a matter of fact, as Lean acknowledged, Laurents "hated the film."[11] In the film's defense, Hepburn said, "[Lean] deleted all of the rather complicated and extraneous happenings [from the play]." Lean had turned the screenplay into the story of Jane Hudson, "a woman over forty, who vacations in Venice one summer and is flirted with by a fascinating Italian," and "he was going to keep it just that."[12]

It was Ilya Lopert who first approached Hepburn for the role of Jane. Lean hesitated to contact her because, by then, she was not just a movie star but a Hollywood institution. In working on *Summertime,* a mutual admiration between Lean and Hepburn developed, flowering into a lasting friendship. In an essay on her favorite directors, Hepburn made the following observations about David Lean: "I think he knows more about film than a banker knows about money. He wants perfection, and that is what he gets. It's always there if you work hard enough."[13] Elsewhere, Hepburn added that making a Lean picture was a rough ride: "He doesn't care if everyone dies around him; he'll just take over the camera, prop up the actor, and get what he wants." In sum, Lean "cannot help being a perfectionist."[14]

As for choosing the rest of the cast, since many of the roles would be filled by Italian actors, Lean held casting sessions at the Excelsior Hotel in Rome. Rosanno Brazzi, an Italian star who had just appeared in Joseph L. Mankiewicz's *The Barefoot Contessa* (1954), opposite Ava Gardner and Humphrey Bogart, was picked to play Renato. Isa Miranda had impressed Lean as a world-weary waitress in René Clément's *Au-delà des grilles* (*The Walls of Malapaga,* 1949), for which she won a best actress award at the Cannes Film Festival, and he chose her to play Signora Fiorini, the widowed concierge of the Pensione Fiorni, where Jane Hudson stays. When Miranda showed up on the set, Lean was exasperated to see that she had had a face-lift since he saw her last and no longer looked like the matronly concierge he wanted her to play. But it was too late to recast the part. In reality, Lean seems to have exaggerated the fact that Miranda looked too young for the role; she was nearly as old as Hepburn and looked her age in close-ups.

Lean did not find the right boy to play Mauro, the streetwise urchin who acts as Jane's self-appointed guide, until he reached Venice. There he found ten-year-old Gaetano Audiero, who had not answered any casting calls—and even then Lean had to persuade him to take the part. The irrepressible youngster resembled a pint-size Chico Marx, speaking broken English with a pronounced Italian accent, and punctuating his chatter with Italian phrases like *Mama mia*.

Principal photography took place in Venice throughout the summer of 1954. Lean and Hepburn got along like shipmates; to Lean she was just one of the chaps, as the English saying goes. But the headstrong actress had several run-ins with members of the cast and crew, who thought her too bossy. (Shades of Charles Laughton.)

Admittedly, Hepburn was not always in good spirits during filming. If Charles Laughton had boyfriend trouble of one kind during the shooting of *Hobson's Choice,* Katharine Hepburn had boyfriend trouble of another kind on *Summertime.* She had maintained a relationship with Spencer Tracy off-screen as well as onscreen for several years. Cukor once told me in conversation that Tracy would not divorce his wife because, as a Catholic, he did not believe in divorce, and his lifelong affair with Hepburn was an open secret in Hollywood.

Tracy's visit with Hepburn during shooting was fraught with tension because she suspected him of carrying on with a younger actress back in Hollywood during her absence. Tracy resented her insinuations and was, consequently, grumpy and short-tempered throughout his stay. Because of the discord, Hepburn tended to be moody and ungracious for some time after Tracy departed.

Summertime was one of the first British films to be shot entirely on location. It was customary in the 1950s for a British director to film some exteriors on location in a foreign locale; this footage would then be carefully interspersed throughout the film to enliven the material that was shot on the studio back lot. By contrast, Lean was convinced that the authentic atmosphere of Venice could be achieved—that he could make Venice the star of the picture, which was his goal—only by shooting *Summertime* entirely in Venice, both exteriors on location and interiors in a studio. Hepburn totally agreed with him. "When you film on location," she said, "the climate and the terrain affect a performer's interpretation of a role."[15]

The interior scenes set in the Pensione Fiorini, where Jane sojourns, would be shot in the studio. But the terrace of the pensione, which adjoins

Jane's room, was built in an empty lot overlooking the Grand Canal. Vincent Korda, the production designer, erected a terrace facing the canal so that real gondolas would be visible in the background as they passed. The Pensione Fiorini is a small, second-class tourist hotel that has seen better days, so Korda designed the interiors with a somewhat frayed, tacky look. His attention to detail matched Lean's; he had a talent for establishing just the right atmosphere for a scene with a set he designed.

Lean was experiencing some problems on his first foreign shoot. Some of the shopkeepers around St. Mark's Square demanded substantial compensation, claiming that the filming obstructed tourist traffic and caused their business to fall off. So they threatened to disrupt shooting. The merchants blackmailed Lean into reimbursing them for the imagined loss of business.

To make matters worse, Michael Korda, Vincent Korda's son, writes, "Rumors had preceded the arrival of the company for *Summertime:* that it was the story of unmarried love, and that there would be scenes of indecency, offensive to the sensibilities of the Venetians."[16] Lean did, in fact, receive a complaint from the local Catholic authorities that Hepburn was observed appearing in one scene wearing a sleeveless dress while standing outside St. Mark's Basilica. Lean dutifully guaranteed the cardinal patriarch of Venice that "there would be no bare arms or short skirts in and around the holy places." He accordingly reshot the scene, with Hepburn "in a long-sleeved blouse tucked demurely into a full skirt."[17]

There were also delays in shooting. While some (such as that caused by having to reshoot the basilica scene) were no fault of Lean's, other were the result of his quest for perfection. "He can't be hurried," Hepburn remembered. He would not budge until a scene was done to his satisfaction.[18] Lean had a preconceived notion of what he expected from any given location. He would shoot a love scene, for example, only at a certain hour of the day, when the sun was over a narrow back street, casting shadows in just the way he wanted. "It was David Lean at his most maddening," says Norman Spencer, the associate producer. Gradually, Lean slipped behind schedule, just as he had when filming *The Passionate Friends* on the Continent.[19]

One time-consuming location scene occurred when Jane goes sightseeing with Mauro, her young sidekick. Jane photographs Renato's antique shop with her ever-present Bell and Howell home movie camera. She steps back to get a wider angle, loses her footing, and tumbles into the canal. Mauro realizes that Jane can swim but that the camera cannot float, so he has the presence of mind to snatch the camera from her hands before it sinks into the water.

When preparing Hepburn to film this scene, Lean informed her that the civil authorities suggested that he stage it in a swimming pool since the water in the Venetian canals is an unsavory mixture of garbage, mud, and excrement. But, given Lean's thirst for realism, he was determined to shoot it in a canal, and told Hepburn so. She surveyed the canal and then said, "What the hell! I'll fall into the goddamned canal! That's what I'm paid for."[20]

Lean arranged to barricade the shooting area around the canal with screens, to keep the locals and the tourists from getting in the way. He also flooded the water in the enclosed area with disinfectant, to prevent Hepburn from contracting dysentery or some other disease. Furthermore, Hepburn's face and the exposed parts of her body were smeared with Vaseline as protection for her skin. With two cameras turning, Hepburn fell backward off the quay into the canal with a resounding splash. She was then pulled out of the water by a passing gondolier, who thought she was drowning. (The rescue did not make the final cut.) "The water was lousy," she recalled; because of the disinfectant "it was like the water in the swimming pools in California, with all that chlorine."

Anne Edwards, Hepburn's biographer, claims that Hepburn had to fall into the water backward no less than five times, and Michael Korda states that she had to do it "repeatedly."[21] But Peter Newbrook, the camera operator, declares that she took the plunge only once. Lean had chosen the precise place where Hepburn would fall into the canal; the spot was adjacent to some steps that were actually visible on-camera throughout the scene. After her fall, Hepburn did additional shots of Jane floundering in the water, but, according to Newborn, for these shots she got in and out of the water by means of the steps.[22]

That night, according to Edwards, "Kate's eyes began to itch" and became teary. "She had infected them with a form of conjunctivitis."[23] Lean refused to take the blame, however. He contended that Hepburn frequently went swimming in the Grand Canal at the end of the shooting day and that that was how she contracted her eye infection. "She was absolutely mad."[24]

When Lean photographed Jane's farewell to Renato at the train station, he was gratified to see that Hepburn generated genuine tears. He never caught on that it was thanks to the eye infection that she could easily produce a teary look. In any case, it was worth all the trouble to shoot the canal scene on location. Venetian tour guides to this day point out the historic place where Katharine Hepburn made her legendary plunge into the canal.

Nevertheless, Ilya Lopert, the producer, was infuriated that Lean was spending too much time on sequences. He thought that the canal scene could have been staged much more quickly and economically in a swimming pool, as the authorities had suggested. He urged Lean to take shortcuts to get back on schedule. To emphasize his point, Lopert picked up a copy of the shooting script, tore out a couple of pages, and handed it back to Lean, saying that this was one way of catching up.

Lopert, we remember, had said from the outset that Lean needed to be managed by a strong producer if he was not to go considerably over budget. He continued to be on the warpath during the final days of shooting. Over the objections of the production manager, Ray Anzarut, he ordered some workmen to dismantle the terrace of the pensione as soon as Lean finished shooting on that set. "He ripped down a major set before any reports of the rushes came back from the lab to confirm that the processed film was satisfactory."[25] If some of the footage did not turn out, it would have to be reshot. The disgruntled Anzarut sent a phony telegram to Lopert, ostensibly from the film lab in Rome, stating that the footage for one of the scenes shot on the pensione terrace was unusable and would have to be reshot. Lopert's face was scarlet when he read the telegram and showed it to Lean, who recognized it as a practical joke. Lopert never learned who sent the telegram, but Lean warned him that the jokester was making a valid point: the producer should never pull down a set until the rushes are approved.

Undeterred, Lopert later warned Lean that, if he did not finish principal photography posthaste, he, Lopert, was going to take away the cameras. He shortly afterward made good his threat by sending the huge thirty-five-millimeter Mitchell cameras back to the company in Rome from which they had been rented, leaving Lean with "just a 35mm Arriflex for the last week of shooting."[26] So he had to finish a major motion picture with his own camera.

Throughout the shooting period, Lopert employed what is known in the film industry as a front-office spy—someone delegated by the producer to monitor the director's progress and report regularly to the producer. Lean observed Lopert's assistant timing how long he spent rehearsing a scene and actually shooting every camera setup. Lopert's spy even eavesdropped on a conversation between Lean and Hepburn, in which she promised to work for nothing after her contract ran out until the movie was completed to Lean's satisfaction.

When Lopert heard that Lean and Hepburn were conspiring to continue shooting, if need be, after the official wrap date, "he bribed the Italian authorities to say that David's work permit had run out" and that he must leave Italy.[27] Lean was summoned to the police station, where he pleaded in his own behalf that his movie would undoubtedly boost tourism in Venice and that he should be allowed to finish it. Finally, a police official intervened and told Lean to take a train to the Italian frontier, then surreptitiously turn around, take another train back to Venice, and remain in town unofficially. By that time, Lopert had himself left Venice, so he would not know of Lean's subterfuge. Hepburn later summed up Lopert as an "untrustworthy, somewhat crooked character."

Despite all Lopert's fears, Lean came fairly close to finishing the picture on schedule and on budget. Still, after Lopert confiscated his equipment and attempted to have him deported, Lean was in the market for a new producer.

Knowing about Lean's stellar reputation as a film editor, Hepburn asked him if she could sit in with him and the editor, Peter Taylor, in the cutting room for a couple of days. "I watched him cut some of it together," she said. "He seems to understand film in much the same way as a painter understands his canvas. He is a miracle of precise knowledge and sensitive feeling."[28]

Lean's third color film turned out to be the most beautiful, picturesque movie he had made up to that time. The luminous images that pervade it reveal for the first time his eye for the kind of sumptuous imagery that would characterize his later superspectacles. Jack Hildyard's color camera "brilliantly captures the awesome monuments and sights of this magnificent Renaissance city" in all its grandeur. If the film resembles a travelogue at times, it is because "our view of Venice is Jane's view," and her view is through the lens of a Bell and Howell, her home movie camera.[29] Jane's picture-postcard concept of Venice suggests that she naively sees the city through rose-colored glasses, as a kind of storybook land.

In fact, just as Jane arrives in the Venice terminal on the Orient Express, she photographs a travel poster depicting "Venice, City of Romance." She introduces herself to a British traveler as "a fancy secretary from Akron, Ohio." He tells her that he hopes she will like Venice. Jane answers, "I've got to! I've come such a long way; I've saved up such a long time for this trip."

On her first evening in Venice, Jane sits alone at a table in a sidewalk café near St. Mark's Square, the hub of the tourist trade. She notices a handsome Italian peeking at her from behind a newspaper, and she bashfully dons her sunglasses in a kind of symbolic concealment. For good measure, she slides her cup and saucer over to the other place at the table, a ploy indicating that she is waiting for a companion, and drinks water from the tumbler in front of her. It later develops that the man with the newspaper is Renato. Jane is initially afraid that some Italian male will press his attentions on her, but the following evening she hopes that some eligible bachelor will notice her. Loneliness has overtaken her, once the excitement and novelty of sightseeing have worn off.

Jane, alone and forlorn, strolls on the terrace of the Pensione Fiorini one evening, after all the other guests have gone out on the town. Hepburn captures Jane's aching loneliness and yearning, as she is brought to the brink of tears. Alessandro Cicognini, who composed the film's score, provides a lush romantic theme, which fills the air; it serves as a poignant counterpoint to Jane's solitude. This romantic melody, which recalls Lean's use of the Rachmaninoff piano concerto in *Brief Encounter*, is repeated throughout the movie in various orchestral configurations. Here, a mandolin and a guitar are featured, lending the music a Mediterranean flavor.

This is a touching moment in the film, and Hepburn said that this scene paralleled a similar experience she had during shooting. She often socialized with Lean and the other actors in the evening, but, on this particular occasion, no one had asked her to join them. "I suppose they all thought I had madly exciting things to do and left me to it. . . . I wandered off by myself, feeling lonely and neglected."[30] It was just this sort of experience that helped her play the terrace scene so authentically.

Jane has a confab with Signora Fiorini, in which she expresses the hope that a "magical miracle" will happen to her while she is in Venice. The signora cautions her not to expect too much and confesses that she herself is involved with a younger man, whom she is afraid she is losing. Subsequently, Jane observes her with her inamorato, Eddie Jaeger (Darren McGavin), a young married man who has been staying with his wife at the pensione for some time. There are tears in the signora's eyes as he says to her coldly, "I don't love you." This makes Jane wonder whether she has any hope of having a romantic encounter before she goes home.

It seems that, since Lean was convinced that Isa Miranda did not look old enough to play the slightly faded concierge, he was never satisfied with her performance. According to Hepburn, when Lean came to rehearse the scene with Miranda and McGavin, he grew impatient and testy with her. He said, "If she doesn't get the scene right, I'll shoot myself!" Hepburn intervened and suggested that she take Miranda aside and coach her. Hepburn recalled, "She was supposed to cry but couldn't muster any tears on her own, so I suddenly slapped her a good one. At first she looked stunned; then she began to get weepy; and David shot the scene." Lean chuckled afterward, saying to Hepburn, "You are a tougher director than I am."

As the story unfolds, Jane does connect with Renato. Like a dreamy schoolgirl, she becomes enchanted with him. Though, as a career woman, Jane has a somewhat patrician manner, prim and starchy, she nevertheless bewitches Renato. The feeling is mutual. She tours Venice with Mauro, the cute kid who hustles tourists, whom she calls "Cookie," and they happen on Renato's antiques store. It is then that Jane, when she attempts to photograph the shop's display window, falls ignominiously into the canal. Jane's embarrassment is underscored by her feeble quip to the bystanders about "trying out for the Olympics." After she is hauled out of the water, "she slips through the crowd and hurries away, fearful of Renato coming out and seeing her."[31] This scene, of course, brings to mind Alec's getting dunked in the drink while rowing Laura across the park pond—yet another reminder of *Brief Encounter.*

On another foray to Renato's antiques shop, Jane is waited on by Vito, a teenaged boy who turns out to be one of Renato's children. Renato had earlier referred to the lad casually as his nephew. Jane is devastated to discover that Renato is both a husband and a father. But he subsequently explains that he has been separated from his wife for some time—divorce was strongly disapproved of in Italy in those days.

As Jane hashes out her relationship with Renato, she endeavors to conceal her wounded heart behind a show of bravado. She struggles to uphold her moral code, which dictates that she not dally with a married man. But, in the atmosphere of exotic, sensual Venice, she finally decides to risk a passionate love affair that will inevitably be as fleeting as a shipboard romance. She explains to Renato that she wants to find out what she has been missing all her life. Extended interchanges between Jane and Renato like this one were incorporated intact into the script right from the play. So Laurents's complaint that Lean threw the play away when he wrote the screenplay is an exaggeration.

As Jane and Renato take a walk through St. Mark's Square, he buys her a gardenia from a flower seller. Jane muses that, when she was young, she wanted to wear a gardenia to a college dance. But gardenias were expensive, and her beau could not afford one. Now that Renato has given her one, it seems that romance has come to full flower in her life. "Everything comes to you if you wait," she concludes.

Renato invites Jane to his apartment for a tryst, and she goes on a shopping spree beforehand for some new clothes, including a pair of flashy, red high heels with gold trimmings. These shoes provide a sharp contrast to the drab, sensible ones she has been wearing up to now. The filmgoer must overlook the fact that the elegant fashions that Jane purchases are beyond the means of a secretary from Ohio, no matter how much she earns.

That night, Jane and Renato embrace on his balcony as the movie's love theme swells to a peak. As we have seen, Malcolm Arnold once noted that a Lean film must always have a "big tune." Renato and Jane disappear into his bedroom to make love in a seduction scene climaxed by a fireworks display, an incandescent cascade of color in the night sky. The exploding fireworks, which salute Jane's night of love, constitute one of the most playfully discrete sexual metaphors in the Lean canon. By coincidence, Alfred Hitchcock employed the same imagery in *To Catch a Thief,* released the same year as *Summertime.*

The next morning, Jane inadvertently leaves one of her red shoes behind on Renato's balcony, just as Cinderella loses one of her glass slippers at the ball. Jane's Prince Charming, like the one in the fairy tale, wishes to pursue his relationship with his Cinderella. But, after her night of love, Jane realizes in the sober light of day that their relationship can never be anything but transitory. She therefore resolves to cut her vacation short and return to Akron. "All my life I've stayed at parties too long because I didn't know when to go," she reflects. "Now I'm grown up, and I do know when to go." The affair ends "because Jane, knowing the situation to be impossible, . . . wills that it must."[32]

Jane boards the Orient Express at the train station where the movie began; just as the train pulls out, Renato comes running down the platform. He tries to give her a gardenia as a souvenir of their love. She reaches for it, but it is beyond her grasp, like the gardenia at the college dance. So too, many of the hopes and dreams that she nurtured when she was young have eluded her grasp. Jane waves tearfully and frantically out of the coach window as the train gains speed and Renato gradually disappears from view. But "Jane has seen the flower and noted the gesture, and we know that she is returning home comparatively happy"—and somewhat the wiser, no doubt, for the experience.[33]

This closing episode is truly a virtuoso sequence: "In ten years Lean has moved from the streets and railway platforms of Milford Junction in *Brief Encounter* to the color and splendor of Venice."[34] We cannot but sympathize with Jane Hudson, a middle-aged puritan, whose clinging to respectability links her to Laura Jesson. She thus exemplifies Lean's recurring theme, for she refuses to be crushed by disappointment: She has lost her love, but she somehow grasps that it is better to have loved and lost than not to have loved at all. She is determined to get on with her life.

Ilya Lopert held the gala world premiere for *Summertime* in the seventeenth-century Palazzo Grazzi—which is open to the sky and situated on the Grand Canal—on May 29, 1955. In attendance were film critics from Europe and America, but Lean and Hepburn, who always shunned enormous public events of this sort, were conspicuous for their absence. (Neither of them showed up for the 1956 Academy Award ceremonies, though both had been nominated for *Summertime*.)

The premiere was a triumph, and critics on both sides of the Atlantic bestowed mostly first-rate reviews on the picture. *Summertime* was hailed for blending the talents of a resourceful director and a sensitive actress in the filming of a charming, bittersweet comedy. At the very least, it was rich, creamy hokum. Though Lean and Hepburn did not win Oscars, Lean won the New York Film Critics Award as best director of the year—for a film that he was forced to finish with his own Arriflex movie camera.

Pauline Kael declared in 1969 that Hepburn's superb performance in *Summertime* was proof positive that she was "probably the greatest actress of the sound era" up to that time. In a career that spanned talkies almost from the beginning, Hepburn began, when she was close to fifty, to play "plain Janes" like Jane Hudson, a gaunt Yankee old maid. Kael concluded that Hepburn had the perfect costar in *Summertime:* Venice, which emerged as a great setting for visual appeal.[35]

Lean handles the story line that he develops in his low-key, literate screenplay with tremendous conviction and dexterity. He is aided by Alessandro Cicognini's lush background music and by Jack Hildyard's inventive camerawork, which propels us through a fascinating, neon-lit Venice. (Though Lean did not do a Hitchcockian walk-on in the film, he rewarded Hildyard with a cameo appearance as a tourist in St. Mark's Square.) Moreover, the movie is a minifestival of naturalistic performances. Hepburn gives an extremely focused portrayal in the lead, with terrific backing from Rossano Brazzi, Isa Miranda (pace David Lean), and little Gaetano Audiero.

There are moments when the movie oscillates between an old-school farce (Jane's dunking in the canal) and a more knowing, intimate depiction of relationships in modern society. *Summertime* is a delectable treat, a smart and witty journey of self-discovery from a director who seldom served the comic muse—"one of the rare times when the movie is better than its source material."[36] Lean subsequently singled it out as a personal favorite among his own movies. "I've put more of myself in that film than any other I've ever made," he said, adding that working with Katharine Hepburn was a revelation of professionalism in action.[37]

When Lean returned to Venice on vacation a year or so later, he was told by the manager of the hotel where he was staying that the Venetians should erect a monument in St. Mark's Square in his honor because tourism in Venice doubled in the year following the movie's opening. The monument was not forthcoming, but Sandra Lean records that, on Lean's subsequent visits to Venice over the years, the municipal band, which plays in the square in the film, struck up the main theme from *Summertime* whenever he walked there: "A wonderful consequence for a film director, to be admired by a whole city."[38]

Summertime fared well with audiences throughout the world when it was released and rarely ran into censorship troubles. The picture, as expected, received an adult classification from the British censor. Lean noted that some cuts were made by the German censor, though he did not specify what was excised. "In my experience, the Indian Censor Board is the most backward in the world," he continued. "They banned *Summertime* in its entirety, presumably because it showed a brief encounter between an American spinster and a married Italian, in spite of the fact that he was separated from his wife. I have several good friends in the Indian film world, whose work . . . is being badly hampered by these no doubt worthy Victorian moralists at the top."[39]

In the spring of 1955, after finishing postproduction on *Summertime*, Lean was called on the carpet by the income tax office in London. He was informed that he owed the government £20,000 in back taxes and that he was expected to pay up. It seemed that his finances had become inextricably entangled with those of Ann Todd during the period of their marriage. Lean—although the son of an accountant—was never good at managing money; to the end of his days he counted on his fingers when he tried to add up a bill. There was no hope of his consulting with Todd over the matter. Had Lean turned over such a huge sum to the tax office, he would have been bankrupted for the foreseeable future. Furthermore, the annual taxes in England for someone in a high income bracket like Lean were decidedly steep anyway.

As he saw it, he had no choice but to leave England and become a tax exile, meaning that he maintained no domicile anywhere in Great Britain. Lean was following in the footsteps of Noël Coward, who, a few years earlier, likewise had become a tax exile, taking up permanent residence in Jamaica. On April 2, 1955, Lean left London, bound for Paris, assuring himself that life begins at forty-eight.

What is more, Ann Todd had, as mentioned earlier, received an extremely lucrative divorce settlement, which left Lean nearly broke. She laid claim to their house in Ilchester Place, with all the treasured paintings and antiques therein. In fact, Lean had been so cleaned out by the divorce settlement that he could not afford to have his teeth fixed. In addition, the tabloids, as noted already, covered the divorce case in a highly sensational manner, so Lean continued living abroad, where the British press could not hound him. Once he moved to the Continent, then, he had no compelling reason to return to England, and he continued to live abroad for the next three decades.

Living in foreign climes was very congenial to Lean. From boyhood on, he had always loved to travel. In the summer of 1954, for example, after completing *Hobson's Choice,* he went on an extended vacation to India, his first visit to that country. It was there that he met a native Indian, Leila Matkar, who was at the time married to an Indian civil servant. They began an affair that would eventually lead to marriage. Norman Spencer, Lean's close associate, could never understand what Lean saw in her. He called her "an Eastern Ann Todd" because she never stopped talking.[40] What is more, Spencer wondered why Lean would take up with a woman who experienced serious bouts of depression with some regularity. Apparently, Lean naively believed that his love and affection would be all that was required to cure her. In any event, Lean returned to Europe to direct *Summertime* and did not see Leila again until after he had finished that picture.

After filming *Summertime* in sunny Venice, Lean was prompted to continue shooting movies in outdoor locations in far-flung foreign lands. He felt that making films in the insulated atmosphere of a studio was like filming "in a pitch-black mine": "I prefer the sun."[41] Consequently, when the Hollywood producer Sam Spiegel offered him *The Bridge on the River Kwai,* a film that was based on the Pierre Boulle novel and was to be shot on location in Southeast Asia, he jumped at the chance.

It is an index of the way in which Alexander Korda was losing touch with the public's taste toward the end of his life that he had refused absolutely to consider making a picture from the book. He declared, "To show British prisoners of war helping their enemies to build a bridge over the River Kwai was thoroughly anti-British."[42] Korda, a Hungarian émigré, was being almost more British than the British; Lean, at any rate, did not share his reaction to the novel at all. Anyway, Korda could not have been more wrong about the project, as we shall shortly see. "Although Korda had played a decisive role in the rise of the prestige British film," as Roy Boulting told me in conversation, "the parade had passed him by."

Lean wisely accepted Spiegel's offer. His association with Spiegel on this picture signaled a new phase in his career. No one could blame him for becoming associated with the American film industry. The steady decline of the British film industry as a significant force in world cinema during the period in which Lean's career developed, as evidenced by the crumbling of the Rank organization and Korda's London Films, indicated that it was time for him to move on.

"The British film industry was making films that were underfinanced," the British director John Schlesinger (*Darling* [1965]) told me in conversation. "The filmmaker had to go cap-in-hand to the movie executives to try to obtain financing; moreover, British films received narrow distribution, in comparison with Hollywood pictures." Consequently, it was not surprising that, in the mid-1950s, Lean allied himself with major Hollywood studios like Columbia Pictures. They guaranteed him bigger budgets than had ever been available to him in Britain; furthermore, they afforded him the chance to reach the vast international audience that American films more readily commanded.

What is more, Schlesinger continued, "Hollywood was becoming the principal source of financing for production, both in England and in America." Thus, as we have seen, much of the backing for *Summertime* came from American capital. In sum, once Lean became aligned with an American producer, Sam Spiegel, and an American studio, Columbia Pictures, "it became abundantly clear to him," said Schlesinger, "that it was in the United States, to an ever-increasing degree, that decisions about film projects were being made and that therefore it was in Hollywood that financing was to be found." So Lean would continue making pictures for Hollywood studios. And other British directors would join the exodus, Carol Reed, for example, making the 1956 Burt Lancaster vehicle *Trapeze* there.

But Lean had no intention of being swallowed up in the glossy factory system of American moviemaking, turning out films that rolled off the studio conveyor belt as anonymous studio products. An auteur at heart, he aimed to maintain considerable creative control over his productions, just as he had done while working for Rank and Korda.

Part Four

THE PEAK YEARS IN HOLLYWOOD

Chapter Eleven

THE UNDEFEATED

THE BRIDGE ON THE RIVER KWAI

Everyone has a destined path. If it leads him into the wilderness, he's got to follow it.
> —*Charles Laughton as Rembrandt van Rijn in the film* Rembrandt

A warrior's glory walks hand in hand with his doom.
> —*Ulysses in the film* Troy

With the gradual collapse of the studio system in the 1950s, independent producers began to come to the fore in Hollywood. Sam Spiegel, who was an eminent independent producer, would produce Lean's next two films. He was born in 1901 in Galacia, in southwestern Poland, which was then part of the Austro-Hungarian Empire. In the early 1930s, he worked in the Berlin branch of Universal Studios, preparing its films for European distribution. He fled Hitler's Germany in 1933 and emigrated to England, along with other producers like Gabriel Pascal and Alexander Korda.

Spiegel did not immediately succeed in the film business; he had a short-lived career as a con man and check forger. Specifically, when he ran out of money while making *The Invader* (Adrian Brunel, 1935), a vehicle for the has-been silent comic Buster Keaton, he issued some rubber checks to get the movie finished. He served a brief sentence for fraud in a London jail; deported from Britain, he went to America. With tenacious salesmanship and chutzpah—and the help of Harry Cohn, who ran Columbia Pictures—he gained a foothold in Hollywood. He set up Horizon Pictures, his own independent film unit in New York. The going was tough, and he referred to his nascent company as "Shit Creek Productions" at times—until he had a hit with *The Stranger* (1946), a thriller directed by and starring Orson Welles.[1]

Spiegel became an autocratic, bullying wheeler-dealer as he grew more successful. The director Fred Zinnemann (*High Noon* [1952]) described him to me as an impressive man, saying, "His eagle-like nose made him resemble a Roman emperor in profile; all prominent men have prominent noses."

It had been customary in the past for Hollywood producers to work for one studio and simply carry out the orders of the top executives. Spiegel came to epitomize the independent producer of his era. He was an entrepreneur, packaging a limited number of projects and, usually, releasing them through a major studio like Columbia. He engaged top directors and big-name stars.

Like Rank and Korda before him, Spiegel realized that rising production costs and falling box office receipts meant that a picture could no longer recoup its costs in the home market. Yet, as noted, so much of British cinema at the time was parochial. Many films made for British audiences did not translate well for international audiences. So Spiegel aimed at producing films for the world market. Hence, along with the main Horizon Pictures office in New York, he maintained a branch office in London. He often said that he had no real American roots, "only permanent refugee status" in the United States. Consequently, he loved to roam the world; whenever he was asked where his home was, he replied that it was "in a valise." As a matter of fact, Spiegel loathed Hollywood, calling it "a factory town in the sun." He returned to Hollywood only for short periods, to arrange the financing and distribution of pictures that he was producing. He once said, "I never stay in Hollywood more than five days [at a time]."[2]

By the time David Lean encountered Spiegel, the latter had already produced some Oscar-winning blockbusters, like John Huston's *The African Queen* (1951) with Katharine Hepburn and Elia Kazan's *On the Waterfront* (1954) with Marlon Brando.

Carl Foreman, a blacklisted expatriate American screenwriter who was employed by Alexander Korda to find potential projects for filming, had optioned Pierre Boulle's *Pont de la rivière Kwaï,* or *The Bridge on the River Kwai,* which deals with British soldiers in a Japanese prisoner-of-war camp. But, we recall, Korda had rejected the proposed project, seeing the central character, Colonel Nicholson, as an unstable officer who commands his men to help the Japanese build a railway bridge. He assumed that British audiences would be offended by the story. Spiegel disagreed.

Spiegel, who read several European languages, had picked up a copy of the novel in Paris and read it with interest. So, after contacting Boulle and being directed to London Films, he purchased the screen rights from Korda. He first solicited directors like Carol Reed and Fred Zinnemann to direct the picture, sending them the recently published English translation of the novel by Major Xan Fielding, a British officer who saw action in Crete and northern France during World War II. But, as they later told me, Reed found the ending—in which most of the principal characters are killed—too much of a downer, and Zinnemann too found it disappointing.

Spiegel likewise mailed a copy of the book to Lean—by way of the London office of Horizon Pictures—while he was still making *Summertime*. When Lean expressed interest, Spiegel invited him to New York to discuss the project. Lean, who was renowned in the British film industry, was relatively unknown in Hollywood, but Spiegel had heard of him through his London office. He knew that Lean had codirected the successful World War II movie *In Which We Serve*, which Spiegel thought reflected Lean's keen grasp of the military mind. He was also aware that Lean had recently won the New York Film Critics Award as best director for *Summertime*. On February 4, 1956, Spiegel officially asked Lean to direct *Kwai*. Lean agreed.

The Bridge on the River Kwai (1957)

Lean had no project on the front burner at the time; moreover, as we know, he was down on his luck. Because of his costly divorce from Ann Todd, he was broke and needed work; he had even pawned his gold cigarette case. Another incentive for Lean to make *Kwai* was that Spiegel planned to shoot the film in Southeast Asia. Lean found the prospect of shooting the movie in a foreign land appealing taxwise (see chapter 10). Also, he had always, we recall, loved traveling to the far corners of the earth.

Nevertheless, when Lean and Spiegel met in the New York townhouse of their mutual friend Katharine Hepburn to discuss the project, Lean made certain demands. He chiefly wanted a say in the composition of the screenplay. He assured Spiegel that he would work with the screenwriters to "rescue Col. Nicholson from being depicted either as a lunatic or a traitor . . . and give his character a sympathetic and heroic dimension."[3] Fred Zinnemann told me that he expected Lean to have some disagreements when working with Spiegel "since Spiegel was a creative producer who initiated his own projects and expected to run the show." Lean would not always see things Spiegel's way, but he admired Spiegel because he had a keen mind and loved making movies.

Spiegel had a solid relationship with Columbia Pictures, which financed his films and distributed them worldwide. The studio boss of Columbia was, as we have seen, Harry Cohn, an obstreperous, volatile Hollywood mogul. He had a vulgar tongue. For example, David Thomson points out that Cohn claimed that his butt began to itch when a movie went on too long, which is, Thomson noted, "like a witch doctor making a cult out of hunches." The screenwriter Herman Mankiewicz observed, sarcastically, "Imagine the whole studio wired to Harry Cohn's butt."[4]

Because of his volcanic temper, Cohn inevitably made a lot of enemies in Hollywood. Carol Reed told me that Bette Davis admitted attending Cohn's funeral just "to be sure that the son of a bitch was dead." But even Cohn's enemies acknowledged his uncanny ability to recognize promising projects. He agreed to have Columbia finance and distribute *On the Waterfront* for Spiegel after other studios had turned it down, and the film went on to win eight Academy Awards.

Similarly, Cohn made a deal with Spiegel for Columbia to provide financial backing for *Kwai* and to release it. With Spiegel and Columbia behind *Kwai*, it was clearly an American production. Yet some journalists insisted on assuming that it was a British film because of the English director and the largely British cast. That *Kwai* was a Hollywood picture was important to Lean's career since it was only when he started working for the American majors that he became a filmmaker of international magnitude. Both Lean and Spiegel realized that parochial British films like *Hobson's Choice* were less popular in America than in Britain. So *The Bridge on the River Kwai* was designed from the get-go first and foremost as a colorful Hollywood spectacle: "Its British subject matter was incidental."[5]

Spiegel was strong-willed and, therefore, always wary of placing too much power in a director's hands; he liked to think of himself as the guiding force behind the films he produced. Nonetheless, he did not really cramp Lean's directorial style. In fact, in all the years he worked with Lean, he granted him considerable creative control—often allowing him to modify screenplays and to cast and edit films as he saw fit—in no way keeping him from meriting the status of an auteur director. Still, there was, as we will see, some friction between Spiegel and Lean over the screenplay for *Kwai* as Lean sought to keep it as close as possible to Boulle's novel, which drew in part on his experiences as a prisoner of war.

Pierre Boulle was born in Avignon in 1912 and worked on a British rubber plantation in Malaya before World War II. He entered the French army when war broke out in 1939 and was posted to French Indochina, which encompassed present-day Laos, Cambodia, and other countries. After the fall of France in 1940, Boulle joined the French resistance, de Gaulle's Free French forces, in Singapore, where he received training as a spy and saboteur, learning the art of derailing trains and blowing up bridges from a British commando team, Force 136. "When I was of university age, I dreamed of building bridges," Boulle mused in later life. "A little later, during the war, I learned how to destroy bridges. . . . I never had the opportunity, alas, either to build or to destroy a bridge."[6]

When the Japanese overran Singapore in 1942, Boulle was ordered to return to Indochina, which was by then ruled by pro-Nazi Vichy France. He was assigned to establish contact with the French resistance fighters there, but he was captured by Vichy partisans and spent two years in a prisoner-of-war camp. He finally escaped in 1944, and, at the end of the war, he was repatriated to France. In 1948, he moved to Paris and became a novelist. In his autobiography, *My Own River Kwai,* written nearly twenty years later, he reflected that his decision to become a writer "still strikes me today as the worthy conclusion" of his wartime adventures.[7]

In 1952, Boulle published *Pont de la rivière Kwaï,* which drew in part on his own experience as a prisoner of war, transposed to a Japanese prison camp. It also drew on the infamous Death Railway—the three-hundred-mile-long Thailand-Burma Railway built in 1942–43 with slave labor by the Japanese at the cost of the lives of some fourteen thousand Allied prisoners.

Though Boulle had served in Indochina during the war, he was admittedly unfamiliar with the area in which the novel is set. As he told Lucille Becker, his biographer, "I took an atlas and I looked for the river where they were building the Siam [Thailand]-Burma Railway. I didn't know the River Kwai before I wrote the book."[8] On finding the river, he decided to place his fictional bridge near the Burma frontier, not knowing that the Kwai was little more than a trickling stream at that point. Nor did he discover that the actual bridge over the Kwai was constructed near Bangkok, some two hundred miles to the east. Still, there was some truth to his fictional account. As Ian Watt, one of the Allied prisoners who toiled on the Thailand-Burma Railway, noted after the war, in order to survive the prisoners could not avoid "collaborating with the Japanese."[9]

In the novel, Colonel Nicholson, the senior British officer in a Japanese prison camp, gets the chance to have his men construct an important bridge on the emperor's railway from Bangkok to Rangoon, a project that the Japanese have so far botched. Nicholson and his men see the project as a chance to demonstrate British know-how and the dauntless British spirit. Consequently, they undertake it willingly. To put it simply, they see this as the chance to create something that will outlast the war.

Boulle told Becker that the character of Colonel Nicholson was modeled in part on the Vichy French colonel who, after Boulle's capture, presided over his trial and sentenced him to hard labor. Like that colonel, Nicholson had a curious conception of honor, one "that allowed him to collaborate enthusiastically with the enemy at the expense of his compatriots."[10]

Watt suggests that Nicholson was also based on Philip Toosey, a British officer captured by the Japanese in 1942. Toosey, the senior officer in his prison camp, was known for negotiating with the enemy on behalf of his men. But he did not collaborate with the enemy to the degree that Nicholson does.[11] Be that as it may, Boulle never mentioned Toosey to Becker as a source for the Nicholson character.

Boulle portrays Colonel Saito, the commandant of the camp, as a drunken, sadistic tyrant, describing him as "a grotesque figure," subject to "fits of raving hysteria."[12] Becker explains, "Saito is a caricature meant to heighten the contrast between Japanese barbarous brutality and English civilized behavior, represented by Nicholson."[13]

Boulle's novel—which went on to win the Prix Sainte-Beuve—has been called "a stirring adventure story about men at war."[14] The plot consists of two interlocking stories. The first centers on Nicholson and the battalion of prisoners who build the bridge. The second centers on a small British commando team led by Major Warden, along with Major Shears and Lieutenant Joyce, that has been ordered to destroy the bridge. (The commando team is known as Force 316, an inversion of Force 136, with which, as we have seen, Boulle trained.) So the struggle at the heart of the novel is, ultimately, not between East and West but between two British forces: one committed to constructing the bridge, the other to demolishing it.

When the commando team reaches the bridge, Joyce kills Saito and struggles with Nicholson, who attempts to keep him from destroying the bridge. One of the charges does go off just as a Japanese troop train is crossing the bridge, and the train plunges into the ravine below. But the bridge remains virtually unharmed. Joyce, Shears, and Nicholson are all killed in the exchange of gunfire between the Japanese guards and the commandos, but Warden manages to escape. Boulle wrote this final scene first: "The rest was written to lead up to it."[15]

Boulle always had a sense of compassion for his characters, and his final judgment of Nicholson is rendered by Warden, who writes in his official report, "Some damage done, but bridge intact, thanks to British colonel's heroism." Warden goes on to comment that, in retrospect, it seems that Nicholson was acting according to his own lights: "He had probably spent his whole life dreaming of constructing something which would last. In the absence of a town or a cathedral, he plumped for this bridge. He had a highly developed sense of duty and admired a job well done." Perhaps, in the end, Nicholson "was really quite a decent fellow at heart."[16] No wonder, then, that, on hearing that Korda considered the novel anti-British, Boulle was indignant. "Anti-British?" he declared. "Who has dreamed that one up?" He went on to say that, in *Kwai*, he had sought to portray British courage, ingenuity, and fidelity to principle.[17]

Interestingly, it was Boulle's name that appeared on the screen adaptation of the novel that Lean was handed when he arrived in New York for story conferences with Spiegel. But the real author was Carl Foreman, as Spiegel told Lean privately. Once Spiegel had bought the screen rights to the novel, Foreman had written a screen adaptation and submitted it to him. But, because Columbia would not employ blacklisted writers, Spiegel had put Boulle's name on the title page—a ploy that, because Boulle had no skill at all in writing English, was hardly credible.

Lean thoroughly disliked Foreman's draft and lost no time telling Spiegel so.[18] For one thing, it starts out with English saboteurs being rescued by a British submarine after having destroyed a Japanese train in the Malayan jungle. Lean pointed out that this whole episode had precious little to do with the ensuing story of the building of the bridge.[19]

When Foreman's script finally gets around to dramatizing the clash of wills between Colonel Nicholson and Colonel Saito, Foreman depicts Saito as a drunken despot. To be fair, Foreman was following Boulle's portrayal of Saito. Be that as it may, Lean maintained that Saito behaved throughout like a B-movie villain.[20] Indeed, his first address to the British prisoners of war begins, "I hate the British!"[21] As a matter of fact, Lean thought that most of the characters in Foreman's draft were "cardboard cutouts" like Saito. In short, Lean was convinced that, in Foreman's screenplay, "the whole spirit of the book" had been lost.[22]

Norman Spencer, who had been the associate producer on Lean's last three films, states that Lean phoned him in London and asked him to come to New York to work on the scenario. Lean said, "We will produce a prose treatment from the book."[23] Spencer arrived in New York on February 15, 1956. Lean, says Spencer, chose which episodes from the book would be in the film and which bypassed. Lean and Spencer finished their prose treatment on March 20.

Like Alexander Korda, Sam Spiegel, as the executive producer of his pictures, was inclined to deal personally with a filmmaker and not use another producer as an intermediary. He particularly objected to Spencer's presence because he "refused to tolerate the idea of a former relationship of

Lean's threatening his own."[24] Hence, he sought to separate Spencer from Lean by informing him that Lean did not need him as his associate producer on *Kwai*. But, the title *associate producer* not being important to him, Spencer stayed on as Lean's production assistant—at Lean's request.

Spiegel insisted—over Lean's objections—that Foreman, who had, after all, written the classic *High Noon*, continue working on the screenplay. Consequently, when Lean went to Ceylon (now Sri Lanka), where the film was to be shot, to labor over the script, Spiegel sent Foreman along. En route, Lean paid a courtesy call in Paris to Pierre Boulle, who was most cordial to him. Lean arrived in Ceylon on May 28, 1956.

Spiegel was a firm believer that the best scripts emerge from the friction between the writers who collaborate on them. Lean, of course, wanted to employ the treatment that he and Spencer had put together in New York as a guide to reworking Foreman's draft. Foreman, for his part, balked at "slavishly" following the treatment in revising his own draft. At one point, Spencer says, Foreman fumed at Lean: "David, you are a good art house director; you've made some small British films. But you have no experience of the big international market." Lean later told Spiegel about the incident, saying that he retorted that Foreman could say what he liked about Lean's inexperience but that he, Lean, could not direct Foreman's script as it stood—starting with the opening sequence aboard "an American submarine" (actually a British one).[25] So Lean and Foreman soldiered on, Foreman scuttling his opening sequence.

Because *Kwai* was a Hollywood movie designed first and foremost to appeal to the mass audience in America, Spiegel requested the introduction of an American commando. So Foreman transformed Major Shears from a British commando into an American sailor. Lean acquiesced, but he still believed that Foreman's Shears smacked too much of the standard Hollywood hero such as the one Errol Flynn played in *Objective Burma* (Raoul Walsh, 1945). Foreman even introduced an action sequence in which a herd of elephants charges Shears and his fellow commandos during their jungle trek to reach the bridge. Furthermore, Lean was convinced that Foreman was focusing too much on Shears, at the expense of Nicholson. All in all, he believed that Foreman's adaptation seemed more like a blood-and-guts adventure picture than a thought-provoking antiwar movie.

Lean telegraphed Spiegel that he had finally given Foreman his walking papers. "Carl," he said, "either you go or I go." Spiegel reluctantly terminated Foreman, who left Ceylon on June 25. In an overall progress report on the screenplay sent to Spiegel much later (August 10, 1956), Lean reiterated that he could not have filmed Foreman's script. Some of the scenes were "awfully rough," Lean explained, and, perhaps with *Objective Burma* in mind, he added that other scenes were "even derivative."[26]

Read today, Foreman's draft can be seen to contain some material obviously supplied by Lean, as when Lieutenant Joyce reminisces about his dull life as an accountant, which was undoubtedly based on Lean's own brief period with his father's accounting firm (see chapter 1). But Lean exaggerated when he contended that "there is not a single word of Foreman's script in the picture."[27] If one compares the final shooting script with Foreman's draft, one finds that, while much of his dialogue was heavily revised or deleted, some of it was retained. To take one salient example, Colonel Nicholson's congratulatory speech to his men after the bridge is completed survives in the shooting script just as Foreman wrote it.[28] And the plot and cast of characters in both Foreman's draft and the shooting script are fundamentally the same.

At any rate, in July, Spiegel sent the screenwriter Calder Willingham (*Paths of Glory* [Stanley Kubrick, 1957]) to Ceylon to replace Foreman. Lean found Willingham even a cut below Foreman when it came to writing dialogue. Willingham submitted to Lean a sample scene that depicted a quarrel between Saito and Nicholson; Lean thought it was dreadful. Saito called Nicholson a "stupid English donkey," and Nicholson replied that Saito was a "beastly, uncivilized, repulsive bounder." Lean told Willingham in no uncertain terms that his stilted dialogue would not wash, and the furious writer accordingly wired Spiegel on July 17, 1956: "I feel Lean not very responsive and meet considerable resistance."[29]

After two weeks, Willingham threw in the towel and flew to London. In his August 10 progress report to Spiegel, Lean also included his estimate of American screenwriters like Foreman and Willingham: "These American writers really frighten me. . . . I don't mean to be offensive, but they are *so* touchy."[30]

After Willingham's departure, Lean took a crack at reworking the screenplay on his own. But he had trouble writing the dialogue for the newly Americanized Shears. He asked Spiegel for yet another writer to help him out, preferably not an American. Spiegel asked the advice of Carl Foreman, who suggested Michael Wilson, another blacklisted American screenwriter. Wilson had received an Academy Award for coauthoring the script for George Stevens's *A Place in the Sun* (1951) and had continued to write scripts for Hollywood movies anonymously while living as an exile in Paris. Spiegel took Foreman's advice, and Wilson arrived in Ceylon on September 9. As luck would have it, Wilson and Lean got along famously.

It helped that Wilson had seen action in the South Pacific as a marine during World War II; that experience aided him in writing about the war in Burma. Because of Columbia's strict policy of not employing blacklisted writers, the New York and London offices of Spiegel's Horizon Pictures circulated an interoffice memo stating that Wilson was to be referred to in all subsequent memos as "John Michael" and that on no account "was his real name to be divulged to Columbia Pictures."[31] In general, Wilson, with Lean's supervision, sought to bring the second draft of the screenplay closer to Boulle's book. For example, Wilson restored Nicholson's character to the prominence that he has in the novel.

Meanwhile, back in Hollywood, Harry Cohn was having second thoughts about *Kwai*. "Cohn had even considered canceling the production when Michael Frankovich, head of Columbia's London office, had invested $600,000 in preproduction money."[32] Cohn cabled Frankovich: "How can you idiots in the London office give a crook like Sam Spiegel [$600,000 to go to some] God-forsaken [place like Ceylon] to shoot a picture?"[33] (The reference to Spiegel as a crook probably referred to Spiegel's reputation in Hollywood as a wheeler-dealer, not to the fact that he had done jail time for fraud in London years before—something Cohn most likely was not aware of.)

To make matters worse, Cohn took one look at Foreman's draft of the screenplay, which Spiegel had submitted to the studio prior to hiring Wilson, and threw a fit. He complained to Spiegel that there was no love interest. More specifically, he pointed out that the only women in the picture were natives. Cohn was threatening to shut down the picture altogether because, as he put it in his typically blunt fashion, "there were no white women" in the script.[34] He demanded that there be a love scene between one of the soldiers and an army nurse. So Spiegel directed Lean to revise the screenplay accordingly.

According to the assistant editor Teddy Darvas, Lean confessed that he had to give in and shoot the scene. But having to do so was "bloody awful" since the scene represents a disconcerting intrusion of a love story into the male world of prison camps and commando raids. As scripted, the love scene between Shears and a nurse plays out on a tropical beach in less than two minutes. Its success testifies to Wilson's ability "to adjust continuity, plot, and characterization without compromising the integrity of the story."[35]

Though Lean went along with the love scene reluctantly, he did not in general mind the Americanization of Shears. The American sailor, he commented, "softens the Yorkshire pudding effect of the whole," thereby giving American audiences a hero to root for.[36] Lean and Wilson continued to finalize small details in the definitive version of the script almost up to the time principal photography began.

Lean was very pleased with the final shooting script. Though he tended to minimize Foreman's contribution to it, he made a point of emphasizing Wilson's. "It was really Mike's and my script," he insisted; Wilson not only composed much of the dialogue but also edited and tightened the whole screenplay.[37] Wilson would subsequently adapt another of Boulle's novels, *La planète des singes* (1963), for the 1968 Franklin J. Schaffner film *Planet of the Apes.*

While Lean was toiling on the screenplay in the summer of 1956, Spiegel was conferring with him from time to time about casting, in order to line up an impressive roster of actors for the picture. Alec Guinness was not Lean's first choice for Colonel Nicholson. Since appearing as Fagin in *Oliver Twist,* Guinness had gained fame by playing in a series of British comedies like *The Lavender Hill Mob* (Charles Crichton, 1951), and Lean wondered whether audiences would accept him in a deeply serious role.

Lean had initially considered Charles Laughton (*Hobson's Choice*) for Nicholson. But Laughton was too unfit to be underwritten by the studio's insurance company, which judged that he could not withstand several harrowing months in the jungles of Ceylon. Spiegel then encouraged Lean to opt for Guinness and mailed Guinness a copy of the first draft of the screenplay by Carl Foreman, Lean and Wilson not yet having finished the second draft.

As Guinness writes in the foreword to this book, he rejected the Foreman draft "because it was rubbish—filled with elephant charges and that sort of thing." Foreman's reduction of Nicholson to a secondary character further alienated Guinness. Spiegel eventually shipped Guinness the second draft, but he rejected the role a second time because he still found Nicholson to be "a blinkered character," whom audiences might not take seriously. Moreover, he had read in the trade papers that Laughton had been Lean's first choice for the role.[38]

Lean later denied that he had ever seriously considered Laughton for Nicholson. And, in fact, Teddy Darvas remembers Lean saying, "The idea of Laughton was ludicrous—you could not believe that a fat man like Laughton was living on starvation rations in a prisoner-of-war camp." Yet Lean wrote Spiegel on August 10, 1956, that he believed that Laughton was "the best choice." Lean continued to nurture the idea that Laughton would be willing to lose weight before shooting commenced, though Spiegel had already tried to disabuse him of that notion. "I frankly feel that Laughton is unable to go through with a diet," he had written Lean as early as July 6. "He looks like a big Moby Dick!"[39] So Lean's assertion that he never seriously wanted Laughton for the role does not ring true.

Finally, Spiegel took Guinness to dinner and convinced him to play Nicholson. As Guinness writes, "By the end of the evening we were discussing what kind of wig I would wear." Guinness in due course flew to the location site in Ceylon. He told me that, when he arrived at the airport in Colombo, Lean met his plane: "As soon as I got off, David blurted out: 'Of course, you know I really wanted Charles Laughton.' I felt like turning around and getting back on the plane and paying my own fare home!"

Told that Guinness was mortally offended by his remark, Lean categorically denied making it: "I never said a word about Charles Laughton." Later on, he watched while Guinness repeated the anecdote on television: he said he bristled and "shut the damned thing off."[40] When I told Guinness that Lean vehemently denied the airport incident, he replied, "I saw David deny it on television, but it really happened."

Asked why Lean would say such a tactless thing to him at the beginning of a long and arduous shoot, Guinness answered, "I suppose David was nettled because I refused the part twice." Guinness wrote of Lean in his autobiography, "Let me make it clear that I admire his work enormously. . . . The fact that he didn't particularly want me for *The Bridge on the River Kwai* is understandable but of no consequence."[41]

Spiegel had a much easier time signing up the rest of the principals. Jack Hawkins, who had starred in Carol Reed's *The Fallen Idol* (1948), took on the part of Major Warden. Spiegel wanted Cary Grant to play Major Shears, but Lean was dead set on William Holden, who had given an Oscar-winning performance as a prisoner of war in Billy Wilder's *Stalag 17* (1953). Because of Holden's box office pull, Spiegel offered him a sweetheart contract, including a $300,000 salary (twice what Lean was receiving), plus 10 percent of the gross box office receipts. Holden immediately accepted the role. "I'm like the chorus girl who was offered an apartment, a diamond necklace, and a mink coat," he quipped.[42] Lean acknowledged, "He was worth it." Besides being a top star, Holden was "very dependable, was never late, and always knew his lines."[43]

Spiegel coaxed the Japanese actor Sessue Hayakawa out of retirement to enact the role of Colonel Saito. Hayakawa had been a Hollywood star in the silent era, from 1914 to 1923, appearing most notably as the villain in Cecil B. DeMille's *The Cheat* (1915). More recently, he had played a Tokyo police detective in Samuel Fuller's *House of Bamboo* (1955). In a surprise move, Spiegel signed Geoffrey Horne, a twenty-three-year-old unknown, to play Lieutenant Joyce. Horne had played a cadet in a military school in *The Strange One* (Jack Garfein, 1957), which Spiegel had produced. James Donald rounded out the cast of *Kwai* as Major Clipton, the British doctor in the camp. Lean remembered him from *In Which We Serve,* in which he essayed the role of a Navy medico.

Lean held on to the cinematographer Jack Hildyard and the editor Peter Taylor from previous pictures as well as the composer Malcolm Arnold, who would be scoring his third Lean film. New to Lean's team was the production designer Donald Ashton, who was familiar with Ceylon, where he had been stationed during World War II. Ashton chose a site sixty miles from Colombo, near the village of Kitulgala, to construct the bridge. Construction began several months before shooting started.

The design of the bridge was based on an authentic document. One day, while Lean and Ashton were scouting locations, "a man came to them with a faded scrap of rice paper, which had been smuggled out of Burma during the war": "On the paper was a sketch of a bridge on the Death Railway, to be passed on to commandos, to help them seek out and blow up the bridge."[44] (The real bridge was never destroyed.)

Soon after arriving in Ceylon, Ashton discovered that an engineering firm called Hubbard and Company, from Sheffield, England, was building a dam in Ceylon. He contacted Keith Best, the chief engineer, and engaged his company to help him design the bridge, which was erected by the Equipment and Construction Company, a local Ceylonese firm. It took eight months to design and build the wooden bridge, with forty-five elephants to haul fifteen hundred huge trees—most from the banks of the river—to the building site, where they were shaped into pillars.

The bridge was ready by January 1957 and stood 425 feet long and 90 feet high. Spiegel announced in a press release that it cost $250,000—in order to emphasize that *Kwai* was a big-budget Hollywood picture, says Ashton. But, in reality, it cost only $52,085, not a huge slice of the movie's $2 million budget. "It was cheap," Ashton explains, "because we used local labor and elephants; and the timber was cut nearby."[45]

Lean and Ashton discovered an abandoned stone quarry that possessed an appropriately grim, scorched ambience to serve as the setting of the prison camp. The Japanese government supplied a military adviser for the scenes in the camp. Japanese officialdom cooperated with the production because Spiegel had the foresight to submit the script to the Japanese government and convinced the officials that "the movie was not intended as a bitter, hate-inciting document against the Japanese, but rather as a reflection of the general folly and waste of war."[46] Similarly, Spiegel personally engaged Major General L. E. M. Perowne, a retired English officer who had served in the Far East as a commando in World War II, as the British military adviser on the movie.

Lean had some preliminary thoughts about the film's score during pre-production. For the scene in which the British prisoners march into the camp for the first time, he wanted them to be singing a spirited marching song. Spiegel favored "Bless 'Em All," a popular ditty from World War II used in *The Sound Barrier*. But he soon learned that, by this time, the rights to the song had become prohibitively expensive. Then Lean came up with a marching song that he remembered hearing as a boy during World War I: "The Colonel Bogey March," composed in 1914 by Kenneth Alford, who had been the conductor of a military band.

Lean discovered that, during World War II, the tune had been set to saucy lyrics that were still widely known among British servicemen: "Hitler has only one right ball / Goering has two, but they are small / Himmler has something sim'lar / but Goebbels has no balls at all."[47] Lean knew that these lyrics would not pass muster with the censor and, therefore, decided to have the soldiers whistle the melody instead. Alford's widow granted permission for the song to be employed in the film, with the understanding that the crude lyrics would not be used. Norman Spencer adds that, later on, when Lean asked Malcolm Arnold to work "Colonel Bogey" into his score, he said, "I will write a counter melody which will fit with the original melody, and these themes will be incorporated into the film's underscore."

Larry Timm, in his book on film music, opines that Arnold should not have been eligible to be nominated for an Academy Award for his score because "the march song contained within the film was actually composed by someone other than Arnold."[48] That is like saying Max Steiner should not have been nominated for his music for *Casablanca* (1942) because he made use of "As Time Goes By" in the score. Film composers frequently weave preexisting music into their movie scores; as a matter of fact, the rules governing the eligibility of a film score for Oscar consideration state that only half the score must be original music.[49] Arnold's score for *Kwai* certainly meets that criterion—and then some.

Principal photography commenced in November 1956 and continued until May 1957. This added up to a gruelling 251 days in the jungle for the film unit. During this period, Lean became totally engrossed in filming a wide-screen epic in the wilds of Ceylon. He was operating not on fully equipped studio soundstages but in the wilderness, where technical equipment was more apt to break down.

"I do become obsessed by a movie, in a sort of maddening way," he confessed. "I become immensely focused when shooting a picture." If he could not expect the cast and crew to share his obsession with making a movie, he did expect their total commitment. He sometimes scolded the technical crew for their lack of efficiency, and some of them groused that he was too much of a perfectionist.

Hayakawa reported that he and Lean got along very well indeed: "We never found ourselves in opposition. But he was less than slightly beloved by some of his associates, being broiled in the hot sun and infernal humidity of Ceylon during the stifling months we were isolated there." Sometimes at the end of the day, Lean would sit by himself on a rock and contemplate the bridge while mulling over production problems. On one occasion, Hayakawa overheard one of the technicians exclaim, "Lean the bloody perfectionist! He shot thirty seconds of film today and then sat on a rock and stared at his goddamned bridge!"[50]

Lean was aware of the dissonance in the ranks; members of the camera crew made snide remarks about their "genius director" that sometimes he overheard. He even had a falling out with Jack Hildyard, with whom he had had a good working relationship on previous pictures. Hildyard declined to stay around each evening to compare notes on the day's shooting; as a result, Hildyard never shot another Lean picture.

Lean felt miserable about this lack of rapport since, on his previous pictures, he had often found the technicians more congenial than the actors. In fact, as we have seen, Lean sometimes slighted the actors by consulting not with them but with the camera crew (see chapter 3).

He was also unhappy that some of the cast had little confidence in his ability to direct actors. Guinness remembered that James Donald, "who played the sympathetic doctor so admirably," was often at loggerheads with Lean about how to play a scene. One day, he told Lean that he knew nothing about acting and that George Cukor, who had directed him in *Edward, My Son* (1949), was superior in that regard. "Don't dare speak to the director like that!" one of the crew snapped at Donald. Guinness concluded: "But James was not one to be put down easily."[51] Neither was Guinness; he had his own disagreements with Lean, as we shall shortly see. Asked about Donald's observation, Cukor told me: "I would be flattered to be compared favorably to David; as for my being a better director than he, oh, my, no!"

William Holden usually lived up to Lean's expectations as an agreeable and cooperative actor, except for those few occasions when he was in his cups. (Holden had a drinking problem, which would grow more serious as he got older.) It seems that Holden was not satisfied with the living accommodations that Spiegel had provided for the production unit. Spiegel had erected a compound in a jungle clearing; it included a makeshift bungalow "which looked like a mock-Tudor-type house" for Guinness, Holden, and the other major players.[52] Everyone else had to make do with the tin shacks that surrounded the bungalow. Neither the bungalow nor the shacks were air-conditioned. Furthermore, the quality of the food dished up by the catering service steadily eroded as Spiegel made cuts in the budget allocated for living expenses. Yet, whenever Spiegel showed up in Ceylon, he stayed in an air-conditioned hotel suite in Colombo.

During one such visitation, Spiegel and his wife, Betty, hosted a dinner party for William Holden and his wife, Ardis, and Jack Hawkins and his wife, Doreen, while Mrs. Holden and Mrs. Hawkins were paying their husbands a visit. When Betty Spiegel owned that her husband found coming out to Ceylon very trying, the inebriated Holden pointed out that Lean, along with the rest of the cast and crew, was "working his ass off in a hundred per cent humidity" and that he, Holden, had no sympathy for Spiegel, sojourning in a luxury hotel suite in town. Holden then announced, "You know what, Betty? You're a bitch!" When Doreen Hawkins and Ardis Holden attempted to intervene, Holden turned to them and assured them that they too were bitches.[53] The next day, the contrite Holden had baskets of fruit delivered to the offended ladies.

The spartan living conditions did not bother Lean in the least since material comforts were never a priority for him. He did confront Spiegel about budget cutbacks that affected filming, however. When Spiegel would warn him that he was going over budget, Lean would respond, "What budget? I've got to get this shot!"[54] A meticulous, painstaking filmmaker, Lean was not concerned about going beyond the schedule and the budget; if the picture turns out well, he reasoned, no one will remember the schedule or the budget.

Lean complained that he was forced to "skimp, skimp, skimp," all along the line during the production period. For example, he noted that Spiegel would not pay to have British soldiers flown to the location in Ceylon to act as extras in the prison camp scenes. Instead: "We used a lot of Ceylonese natives done up in white face."[55] The location manager beat the bushes to corral local residents, including businessmen and planters, who were willing to serve as extras. According to Don Ashton, "The extras recruited to play British soldiers were a mixed bag of civilians: Malaysians, Europeans—anyone who was half white was pressed into service."

In justice to Spiegel, it must be stated that this was one bit of "skimping" that was not his fault but, instead, the result of a stricture imposed by General Percival of the British War Office. Norman Spencer explains that Percival, who had served in the Far East during World War II, was anxious that Britain maintain good relations with Japan. "After he read the screenplay," says

Spencer, "he thought it was terrible that a Hollywood movie was being made about the wretched way the British prisoners of war were treated by the Japanese in Burma while they were building the railway." He therefore would not allow the War Office to cooperate with the film even to the extent of having British troops appear in the movie.

It was pointed out to Percival that the Japanese government had approved the same script that he had read. Indeed, a decade after the war was over, the Japanese formally apologized to the British government for the mistreatment of British prisoners of war, declaring, "Japan, through its colonial rule and aggression, caused tremendous suffering. Japan squarely faces these facts of history in a spirit of remorse."[56] But Percival remained adamant.[57]

Lean's most vociferous disagreement with Spiegel during shooting had to do with a personal matter. As a rule, Spiegel frowned on the presence of wives and loved ones on location. Nevertheless, Lean wrote Spiegel on November 16, 1956, that he wanted Leila Matkar, his inamorata, to come over to Ceylon for Christmas. Lean had been involved with her for two years and would eventually marry her (see chapter 10). He promised Spiegel that he would not neglect his work while Leila was around.

Spiegel was not so sure that Leila's visit would be a good idea; he had heard through the grapevine that she had a history of mental illness and had undergone electroshock treatments. He did not want her distracting Lean with her problems. Accordingly, he had a private meeting with her in the New York office of Horizon Pictures and advised her that Lean was filming in remote areas of the wilderness, making a visit unsafe. Leila did not suspect that Spiegel was lying to her.

When Lean learned that Spiegel had sold Leila a bill of goods, he fired off a broadside on November 22: "You obviously believe that a film contract entitles you to complete ownership of a human being. You are a dictator with no respect for human dignity." He accused Spiegel of not trusting him and of endeavoring to manage his private life. Spiegel cabled Lean on November 29 that Lean's letter was degrading and unconscionable: "I am washing my hands of entire issue and hope you will learn to appreciate friendship in future."[58] Leila did spend Christmas with Lean in Ceylon, and Spiegel made amends for his interference by arranging for her to continue her therapy with a Manhattan psychiatrist.

Another battle with Spiegel that Lean won concerned the rushes. They had to be sent to London to be processed, and Spiegel wanted them kept at Horizon's London office. But Lean insisted that they be returned to him in Ceylon so that he could see them. "I must see what I am getting on the screen," he wrote Spiegel on November 16, in order to decide whether any retakes were necessary. "I'm a cutter, Sam, first and foremost; don't take that away from me."[59] Spiegel acquiesced.

One of the reasons that Lean desired to see the rushes as soon as possible was that he had never worked in the CinemaScope wide-screen process before, and he was still to some degree feeling his way. Lean had had the foresight to experiment with a sixteen-millimeter Arriflex camera that had been fitted with a wide-screen lens before he started filming *Kwai*. He quickly learned that the first rule in employing this format is that, if the action in the center of the frame is blocked out properly, the action taking place on either side will pretty much take care of itself. He was not particularly alarmed by this new technique. When Spiegel expressed concern that he was inexperienced in employing CinemaScope, he reminded Spiegel that he had always had an eye for composition.

Lean was annoyed by Spiegel's occasional visits to Ceylon, resenting Spiegel looking over his shoulder; filming a scene under the watchful eye of the producer made him uncomfortable. Jack Hildyard said that Lean and Spiegel had a love-hate relationship: "They treated each other with respect and animosity." Still, Spiegel's forays into the field to check up on Lean were few and far between. Spiegel was for the most part content to have William Graf, a Columbia executive, as his on-site representative. Unlike the sneaky production assistant that Ilya Lopert had spy on Lean during the shooting of *Summertime,* Graf was no undercover agent for Spiegel. He possessed "the experience, diplomatic skills, and toughness to be able to ride out the storms."[60]

Besides his running battle with Spiegel, Lean also had his dog days with Alec Guinness over their differing approaches to the character of Colonel Nicholson. Though Guinness makes little of their altercations in his autobiography, Sessue Hayakawa writes, "The coolness with which each man regarded the other was almost solid enough to be seen."[61]

Nicholson is a deeply neurotic man, madly drawn to building a bridge that will, ultimately, be a monument to himself. Lean therefore wanted Guinness to play the part with some intensity, thereby suggesting overtly that Nicholson was ruled by obsession. But Guinness was not given to emotional displays in delineating a character. He was inclined to render a character's inner turmoil in an understated manner. As Kenneth Tynan states, "The people whom Guinness plays best of all are iceberg characters, nine-tenths concealed. . . . Guinness can convey, by his voice and bearing, the existence of little fixed ideas frisking about behind the deferential mask of normality."[62]

"I knew officers like Nicholson when I was in the navy," Guinness told me, "men who were a bit thick between the ears." Still, on the surface they could seem quite sensible. Guinness even wanted to inject a little tongue-in-cheek humor into his portrayal of Nicholson, to make him more sympathetic to the audience. "But, of course, David wouldn't allow it," he told me, "because David has no sense of humor." Guinness saw Nicholson as a case study of a military man who possessed too much grit and obstinacy to indulge in emotional outbursts, either before his men or before the Japanese. Guinness told Lean that he wanted to rely on nuance and suggestion to give fitful hints of Nicholson's inner conflicts. When Lean wanted Guinness to put more emotion into his performance, Guinness would remind him that the film actor's first rule is "Less is more."

One day Lean and Guinness had an especially acrid confrontation about a scene near the end of the movie. Nicholson is photographed against the setting sun as he surveys the completed bridge, which prompts a reverie about the past: "It's been a good life; but there are times when suddenly you realize you're nearer the end than the beginning. And you wonder what the sum total of your life represents. What difference your being there at any time made to anything. . . . But tonight!" Lean wanted Guinness to give a reading of the speech that reflected deep feeling on Nicholson's part. But Guinness insisted on underplaying the monologue, which, Lean contended, undermined the significance of the whole scene. Spiegel recalled that Guinness's stubborn refusal to do the speech in the manner that Lean wanted caused Lean "literally to shed tears." For his part, Guinness recalled that delivering this extended monologue was "torture for me": "David wanted me to finish this long speech just as the sun tipped the tops of the trees on the horizon down the river."[63] So Guinness had to time his delivery to the setting of the sun. Lean spent five consecutive evenings getting the speech timed to the exact second.

Another bone of contention during the filming of this scene was that Lean had Guinness play the scene with his back to the camera, leaning on the railing of the bridge. Guinness curtly inquired why the camera was focused on his back instead of on his face; Lean went ballistic and told Guinness to play the scene the way he directed it. Their disagreement degenerated into a shouting match that peaked with Guinness telling Lean, "Look here, I haven't cared for the way you've directed a single scene in this picture." Lean was beside himself. "If that's the way you feel," he bellowed, "you can jolly well pack up and fuck off."[64] In the end, Lean compromised by giving Guinness a close-up, but in profile, not full face, as Guinness demanded.

"I suppose we are both strong-willed, and his will is the stronger," Guinness writes in his autobiography. "Let me make it very clear, that I am

241

very fond of David."[65] Indeed, after seeing the finished film, Guinness wrote Lean, testifying that he was proud to be associated with the picture.

Hayakawa, unlike Guinness, never sparred with Lean. But Peter Newbrook says that Lean felt a little uncomfortable with Hayakawa at times. Lean thought of Hayakawa "as quite old and going a bit ga-ga." Actually, Hayakawa was only sixty-eight and quite spry. His principal problem was that he had lost his mastery of English since his days in Hollywood in the silent era. So he had to deliver some of his lines phonetically, without really grasping the full import of what he was saying. Moreover, because of Hayakawa's heavy accent, he had to do up to twelve takes of a given shot before it was recorded satisfactorily on the sound track.

In order to focus on his lines exclusively, Lean remembered, Hayakawa marked all the scenes in the script in which he had dialogue. "He had bound his scenes all together and thrown out all the rest." This caused no problem until filming reached the scene at the end of the picture when the commandos show up to destroy the bridge. Nicholson and Saito are standing on the bridge, and Saito is to follow Nicholson when he goes to investigate the presence of the saboteurs. But Hayakawa stayed on the bridge, as immovable as a rock. "Go on, Sessue, follow him," Lean yelled. "This is where you get killed!" Hayakawa shouted back in disbelief, "I get killed?" Lean concluded: "He had thrown the rest of the scene away because he had no dialogue." Hayakawa had not known until that moment that he was to die at the end of the picture.[66] Despite all the problems involved in his appearing in an English-language movie, Hayakawa was nominated for an Academy Award for his role.

But Hayakawa was the least of Lean's worries when he shot the scene in which Warden and his demolition squad destroy the bridge. In the novel, the bridge is left standing, as mentioned above. But Lean was convinced that, in the movie, it was essential that the bridge be demolished to provide a spectacular climax; otherwise the audience would feel cheated.

Boulle seemed to be of two minds about the destruction of the bridge in the picture. Becker quotes him as saying, "In my book the bridge is not blown up; the colonel saves his bridge. I do not agree with the movie's end."[67] And elsewhere, describing his meeting with Spiegel and Foreman to discuss the film version of his novel, before Lean was involved in the project, he states, "I fought them over the change. In the end I gave up."[68]

Yet the Lean biographer Kevin Brownlow quotes Carl Foreman as saying that Boulle told him and Spiegel that he had wanted to destroy the bridge in the book but could not work out how to do it. "If you can do it, God bless you," Boulle concluded.[69] Peter Newbrook supports Foreman in this regard, stating that he met Boulle some years after the picture was released and that the novelist said that he was intrigued by the material added to the plot in the movie, including the way in which the bridge is destroyed. "I wish I had thought of that," Boulle told him, "because I would have written that myself in the book if I had." After exchanging letters with Kevin Brownlow about this double-mindedness, I came to the conclusion that, initially, Boulle thought that the film should follow the book but that, ultimately, he became reconciled to the plot change.

In any event, the grand finale of the movie was to be the destruction of the bridge, just as a Japanese troop train was crossing it for the first time. The sixty-five-year-old train, which Spiegel had obtained from the Ceylonese government, had once belonged to an Indian maharaja. The destruction of the bridge was scheduled for March 10, 1957.[70] The operation was being coordinated by Peter Dukelow, the construction manager, who would now be destroying the bridge he had helped build. Spiegel arrived in his air-conditioned limo to witness the spectacle. Three explosive experts from Imperial Chemical Industries in Britain were on hand to set off the charges. Five CinemaScope cameras were planted in dugouts at strategic points around the bridge, to photograph the explosion. The five cameramen were to retreat to five nearby trenches to shelter themselves from the blast. The explosive experts had warned Lean that big chunks of wood, traveling at one hundred miles an hour, would be hurtling through the air as soon as the explosives went off. A control panel had been rigged in the central control hut, where Lean and Spiegel were ensconced. The panel consisted of five lights, one for each camera operator. Each cameraman was to press a button after he had started his camera, to tell Lean that he was proceeding to his trench a few moments before the blast. Then Lean could give the signal to blow up the bridge.

One cameraman, Freddy Ford, was in such a hurry to escape the explosion that he forgot to press the button to give Lean the signal that he was safe in his trench. Lean feared that, if one cameraman had not reached safety, he might still be close enough to the explosion to sustain serious injuries. Consequently, he did not give the signal to detonate the explosives. He had no way of notifying the stunt man who was driving the train that the operation had been aborted. So the ancient train, pulling six coaches, trundled across the bridge, and the locomotive jumped the tracks, after the engineer had leaped from it.

Newbrook recalls that Spiegel was apoplectic and would have had Ford executed if he could. But Lean took Ford's part when he was jeered by the rest of the camera crew. Spiegel was furious that Lean was supportive of "the idiot who fucked up the shot."

Fifteen stalwart laborers, aided by several elephants, worked until 2:00 A.M. to jack the train back onto the track. On March 11, Lean restaged the explosion. When the stuntman who had engineered the train the previous day begged off from doing it again, Eddie Fowlie, the property master and Lean's factotum, volunteered to take the controls. "I set the throttle to make sure the train would stay on course, then I jumped off the engine at the opposite end of the bridge," Fowlie explained. All the lights on Lean's control panel were illuminated this time, and he gave the order to detonate the explosives. Everything went according to plan; the bridge collapsed, and the train plummeted into the ravine for a spectacular climax to the movie.

On this, his last visit to the location, to see the fireworks, Spiegel took the opportunity to inform Lean that Cohn was upset that he had gone $800,000 over budget in the final months of the shoot, with the result that the budget would reach $2,800,000. Admittedly, some of the overages were Lean's fault, as when he spent no fewer than five nights filming Nicholson's valedictory speech on the bridge. But some of the delays could not be laid at his door. For example, "shooting was delayed for eleven days" when heavy rains lifted the river to flood level and no scenes could be shot on the river or its banks.[71] Be that as it may, Spiegel emphasized that the word from Cohn was that Lean was to wrap up principal photography as soon as possible so that the cast and crew, and the CinemaScope equipment, could be shipped back to London.

Holden's time on the movie was running out, so Columbia's front office in Hollywood decreed that Lean must complete his scenes posthaste. The studio was not prepared to pay the star overtime for staying on to work after his contract had expired. "I finished with Holden by means of a hectic rush," Lean wrote Spiegel on April 14, 1957. "I hope this does something to mitigate my 'criminal expenditures' [of Columbia's funds]. . . . I am an exhausted wreck, and I am so longing to . . . rest after this marathon."[72]

But the marathon was not yet over. Though Spiegel was having the CinemaScope cameras sent back to London to discourage further shooting, Lean negotiated with Spiegel to allow him to stay behind for a couple of weeks with an Arriflex camera and a skeleton camera crew. His purpose was to film some establishing shots of panoramic vistas, in order to give the movie more scope. History was repeating itself: as with *Summertime*, Lean was finishing a major motion picture with his trusty Arriflex, using available light. Peter Newbrook stayed on as his cameraman, as he had done on *Summertime*.

Among the images captured by Lean with his Arriflex were those book-ending the film. The picture begins with "a shot of a hawk soaring above the jungle": "This archetypal image of a free spirit . . . provides an immediate contrast with the prisoner-of-war camp [seen] below."[73] Lean matched that shot with a similar shot of a hawk at the final fade-out.

When planning the final fade-out, Lean asked Newbrook, "How can we show the devastation at the end from the bird's point of view?" Newbrook suggested a helicopter shot, so Lean borrowed a helicopter from the Royal Ceylonese Air Force. Newbrook explains, "I did a long shot as the helicopter pulled up and away from the ruined bridge, with Clipton, the camp medico, standing on the bank surveying the devastation." In this aerial shot, a double had to stand in for James Donald, who had already been packed off to London. "The final image of a hawk circling in the peaceful sky, which follows the helicopter shot, takes us back to the beginning, to the world of nature." The encroaching, primordial jungle implicitly reasserts itself and dwarfs all human endeavors.[74]

Since Lean was now living on the Continent, the picture was cut in Paris, with Lean again working closely with the editor Peter Taylor, as he had on *Summertime*. Lean was concerned that the film would be overlength, so he took to trimming some of the scenes in the rough cut. He pointed out that Lean the editor would cut scenes that Lean the director had very much liked: "This may be partly due to the fact that I was an editor for many years and am generally more ruthless [when it comes to shortening scenes] than the producer."[75]

In this particular instance, Lean was more ruthless than even Spiegel. "I had quarrels with David in the cutting room because he wanted to cut too much," said Spiegel.[76] Lean ultimately came in with a cut that ran 161 minutes. When it was shown to Columbia executives in Hollywood, Harry Cohn complained that the picture was still too long. "Spiegel fought for every inch of the film to be kept in the final cut of two hours and forty-one minutes that he had approved," the Columbia executive Leo Jaffe said. "When he thought he was right, nothing could shake him"—not even Harry Cohn.[77] Spiegel was convinced that the epic quality of the movie would sustain its length.

Lean finished his final edit in mid-August 1957 in Paris. He would, of course, be unable to attend the dubbing sessions at which the sound track was to be recorded since they were to take place back in England at Shepperton Studios, but he had great faith in Winston Ryder, the sound editor supervising the sound track. He made voluminous notes for Ryder, indicating even every buzzing insect and creaking tree branch. Malcolm

Arnold had only three weeks to compose his final score before it was scheduled to be recorded by the Royal Philharmonic. He insisted that "The Colonel Bogey March" be played by an army brass band, to make it sound like an authentic military march. The final mix of the sound track was completed in time for Spiegel to deliver the finished film to Columbia by the end of September.

"The Colonel Bogey March" figures in the movie's first major sequence. A new batch of prisoners, led by Colonel Nicholson, arrives at Colonel Saito's Camp 16. They stride briskly into the compound, whistling "The Colonel Bogey March" with a bravado that belies their wretched condition. Lean cuts to their muddy shoes, "barely holding together, soles flapping and without laces."[78] Their battered footwear contrasts sharply with the shining boots of Colonel Saito, seen as he looks down on his new charges from the porch of his quarters. This shot further implies that the grimy, sweaty prisoners are beneath Saito in every sense of the word.

Saito jumps onto a soapbox and addresses the new "recruits" as they stand at attention on the parade ground. He informs them that escape is impossible since the camp is "an island in the jungle." The intrepid Shears gives Saito's boast the lie by soon making good his escape from the camp. In what Becker terms "an obligatory adventure scene," typical of Hollywood spectacles, Shears eludes the prison guards, jumps into the river, and is washed downstream.[79] He crawls through the steaming jungle, is finally rescued by some friendly villagers, and eventually makes it to a British training post in Ceylon. Saito assumes that Shears has drowned.

Meanwhile, back at the camp, Saito insists that all Nicholson's men—officers included—contribute to the building of a bridge to accommodate the Thailand-Burma Railway. Nicholson absolutely refuses to permit his officers to do hard labor, which is contrary to the Geneva Conventions' code of conduct. Saito threatens to order the prisoners in the camp hospital to work on the bridge if Nicholson will not allow his officers to do so. Visibly unperturbed, Nicholson hands his copy of the code to Saito, who furiously slaps him across the face with it and throws it to the ground. Nicholson solemnly picks it up and dusts it off, implying that the code is still very much in force.

Guinness writes in his autobiography that, at the moment Hayakawa smacked him—"which he did very lightly"—"I crushed a capsule of what looked like blood that I held in my mouth." The Japanese military adviser assigned to the film was dismayed because he assumed that Hayakawa had actually "drawn blood." He reported the incident to the Japanese ambassador in Colombo, who "wrongly hauled Sessue Hayakawa over the coals" and required that he make a public apology to Guinness.[80]

As the film unspools, Nicholson and Saito are both intransigent. "I'm fascinated by these nuts," Lean commented; "Nicholson was certainly a nut," and so was Saito.[81] Both wind up confiding in Clipton. Saito says, "He is mad, your colonel; quite mad!" Shortly afterward, Nicholson says to Clipton, "Actually, I think the colonel is mad." Clipton mutters to himself, "Are they both mad? Or am I going mad?"

Lean stresses in the film, more than Boulle does in the novel, that "Saito in many ways is the counterpart of Nicholson." Saito is not a savage but an alumnus of a London university. Like Nicholson, he is "a man molded by a military tradition, guided by an inflexible code."[82] His sense of duty is that of a samurai serving his emperor. "You speak of a code," he snaps at Nicholson. "Yours is the coward's code. What do you know of *bushido*, the soldier's code?" Nicholson has been trained "to go by the book," and the book for him is the code of conduct, by which he serves his king. "Without law," he answers Saito, referring to the code, "there is no civilization."

The enlisted men are put to work, but Nicholson himself is prepared to endure torture, rather than endorse a breach of the Geneva Conventions. As he confides to Clipton, "If we give in on this, there'll be no end to the concessions we will be expected to make." He is, accordingly, isolated in a suffocating, cage-like tin sweatbox, under the relentless tropical sun. "His attempt to maintain a proper gait when he is summoned from his torture chamber to see Saito is a devastating sight."[83]

In a BBC-TV interview, Guinness recalled filming that scene: "My son had polio at the age of twelve; when he was recovering, he had a stiff, strange walk. When I was filming that scene of Nicholson emerging from the sweat box, I found myself doing the identical walk that I had seen my son doing some six years previously—a curious, slightly lurching, bent walk."[84]

Saito has summoned Nicholson to inform him that he has declared "a general amnesty" on the occasion of a Japanese national holiday: Nicholson's officers will not be forced to do hard labor. Actually, Saito has faced the fact that, if Nicholson and his officers supervise their own men, the bridge can be completed on time. He correctly reasons that, whereas the British enlisted men have resisted obeying Japanese officers, they will willingly obey their own officers. So Saito has, in effect, caved in, and Nicholson has won the day.

When Nicholson stands erect and marches as best he can out of Saito's office onto the parade ground, his men intuit that he has won a moral victory. They carry him aloft on their shoulders, cheering deliriously, and a triumphant rendition of "Colonel Bogey," all snappy snare drums, blaring trombones, and chattering clarinets, plays in the background.

With that, Nicholson takes charge of the building operations; he is totally committed to finishing the bridge on schedule even though the chances of that happening are slim. Nicholson thus embodies the recurring theme of Lean's films, in that he is one of those Lean characters who refuse to accept the possibility of failure, even when it stares them in the face. He becomes increasingly obsessed with making the bridge a tribute to British know-how and resourcefulness that will put the Japanese to shame. He discovers that the bridge is being built with elm trees, like those used in the erection of London Bridge, which lasted for six hundred years. "Six hundred years," muses Nicholson, who surely has delusions of grandeur; "that would be something." He has patently lost sight of the bridge's strategic importance to the Japanese war effort.

The positions of Saito and Nicholson are now reversed. Saito becomes passive and defers to Nicholson, while Nicholson becomes the personification of the fascist leader that Saito was earlier. In order to finish the bridge on time, Nicholson does an about-face, asking all his officers to "volunteer" to "pitch in."

Nicholson even solicits Clipton to let some of the wounded in the camp hospital help out—something Saito had threatened to do. He explains that they will be asked "to do some light duties, to fetch and carry," and that "they'll get some fresh air." Clipton balks, reminding him that he is implicitly collaborating with the enemy by constructing a first-class bridge for them. Nicholson responds testily, "If you had to operate on Colonel Saito, would you do your best, or let him die?" Nicholson, acting according to his lights, firmly believes that his men are demonstrating "what British soldiers can accomplish, even in captivity."

This interchange is reminiscent of the opening paragraph of the book. "The conduct of each of the two enemies was superficially dissimilar," Boulle writes. "Perhaps the mentality of the Japanese colonel, Saito, was essentially the same as that of his prisoner, Col. Nicholson."[85] Both men, in the last analysis, were martinets who manipulated their subordinates for their own purposes.

Meanwhile, at the British commando training post in Ceylon, Major Warden has been put in command of a strike force charged with destroying the bridge. He pressures Shears, who has been recuperating from his jungle ordeal in the base hospital, into joining his demolition team since he is familiar with the terrain around the prison camp and with the bridge, which was already under construction before he took off. "Since I'm hooked," Shears quips to Warden, "I might as well volunteer."

Commando Force 316 sets off on its mission with Warden in the lead, along with Shears, Joyce, and some other commandos, plus some female native bearers. After several days of hacking their way through the wilderness, the saboteurs reach their objective on the eve of the very day the first Japanese troop train is scheduled to cross the bridge. The commandos spend the night setting their charges, which are positioned under water so that they will not be detected by the enemy.

The following morning, however, the demolition squad is chagrined to see that the waters of the river have receded, to the point that the explosive wires leading to the charges are quite visible. Nicholson admires the plaque he has posted on the bridge: "This bridge was designed and constructed by soldiers of the British army." As he surveys the bridge from his hidden command post, Warden is alarmed to see Nicholson spy the wires.

Nicholson, with Saito at his heels, scrambles down the bank to the river, where he spots the telltale cable leading to the detonator and alerts Saito. Warden cannot believe his eyes: "Nicholson has gone!" Warden blurts out. "He's leading Saito right to it—one of our own men!" Shears likewise picks up on Nicholson's complicity with the Japanese, but Joyce does not.

Joyce, observing the proceedings from his hidden vantage point, fears that the mission will be jeopardized if the detonator is discovered, so he races from his cover with a knife, grabs Saito, and slits his throat. Nicholson pounces on him in a frenzy, and Joyce shouts, "You don't understand! We're British commandos, here to blow up the bridge!" Nicholson is not prepared to have his achievement annihilated and struggles fiercely with Joyce, to keep him from reaching the detonator. Shears hollers ferociously at Joyce, "Kill him!" But the uncomprehending Joyce cannot bring himself to slash the throat of a British officer, and he is himself struck down by a Japanese sniper. So it is up to Shears to kill Nicholson.

Lean recalled in a television interview: "I had told Bill Holden to jump into the water at that point and swim over to Alec Guinness. I knew what he was going to do; but when he plunged into the river and swam over to Alec, I jumped out of my chair beside the camera. Such was the force of Bill's concentration when he did that scene, that it made me jump—that's real star stuff."[86]

When Shears confronts Nicholson on the riverbank, Nicholson gasps, "You!" Like Saito, Nicholson had assumed that Shears had perished. In a blind frenzy, Nicholson is dead set on preventing Shears from reaching the detonator and demolishing his beloved bridge. Both men are hit by a mortar shell fired by Warden from his command post on the opposite shore. Shears is killed instantly. Nicholson is fatally wounded, but, still conscious, he mumbles, "What have I done?" Then he stumbles forward and collapses on top of the detonator just as the train crosses the bridge. The bridge is totally destroyed, and the train plunges into the ravine. Nicholson and his bridge are annihilated together.

According to Peter Newbrook's eyewitness account, "In the script it was never really decided whether Nicholson fell on the detonator on purpose, in a moment of repentance, or whether he fell on it accidentally." Newbrook explains that, even after a prolonged discussion on the day of shooting, Lean and Guinness could not resolve the matter. Finally, Lean told Guinness, "You are stunned by the mortar blast that's just gone off; spin around and fall on the detonator. The motivation can remain enigmatic."

Commentators on the film are divided on this issue. On the one hand, Silver and Ursini contend that Nicholson would never willingly blow up his bridge; he just happens to fall on the charging handle and sets it off accidentally, "thereby taking the issue out of his hands."[87] On the other hand, Michael Sragow affirms that Nicholson sees the error of his ways. "He even asks himself, 'What have I done?' before he moves toward the plunger that will detonate the explosives under the bridge."[88]

Lean subsequently regretted not delineating Nicholson's motivation more precisely. "The film's ending was too ambiguous," he declared. In retrospect, he was inclined to think that Nicholson realizes his mistake and is attempting to blow up the bridge when he himself is killed. Lean said that Nicholson is thinking in effect: "There's the plunger; I'm going for it." But, adds Lean, "He gets hit, and without him knowing it, he does succeed. His dead body does it."[89] Moreover, Guinness came round and ultimately agreed with Lean on this point.

Warden's native bearers recoil in disgust at the role he played in killing Shears, his own comrade, as well as Nicholson, whom they assume was likewise Warden's ally. "I had to do it," he exclaims in anguish. "They might have been captured *alive!*" His implication is that they would have been tortured and forced to give up military secrets. This chilling moment is not in the novel and is one of the things in the movie that Boulle told Newbrook he wished he had thought of.

"Madness! Madness!" shouts Clipton as he sees Nicholson's commemorative plaque floating away with the rest of the debris. The camera pulls back for a wide shot as Clipton, picking his way through the wreckage along the beach, observes the high body count. Clipton, who all along suspected that both Nicholson and Saito were insane, is referring not just to the madness of war but to fanatics with distorted values.

But perhaps Nicholson was not entirely deranged in his unswerving determination to erect the bridge. As Sam Spiegel put it, "Man came into this world to build, and not to destroy. Yet he's thrown into the necessity of destroying, and his one everlasting instinct is to try to save himself from having to destroy."[90] Spiegel's statement is totally consistent with Lean's approach to the film, throughout which Nicholson is presented as a character who deserves our compassion, even though he is eccentric to the point of neurosis.

The strains of "The Colonel Bogey March" are heard one last time. The music—accompanied by the soldiers' earlier triumphant cheers occasioned by Nicholson's release from the punishment hut—is in sharp contrast to the spare strains of most of Arnold's score and leads to the grandiose musical finale.

The Bridge on the River Kwai premiered in New York City on December 18, 1957, and became an instant critical and popular success. In some ways, it is odd that the movie became such an international blockbuster. While it is on the surface "a celebration of courage, daring, and recklessness," it is underneath a movie "founded in uncertainty, melancholy, and the hard presence of unshakable fate."[91] It both challenges and entertains an audience—and at a variety of levels. Indeed, what helps set this film apart from other historical epics are the bravura visuals—the skillful camerawork, the evocative lighting, and the elaborate sets. These show a director fully exploring the potential of his medium.

In short, *The Bridge on the River Kwai* is a majestic work that boasts rich performances, a haunting musical score, and no end of directorial flair. It tells the story of men who possess a perverse need to cling to a show of honor; what remains preeminent is the immensity of the drama. Thus, the army doctor surveying the corpses littering the shore in the final scene represents an accomplished piece of broad-stroke storytelling, the entire narrative boiled down to a few telling shots.

Kwai had cost $2,800,000 and chalked up a worldwide gross of over $22,000,000. Brewer calls the picture "the first British film to be the top moneymaker in the U.S."[92]—thus perpetuating the myth that, because many of the cast and crew were English, the movie was a British production. Yet *Kwai* was produced by an American producer under the aegis of an independent Hollywood production unit, and it was financed and distributed by a major Hollywood studio. The inescapable reality is that an ambitious production like *Kwai*, and the Lean spectacles to follow it, simply could not have been financed by the all-but-moribund British film industry. After all, by 1957, both the Rank organization and Korda's London Films had ceased to be mainstays of the English movie industry.

Columbia's studio chief, Harry Cohn, who had attempted to abort the production of *Kwai,* suffered a fatal heart attack shortly after the film's triumphant premiere. He did not live to see it win seven Academy Awards the following March.

In fact, *The Bridge on the River Kwai* represents the climax of Lean and Guinness's professional association. Both Lean and Guinness received Academy Awards for their work on it, as did the director of photography, Jack Hildyard, the editor, Peter Taylor, and the composer, Malcolm Arnold (Lawrence Quirk baldly asserts that "the striking cinematography was by Malcolm Arnold"),[93] and the film itself was voted best picture. "The Colonel Bogey March," in Mitch Miller's jazzed-up version, rose to the top of the hit parade. This presaged the day when films would frequently feature marketable theme songs.

The film also won the Oscar for best screenplay. But that award was surrounded by controversy since it went to Pierre Boulle, who spoke not a single word of English! (As a silent protest, Michael Wilson sardonically placed a black hood over the head of his Oscar for *A Place in the Sun.*) Insiders in the industry knew that Carl Foreman invariably named two minor characters in his screenplays Grogan and Baker, after his agents, John Grogan and Herbie Baker. There are, in fact, two British soldiers in *Kwai* named Grogan and Baker. When a couple of journalists, including the Hollywood gossip columnist Hedda Hopper, noticed this, they inquired whether the blacklisted Foreman had coscripted the movie. Actually, *two* blacklisted writers, Foreman and Wilson, were involved, as we know.

Spiegel said that he had phoned Boulle during postproduction and asked him to accept the script credit because the screenplay "was taken directly from his contribution—the book." That is, the story line and the characters came from his novel.[94] What the crafty Spiegel did not mention was that he could not list the real authors. Lean wrote Michael Wilson on January 30, 1958, that, in giving interviews at the time he won the Screen Directors Guild Award for the movie, he had maintained the deception because "Sam was worried that your wicked name might get out of the bag and 'ruin our chances, baby.' . . . I lied like a trooper and . . . made up a story [about collaborating with Boulle in Paris]." Spiegel, Lean continued, explained to the press that Lean did not want a cowriter's credit because "directors take it as part of their job" to work on screenplays.[95]

That Lean did not want a script credit on his movies was manifestly not true. To begin with, he had already received no fewer than five screen credits—for coscripting *Brief Encounter, Great Expectations, Oliver Twist, Hobson's Choice,* and *Summertime.* In addition, he stressed in a letter to Mike Frankovich at Columbia Pictures that the screenplay was written by "Michael Wilson and myself." He continued: "I am certainly responsible for the anti-war angle and the general tone and style." In addition, some of the dialogue was his. He had also "thought of the big camp scenes," such as the one in which the soldiers whistle defiantly as they enter the prison camp and the one in which Nicholson is being released from solitary confinement "and is being greeted by all the men racing across the parade ground." Lean thought the latter the "best thing" he had done.[96]

Lean declared that he had totally scuttled Foreman's draft. The screenwriter-director Bryan Forbes told me in correspondence that Lean told him that Foreman was going around saying that his draft was the basis of Wilson's script. Lean threatened, "If he persists any more, I'll show people the script he wrote!" That was a bluff on Lean's part since he had not saved a copy of Foreman's draft. Wilson affirmed that Foreman's work had not been scuttled, "although I did alter it considerably and introduce new elements."[97]

Forbes told me: "I was asked to be one of the arbitrators by the British Writers Guild to try and establish the true final authorship of *The Bridge on the River Kwai.* I came to the conclusion, after having read and studied half a dozen drafts of the script, that Wilson should be accorded credit for sure." He also concluded that Foreman's contribution to the final shooting script was minor by comparison. Asked if he thought Lean should have been accorded a script credit, Forbes replied, "David always contributed a great deal himself to any script that he directed." But, once again, Forbes believed that Wilson was the principal author of the *Kwai* screenplay.

Lean was miffed, not only because of the Boulle script credit for the film, which he deemed "a farce," but also because the publicity layouts all proclaimed, "A SAM SPIEGEL PRODUCTION."[98] Lean contended that he and Spiegel had an agreement, whereby the film would be called "A SAM SPIEGEL–DAVID LEAN PRODUCTION" and that they had shaken hands on it. As Fred Zinnemann commented to me about this incident, "The day when a handshake meant anything in the picture business was gone forever." Zinnemann then quoted another producer, Sam Goldwyn, who had once quipped, "Verbal contracts aren't worth the paper they're written on." On their next production together, Lean would demand a clear contractual statement that the film would be billed as a Sam Spiegel–David Lean production.

As we have seen, *The Bridge on the River Kwai* swept the Oscars. Among the *Kwai* nominees, Guinness was a no-show at the March 26, 1958, ceremony because he did not think he had any chance of winning. (He learned of his win over the radio and subsequently picked up his Academy Award at a luncheon in the Savoy Hotel in London.) Boulle was a no-show as well.

After the ceremonies, a radio reporter asked Lean point-blank who really wrote the screenplay. Lean waffled and finally said, "I'm not prepared to tell you." He had wanted the script credit—and the Oscar—to go to Wilson and himself, and he refused to acknowledge Boulle. Spiegel, who had accepted the award for best picture, overheard Lean's response. "Sam went berserk," Lean recalled. "I remember standing outside the theater after the Oscar ceremony, with Sam holding his Oscar for best picture and shaking it at me in fury; and I shouting back at him, brandishing mine. It was a ridiculous scene."[99]

Boulle told his biographer that, when he learned too late that he was given the Oscar for the screenplay because Foreman and Wilson were blacklisted, he was appalled. As Becker noted, "Had he known the real reasons, he would never have permitted his name to be used." Boulle subsequently added, "I have never claimed to have written the script. In fact, I did not care a damn about the script!"[100]

Finally, in 1985, the Academy of Motion Picture Arts and Sciences got around to honoring Wilson and Foreman with posthumous Academy Awards for *Kwai*. Lean had always wanted Wilson's name in the film's credits, writes Sandra Lean, "And before he died he insisted that this happen." In 1994, when the movie was released in wide-screen (letterbox) format on videocassette, Sandra Lean made certain "that the name of Michael Wilson," along with that of Carl Foreman, "appeared for screenwriting."[101] Similarly, their names appear in the credits of the subsequent DVD version of the film (released in 2000).

The Bridge on the River Kwai has continued to be a popular movie over the years. When, on September 23, 1966, it was first broadcast on network television in the United States, it was watched by 60 million viewers. A fully restored version was released on DVD in 2000, digitally remastered, both the images and the sound meticulously repaired.

The recognition accorded the film has also continued. *Premiere* magazine conducted a nationwide poll in 2003 to determine the best action movies of all time. *Kwai*'s citation declared, "David Lean's meditation on the futility of war is also an amazing adventure tale."[102] A 2004 nationwide *Premiere* poll lists *Kwai* as one of the most influential films of all time because it demonstrates that a wide-screen spectacle can be both an entertaining movie and a serious work of art: "It is the tip of the pyramid."[103]

Thailand is still associated with the picture. Vannthret Dhihntravan, a native of Thailand, told me in conversation that "tours are regularly organized from Bangkok to visit 'the Bridge on the River Kwai.'" She gave me a travel brochure from Thailand Tours that indicates: "Each year thousands of tourists visit the historic spot where the actual bridge over the River Kwai was built by British prisoners of war. The site of the bridge is a two-hour drive from Bangkok."[104] Moreover, she adds, "There is an annual memorial ceremony held on the bridge to commemorate those who died while building the bridge and the railway from Burma to Siam for the Japanese." Interestingly enough, the real bridge and Lean's bridge are identical, having been built from the same set of plans.

Furthermore, in a 2003 interview, the filmmaker Steven Spielberg paid tribute to Lean by acknowledging that he filmed part of *Indiana Jones and the Temple of Doom* (1984) in Sri Lanka near where Lean shot *Kwai,* as a private homage to Lean. "I wanted to walk in David's footsteps," Spielberg said. "If I work very hard, I can put one-tenth of a David Lean image on the screen."[105]

After *Kwai* was released, Lean was hailed as a director who could fashion every aspect of an epic movie with great care and competence. To put it another way, Lean was a thoroughgoing auteur. He received numerous offers to direct another historical spectacle. Spiegel, for example, suggested T. E. Lawrence as a subject. In fact, Lean had for some time been intrigued by the legendary Lawrence, the English officer who participated in the revolt of the Arabs against the Turks during World War I. While on a visit to London, he met with Spiegel, and they agreed on the Lawrence project. They accordingly raided a bookshop in downtown London and acquired every book about Lawrence in sight. Lean said jokingly, "*Kwai* was about a stupid nut, while *Lawrence of Arabia* was about a brilliant nut; and that is why I was drawn to do a film about Lawrence next."[106]

Alec Guinness, who quite by accident happened to be in the bookstore at the same time as Lean and Spiegel, told me that he later asked Spiegel why, in the wake of their quarrels on *Kwai,* he was willing to work with Lean again. Spiegel had an answer ready: "The devil I know is better than the devils I don't know."[107]

Chapter Twelve

PILLAR OF FIRE

PLANNING *LAWRENCE OF ARABIA*

Wisdom has built herself a house; she has erected her seven pillars. . . . She has proclaimed from the city heights, "Who is ignorant? Let him step this way."
—Prov. 9:1–4

God led the people by night in the form of a pillar of fire . . . to light the way ahead of them through the desert.
—Exod. 13:21–22

The first indication that David Lean was interested in making a picture about T. E. Lawrence surfaced in 1952. After seeing *Oliver Twist,* Harry Cohn, the head of Columbia Pictures, was impressed with the way in which Lean had been able to make a quality period picture on a relatively modest budget. Cohn accordingly wrote Lean, inquiring whether he would make a film about Lawrence for Columbia.

Lean had been intrigued by the legend of Lawrence for years. "During the First World War," the historian John Kifner writes, "Lawrence had been present at the birth of modern Arab nationalism and fought alongside the guerrillas to victory against the Ottoman Empire of the Turks."[1] Little wonder that to Lean he seemed the perfect subject for a historical picture. In fact, he had been a hero of Lean's from his school days. "He was to young English boys the last word in exotic heroes," Lean recalled. "We saw pictures of him in that exotic head gear. But then Lawrence is an enigma, and I've always been fond of enigmas. I like the 'flawed heroes.' Perfect heroes are dull."[2]

Lean replied to Cohn on May 2, 1952: "This is to tell you how excited

I am by the Lawrence of Arabia idea. . . . I can't think of a better subject for my first picture for America."[3] It is significant to note that, from the get-go, Lean thought of the Lawrence project as an American production since, despite the fact that the production company and the distributing company were both American, the trade press insisted on dubbing it a British production. As with the confusion over *The Bridge on the River Kwai,* this was because Lean was British, as were a number of the cast members.

At any rate, Columbia contacted Professor Arnold Walter Lawrence of Cambridge University, T. E. Lawrence's surviving brother and the executor of his estate, to purchase the screen rights to *Seven Pillars of Wisdom,* Lawrence's memoirs about the Arab Revolt. But A. W. Lawrence mistrusted Hollywood and feared that the resulting film would be an empty sword-and-sandal spectacle. So he refused unless he was granted script approval. Cohn, a strong-willed movie mogul, was not prepared to make such a substantial concession, and the project was aborted. Lean then went on to make *Summertime* for Alexander Korda.

Lean may have placed the Lawrence project on a back burner, but he never gave up hope of reviving it. After finishing *Kwai,* he became even more intrigued with Lawrence's character, seeing a continuity between *Kwai*'s Colonel Nicholson and Colonel Lawrence. Both are Englishmen placed by fate in a foreign locality and made to face enormous challenges to accomplish a mission. This was a fascinating situation that Lean wanted to explore again and in greater depth.

Thomas Edward Lawrence was born on August 16, 1888, Napoléon's birthday, in Tremadoc, Caernarvonshire, North Wales. His father, Thomas Chapman, had earlier deserted his wife and four daughters; when his estranged wife refused to divorce him, he established a new home with his daughters' former governess, Sarah Junner. (Recall that Lean's own father likewise left his family for another woman; see chapter 1). Chapman's wife and daughters continued to live in the Chapman house on the outskirts of Dublin.

Chapman kicked over the traces by adopting an assumed name, Lawrence, and moving to England, where he proceeded to sire five illegitimate sons; eventually, in the summer of 1896, the Lawrence family settled in Oxford. When Thomas Edward "Ned" Lawrence was ten years old, he discovered quite by chance that he was illegitimate. So distraught was he at this revelation that he vowed to rise above the stigma and prove himself superior to his peers. He became an outstanding student at Oxford City High School for Boys, for example. Nevertheless, he cut an unprepossessing figure as a slightly built, pale young man with a schoolgirl giggle.

Ned Lawrence went on to Jesus College, Oxford, where he developed an interest in medieval history and the Crusades and a fascination with the Middle East. Characteristically, he would later view his participation in the Arab Revolt as a crusade. In 1909, he graduated from Oxford with an honors degree in history. That same year, at age twenty, he went on a walking tour of Syria, in order to study medieval history on his own. He lived among the Arabs and learned colloquial Arabic.

Lawrence returned to Syria from 1911 to 1913 as a member of an archaeological expedition, doing excavations along the Euphrates River. He immersed himself in Arab culture and social mores and learned several Arabic dialects. The British historian Stephen Foster told me in conversation that, during this period, Lawrence acted as a covert British espionage agent, helping with a secret military survey of the region. There were already rumblings of war, and he was put to spying on the Turks, who would, British intelligence suspected, cast their lot with Germany when the time came.

At the outbreak of World War I in 1914, the Turkish caliph, who presided over the faltering Ottoman Empire from its capital in Damascus, did, in fact, side with Germany. Sharif Hussein, the emir of Mecca, formed an alliance between Arabia and Britain. Lawrence enlisted in the British army. At just over five foot five, he was below standard height for active duty. Nevertheless, his knowledge and experience of the Middle East qualified him for British intelligence, and in December 1914 he was posted to the Arab Bureau, the Military Intelligence office in Cairo. He was assigned by his superior officer, General Edmund Allenby, the commander in chief of British forces in the Middle East, to the Geographical Section, to make maps of strategic areas.

The Ottoman Empire still ruled most of the Middle East. Turkish brutality to the Arabs incited Sharif Hussein to instigate in June 1916 an Arab uprising against the Ottoman Turks, an endeavor that received the aid of the British. Lawrence then volunteered to help the Arab Bureau solidify a closer liaison between the British and the Arabs against their common enemy, the pro-German Turks. It was at this time that the British government promised to endorse Arab independence if the Arabs assisted Britain in winning the war.

In October 1916, Lawrence formed an association with Prince Feisal, Sharif Hussein's son, who was to be the heart and soul of the revolt. Lawrence also became a moving spirit in the revolt, assisting Feisal in fostering the insurrection. In June 1917, Lawrence was appointed British liaison officer to Feisal and soon became his chief adviser and close friend.

Lawrence, who had lived among the Arabs during his prewar stints in

Arabia, now affected Arab dress and mingled freely with Bedouin tribesmen. He saw himself as the bridge between Arabia and the British Empire, and, hence, he sometimes wore a British uniform with an Arab headdress. (This is how Lean remembered seeing Lawrence's picture when he was a boy.) He became expert during the Arab Revolt in blowing up Turkish trains. The Bedouin therefore nicknamed him "Emir Dynamite"; they also called him "El Aurens," their pronunciation of his surname. He also became known as "the uncrowned king of Arabia" and "an Arabian knight." He styled himself as a modern-day Crusader, championing the Arab cause in the name of his high-minded ideals.[4]

Lawrence became allied with Auda Abu Tayi, the courageous, ruthless chief of the Howeitat tribe. Together they led Auda Abu Tayi's guerrillas, a band of cutthroats, in successful raids on Turkish strongholds. They ultimately crossed the desert to seize the vital Turkish port of Aqaba on the Red Sea for Feisal on July 6, 1917, with barely a shot being fired. Lawrence's crown of glory was somewhat tarnished, however, when, "at the end of November 1917, during a spying mission in Deraa," a crucial Turkish outpost, he was temporarily captured by the enemy: "He was tortured by order of the Turkish bey [provincial governor], then sexually assaulted."[5] This was a traumatic experience for Lawrence, one that would provide the most controversial sequence in Lean's film.

Later on, Lawrence, in concert with Allenby, endeavored to coax Feisal to join forces with the British in advancing on Damascus. Huda Krad, a native of Syria, told me in conversation that Lawrence pointed out to Feisal that they had already occupied Aqaba, which was the gateway to Damascus. Lawrence assured Feisal that, once the Arabs marched into Damascus, they could effectively negotiate with the British to grant the Arabs independence and self-rule, Krad concluded. Feisal acquiesced. By now "Emir Dynamite" had a price on his head, yet he personally led Feisal's camel corps as they marched triumphantly into Damascus on September 30, 1918, having brought off a coup d'état.

The British promised to set Feisal up in Damascus as king of Syria after the war, and Feisal arrived at the Paris Peace Conference in the spring of 1919 as the chief Arab spokesman. Lawrence served as his adviser and interpreter during the conference, which would hammer out the Treaty of Versailles.

The British did not, however, keep their pledge to Feisal. During the conference, "Britain and France had secretly agreed to divide up the Middle East." Thus, "Feisal's reign lasted only a few months"—until the French drove him into exile.[6] Even before he left Arabia during the war, Lawrence was painfully aware of the backroom deals being struck regarding postwar territorial claims in the Middle East—the result of oil having been discovered in Arabia. And Lean does imply this in his film.

As a matter of fact, during the peace conference, Lawrence was advised privately by the British delegation that, fight as he might against French plans to annex Feisal's domain, he would not prevail. But Lawrence never told Feisal this. Lawrence was committed to both Britain and Arabia, but he was first and foremost a British officer. The fact remains, however, that, "when Britain and France redrew the map of the Middle East to suit their own needs," Lawrence's belief that he had betrayed his Arab friends and his ideals was reinforced.[7] Hence, he was deeply depressed by his failure to help establish Arabia as a sovereign state with Feisal as its permanent ruler. He felt that the mantle of fraud had descended on his shoulders because he had been privy to Britain's double-dealing with the Arabs.

Lawrence "promised freedom to the Arabs, knowing that it was a promise that would not be honored, and one which was not, anyway, in his gift."[8] Therefore, when he returned to England after the peace conference, he tossed the Victoria Cross and all the other medals he had been awarded into the Thames in disgust. Even before the Paris Peace Conference, Lawrence could not shake the nagging suspicion that he had been hugely presumptuous to think that he could "lead a national uprising of another race." Now he thought, "Men bust themselves trying to be bigger than they are."[9]

As a result, Lawrence was not inclined to boast about his adventures in the Middle East when he returned to England. But the American war correspondent Lowell Thomas had other ideas. Thomas had been commissioned by the U.S. government to put together a lecture, illustrated with footage shot by his cinematographer, Harry Chase, in the war zones, "to help in the work of stimulating enthusiasm for the Allied cause."[10] He was eventually drawn to the Middle East and the desert campaign, which—much to his surprise—was being spearheaded by an English officer, one T. E. Lawrence. Thomas soon discovered that the segment of his illustrated lecture that was entitled "With Lawrence in Arabia" was the highlight of his media spectacular.[11]

It is significant that Lawrence was first introduced to the world at large via the medium of film. Lawrence's exploits in the Middle East had not been generally known until Thomas unveiled his travelogue—first in America, then in England—in 1919. One night, during the run of Thomas's show in London, Lawrence, incognito, slipped into the back row at the Royal Albert Hall and saw the show.

Lawrence had a private powwow with Thomas afterward, in which he upbraided Thomas for turning him into "a kind of matinee idol" and making him appear to be a "self-advertising mountebank." Lawrence was convinced that Thomas had exaggerated his contribution to the Arab cause, noting that journalists preferred to accept the marvelous rather than the true. It seems that Lawrence thought of celebrity as something that was happening to him, rather than who he was. Thomas, somewhat miffed by Lawrence's failure to appreciate the fame he had brought him, later commented sardonically that Lawrence "had a genius for backing into the limelight."[12]

Undaunted by Lawrence's admonition, Thomas would expand his lecture into the first biography of Lawrence ever published, utilizing the same title as the lecture, *With Lawrence in Arabia*. His book was subsequently used by the screenwriter Michael Wilson in preparing a preliminary prose treatment for the screenplay of Lean's film.

For his part, Lawrence was himself working on a book about his role in the Arab Revolt. As a matter of fact, he was temporarily staying in London at the time he saw Thomas's show, in the attic apartment of a friend's home near Westminster Abbey, laboring over the first draft of his manuscript. He had actually begun the book, entitled *Seven Pillars of Wisdom*, during his free time at the Paris Peace Conference. He had recently been named a research fellow of All Souls College, Oxford, for the purpose of pursuing his project. *Seven Pillars* would become the principal source of the screenplay of *Lawrence of Arabia*; indeed, the working title of the film script was *Seven Pillars of Wisdom*.

Seven Pillars of Wisdom

Lawrence took the title of *Seven Pillars of Wisdom* from Prov. 9:1–4 (see the first of this chapter's epigraphs). In another biblical reference, he called dust devils (swirling clouds of sand stirred up by the desert winds) "pillars of fire," referring to the pillar of fire of Exod. 13:21–22 (see the second of this chapter's epigraphs) by which God led Moses and the Israelites through the desert at night. He implied that God was leading him and his Arab band in their crusade in the desert.

Lawrence studiously applied himself to the task of writing his memoirs, mostly at Oxford. In December 1919, he suffered a major setback when he lost the nearly completed manuscript while changing trains at Reading, on the way back to Oxford from London for Christmas. He had inadvertently left the satchel containing the manuscript under a table in the refreshment room at Reading station while boarding the Oxford train. "I've lost the damned thing!" he wrote George Bernard Shaw, who insisted that he rewrite the whole manuscript.[13]

Wendy Hiller as Eliza Doolittle is subjected to a long-overdue bath in *Pygmalion*. Lean edited the film. (Larry Edmunds Bookshop.)

Professor Higgins (Leslie Howard) monitoring the speech exercises of Eliza (Wendy Hiller) in *Pygmalion*. Lean directed the montage sequences in the film that show Higgins transforming Eliza into a lady, but only Anthony Asquith and Leslie Howard were listed as codirectors of the film. (Larry Edmunds Bookshop.)

Rex Harrison as Adolphus Cusins, a Salvation Army recruit in *Major Barbara*. Lean edited the film. He also codirected it with Gabriel Pascal, but only Pascal was listed as director. (Larry Edmunds Bookshop.)

Noël Coward as Captain Kinross (center) clings to a raft in an oil-grimed sea after his ship has been sunk by the enemy in *In Which We Serve*. Lean was officially credited as codirector of the film with Coward. (Ohlinger's Movie Material Store.)

Charles Condomine (Rex Harrison) and Elvira (Kay Hammond), the ghost of his deceased wife, go for a joyride in *Blithe Spirit*. By now Lean was a full-fledged director in his own right. (Ohlinger's Movie Material Store.)

Laura Jesson (Celia Johnson) and Alec Harvey (Trevor Howard) in Lean's
classic love story *Brief Encounter*. (Museum of Modern Art/Film Stills Library.)

Laura (Celia Johnson) and Alec (Trevor Howard) in *Brief Encounter* walk out of a film called *Flames of Passion*. The title refers to a movie produced by Herbert Wilcox, one of Lean's early mentors. (Museum of Modern Art/Film Stills Library.)

Jean Simmons as the young Estella, Martita Hunt as the mad Miss Havisham, and Anthony Wager as the young Pip in *Great Expectations*. (Ohlinger's Movie Material Store.)

John Mills as the adult Pip enters Miss Havisham's crumbling mansion at the climax of *Great Expectations*. (Larry Edmunds Bookshop.)

Nancy (Kay Walsh), a doxy, Oliver Twist (John Howard Davies), and Fagin (Alec Guinness), a Jewish fence, in Lean's *Oliver Twist*. Guinness's performance triggered charges of anti-Semitism in America. (Museum of Modern Art/Film Stills Archive.)

Trevor Howard at the time he played Steven Stratton in *The Passionate Friends*. Like Alec Harvey in *Brief Encounter*, Stratton is drawn into an adulterous affair. (Larry Edmunds Bookshop.)

The defense attorney (Andre Morell) defends Madeleine Smith (Ann Todd, center), an accused murderess, in *Madeleine*, based on a true story. (Larry Edmunds Bookshop.)

Susan Garthwaite (Ann Todd) and her husband, Tony (Nigel Patrick), in *The Sound Barrier.* (Ohlinger's Movie Material Store.)

Sir John Ridgefield (Ralph Richardson), an aviation pioneer, and Tony Garthwaite, a test pilot (Nigel Patrick), in *The Sound Barrier.* (Ohlinger's Movie Material Store.)

Henry Hobson (Charles Laughton) on a spree in *Hobson's Choice*. (Ohlinger's Movie Material Store.)

Henry Hobson (Charles Laughton, center) is surrounded by his daughters—Alice (Daphne Anderson), Vicky (Prunella Scales), and Maggie (Brenda de Banzie). Freddy Beenstock (Derek Blomfield, standing) is courting Vicky. (Larry Edmunds Bookshop.)

Jane Hudson (Katharine
Hepburn) and Renato de
Rossi (Rossano Brazzi),
her Italian lover, in
Summertime. (Larry
Edmunds Bookshop.)

Jane (Katharine Hepburn) at the climax of *Summertime*. (Larry Edmunds Bookshop.)

Alec Guinness as Colonel Nicholson in *The Bridge on the River Kwai,* for which David Lean and Guinness both won Academy Awards. (Cinema Bookshop, London.)

Major Shears (William Holden) and Major Warden (Jack Hawkins) plot to blow up the bridge in *Kwai.* (Ohlinger's Movie Material Store.)

David Lean (right) directs Peter O'Toole as T. E. Lawrence on location in the Arabian desert for *Lawrence of Arabia,* for which Lean won an Oscar. (Cinema Bookshop, London.)

T. E. Lawrence dressed as an Arab chieftain, photographed by the American journalist Lowell Thomas's cameraman, Harry Chase. (Photography Collection, Harry Ransom Humanities Research Center, University of Texas, Austin.)

T. E. Lawrence (Peter O'Toole) in the robes of a Bedouin chief in *Lawrence of Arabia*. (Museum of Modern Art/Film Stills Archive.)

Alec Guinness as Prince Feisal in *Lawrence of Arabia*. Arthur Kennedy plays a war correspondent based on Lowell Thomas. (Larry Edmunds Bookshop.)

Lara (Julie Christie) and Yuri Zhivago (Omar Sharif) in *Dr. Zhivago*. (Ohlinger's Movie Material Store.)

Yuri (Omar Sharif), a doctor, and Lara (Julie Christie), a nurse, tend the wounded in *Dr. Zhivago*. (Larry Edmunds Bookshop.)

Rosy Shaughnessy (Sarah Miles) visits her husband, Charles (Robert Mitchum), in his classroom in *Ryan's Daughter*. (Larry Edmunds Bookshop.)

Rosy (Sarah Miles) and Major Randolph Doryan (Christopher Jones), her lover, in *Ryan's Daughter*. (Larry Edmunds Bookshop.)

Rosy (Sarah Miles) and Charles (Robert Mitchum) face the storm in *Ryan's Daughter*. (Ohlinger's Movie Material Store.)

Adela Quested (Judy Davis) and Dr. Aziz (Victor Banerjee) in *A Passage to India*. (Museum of Modern Art/Film Stills Archive.)

Dr. Aziz (Victor Banerjee) is arrested in *A Passage to India*. (Museum of Modern Art/Film Stills Archive.)

Dame Peggy Ashcroft as Mrs. Moore in *A Passage to India*, for which she won an Academy Award. (Ohlinger's Movie Material Store.)

The screenwriter Robert Bolt, Robert Mitchum, David Lean, and the cinematographer Freddie Young on the set of *Ryan's Daughter*. Bolt and Young were veterans of previous Lean films. (Ohlinger's Movie Material Store.)

Lawrence completed a second draft of the manuscript in the spring of 1920. At 400,000 words, however, the manuscript was, he thought, too verbose, so he spent the next year or so whittling it down to 280,000 words (the published volume would run 670 pages). In 1922, he had eight copies of this revised text printed at the *Oxford Times* so that he would never again risk misplacing it. He circulated some of the copies among his friends, including Shaw and E. M. Forster.

In August 1922, Lawrence joined the Royal Air Force (RAF) as a recruit, but under the name John Ross, in order to avoid the incessant glare of publicity. He therefore demoted himself from his status as an officer to the ranks. "He sought anonymity," writes Robert Bolt, a coauthor of the *Lawrence of Arabia* screenplay, by escaping into "what he called the 'monastery' of an Air Force barracks."[14] In January 1923, the London *Daily Express* exposed Lawrence's deception. The result was his dismissal from the RAF, his fame being an embarrassment to his superior officers. His reaction? "Damn the press!"[15] Disgruntled, Lawrence canceled plans to publish his memoirs, at least for the time being.

Two months later, Lawrence enlisted in the Royal Tank Corps under the name of Thomas Edward Shaw. He wrote Bernard Shaw (whose surname he had appropriated) that he was spending his spare evenings reworking his manuscript but was convinced that it was "careless in style" and "irredeemable muck."[16] Lawrence's indecisiveness about publishing his book was typical of him, writes Bolt: "One half of him was a scholar, thinker, gentle, retiring. The other half was a man of action, decisive, and it must be said, flamboyant." Perhaps it was the second half from which he was in flight "when he sought anonymity."[17]

Lawrence finally reached a compromise with himself by opting to have Jonathan Cape publish a privately printed subscription edition of 212 copies. But the showman in Lawrence required that the book be lavishly illustrated, and he commissioned Eric Kennington to make pastel sketches of each of the principal players in the drama of the Arabian Desert campaign.

In the meantime, Lawrence had petitioned the RAF for reinstatement. In 1925, the British government finally honored that petition, reinstating him as an aircraftsman, the lowest rank. He still went by the name Shaw, having had his surname legally changed to dissociate himself from Lawrence of Arabia. Anthony Nutting, one of Lawrence's biographers, who was to be the Oriental consultant (technical adviser) on Lean's film, writes that Lawrence was torn between the desire to see himself in print and the fear that the book would receive a negative response from his friends and war comrades—"the old craving for fame battering with the dread of being exposed as a failure."[18]

By the summer of 1925, Lawrence was exhausted from his five years of editing and tightening the manuscript. He was deeply disturbed by reliving his harrowing wartime experiences. And he was still worried about the book's reception. In retrospect, it was no surprise that he suffered a nervous break-down "and talked of suicide."[19] The writer Edward Garnett, whom Lawrence had consulted about the manuscript, was dismayed when Lawrence wrote him on June 13, 1925: "I'm no bloody good on earth. So I'm going to quit."[20] Lawrence had even composed a suicide note. So Garnett contacted Shaw, who managed to dissuade Lawrence from carrying through on his threat.

Lawrence needn't have worried on one count at least. The subscribers' edition of *Seven Pillars* was enthusiastically received when it appeared in 1926. Nevertheless, the extravagance with which the handsome limited edition was produced meant that sales did not cover publishing costs. So Cape persuaded Lawrence to publish a condensed, mass market edition, entitled *Revolt in the Desert*. "This abridgment of *Seven Pillars* contains 130,000 words. It was made by myself in 1926," Lawrence wrote.[21] The abridgment was produced by the simple expedient of excising passages of personal reflection and self-analysis. It was published in 1927, in England by Jonathan Cape and in America by Doubleday Doran.

Revolt in the Desert sold like hotcakes and paid off the overdraft occasioned by the subscribers' edition. Lawrence then withdrew it from publication. He declined to make a personal profit "from a best seller written in British and Arab blood."[22] He had already decreed in a postscript to the subscribers' edition: "No further issue of *Seven Pillars of Wisdom* will be made in my lifetime."[23] And he was as good as his word. It was the subscribers' edition, incidentally, that Sam Spiegel read when it was published. At a time when he was still a fledgling producer, he made a mental note that the book would make a great movie someday.

Over the years, historians have questioned the reliability of Lawrence's account of the Arab Revolt. Lawrence himself cast doubt on the accuracy of his memoirs at the outset. In the preface to the subscribers' edition, he states flatly that the book "does not intend to be impartial": "Please take it as a personal narrative pieced out of memory. There were many leaders and rank-and-file fighters to whom this self-regardant picture is not fair."[24] He wrote Walter Stirling, a fellow veteran, on October 15, 1924, while he was still reworking the text, that he mistrusted the accuracy of his account because it contained conversations reconstructed after several years: "If people read it as a history, then they mistake it."[25]

Lawrence's insistence that his is a subjective view of the Arab Revolt has led some commentators to dismiss *Seven Pillars* as fact hopelessly intertwined with myth. Admittedly, Lawrence at times lapses into passages of purple prose that seem contrived and inflated; for example, his description of his torture by Turkish soldiers is needlessly detailed and overwritten.

But the comment by Lawrence that troubles historians and critics the most is his admission early in the book that, at times, he "conceals" certain facts.[26] Nutting judiciously comments, "There is no doubt that Lawrence left out certain facts he did not wish to acknowledge." For example, he is "reticent" about the British army's contribution to the success of the Arab Revolt, presumably because he wished to emphasize the role of the Arabs in fighting for their own independence. As a result, "the unwitting reader is left with the impression that the Arabs received little Allied help"—except maybe for some guns supplied by the British army at Lawrence's behest. If the narrative appears biased at times, it is because Lawrence is writing subjectively about his role in the Arab movement "and certainly not about the Middle Eastern campaign as a whole."[27] Despite Lawrence's disclaimers that his book is not objective history, *Seven Pillars* would become the cornerstone of both Wilson's and Bolt's script drafts for Lean's film: it is, after all, a firsthand account of the Arab war.

Lawrence retired from military service in February 1935 and settled down in Clouds Hill, a country cottage in Dorset, near the Bovington military camp where he had been stationed earlier. On May 13, he was injured in a motorcycle accident that would be reenacted in Lean's film. He was on his way home from mailing a letter to his friend Henry Williamson when the crash occurred; his papers identified him as T. E. Shaw, late of the RAF. But Winston Churchill, who had known Lawrence when he, Churchill, was colonial secretary, made inquiries that proved T. E. Shaw was, in fact, T. E. Lawrence. On May 19, 1935, Lawrence died in Bovington Military Hospital, without ever regaining consciousness.

There was widespread speculation as to whether Lawrence had killed himself. At the inquest on May 21, the sole witness to the accident testified that there was a rise in the road, high enough to hide approaching traffic from a cyclist or motorist. Lawrence suddenly saw before him on the crest of the narrow road two boys on bicycles who were in the wrong lane: "He swerved to miss them and was going too fast for it."[28] He lost control and was hurled from his motorcycle. Nonetheless, speeding on a motorbike on a backcountry English lane—going too fast to slow down in time to avoid an accident—seems to qualify as reckless endangerment.

Could Lawrence have been the victim of a death wish? Because life no longer held any appeal for him, he was certainly self-destructive—and in this instance quite literally suicidal. He had, we recall, contemplated suicide in the past. Indeed, on one occasion he had said, "I want to lie down and go to sleep and not wake up."[29] So perhaps he had developed a death wish as he got older. At any rate, the mystery surrounding Lawrence's death would not be entirely solved in Lean's film, which portrays the accident in an ambiguous fashion.

Lawrence was accorded a state funeral at St. Nicholas Church, Moreton, Dorset, and he is buried in the cemetery there. He was fondly remembered by many of those who knew him. Winston Churchill pronounced the following encomium for Lawrence: "His name will live in English letters; it will live in the annals of war; it will live in the legends of Arabia. We shall never see his like again."[30] In a somewhat lighter vein, Noël Coward described him as "strange and elusive, painfully shy, gay, and loquacious."[31]

A. W. Lawrence authorized a mass market edition of *Seven Pillars* that appeared on July 29, 1935, a scant three months after his brother's death. The trade edition, of course, was widely reviewed and discussed. Bernard Shaw called it a masterpiece, as did the novelist E. M. Forster, who, like Shaw, had been a loyal friend to Lawrence over the years.

Still, the book left some unanswered questions about its author, questions that Lean would have to address in the film. For one thing, it had been rumored for years that Lawrence was homosexual, that he had never came to terms with his homosexuality, and that he sought in various ways to suppress it. The British film director Anthony Asquith, for whom Lean had edited *Pygmalion,* believed that Lawrence was homosexual. Asquith was himself homosexual (see chapter 6). Lawrence and Asquith had mutual homosexual friends, and, when Asquith was asked whether Lawrence was homosexual, he replied laconically, "Not practicing."[32]

Certainly, Lawrence was very partial to Arab boys while he was serving in the Middle East. For example, when he went on an archaeological expedition to Syria in 1911, he chose an Arab waterboy, Salem Achmed, known as Dahoum, as his personal assistant. They developed a close, long-lasting relationship; Lawrence even took him back to Oxford for a visit. However: "There is no conclusive evidence that he had a sexual relationship with any of [the Arab boys he befriended]."[33]

Still, when Salem Achmed succumbed to typhoid in 1917, Lawrence was left desolate. He later dedicated *Seven Pillars* to "S.A." Stephen Tabachnick writes that there is little doubt that the dedicatee is Salem Achmed.[34] The dedication begins, "I loved you," indicating Lawrence's enduring devotion.[35] Lean would imply Lawrence's homosexual nature in the film by showing that two Arab boys were Lawrence's constant companions.

Lean also wanted to cope with Lawrence's alleged sadomasochism. John Bruce, a Scots soldier whom Lawrence knew while he was in the tank corps, came forward thirty years after Lawrence's death with evidence about this disputed point. Bruce testified that he administered ritual floggings to Lawrence while they were stationed at the Bovington Tank Corps station. Lawrence explained to Bruce that he sometimes received letters from someone whom he cryptically referred to as "the Old Man"; whenever the Old Man was displeased with Lawrence, he was to be thrashed with a birch cane.[36]

Bruce strongly suspected that the Old Man was "a fantasy figure created by Lawrence," perhaps modeled on Lawrence's stern father, and that Lawrence himself wrote the letters that he showed Bruce. After Lawrence returned to the RAF in 1925, he and Bruce were separated. But Lawrence continued to meet with Bruce intermittently for additional floggings until 1934. Bruce insisted to his dying day that he beat Lawrence at Lawrence's own request and that Lawrence never wavered from his explanation for the beatings over a period of eleven years. "Lawrence scholars now accept Bruce's main claims."[37]

Asked by an interviewer why his brother evidently had a masochistic love of pain inflicted on himself, A. W. Lawrence responded, "My older brother had read any amount of medieval literature when he was at Oxford, about saints who quelled temptation by beatings; and that's what he did." He wanted to subdue his body by methods advocated by the saints. "I knew about the floggings after his death, but of course I said nothing. They were too amenable to journalistic sensationalism."[38]

Kevin Brownlow, the author of Lean's definitive biography, told me in correspondence that A. W. Lawrence's explanation of his brother's behavior is credible. Brownlow said that there is considerable evidence that Lawrence enjoyed being thrashed because he believed that he achieved spiritual exhilaration through pain: "Lawrence was like a medieval saint who felt that his sins had to be beaten out of him." Robert Bolt's screenplay, following Michael Wilson's original draft, would deal with this aspect of Lawrence's psychological makeup in the notorious episode in which Lawrence was beaten and raped by the Turks in Deraa.

Lean's project was not, however, the first attempt to navigate the treacherous waters of Lawrence's psychological makeup. As early as 1926, the year *Seven Pillars* was first published, Rex Ingram (*The Four Horsemen of the*

Apocalypse) wrote Lawrence, saying that the book seemed tailor-made for epic cinema. Lawrence answered on October 5, 1926, discouraging Ingram by dismissing his book as an inferior work—"but the best I can do."[39] Ingram renewed his offer in 1927 when *Revolt in the Desert* became a best seller. "[Film producers] babble sometimes to me of making a film of *Revolt in the Desert*," Lawrence replied, "but I'd hate to see myself parodied on the basis of my record of what the fellows with me did."[40] With that, Ingram gave up.

Lawrence told his friends that he was against either version of his book being filmed. As he also acknowledged, however, "I have no control or ownership or copyright of the Arab Revolt, as it happened to be an event, and not a fiction."[41] And after fending off other offers for the film rights to *Revolt in the Desert*—including one from the British director M. A. Wetherell in 1928—he noted stoically: "If they want to film the rotten book they must."[42]

By 1934, his resistance having apparently been worn down, Lawrence sold the screen rights of *Revolt in the Desert* to Alexander Korda. Korda would produce the picture for London Films, and Leslie Howard would star. Lawrence joked that he endorsed Howard's casting because Howard was better looking than he was—"which would be an advantage!"[43]

Not surprisingly, Lawrence began to have misgivings about green-lighting the project. He wrote his friend and biographer Robert Graves on February 4, 1935, that he met with Korda and explained that he disapproved of the "superficial falsity and vulgarity" of the movies and was, therefore, opposed to the filming of *Revolt in the Desert*. The result of the meeting? "Korda agreed to put it off till I die."[44] Korda must have assumed that Lawrence was being facetious when he mentioned his own death, but three months later Lawrence was dead. Korda tried to resurrect the project, but he eventually experienced yet another of his periodic financial crises (see chapter 10) and could not raise the funding for a costly costume drama.

The playwright-screenwriter Terence Rattigan, who had written the script for *The Sound Barrier* for Lean, entered the lists in 1958. He had composed a screenplay derived from Basil Liddell-Hart's authorized biography of Lawrence. He was particularly interested in how Lawrence sank into seclusion as an enlisted man after World War I. His scenario began and ended at the RAF base where Lawrence was known as Ross, with an extended flashback to the Arab campaign making up the bulk of the story.

But Rattigan could not interest any British studio in backing an expensive "camel opera." One of the reservations that studio executives had about the scenario was that it had no love interest or romance. Lawrence himself had quipped, "There was nothing female in the Arab movement but the camels."[45] So Rattigan gave up the idea of selling his Lawrence project to the movies and decided to turn his screenplay into a stage play called *Ross*.

Because the project was derived from Liddell-Hart's biography, not *Seven Pillars*, Rattigan sidestepped the necessity of securing A. W. Lawrence's approval. Alec Guinness was chosen to play Lawrence, and he accordingly interviewed some of Lawrence's friends. One of them, Sir Sydney Cockrell, gave Guinness a coarse, striped robe that had once belonged to Lawrence. "I handed it on to Clouds Hill, Lawrence's hideaway cottage, as a memento," Guinness said.[46]

Though nothing is explicitly stated in the play's dialogue, *Ross* does depict Lawrence as a homosexual. Indeed, the drama presents the rape of Lawrence offstage, with the implication that Lawrence was a homosexual masochist. Guinness's authorized biographer, Piers Paul Read, states, "Guinness must have been aware that he was portraying a historical figure with whom he felt some degree of affinity." Specifically, Read depicts Guinness as a latent homosexual who maintained a circle of homosexual actor friends, including Noël Coward and Michael Redgrave. On the one hand, Guinness, like Lawrence, "engaged in . . . flirtations with handsome young men." On the other hand, like Redgrave, he was a husband and father who was "determined that he should never be taken as homosexual."[47]

Ross opened at the Theatre Royal Haymarket on May 12, 1960. It came across like a discarded film script, one from which the location sequences had been cut—which is precisely what it was. Still, Guinness was commended for the wit and pathos that he brought to the role. *Ross* had a substantial run of 762 performances in London and was transferred to Broadway with John Mills in the lead.

The success of *Ross* both in London and in New York stimulated Rattigan to turn it back into a screenplay. And, once the screenplay was completed, Herbert Wilcox expressed interest in filming it. On October 10, 1960, Wilcox published a press release, stating that he had purchased the screen rights to Rattigan's *Ross* for £100,000.

Sam Spiegel was startled by this news. Despite the failure of his first attempt in 1952, he had, as we will see, subsequently managed to acquire the screen rights to *Seven Pillars*. Consequently, through Horizon Pictures, he slapped Wilcox with an injunction, contending that all the major dramatic incidents in *Ross* "must ultimately have been derived from *Seven Pillars*" and that any film based on *Ross* would, thus, constitute copyright infringement.[48] Spiegel's own solicitor warned him that his case against Wilcox was weak. Lawrence himself had, as we have seen, admitted not holding the copyright on the Arab Revolt. Furthermore, Rattigan had based both his stage play and his screenplay on Lidell-Hart's biography, not *Seven Pillars*.

"I could have gone ahead and made *Ross*, defying Spiegel," Wilcox writes. "I could have shown my film a year ahead of his, since David Lean, although a great director, is very slow. But I had to let the whole subject drop, since no distributor would finance me with an injunction hanging over my head. Not a penny of the £100,000 did I recover."[49] That is not quite true. Since Spiegel wanted to prevent some other producer from mounting a film production of *Ross*, Wilcox was able to sell him the screen rights to the play—for an undisclosed sum. Still, in 1964, Wilcox declared bankruptcy; he never made another movie. And Spiegel and Lean at last went on to make *Lawrence of Arabia*.

Lawrence of Arabia (1962)

In the fall of 1959, Spiegel contracted with Michael Wilson, who had done yeoman's service on the screenplay for *The Bridge on the River Kwai*, for Wilson to construct a prose treatment of the life of T. E. Lawrence, which Spiegel would then submit to A. W. Lawrence. Wilson was then to prepare a complete screenplay. He was to be paid in all $100,000, in installments.

Wilson was still blacklisted by the House Un-American Activities Committee. Hence, Spiegel saw to it that there was a clause in Wilson's contract specifying that he would receive a screen credit for his script once he had formally denied any association with the Communist Party. Though Wilson had, in fact, terminated his affiliation with the party in 1957, he was not prepared, then or later, to renounce his political beliefs. The dispute about his screen credit was placed on the back burner for the time being.

On September 20, 1959, Wilson submitted to Spiegel a preliminary sketch of the scenario with the title *Lawrence of Arabia: Elements and Facets of a Theme*. In it, Wilson writes that Lawrence became a legend in his own time: "The prime mover in the creation of the legend was, of course, Lowell Thomas. But Lawrence himself, wittingly or unwittingly, contributed to the myth. . . . Lawrence needed the legend; he fed on it." In fact, as Lawrence admitted in *Seven Pillars*, he had a craving to be famous and a horror of being known to like being famous. Consequently, Wilson continues, "Our story should develop as a slow revelation of the man behind the myth." Lawrence's tragedy was that of a man who tried to follow two masters, "neither of whom he could satisfy": "He championed Arab independence; yet he was a British officer who was committed to serving the interests of the British Empire in the Middle East."[50]

Wilson—working in his apartment in Paris, where he was living in exile—then proceeded to fashion a detailed screen treatment. He was barred at this point from drawing on *Seven Pillars,* for which Spiegel had yet to obtain the screen rights. So he was forced to depend on Thomas's biography, which was sketchy and excluded several significant events covered in—as well as all the confessional elements of—*Seven Pillars.* He had hoped to shape a much franker, more in-depth portrait, for which recourse to *Seven Pillars* would be necessary. But, in the meantime, he completed his treatment, dispatching it to Spiegel on December 10, 1959. He later wrote Lean: "The next day [A. W.] Lawrence informed Sam that he was authorizing his lawyers to negotiate the sale of the rights to your outfit. So it is perhaps not immodest to assume that my approach to *Seven Pillars* helped to bring the old boy around."[51]

Lawrence expressed his satisfaction with the screen treatment, which he mistakenly assumed Spiegel had written. "Spiegel has done a first-class job of abridgement," he said. It was, he felt, the only accurate film scenario based on his brother's life that he had ever read. He concluded, "Spiegel's script doesn't lose balance, neither does it distort characters or incidents."[52] Only time would tell what he would think of the final shooting script, which, now that the rights to the material in *Seven Pillars* had been obtained, would contain problematic material that Thomas had skirted. And Lawrence's opinion still mattered because permission to use the title *Seven Pillars of Wisdom* depended on his approval of the final shooting script.

Lean came to London for the official signing of the contract between Lawrence and Horizon Pictures on February 11, 1960. Also present was Sir Anthony Nutting, one of the film's technical advisers, who, as a former minister of state who had represented the British government on diplomatic missions to the Middle East as well as one of T. E. Lawrence's biographers, was someone whom A. W. Lawrence respected. Spiegel asked A. W. Lawrence to suggest a fee for the screen rights to the book, for a film to be entitled *Seven Pillars of Wisdom.* The professor, who was not wise in the ways of Hollywood dealmaking, answered that he had no specific sum in mind. With that, Spiegel cagily offered him £22,500. "Done!" Lawrence instantly replied. (Lean later observed that Lawrence could probably have gotten away with asking for as much as £100,000.)[53] Spiegel—who drove a hard bargain—also had inserted in the contract a clause whereby, if Lawrence subsequently withdrew his permission for the title of his brother's book to be used as the film's title, he would forfeit £5,000 of the amount payable to him by Horizon Pictures.

Spiegel and Lean jointly hosted a reception at Claridge's Hotel on February 17, 1960, to formally announce the launching of their film *Seven*

Pillars of Wisdom. Spiegel also announced that Marlon Brando, who had won an Academy Award for his performance in Spiegel's *On the Waterfront,* would play Lawrence. As things turned out, Brando withdrew from the Lawrence film because he preferred to spend time in the tropics making *Mutiny on the Bounty* (Lewis Milestone, 1962), rather than in the desert making *Seven Pillars.* In retrospect, Lean was relieved to get shot of Brando, who was too bossy in dealing with directors: "Lean feared the actor might impose his style and character on the part." He did not want the movie to turn out to be "*Brando of Arabia.*"[54]

Now that Wilson had full access to *Seven Pillars,* he was ready to develop his scenario into a full-scale screenplay. Lean assured him, "I am mad keen to work with you again. Hope you feel the same."[55] He also warned him that capturing Lawrence on film would be a tall order: "Lawrence and his book have endured the comments and interpretations of scores of historians, . . . often with an axe of their own to grind."[56]

Wilson worked on the first draft of his screenplay for eight months, sending it off to Spiegel on August 4, 1960. It begins with a prologue portraying Lawrence's death and then his memorial service at St. Paul's in London. An intrepid reporter asks various celebrities in top hats their estimation of Lawrence. One veteran states that he was "a glorious hero"; a war correspondent, representing Lowell Thomas, says sotto voce, "He was a shameless exhibitionist." This scene leads into an extended flashback portraying Lawrence's participation in the Arab Revolt that constitutes the balance of the film.

Wilson's first draft emerges as a complicated political drama, with an enormous gallery of characters. To his chagrin, Lean figured out that, as it stood, the draft would make a film of seven hours' running time. Disappointed, Lean insisted that he and Wilson collaborate more closely on the second draft.

Lean peppered Wilson with voluminous suggestions: "Lose the *Desert Song* quality wherever it exists." This was a reference to Roy Del Ruth's 1929 film version of Sigmund Romberg's operetta, a highly romantic movie musical with John Boles as a swashbuckling desert Robin Hood. Lean also cautioned Wilson against too many action sequences: "Do we want to make a western?" he asked wryly. In essence, Lean was looking for more of a character study of a complex personality, one with inner conflicts simmering underneath the surface behavior. "Many faceted aspects of Lawrence's character not yet in the screenplay," he complained—for example, "Lawrence's masochism." He continued: "Let us not avoid or censor out the homosexual aspects of Lawrence's relationships. . . . The incipient homosexuality of Daud and Farrij [two Arab boys whom Lawrence befriended] must be emphasized." Daud and Farrij are modeled on Ali and Othman, respectively, a pair of homosexual lovers. Lawrence's sympathetic treatment of them in his memoirs aroused his biographers' suspicions about his own sexuality. Indeed, these lads bring to mind the Arab youngster Salem Achmed, to whom Lawrence dedicated *Seven Pillars*.[57]

From the outset, it was clear that, in making *Lawrence*, Lean was determined to evolve a new concept of film biography that would liberate the genre from the conventions of the highly romanticized Hollywood biographies of the past. His approach to the project was designed to come to grips with the problems of his hero's life in a way that would make for a much more challenging and entertaining picture than the sugarcoated kind of conventional screen biography ever did.

The British director Ken Russell endorsed Lean's "warts-and-all" approach to Lawrence. Russell himself, who made controversial biopics like *The Music Lovers* (1970), his life of Tchaikovsky, told me in conversation: "According to the accepted textbook idea of a biopic, you were supposed to extol the hero's accomplishments. But I tried to dispel the preconceived idea of what a biopic should be by presenting the life of the hero in a way that showed how he transcended his own personal problems and weaknesses in order to meet the challenges he had to face." Standard biopics present someone with no inner conflicts. But, according to Russell, "Showing the personal struggles out of which the hero's accomplishments grew is more of a tribute to him." This is what Lean attempted in *Lawrence of Arabia*.

Wilson finished his second draft of the script in September 1960 and mailed it to Lean, who was scouting locations in Jordan. Lean summoned Wilson to Amman in mid-December, where he candidly informed Wilson that his screenplay was just not working out. For one thing, it was still in need of massive cuts. For another, the dialogue was perfunctory; for example, there were far too many scenes set in offices, with the characters engaged in dry political discussion. In fact, Lean wanted to get away as much as possible from the heavy dose of politics that Wilson had injected into the script. Wilson was contractually obligated to submit a third draft, but it was almost a foregone conclusion that it would not be acceptable to Lean.

Lean complained about Wilson's script to Spiegel in a letter of January 5, 1961: "The character of Lawrence, which is what fascinated us in the first place, hardly peeps through at all." Wilson was concentrating too much on external action, such as the capture of Aqaba and Damascus by Lawrence's troops, and not enough on an in-depth psychological portrayal of Lawrence's character. Lean grimly declared on January 7 that Wilson "has shot his bolt as far as this script is concerned." For his part, Wilson was thoroughly fed up with the whole project; after he had labored for a year on the screenplay, Lean was still dissatisfied with it. So, after delivering his third and final draft of 273 pages on January 31, 1961, Wilson threw in the towel. He commented at the time that, if he lived to be a hundred, he could not satisfy David Lean. He was bitter and disappointed since he knew that he would inevitably be replaced.[58]

In point of fact, even before Wilson's final draft landed on his desk, Spiegel was already searching for his replacement. Moura Budberg, a close friend of Spiegel's, who had been a reader in Alexander Korda's story department at London Films, recommended Robert Bolt. His play *A Man for All Seasons,* which had opened to rave reviews in the summer of 1960, had demonstrated that Bolt could pen witty and literate dialogue and that "he had an extraordinary ability to telescope and clarify history in dramatic form."[59]

Spiegel invited Bolt to his London office and arranged for him to rework Wilson's screenplay, starting in January 1961. He told Bolt that he particularly wanted him to write some classy dialogue. After dipping into Wilson's script, Bolt told Spiegel that some of the major characters lacked substance. Clearly, Bolt had his work cut out for him.

Spiegel sent a note to Lean in Amman, informing him that he had engaged Bolt. Lean knew so little about Bolt that he misspelled his surname as "Boult" in his reply to Spiegel. In his letter of January 5, already cited, Lean said that he was uneasy that he, the director, had had no say in Spiegel and Bolt's story conferences. He moaned that he was thousands of miles away and that "the whole film is drifting away from me." "That," Spiegel promptly replied, "is why Bolt is being brought in chains to Amman to join you"— as soon as it would be feasible for him to do so. The fact of the matter was that Spiegel saw Bolt as his personal discovery and did not want Bolt to meet Lean until the last opportunity; he was, as one of his colleagues put it, "very possessive." Indeed, Spiegel did not send Bolt to Jordan until April, after Bolt had finished the first half of his screenplay. To reassure Lean that Bolt was doing good work in the interim, Spiegel forwarded to Lean in due course the first few pages of Bolt's script. Lean responded that he was "madly impressed" by Bolt's preliminary work.[60]

Spiegel was anxious to start principal photography, but on January 7 Lean cautioned him that "no one but a madman would start a film without a script."[61] Spiegel finally issued Bolt a contract on February 17, 1961, commissioning him to write "a screenplay with reference to a script by Michael Wilson."[62] Significantly, this statement implicitly acknowledges that Wilson's screenplay had laid the groundwork for the entire film, a fact that Bolt would later dispute. Wilson had incorporated in his draft every episode from *Seven Pillars* that Lean deemed indispensable, and Bolt had followed suit by keeping all of them in his script. Consequently, the narrative structure of Bolt's script was well-nigh identical with that of Wilson's draft.

Like Wilson, Bolt had found that Lawrence's biographers contradicted each other in dealing with their controversial subject. So, like Wilson, Bolt said that he made *Seven Pillars* his principal source, even though "it contains long passages of dubious veracity." Still, he took as essentially true "[Lawrence's] account of what had happened, or what he passionately wished had happened."[63] Lean and Spiegel both agreed with this approach. "I don't believe that Lawrence was ever a liar," said Spiegel. "He was a poet who colored things with his own impressions."[64] As the newspaper editor says in John Ford's *The Man Who Shot Liberty Valance* (1962): "When the legend becomes the truth, you print the legend."

Since Wilson's screenplay was overlength, Bolt slimmed it down by omitting some minor incidents and combining some characters. For example, he condensed the various British diplomats with whom Lawrence had to cope into a single intelligence agent of the Arab Bureau named Dryden, a character based primarily on David Hogarth, the deputy director of the Arab Bureau.

At long last, in April 1961, Bolt arrived in Jordan. When Lean and Bolt finally met, they struck up an instant rapport. For his part Bolt was very impressed by Lean's suggestions. There is, for example, the scene in which Lawrence is forced to execute Gasim, a former friend who has murdered a member of another tribe, in order to avert a tribal feud. Lawrence tells General Allenby how guilty he feels and then mentions, "There's something else." Because Bolt feared a censorship problem, he did not have Lawrence elaborate on what that "something else" was. Lean insisted that he do so, asking, "What is that something else, Robert?" Bolt replied, "Well, he sort of enjoyed it." Lean threw his script in the air and exclaimed, "For heaven's sake, why don't you put it in?"[65] In this manner Lean encouraged Bolt to explore Lawrence's personality in more depth than Wilson had done, in this instance by implying his sadomasochistic streak.

Bolt in turn made some felicitous contributions to the screenplay that impressed Lean. For example, he added a salient detail to the final scene, in which Lawrence is departing by car for the ship that will take him home. Bolt added a shot of a motorcyclist roaring past Lawrence's car; this is an implicit reference to Lawrence himself speeding down the road on his motorcycle in the film's opening scene. In this manner, the film ends by reminding us how Lawrence will die in a motorcycle accident, thereby bringing the movie full circle.

Spiegel finally insisted that shooting would have to begin on May 15, 1961; further delay might mean that the contracts of some of the cast and crew would expire before shooting was completed, as almost happened with William Holden on *The Bridge on the River Kwai*. At this point, Bolt returned to London to continue work on the second half of the script throughout the summer and fall.

Lean had to send the footage shot every day to London to be processed, and the rushes were delivered to the Horizon office, where he would catch up on viewing them on his periodic visits there. Bolt and Spiegel watched the rushes too, and Bolt took to sending suggestions to the actors on location as to how to speak their lines. He would enclose copies of his memos for Lean, who was apoplectic when he read them.

"He hasn't yet finished his first film," Lean wrote Spiegel. Yet there he was, acting like "the guiding hand behind the direction of this film." Lean demanded that Spiegel instruct Bolt to send his comments directly to him alone: "But please allow me to pass on what I see fit to the actors."[66] Bolt complied.

But Bolt was not finished making mischief. He was absolutely opposed to the making of atomic weapons. He participated in a massive anti–nuclear war rally, organized by Bertrand Russell and other left-wing intellectuals, in Trafalgar Square on September 17, 1961. The protestors carried placards saying, "BAN THE BOMB!" Bolt was arrested and given a thirty-day sentence for civil disobedience. Spiegel wired Lean that he personally showed up at Drake Hall prison in Staffordshire and pleaded with Bolt to recant and go back to work on the screenplay. Spiegel claimed that Bolt's losing several days' work on the script would, ultimately, disrupt the shooting schedule, close down the production indefinitely, and put hundreds of studio employees on the breadline. When Spiegel burst into tears—he could shed crocodile tears on demand—Bolt relented and signed a statement promising not to take part in future political demonstrations.

Bolt was released, after serving half his sentence, and spirited away from the prison in Spiegel's Rolls-Royce. "I felt ashamed," he commented, referring to the fact that he had caved in to Spiegel and renounced his ideals while Michael Wilson had stood firm and suffered the consequences.[67] In the end, Bolt never forgave Spiegel. Later on, he agreed to write the script for *Dr. Zhivago* only on the condition that Spiegel not produce the picture.[68]

Bolt joined Lean in Spain, where the film unit had moved for further location work, in a last-ditch effort to complete the remaining scenes on time. He finished the second half of the screenplay at the end of December 1961; he had worked on the script for a year, the same amount of time that Wilson had devoted to it. Despite the additional nuances and clarifications of Lawrence's characters that surface in Bolt's revised screenplay, the fact remains that it was never the intention of Lean and his collaborators to explain away all the ambiguities that surround the enigmatic T. E. Lawrence. For example, the film does not explicitly deal with the question of Lawrence's homosexuality. For one thing, censorship restrictions in the early 1960s were tougher than later on and did not permit a director to be very frank in dealing with homosexuality.

Still, a clever director like Lean could get around such restrictions. As the screenwriter-novelist Gore Vidal says, "It would be perfectly clear to the cognoscenti who were on the right wave length that a particular character was homosexual."[69] In the case of *Lawrence of Arabia*, Lean shows Lawrence enjoying what appears to be something more than an avuncular relationship with Daud and Farrij, the two orphaned desert urchins who become his constant companions, without exploiting the homosexual implications of the situation. In fact, as Roger Ebert observes, "None of the other characters in the movie seem to notice."[70]

Lean later stated that he addressed Lawrence's sexuality as forthrightly as the censorship laws of the day would allow: "Lawrence was very, if not entirely, gay. We thought we were being very daring at the time; for example, Lawrence and the Arab boys."[71] In their tightly reasoned essay on the film, Vankin and Whalen write that, given the censorship regulations of the time, "there was only so much Lean could do to show this rather dark aspect of Lawrence's enigmatic personality."[72] But there were sufficient hints for those in the know.

Bolt remembered that the question he was most often asked when the film was released was whether he thought Lawrence was homosexual. His opinion: "That he was more or less homosexual by nature, I think most certain." He also agreed that Lawrence seemed to have a craving for pain: "There does seem to have been in his psyche an element of sadomasochism, some special regard for suffering, inflicted or received."[73] The scene in the film that most directly addresses both these character traits is that during which, during a scouting expedition to the strategic Turkish garrison town of Deraa in November 1917, Lawrence is captured by soldiers of the Turkish bey Nahi (a pseudonym for Hajim).

In *Seven Pillars,* Lawrence writes that the bey, who did not know Lawrence's real identity, had him pinioned by his guards and stripped and that he then made homosexual advances toward him, which Lawrence rebuffed with a knee to the groin. In retaliation, the bey commanded his guards to beat the prisoner senseless. Lawrence was then taken to another room, spread-eagled on a table, and lashed savagely: "I remembered a delicious warmth, probably sexual, was swelling through me."[74] He was released the following morning.

"The description of the beating at Deraa," one of Lawrence's biographers explains, "shows an abnormal fascination with physical suffering; his lingering over the color and texture of his wounds, and the detailed description of the instrument of torture—the whip—is typical of masochistic reveries." As a matter of fact, the torture that Lawrence endured at Deraa perhaps turned him into "the full-blown masochist he later became."[75]

Lawrence concludes his own account by saying, "In Deraa that night the citadel of my integrity had been irrevocably lost." This remark has puzzled historians and biographers; it can refer neither to his being sodomized by the enemy soldiers nor to the bey's sexual advances, which he rejected. It therefore most likely refers to his statement that he was "completely broken" by the torture "and left sobbing for mercy."[76] Lawrence was humbled by the realization that, had the bey subjected him to interrogation at that point, he would, for a respite from pain, have revealed military secrets and betrayed his comrades in the bargain.

Lawrence's biographers mostly agree that his account of how he was beaten and raped is essentially true. Turkish brutality toward prisoners has been well documented. In allowing his soldiers to abuse Lawrence, the bey was primarily interested in degrading a handsome white man. But some of his biographers feel that Lawrence's allegation that the bey himself attempted to assault him sexually rings false. Tabachnick writes that Hajim's diaries reveal him to be a rabid heterosexual who had a steady supply of females in Deraa and that the bey's attempt at seduction was very likely Lawrence's invention—he had to present himself as a victim in this manner to explain away his homosexuality. By the same token, "Lawrence stated that he allowed himself to be raped by the bey's soldiers when he could no longer stand the pain of their beating."[77]

Scholarly controversy aside, Wilson took *Seven Pillars* as gospel and portrayed the bey as bent on seduction. Nevertheless, in his notes, Wilson observes that Lawrence's homosexuality should not be "placed at the center of the riddle" of his personality. Therefore, in the torture scene, there was, he felt, "little to be gained from dramatizing the notion that Lawrence finally succumbs to the bey's advances," as a couple of his biographers have alleged. "This does not mean," he continues, "that one should omit any suggestion of the bey's homosexuality." Wilson is further convinced that Lawrence's statement regarding his lost "integrity" means that he had previously believed that he had the willpower to endure any physical pain but "found that he too had his breaking point and finally whimpered for mercy": "Is that not enough for our story?"[78]

Bolt followed Wilson's approach to the flogging sequence in the shooting script; in fact, Bolt's handling of the whole sequence in the bey's quarters differs very little from Wilson's. Both exercise discretion in suggesting the bey's supposed homosexuality, in order to satisfy the censor.

A. W. Lawrence finally obtained a copy of Bolt's screenplay in July 1962. Wilson's preliminary screen treatment, which he had read two years earlier, was, we remember, based on Thomas's bland, laudatory biography. Hence, he was livid when he saw that the final screenplay implied that his brother was both homosexual and sadomasochistic. In addition, there was a scene in which Lawrence discussed his illegitimate birth.

As Tabachnick puts it, "A. W. Lawrence was a firm guardian of [T. E.] Lawrence's reputation, especially when disagreeing with some aspect of the 1962 David Lean film." He therefore summarily fired off a letter to Spiegel on August 16, 1962, declaring that to say that he was disappointed with the script would be a gross understatement. He forthwith denied permission for the film to be entitled *Seven Pillars of Wisdom*.[79] Spiegel reminded him that, according to their contract, such a decision would cost him £5,000. Ironically, Lean had wanted to call the film *Lawrence of Arabia* all along, so Lawrence's change of heart was not a problem for him.

Interestingly, where the film only implies that Lawrence was homosexual and masochistic, it more directly "accuses him . . . of sadism."[80] Surprisingly, A. W. Lawrence did not attack the movie on that score. After all, as we have seen, in the final shooting script Lawrence admits to having enjoyed killing Gasim. What is more, he launches a massacre of Turkish soldiers—who are retreating from Tafas—with maniacal glee and manifestly enjoys the bloodbath. This sequence in the film coincides with Lawrence's own account—though other eyewitnesses claimed that he grossly exaggerated the carnage. It appears that, "in the deeper recesses of his psyche, he may have fancied himself . . . a thrill killer" and that that led him to exaggerate his own apparent sadism.[81] In any case, these scenes dramatize how far the screenplay departs from Wilson's preliminary prose treatment.

A. W. Lawrence was not the only one upset about the shooting script. Michael Wilson was too; he had requested a copy of the final draft of the screenplay from Spiegel, in order to ascertain whether he was entitled to a screen credit as coauthor. In examining the screenplay, he estimated that, while only about 10 percent of his dialogue remained, 90 percent of the narrative structure was derived from his draft.

Wilson promptly wrote Spiegel on November 11, 1962, declaring, "The overall narrative structure of the shooting script is mine." He maintained that his final script had provided Bolt with the blueprint for his entire screenplay. He further contended that nearly all the dramatic episodes in his screenplay survived one way or another in Bolt's. Moreover, incidents that he had invented, and that are not to be found in *Seven Pillars*, "were retained by Bolt." He therefore petitioned Spiegel for a joint screenplay credit with Bolt.[82]

Spiegel responded through his lawyers on November 23, 1962, that Wilson had no contractual right to a shared screen credit with Bolt because Bolt had substantially revised his work. Wilson therefore submitted his case to the British Screenwriters Guild (BSG), to which both he and Bolt belonged, for arbitration. In a letter dated November 28, 1962, he compared his draft of the script with Bolt's shooting script, enumerating several parallels between the two drafts.

For starters, Wilson points out that his script begins with Lawrence's death and subsequent memorial service, events that were, of course, not in *Seven Pillars* and that Bolt had clearly appropriated, even though condensing the memorial service dialogue.[83] He further draws attention to the scenes depicting Lawrence's rescue of Gasim, lost while crossing the desert, and Gasim's subsequent execution. "Both of these incidents are recorded in *Seven Pillars*," Wilson explains. But, there, the man Lawrence rescued, Gasim el Shimt, was not the man he shot, Hamed the Moor. Wilson "conjoined them," he indicates, in order "to dramatize (my invention)" of how Lawrence is forced by circumstances to kill someone he had once considered his comrade—a conjunction that Bolt retained.[84] Wilson also notes how close Bolt's handling of the torture scene is to his[85] and that Bolt retained his introduction of Lowell Thomas (never mentioned in *Seven Pillars*) as a character, albeit changing the name to Jackson Bentley. In short, Wilson insisted that his screenplay was the structural edifice on which Bolt built.

While waiting for a response from the BSG, Wilson addressed himself to Bolt in a letter of November 29, 1962. He began by saying that he had spent a year on the script and deserved some recognition for his labors, then repeated the arguments he had made to the BSG. Referring to his status as a blacklisted writer, he observed that film executives should have the courage to give credit to the writers they engage: "The men in control of *Lawrence of Arabia* lack that courage." This was a not-so-veiled reference to Spiegel and his cohorts at Columbia Pictures. As we have seen, Wilson's contract with Spiegel declared that Wilson would be granted a screen credit only if he formally denied any association with the Communist Party, something that Wilson had categorically refused to do.[86]

Bolt answered Wilson on December 3, 1962. He said he was startled by Wilson's "bombshell" because he never thought that his sole authorship of the screenplay would be questioned, given the fact that he had devoted a year to working on it. As for the parallels between the narrative structure of his screenplay and Wilson's, he protested that he had scrupulously followed the narration of events as laid out in *Seven Pillars.* "I don't know of any account of Lawrence's life which does not follow that storyline."[87]

Bolt's response seems somewhat disingenuous. To begin with, Bolt's contract, we recall, stated that he was to compose a screenplay "with reference to a script by Michael Wilson," and he did follow Wilson's script. Indeed, as we have seen, some of the incidents in Bolt's screenplay come directly from Wilson's draft, not *Seven Pillars.* In general, Bolt's defense masks the fact that, while he had stood on Wilson's shoulders, Wilson's contribution was to go unrecognized.

The BSG appointed a committee of three screenwriters to arbitrate the case. The most prominent member was the screenwriter-director Bryan Forbes (*Whistle Down the Wind* [1961]), who, as we have seen, had also been involved in the consideration of Wilson's plea for a screen credit on *The Bridge on the River Kwai.* Forbes told me in correspondence that he had decided in Wilson's favor on *Kwai* and that he supported Wilson's petition on *Lawrence.* So did the BSG committee. In essence, it stated that, while, admittedly, history is not copyrightable, if the way in which an author narrates a particular historical event is peculiar to that author, his account *is* copyrightable. Moreover, Bolt had access to Wilson's work, and the two screenplays are substantially similar. Hence, when the committee finished its deliberations in June 1963, it voted unanimously to uphold Wilson's claim.

Meanwhile, the BSG had in March 1963 already bestowed on Bolt its award for the best screenplay of 1962 for *Lawrence of Arabia.* (The film had premiered in London on December 10, 1962; see chapter 13.) And, on the recommendation of Forbes and other members of the committee, Wilson belatedly received his own bronze plaque, one identical to Bolt's, from the BSG on December 18, 1963.

Spiegel, however, was not obligated to abide by the BSG's verdict—and, in fact, did not. Even though the Communist witch hunt had largely died with Joe McCarthy in 1957—and the Hollywood blacklist shortly thereafter—he was still afraid that the open association of a blacklisted writer with *Lawrence of Arabia* would hurt the film's Oscar chances. But Spiegel was not the only stumbling block in Wilson's way. David Lean thought that Wilson's script was "just awful" and that in no way did he deserve a screen credit for it.[88]

Michael Wilson succumbed to a heart attack on April 9, 1978. By then, he had finally received an official screen credit for cowriting the 1968 *Planet of the Apes*. Nevertheless, he became increasingly despondent during his last years over the way the blacklist had wrecked his career, and he took to drinking heavily. Indeed, his last illness was exacerbated by his alcoholism.

When the restored version of *Lawrence of Arabia* was being prepared in 1989, Forbes and the rest of the original BSG arbitration committee appealed to Columbia for a screen credit for Wilson. Columbia declined, on the grounds that "the director was adamant in refusing to acknowledge [Wilson's] claims."[89] (Forbes later told me that Columbia never even contacted Lean about the committee's request.) Finally, in 1995, spurred by studies of Wilson's case published by film scholars,[90] the Screen Writers Guild of America took up the cause, declaring Wilson's contribution to *Lawrence* "substantial."[91] This appeal proved successful, and, when the restored version of *Lawrence* was released on home video in 2000, in the opening credits the screenplay was officially attributed to Robert Bolt and Michael Wilson.

Similarly contentious—though not nearly so long drawn out—was the decision of whom to cast as Lawrence. After Brando turned down the role, Lean and Spiegel briefly considered Alec Guinness, who had played Lawrence on the London stage in *Ross*. (Guinness told me jokingly that he was thinking of forming an exclusive fraternity of all the actors who had at one time or another been considered to play Lawrence on the screen.) But Guinness was getting too old for the part. And the same could be said of John Mills, who had played Lawrence in the Broadway production of *Ross*. Both were also well-known, and Lean wanted a relative unknown for the part because, when Lawrence turns up in Cairo at the beginning of the picture, he is an unknown quantity, both to his fellow British officers and to the Arabs. As the director John Schlesinger told me in conversation, "David wanted . . . a fresh face for the role [because] it would be hard for an audience to accept an established star like Brando as an unknown quantity." Lean would then surround the newcomer with the supporting cast of seasoned professionals that would, he felt, be necessary if he was carry the picture.

The main contender at this point was Albert Finney, a young British actor who had played a rebellious factory worker in Karel Reisz's *Saturday Night and Sunday Morning* (1960). In August 1960, Spiegel arranged for a screen test, with Finney dressed in various Arab and British army costumes. Lean and Spiegel were favorably impressed, but Finney balked when Spiegel insisted on tying him down to a five-year contract. "I hate to be committed to a girl or a film producer," he later said. "Plenty of people have been ruined by Hollywood. I want to be an actor, not a marketable property like a detergent."[92]

Lean happened to see a heist film called *The Day They Robbed the Bank of England* (John Guillerman, 1960), in which Peter O'Toole played a British officer. "That's it. I've got to test him," he told himself. "One of the first things about actors is screen presence." That means that all the actor has to do in order to dominate a scene is to enter it. "O'Toole had screen presence."[93]

Peter O'Toole was the twenty-seven-year-old son of Irish immigrants; in this he resembled Lawrence, whose parents were also from Ireland. For his screen test on November 7, 1960, O'Toole, decked out in Arab garb, acted out a couple of scenes from Wilson's draft script, which was all that was available at the time, Lean feeding him cues off-camera. He also recited passages from *Seven Pillars*. Before the test was over, Lean stopped the camera and announced, "No use shooting another foot of film. The boy *is* Lawrence!" O'Toole quipped disingenuously, "Is it a speaking part?" This was a jab at Brando, who had a habit of mumbling his lines.[94] Little did O'Toole realize that he was going to have to memorize 648 lines, the longest speaking part in the history of cinema.

Spiegel officially announced that O'Toole had gotten the lead in the film on November 20, 1960. Still, he had heard gossip that the rowdy Irishman indulged in binge drinking. So he asked Anthony Nutting, officially *Lawrence*'s technical adviser but really a factotum, to monitor O'Toole's behavior during filming. "I had to keep Peter off the bottle," Nutting recalled. One day, O'Toole showed up on the set in Jordan with a hangover. Nutting gave him a stern lecture: "Look, if you don't stay sober, you're going to leave Jordan on your ass. . . . You're the only actor we've got for Lawrence; and if you get bundled home, that's the end of the film; and that's probably the end of you. So you'd better behave yourself." Nutting conceded that O'Toole could do his drinking in Beirut, known as "sin city" in the Middle East, when there was a break in filming.[95]

Lean was now more convinced than ever of the need for a solid supporting cast, and Spiegel agreed. Spiegel asked Alec Guinness to play Prince Feisal. The prince was actually close to Lawrence's age, but his grave, deeply lined countenance and regal bearing made him seem older, as is evident from contemporary newsreel footage.[96] Hence the choice of the older Guinness, who was very imposing in the role.

Because Lean and Guinness had quarreled frequently during the filming of *Kwai*, a rumor spread in the industry that Lean did not want Guinness in *Lawrence*. According to Andrew Sinclair, when Spiegel advised Lean that he had signed Guinness, a scene ensued: "Lean immediately stopped work and announced he was leaving the picture. According to legend, Spiegel fell to the ground, the apparent victim of a heart attack." The repentant Lean visited Spiegel in the hospital and assured him that he would do anything to help Spiegel recover. Spiegel made an instant recovery and said, "You're so nice. So we cast Guinness."[97]

The story is hardly credible. Guinness told me that it was Lean, not Spiegel, who asked him personally to play Feisal—which gives the lie to this apocryphal tale. Nevertheless, Spiegel was not above feigning a heart attack in order to get an associate to see things his way; indeed, he later told Lean that he had had a heart attack when Lean was going over schedule, and Lean did not believe him for a moment.

In any case, Lean and Guinness had long since patched up their falling-out over *Kwai*, and Guinness looked forward to working with Lean again. "I like to work with people I know," he explained. "Lean is very keen. He has a firm picture in his mind of what he wants, though he will occasionally listen to suggestions."[98] In fact, Guinness and Lean got along extremely well while filming *Lawrence*.

Guinness said that he preferred to play Feisal, rather than Lawrence, the part he had been considered for earlier. The more he learned about Lawrence, the more disenchanted he became. Like Lean, Guinness had idolized Lawrence when he was a youngster. "I was endlessly throwing a towel over my head and tying a tie around it and pretending to be Lawrence of Arabia," Guinness recalled.[99] But, when he interviewed some of Lawrence's friends prior to playing in *Ross*, he got a somewhat problematic picture of him. "He was a terrible fibber, you know," one of Lawrence's friends, Sydney Cockrell, declared. When Cockrell once asked Lawrence why he lied so much, Lawrence answered, "Because my lies are more interesting than the truth." Guinness commented, "I find fibbers tiresome."[100]

By contrast, Guinness viewed the ascetic Prince Feisal as a gentleman. According to Garry O'Connor, Guinness felt that the prince "had a code of honor which was in many ways superior to that of Lawrence." Thus, in his performance, he displayed his wholehearted and unreserved admiration for Feisal. But Guinness certainly had a "disdain for the self-centered virtues of Lawrence."[101]

Spiegel wrote Lean that he hoped to cast the ever-popular Cary Grant as General Allenby. "Bugger and blast the star system!" Lean responded vehemently on February 21, 1961. Jack Hawkins, who had played a British officer to perfection in *Kwai*, would make "a mighty good stab at the Allenby part."[102]

Spiegel conceded in this case. But he was determined to corral one big

Hollywood star to give the picture more box office pull in the United States—as William Holden had done for *Kwai*. He chose the Oscar winner Anthony Quinn (*Lust for Life* [Vincente Minnelli, 1956]), the Mexican-born actor, to play Auda Abu Tayi, the impetuous, rough-hewn Arab pirate who had become a folk hero to the Arabs. Quinn had just scored a triumph as a resistance worker in the World War II adventure film *The Guns of Navarone* (J. Lee Thompson, 1961); for his part, he was anxious to be in a David Lean film, being a big fan of Lean's.

According to Quinn, he first met Lean in Jordan, where filming had already begun.[103] When he arrived on location in the desert, Quinn first got into an Arab costume, then went to the makeup tent, where he was given cocoa makeup for his face plus a beak-like nose. His makeup was modeled after the pastel sketch of Auda Abu Tayi in *Seven Pillars.*

When Quinn emerged from the makeup tent, the Arab extras standing around suddenly exclaimed, "Auda Abu Tayi!" Lean took one look at him and said, "He *is* Auda Abu Tayi!" Then he turned to an assistant and said, "Screw this man Quinn; hire this fellow instead!" Robert Bolt, for one, was never impressed by Quinn's portrayal of the desert brigand. He later said that he thought Quinn's acting was over the top; he was obvious, not subtle. Quinn, noted Bolt, belonged to that class of virile Hollywood actors "who wear their balls on their sleeves."[104]

Another Oscar-winning actor, José Ferrer (*Cyrano de Bergerac* [Michael Gordon, 1950]), agreed to do a cameo as the sadistic Turkish bey. Ferrer noted afterward that he did the best work of his career as the infamous bey. Claude Rains, who had appeared in Lean's *Passionate Friends,* took on the role of the devious Mr. Dryden, an espionage agent attached to the Arab Bureau. Rains's rich, throaty voice perfectly captured Dryden's urbane villainy.

Spiegel had real difficulty finding an actor to play Sherif Ali, a gallant young Arab aristocrat based primarily on Sherif Ali ibu el Hussein, a spirited leader of the Arab Revolt and Lawrence's closest friend and confidant. Spiegel had originally cast the French actor Maurice Ronet, but Lean complained that Ronet had a thick French accent and possessed little command of English. Moreover, Lean felt that Ronet had no feel for the role: "When I put him in Arab dress, it looked like he was walking around in drag."[105]

Having decided to replace Ronet, Lean leafed through a catalog of Egyptian actors until he found one—Omar Sharif—who was listed as speaking English. He told Spiegel to bring Sharif out to the desert location for a screen test. Sharif says, "I was a star in Egypt; I wasn't really interested in making a Hollywood film; but I went really to meet David Lean." He was flown in a private plane directly to the location site in Jordan. The plane landed in the desert and taxied over to a lone figure standing in the desert sand—David Lean. "I noticed that he had piercing eyes, like a hawk," Sharif continues, "the first time I met him."[106]

Sharif did a screen test with O'Toole, and Lean sent the results to Spiegel on May 15, 1961, noting that he thought Sharif "could play Ali" but did not quite have "the desert hawk quality" of an Arab chieftain.[107] Spiegel encouraged Lean to go with Sharif. Ronet was given his walking papers, and Sharif went to London for a conference with Spiegel. He had neither an agent nor a lawyer, so the wily Spiegel got him to sign a seven-year contract, with a paltry $15,000 for his salary on *Lawrence*. This was precisely the sort of slave contract that Albert Finney declined to sign; Lean was beside himself when he heard.

When he returned to Jordan, Sharif asked Lean about Sherif Ali's friendship with Lawrence. Lean answered that, though Ali and Lawrence were good friends, there is no indication that they shared a homosexual relationship, as a couple of commentators on Lawrence's life have suggested. Indeed, Lean said, in *Seven Pillars* Lawrence compares their friendship to that of "David and Jonathan in the Old Testament." In fact, Lean encouraged O'Toole and Sharif to become good friends during filming because Lawrence and Ali were "great mates."[108] Guinness personally liked Sharif, he told me, finding him very friendly. But he also had a special interest in chatting with him. "I listened carefully to Omar's accent," Guinness recalled, "and used it for Feisal, who was, like Omar, an Arab speaking English."

Another actor had to be replaced besides Ronet, but for reasons of ill health. Edmund O'Brien had taken the role of Jackson Bentley, the opportunistic American journalist modeled on Lowell Thomas, but he suffered a heart attack after filming only a few scenes. As a matter of fact, O'Brien can still be seen in the background of the scene in which Lawrence discusses his ill-fitting uniform in the British officers' club. Arthur Kennedy, who had appeared with Anthony Quinn in *Barabbas* (Richard Fleischer, 1962), took over for O'Brien.

Lean was wise in changing Lowell Thomas's name to Jackson Bentley since Thomas had no wish to be associated with the movie. He later sneered, "The only true things in it are the sand and the camels." For example, O'Toole was a head taller than Lawrence.[109] But, since few people knew Lawrence was short, only the purists were troubled.

Lean was as careful in casting the production crew of a movie as he was in casting the actors. Moreover, Spiegel had an unerring knack for marshaling first-rate talent on both sides of the camera. He understandably suggested that Lean rehire Jack Hildyard, who had won an Academy Award for

Kwai, as director of photography. But Lean demurred because Hildyard had balked at all the overtime Lean had demanded on *Kwai.* Lean preferred to work with "dedicated maniacs" like himself. William Graf, chief of the Columbia Pictures London office, who had been the studio's representative on *Kwai* as well as on *Lawrence,* then suggested Freddie Young, who had photographed Mark Robson's *Inn of the Sixth Happiness* (1958), starring Ingrid Bergman as an English missionary in China, and other cinematic epics. Spiegel was much in agreement with Graf.

But Lean was hesitant because he and Young had not gotten along while they were working on *Major Barbara* twenty years earlier. Lean, as we have seen, was editing that film. But the director, Gabriel Pascal, knew nothing about directing and asked him to be present on the set as his personal assistant, to advise him on selecting camera setups. And the feisty Young, the cinematographer, resented being given directions by an upstart. At the end of the first week of shooting, Young exploded at Lean, telling him "not to try to teach his grandmother to suck eggs"—an old English proverb meaning that one should not presume to offer advice to an expert.[110] As a result, Lean demanded that Pascal replace Young. He also resolved to steer clear of Young in the future.

But Spiegel and Graf insisted that Lean bury this ancient grudge because Young was at the head of his profession. And so Lean began a professional relationship with Young that would win Young Oscars on three Lean pictures in a row, starting with *Lawrence.* As it happened, Young was to have been the cameraman on Wetherell's abortive *Revolt in the Desert* project of 1928. So this was his second crack at a film about Lawrence. Despite their past differences, Young emphasized that he had always liked Lean and wanted to work with him.

When Young met with Lean to discuss Lawrence, the two got along like a house afire. Still, they managed to establish a work relationship. Lean acknowledged that, while he knew more than a bit about camera lenses and lighting a set, Young knew still more. Hence, Lean would describe a shot in minute detail, disappear into his trailer, and let Young arrange the camera setup. "The compositions were worked out between us," Young said. "I never felt he was trying to do my job for me."[111]

Lean informed Young that he planned to shoot *Lawrence* in seventy-millimeter Panavision, which provided a larger image even than CinemaScope, which was used for *Kwai.* When projected on the giant screen of a movie palace, the seventy-millimeter image was awesome. Young went straight to Hollywood, where he obtained equipment from Robert Gottschalk, who had invented the Panavision process. He also got Spiegel to engage Ernest

Day as a camera operator because Day had worked on Otto Preminger's *Exodus* (1960), which had also been shot in Panavision. Peter Newbrook, who had previously been Lean's camera operator, became a cinematographer for the second unit.

For the production designer, Lean asked Spiegel to get John Bryan, who had designed Lean's two Dickens films, but Bryan had to beg off because of ill health. So John Box, who was to have collaborated with Bryan, took over as production designer. Box had already designed *The Inn of the Sixth Happiness* (which had been photographed by Young), managing to make North Wales look like China. He went off to Jordan to help scout locations.

Armed with a copy of *Seven Pillars*, Lean and Box made an extensive reconnaissance trip, accompanied by an Arab guide who was a member of the Desert Patrol. They journeyed to the areas through which Lawrence had traveled, making, for example, an excursion to Wadi Rumm, a valley in the desert surrounded by towering cliffs rising two thousand feet into the air from the desert floor. Lawrence described Wadi Rumm as "vast and echoing and God-like."[112] Box called it the Middle East's Grand Canyon, and he and Lean made ample use of it in the film. They also found an abandoned fort where Lawrence and his brigade had holed up for a spell. According to Box, he and Lean even discovered "the remains of a Turkish railway which Lawrence and his raiders had demolished, with wrecked carriages still lying in the sand on the side of the twisted railroad tracks."[113] In sum, Lean and Box found *Seven Pillars* quite accurate when it came to Lawrence's descriptions of places that had figured in his adventures.

Phyllis Dalton, who had provided the costumes for Albert Finney's screen test on a moment's notice, came aboard as costume designer for the film. Dalton studied the photographs taken by Lawrence himself that were available in the Imperial War Museum, as well as Kennington's pastel sketches in *Seven Pillars*, to get a fix on the costumes associated with the period. She then went to Hawkes, a men's clothing store in London, where she found the tailor who had made General Allenby's uniforms still employed. "I had Peter O'Toole's officer's uniform made to be deliberately ill fitting because it was immediately clear that Lawrence was a misfit in the regular army," Dalton says. "For the Arab costumes I raided the bazaars in Damascus, which is thought to be the oldest city in the world."[114]

Like Phyllis Dalton, the film editor Anne V. Coates was engaged for *Lawrence* by Spiegel because she had worked on Finney's screen test. A niece of J. Arthur Rank, she came from a strong film background. She had already edited the 1958 Alec Guinness vehicle *The Horse's Mouth* for Ronald Neame.

She actually volunteered to edit the Finney screen test, which she watched with Lean. She had a panic attack while sitting next to Lean: "To be cutting for David, who was known to be one of the greatest editors, was nerve-threatening," she remembers. After the screening, Lean turned to her and said, "That's the first piece of film I've ever seen cut exactly the way I would have done it!" A couple of days later, Spiegel called her to say: "David Lean would like you to edit *Lawrence of Arabia*."[115]

The production crew that Lean and Spiegel had assembled were all "dedicated maniacs," the kind that Lean sought out. In addition to those already named, the property master Eddie Fowlie, Lean's production assistant Norman Spencer, and the cameraman Peter Newbrook, all veterans of previous Lean films, likewise fit that profile—individuals who displayed "a singular dedication to the job."[116]

Not all aspects of the project went so smoothly. Lean and Spiegel always seemed to be at loggerheads about something, and Bill Graf tried to arbitrate between them, as he had done on *Kwai*. At least Lean had a much better rapport with the film crew than he did on *Kwai*. By this time the technicians recognized him as a topflight director and made allowances for his being a perfectionist. He was now in a position to chide Spiegel, in a letter of April 28, 1961, shortly before principal photography began, for being high-handed and impatient with the crew: "It creates awful resentments of which you seem quite unaware."[117]

Spiegel answered on May 5 that his purpose was to keep the crew from wasting time and money; he added that he resented Lean's assuming the role of "valiant champion." He also noted that, as far back as *Great Expectations*, producers like Ronald Neame said that Lean was suspicious of them. Still, with filming soon to begin, Spiegel thought it diplomatic to bury the hatchet with Lean once more. He followed up with a note of reconciliation: "I promise to keep the provocations to a minimum."[118]

The endless problems with the screenplay had made the preproduction period especially stressful for both Lean and Spiegel. Then too there were the manifold difficulties involved in getting the right actors and even having to replace some cast members. Lean had set up shop in Jordan, the first major location site for the production, in April 1960. So Lean and Spiegel frequently had to negotiate with each other via cables and letters, except for those rare occasions when Spiegel visited Jordan to confer with Lean personally.

On his visit to the Horizon production office in Amman in the spring of 1961, Spiegel was apprehensive about the numerous obstacles inevitably to be faced when shooting a huge spectacle with a production unit of several hundred people in such a remote and primitive locale. "There's going to be no picture," he moaned ruefully. Lean was furious at Spiegel's panicky outburst and replied that they had weathered similar storms while making *Kwai* in the jungle and that they would surmount the problems they faced in making *Lawrence* in the desert. "So let's stop this fucking around and get on with the picture."[119]

Chapter Thirteen

IN SEARCH OF A HERO

FILMING *LAWRENCE OF ARABIA*

His life was rather pathetic. But it is by folly alone that the world moves; and so it is a respectable thing, upon the whole. And besides, he was what we could call a good man.

—*Joseph Conrad*, Victory

All men dream. Those who dream by night in the dusty recess of their minds wake in the day to find that it was vanity. But the dreamers of the day are dangerous men, for they may act their dream, with open eyes, to make it possible. This I did.

—*T. E. Lawrence*, Seven Pillars of Wisdom

"Bernard Shaw once said that no one has satisfactorily placed a boundary between myth and history," Peter O'Toole said in a 2004 interview. "You can see the enormous attraction of a historical film which has an aura of myth." He further indicated that no epic film mingles history and myth quite the way *Lawrence of Arabia* does. O'Toole recalled the first day of shooting on *Lawrence*, when David Lean said to him, "Pete, this could be the start of a great adventure." Concluded O'Toole, "And for the next twenty months, it was."[1]

Principal photography on *Lawrence* commenced in Jordan on May 15, 1961, in one of the most remote locations ever selected for a commercial Hollywood film: the arid, desolate area in the Jordanian desert called Jebel el Tubeiq, which had been uninhabited since some monks abandoned their dwelling there in the seventh century. Yet here was Freddie Young with his seventy-millimeter Panavision camera, recording the first shot for the film, which was in the can by midafternoon. It was a spectacular image of the desert, radiating heat as if from a blast furnace. With the temperature rising to 120 degrees, Young had already learned that he had to drape damp towels over the camera and place a beach umbrella over it, in order to keep the camera from getting overheated. Furthermore, the film stock had to be preserved in a refrigerator truck to keep it from wilting.

Lean remembered that, on the first evening in the desert, he turned on his portable Zenith shortwave radio, to listen to the news. The first thing he heard was "The Colonel Bogey March" from *The Bridge on the River Kwai*. He reflected, "If that's not a good omen!"[2]

The ruler of Jordan, King Hussein, was the great-grandson of Sherif Hussein, who was, in turn, Prince Feisal's father. It was Sherif Hussein who instigated the Arab Revolt against Turkey in 1916. King Hussein proved most cooperative with Lean and the film unit; he was, of course, confident that the film would give a tremendous boost to tourism. Anthony Nutting served as the chief liaison between the king and the production unit, and he negotiated the Jordanian army's participation in the film for £150,000, considerably less than Spiegel had anticipated.

Spiegel, as producer, set up a location headquarters near the seaport of Aqaba, 250 miles north of Amman. A dilapidated army barracks served as the base of operations from which the film unit would set out for the far-flung desert locations where Lean was shooting. Most of the cast and crew lived in canvas tents with wooden floors. The same British catering service that Spiegel had employed in Ceylon to feed the *Kwai* unit was on hand once again in the desert. There were few creature comforts at the camp, but Lean observed that "physical discomfort is the price of authenticity."[3] The crew christened the tent city "Camp David" (perhaps a reference to the U.S. presidents' hideaway).

Lean had a caravan-type trailer, known as the command van, all to himself, from which he ruled the roost. Anthony Quayle, who was playing Colonel Brighton, one of Lawrence's superior officers, says that Lean was in his element, shooting in the desert. One day, while watching Lean issuing orders to cast and crew, Quayle exclaimed, "You're like a bloody general out here; you've got a huge army under your command. I'm madly impressed!"[4]

Because there were no adequate projection facilities on location, as noted before, Lean could not see any of the footage that he had shot. So the rushes were sent to London to be processed, after which Spiegel and Anne Coates would watch them at the Horizon office. A few months later, Lean would view the rushes, when he touched base with Spiegel in London during a break in shooting. The lab, of course, would notify Lean directly if any footage was damaged and had to be reshot. For example, sand sometimes got inside the camera and ruined a take, but this seldom happened.

Freddie Young was impressed with the careful preparation that Lean put into composing a shot. "Some directors shoot masses of stuff from different angles, hoping that it will all cut together in the end," Young explained. "But David wasn't like that; he had the mind of a trained editor." Lean would visualize a scene in his mind's eye before he shot it. "Once having decided how to shoot a scene, he shot it in one way—his way." Thus, Lean did not see the need to supply the editor with a great variety of surplus footage, in order to ensure sufficient material to assemble a scene in final form. But he always saw to it that there was enough footage to put together a coherent sequence. In brief, he shot only as much as he felt he would use in the completed scene. "Although David took a lot of time to make a film, he was neither indecisive nor wasteful," Young concluded.[5]

Still Lean sometimes seemed to be spending too much time looking through the viewfinder while he prepared a shot, as if he were in a trance. Barbara Cole, the script supervisor, would tap him on the shoulder and tell him to get a move on. The script supervisor is responsible for seeing to it that the actors follow the dialogue and action dictated in the script exactly and for keeping a detailed record of everything that is shot. It was an open secret that Barbara Cole was also his inamorata. Once Lean and Cole became lovers, they frequently shared his caravan. Things got dicey when Leila, Lean's wife—they had married in 1960—came to stay at the base camp in Aqaba for a few days. But the cast and crew never breathed a word to Leila Lean about Barbara Cole.

Phyllis Dalton said frankly, "Leila was very fond of David; but by the time of *Lawrence*, David had no further use for her." Leila characterized her relationship with her husband as a series of partings. Leila, as we know, was mentally disturbed (see chapter 11). Whenever Lean broached the possibility of divorce, Leila inevitably threatened suicide, and Lean knew her well enough to believe that she meant it. So he remained married to her while continuing his affair with Barbara Cole. As Bill Graf put it, "David played musical chairs with his women."[6] But the women in Lean's life always took a backseat to his preoccupation with his work.

Lean, we remember, never welcomed Spiegel's visits on location, and he was relieved that Spiegel did not show up in Jordan very often. Spiegel did arrive on one occasion with a fleet of photographers, Lean recalled in a television interview. They snapped endless pictures of him "stroking camels, stroking me, and going around with the cast." These photographs were released to the trade press in England and America and gave the false impression that Spiegel spent a great deal of time on location.[7]

There was one difficult shot in particular that Lean was concerned about; he had discussed it with Young even before principal photography started. When Young was leaving for Hollywood to acquire Panavision equipment, Lean said to him, "Freddie, I'd like to get a mirage in this film. I don't know how in bloody hell we are going to do it, but I want you to give it a bit of thought." Young found the solution when he was selecting equipment in the Panavision plant. He spied a 450-millimeter telephoto lens on a bench; it was shaped like a fire hose nozzle. "I immediately got the idea that, with that telephoto lens, I could get a close-up of a mirage," he recalled. So he acquired it. "A mirage in the desert is always seen in the distance, looking as though the sea is lying on top of the sand," Young explained. "With a telephoto lens you can film this in close-up, which enables the audience to see the details of the heatwaves that are invisible to the naked eye."[8]

The mirage shot was conceived for the entrance of Ali (Omar Sharif) into the film. "We chose a spot which we knew normally produced a mirage at the hottest time of the day," Young continued. "There we built a dummy well; Lawrence and his Arab guide, Tafas, who is drawing water from the well, were in the foreground. Omar Sharif, on his camel, was placed a quarter of a mile into the distance. At a given signal, the camera rolled, and Sharif's camel began trotting forward. We shot a thousand feet of film, ending with the arrival of camel and rider at the well." The haze of heat given off by the hot desert sand causes a distant figure to materialize like the apparition of an eerie, bobbling specter. "On the screen you see at first just the mirage, then on the horizon a shimmering blur of a figure," Young went on. "As he comes closer, you get a distinct image of his camel trotting, it seems, through waves of water; and finally a clear view of Omar Sharif, approaching the last few yards."[9] Sharif rode out of infinity in a flame-like, flickering image in long shot, continuing on into a close-up, and this was all accomplished in a single take. Young had captured an optical illusion on film.

When Spiegel and Coates saw the mirage scene in the rushes, they were overwhelmed. In general, Spiegel was satisfied with the footage that Lean shipped to him. But Robert Bolt, who often watched the rushes with Spiegel and Coates, was not as impressed as the other two. Bolt, who had never been involved in a film before, did not quite appreciate the logistics of shooting a huge motion picture spectacle. He was often bored watching endless footage of actors trekking around the sand dunes. Never, he thought, had so little been shot in so much time.

Bolt told a London gossip columnist that, after visiting with Lean and Spiegel in Jordan, he was convinced that life on location was "a continuous clash of egomaniacal monsters, wasting more energy than dinosaurs and pouring rivers of money into the sand."[10] Spiegel, who was already worried about Lean going over both schedule and budget, went ballistic when he read Bolt's condescending remarks. In a fit of pique, he fired off a cable to Lean, warning, "If you do not move faster, I shall have to come out there with a big broom and make a clean sweep—and replace the whole crew."[11]

Lean was livid when he read Spiegel's wire. In order to reply properly, he got a big broom from the property department and filmed a shot of himself in seventy millimeter while he swept sand in the desert. Then he spoke directly to the camera: "Well, here I am in this fucking desert, making this fucking film. You come out here, you bugger, and try having a go in my place. You wouldn't last an hour. We're going as fast as we can." He wrote Spiegel a follow-up letter on August 17, 1961, indicating that he had heard that Bolt had issued a retraction and hoped that Bolt would shut up in the future.[12]

Not surprisingly, Spiegel and Graf were not amused when they took a look at Lean's seventy-millimeter "memo." Graf contacted Mike Frankovich in Hollywood—Frankovich was in charge of international production for Columbia—and alerted him to the fact that Lean had been filming in Jordan throughout the summer, with no end in sight, and would have to be confronted.

In Lean's favor, it must be stated that the production was originally underfinanced. Spiegel's initial budget of $3 million was totally unrealistic for such a project. So overages were inevitable. Spiegel now projected a revised budget closer to $10 million. Frankovich and the front office in Hollywood decided that the Jordan shoots should be terminated as soon as possible, the funds allocated for filming there having been used up, and the production moved to Spain, where the studio had funds frozen.

Spiegel accordingly shut down filming in Jordan on September 18, 1961. By that point, Lean had been shooting in the desert for twenty-one weeks, not the sixteen weeks originally scheduled. "When the decision was made to pull up stakes in Jordan," says John Box, "David had to be dragged screaming from his caravan."[13] According to Roy Stevens, the assistant director, there was good reason for the move to Spain: "Spiegel was quite convinced that, if he didn't pull the rug out from under David's feet, he would still be in Jordan, shooting pretty pictures."[14]

Lean was upset primarily because Spiegel did not tell him personally that he was terminating the Jordan shoot. He had Box, who was at the production office in Amman, send Lean a memo with the bad news. In a letter of

September 29 to Spiegel, Lean chided him that he had to learn from Box secondhand that the order had already gone out to ship the cameras and other equipment to Spain. "Not a word from you," Lean pouted. "As Alex Korda once said in his early days in Britain, 'I know fuck all' about what's going on!"[15]

Spiegel negotiated a six-week hiatus for the film unit before resuming production in Spain, where accommodations would be a full-service hotel, conditions considerably upgraded from those of the desert camp. The exodus from Jordan to London took place on October 1, 1961. The respite from filming allowed Lean the opportunity to see the ten hours of rushes that he had sent to the Horizon office so far and to give Coates specific instructions on cutting all the footage together. Coates was, thus, able to make a rough assemblage of all the Jordanian footage at this juncture. Thereafter, she would make periodic forays to Spain, in order to confer with Lean about the edit of the material he shot there.

Lean proceeded to Spain to help John Box scout locations. They chose buildings in Seville that featured Arab-Moorish architecture suggestive of the Middle East. They even searched out areas in the hinterlands that could pass for the Arabian Desert. Moreover, Bolt had come to Spain, and he and Lean made further revisions to the script. Meanwhile, the cast and the rest of the crew relaxed in England.

On December 18, principal photography resumed. Bolt got to do a brief cameo before returning to London to put the finishing touches on the screenplay. There is a scene in which Lawrence shows up in the officers' bar at British headquarters in Cairo in his grimy Arab garb. A starchy officer taps his pipe against his chin as he stares disapprovingly at Lawrence. That officer is Bolt. "No rehearsal; no pay, just a bit of fun," Bolt commented.[16]

A bit of fun was to be had off the set as well. On one occasion, for example, Guinness and O'Toole were invited to have dinner with a Spanish grandee: "O'Toole got drunk, quarreled with his host, and threw a glass of champagne in his face." Guinness admired O'Toole's acting abilities—but not his drinking abilities, especially when Nutting was not around to keep an eye on things. O'Toole could have been shot for his gross insult to a dignitary, Guinness commented, "And I am beginning to think it's a pity he wasn't."[17]

Still, filming proceeded apace. Whereas in Jordan many of the exterior scenes had been shot—"all the big, spectacular desert material," according to Lean—in Spain things moved inside: "We did a lot of the interiors—interiors of authentic Moorish buildings—in and around Seville."[18]

As the filmmaker Stanley Kubrick (*Barry Lyndon* [1975]) once told me,

"Most of the interiors of a period film can be shot in castles and mansions that are still preserved in Europe, where the furniture and decor are already there. You only have to move in your cast and crew and get to work." This was certainly true in Seville, where many of the buildings showed medieval, Moorish influences—particularly the buildings in the Plaza de España (erected for the 1929 Seville International Exhibition), which Lean and Box commandeered for use in the film. For example, one building served as the setting for the Arab Bureau in Cairo.

Other locations were used as well. For example, the Casa del Pilato (so called because it resembles Pilate's villa in Judea) was utilized as General Allenby's headquarters in Cairo. As for the bey's headquarters: "The town of Deraa, where Lawrence was apprehended and tortured . . . , was in reality a wretched place," said Box. So: "We picked a terrible slum."[19]

Box worried about the difficulty Young would have in rigging his lamps to light the interiors where they were filming. Movie sets are designed to accommodate the cameraman's lights, but real rooms in real houses are not. When the crew was filming in a small room, such as the bey's austere office, it was hard for Young to keep his lamps out of camera range. But he managed skillfully to conceal his lights from the camera. "I acknowledge the sheer technical ability of Freddie Young in this regard," says Box.[20]

Alec Guinness told me that Lean was known for his no-nonsense approach to shooting a scene; he would tolerate no horsing around on the set. Guinness watched Lean filming a tense scene between O'Toole and Jack Hawkins, in which General Allenby asks Lawrence about his sordid experience in Deraa. During one take, Hawkins asked O'Toole, "What precisely happened at Deraa?" O'Toole, who was getting giddy after several takes, blurted out, "I was fucked by some Turks!" "What a pity," Hawkins replied, going along with the gag. Lean blew his top and berated the two actors for their "disgraceful behavior."

Guinness did not approve of rude language; still, he thought that Lean had overreacted and noted that Roy Stevens, the first assistant director, thought that Lean liked the set tense and quiet. Guinness quoted Stevens as saying, "It was like going to church when you went on a David Lean set." In justice to Lean, he was convinced that the best way to ensure that the actors and the director could fully concentrate on the scene at hand was to run a tight ship.

On March 19, 1962, Lean finished shooting interiors in and around Seville. He moved the production unit to Almeria, where there were some sand dunes that looked like the Jordanian desert, in order to shoot more exteriors. At Almeria, Spiegel brought in another second-unit director, André de Toth, in addition to the two already on board, André Smagghe and Noel Howard. Lean continued to fall behind schedule, so Spiegel wanted to provide Lean with additional help.

Unlike Smagghe and Howard, de Toth had been directing feature films—like the hard-boiled western *Ramrod* (1947)—for two decades. Known for his predilection for violence, de Toth seemed suitable to work on the battle scenes coming up in the schedule. Asked why he wore a black eye patch over one eye, he would reply, "I sometimes visit the grave of the one responsible."[21] But Lean was not particularly impressed by the formidable de Toth.

De Toth and Box found a hot, barren canyon near a bay where Box could build a replica of the seaport of Aqaba—the real Aqaba was too modernized to be used in the film. "We needed a long, straight section of desert," Young writes, "to film the charge by the Arabs on the Turkish defenders of Aqaba. . . . At Almeria there was an isolated stretch of sand similar to some of the locations we used in Jordan."[22]

"The whole point about Aqaba," Box says, "was that the Turks expected an invasion from the sea because invaders attacking Aqaba on land would have to cross the desert. I wanted to do a shot that would pan across the garrison town toward the sea, with the big cannon in the foreground, pointing toward the sea, where the invasion was expected to come from."[23] The gun could not be turned around and aimed at Lawrence's forces when they entered Aqaba from the rear. Box designed the reconstruction with three hundred separate buildings—which were actually a series of skillfully constructed facades—crowned by the forty-foot Turkish cannon.

"When the day came to shoot the big charge to capture Aqaba," Omar Sharif says, "Peter O'Toole and I had to lead about five hundred extras galloping on camels and horses. I realized that, if I fell off my camel, I could be trampled by the whole troop of charging Arab cavalrymen. Hence I tied myself to my saddle so I wouldn't fall off." O'Toole did not take that precaution, and he did fall to the ground—right in the path of the oncoming cavalry troops. "His camel planted its four legs around where Peter had fallen, as it was trained to do, and protected him," Sharif concludes. "And the whole troop passed him by."[24]

On May 15, 1962, in observance of the first anniversary of shooting, Lean hosted a party for the production unit at the yacht club in Almeria. Spiegel made a junket to the location site around this time. He had dinner with Lean in Almeria on May 21. He started off by tactfully telling Lean that he needed help getting back on schedule and that, henceforth, the "big action stuff" would be handled principally by the second-unit directors.

Consequently, de Toth was assigned to stage the train wreck carried out by Lawrence and his raiders.

Lean was quite nettled by this development. De Toth's cameraman, Nicholas Roeg (later the director of psychological thrillers like *Don't Look Now* [1973]), recalls that Lean delegated scenes to second-unit directors very grudgingly; he wanted to shoot everything himself, suspecting that "a second-unit director really wants to make his own film."[25] Lean accused Spiegel of "sacrificing the quality of the picture" just to get the shooting over with. Spiegel countered that Lean was too slow and meticulous and that he needed the second-unit directors to complete the filming in Spain with dispatch. Spiegel set a target date of June 22 for Lean to finish up before moving on to another location. Lean stubbornly maintained that this was impossible. The discussion became a shouting match that ended with a red-faced Spiegel screaming in Lean's face, "You perfidious Englishman!" The next day, Lean very reluctantly advised the second-unit directors that, "under pressure of time and money," he would allow them to shoot "a certain amount of film."[26]

Lean, still angry, blasted off a vitriolic letter to Spiegel on May 22: "The harder I've worked and the more compromises I have made, the more you have harassed me. You cannot imagine how galling it is to have you nagging me to go faster and faster, while you have weekends in Paris." As a matter of fact, Spiegel was weekending in Monte Carlo. "At times there was more than slight friction between Sam Spiegel and David Lean that someone had to deal with," says Terrence Marsh, who assisted Box as art director on the film, "and so John was the figure." Lean asked Box to deliver his letter by hand to Spiegel. When he did so, Box asked whether Spiegel wished to reply. Spiegel answered laconically, "Tell him to go fuck himself."[27]

Meanwhile, de Toth was preparing for the destruction of the Turkish train by Lawrence's Arab band. The extras playing the Arab raiders were Gypsies, many of whom were descendants of the Moors who had once overrun Spain and, thus, looked very much like Arabs. De Toth and Box laid twenty-two miles of railroad track near some sand dunes some distance from Almeria. They collaborated with the construction foreman Peter Dukelow, who was involved in the destruction of the bridge in *Kwai*. They had commandeered an ancient steam engine and some old carriages for the scene.

The scene in which the train explodes was shot on June 20, 1962. "We had to use ten pounds of gunpowder to derail the train," de Toth said. He instructed the train engineer when to jump away from the locomotive, just before the blast went off. Everything went according to plan.[28]

De Toth covered the explosion with three cameras since the shot could not be repeated. Box recalls that, when the blast went off, the boiler of the steam engine exploded, and the locomotive careened off the track in a dense cloud of steam: "The engine plowed right through the sand toward the camera that was close by and stopped dead—without crashing into the camera."[29] When the steam had evaporated and the smoke had cleared, Roeg checked all the cameras. He found that all had gotten the shot and reported this to Lean, who arrived at this point to shoot the aftermath of the wreck with the actors.

Lean filmed the last location scene in Spain on July 4, 1962, only two weeks over Spiegel's deadline of June 22. He had already convinced Spiegel that the patches of sand dunes around Almeria would not suffice to serve as the locales for the battle scenes involving the Arab and Turkish armies but that the panoramic desert vistas in Morocco would. Moreover, these scenes required many more soldiers as extras and many more camels than Spain was prepared to supply. Spiegel agreed that they must move on to Morocco.

Spiegel was cognizant of the fact that Norman Spencer was Lean's most trusted production assistant, so he deputized him to be in charge of the location filming in Morocco. Spencer set up a production office in Casablanca. He and Spiegel paid their respects to King Hassan II, who allowed the Royal Moroccan Cavalry and the Camel Corps to participate in the film, along with one hundred nomads from the Sahara Desert, who would form part of Lawrence's Arab forces.[30]

It was Spencer who had to arrange to have all the equipment packed up and shipped by coastal freighter from Almeria to the port of Casablanca and then transported by a fleet of British army trucks to the location at Ouarzazate, a town in the Moroccan desert. Spiegel took no part in overseeing this enormous operation. Spencer recalls that Spiegel merely said to him, "That's what you employ people for."[31]

Ouarzazate was fiendishly hot, "a terrible place," Lean wrote. "The production office was in a building that was once occupied by the French Foreign Legion. When we were there, they were still sending Legionnaires there as a punishment. The heat was tremendous, and we shared the punishment with the Legionnaires."[32]

Filming resumed on July 18. When Lean was shooting in desert locations, the unit was again living in tents on the desolate plains, as in Jordan. "There were the most appalling living conditions," Spencer recalls—not to mention the oppressive heat—"and everybody went a bit mad out there." The Moroccan army officer attached to the film unit as military adviser went off his head and took to shooting live bullets out of his tent at night. "Anything he saw, he shot at," says Spencer, "so he had to be taken away."[33]

To make matters worse, the troops serving as extras were disgruntled; they hated standing around among the sand dunes, waiting for the cameras to turn. Lean remembered them as a tough lot, and their officers had little control over them. One day, while Lean was setting up a shot, he was startled when bullets whistled over his head. He investigated, only to find that the soldiers had fired the shots in protest because they had not been paid.

Lean at first blamed Spiegel but eventually learned that King Hassan had delegated his brother, Crown Prince Moulay Abdullah, to be the liaison between the government and Horizon Pictures (which the Moroccans pronounced phonetically as "Rice and Pitchers"). Spencer told Lean that the crown prince was "a complete playboy"; apparently, he was sending the checks destined for the soldiers to a private bank account in Paris. There was really nothing Spiegel could do.[34]

The military extras were needed primarily for the staging of the barbarous massacre of the retreating Turkish soldiers by Lawrence's forces at Tafas. The incident—which was known as the bloodbath—was designed to show how Lawrence's high ideals had degenerated into bloodlust. De Toth was to lay out the action for the massacre as it was described in the screenplay.

Lean, as we know, was suspicious of second-unit directors and not very open to their suggestions. Nevertheless, the intrepid de Toth proposed that the shot begin with a torrent of blood exploding across the screen, to underscore the savagery of the scene. Roeg, who observed Lean's interchange with de Toth, reported that Lean snapped, "That's disgusting!" De Toth was crushed and left the picture in a huff the next day. (He went on to direct more movies, most notably the Michael Caine vehicle *Play Dirty* [1969], a war picture about British soldiers fighting in the African desert.) Roeg took his place. Having seen de Toth bite the dust, he decided to keep a respectful distance from Lean and "just shoot what was asked for." "David frightened people, and demanded obedience, rather than allegiance. No one dared question him," said Roeg. "He was absolutely in command."[35]

But Lean still had to contend with Sam Spiegel, who was not so easily intimidated. Spiegel was beginning to fear that filming would never end. Lean was at this point shooting only a page of script a day, when three pages a day was the norm for a feature film. For the record, shooting this movie had taken as long as the actual Arab Revolt that it portrayed. Spiegel accordingly flew to Ouarzazate, determined to get Lean to expedite things.

There was a full unit call on the patio of the local hotel so that Spiegel could address the entire production unit. "Spiegel was like Napoleon," Roeg remembers. "He had learned everybody's name and could address them personally." Spiegel delivered his pep talk seated on a kitchen chair. He said that he was impressed with the tremendous effort spent on the picture and implored everyone not to quit or go on strike. "Boys, we've got to go faster!"[36]

The next morning, Lean watched Spiegel's plane take off. "Bastard!" he muttered to Roeg. "Last night he told me he'd had a heart attack"—from worrying about the film. Spiegel made Lean promise to wrap the shooting by mid-August. "Heart attack! He's a better actor than I've got on the set." Lean knew that Spiegel was fibbing about the heart attack; like T. E. Lawrence, Spiegel was a great fibber.[37] Nevertheless, Lean did finish by mid-August.

What really convinced Lean to cooperate was that Spiegel had informed him that he had already set the dates for the British and American premieres of the picture. The London premiere would be on December 10 and the New York premiere on December 16—meaning that Lean had only four months for postproduction. As far as Lean was concerned, this was the straw that broke the camel's back. Being pressured by Spiegel to supervise the editing and scoring of a mammoth historical spectacle in a mere four months was really daunting.

O'Toole saw things differently. "I must say it was a master stroke on Sam's part, fixing the premiere dates before we were even through," says O'Toole. "Sam knew we were going on too long; David and I had begun to forget we were making a film. After two years it had become a way of life. So Sam nailed us with the dates and that was that."[38] "When we finished in Morocco," Norman Spencer recalls, "we had a celebration at a hotel in Casablanca." O'Toole, who was no longer under an interdict to stay sober during shooting, got smashed. He marched into the hotel lobby and shouted, "The fucking picture is finished!"[39]

Lean and the whole film unit decamped for London on August 18. By that time, Lean and Spiegel were barely on speaking terms, says a mutual friend, Nina Blowitz. Blowitz attended a dinner party hosted by Spiegel for members of the production unit. Spiegel said to her, "Ask David if the wine is alright." Then Lean answered, "Tell him the wine is alright." Says Blowitz, "This went on all night! They were like a couple of kids."[40]

Despite O'Toole's loud lobby proclamation, the film was not, in fact, finished. Back in England, Lean had to shoot the movie's prologue. On September 14, he took a small crew to Chobham, Surrey, to film the motorcycle crash, utilizing Lawrence's own Brough motorbike. Lawrence had owned two cycles and christened them *Boenerges*. This is a Hebrew term used in the New Testament meaning "sons of thunder"; that is what Christ called the apostles John and James, who had volatile tempers. Lawrence had in mind the motorbikes' thunderous noise.

While filming the accident, O'Toole took a spill. Though he sustained no serious injury, he joked that Lawrence was "teasing him from heaven."[41] Then, on September 21, Lean proceeded to London to shoot the memorial service at St. Paul's. With that, he officially finished principal photography on what was one of the longest shooting schedules for a single film in cinema history, from May 1961 to September 1962.

"Owing to the December premiere of the picture," Anne Coates remembers, "we had to have the film fine cut, music written, and a six-track stereo sound track dubbed in under four months." She concludes, "On paper the finishing schedule seemed impossible." Barbara Cole wrote Coates, "Hope you are gathering your strength for the final rush. I will come around handing out pep pills and black coffee."[42]

Coates took over a postproduction facility on South Audley Street in London, near the Dorchester Hotel. Lean himself occupied the apartment above the editing suite, where he had his own Moviola editing machine. "As I was an editor, it's hard to keep my hands off the celluloid," he explained. He had learned to preplan his films so that he shot only what he needed; this amounts to precutting the movie in the camera, insofar as that is possible, by making dramatic selections in advance. "Nobody can prophesy at the script stage how a film is going to be cut, but I try to get the shots I know will be needed."[43]

Lean and Coates, faced with miles of film to edit, worked seven days a week from 9:00 A.M. to midnight, in order to complete the edit on time. "David was happy and relaxed in the cutting room," says Coates; there were no actors to talk back to him there, as there had been on the set. Coates's assistant, Willie Kemplen, found Lean totally obsessed with the work at hand. Kemplen felt that, had he suddenly keeled over dead, Lean would have said, "Oh what a shame. Could you get him out of the way? I must look at this shot."[44]

Lean and Coates had during the late 1961 hiatus from shooting already examined all the footage that had been shot in Jordan, Lean leaving behind detailed instructions with which Coates had prepared a rough assembly of the first half of the picture. Hence, they now decided to work first on the footage for the second half of the film, which had not yet been touched. "Only after we finished with the second half did we go back for the fine cut of the first half," Coates says.[45] Meanwhile, Win Ryder, who had dubbed the sound track for *Kwai*, was mixing the sound track with John Cox, the chief sound editor, at Shepperton Studios.

Lean and Coates worked together closely because they had a tight schedule. "In four months there was no way that one single editor could have actually cut that film. You had to have two people," Coates declares. "David was cutting scenes, and I was cutting scenes; I was altering his stuff, and he was altering my stuff. I mean, the last word in the editing was David's; but then the last word in any film is the director's."[46]

Coates was personally responsible for what has become the most famous visual transition in film history. "I thought of Lawrence lighting a match, and, as he blows it out, I cut directly to the desert sunrise," Coates says.[47] Thus, Lawrence blows out the fire of the match and is suddenly plunged into the fire of the desert sun. Specifically, a close-up of Lawrence and the match is followed by a breathtaking shot of the flaming Sahara sun; it is slowly rising on the horizon over the rim of the desert, which stretches into the measureless reaches of space, dwarfing man and his petty pretensions by comparison. This single shot creates the entire scope of the infinite desert.

Lean told Coates that he firmly believed that "part of what makes a great editor is what you take out, not just what you leave in." As we have seen, Lean could be more ruthless than any producer in trimming scenes. "You've got to be ruthless to get down to the actual core of a picture," says Coates. "He threw a whole heap of stuff out that broke my heart, and he was right."[48]

When it came to engaging a composer for the movie, Lean had always assumed that Malcolm Arnold, who won an Academy Award for his score for *Kwai*, would write the music for *Lawrence*. Spiegel, who wanted the list of collaborators on the film to be as prestigious as possible, opted to commission two of Britain's leading composers to write the underscore: not only Arnold, but also William Walton, who had scored *Major Barbara*.

Spiegel arranged for Coates to run two hours of the rough cut for Arnold and Walton at the South Audley Street screening room. They arrived after a long lunch, in which they had imbibed copious amounts of vino. "They were a little the worse for wear," according to Coates; they began giggling and nudging each other like schoolboys during the screening. Afterward Arnold pronounced the movie "terrible," and Walton added that it was "a travelogue that would require hours of music." Considering that they both intermittently napped during the screening, they were in no position to judge.[49]

Both Lean and Spiegel were deeply offended when Coates reported the composers' verdict. But Spiegel had another game plan. He remembered that the Broadway composer Richard Rodgers had done an "Oriental" musical set in Siam entitled *The King and I* (1951–54) and that he had also written the score for the World War II television documentary *Victory at Sea* (Isaac Kleinerman, 1954). That qualified Rodgers, in Spiegel's mind, to write the score for *Lawrence*. Spiegel also remembered a young French composer named Maurice Jarre who had just written the underscore for *Sundays and Cybele* (Serge Bourguignon, 1962), a French film in which Spiegel had a financial investment. He decided to have Rodgers write the music for *Lawrence* and Jarre orchestrate it.

Rodgers, who remained in New York, looked at none of the footage shot for *Lawrence,* depending exclusively on Bolt's screenplay to assist him in creating themes for the film. Meanwhile, Jarre looked at as much of the rough cut as Coates could provide in the screening room at South Audley Street. In September 1962, Spiegel received by mail at Horizon Pictures in London the themes that Rodgers had worked up for the movie. He got a pianist to play them for Lean, Jarre, and himself in a rehearsal room at the Berkeley Hotel.

Jarre recalls that Rodgers's "Oriental Theme" sounded like "something left over from *The King and I.*" The pianist then launched into Rodgers's "Love Theme." Besides being atrocious, Jarre says, the theme disturbed him; he asked himself in what context this theme would be played in the picture since Lawrence was thought to be homosexual and there were no women in the cast of characters.[50]

At this point, Lean rose from his chair and addressed Spiegel impatiently: "Sam, what is all this rubbish? I am supposed to be editing the film, and you take up my time with the nonsense!" According to Larry Timms, Rodgers was present on this occasion, but Jarre emphatically declares that he was not; Lean would not have denounced the music in such scabrous terms had the composer been on hand. Lean then turned to Jarre and inquired whether he had created anything for the score. Jarre obliged him by playing a haunting melody that he called simply "The Theme from *Lawrence of Arabia.*" Lean put his hand on Jarre's shoulder and announced, "Sam, this chap has got the theme. Maurice, *you* are going to do it!"[51]

As Jarre later remembered, "Now I was faced with writing two hours of music for a four-hour film, scored for one hundred instruments." Not only that, but the postproduction schedule allowed him only six weeks in which to do it. He accomplished this arduous task working round the clock and napping at intervals on the couch in his tiny office in Berkeley Street. "After watching several hours of Lean's unedited rushes," Jarre continued, "I was transfigured by the beauty of the film. My imagination is directed by what I see; the images were superb. I really entered into each sequence so that the themes came to me quite naturally. When Lawrence snuffs out the match and we cut to the burning sun rising over the desert, I used muffled kettle drums," as well as shimmering strings and soft brass. "Then the music explodes into an enormous crescendo as the sun blazes in the sky. This was one of the film's climaxes. This scene shows the genius of David Lean: his visual imagery can have an extraordinary poetic quality, and that really inspired me."[52]

Though Jarre was accustomed to orchestrating his own film music, because of the tight schedule he had to turn over this task to Gerard Schurmann, who had orchestrated Ernest Gold's score for Otto Preminger's *Exodus,* another large-scale epic. Because Kenneth Alford's "Colonel Bogey March" was employed to such good advantage in *Kwai,* Lean requested that Jarre incorporate another Alford march, "The Voice of the Guns," into his music for *Lawrence.* Jarre, in turn, asked Schurmann to score "The Voice of the Guns" specifically for military brass band, which is the same approach that Arnold took to "Colonel Bogey" in *Kwai.*

Jarre was also used to conducting his own scores at recording sessions. But Spiegel, desiring to add another prestigious name to the screen credits, engaged Sir Adrian Boult, the director of the Royal Philharmonic, to conduct the orchestra for the sound track, which was set to be recorded at Shepperton Studios.

It became painfully obvious at the first recording session that Boult had absolutely no experience in pacing the tempo of the music to fit the action on the screen with a stopwatch. He turned to Spiegel and declared that he was incapable of conducting a motion picture film score. With that, Boult graciously turned his baton over to Jarre and walked out of the studio. Spiegel still insisted that Boult's name appear in the screen credits as conducting the score. Jarre made that concession to Spiegel, and Spiegel, in turn, honored his demand that his name appear as conductor of the score on the sound-track album. "I told Sam," Jarre declares, "that I would not stand for having Boult listed as conducting the score for the disk when he didn't do anything! Sam agreed."[53]

Jarre collaborated with Schurmann on the orchestrations. Attempting to capture the feeling of the Arabian Desert, Jarre utilized unearthly, unorthodox instruments. For example, he wrote solos for the ondes martenot—"an electric keyboard instrument which produces an eerie, metallic sound"—that were blended with sweeping strings to create the deliriously lush "Lawrence Theme."[54] This theme is paired in the film's overture with Alford's "Voice of the Guns" march. The overture includes generous helpings of brass and percussion; snare drums crackle with intensity, while trumpets and trombones blast away, joined by crashing cymbals, throbbing kettledrums, and strident strings. Jarre would score all Lean's films from *Lawrence* onward, winning Oscars for *Lawrence, Dr. Zhivago,* and *A Passage to India.*

Lean went right to the wire fine-tuning the final cut, finishing just in time for the premiere. The Columbia executives were chagrined that the final cut that Lean delivered was three hours and forty-two minutes long. They feared that audiences would become restless sitting through one of the longest movies ever released by a Hollywood studio. Consequently, Columbia pressured Spiegel to have Lean shorten the movie. But Spiegel fought the studio for Lean's final cut, finally winning by simple intransigence. Contractually, Spiegel and Lean had final say, so the studio gave in, for the time being at least.

As we have seen, the finished film begins with a prologue set in 1935 portraying Lawrence's death. While the film does not seek to settle the dispute about whether his death was a suicide, certainly it suggests that perhaps it was not entirely accidental. There is a curious smile on Lawrence's face as he recklessly careens along, gathering speed all the while. When he swerves to avoid hitting the two boys, he inevitably loses control and crashes into a ditch. As Anderegg notes, Lawrence comes across in this scene as "brave but foolhardy," "a thrill-seeker who seems to invite disaster," someone possessed of self-sacrificial bravado.[55] In short, the scene suggests Lawrence may, to some degree at least, have been unconsciously courting death.

This is followed by a scene of the impressive memorial service held shortly afterward. With that, the film goes back to World War I, when Lawrence was a British intelligence officer stationed in Cairo, and then proceeds to dramatize Lawrence's life from that point on.

We discover Lawrence demonstrating his stoicism by smiling as he puts out a lighted match with his finger and thumb without flinching. An admiring private attempts to imitate him and yelps in pain when he is burned. "What's the trick, then?" he asks Lawrence. "The trick," Lawrence answers, "is in not minding that it hurts." Ken Russell writes, "This scene is the first clue as to the true nature of Lawrence's character." In this instance, what is revealed is that Lawrence enjoys suffering pain, a masochistic strain in his personality that will become more obvious later on.[56]

As mentioned already, Lawrence's masochism seemed to be linked to his attempts to repress his homosexual impulses. In *Seven Pillars of Wisdom*, he writes that certain homosexuals in the Arab army, "thirsting to punish appetites they could not wholly prevent, took a savage pride in . . . enduring physical pain."[57] There is little doubt that he implicitly included himself in this observation.

At any rate, Lawrence manages to convince his superiors to let him seek out the Bedouin chief Prince Feisal in the desert and help him unite the Arab tribes against the Turks, with whom the British are also at war. En route to Feisal's desert camp, Lawrence and his Arab guide stop to drink at a water hole. Sherif Ali materializes out of a mirage. Lawrence's guide, who belongs to a rival tribe, pulls a gun on Ali, who shoots first and kills the guide. Lawrence, who is appalled, remarks acridly to Ali, "So long as the Arabs fight tribe against tribe, so long will they be a little people—greedy, barbarous, and cruel." Ali shrugs off his remark and goes on his way, but he and Lawrence will eventually become allies.

Anthony Nutting strongly objected to this scene. "An Arab would never shoot another Arab at a well," he said, contending that it would not be honorable.[58] Lean nonetheless retained the scene, arguing that the guide reached for his gun first and that Ali acted in self-defense.

Lawrence finally meets up with Feisal and becomes the charismatic leader of the Arab forces, spurring them on to victories against the Turks. The first time he dons his chieftain's robes, he wants to see what he looks like. Lacking a mirror, he stares narcissistically at his own reflection in the blade of his knife. Dressed in white, the traditional sign of purity and innocence, he admires his handsome reflection in his shiny new dagger. Actually, Lawrence's self-conscious strutting about in his new outfit borders on exhibitionism. O'Toole joked in an interview about being terribly in awe of his finery: "I practically turned into a transvestite! I thought I'd literally end up running around in a nightie for the rest of my days!"[59]

In any event, Lawrence and Ali, with their contingent of warriors, join up with the ferocious Auda Abu Tayi and his band of desert marauders. Together, they traverse the boiling Nefud Desert, known as the "sun's anvil," and seize the strategic port of Aqaba.

Lawrence's assault on Aqaba proved that he had more faith in the Arabs than did the British high command, who saw them as hotheaded rabble, "incapable of disciplined, large-scale tactical warfare." But Lawrence knew that the Arabs excelled at guerrilla warfare. Desert warriors had always viewed battle as a series of swift, aggressive surprise attacks; these were "perfect tactics against enemies with superior weapons and more men." In the movie, Lawrence puts his theories to the test as he hurls his raging Arab guerrillas at the superior forces at the Aqaba garrison, "which surrenders meekly."[60]

Lawrence then tells Auda that he is going to cross the Sinai Desert, accompanied by his two young body servants, Farraj and Daud, his constant companions. He intends to report in person to the high command in Cairo on the taking of Aqaba. "You will cross the Sinai?" asks Auda. "Moses did," Lawrence replies. "Moses was a prophet and beloved of God!" Auda responds, implying that Lawrence is no Moses.

Dryden, an agent of the Arab Bureau, thinks that Lawrence is nurturing delusions of grandeur, as does Auda. When Lawrence says to Dryden that the desert campaign is an adventure, Dryden snaps, "Only two kinds of creatures get fun in the desert—Bedouins and gods. And you are neither." Lawrence disregards Dryden's remark, just as he ignored Auda's.

During the trek across the Sinai Desert, Daud loses his life in quicksand, and Lawrence arrives at journey's end with just Farraj. As Lawrence and Farraj emerge from the desert, an army motorcyclist parked on the road some distance away notices that Lawrence is a white man dressed in Arab regalia. He shouts at him, "Who are you?" It is significant that Lean himself dubbed this line of dialogue for the cyclist. Adrian Turner comments, "It is the director puzzling over the nature of his hero, and the film never really answers that question, 'Who are you?' Lawrence himself remains confused about his own identity."[61]

When Lawrence enters the officers' club at the British military post in Cairo, his fellow officers eye him disapprovingly. Not only is he dressed as an Arab, but he is also accompanied by a young desert outcast whom they assume is his "tent boy" (camp follower). Lawrence blithely puts his arm around Farraj affectionately, as he orders the barman to give the lad a glass of lemonade. Soon after, he greets General Allenby with the news of the Aqaba victory. In light of Lawrence's news, Allenby is prepared to overlook the impropriety of Farraj's presence, as are the other officers. As the first part of *Lawrence of Arabia* draws to a close, Allenby authorizes Lawrence to ambush Turkish troop and supply trains. He comments to Dryden, "Lawrence is riding the whirlwind." Dryden responds ruefully, "Let us hope that we are not."

As the second part of the movie begins, Lawrence is at the peak of his popularity with the Arabs; his success in destroying Turkish trains wins him the title "Emir Dynamite" from the Arab hordes. But Lawrence unfortunately turns out to be a man defeated by his own capacity for greatness. As the Arabs begin to treat him like a god, he becomes vain, egocentric, and erratic. The most brilliant scene in the film shows how Lawrence has become mesmerized by the adulation of his Arab warriors. After he and his men destroy a Turkish train, he jumps atop one of the cars to accent the cheers of his men. As he stands there wearing the dazzling white robes of a Bedouin chief, he is suddenly stunned by a bullet that just misses wounding him critically. He looks down to see that a dying Turk is firing at him from the ground. An expression of amazement crosses his face; he has been jolted into realizing that he is, after all, still a mortal.

Lawrence comes to an even deeper realization of his limitations when he is captured by the Turkish bey, a local official in Deraa, a town occupied by the Turks. He is taken into custody while wandering incognito through the town on a scouting expedition. This is one of the most crucial sequences in the entire picture. When Lawrence repels the bey's advances, the bey has him tortured. As mentioned, the bey orders that he be beaten and sodomized because he has discerned the homosexual masochism that Lawrence has hidden from himself; he does not have him executed because he does not want to make him a martyr. During the beating itself, Lean has the bey go into another room, deliberately leaving the door ajar so that he can watch. The beating resembles a sadomasochistic ritual; indeed, the nearly naked Lawrence seems to enjoy being tortured.

Lawrence's subsequent rape by the soldiers is not shown; the lascivious leer of one of the guards beforehand, plus Lawrence's dazed looks and gestures afterward, imply what has taken place. Finally, the guards throw Lawrence into a mud puddle in the gutter outside. The dirty water that splashes on him signals his violation. This episode has been called "one of the most daring homosexual scenes of indecent assault ever to be filmed decently."[62]

The experience is profoundly disillusioning for Lawrence, for it forces him to recognize not only the fundamental frailty of human flesh but also the fact that he, like other men, has a breaking point. Indeed, he admits to Ali afterward that, under torture, he would have told the enemy whatever he wanted to know. As Michael Anderegg writes, "Lawrence finally comes face to face with his simple mortality." Lawrence also faces what he himself terms his "ration of common humanity."[63] Filled with self-doubt, Lawrence asks General Allenby to allow him to return to regular military service. But Allenby sends him back to lead his Arabs once more, telling him that his mission is too vital to the war effort.

The subsequent attacks on the Turks become increasingly savage as Lawrence "resorts to barbaric violence after he loses faith in himself."[64] He participates in the senseless slaughter of a whole caravan of Turkish soldiers at Tafas, an attack that he launches with the cry: "No prisoners!" Admittedly, these same Turks have themselves just destroyed a nearby Arab village, yet Lawrence realizes that he is becoming as sadistic as the enemy.

Lawrence of Arabia is a masterpiece of understatement. Often feelings are only hinted at and words left unarticulated, in order to let the viewer gradually discover the full implications of the story as it unfolds. Characteristically, Lean has succeeded in compressing much of the meaning of a given scene into cinematic imagery, as when Lawrence faces up to his own streak of sadism after the massacre at Tafas. As the scene develops, Lawrence stares fixedly at his own reflection in the blade of the knife that he has just used in the course of the slaughter. This image is meant to recall an earlier scene in which he does the same thing—right after he dons his snow-white Arab apparel. The difference is that now the knife blade is blood smeared and his once-spotless robes are caked with blood and dirt, just as his character has been soiled by vile, savage deeds. Moreover, the visage he now stares at is no longer that of the heroic figure he gazed on before but that of the chieftain of a marauding band of desert thugs.

At this point, *Lawrence* illustrates Lean's ongoing theme: Lawrence declines to accept defeat even when it seems that his original goals have been compromised. That this theme continues to turn up in his films, regardless of their varied subject matter, is one sure sign that David Lean is an auteur.

Lawrence seeks to blot out the bloodbath at Tafas by going on to lead his victorious forces into Damascus, followed soon after by Allenby's troops. He champions Arab nationalism, Arab independence, after he discovers that his own countrymen are using the Arabs as pawns in their political maneuvers in the Middle East. He also sees, however, that his attempts to form a Pan-Arabia are doomed to frustration by the factiousness of the Arab tribes and the continued meddling of the British. He therefore decides once and for all to return to the ranks of the British army and go back to England, to live out the balance of his military life in obscurity.

Even Feisal is not sorry to see Lawrence go. "There is nothing further for a warrior here," he tells him. "Young men make wars, and then old men make the peace." Shortly after, Feisal says to Allenby laconically, "Lawrence is a sword with two edges; we are equally glad to be rid of him, are we not?" As Lawrence is driven to the pier, a truckload of British soldiers and a group of Arabs on camels pass; no one recognizes him, implying that he has already been forgotten. Lean underscores this point by cutting to a shot of Lawrence's face as seen through the dusty windshield of the car. His tarnished image has already begun to fade, his moment of glory having passed.

Lawrence returns home, ultimately to die, his motives in death as well as in life remaining ambiguous. But that is as it should be, for, in the last analysis, *Lawrence of Arabia* endures as a thought-provoking motion picture precisely because the central figure continues to be something of a mystery to the end.

Lawrence's tragedy, like that of Colonel Nicholson, lies in his being robbed of the dignity that might have accompanied an honorable defeat by the fatal flaws in his character that have been exposed by the crises he has faced. Lawrence, the would-be hero, is stubbornly determined to surmount staggering odds, but he is revealed in the process to be a self-deluded man who is as dedicated to his own self-esteem as to the principles he is championing. Lean never ceased to be concerned with the individual and his ability—or lack thereof—to measure up to life's demands. Lawrence is a case in point. Yet Lean presents him throughout as a character who deserves our compassion, even though he is eccentric to the point of neurosis.

The world premiere of *Lawrence of Arabia* was held in London on December 10, 1962, in the presence of the queen and the royal family. The picture's reception was all that Lean could have hoped for, except for the fact that his father, who never considered motion pictures as a worthy career for his son, declined to attend the premiere. He lived in Marlow, in the Thames Valley, and he tactlessly told his son that London was too far to go, just to see a movie.

Lean was consoled for his father's absence by the presence of fellow directors like Fred Zinnemann, who told me, "I congratulated David for making a stupendous historical picture, filled with grandeur, and added that it was simply out of my league." Zinnemann's point was that open-air scenes often defeat a director's efforts to create dramatic tension. But Lean created dramatic set pieces staged in the sunbaked desert that were fraught with dramatic tension.

Noël Coward loved the movie but had to have his little joke. He quipped to Lean at the postpremiere party that, if O'Toole had been any prettier in his Arab finery, "the picture would have had to be called *Florence of Arabia*." Another humorous incident involved a self-proclaimed industry insider who commented to a friend, "They didn't go to the desert at all; they simply poured sacks of sand on the studio floor."[65] When this was reported to Lean, he said that the individual must have been thinking of O'Toole's screen test, which was done in just such a makeshift fashion on a soundstage strewn with sand. But that was hardly the way the picture was shot on location.

The response to the American premiere on December 16 was just as enthusiastic. In general, the American critics, like the British reviewers, pointed out that Lean had expanded the horizons of the epic film by combining the visual splendor of a momentous spectacle with a searching psychological character study. As such, Pauline Kael wrote that *Lawrence* was "the most literate, tasteful, and exciting . . . of the modern expensive costume dramas."[66] Perhaps the filmmaker Martin Scorsese (*Taxi Driver* [1976]) said it best when he wrote: "*Lawrence* was the first grand-scale film constructed around a character who was not a traditional hero. Lawrence is a tormented man, . . . a flawed character full of psychological shadings and honest weakness—a tragic figure."[67]

After the film opened, Peter O'Toole was the man of the hour. Yet British journalists complained that they had to scour the alehouses and pubs in London to snag an interview with him. What is more, O'Toole's behavior did not improve when he and Omar Sharif went on a press junket to the United States to promote the movie. Sharif was gracious and friendly in dealing with the American press while O'Toole was often slightly tipsy when giving interviews.

Disaster loomed the night before the Los Angeles premiere, when O'Toole took Sharif to see Lenny Bruce, the controversial stand-up comedian, perform at a small bistro near Sunset Boulevard. After the show, Bruce invited O'Toole and Sharif back to his pad. The local police had been keeping Bruce, a suspected drug addict, under surveillance. As luck would have it, the drug squad raided Bruce's digs that very night. Bruce was charged with possession of an illegal substance, and O'Toole and Sharif were carted off to the drug tank along with Bruce.

Spiegel, we remember, had sprung Robert Bolt from a jail in England, and he again went bail, this time for Sharif and O'Toole in Los Angeles. He showed up at the police station flanked by a battery of pricey lawyers. After a confidential confab with the cops, O'Toole and Sharif were released. "The story never hit the papers," Sharif says, "but it must have cost Sam Spiegel an arm and a leg."[68]

Another source of negative publicity for the film, one that Spiegel could not hush up, revolved around A. W. Lawrence. He had already, we remember, rejected the shooting script as historically inaccurate and, accordingly, denied permission for the title *Seven Pillars of Wisdom* to be used for the film. Lean and Spiegel nevertheless thought Lawrence might still be favorably impressed by the film itself. They invited him to a private screening of the rough cut at South Audley Street prior to the film's opening. Lawrence was outraged by the movie, however; he stood up at the end of the screening and shook his fist at Spiegel, roaring, "I should never have trusted you!"[69] Then he stormed out while Lean, totally abashed, sank down in his seat.

Privately, Lawrence described the film sardonically to one of his brother's biographers: "They have used a psychological recipe: take one ounce of narcissism, a pound of exhibitionism, a pint of sadism, a gallon of bloodlust, and a sprinkle of other aberrations; and stir well."[70] He did not make a public pronouncement immediately; he held his fire until the picture was premiered. Then he published an article in the London *Observer.*

Lawrence damned the film "for attempting to tell an adventure story in terms of a psychological study which is pretentious and false." He went on to criticize the scene in which Lawrence "forces his way with an Arab boy into the officers club in Cairo" since he felt it unfairly implied an inappropriate relationship between the two. "The real key to the film is sadism," he continued. Lawrence tells Allenby he "enjoyed" killing an Arab renegade.

This "prepares the audience for a grand-scale glutting of bloodlust upon a mob of Turks." (For the record, this incident *is* described in *Seven Pillars*.) He concludes: "I do not want to give the impression that I consider the Lawrence of the film entirely untrue. I need only say that I should not have recognized my brother."[71]

Lawrence's article was widely circulated both in England and in America, and Spiegel had no choice but to reply. He did so diplomatically: "I quite understand what the movie must mean to someone who has lived in the shadow of a legend of an older brother for some fifty years. Prof. Lawrence did not want family skeletons rattled. He wanted to preserve the Lawrence of Arabia legend in Victorian cleanliness. But anyone who dramatizes the life of Lawrence of Arabia cannot ignore that he was illegitimate or avoid the conflict of this man who was aware of homosexualism. This was a man who became involved in all sorts of masochism as the result of his conflicts." In closing, Spiegel stated that the filmmakers had not proposed to explain away the enigmas that are part and parcel of Lawrence's life: "We did not try to resolve the legend of Lawrence of Arabia; we tried to perpetuate it."[72]

George Staples, a cavalry commander who fought the Turks with Lawrence in the battle for Damascus, came forward to challenge A. W. Lawrence's diatribe against the film, giving an interview to the *Toronto Telegram* when the movie opened in Toronto on January 30, 1963. His point was that Lawrence was not with his brother in Arabia and did not know what he was like over there.

One blistering hot day on the road to Damascus, Staples, who was with a detachment of Allenby's British soldiers, spied a white man dressed as an Arab coming around a sand dune on a camel. "I'm Lawrence," the man proudly proclaimed in an Oxford accent. "Where is your division commander?" Staples remarked, "He acted as if the whole world should know who he was." Then, regarding A. W. Lawrence's point that he did not recognize his brother in the film version of his life, Staples commented, "I don't think A. W. Lawrence knew the Lawrence of Arabia that we in Arabia knew. The man in the film was very much like the Lawrence we campaigned with."[73]

Most commentators have defended the movie against A. W. Lawrence's charges that the picture was not a historically valid portrait of his brother. They note that, in any highly literate biopic, the established facts of chronology are modified and characters combined or simply invented—and that *Lawrence of Arabia* is no exception to this rule. As Robert Bolt put it, the film's "triflings with reality" are merely meant to streamline the plot. *Lawrence of Arabia*, in brief, jettisons pedestrian accuracy for mythic truth.[74]

On April 8, 1963, the Academy Award ceremonies were held in the

Santa Monica Civic Auditorium. *Lawrence of Arabia* led the field with ten nominations. It went on to repeat the triumph of *The Bridge on the River Kwai* by also winning seven Oscars. Lean again won as best director, and Spiegel again won the best picture award. In addition, Oscars went to the cinematographer Freddie Young, the film editor Anne Coates, the production designer John Box, the sound editor John Cox, and the composer Maurice Jarre.

Jarre says that he asked Spiegel to pay his way to the Oscars in America and that Spiegel replied, "Foreigners don't have a chance of winning in Hollywood." Spiegel told Coates and the other Europeans who were nominated the same thing. Spiegel, said Jarre, was a tightwad, just as Lean had always maintained.[75]

Lean, whose win for *Kwai* marked him as the first British director to receive an Academy Award, said in his acceptance speech, "This Limey is deeply touched and greatly honored." Spiegel was equally gracious in accepting his Oscar: "On behalf of all those who sweated in the desert for months, I sincerely thank you."[76]

Shortly after the New York premiere, Lean was strolling down Fifth Avenue with David O. Selznick, the producer of *Gone with the Wind*. Selznick told Lean that, all through the years, the studio had wanted him to cut *Gone with the Wind*, which was exactly the same length as *Lawrence of Arabia*. "I would never let them cut it. Tomorrow morning you're going to start getting phone calls from people telling you to cut it. Don't do it!"[77] Sure enough, Spiegel, with Columbia's support, phoned Lean the very next morning to ask him to think about making some excisions.

At the time of the premiere in December 1962, the picture ran 222 minutes. When the film was about to go into general release in February 1963, after its initial road-show engagements, Spiegel hoped that strategic cuts would increase the tempo of certain scenes that seemed to develop too slowly. Lean recalls Spiegel saying to him, "If we can take twenty minutes out of this thing, we'll really have something."[78] Anne Coates attests that she and Lean worked together to make deletions in the film. When they started, Lean assured her that the cutting would not be done rashly: "The cuts will be made with a scalpel, not an ax."[79] He aimed to shave away twenty minutes so carefully that the audience would never notice. He and Coates thus brought the running time to 202 minutes. Afterward, Lean said, "I defy anyone to find the places where the cuts were made."[80]

"Seven years later, in 1970, Columbia was preparing to release the film to television," Coates says. They wanted us to whittle down the movie a little more. So David and I took out another fifteen minutes."[81] Now *Lawrence* had a running time of 187 minutes (in a version that first aired on television in 1972).

Yet a rumor has persisted for years in the industry—a rumor that Lean never bothered to squelch—that most of the cuts in the film were made by Spiegel without Lean's knowledge or consent. Coates states flatly that all the cuts were made, both in 1963 and 1970, with Lean's cooperation. In fact, he suggested and sanctioned them.[82]

Still, Spiegel was not entirely honest with Lean about the various versions of *Lawrence*. When Lean shortened the film for television, he insisted that, when the picture was reissued to theaters in 1971, it would be the 202-minute version of 1963, and Columbia and Spiegel agreed. Yet it was the television version, which was ready to hand, that was rereleased in 1971, something Lean did not find out about until it was too late for him to do anything about it.

A quarter of a century after *Lawrence*'s initial release, the film archivist Robert Harris got permission from Columbia to restore the film to its original length. Lean was euphoric. "Of course I want it to be restored," he declared. "I'm afraid the rats have gotten at it."[83] The rats had, indeed, gotten at it—in the sense that the master print languishing in the Columbia vaults had become warped and torn and the color had begun to fade. The project was green-lighted by David Puttnam, the British film executive who was president of Columbia Pictures at the time. Harris eventually recovered the missing footage from the studio vaults, and a restored version in the original seventy-millimeter format was released theatrically in 1989, to renewed critical and popular acclaim. More than one critic noted that, to be fully appreciated, the film's awesome images need to be seen on the wide screen of a movie theater.

The restoration of *Lawrence* to its original length was no easy task. Harris, who supervised the undertaking, aided by Lean and Coates, had to sift through more than two tons of film cans to piece together the missing footage from various prints, some of them imported from Europe.[84] Harris told me in conversation that, when all the missing footage was finally tracked down, "we discovered that the sound track for this material had not survived. Accordingly, we had to get the actors back to redub their dialogue." Lean was present for the recording sessions in London. "I hadn't seen Peter O'Toole for twenty years," he says. "After one scene was rerecorded, I said that I thought that he was even better than he had been in the original film." O'Toole agreed, telling Lean, "After twenty-five years I think I have learned enough to play the scene properly."[85]

"Most of the additions are transitional passages or establishing shots, rather than new scenes," notes Janet Maslin, "more like clauses in a sentence than whole sentences themselves."[86] For example, some transitional footage was restored at the end of the motorcycle sequence and at the beginning of the following scene, the memorial service, and this material provides an excellent example of Lean's acute visual sense. The fateful death scene concludes with a restored close-up of the goggles Lawrence was wearing when he crashed; they are seen dangling from the branch of a tree. This shot is succeeded by a restored close-up of Lawrence's bust in the crypt of St. Paul's. It is a replica of the bust that Eric Kennington, who illustrated *Seven Pillars*, made of Lawrence in 1926. Then the camera pulls back to show two of the mourners attending the ceremonies as they discuss whether Lawrence really deserves all the pomp and circumstance that have surrounded his passing. By juxtaposing Lawrence's death with the memorial that followed it, Lean ironically contrasts the inglorious demise of a forgotten war veteran on a backcountry lane with the "instant immortality" conferred on him by the elaborate service, along with the heroic bust so prominently on display.

Admittedly, none of the segments that Harris reinstated are particularly significant in themselves, but each contributes additional details that help fill out Lawrence's portrait. For example, in its depiction of the aftermath of the massacre of an Arab village by Turkish soldiers, the film now lingers at greater length on shots of the victims, with women and children clearly visible among the dead. Lawrence is appalled at the sight of these innocent victims, left behind to rot by the Turkish soldiers who can still be seen marching away into the distance; this restored footage helps explain, if not excuse, his later slaughter of that same Turkish regiment.

By the same token, Janet Maslin adds, "The torture scene, though essentially the same, now includes outdoor reaction shots of Lawrence's friend Ali that indicate that the episode lasted from morning until night."[87] The indication of the prolonged duration of Lawrence's torture by the Turkish bey's men further explains why the experience had such a lasting effect on Lawrence, psychologically as well as physically.

When Lean took a look at the restored print of his film, he decided to snip out a few frames here and there that he thought slowed down the pace; by doing so he brought the running time to 217 minutes, slightly under the original 222 minutes. Lean explained that, since he was an editor before he became a director, he had always been perceptive in spying out superfluous footage in his films. In fact, when he trimmed one particular shot from *Lawrence*, Harris begged him to leave it in. "David," he pleaded, "that's such a gorgeous shot; how can you cut it?" Lean responded, "This movie is *full* of gorgeous shots. One less won't ruin it." After finally viewing the finished print, Lean remarked laconically, "I must say, it looks *damn* good!"[88] The premiere of the restored version was on February 4, 1989.

When one considers the positive public response to many of Lean's movies, underscored by the successful theatrical rerelease of *Lawrence* some twenty-five years after its premiere, it is evident that few directors have commanded such a large portion of the mass audience. Indeed, Lean seems to have possessed a sixth sense that, over the years, enabled him to guess what the public would like. In the case of *Lawrence,* he had the foresight to gamble $10 million on a project that at the outset seemed at best unpromising. "It was a very expensive film," Omar Sharif observed, "with no love story, no action really, if you come to think of it—no great battles—just a lot of Arabs going around the desert on camels." Moreover, the actor playing the title role was not yet an established star, "and the leading character was an anti-hero." Hence, Sharif concludes, he would never have guessed, while making the film, that it would be such an enduring success.[89]

It is, of course, the restored version that was released on videocassette in 1990 and again in 2000 as well as on DVD in 2000. On the occasion of the 2000 release to home video, the film was reviewed all over again and called the ultimate cinematic spectacle, the like of which we would probably never see again.

Lean's film has continued to be singled out as a masterpiece over the years. In 2003, *Premiere* magazine, in a poll of its readership, chose *Lawrence of Arabia,* along with *The Bridge on the River Kwai,* as one of the best action movies ever made. It was termed a spellbinding, gargantuan biopic, "the yardstick by which all other visual epics are measured."[90] In another nationwide poll the same year, *Premiere* picked *Lawrence* as one of the hundred "greatest movies," a film "filled with memorable moments."[91] The American Film Institute honored the best hundred heroes and villains in cinema history with a television special broadcast on CBS on June 3, 2003; T. E. Lawrence was cited as one of the top ten heroes of all time.

Also in 2003, a banner year for *Lawrence,* John Cape selected Jarre's score as one of the all-time best: "This minimal score to a maximal epic employs the ondes martenot and other electronic sounds to great effect in the desert landscape."[92] To top off 2003, Peter O'Toole was given an honorary Oscar, celebrating his lifetime in films. The focus of the tribute was, of course, O'Toole's soaring performance as Lawrence.

The fact that the trend toward darker, more critical biopics originated with *Lawrence of Arabia* demonstrates the film's lasting influence. The tormented Lawrence prepared the way for later troubled heroes. The year 2004 alone showed us Cole Porter being unfaithful to his wife with other men in

Irwin Winkler's *De-Lovely,* Ray Charles's womanizing and heroin addiction in Taylor Hackford's *Ray,* and Howard Hughes's obsessive-compulsive neuroses in Martin Scorsese's *The Aviator.* Whenever biopics knock favorite figures off their pedestals, recall that it all started with *Lawrence of Arabia.*

In 2005, *Time* magazine released on the Internet its list of the hundred all-time best movies. Not surprisingly, *Lawrence of Arabia* was among them. The film continues to be esteemed as Lean's finest achievement. As Richard Corliss stated in *Time,* the film reveals the madness that made T. E. Lawrence great and the greatness that made him mad. Lawrence's "elusive charisma is perfectly captured in screenwriter Robert Bolt's epigrammatic dialogue, in Peter O'Toole's brilliantly bold portrayal, and in Lean's images of a vast desert that one small Englishman filled with his idealism and his ambition."[93] Finally, in its April 2006 issue, *Premiere* chose the hundred greatest performances of all time; heading the list was Peter O'Toole in *Lawrence of Arabia.*

T. E. Lawrence retains some of his heroic stature in the popular mind. Matthew Paschke, who participated in an archaeological dig in the Middle East under the aegis of the University of Chicago, told me that commemorative plaques still identify historical sites associated with Lawrence in Arabia. For example, there is a plaque on Lawrence's house in Yenbo on the Red Sea coast stating that he lived there for a time during the Arab Revolt of 1917.

Lawrence is, of course, well remembered in Britain. As a matter of fact, to commemorate the seventieth anniversary of his death, the Imperial War Museum in London mounted a major biographical exhibition. "Letters, diaries, [Lawrence's] Arab robes, photographs, film, paintings, and memorabilia" were on display from October 2005 through the following April.[94]

After the triumph of *Kwai* and *Lawrence,* it was assumed in Hollywood that Lean and Spiegel would collaborate on another major movie. But it was not to be. After Spiegel got his third Academy Award, he was the "uncrowned king of Columbia." But success had gone to his head. "After *Lawrence* he became impossible." When producing his later films, he became a dictator whom no one dared oppose. "He forgot the teamwork behind his extraordinary productions, and began to believe that he was the sole reason for their success." As for his partnership with Lean, Norman Spencer called it "a marriage that had run its course."[95]

Spiegel would never again work with a director of the caliber of David Lean, and his subsequent pictures never repeated the success of *Kwai* and *Lawrence.* Even *Night of the Generals* (1967), in which he once again paired Peter O'Toole and Omar Sharif, this time as Nazi generals, turned out to be an overheated potboiler. Spiegel incessantly interfered with the direction of the picture by Anatole Litvak (*Anastasia* [1956]). The movie performed in a lackluster fashion at the box office.

"We were a great team," Lean reminisced, "but I couldn't go on with Sam"—whom he called his sparring partner. "I couldn't trust him."[96] Lean discovered that Spiegel had been skimping on the amount of money he had been sending Lean at intervals as his share of the profits of *Lawrence*. Lean pointed out to Spiegel that the picture was making a mint of money at the box office. But Spiegel would invariably reply that it did well only in big cities—otherwise, the picture was a flop. And that was certainly not the case.

It is true that Lean eventually received $1.1 million from Spiegel as his percentage of the gross, in addition to his $200,000 director's fee. But *Lawrence* had finally cost $13 million to make and had grossed $17 million in its first-run engagements in America alone, going on to make $70 million worldwide. So Lean felt that his share of the film's profits should have been close to $4 million. But it was impossible for Lean's lawyer to unravel Spiegel's complex financial records and murky tax maneuvers, so Lean had no way of making Spiegel pay up. Hence, Lean's last quarrel with Spiegel in 1963 was over money. "All right, Sam," Lean fumed. "You have cheated me for the last time. I'll never work with you again." Lean later added, "Sam Spiegel was a two-edged sword; he couldn't keep his hand out of your pocket."[97]

If Lean was finished with Spiegel, he did want to continue working with Robert Bolt. He wrote Bolt on December 23, 1962, after the Los Angeles premiere of *Lawrence:* "We must work together again. I think we could spark well together, especially after having done this picture. . . . I'm just about at the top of my form." He concluded: "I'm—for the first time—anxious not to allow too long to go by before making another attempt on something ambitious."[98] Lean was looking for a project that would take him as far away from Spiegel as possible.

Philip Kellogg, Lean's agent at the William Morris Agency in Hollywood, suggested that he might consider Boris Pasternak's *Dr. Zhivago,* a novel that had won the Nobel Prize. The screen rights were owned by Carlo Ponti, who had arranged to produce the picture for Metro-Goldwyn-Mayer. Kellogg gave Lean the book, which Lean read while crossing the Atlantic back to Europe. It was a bulky historical novel that made Lean think of his two Dickens films. By the time he finished it, Lean said to himself, "I don't see how it is to be done, but we must do it."[99] So he wired his agent that he was interested in filming *Dr. Zhivago.*

Chapter Fourteen

KNIGHT WITHOUT ARMOR

DR. ZHIVAGO

The soul of our country is being destroyed.
                    —*Curtis Zampf, a political activist in the film* The Believer

I haven't written a good poem since the Revolution began. Politics sure play
hell with your poetry.
                    —*John Reed in the film* Reds

After reading Boris Pasternak's internationally acclaimed *Dr. Zhivago*, Lean
wrote John Box that it was the best novel he had read in a long while: "It's
wonderfully written with great compassion and understanding for human
beings."[1] The producer Carlo Ponti owned the screen rights and was keen
on having Lean direct it.

The novel, first published in 1957, had gained international attention
when Pasternak was forced by the Kremlin to decline the 1958 Nobel Prize
for literature. The Soviets condemned the novel, which dealt with the Russian
Revolution, for not following the Communist Party line in the portrayal of
the Revolution of 1917.

Boris Pasternak was born in Moscow on February 10, 1890; he was fifteen when the first, abortive Revolution of 1905 broke out. He never forgot
the atrocities committed by Czar Nicholas II in the process of crushing the
uprising. The Russian filmmaker Sergei Eisenstein's silent film *Potemkin*
(1925) dramatized the mutiny of the sailors of the battleship *Potemkin,* one
of the episodes of defiance that took place during the 1905 rebellion.
Eisenstein created a scene in which the czar sent Cossacks to slaughter the
citizens of the town of Odessa, who had demonstrated in favor of the muti-

neers. The film historian Kevin Brownlow has told me in correspondence that, though the mutiny was a fact, "the Odessa Steps massacre did not take place; it was Eisenstein's invention." Nevertheless, the Odessa Steps massacre in *Potemkin* inspired a similar scene in Lean's *Dr. Zhivago*. In any case, the Revolution of 1905 was the beginning of the end of the Russian monarchy. As Roquemore puts it, "The smoldering malaise festered for a decade."[2]

In 1912, Pasternak was enrolled in the University of Marburg in Germany; he returned home two years later to find conditions growing steadily worse. After the outbreak of World War I in 1914, the excessive number of Russian casualties at the front, plus severe wartime shortages at home, caused widespread discontent with the czar's regime. By 1917, riots were breaking out, most notably in Petrograd on March 8, when seven thousand workers poured into the streets. On March 15, Czar Nicholas II abdicated; he and his family were eventually shot by a band of Communist insurgents.

By October 1917, after more riots and mutinies, Vladimir Lenin, the leader of the Bolsheviks, a cadre of Marxist fanatics, was fully prepared to take over the government. On October 25, Lenin's forces stormed the Winter Palace and seized power. John Reed, the American journalist-poet, wrote an eyewitness account of the coup d'état, which he published in 1919 as *Ten Days That Shook the World*. When Lenin turned out to be a tyrant, however, Reed, whose life was dramatized in the film *Reds* (Warren Beatty, 1981), had second thoughts about his endorsement of Lenin's insurrection.

The October Revolution was in due course followed by a civil war pitting the Bolsheviks (Reds) against the czarist counterrevolutionaries (Whites). Between 1918 and 1921, the White Guards fought "an endless series of isolated, bloody brawls" against the Red Guards. By 1921, the Bolsheviks finally prevailed, "quickly building a gigantic, bureaucratic apparatus of centralized control throughout Russia."[3]

When the Bolsheviks took over, tight censorship was imposed on Russian writers. Lenin died in 1924, but his successor, Joseph Stalin, was, if anything, more brutal. Dissident writers were shipped off to the gulags (internment camps) that Lenin had instituted. Some of Pasternak's short fiction and essays from the early 1930s implied his growing disillusionment with the repressive Communist regime and, thus, met with official disapproval. As a Communist official ruefully remarks to the outspoken Yuri Zhivago in Lean's film version of *Dr. Zhivago*, "Your attitude is noted; oh yes, it is noted."

So Pasternak curtailed his creative writing and from 1934 to 1944 turned to translating Shakespeare's plays, many of which were presented at the

Moscow Art Theater by the renowned Russian stage director Konstantin Stanislavsky. He also translated other Western writers as well, to make a living. Pasternak's sister, Lydia, states that he had certainly begun thinking in terms of composing a big novel by the early 1940s and that "the characters in it grew and matured" until in the winter of 1945 he began working on what would become *Dr. Zhivago*. "I want to write something deep and true," he said at the time.[4]

Yuri Zhivago, the novel's central character, is a physician and a poet who marries his childhood sweetheart, Tonya Gromeko. But he then falls in love with Lara Guishar, a nurse, and writes some lyric poems dedicated to her. The novel is semiautobiographical, in that it is informed with Pasternak's personal experiences. Like Pasternak, Yuri lives through the great social upheavals of the First World War, the Russian Revolution, and the fierce civil war that followed.

Yuri at first believes firmly in the Revolution. When the czar abdicates and the Revolution takes hold, he exclaims to Lara, "Just think of it, the whole of Russia has had its roof torn off. . . . Freedom! Freedom dropped out of the sky, freedom beyond our expectations."[5] He sees the Revolution as guiding the Russian people to a better future.

But, as time goes on, Yuri's positive attitude gradually changes to one of profound disillusionment with the Bolshevik brand of communism. As Kudova explains, "Material deprivation, hunger, epidemics, brutality, and the bureaucracy of the Bolshevik regime all inexorably lead Zhivago to change his view of the Revolution."[6] As Yuri puts it in the novel, the people "had only exchanged the old oppression of the czarist state for the new, much harsher yoke of the revolutionary superstate." It is always the same, he concludes, with those possessing absolute power.[7]

Some of the characters in the novel were based on individuals whom Pasternak knew. Thus, Lara was modeled on Olga Ivinskaia, whom Pasternak met in the fall of 1946, after he had begun writing the novel. Olga became his mistress; hence, Pasternak became caught up in the moral dilemma of being torn between her and his wife. In the only filmed interview she ever gave, Olga states, "This was a difficult situation for Boris. He loved me; but he didn't want to leave his family."[8] Pasternak never resolved this conflict, and Olga remained his mistress for the rest of his life. Indeed, she greatly influenced the creation of the character of Lara. As Pasternak declared, he gave the endearing characteristics of his wife, Zinaida, to Yuri's wife, Tonya, but "Olga is the Lara of this book."[9]

The secret police discovered Olga's liaison with Pasternak, who was out of favor with the government. She was arrested and served five years in a prison camp, being released in 1953. "I paid very dearly for my love of Boris," Olga states. "I have been asked why they sent me to the camp rather than Boris. It was because the authorities wanted to punish him indirectly; they thought they could get the better of him by the pain they caused me."[10] A similar fate befalls Lara.

When Stalin died on March 14, 1953, Pasternak noticed that government censorship of literature was somewhat relaxed. That provided fresh impetus for him to finish his novel, which he did in 1956. But the post-Stalin thaw was short-lived, and, in 1957, the Kremlin forbade publication of Pasternak's manuscript, terming it contrary to the Soviet cause because of the author's negative view of the Bolshevik Revolution. As a result, no Russian publisher could touch it. Nevertheless, Pasternak never ceased to be convinced of the book's worth. He ends his brief 1957 autobiography, *I Remember,* with this declaration: "I have completed my chief and most important work, the only one I am not ashamed of, and for which I can answer with utmost confidence, a novel in prose, *Dr. Zhivago.*"[11]

In March 1956, the Italian journalist Sergio D'Angelo, who much admired Pasternak's work, visited him at his house in Peredelkino, a writers' colony fifteen miles southwest of Moscow where Pasternak lived the last twenty-five years of his life. Pasternak arranged for D'Angelo to smuggle his manuscript out of Russia and submit it to a publisher in Milan, Giangiacomo Feltrinelli, who was willing to publish it in an Italian translation. The Kremlin attempted to pressure Feltrinelli into abandoning his plans, but Feltrinelli reminded the Kremlin that it had no jurisdiction in Italy.

The publication of *Dr. Zhivago* in Italy on November 15, 1957, greatly disturbed the Khrushchev regime. Pasternak was expelled from the Union of Soviet Writers for betraying his country, though it is doubtful that any of the membership had read the book. Outside Russia, the book caused an international sensation, and *Dr. Zhivago* was soon translated into English and several other languages. On October 23, 1958, Pasternak was awarded the Nobel Prize for literature, for writing a lyrical historical novel in the great Russian epic tradition of Tolstoy's *War and Peace.*

Pasternak was warned by the Soviet government that, if he went to Stockholm to accept the Nobel Prize, he would not be allowed to return to his native land. Pasternak did not wish to be forced into exile, so, on October 29, he sent a telegram declining the prize: "Because of the significance attached to this award in the society to which I belong, I must give up this undeserved prize. Please do not be offended by my voluntary refusal." He followed up on October 31 with an open letter to Khrushchev, begging not to be deported: "I am linked with Russia by my birth, life, and work. I cannot imagine my fate separate from and outside Russia. For me to leave my country would be to die."[12]

Despite his capitulation to the Kremlin, Pasternak remained under a political cloud for the rest of his days. He died on May 30, 1960, at the age of seventy. But he had lived to see his saga of the Revolution published throughout the world, if not in his own country.

When *Dr. Zhivago* appeared in the United States, the distinguished literary critic Edmund Wilson led the chorus of praise, pronouncing the novel "one of the great events in man's literary history." While other reviews in America were not quite so extravagant, the book was well received.[13] Finally, in 1985, Pasternak was posthumously reinstated in the Union of Soviet Writers, paving the way for the publication of *Dr. Zhivago* in Russia in 1987.

Carlo Ponti, an Italian film producer, purchased the screen rights to the novel from Feltrinelli. He intended to cast his wife, the Oscar-winning superstar Sophia Loren (*Two Women* [Vittorio De Sica, 1960]), as Lara. Ponti was born in Milan in 1910. He made a name for himself as a producer in Italy after World War II, and his reputation spread beyond Italy when he produced Federico Fellini's classic *La Strada* (1954), with Anthony Quinn as a brutish circus strongman.

Ponti turned more and more to international productions like King Vidor's epic film of Tolstoy's *War and Peace* (1956). He eventually approached Robert O'Brien, the president of MGM, about funding a film of *Dr. Zhivago*. Ponti maintained an office in Rome, but, like Sam Spiegel, he went to Hollywood whenever necessary to confer with studio executives there. Thus, he met with O'Brien in the offices of MGM in Culver City, California. He made his pitch, indicating that he hoped to get David Lean to direct. O'Brien agreed to green-light the project—so long as Ponti snagged Lean.

Dr. Zhivago (1965)

King-size spectacles were going out of fashion at the time, as evidenced by the box office failure of epic movies like the Brando vehicle *Mutiny on the Bounty*. But O'Brien had a deep respect for great directors, and he clearly thought that Lean belonged in that class. Moreover, topflight filmmakers admired O'Brien. Stanley Kubrick, who made *2001: A Space Odyssey* (1968) for MGM, told me in conversation, "Bob O'Brien was a wonderful man and one of the few studio bosses who inspired loyalty in his directors; he trusted your judgment."

Lean set sail on the *Leonardo da Vinci,* bound for Europe, in May 1963, after doing second-unit work on *The Greatest Story Ever Told* (1965) as a favor to George Stevens. He had with him a copy of *Dr. Zhivago* that Ponti had sent him from his Rome office. Lean, as we know, was captivated by the book. Nevertheless, before he signed on to direct, he made some stipulations when Ponti conferred with him at his hotel in Madrid in June.

Mindful of how Spiegel had underpaid him more than once, Lean demanded a substantial portion of his salary up front, in addition to a percentage of the gross. It was the kind of sweetheart contract that William Holden—but not Lean—had for *Kwai.* Furthermore, Lean insisted that Robert Bolt write the screenplay and that Ponti—unlike Spiegel—not interfere while Lean was shooting the picture. Ponti, with O'Brien's approval, acquiesced to all Lean's demands.

Ponti had discussions with Lean during preproduction about casting and location sites, but, once shooting had started, Ponti kept a low profile. Lean recalled that Ponti "never came near the picture until he arrived at the music recording sessions" at MGM: "That was the first time he saw any of the footage."[14]

For his part, Sam Spiegel was most unhappy that Lean was making *Dr. Zhivago* for Ponti and not for him. In 1971, Spiegel produced Franklin Schaffner's historical spectacle *Nicholas and Alexandra,* which was about how the Russian Revolution destroyed the czar. *Nicholas and Alexandra,* of course, was Spiegel's *Dr. Zhivago.* It was a typical Spiegel showpiece, done on a grand scale. But it turned out to be an inflated pageant that was no match for Lean's film. It was becoming apparent that, without Lean as a partner, Spiegel was losing his touch.

Lean said that he admired the breadth and scope of Pasternak's *Dr. Zhivago,* which reminded him of Dickens. Pasternak's reliance on coincidence as a handy way of bringing together characters likewise recalled Dickens (see chapter 5). For example, after Yuri has lost track of Lara for some time, he eventually encounters her one day in a public library in a mountain village, and they renew their relationship.

Bolt loved the book, which he had read at Lean's urging, as much as Lean did, but he had some reservations. "As a story, it's second rate," he wrote in his preliminary notes for the script on July 9, 1963. "It's melodramatic and full of coincidences. But in the manner of the telling, it is superb. . . . How marvelously unsentimental Pasternak is."[15]

"The story of *Dr. Zhivago* is very simple," Lean commented. "A man is married to one woman and in love with another. The trick is in not having the audience condemn the lovers."[16] Since Lean was, at this juncture, married to Leila Lean and in love with Barbara Cole, he was inclined to sympathize with Yuri's plight. Furthermore, he was attracted to Yuri's story because he never ceased to be concerned with the individual and his ability, or lack thereof, to measure up to life's demands, and this is borne out in *Zhivago*.

"Making a film from a novel is not simply stringing bits of the book together," Bolt explains. "One must know the author's intent, story, and characters before attempting it. This is particularly true of Pasternak's monumental novel. Pasternak's intent is to make a strong affirmation of his belief in life and in the individual."[17] Bolt began work on the screenplay in the summer of 1963. "I've never done anything so difficult," he complained. "That bugger Pasternak! It's like straightening cobwebs."[18]

Bolt conferred with Lean, who was at that point sojourning in a hotel in Venice (since becoming a tax exile, "home" for him was a series of Continental hotels). Then he returned to England to toil on the prose treatment, a preliminary outline of the scenario, which he was hammering out in consultation with Lean. It was slow going. Bolt found it hard to give his full attention to the project because his marriage was falling apart and he was depressed and distracted by his home situation. In addition, he was also working on a new play.

The upshot was that Bolt did not submit the fifty-page treatment, entitled *An Account of the Intended Script,* until April 1964. The response from MGM's story department was fundamentally positive. Lean accordingly urged Bolt to join him at the Hotel Richmond in Madrid, his favorite hotel in Spain, to continue work on the screenplay. Lean was sure that, given his domestic problems, Bolt would accomplish more in Madrid, in collaboration with him, than at his rural home in Hampshire. But Bolt declined the invitation; he wanted to work on his own for as long as possible.

Nevertheless, Ponti was getting pressure from MGM to make progress on the screenplay, and he told Lean to make Bolt get down to work in earnest. So Bolt put aside the play and concentrated solely on the script. To mollify Lean, Bolt sent him the early pages of the script in May and told him to inform MGM that he had done so. Lean responded that Bolt was for the most part doing a wonderful job in fleshing out the principal characters but that his treatment of Lara was of some concern. "Look here, Robert," Lean wrote Bolt, "you've made Lara an absolute bitch." She seemed to be behaving like a selfish, temperamental female. Lean suspected that Bolt was subconsciously modeling Lara on his estranged wife.[19] When his marriage finally ended in November 1964, Bolt wished to get away from home for a while, so he accepted Lean's long-standing invitation to come to Madrid.

Bolt later wrote that he and Lean revised the screenplay several times:

"We fought our way, line by line and even sometimes shot by shot, from one end of the screenplay to the other many times over. The result goes under my name, but it is really our joint effort."[20] Adapting *Zhivago* for film was an arduous task because the story line encompasses a world war and a revolution and develops over a period of more than three decades. Consequently, it had to be rigorously condensed and many of the minor characters combined or dropped.

A particularly prickly problem with the plot is evident toward the end of the book. The main story concludes in chapter 15, with the report of Lara's death. There follows an epilogue—chapter 16, set several years later, during World War II—that focuses on the life of the lost child of Yuri and Lara. The girl, who is now grown up, is ironically named Tonya, after Yuri's wife. As far as the screenplay was concerned, this sudden leap over many years presented an awkward gap in the narrative, as Bolt explains: "In the film, with the overriding need for continuity, we felt that it would be hard to keep the audience in the cinema when the main story had ended." That is, to interest them in the emergence of an entirely new character, the daughter, so late in the movie would be very difficult. "The device we employed was the well-tried one of the narrator. . . . We promoted the shadowy figure of Yevgraf, Yuri Zhivago's half-brother, to this post."[21]

Lean and Bolt started out with a prologue in which Yevgraf meets Tonya, the illegitimate daughter of Yuri and Lara, so the audience knows from the outset that the lives of Yuri and Lara are going to intersect. The prologue leads into an extended flashback, in which Yevgraf narrates the story proper. The film ends with an epilogue, which returns to Yevgraf and Tonya.

Lean had employed a flashback structure as early as *In Which We Serve*, as a way of telescoping the action of an episodic narrative by jumping from one flashback to another. In the present instance, Lean and Bolt selected the episodes from the book that they wanted to utilize in the flashbacks—beginning with Yuri's childhood—and scrapped the rest. The love triangle, involving Yuri, Tonya, and Lara, would be played out "against the background of the Revolution," Bolt emphasized, "but it is a background only."[22]

As a matter of fact, the first edict that Lean gave Bolt was to focus on the love story and downplay the politics. Lean stressed that he was not interested in making a political statement about war and revolution. "I'm not mad about messages," he said. "I think that belongs to the philosopher. I consider myself an entertainer." He continued, "The Russian Revolution itself was a towering historical event; but *Dr. Zhivago* is not the story of the Revolution. The drama, the horror, and the turbulence of the Revolution simply provide the canvas against which is told a moving and highly personal love story."[23] In *Zhivago*, Lean zeroes in on a group of individual human beings, heroic in their efforts to survive the onslaughts of historical events that are shaping their lives but over which, ironically, they have no control. The Revolution itself remains in the background, but it is always there. Bolt quotes Lean as telling him, "I'm not saying the political conflict should be ignored, but it is the love story that will touch the mass audience."[24]

Lean and Bolt also added to the screenplay two brief incidents that, like the prologue, are not in the book. These are the first meeting of Yuri and Lara on a trolley car and Yuri's last sight of Lara from a streetcar as she walks down a Moscow street at film's end. These rhyming episodes provide a narrative frame for the romantic story, which is central to the plot. By centering the film on the love story, Lean and Bolt drastically contracted Pasternak's narrative.

It was incumbent on Lean and Bolt to compress the novel's plot for the screen as much as possible. "If you took the novel as a shooting script, shooting it, in so far as possible, page by page as it stands," Bolt surmises, "the resulting film would run about forty-five hours." Therefore, in the movie "you can only have one-twelfth of the book." "You have to digest the whole work"—choosing the dramatic peaks that emerge from the vast panorama and developing in-depth portraits of the key characters. "Then you say, 'These are all I can deal with in dramatic form.'"[25]

As Lean himself put it, "We naturally cut masses out of the book; but if we have made good cuts, nobody should be able to tell."[26] As a matter of fact, Bolt, with Lean's consultation, ultimately managed to pare down the 500-page book to a 284-page screenplay. By retaining only the more compelling incidents and by "creating vivid characters from vague shadows," Anderegg contends, Lean and Bolt's script "improves on the novel." Moreover, Anderegg reminds us that the screenwriters made some significant contributions to the script that do not have their origins in the novel: "The flashback structure, along with Yevgraf's voice-over narration, . . . and virtually all of the dialogue are original with the filmmakers."[27]

Bolt stayed on at the Hotel Richmond in Madrid, collaborating with Lean on the screenplay, until February 1965, at which time he headed for home. "I'm proud of our script," he wrote Lean at the time—"*ours,* not *mine.*" He ended by saying that he had every reason to believe that Lean could make an exceptional film from the script.[28]

Though Ponti seldom intervened during the production period, he did make some suggestions about casting. First off, as we've seen, he thought that Sophia Loren was right for the part of Lara. In fact, he even went to the trouble of bringing her to visit Lean in Madrid. She appeared in a simple frock with a lace collar, looking very fetching. But Lean was not impressed.

Omar Sharif, who plays the title role in the film, says that Lean believed Loren too voluptuous, "too amply endowed," to play the seventeen-year-old Lara at the beginning of the movie. According to Sharif, Lean phoned Robert O'Brien the next day with his verdict, not wanting to tell Ponti or Loren personally. He declared that he could cast Loren as Lara only "if she can convince me that she can play a seventeen-year-old virgin." O'Brien replied, "David, I have talked to my people; you are free to cast whomever you want in the movie." Sharif concludes, "Ponti never raised the issue again."[29]

"As the characters took shape in the screenplay," says Lean, in a filmed interview, "we naturally began to think of who was to play them on the screen." He began watching current movies, in search of promising actors—the method that had found him Peter O'Toole for *Lawrence*. He happened to see John Schlesinger's breezy comedy *Billy Liar* (1963) and noticed a girl walking down the street, casually swinging her handbag. "I couldn't take my eyes off her," Lean says. "She had this extraordinary screen presence."[30] The actress was the twenty-four-year-old Julie Christie; she was still relatively unknown when she got the part of Lara.

Lean spotted Tom Courtenay in the title role of *Billy Liar*, opposite Christie. He tapped Courtenay to play Pasha Antipov, a young revolutionary who resurfaces as the dreaded General Strelnikov late in the film. Once on the set, Courtenay was awed in the presence of fellow cast members Sir Ralph Richardson and Sir Alec Guinness. "I hadn't done enough on stage or screen to be in their company," he explained. "It wasn't right. I felt like an imposter." Because his character appears only intermittently, Courtenay remembers doing only about three weeks' work, spread out over six months. Asked at the time what he did for a living, Courtenay reportedly quipped, "*Dr. Zhivago.*"[31]

In the course of the movie, Lara becomes entangled with a corrupt lawyer and politician, Victor Komarovsky, who was to be played by Rod Steiger (*On the Waterfront*). Steiger was singled out in publicity layouts for the film as the only American in the cast. Actually, Geraldine Chaplin, the daughter of Charles Chaplin, who was to play Yuri's wife, Tonya, was born in Santa Monica.

Chaplin was only twenty when Lean chose her to play opposite Omar Sharif. "My eye had been caught by some publicity pictures of Geraldine Chaplin in some fan magazines," Lean says. He gave her a screen test on October 29, 1964. "She looked far too young, but she had a kind of dignity, which I liked." Lean wrote her parents, Charles Chaplin and Oona O'Neill, that he was "madly impressed" by Geraldine's talent and was pleased to be able to give her her first screen role.[32] Lean had, as we have seen, admired her father from childhood. Geraldine Chaplin later said that she based her performance on her mother, who was devoted to her father in much the same way that Tonya was devoted to Yuri.[33]

Omar Sharif was not the first choice to play Yuri. Lean originally considered Peter O'Toole and had a copy of the script sent to him from Ponti's office in Rome. O'Toole replied frankly that, after enduring the rigors of shooting *Lawrence* for nearly two years in the desert, he was not prepared to make another picture with David Lean for the foreseeable future. He had, instead, accepted the title role in Richard Brooks's film adaptation of Joseph Conrad's *Lord Jim* (1965). Lean, as said before, was easily offended, and he felt that O'Toole did not appreciate the career-making role that he had given him in *Lawrence*. Having been turned down by O'Toole, Lean blurted out, "Damn it! I'm going to use Omar Sharif. He's easy to work with."[34]

Lean notified Sharif that he wanted him to be in *Dr. Zhivago*. Sharif, who had read the novel when he got wind of Lean's plans to film it, could not see himself—an Egyptian—playing the lead in a Russian epic. He thought he might get by in a smaller role like Pasha. After making this suggestion to Lean, the director wired back that he would rather have Sharif play Yuri.

"I have round eyes," says Sharif. Hence, Lean decided to give a Slav-like slant to his eyes. "I'm convinced they will believe he's a Russian," said Lean. So, every day during shooting, according to Sandra Lean, a makeup artist "would pull his eyes into an almond shape": "The skin was stretched and then taped to his temples." "David did not think of the discomfort this would cause Omar," she continues. But it was worth it: "One actually believed that he was Russian."[35]

Besides Sharif, other members of the cast were veterans of previous Lean films. Ralph Richardson (*The Sound Barrier*) was to play Alexander Gromeko, Yuri Zhivago's adopted father. Alec Guinness, appearing in his fifth Lean movie, was to play Yevgraf Zhivago, Yuri's half brother and a commissar in the secret police. But Guinness did not accept the part immediately. His wife, Merula, advised him against it, saying that he should not allow himself to be sucked into another David Lean monster epic, in which the actors are totally smothered by the scenery.

As it happened, Ponti's office sent Guinness a preliminary draft of the screenplay, which was missing several of the later scenes. On the basis of what he read, Guinness rejected the part of Yevgraf. (We recall that he initially turned down the role of Colonel Nicholson in *Kwai* after reading an early draft of the script.) He replied to Lean that Yevgraf was an "enigmatic character" who appeared in only a few scenes. He functioned principally as the movie's narrator, and, as Guinness noted, "The commentary stuff is irritating." He further noted that Alexander Gromeko was a meatier role and much more to his taste. That part, however, was to be played by Ralph Richardson. (Guinness's biographer Piers Read says that Richardson "appeared with Guinness in *Lawrence of Arabia*."[36] This is, of course, incorrect.)

After Guinness received the rest of the script, Lean followed up with a letter on November 11, 1964, pointing out that Yevgraf commented on the action: "And I love so-called commentary in films." Laura's compelling commentary in *Brief Encounter*, he went on, was one of the outstanding qualities of that picture. Lean described Yevgraf as just the sort of complex figure Guinness loved to play. He can be cruel, as when he says that he has executed better men than himself with a pistol; yet he can be kind, as when he talks with the girl Tonya, who is very probably his niece. Lean assured Guinness that Yevgraf was a more challenging part than Gromeko. Gromeko was not, he continued, a demanding role. "He's not in *the same fucking street as Yevgraf!*"[37] Guinness told me that he cabled Lean that he would take the role of Yevgraf, explaining that his "shillyshallying was because he had received the script in two sections, separated by several days": "Reading the screenplay straight through changed my mind." Moreover, Lean had persuaded him that the commentary would work.

Rita Tushingham, a young British actress, played the love child of Yuri and Lara as an adult. All her scenes, which were exclusively in the prologue and epilogue, were with Guinness. "We did all of our scenes in one block; it took a whole month, which is rather slow filmmaking," she told me in conversation. "I enjoyed working with Alec Guinness, who had a fine sense of humor." Though, as a rule, Guinness was not prone to joking around on the set between takes, he was aware that Tushingham had only been in some low-budget independent films like Tony Richardson's *A Taste of Honey* (1961) and found being part of a huge superproduction rather daunting. "So Alec kidded with me," she said, "just to put me at ease."

"I admired David Lean and loved being directed by him," said Tushingham. "But some of us in the cast were quite young; so Geraldine and I and some others found it hard to think out a scene the way he wanted us to." To Tushingham, Lean seemed too reserved: "But I guess he was preoccupied with choosing the right way to shoot a scene." She concluded that Lean once said in his own defense: "I'm often thought to be rude on the set, where I'm really anxious about solving some problem in filming a scene."

Lean was, indeed, using some young players in the film as well as some seasoned performers. The director "is responsible for the casting," he explained at the time, so it was his decision "to take a risk with unknowns, as indeed we've done with *Zhivago* in several cases." Besides Tushingham: "We've got Julie Christie, who's not all that well known, and Geraldine Chaplin, who's only done this film; and that's quite a gamble—they really are big parts."[38]

Lean agreed with the principles of the auteur theory concerning the crucial role of the director in shaping a movie, in terms of casting and other production decisions. But he also believed that the filmmaker must earn the right to exercise artistic control: "It is the first time I've worked with MGM, and I've had no quarrels with them at all. They've let me do just as I like. . . . If a large company is going to put a vast amount of money into a film project, I suppose they naturally entrust that money to people who have proved themselves in the past; and I suppose I have had a fairly good record that way."[39]

Lean as usual rounded up a talented crew, many of whom he was familiar with from previous pictures. He still referred to them as his dedicated maniacs. The production designer John Box and his right-hand man, the art director Terence Marsh, the costume designer Phyllis Dalton, the property master Eddie Fowlie, and the composer Maurice Jarre were all veterans of *Lawrence of Arabia*. So were the film editor Norman Savage and the script supervisor Barbara Cole (who also continued to be Lean's mistress). Norman Savage, a protégé of Anne Coates's, had been an assistant editor on *Lawrence*. Since Coates was committed to edit John Ford's *Young Cassidy* (1965) and other films, she recommended that Lean promote Savage to be principal editor of *Zhivago*. Lean had hoped to have Freddie Young once again as director of photography, but Young had signed to photograph *Khartoum* (1966), another historical spectacle, for Basil Dearden. Hence, he selected Nicholas Roeg, a second-unit director on *Lawrence,* as cinematographer.

Lean had little hope of shooting the picture in Russia since the novel was forbidden there, but he sent up a trial balloon anyway, inquiring through diplomatic channels. His hopes were soon dashed by the scorching response he got from the Kremlin. The Russian government denounced Pasternak's book, which implies that the Bolsheviks betrayed the Revolution, as a "pack of lies" and warned that any film unit from the West making a movie of that novel in Russia would be operating under a cloud of suspicion.[40] That was enough to scare off Lean.

Lean and Box then embarked on a four-month journey to scout possible locations, covering ten thousand miles all told. Lean favored Finland, where the winter weather was the same as in Russia. But Box threw cold water on the idea because Finland did not have a film studio capable of handling a huge production. "So I suggested Spain," Box recalls. After shooting some of *Lawrence* in Seville, it was evident that Spain boasted well-equipped studio facilities, staffed by competent technicians. Furthermore, says Box, "Spain had landscapes within easy reach of a studio, so the Spanish plains could become the Russian steppes."[41]

Consequently, *Dr. Zhivago* would be primarily shot in and around the CEA Studios in Madrid, with a side trip to Finland for a couple of weeks to film snowy exteriors. Few people over the years seem to have noticed the difference. As Freddie Young noted in his autobiography, "I've often been asked in which part of Russia we filmed *Zhivago*."[42] Ponti negotiated with MGM for a budget of $11 million, but the price tag of the picture would eventually climb to $15 million.

Lean and Box decided to build the largest principal set ever constructed for a Hollywood movie on location. It encompassed two Moscow streets and was built on a ten-acre site near Canillejas, a suburb of Madrid. The planning and erection of the Moscow set took eighteen months. Box began construction on August 3, 1964, and employed eight hundred workers to build the set. It consisted of two streets, Box says; the larger one he called "the street of the elite." This thoroughfare, where the well-to-do families lived, was half a mile in length and featured several shops and houses. It was dominated by the Kremlin in Red Square, which was at the end of the block. This street had a tram line, with functioning trolley cars. There was also "the street of the poor," where working-class families lived. It ran parallel to the other street "and led to a factory with smokestacks," says Box.[43]

Most of the houses on the two streets were just facades, Geraldine Chaplin remembers: "But three of them were complete houses, which could be used for shooting interiors."[44] Lean therefore could begin a shot on the street outside a house and then move the camera inside to the interior set in a single take, without cutting from the exterior to the interior. For example, the Gromeko house in the street of the elite, where Tonya lived with her family, had detailed interiors, as did the house in the street of the poor where Lara and her mother lived.

Box's carefully researched, artfully executed Moscow set exemplifies "his sweeping and grand treatment of the past," which influenced later epics like *Nicholas and Alexandra* and *Reds*. Little wonder that Vincent LoBrutto chose *Zhivago* for his list of the one hundred outstanding examples of production design in American cinema.[45]

Principal photography was set to begin in December 1964 and continue until October 1965. The first official day of shooting was December 28, 1964. Lean started off with the burial of Yuri Zhivago's mother when he was a boy. The young Yuri was played by Omar Sharif's seven-year-old son Tarek, so Lean gave Sharif instructions for his son, which Sharif, in turn, passed on to the lad. The scene was set on a grim winter's day; hence, Nicholas Roeg, the lighting cameraman, put a filter on the camera lens to dim down the sunlight and wash the clouds out of the sky. This gave the sky a cloudless, burned-out look, in order to reflect the barren quality of the landscape.

Despite Roeg's remarkable handling of scenes like the burial sequence, he and Lean did not get along. Roeg had been compliant in working with Lean on *Lawrence* because he was conscious that he was merely a second-unit director. But, when he was advanced to the post of director of photography on *Zhivago*, he assumed that he should have more of a say in how a scene was filmed.

Lean said that, given the dark subject matter of the movie, he did not want the picture to look "pretty." Geraldine Chaplin states that she overheard Lean say to Roeg, "I want the love scenes to be drained of color and set in the horrible cold." But Roeg wanted to light them to look warm and beautiful. "They fought bitterly about that one Saturday," says Chaplin. "On Monday we heard that Nick Roeg was out and Freddie Young in."[46] Roeg comments that he usually liked working closely with a director while photographing a picture: "I enjoyed being part of the film that was being made." But his continuing disagreements with Lean made him realize that this time around, "I was on the wrong planet."[47]

Lean once again had a caravan on location that served as his command post. He summoned Roeg to the caravan, where he sat pensively smoking a cigarette in his ever-present cigarette holder. Lean managed the dismissal as tactfully as possible. "I predict that you will be a good director some day," he told Roeg, "but I'm afraid you can't photograph this film." He assured Roeg that he did not have another lighting cameraman in mind to take over, someone he preferred to Roeg. "But I think we ought to change."[48] This, of course, was simply not true; he had wanted Freddie Young from the get-go. In fact, Lean got Ponti to negotiate with United Artists to buy Young out of his contract to shoot *Khartoum* as soon as he decided to let Roeg go.

"Being fired by David Lean did not harm Nick's career," John Schlesinger told me in conversation. "Nick was one of Britain's major cinematographers, and when I heard he was available, I immediately hired him to photograph my film of Thomas Hardy's *Far from the Madding Crowd* [1967], also starring Julie Christie." Roeg went on to direct Christie himself in one of his best directorial efforts, *Don't Look Now*, an excursion into the occult. So Lean's prediction that Roeg would become a good director came true.

Shooting in Madrid in a studio that was not air-conditioned caused a good deal of discomfort for the actors during the spring and summer months. The cast was enduring temperatures up to 116 degrees, "muffled up to the ears in Russian furs," as Alec Guinness writes in his foreword to this book. "We just wanted to say our lines and get out of that heat!"

For the long train sequence, in which Yuri transports his family to their country home in the Ural Mountains, Box constructed a mock-up of a railway car in the studio, in order to film the interior scenes. "The whole set was on rockers, so that we could simulate the motion of the train," Lean remembered. "It was the middle of summer; and these poor wretches were wearing overcoats, as if they were muffled up against the cold."[49] The costumer Phyllis Dalton adds, "I became a policeman, going around the set bullying the actors into keeping their layers and layers of clothes on."[50]

Though Lean usually left Dalton to her own devices when she was dressing the extras, when it came to the costumes for the actors, he sometimes kibitzed. Dalton designed a gray traveling outfit for Geraldine Chaplin to wear when Tonya arrives back from a trip to Paris at the Moscow station. But Lean was adamant that she wear pink. So Dalton remade the exact same costume in pink. She tactfully told Lean that she had originally chosen gray because Tonya would not travel all the way from Paris in a pink dress—it would appear grimy after a long train journey. Lean answered that, if Tonya looks great in pink, the audience "will never question whether she's spent hours on a train or not." Dalton admitted that she was being too practical: "David was right; he nearly always was."[51]

Lean was just as insistent about the scarlet gown that Lara wears for an assignation with Victor Komarovsky. But Julie Christie balked at wearing it; she thought it made her look too much like a scarlet woman. Box recalls that he took her aside before she got into a row with Lean and explained why Lean had approved the costume: "It's not a dress that you would have bought or Lara would have bought. But it is just the kind of gown that Komarovsky would make her wear because Komarovsky treats her like a whore in the scene. So please play the scene in it."[52] Christie acquiesced.

Like Rita Tushingham, Julie Christie admired Lean, and she endeavored to be cooperative throughout the production period. She was, she says, playing a renowned role, the legendary Lara, for a distinguished director, and she "desperately wanted to bring it off." She continued, "David's presence on *Zhivago* was more paternalistic than that of many directors." She remembers that she viewed him as an authoritarian but kindly father; in fact, he "fathered" her in directing her scenes. "I always understood what he wanted," she said. And she would always strive to deliver the performance he expected. What actors did not like, she concluded, was that Lean perhaps imposed his will on them too much. Nevertheless, "The whole vision of the film was in *his* head; and he used us actors like colors in his painting."[53]

Christie noticed that Lean discouraged the actors from improvising during rehearsals, unlike John Schlesinger, for whom she had recently made *Billy Liar.* Asked about this, Lean answered that he rarely departed from the shooting script. "When I get the actors and I run through the scene, I'm following the script," he explained, "because I rarely find that you can do something better at the last minute. . . . I am personally very wary of improvisation."[54] Lean would discuss a scene in detail the day before he shot it and walk the actors through it, then plot out the camera positions for the lighting cameraman, and they would film the scene the following day, just as rehearsed.

Still, Lean was open to considering an actor's suggestions on occasion, even though, as Rod Steiger says, he thought of the shooting script as the Bible. Steiger recalls that, in an early scene, Victor Komarovsky was to kiss Lara passionately while riding in a sleigh and that "she was supposed to be shocked because she didn't see it was coming." When they rehearsed the scene, Steiger noticed that Christie "anticipated the kiss, which was reflected in her nervousness." Steiger asked for a private word with Lean and suggested that he would kiss Christie as she expected: "But then I won't let go; I will follow the first kiss with a French kiss; and she *will* be shocked." Lean accepted Steiger's suggestion, and Christie was genuinely taken aback. "Lean realized that any suggestion I made to him was always within the framework of the script," Steiger continued. In another scene, Lara angrily slaps Victor across the face. "Nobody slaps Komarovsky and gets away with it," he said to Lean. "So Lean allowed me to slap her right back"—an action that was not scripted. "But I acted like a gentleman and slapped her with my glove, not with an open hand."[55]

While Steiger seemed to have developed a workable, if cautious, professional relationship with Lean, Guinness found coping with him more difficult than before. Lean attempted to coax Guinness into delivering high emotions in a couple of scenes while Guinness insisted on underplaying as always. He stuck to his guns by reminding Lean once again of the film actor's aphorism: "Less is more." Lean appeared to Guinness more than ever before to be playing "the great director." Guinness wrote in his diary on May 8, 1965: "I begin to dislike him and his egoism, which he assumes everyone else has as well." Years later, he looked back on his unhappy stint on *Dr. Zhivago* and found that his opinion of Lean had not changed. "David Lean and I had fallen out quite a bit during that film," Guinness recorded in his diary on May 19, 1973, "he having become so very intense, a slave-driver, tetchy and humorless."[56]

Omar Sharif had his own, somewhat different problems on the set. For example, whenever he viewed the rushes of the previous day's shooting, he noticed that Steiger and Christie and other actors were praised by the members of the cast present—but that no one ever complimented his performance. He gradually became demoralized and asked to see Lean one evening. He told Lean that he was sinking into the background because his performance was consistently overlooked by everyone. Lean explained that Yuri Zhivago is an observer: "You are in almost every scene, and everything is seen through your eyes. Trust me. They won't notice you much in any one scene; but when the curtain comes down, everyone will remember you more than anyone else."[57] Just as in the novel, he is at the center of the action, the link between all the various characters, each of whom is trying to survive the critical period of the Revolution.

One scene in which Yuri definitely plays the role of observer, rather than that of participant in the action, particularly stands out. He witnesses from a balcony overlooking a Moscow street the slaughter of peaceful demonstrators by the czar's Cossacks. Rather than portray the violence directly, as he did in the case of the massacre of the Turks in *Lawrence,* Lean cuts to Yuri's reaction. He believed that, in this instance, Yuri's horrified facial expression would have more emotional impact than would actual images of bloodletting. Only at the end of the scene does the camera explore the consequences of violence, showing bodies in the street. Lean later noted, "Thank goodness it worked; if it hadn't, I'd have been cooked, because I didn't shoot any of the sabre bashing."[58]

Problems were not, of course, confined to the actors. When Freddie Young took over from Roeg as lighting cameraman, Lean informed him that *Zhivago* was not being shot in seventy millimeter, as *Lawrence* had been, because the MGM front office maintained that it was too expensive. Lean remembered being told, "Nobody will notice the difference if you shoot on 35mm widescreen and blow it up [to seventy-millimeter super-Panavision]."[59]

Andrew Mollo, the movie's technical adviser on all things Russian, was faced with a difficulty of another sort. For the scene depicting the peaceful outdoor demonstration, Lean needed a revolutionary song, but one that would not be familiar in the rabidly anti-Communist Spain of Francisco Franco. Mollo selected the "Internationale," which had, he assumed, been forgotten since it had been outlawed in Spain since Franco ascended to power in 1936. But the local chief of police—who was on hand to watch as two thousand extras marched down the main street of the outdoor set—recognized it and immediately intervened to stop the singing. The second assistant director, Pedro Vidal, who was a Spaniard, was delegated to mollify him by reminding him that this was a historical movie. The crowd was demonstrating against the Russian czar in the context of the story, and the song meant nothing more than that. Feeling that he had done his duty, the police chief let the filming proceed.

The intervention of the police chief provided a tense moment on the set, but the grimmest moment of the whole shoot occurred when Lean was filming a scene aboard a freight train transporting refugees to the country, in which Yuri and his family are traveling. The scene was shot on a real freight train steaming down the track, with the camera in the boxcar pointing out the open door. A peasant woman (Lili Murati) is running alongside the train, attempting to get on board. Yuri reaches out to grab her hand. "I realized that she couldn't keep up with the train, which was gathering speed," Sharif says in the sole eyewitness account of this episode. "I didn't want to drag her along; so I let go of her hand, and she tumbled and fell under the train. (This shot is used in the film.)[60]

Lean got on his walkie-talkie and told the engineer to halt the train. When he apprehensively looked beneath the boxcar, he discovered that Murati had doubled up on the track when she fell so that the train wheels did not roll over her legs. But she had broken two bones in one leg. Lean directed one of his assistants to see to it that she was rushed to the nearest hospital, says Sharif. Lean then turned to Vidal and said, "Dress the double in a costume; we had better continue shooting, to keep up morale." Sharif was not alone in being shocked that Lean simply kept going, as if nothing had happened.[61]

Shariff maintains that, the next day, he confronted Lean about his apparent callousness. "The general must keep the troops going, or the whole operation will break down," Lean replied. Sharif comments, "Perhaps David didn't show it on the set, but he was concerned about the actress and phoned the hospital several times, inquiring about her." Moreover, it was not generally known that Lean went to visit her in the hospital. "David felt he was the commander-in-chief, like General Eisenhower on D-day," Sharif concludes. "So he had to keep the show on the road."[62]

"Of all the pictures I've worked on," Freddie Young states, "I think *Dr. Zhivago* is the most memorable and challenging. It has an enormous variety of moods and situations."[63] He pinpoints one challenging scene in particular—that in which Lean wanted to underscore Yuri's grief at parting from Lara, after they have worked together in a military hospital caring for casualties for some time. Young worked out a visual metaphor with the property master Eddie Fowlie, Lean's jack-of-all-trades. There was a vase of sunflowers in the reception area of the hospital, and Fowlie attached fine threads to the flowers' petals. When Lara departs, Young photographed the sunflowers as Fowlie, out of camera range, pulled on the threads. This caused the petals to fall, as if blown by a breeze; it is as if the sunflowers are weeping, just as tears come into the despondent Yuri's eyes.

Zhivago was a demanding picture to shoot, says Young, because in it "all four seasons are represented." For the autumn scenes, for example, Lean had the property department collect tons of leaves, put them in sacks, and load them on the truck. "When the time came, they were scattered on the ground; a wind machine was used to create a flurry."[64]

Winter was even more challenging. "Turning Spanish locations into a wintry Russia," said the *Times*, "represented the essence of cinema—creating the illusion of reality."[65] Lean, of course, wanted Varykino, the hideaway in the country where Yuri and Lara isolate themselves for a few months, surrounded by snow for the winter scenes. The exterior of the house was, as Lean remembered it, "a marvelous set built by John Box in the middle of agricultural land in a place called Soria, . . . about 150 miles north of Madrid, about a four-hour drive." There were pine forests nearby, so it did resemble Russia. "Soria was about four thousand feet high," Lean continued. And it was reported to be the coldest place in Spain, with snow guaranteed from December to March, "sometimes waist-height."[66]

Unfortunately, the winter of 1965 turned out to be the warmest on record for that part of Spain. When Lean wanted to shoot an establishing shot of the house at Varykino, the snow was not nearly deep enough. Young recalls only "a light covering of snow": "And the furrows were plainly visible in the plowed fields. The solution was marble dust. We bought hundreds of tons from a local marble works and spread it on the ground; whitewash was sprayed on the pine trees."[67]

Box called the house at Varykino the Ice Palace. His concept of the interior of the house was that the snow had seeped inside through cracks in the roof. The rooms in the house were covered with snow, thus recalling the rooms in Miss Havisham's ramshackle mansion in *Great Expectations*, which were covered with cobwebs. Actually, Box's inspiration for the interior of the Ice Palace was not *Great Expectations* but a still photograph of the explorer Captain Scott in the Antarctic, shivering in his hut; there was a hole in the roof where the snow had gotten in and covered everything.

The interior of the Ice Palace was constructed on a soundstage in the studio in Madrid. Box had Eddie Fowlie go around the set with a bucket of hot candle wax and a mug and throw the wax on the furniture and the walls.

"I walked behind him with a bucket of freezing water and a spray gun and sprayed the set," Box says, "so that everything looked frozen. And yet the temperature was 100 degrees in the studio."[68]

In the scene in which Lara is viewed from outside a frosted window, Lean wanted to create the effect of a candle flame melting a circle of ice on the glass, allowing the viewer to see through the windowpane. Lara is "regularly associated with warm, golden colors," as with the glowing candle flame here and the sunflowers earlier.[69] Fowlie mapped out the shot. He first put the windowpane in a tub of dry ice, and it frosted. Then he substituted the warm air of a hair dryer offscreen for the warmth of the flickering candle flame, causing a circle of frost to melt on the icy windowpane. The camera moved closer to the window, through which Lara was visible in a luminous close-up. At this moment she is Lara as Pasternak envisioned her, a woman of great devotion and spiritual beauty—stubborn, extravagant, adored.

Lean commented that he never ceased to be amazed at what Fowlie could invent. Consider the scene in which, as Young writes, "the Red Army charges across a frozen lake": "Some of them get shot, and their horses tumble and slither across the ice." Since the scene was scheduled to be shot in the boiling heat of a Spanish summer, the frozen lake would have to be simulated. Fowlie got together with Box, and they decided to spread cement over a huge field. Then they "sprinkled marble dust on it to resemble snow-covered ice": "No one would believe it wasn't a frozen lake."[70]

Lean very much wanted to do a scene that established the coming of spring at long last. This involved Yuri looking through a window at a field of daffodils. "We were growing those damned daffodils for weeks in a green-house," said Lean. He wanted the room from which Yuri looks out at the flowers to be somber. To achieve that effect, "We used a spray gun and sprayed the bright colors in the room with gray paint."[71] Lean said that Young protested, "It's going to look bloody awful!" But Lean responded, "It will provide a stunning contrast with the daffodils, when we get to the next scene; and it will make their bright colors that much more effective."[72]

Young adds: "When the daffodils were coming to flower, we took them out and planted them in a field. We iced up the window that Omar looks through. We took the pane of glass out and put it in an icebox, until it was frosted over; and then we stuck it back in." When Yuri rubs the ice away, the snowflakes on the windowpane dissolve to a shot of the flowers. "You see a flood of daffodils which had been planted that morning."[73]

In early March 1965, while Lean was still shooting on location in Soria, Robert O'Brien came over from MGM for a progress report. Ponti and O'Brien had agreed that, since Lean was spending MGM's money, O'Brien, not Ponti, would visit Lean on location. O'Brien stopped first in Madrid to look at the rushes of the footage that Lean had shot thus far and then came up to Soria for a conference. Lean dreaded the encounter because he was painfully aware that he was considerably over budget and behind schedule. He even feared that O'Brien would demand that he tear the next twenty pages out of the script to save time and money. "Bob, I don't know what to say," he began. "I know that I am $3 million over budget." He explained that, as always on location, there had been a number of delays and setbacks that were beyond his control—too much sun when the script called for snow, rain washing away the artificial snow from the outdoor sets, technical equipment malfunctioning, and so forth. O'Brien answered that he was pleased with the rushes. He quoted the often-repeated Hollywood adage, "You only need three great shots in a movie to get an Oscar," and then indicated that, as far as he was concerned, *Zhivago* already had more than that. "You carry on as you've been doing, and let me look after the money," he concluded.[74] O'Brien was so pleased he even permitted the planned—but expensive— move from Spain to Finland that would be necessary if Lean were to get the panoramic shots simulating Russia's winter landscapes that were impossible in Spain.

Lean and his intrepid band of cast and crew members set out for Finland on March 15, 1965. He planned to film the exterior shots of the train that takes Yuri and his family to their summer home in the Ural Mountains. Ponti obtained the cooperation of the Finnish State Railroad, which supplied thirty-two railway cars and two wood-burning engines, modified to resemble Russian locomotives of the early twentieth century. The railway tracks on which the train traveled had actually been laid in 1940 during the Russian invasion of Finland.

Lean's unit sojourned at Joensuu, a lumber town four hundred miles north of Helsinki, close to the Arctic Circle, and only seventy-five miles from the Russian border. "That was as close to Russia as we could get," says Box. "We shot in Finland, despite temperatures of forty degrees below zero, because Finland best resembled the Russian steppes."[75]

Lean filmed in the snowy, misty, windblown area around the frozen Lake Pyhaselka. Lapland Gypsies, from a nomadic tribe that wandered in the country's northern region, were enlisted to play the Siberian refugees whom the Zhivagos traveled with. Filming was slow going since, in the winter in that remote region, Lean could count on only four to six hours of daylight on any given day.

After two weeks, Lean decided to pack up and return to Spain. He dispatched a second unit to Canada, where Ponti obtained the cooperation of the Canadian Pacific Railway for some additional outdoor footage. "Where second unit work is required," Lean noted, "I do a diagram picture of what I want." He would then give the diagram to the second-unit director, in this case Roy Rossotti.[76] Lean was always at pains to see that every shot in a David Lean film would bear his trademark—hence the blowup with de Toth on the set of *Lawrence* (see chapter 13).

Before departing from Finland, Lean celebrated his fifty-seventh birthday on March 25, 1965, with a cake topped by a model diesel locomotive. The unit decamped on March 28 for the CEA studios in Madrid. Principal photography wrapped on October 7, 1965, after 232 days of shooting, which adds up to nine months. This was an exceptionally long schedule, but still four months shorter than the shooting period for *Lawrence*.

The premiere of *Dr. Zhivago* was originally set for March 1966, but, after principal photography wrapped, O'Brien asked whether Lean might have the film edited and ready for a premiere in December 1965. Lean's first reaction was to state flatly, "Impossible." But O'Brien employed the same logic that Sam Spiegel had used to coax Lean into finishing postproduction on *Lawrence* in four months. He pointed out that he had booked theaters in New York and in Los Angeles for the week of December 20 so that *Zhivago* could qualify for the 1965 Academy Awards. *Zhivago* would surely win some Oscars, O'Brien reasoned, and that undoubtedly would help the film at the box office. In the wake of expensive flops like *Mutiny on the Bounty*, MGM desperately needed a moneymaker. Lean asked for twenty minutes to contemplate O'Brien's suggestion and walked away. When he returned, he said, "All right, Bob, we'll do it."[77]

Lean then faced the prospect of completing postproduction in less than three months; that meant whittling down thirty-one hours of footage to the final running time of just over three hours. MGM invited Lean to its studios in Culver City to edit the film. Though he was a Hollywood director, the only other time Lean had worked in a Hollywood studio was when he did second-unit work on *The Greatest Story Ever Told*. The studio provided him with a bungalow on the lot that had once been the schoolroom for Judy Garland and Elizabeth Taylor when they were child stars at Metro. It was remodeled to include a posh editing room with a plush carpet; Lean also had a luxury suite at the Bel Air Hotel, the kind that he thought only Sam Spiegel could afford.

Lean spent ten weeks, working night and day with the chief film editor Norman Savage, who had come over from England to help out. Lean and Savage had attempted to begin cutting the picture in Spain on weekends while Lean was still filming. That system had worked with Anne Coates on

Lawrence, but this time Lean was not satisfied with the results, so he and Savage started over from scratch during postproduction. Three months would have been enough to edit the average ten-reel Hollywood movie, but Lean and Savage had less than three months to edit this king-size, twenty-reel picture, which involved the mixing and recording of the sound track, including the musical score.

As with editing *Lawrence,* editing *Zhivago* became a race against the clock. Lean and Savage had to work until the wee hours, seven days a week. Sometimes they required "vitamin injections" just to keep going, as they presided over a bevy of assistant editors.[78] They would decide how they wanted a given scene edited, then give detailed instructions to one of the assistant editors, marking the footage with a soft, red pencil, for them to cut. Eventually, the edited footage would be passed on to the sound editors.

Lean always took a great deal of trouble with the sound track of a movie. "Yes, I paid tremendous attention to the sound [on *Zhivago*]," he recalled. "It's one of the great technical weapons I have; and I think sound tracks are frightfully interesting." He usually tried "to shoot the sound when actually filming." What he failed to get during shooting he would hope to get during postproduction. He would then call on the vast library of prerecorded sound effects that every studio has. For example, when he was dissatisfied with the sound of the moving train in one sequence, he lifted the sound of the train "from one of the train shots out of *Brief Encounter.*" He was particularly pleased with one of the sound effects that the sound crew dug up, that of howling wolves. They are heard outside the snowbound house at Varykino. "They are real wolves," said Lean, "recorded in Canada."[79]

Lean had brought the supervising sound editor Winston Ryder, one of his dedicated maniacs from previous films, to Hollywood with him. Ryder reported to Lean that the technicians in the MGM sound department were ignoring Lean's instructions. "They thought we Limeys were bloody idiots," fumed Ryder.[80] Lean responded with a threat to the front office: unless he got full cooperation, he would not guarantee that he would have the film ready for the December premiere. After that, the situation rapidly improved.

Lean took a great interest in the music for his film. When he told the head of the MGM music department that he had decided on Maurice Jarre for the score, the latter responded, "Maurice is very good for open spaces and sand, as on *Lawrence;* but I think we can get a better composer for Russia and snow." Lean did not think so. He warned Jarre that he would be under a time constriction similar to that which he had on *Lawrence*—about ten weeks to compose and record the underscore.[81]

"I don't read or write a note of music," Lean confessed. "But I know where and how it should be used in a film; and what it should express. I think a composer must be told what to do."[82] When Jarre came to Hollywood, Lean showed him the rough cut of the movie and discussed in broad terms how he envisioned the music. Then Jarre went away and composed some themes. "Lean didn't have a great musical background," Jarre remembered, "but he was careful to give me as much information as possible."[83]

Jarre wrote a love theme for Lara that Lean found to be fulsome. "Well, Maurice, I think you can do better," he said. Jarre was crestfallen. Sensing this, Lean said, "Maurice, forget about *Zhivago*; forget about Russia. Go to the mountains with your girlfriend and think about her and write a love theme for her."[84] Jarre adds, "David said that the Lara theme should not be specifically Russian, but a universal theme." So he spent the weekend with his girlfriend in the mountains above Los Angeles. "On Monday morning I sat down at the piano and found the Lara theme in one hour."[85] It is as delicate as spun gold.

Once Jarre had composed "Lara's Theme" to Lean's satisfaction, the rest of the scoring went smoothly. Some of the score, including "Lara's Theme," called for lush orchestration. Jarre derived inspiration from the rich and evocative music of such great Russian composers of the past as Tchaikovsky and Rimsky-Korsakov. He once again chose some unorthodox instruments to give the occasional exotic flavor to his music: an electronically amplified piano; a harpsichord; and a Moog synthesizer (just recently invented). The eerie dissonance supplied by these muted percussion instruments provided apt accompaniment for some of the dramatic scenes, as when Yuri, a solitary figure, is trudging back to Varykino through the vast, snowy wastes.

In order to give passages of his score a distinct Russian sound, Jarre used the balalaika, a popular Russian folk instrument that is strummed like a guitar. No musician in the MGM studio orchestra could play the balalaika, however, so, Jarre says, he paid a visit to a Russian Orthodox church in downtown Los Angeles, "where there were twenty-five people who played the instrument": "But they couldn't read music. I taught them sixteen bars, which they learned to play by ear."[86] Maxford sagely observes that, if one listens carefully to the balalaika passages of the score, "it is always the same sixteen bars of music that are played."[87]

Jarre sometimes displayed a flair for descriptive music. When Yuri's mother is being buried, the unceremonious shoveling of dirt into the grave is accompanied by an appropriate passage. Steven Spielberg comments, "I remembered vividly from *Dr. Zhivago* the heightened sound that Lean produced for the dirt hitting the wooden coffin during the burial."[88] Jarre picked up on the sound effect and reinforced it with "four thunderous claps of music (kettledrums, tubular bells, zither) as the earth hits the coffin." The aural shock is startling "in both its starkness and finality."[89] This is an example of how Jarre tried to say with music what could not be said by the camera alone.

Jarre finished recording the score with the MGM orchestra on December 14, 1965, a mere eight days before the December 22 premiere. Lean and Savage managed to pull together a final cut of three hours, seventeen minutes. Lean was still tinkering with the final cut right up to the last minute. The final reel of the movie was flown to New York just in time for the press preview the day before the premiere. As a matter of fact, I was a member of the audience at that preview. I remember vividly that, when the house lights dimmed, a hush of expectation fell over the journalists present.

Dr. Zhivago, like *Lawrence of Arabia*, starts with a prologue; it is set during World War II. A group of laborers walk under the arch of a hydroelectric dam. General Yevgraf Zhivago, a commissar of the secret police, singles out a girl in the line. He is searching for his niece, the long-lost daughter of his deceased half brother, Dr. Yuri Zhivago. The girl he approaches just may be the love child of Yuri and Lara; Yuri had immortalized Lara in his *Lara Poems*. Yevgraf shows the girl a new edition of the poems and inquires whether the book stirs any memories of her parents for her. She says emphatically no.

With that, Yevgraf launches into the story of Yuri Zhivago; it is presented in a sustained flashback, which Yevgraf narrates. But, since Yevgraf and Yuri rarely crossed paths throughout their adult lives, Yevgraf could not possibly have been present for many of the incidents that he narrates. He has, presumably, pieced his half brother's life together from reports he has heard from others.

The extended flashback begins in 1897 with the funeral of Yuri's mother, when he was a child. The scene recalls the opening cemetery scene of *Great Expectations;* like Pip, young Yuri fearfully watches the wind gusting and shaking the branches of the trees in the graveyard and blowing the leaves away. Then Lean quite unexpectedly cuts to a shot of Yuri's mother lying tranquilly inside her casket. Yuri "is trying to come to terms with Death," Bolt writes in the script at this point. So the shot of the corpse visualizes what Yuri imagines. "He is thoughtful, but not awed [by his fantasy]."[90] It is an unforgettable visual image.

Alexander and Anna Gromeko, affluent friends of his mother's, become the adoptive parents of Yuri, who is now an orphan. Alexander gives to little Yuri the balalaika that his mother had bequeathed to the lad. Yuri cherishes the instrument, which she had played beautifully, though she never had a lesson. "She was an artist," says Alex.

Yuri Zhivago grows up to be both a physician and an accomplished poet; he falls in love with his cousin, the Gromekos' daughter Tonya, and they marry. Yuri sees Lara for the first time on a trolley car but pays little attention to her. Lara is being courted by Pasha Antipov, a dedicated revolutionary. Pasha confines his agitation for revolt at this stage to handing out Communist leaflets on street corners, only later joining a peaceful protest march, one demonstrating for bread and peace.

Though Lean for the most part keeps the Revolution in the background of the film, when he chooses to bring it to the foreground, he does so in the same way that Eisenstein handled the abortive Revolution of 1905 in *Potemkin,* that is, by choosing incidents that are relatively insignificant in themselves but still symbolic indications of the thrust of the entire revolutionary effort. For example, in order to dramatize the tyranny that led to the 1917 Revolution, Lean stages the massacre of the peaceful demonstrators by the Cossacks. Lean suggests the slaughter in a rapid succession of images blended into a superb wedding of sight and sound—the slashing of sabers, the stunned expressions of terrified peasants, the drum of the marching band rolling into the mud, blood speckling the snow. After this catastrophe, Pasha becomes a bitter, obstreperous anarchist. "There will be no more peaceful demonstrations," he vows.

Lara's mother, Amelia, a dressmaker, is the mistress of Victor Komarovsky, an overbearing and cunning lawyer. When Amelia rightly suspects that Victor has seduced her teenaged daughter, she attempts suicide by overdosing on pills. Victor summons Dr. Kurt to the wretched Amelia's bedside, and Kurt brings along his protégé, Dr. Zhivago, to help him in this emergency. Before leaving the house, Yuri Zhivago wanders down a shadowy corridor and comes on a glass partition through which a woman is dimly visible sitting alone. Suddenly, the door opens at the opposite end of the room; Victor enters with a lamp, which sheds a shaft of light on Lara. She is weeping because she fears her mother may die. Yuri observes Lara throwing her arms around Victor's neck when he informs her that Amelia's life has been spared. Victor escorts her out of the room, and the room goes dark again. Lean symbolizes the barrier that Lara's relationship with Victor places between her and Yuri at this moment by photographing them on opposite sides of the glass partition.

But Lara is determined to break off her sordid liaison with Victor. When she informs him that she is going to take up with Pasha once again and eventually marry him, he sneers at her, saying, "You are too much of a slut to marry a high-minded young man like Pasha." To prove his point, he throws Lara on a bed and possesses her; she initially resists him but finally succumbs. "Don't delude yourself that this was a rape," Victor comments sardonically afterward. "That would flatter us both."

In a desperate effort to escape from Victor's power over her, Lara appropriates a revolver and follows him to a Christmas Eve celebration. She bursts in on the festivities and summarily shoots at him. Yuri and Tonya, guests at the party, witness the shooting in shocked silence. Victor is not seriously wounded, and he refuses to press charges. Lara subsequently renews her relationship with Pasha in earnest.

The film traces the ways in which the lives of the principal characters are disrupted "by the wars and revolutions that convulsed the social fabric of Russia in the early twentieth century."[91] With the outbreak of World War I in 1914, Yuri Zhivago is drafted into military service; he becomes an army doctor, Lara an army nurse. Yevgraf and Pasha both enlist.

The whole film is, like *Lawrence of Arabia,* a masterpiece of understatement. Thoughts and emotions are often communicated subtly and with few words, and the audience is left to gradually absorb the full implications of the story. As with other adaptations, Lean hones in on the novel's themes and deftly translates them into the visual language of cinema. In one sequence, as Russian soldiers sporting new boots march across the screen on their way to fight in World War I, Yevgraf comments on the sound track that the boots will eventually wear out. Later, at the close of the scene in which a group of war-weary troops have killed the officers who tried to stop their ignominious retreat, one soldier pauses to pull off the boots of a dead officer to replace his own. The soldiers' boots, Yevgraf observes, have finally worn out—like the wearers' enthusiasm for their cause.

Yuri is working tirelessly as a doctor at the Ukrainian front in a makeshift military hospital when he encounters Lara, whose unflagging zeal for her calling equals his own. They fall in love but do not consummate their mutual passion at this time. In fact, when the hospital is later shut down, Lara urges Yuri to go back to his wife and son. Though, because of the war, she has lost contact with her husband—she has married Pasha since her last encounter with Yuri—she has a daughter to think of.

Events move swiftly. By the end of the war, Lenin and the Bolsheviks are in power, and the czar and his family have been executed. Furthermore, civil war has broken out between the revolutionary Red Guard and the czarist White Guard, who are making a last-ditch stand for a return to the monarchy. Yuri returns to Moscow in the midst of the postwar depression, only to find that the Communists have requisitioned the Gromeko mansion and turned it into a commune. Meanwhile, the civil war continues to rage. Surveying the chaotic situation, Alexander Gromeko exclaims, "I wish they would decide which gang of hooligans is going to run this country!"

Yuri is comforted to find that Tonya has genuinely matured during the wartime upheavals. "Initially little more than a pretty china doll, all dressed up in pink," Tonya has developed into a "strong, self-reliant woman, more than worthy of Yuri's love and admiration."[92] Consequently, he puts all thoughts of Lara out of his mind.

Yevgraf pays Yuri and Tonya a visit. This is the first time the half brothers have ever met, and it is disturbing news that has finally motivated Yevgraf to seek Yuri out. Now a commissar of the Bolshevik secret police, Yevgraf informs Yuri that his poetry has been officially censured as "flagrantly subversive and absurdly subjective"; it has, therefore, been condemned by the Communist Party. Yevgraf urges Yuri to take his family to the Gromeko country estate at Varykino, where they can live safely in obscurity. As part 1 of the movie draws to a close, Yuri and his family embark on their journey to the Urals. Given the austerities of the time, they are reduced to making the trip in a boxcar of a freight train crammed with refugees.

As part 2 gets under way, Yuri, while en route to Varykino, unexpectedly runs across Pasha, who is now known as General Strelnikov. He is rabidly waging war against the surviving units of the White Guard. As the notorious Strelnikov, Pasha is the personification of the idealistic revolutionary who, once in power, turns ruthless fanatic. Now a single-minded zealot, Strelnikov chillingly confides to Yuri that he has long since renounced his relationship with Lara because "the private life is dead in Russia for a man with any manhood": "History has killed it. A man has more important things to do." He adds dispassionately that Lara now lives in the village of Yuriatin, not far from Varykino. In this, his last major scene in the film, Tom Courtenay manages to make Strelnikov's intensity seem to be a distorted form of sainthood.

It seems regrettable that Strelnikov all but disappears from the movie after his early scenes in part 1. John McInerney complains, "Strelnikov should not have been allowed to vanish."[93] Asked why he allowed this, Lean responded, "That is absolutely as it is in the novel." As a matter of fact, Pasternak treats Victor Komarovsky in much the same manner; Victor too vanishes from the book early in the story and then, as we shall shortly see, resurfaces near the end. "People who criticize that had better criticize the novel! If we'd departed from the novel, I'm sure they'd have criticized us on that score too!"[94]

Sometime after Yuri and his family move into the Gromeko country house, Yuri—in one of Pasternak's Dickensian coincidences—runs into Lara by chance in the small public library in nearby Yuriatin. Their wartime romance now blossoms into a full-blown love affair. When Tonya reveals that she is pregnant with their second child, however, Yuri rides to Yuriatin and tells Lara that he must never see her again. Leaving her in tears, he starts home only to be conscripted by partisans of the Red Guard, who are still pursuing the remnants of the White Guard and force him into service as a military doctor again.

After two years of ministering to the partisans in the Siberian forest, Yuri is able to escape from the camp during a blinding snowstorm and trudge across the desolate, windswept steppes. He gets as far as Lara's apartment, which is on the second floor of a shabby dwelling in Yuriatin. Lara gives him a letter that Tonya left with her, before Tonya and her family departed for Moscow. Tonya's letter explains that she gave birth to a baby daughter after Yuri was kidnapped. Tonya, her father, Alexander Gromeko, and the children are being deported to France as undesirables, presumably because her husband's poetry has been banned, and this stigma has extended to his family.

Lara tells Yuri that Tonya entrusted her with his mother's balalaika before she left, and he tells her to hold on to it as a keepsake. Suddenly, Victor Komarovsky, who has been drinking heavily, shows up at the door. Always the political opportunist, he has connived his way into being appointed to the Commissariat of Foreign Affairs for the Bolsheviks. He reveals that Strelnikov, by contrast, has fallen out of favor with the Communist Party and been branded a murderous fanatic. Victor drunkenly explains that Lara is now the wife of an enemy of the state and that Yuri has been declared a deserter by the Red Guard—but that he is, nonetheless, prepared to smuggle them both out of the country. They decline his help, fearing Bolshevik reprisals, and throw him out of the house.

Rod Steiger personally sympathized with Victor in this scene. According to Steiger, "Victor had a compulsive addiction to Lara from the time she was a teenager." He comes back years later and finds her with Yuri, his rival, yet he offers to rescue them both. "Victor's obsession with Lara has driven him to drink, and when Lara and Yuri eject him from her apartment, he stumbles and falls down the steps in a drunken rage." Mustering a kind of inebriated dignity, Victor shouts at them that they will both regret their decision. "On the whole," concludes Steiger, "I thought Victor was rather pathetic."[95]

Yuri and Lara seek refuge in the country house at Varykino, which his wife and family have been forced to vacate. Abandoned for months to the elements, the house is covered inside and out with snow; it has become a crystalline ice palace, topped with glittering Byzantine cupolas. Late one night, Yuri sits at his old writing desk, working on his cycle of "Lara sonnets." Outside he hears wolves howling, "symbolic of the grim realities that are stalking close."[96]

The hostile outer world closes in on them in the guise of Victor, who once again suddenly reappears. He reasserts his ultimatum that they both must leave with him. Now cold sober, he tells them that Strelnikov has shot himself in order to avoid an ignominious execution. Lara, now the widow of the infamous Strelnikov, and Yuri, still the dissident poet and deserter, are both candidates for a firing squad. Victor can offer them asylum in a Far Eastern republic, where he is going on a diplomatic mission for the Commissariat of Foreign Affairs.

Lean chose to have Strelnikov's suicide played offstage, even though Pasternak does depict the episode. In the novel, Strelnikov eludes the authorities and secretly comes to see Yuri; he nostalgically reminisces with Yuri about Lara, who is the one link between them. During the night, Strelnikov takes his own life, and Yuri discovers his corpse the next morning. "Strelnikov lay across the path," Pasternak writes, "with his head in a snowdrift. He had shot himself."[97] Bolt had dramatized Strelnikov's fate, but Lean was concerned that this scene, as Bolt wrote it, would add significantly to the overall length of the film.

In any case, Victor says that he will see that Yuri gets safely out of Russia but that he will then be on his own: "Lara stays with me." Yuri ostensibly agrees to leave Russia with Lara, under Victor's protection; he tells Lara and Victor to precede him to the station, where he will join them. But his pride prevents him from accepting sanctuary from Victor, and he stays behind. As Sarris describes the scene, "Yuri runs up the stairs of the old mansion to get one last look at the departing Lara. Lean's camera follows Yuri; the music swells, Yuri reaches the frosted window, but it's locked." In his impatience to "catch one last glimpse of his beloved," he smashes the windowpane.[98] When the train pulls out of the station without Yuri, Lara reveals to Victor something that Yuri does not know: she is carrying Yuri's child. She forlornly realizes that the price of her accepting Victor's help in fleeing to safety is submitting to his sexual demands.

As Richard Schickel writes, "The action of the film may be described very simply as the disillusionment—but not the souring—of Yuri Zhivago. One by one his hopes of preserving his identity as doctor, as poet, as family man, as unique individual are casually and wantonly destroyed by a Revolution with which he mildly sympathizes, but in which he does not want to involve himself. Finally, and most cruelly, the one thing the Revolution has given him—the opportunity to possess physically his great love, the magnificent Lara—is taken from him too."[99]

Yuri returns to Moscow in 1922, and Yevgraf eventually finds him work in a hospital. He develops heart disease, symbolically suggesting that he is suffering from a broken heart after losing Lara to Victor. Thus, Yuri Zhivago, perhaps better than any other Lean hero, represents Lean's ongoing theme. He is a man who simply refuses to accept that a situation is entirely hopeless; he never despairs of somehow being reunited with Lara. But it is not to be.

In 1929, he is riding in a trolley car and sees Lara through the window. He gets off the train and frantically endeavors to overtake her, but he suffers a fatal heart attack, collapses in the street, and expires. Lara is totally oblivious to Yuri's fate. The film, then, is bookended by the two streetcar scenes, which Bolt devised to portray the first and last times Yuri sees Lara.

The last time we see Lara, she proceeds down a street dominated by an ominous poster of Stalin, and she is finally lost from view. Yevgraf comments, in voice-over on the sound track, "I knew her name from the *Lara Poems,* which I had found among my brother's manuscripts." Yevgraf remains an ambiguous figure. As an officer of the secret police, he maintains the party's official ban on Yuri's poems during his lifetime, but, after Yuri's death, Yevgraf loyally snatches them from oblivion and has them published. "I tried to trace Lara," Yevgraf continues, "but I couldn't. She must have been arrested in the street, as so often happens these days; and she died or vanished somewhere in a Stalinist labor camp, forgotten as a nameless number on a list which was afterward mislaid."

The epilogue returns us to the narrative frame, with Yevgraf interviewing the young girl named Tonya, who is most likely the lost child of Yuri and Lara, at the dam site where she works. Yevgraf makes a final reflection on Yuri's life to the young girl: "We've come very far very fast. But do you know what it cost?" After pondering the implications of the story she has been told for a moment, Tonya says flatly that she is not Yuri Zhivago's daughter. She remembers her mother, Lara, she explains, but was always led to believe that Victor Komarovsky was her father. During a chaotic insurrection in Mongolia, where Victor had been posted temporarily, she was separated from her parents and was orphaned. Her one lasting memory of her mother is the balalaika that Lara gave her.

As Tonya, accompanied by her boyfriend, David, takes her leave of him, Yevgraf notices that she has slung a balalaika across her back. He inquires, "Can you play the balalaika?" David, a young engineer, answers for her: "She can; and no one taught her." Yevgraf replies, "Ah, then, she is an artist; it's a gift." Until this moment, Yevgraf's interrogation of Tonya had proved inconclusive, but now he is certain that he has finally found Yuri and Lara's daughter. The balalaika, which Yuri inherited from his mother, had passed to Lara and then to Tonya, who has likewise inherited her grandmother's gift of playing it intuitively.

The film's last shot is not in the screenplay, which ends with David and Tonya receding into the distance as "the dam gates open and the plunging water fills the screen."[100] But Lean adds a final shot of a rainbow glowing over the huge dam, possibly suggesting that the future will be brighter for Tonya than it was for her parents.

Dr. Zhivago has been called *Gone with the Wind* on ice, but it does not pick the audience up and sweep them along like *Gone with the Wind*. *Zhivago* builds slowly toward its climax. Earlier scenes, apparently unimportant, contribute to the gradual development of characterization and atmosphere and to the impact of the film as a whole. As a result, the audience at the first New York press preview, on the day before the premiere on December 22, did not find *Zhivago* compelling. They were simply not prepared for the unprecedented visual experience to which they were treated. Many of the reviewers did not know what to make of the movie, as the early reviews indicate. Since I attended that press preview, I remember that the audience began to fidget noticeably as the movie unspooled. I also recall the impatience expressed during the intermission by some of my colleagues, who felt that the picture was already too long and too slow. I was among the minority who realized that here was a film that needed discussion and reflection before the breadth of its meaning could be grasped fully.

MGM had laid on a grand party after the premiere the following night, on the roof of the Americana Hotel. It was a festive occasion, until around midnight, when the newspaper reviews arrived. Then a pall settled over the proceedings. "The reviews were the worst I'd ever had in my life," said Lean. Some of the guests shook his hand before hastily departing, murmuring, "Well, David, *I* like it." The dining room, which had shortly before been crowded with well-wishers, was now a sea of empty tables. "I felt absolutely sick at heart and ashamed," Lean concluded.[101]

The notices were decidedly mixed. On the positive side, they acknowledged that the movie offered an eyeful on the level of sheer spectacle. It was termed a gloriously glossy movie, featuring colorful parades and pageantry, as well as exciting battles. Referring to the epic sweep of the grand winter landscapes, one critic quipped, "David Lean's *Dr. Zhivago* does for snow what his *Lawrence of Arabia* did for sand." On the negative side, several critics went on to describe the movie as creaking under the weight of a tedious plot that makes the Russian Revolution just a backdrop for a conventional love triangle. Inside this fat movie, one reviewer opined, there is a Lean film struggling to get out.[102]

Judith Crist's review in the *New York Herald Tribune* was typical of the notices that had nothing good to say about the picture at all: "It is merely a spectacular soap opera . . . filled with cardboard characters, declaring that love and revolution make gloomy bedfellows." What really riled Lean was Crist's observation that his previous two masterful spectacles were produced by Sam Spiegel, while for *Dr. Zhivago* "Carlo Ponti took over the production chores."[103]

Crist's implication seemed to be that Sam Spiegel was principally responsible for the success of *Kwai* and *Lawrence,* an opinion with which Spiegel would certainly have agreed. In fact, Spiegel had been giving interviews to the press, in anticipation of the opening of his next production, *The Chase* (Arthur Penn, 1966). He stated that Lean customarily got too bogged down in details when making a movie and that he, Spiegel, like a benevolent uncle, had to keep the production on track. Lean got his own back when *The Chase* was released; the critics were amiable to *Dr. Zhivago* in comparison with the way that they dismissed *The Chase* as a conventional melodrama about an escaped convict, ineptly directed by Arthur Penn and "overproduced by Sam Spiegel."[104] But that was no consolation to David Lean at the time.

What Lean did find consoling was Richard Schickel's enthusiastic notice in *Life,* already cited. Schickel celebrated Lean's achievement in employing his "careful, conscious artistry" to create "the visual equivalent of Boris Pasternak's novel."[105]

Pauline Kael, writing a few months after the premiere, admitted that *Dr. Zhivago* was directed with "solid craftsmanship." But then she weighed in with the dissenting reviewers: "What makes a David Lean spectacle uninteresting finally is that it's in such goddamn good taste. It's all so ploddingly intelligent, and controlled, so 'distinguished.'"[106]

My own judgment of the film has not wavered since the New York press screening. *Dr. Zhivago* is a thought-provoking picture that repays the reflection one spends on it. It is a movie that the filmgoer does not so much enjoy as experience, as one realizes how all the varied elements coalesce into a somber and moving tapestry of Russian life in war and peace.

Robert Bolt's script sticks reasonably close to the original, as Schickel observes, but without affording the literary source undue reverence. The overall plot structure stays intact, with Pasternak's best lines given due weight. The massive production, boasting grand sets and breathtaking locations, evinces Lean's exquisite eye for spectacle and has a rich, storybook quality.

Omar Sharif gives a magnificent performance, the solidity of which draws attention away from the sometimes too-good-to-be-true aspects of his character. Rod Steiger and Julie Christie stand out among the host of fine actors gathered by Lean for *Zhivago,* giving performances of substance and emotional force. And the reliable Alec Guinness once again contributes a thoughtful character study of great depth. Moreover, where a romantic musical passage is called for, Jarre provides it with lush strings and melodic arcs. In brief, the movie unfolds without the gimmicky, sentimental heart-tugging flourishes of most epics, and, while it is not as emotionally involving as Lean's previous two spectacles, the impressions created by this remarkable film linger long after one has seen it.

Reflecting on the mauling that *Dr. Zhivago* received in its initial release, Lean said that he always suspected that critics are "highly suspicious of anything that costs a lot of money": "If you spend a lot of money and you've got big star actors, I think they tend to sharpen up their razor blades and dive in."[107]

Omar Sharif remembers adjourning with Lean to a small supper club after they retreated from the MGM reception. They sat in silence for quite a while, Lean "smoking with his cigarette holder." All of a sudden he said, "Omar! I know where I went wrong!" The film "suffered from being hastily edited," just to meet Metro's deadline for the premiere; he was confident that he could reedit it properly.[108]

The next day Lean went to see Robert O'Brien, who was in New York for the premiere. He explained that, now that he had watched the movie with an audience, he was aware that the pacing of some of the scenes was slightly off. He assured O'Brien that he could sweat some footage out of the film, to improve the overall tempo. O'Brien responded that he still had faith in the picture: "I'm going to spend another $1 million on a new advertising campaign."[109]

Right after New Year's Day, Lean and Norman Savage returned to their editing rooms at MGM in Culver City and began reediting some scenes. There were no substantial alterations at this juncture; the changes were mostly a matter of tightening things up. Lean shaved 17 minutes from the film's original running time of 197 minutes. "If you ask me what I cut, I find it hard to tell you," he said afterward, "because there were ten seconds here and ten seconds there, getting people upstairs a little bit quicker, through doors quicker, and so forth." There was much speculation at the time as to whether Lean's decision to shorten the film to 180 minutes was a panic gesture that resulted in butchering the movie. "There are no great lumps of film cut out," Lean maintained, "just tiny little snips."[110] Lean noted for good measure that he had willingly tightened *Lawrence of Arabia* immediately after it had opened as well.

After he and Savage had finished reediting the movie, Lean shipped the revised prints to the cinemas where *Dr. Zhivago* was being shown. The first two weeks of the picture's run it was playing to empty houses. Then O'Brien's media blitz began to kick in, and the filmgoers who went to see the modified version of the movie reacted favorably. Word of mouth did the rest, and by the fourth week the picture was doing capacity business.

Lean attended the London premiere in April; the British critics had apparently read the American notices and parroted some of the New York critics' complaints. Lean was particularly offended by Alexander Walker's review in the London *Evening Standard*. Walker applied to Lean the old Hollywood aphorism that, when a director dies, he becomes a photographer. Since Stanley Kubrick was familiar with this often-repeated adage, I asked him to comment on its application to Lean. "It's a clever, not to say glib remark," he answered. "It means that the film has been too beautifully photographed. Alex Walker seemed to be suggesting that Lean included some pretty images in the film for their own sake, and not necessarily to serve the story. That is certainly unfair to David Lean." Later, Lean got even with Walker. When, during the making of *Ryan's Daughter*, Walker requested an interview, Lean responded that, since he was supposedly deceased, he could not see him.

Alec Guinness, on the other hand, told me that he thought the movie was "wonderful to look at" but too lovely at times, as Walker contended. "Zhivago composing his poems with frozen ink in a fairy-tale castle," Guinness remarked, "was a bit much." In contrast, Robert Bolt wrote Lean that he found the finished film powerful and moving. It was a necessarily simplified version of the book, but certainly not a "trivialization" of it. "I can't tell you how proud I am to be your lieutenant in the enterprise."[111]

Lean made a rare appearance on London television to promote the picture; he noted that the critic Kenneth Tynan, known for his acid reviews, had been half an hour late for the picture. "He is no doubt now sitting down to write a caustic review of the proceedings," said Lean. When Tynan phoned Lean to protest his statement, he assured Lean that he would write an even-handed review. Lean did not believe him for a minute. He invoked the old bromide in the film industry: "Beware of the man who is softly whispering in your ear, as he may be pissing in your pocket." In point of fact, Tynan did write a caustic notice, comparing the movie to "an orchestra playing without a conductor."[112]

Despite the disappointing critical response in London, the film went on to be a big hit in England, just as it had in America. *Dr. Zhivago* caught the fancy of the general audience, and people poured in to see it the world over. It seemed that nobody liked it but the public—and other directors. After seeing *Dr. Zhivago*, the Italian director Luchino Visconti (*Rocco and His Brothers* [1960]) whispered to a friend, "Let's go in and see it all over again." He insisted, however, that they hide in the back: "Otherwise they [the critics] will lynch me."[113]

The Academy Award ceremonies took place in the Civic Auditorium in Santa Monica on April 18, 1966. *Dr. Zhivago* received ten nominations, the same number as *Lawrence of Arabia*, but *Lawrence* nabbed seven Academy Awards, while *Zhivago* won only five. *Zhivago*'s awards were for cinematography (Freddie Young), production design (John Box), costumes (Phyllis Dalton), musical score (Maurice Jarre), and screenplay (Robert Bolt). William Wyler told me that he had phoned Lean when the nominations were announced and warned him not to expect the Oscar for best director. "They never give it to you for three pictures in a row," he told him.

Nevertheless, Lean still had hope. In fact, he was so convinced that he would win that he was already standing up as the name of Robert Wise was announced for *The Sound of Music*. He therefore found it awkward to have to go to the podium shortly afterward to accept Robert Bolt's Academy Award in his absence. The U.S. government would not allow Bolt into the country because of his prison record, the result of his arrest in 1961 in an anti–nuclear war demonstration in London while working on *Lawrence of Arabia*. "I'm terribly glad to accept this award for Robert," Lean said when handed Bolt's Oscar. "He had a most fiendishly difficult job; and the film would not have got all this brass [Oscars] but for him." Afterward, Lean was congratulated backstage for showing himself such a good loser.

Julie Christie won the Oscar as best actress, but for John Schlesinger's *Darling*, which she made immediately after *Zhivago*. I asked Schlesinger whether he thought he and Lean had made her an international star. "Julie is creative and inventive on her own," he answered, "but she does respond to sympathetic guidance. Under these circumstances a director like David Lean or myself can work with her to produce a better film."

Dr. Zhivago continued to do brisk business at the box office throughout 1966; it cost $15 million to make and eventually earned $43 million while playing first run in its reserved-seat, road-show engagements. Lean attributed the phenomenal success of the picture in some part to the popularity of "Lara's Theme." Neither Lean nor Jarre could have imagined that it would become so popular in its own right, first in an instrumental version, then, with lyrics added, as "What Now, My Love?" The song version remained on the pop charts for two years.

Dr. Zhivago went on to become, next to *Gone with the Wind*, MGM's top moneymaker of all time. It eventually grossed $200 million worldwide. Furthermore, Lean had negotiated a financial deal with Ponti that gave him a bigger share of the film's profits than he had gotten from Spiegel for the two blockbusters they made together. Lean, as stated before, always insisted that he deserved a bigger slice of the pie than he had gotten from Spiegel for *Lawrence* in particular. By contrast, Sharif claims that Lean "made a lot of money on *Zhivago* because he had a very strong contract—his fortune was made on *Zhivago*."[114] Indeed, Lean's earnings from *Zhivago* made him a princely personal fortune of more than $10 million.

Yet Lean always went on the defensive when anyone mentioned that *Zhivago* diminished his reputation with the critics. Never mind the critics, he would snap back: "I wouldn't take the advice of a lot of so-called critics on how to shoot a close-up of a teapot."[115] Elsewhere he noted, "That film made me more money than all of my other films put together."[116]

Lean's personal life, however, was in disarray. He had continued his affair with Barbara Cole while making *Zhivago*. Nevertheless, he was still enough of a Quaker at heart to feel guilty about his neglect of Leila Lean, who was still his wife. In September 1966, he embarked on a worldwide tour to promote *Zhivago*. So he made a stopover, while in India, to be with Leila at a hotel in Delhi for a while.

But their reunion was an unmitigated disaster, as Leila was still suffering from clinical depression. She was becoming increasingly withdrawn and lapsed into long periods of sullen silence. Lean said she was "taking pills by the dozens . . . and tottering on the edge of a nervous breakdown." He began having nightmares in which Leila was transformed into a venomous snake, coiled around his neck.[117] He was convinced that it would be kinder to make a complete break with her, but, whenever he suggested divorce, she countered with renewed threats of suicide. So he stayed married to her for another twelve years.

Continuing his promotional tour for *Dr. Zhivago* in the fall of 1966, he moved into Laurie's Hotel in Agra, a British colonial-type hotel near the Taj Mahal. There he began an affair with Sandy Hotz, the twenty-year-old daughter of the hotel manager. On November 18, 1966, he penned a tortured letter to Barbara Cole, confessing that he had fallen in love with a girl young enough to be his daughter. In his "bloody arrogance," he admitted, he had previously thought he was immune to such behavior. He expressed his shame and guilt for ending his relationship with Barbara in this fashion and begged her forgiveness.[118] Cole was philosophical about the break; she reflected that, when Lean's sexual relationship with a woman had passed its peak, he abandoned her. She had never deluded herself on this point.

Sandy Hotz's parents were scandalized that their daughter was involved with a man thirty-seven years her senior. In a gesture of propriety, Lean waited until Sandy turned twenty-one on February 21, 1967, before he swept her away from her family. They proceeded on to the Richmond Hotel in Madrid, where Lean preferred to hang his hat in those days. David Lean and Sandy Hotz would be together for the next twenty years, but they would not marry until Lean, of course, finally divorced Leila. A British producer who spoke on condition of anonymity told me that, one night in 1976, when David and Leila were together again for a while at Grosvenor House in London, David told her that he was going down to the hotel lobby for a pack of cigarettes—and he never came back. Leila at long last saw the handwriting on the wall, as Lean's three previous wives had done, and they were divorced in 1978, with Leila receiving a $1 million settlement.

Sandy says that, after she went to live with Lean in Spain, they traveled on the Continent extensively while he searched for his next project. He was still disturbed by the fact that, though he had achieved financial independence with *Zhivago,* critical acclaim had eluded him. Leslie Halliwell, for example, regretted Lean's "submergence of his sensitive talent in pretentious but empty spectacles."[119] Halliwell added insult to injury by listing *Great Expectations* as Lean's only outstanding film. "What was I supposed to do," Lean commented, "stop after *Great Expectations?*"[120]

Halliwell implied that, having begun to make Hollywood spectacles, Lean had long since ceased to make films that bore the stamp of his personal directorial style and, thus, that he hardly deserved the status of an auteur director. On the contrary, like any auteur, Lean oversaw every aspect of the production of a film made on the grand scale of *Zhivago* just as personally as he had in the days when he was making "smaller" films. Consequently, his later epics are just as unmistakably David Lean pictures as his earlier movies. "The highbrows," Lean commented, "say I can't do anything but epics. At any rate, I'll make the best epics."[121]

Though some film historians date Lean's "decline" from *Dr. Zhivago,* that film has held up very well. In 1995, it was released on videocassette in wide-screen format at its original running time of 197 minutes. In 2001, it was released on DVD in a fully restored, digitally remastered edition. The studio technicians who reconstructed the film stabilized some images and repaired scratches on the original negative, which reposed in MGM's vault.

As a matter of fact, they even added three minutes of footage that they found in the MGM archives, footage that had not been included in the original-release prints. Accordingly, the restored DVD version runs an even 200 minutes, slightly over the 197 minutes of Lean's original cut. The release of the restored version on DVD brought renewed attention to the picture and garnered some reevaluations by critics like Alexander Walker that were much more benign than the notices that Walker and others accorded the film in 1965.

The film has continued to receive recognition in recent years. When the American Film Institute celebrated American cinema's greatest love stories with a television special broadcast on July 11, 2002, *Dr. Zhivago*, along with *Gone with the Wind*, was among the top ten films selected by the voters (film critics and film professionals). The following year, Omar Sharif was awarded a Golden Lion for his lifetime achievement in film at the Venice Film Festival, and his playing the title role in *Zhivago* was spotlighted.

In addition, a Russian restaurant named Zhivago's has been opened in the Chicago suburb Skokie, in honor of both Pasternak's book and Lean's movie. The manager, a Russian immigrant, told me that the controversy over the book has long since died down in his native land and that now it is taught in schools. Furthermore, the film, which was banned in Russia for nearly three decades, was finally released there in 1994, six years after the ban on the novel was lifted. In short, *Dr. Zhivago* has received kudos that Lean did not live to enjoy.[122]

After the critical failure of *Zhivago* in 1965, Lean was bound to be very careful about what he chose to do next. While he was staying with Sandy in a hotel in Rome, he exchanged letters with Robert Bolt about adapting another classic novel to the screen. They explored the possibility of doing a film along the lines of Gustave Flaubert's *Madame Bovary*, and that is how Lean's next film, *Ryan's Daughter*, came to be.

Chapter Fifteen

THE LOWER DEPTHS

RYAN'S DAUGHTER AND *THE BOUNTY*

It's the life you made for yourself; and don't act like it's not yours.
—*Annette Jennings, a housewife in the film* The Safety of Objects

The critics never caught on that *Ryan's Daughter* was really *Madame Bovary*.
—*David Lean*

Lean was mulling over possible film projects while residing with Sandy Hotz at the Hotel Parco del Principe in Rome. Robert Bolt was dialoguing with him by mail about adapting Gustave Flaubert's 1856 novel *Madame Bovary* for film. Bolt was working on a preliminary screen treatment of Flaubert's classic tale of adultery. He made no bones about the fact that he was developing the treatment with his second wife, the actress Sarah Miles (*The Servant* [Joseph Losey, 1963]), in mind for the lead.

Commentators on *Ryan's Daughter* have customarily not made very much of the link between it and *Madame Bovary*. Yet Lean himself said that the novel was the inspiration for the film, as noted in one of the chapter epigraphs. It is, therefore, important to examine briefly how Bolt's script for *Madame Bovary* evolved into his screenplay for *Ryan's Daughter.*

To begin with, Lean studied Bolt's proposal for a film adaptation of *Madame Bovary* with great care. Flaubert's novel centers on Emma Bovary, the unfaithful wife of a diffident husband, a country doctor, Charles Bovary. She pursues a handsome rake, Rodolphe Boulanger, while trapped in a humdrum marriage. The plot interested Lean, as it did Bolt. After all, Lean at sixty was living with the twenty-one-year-old Sandy Hotz while still married to his estranged wife, Leila, and Bolt at forty-five had recently married the twenty-seven-year-old Sarah Miles after divorcing his first wife. Both men were no strangers to marital discord, and the story of Emma Bovary resonated with them.

Madame Bovary

Gustave Flaubert was born in Rouen in 1821, and, like Boris Pasternak, began his writing career with short stories, graduating to novels by 1845, while still in his twenties. On September 19, 1851, he began writing *Madame Bovary,* his masterpiece, which occupied him for nearly four years. It was first published in serial form in *La revue de Paris* in 1856. In January 1857, Flaubert and the editors of the *Revue* were prosecuted for foisting on the reading public a decadent novel, one that allegedly offended religion and public morals.[1]

Henry James, who much admired *Madame Bovary,* declared that the novel was not an inducement to adultery, as the prosecution charged. On the contrary, it could just as easily be employed as "a Sunday school text," warning against marital infidelity. It shocked the minions of public morality, James contended, because of Flaubert's "refusal to provide explicit moral judgments about the characters"; Flaubert left such judgments to the reader.[2]

In any event, the defendants were acquitted in February 1857, and the novel was published in book form in April. Because of the notoriety occasioned by the trial, *Madame Bovary* became a succès de scandale (just as the banning of *Dr. Zhivago* in Russia would bring Pasternak's novel worldwide attention).

Since his death on May 8, 1880, Flaubert's approval rating in literary circles has steadily risen; he has been recognized as a master of the European novel. James was one of several literary figures who continued to champion the novel; he wrote in 1902 that Flaubert's searching portrait of Emma Bovary and his perceptive picture of her provincial neighbors were impeccable (the full title of the novel is *Madame Bovary: Provincial Manners*). In 1946, the novelist Vladimir Nabokov stated that Flaubert had elevated a banal story about a bourgeois marriage and an adulterous wife to the level of high art.[3]

Flaubert's descriptive language is quite vivid, as when he portrays Emma and Rodolphe's lovemaking: "The chill of the night spurred them to more passionate embraces; the sighs on their lips seemed to them all the more ardent."[4] When Emma's clandestine affair inevitably comes to light, she takes poison to forestall a dreadful scandal. Flaubert describes movingly how, as she lies dying, she looks forward to death: "They were behind her forever, thought Emma—all the betrayals, the infamies, and the myriad cravings that had tormented her."[5]

In the last analysis, Flaubert shows how Emma, an incurable romantic, had derived her longings for the perfect love affair from the penny press of the time, the equivalent of any issue of a woman's magazine like *True Confessions* today. She idealized Rodolphe—who, in reality, was nothing short of a cad—turning him into her knight in shining armor. Flaubert thus depicts how "we live at the mercy of the fictions we ourselves create."[6]

Lean was rightly impressed with Flaubert's celebrated novel, but he had misgivings about making yet another screen version of a book that had already been filmed at least four times. Two of the films—a Hollywood effort entitled *Unholy Love* (Albert Ray, 1932), with Lila Lee, and the German *Madame Bovary* (Gerhard Lamprecht, 1937), starring Pola Negri—were, admittedly, forgotten. But the other two versions—those of Jean Renoir (1934) and Vincente Minnelli (1949)—were the work of major filmmakers and could not be overlooked.

In the summer of 1967, Bolt sent Lean the draft of his screenplay for *Madame Bovary*. With the previous screen versions of the novel in mind, Lean approached the reading of Bolt's script. In general, he found Bolt's necessary compression of the novel to be intelligently done, and he thought that there were some good things in the script. He pointed out positively that Bolt had incorporated Flaubert's "Greek Chorus" of nosy crones. These busybodies represent the village's judgment on Emma—though not Flaubert's assessment of her. They openly disapprove of her indiscretions in the stiffest, most conventional terms. Rodolphe's seduction of Emma in the forest also found its way into Bolt's screenplay.

Nevertheless, Lean was, ultimately, dissatisfied. He wrote Bolt a twelve-page, single-spaced letter, noting regretfully that, for the most part, the script simply recounted in rather banal terms the story of a bored provincial housewife who cuckolds her husband by pursuing a cad—a respectful, but fairly lifeless, rendering of a great novel. It had the feel of a soap opera, which would appeal to the washboard weepers, but not to a large audience. He ended by saying that the script would need an enormous amount of revision and that, under the circumstances, he could not consider undertaking yet another remake of the classic novel.

Then Lean offered a counterproposal. He suggested that Bolt prepare an original screenplay, inspired by *Madame Bovary*, but not a literal film adaptation of it. And so it was that *Ryan's Daughter* gradually came into being.

Interestingly enough, Pauline Kael was the only major critic who recognized the debt that *Ryan's Daughter* owes to *Madame Bovary*. "Bolt and Lean have given us Flaubert's Emma Bovary," wrote Kael in her review of *Ryan's Daughter*. "At the beginning we see the dreamy Rosy Ryan reading a cheap romance"—just like the ones that Emma reads. Like Emma, the sex-starved Rosy yearns for a rapturous love affair. In both the novel and the film, there is "illicit bliss with a classy lover; ruin and suffering; forgiveness from the devoted, betrayed husband."[7] In brief, Rosy Ryan is Emma Bovary.

Ryan's Daughter (1970)

Lean asked Bolt to set the film in twentieth-century Ireland, rather than in nineteenth-century France. He did not hesitate to update the story to World War I because he was convinced that the relationships of men and women had not changed appreciably since Flaubert's time. Bolt concurred.

Lean chose the rugged terrain of Ireland for the setting because the story involves a wild, dark side of human nature. "I think the wildness of this country, Ireland, is rather good as a background for that sort of thing," he explained. Lean hoped to make a love story that would demonstrate to those critics who dismissed *Dr. Zhivago* as a romance à la women's magazines that he still possessed the same talent that created a human drama like *Brief Encounter*. Nevertheless, he wanted to make not a "little gem" of a domestic drama, which is how he viewed *Brief Encounter*, but a film of "some size."[8] He thus wanted the plot to involve some national conflict that affected the lives of the characters, just as *Dr. Zhivago* employed the Russian Revolution as a backdrop. The Irish Easter Rebellion of 1916, known as "the Troubles," which occurred during World War I, would fill the bill.

Lean and Bolt toiled in Lean's penthouse suite at the Hotel Principe in Rome for ten months. John Mills, who was in Rome to appear in an Italian film, stopped by the hotel to say hello. He found them laboring in a room enveloped in a blue haze of cigarette smoke. Looking out the window, he ventured cheerfully, "What a nice pool outside." Lean responded, "What pool?" Lean and Bolt were so preoccupied that they had not noticed the hotel swimming pool beneath their window.[9]

Lean preferred not to start to shoot a picture until he was satisfied that the script was in good shape. The film director Howard Hawks (*To Have and Have Not* [1944]) told me in conversation that, while he was shooting a picture, he would frequently "make changes in the dialogue in the script that no longer fit the flow of the action as it had been progressing." But Lean was categorically opposed to going back and revising a scene in the script on the set because he was convinced that such hasty work would not pay off.

Lean did revise the title of the screenplay after shooting commenced; it was originally entitled *Michael's Day*, a reference to Michael, the mute village idiot, who observes everything that transpires in the town. But that title seemed to give too much weight to Michael's character. So the title was finally changed to *Ryan's Daughter*, which refers to the heroine, Rosy Ryan, the daughter of a local pub owner. As a matter of fact, the screenplay on file in the MGM script repository, dated October 7, 1970, bears the title *Michael's Day*, which is crossed out, with *Ryan's Daughter* written above it.

In reshaping Flaubert's novel to fit their own conception of the story, Lean and Bolt developed the tale of a young girl who marries an older man and then has a love affair with a shell-shocked English officer closer to her own age. The Irish Troubles form a tumultuous background to Rosy's personal story. On the surface, it seems that Flaubert's novel is very different from Lean's film, especially in terms of setting and historical background. Still, there are some noteworthy parallels.

For example, each tale centers on a young wife who is bored with married life. In addition, the husband in each case is "a learned but ineffectual man" named Charles. Emma's husband, Charles Bovary, is a physician, while Rosy's husband, Charles Shaughnessy, is a schoolmaster. (For the record, Robert Bolt was a teacher before becoming a writer.) Moreover, each heroine takes a lover who temporarily fulfills her romantic fantasies: Emma is infatuated with *Rodolphe* Boulanger, and Rosy is enamored of *Randolph* Doryan. Furthermore, each heroine succumbs to her lover's blandishments "in a misty forest among flowers and ferns."[10] Finally, each young woman pays dearly for her indiscretions: Emma takes her own life, while Rosy must endure public humiliation.

In summary, it is evident that *Madame Bovary* provided the fundamental structure of *Ryan's Daughter*. What is more, Bolt, like Flaubert, eschewed an intrusive "know-it-all, voice-of-God narrator."[11] Nor does he have Rosy herself comment on her plight. "I deliberately wrote the part of Rosy so that she had no confidante, nobody to whom she could talk, which meant that she couldn't talk to the audience [and express her feelings]," says Bolt. "The audience simply have to watch her sweating it out herself, and draw their own conclusions."[12]

As luck would have it, while Lean and Bolt were writing the script, Lean's old Cineguild partner Anthony Havelock-Allan happened to be in Rome. He had just finished coproducing Franco Zeffirelli's *Romeo and Juliet* (1968) for Paramount. Since the breakup of Cineguild, Havelock-Allan had produced some important pictures, including another Shakespeare movie, Laurence Olivier's *Othello* (1965).

Lean showed Havelock-Allan the rough draft of the screenplay of *Ryan's Daughter*, which was still called *Michael's Day*. In fact, it was Havelock-Allan who suggested that the title be changed to *Ryan's Daughter*. (To avoid confusion, I use *Ryan's Daughter* only, even at this early stage of the production process.) Lean in due course got around to asking Havelock-Allan to come on board as producer—but not just for old times' sake. Lean had always respected Havelock-Allan. One important reason for this was "the warmth and sophistication [Havelock-Allan] brought to their partnership," which served to balance Lean's sometimes rather cold, technical expertise.[13]

Havelock-Allan in turn admired Lean, who reminded him of Michelangelo, that is, an artist totally absorbed in his work. He once said of Lean, "What he liked doing was to tell great adventure stories; and of this he was a master. . . . In another age David would have sat around a fire and told stories." David Lean was, he concludes, essentially "a teller of tales."[14] When I mentioned Havelock-Allan's remark to Stanley Kubrick, he replied, "Filmmakers are essentially storytellers. The public likes a good story; it started in the caves. A caveman would tell his friends a story as they sat around the camp fire. They either fell asleep, threw a rock at him, or listened; mostly they listened. David and I are tellers of tales."

Lean told Havelock-Allan that he saw Rosy's story as that of a young girl whose adolescent fantasies of her ideal mate are not fulfilled in the older man she married and who thus takes up with a younger man. "We are dealing with primitive emotions," he continued. Rosy cannot square her infatuation with a handsome young stranger with her role as the decent wife she believes herself to be. In short, *Ryan's Daughter* is about "the difficulty of growing up, the doors opening on adult life."[15]

Lean was aware that he was, perhaps, leading with his chin in making a movie that was "intentionally over-romantic," centering as it does on an immature girl with dreams of a storybook prince. To that extent, he saw it as something of "an old-fashioned picture"—until the girl has a "frightening fall back to earth, and realizes that her heaven does not indeed exist."[16]

As Lean and Bolt soldiered on with the screenplay, certain turns of the plot had them stymied. "Robert and I were in a mess on *Ryan's Daughter*," Lean recalled. In setting up the fundamental love triangle that fuels the plot, they had a problem about how to introduce Randolph Doryan into the story effectively. It is obvious, as soon as the handsome British officer arrives at the nearby garrison, that Rosy will be smitten with him. Lean and Bolt had to come up with a way of getting the young couple together quickly. "Otherwise the audience will be way ahead of us in guessing they are in love; and that would be fatal."[17]

One night, Lean woke up in the wee hours with an inspiration. He would have Michael, the village idiot, hanging around the local pub, which is owned and operated by Rosy's father, Tom Ryan. Michael is aimlessly kicking the bar; Major Randolph Doryan, the shell-shocked war hero, who was awarded the Victoria Cross for valor in the trenches on the western front, is also in the pub. Randolph becomes dazed and confused by Michael's racket; to Randolph, the noise sounds like a shell going off on the battlefield. Obviously disturbed, he dives under a table. Lean then cuts to a shot of him seeking cover in a trench during battle. Rosy, who is filling in for her father, sees that Randolph is overwrought. She kneels beside him and cradles his head in her arms. Randolph snaps out of his trance, and he and Rosy kiss. After considering this inspiration, Lean leaped out of bed, grabbed a pencil and pad, and scribbled down what he had just imagined. "It is one of the sequences I'm most pleased with," he said afterward, "because it's one of the best scenes I've ever done."[18]

Bolt too liked the scene. But he and Lean had some heated arguments about other elements of the screenplay. One sore point was the ending. Lean wanted the film to end happily, and Bolt did not. Bolt thought it highly unlikely that Rosy and Charles could be reconciled.[19] In his view, Rosy's affair has driven a permanent wedge between them, even though the despondent Randolph finally kills himself.

Bolt even went so far as to compose a memo on the subject: "I can see them as credible human beings caught in a vice, can see no happy outcome—in short tragedy." He then went on to tell Lean that, "in the teeth of your conviction that it ought not to be so," it would be out of the question for him to write the ending as he envisioned it, that is, Rosy alone, bereft of both her lover and her husband.[20] In the end, however, Bolt decided against giving the memo to Lean and reluctantly composed the ending that Lean envisioned, one in which Rosy and Charles are still together at the final fade-out. Then he shipped the script off to Robert O'Brien at MGM in Hollywood.

Bolt heard through the story department at Metro on October 21, 1968, that O'Brien had officially approved the screenplay. O'Brien had one reservation, however; he thought that the suicide of Randolph would come off as a letdown for the audience. Bolt replied to the story department on October 24, defending Randolph's suicide as a plot point. The shell-shocked Randolph has been dispirited by his traumatizing experiences at the front. His love affair with Rosy is his "last blaze of natural life"; both he and Rosy—and, it was to be hoped, the audience—understand that their romance is "foredoomed."[21] Lean endorsed Bolt's stance on Randolph's suicide, which, therefore, stayed in the script. O'Brien, after all, had usually deferred to Lean before. In the last analysis, Bolt had simply shifted the suicide from Emma Bovary to Randolph.

Lean and Bolt naturally discussed casting intermittently while working on the screenplay. Lean had considered Sarah Miles for the role of Lara in *Dr. Zhivago*, but Bolt, who did not know Miles at the time, vetoed the idea. Miles had played a flirtatious student who seduces her teacher in *Term of Trial* (Peter Glenville, 1962) and a maidservant who seduces her employer in *The Servant* (1963). Consequently, Bolt maintained that her screen image was that of a "North Country slut." Lean answered, "You have believed her publicity, Robert." He insisted that she could play other kinds of roles.

By 1967, however, Bolt had met and married Miles. As we have seen, he had even written his adaptation of *Madame Bovary* with her in mind. Now he wanted her for the title role of the present picture. It was Lean's turn to object to casting Miles, precisely because she was now Bolt's wife. Having experienced difficulties in directing Ann Todd when they were married, Lean had misgivings about taking on the screenwriter's spouse on the set. He feared that Miles would think "she knew more about Robert's intentions in the script than I did." But Lean eventually relented, deciding that Miles "was a good actress and would be perfect in the part."[22]

Casting the other roles went more or less smoothly. Over dinner with Lean during the visit to Rome mentioned earlier, John Mills reminded Lean that they had made four pictures together and wondered whether there was a part for him in the present film. Lean did not respond immediately, as most accounts of this anecdote state, but let the remark pass for the moment. He phoned Mills a couple of days later and offered him the part of Michael, explaining that Michael was "a village idiot." Mills swiftly replied that he would take the part: "Of course, David; it's type casting!"[23]

Metro's management in Hollywood considered Mills too short for the role; they were looking for a tall, ungainly actor. So Lean asked the makeup man Charles Parker to prepare Mills for a screen test. Lean wanted Parker to lay on the makeup with a trowel. But Mills asked Parker to get away with as little makeup as possible; he wanted Michael to look homely, but not bizarre. In the end, Parker gave Mills a bulbous putty nose and also fashioned him a dental plate in order to give the impression that Michael had buck teeth. To top it off, Mills had a "horrific" haircut, with strands of hair hanging down.[24] Lean sent the makeup test to the front office at MGM, and they ratified Lean's choice of Mills for Michael. Stephen Silverman notes that Lean directed Mills to play Michael like Charlie Chaplin's Tramp: "Mills registers

Michael's feelings with his facial expressions, as the Tramp did. He makes us sense what Michael feels, such as his devotion to Rosy."[25]

Trevor Howard, like Mills, was a veteran of Lean's British films who had not appeared in a Lean film for several years. Lean tentatively considered him to play the village priest, Father Hugh Collins, but was more inclined toward Alec Guinness as his first choice. Guinness told me that, in September 1968, Lean wrote him that he regretted that, in the role of Yevgraf in *Zhivago*, Guinness had been underused. He sought to make amends by offering Guinness the pivotal role of Father Collins in *Ryan's Daughter*. Lean forthwith mailed Guinness the first draft of the screenplay, saying that he would welcome Guinness's comments.

"I'm afraid I raised quite a number of objections to the way that Father Collins was portrayed," Guinness told me. For a start, Guinness questioned that the priest, a practical man, would go fishing in a small boat with the village idiot when a fierce storm was brewing. Collins, if not the half-wit, would have had sense enough to wait until the storm had abated. "You don't try to cope with ten-foot waves in a skiff," Guinness pointed out to Lean. A convert to Roman Catholicism, Guinness was offended that Collins was portrayed as a gruff old curmudgeon, too often barking at his parishioners like a top sergeant.

Guinness also admonished Lean that the script had the priest constantly wearing his cassock, a floor-length black robe. In those days, Guinness contended, the British occupation forces banned the cassock in Ireland and made priests wear black clerical suits. In point of fact, Guinness was right—to the extent that Catholic priests in Ireland were prohibited from wearing the cassock in public, outside church grounds. They had to wear a black clerical suit in the street.[26] For the record, Lean disregarded Guinness's admonition and had Father Collins dressed in his cassock at all times because it tended to make him stand out as an important, influential figure in the village community.

Lean saw storm clouds ahead if Guinness played Collins. Lean remembered "various tribulations with Alec" over the years: "He's a convert to Catholicism; and he wrote me two or three pages of things that would have to be altered for him to play the priest." Lean did not welcome his suggestions, as he had promised. He replied, "Thank you very much for being so frank." Then he gave the part to Trevor Howard.[27]

When they first met on the set, Howard chided Lean for not casting him in any films since the late 1940s. "Trevor, the poor old dear, went for me," said Lean. Howard thought that Lean should have at least cast him as a British officer in *Kwai* since he had specialized in playing English military types. "I'm only doing this part because of you!" Howard went on. Asked why, he answered that it was a very unsympathetic role, which is just what Guinness had thought. Lean mollified him by pointing out that Father Collins's bark is worse than his bite. Collins, according to Lean, "strides about in great clumping boots, putting the fear of God into the villagers, but always with an undercurrent of devotion and compassion for his flock." What is more, he acts as the voice of conscience when Rosy has her "brief encounter" with Randolph.[28] Howard took to heart what Lean said.

As Father Collins, Howard was really cast against type. Indeed, the role was far removed from the romantic leads that he had previously played for Lean in *Brief Encounter* and *The Passionate Friends*. As Collins, he appeared with his hair cropped and his craggy face covered with stubble since the priest cared not at all about personal grooming. As time went on, Lean was convinced that Howard completely inhabited the role. Howard felt that donning his great cassock every morning helped put him in the mood for his part. But playing the priest was essentially no great trick for him, he said. The character was there in the script.

Lean was very concerned about casting the key role of Charles Shaughnessy, who was based, of course, on Charles Bovary, Emma's husband. Robert Bolt drew on his own experience as a former teacher in creating Shaughnessy, a schoolmaster. There were also traces in the character of Scott Goddard, Lean's mentor at Leighton Park boarding school. For example, Goddard had a passion for music, so in his living room Charles Shaughnessy has a gramophone, which he often plays.

Havelock-Allan, as producer, conferred with Lean about casting. The picture was originally budgeted for $9 million, which, Havelock-Allan recalled, was a substantial amount for the time. So MGM wanted at least one established Hollywood star with marquee value in the States to appear in the picture. Sarah Miles was not well-known outside England. Lean accordingly sought a Hollywood superstar to play Charles Shaughnessy.

It was Robert Bolt who nominated Robert Mitchum. Mitchum was known for his tough-guy screen image in films like the classic film noir *Out of the Past* (Jacques Tourneur, 1947), which Lean had seen. He wanted to cast Mitchum against type as the mild-mannered, meek Charles Shaughnessy because he knew Mitchum could play him, not as merely a weak, boring character, but as a man with "potential inner strength." In fact, he saw Mitchum as a very capable actor. "Other actors act; Mitchum is," Lean noted. "Simply by being there, Mitchum can make almost any other actor look like a hole in the screen."[29] Furthermore, Mitchum had appeared in *The Night Fighters* (Tay Garnett, 1960), a tale of an Irish Republican Army (IRA) volunteer during World War II, which proved that he could master an Irish accent.

Bolt phoned Mitchum in Hollywood after he had sent him the script. Mitchum declined the role because of the long shooting schedule involved. Bolt reassured him that he would have some time off during the shooting period for rest and relaxation. Mitchum, who disliked being pressured, wryly responded that he was thinking of retiring. He then added the outrageous statement that he might perhaps even commit suicide. Aware that Mitchum liked to affect a world-weary pose, Bolt replied, "Well, if you would just do this wretched little film of ours, then do yourself in, I'd be happy to stand the expenses of your burial!"[30] Nonplussed, Mitchum chuckled and accepted the role.

In a bid to obtain another superstar in the film, Lean offered Marlon Brando the part of Randolph Doryan. But *Burn!* (Gillo Pontecorvo, 1969), a film about a nineteenth-century slave revolt that Brando was shooting in Colombia, was way behind schedule. So, having passed up playing Lawrence, Brando turned down yet another Lean movie.

John Box, Lean's erstwhile production designer, was now a producer, and he invited Lean to an advance screening of his production of John le Carré's *The Looking Glass War* (Frank Pierson, 1969). Lean spotted the newcomer Christopher Jones in the picture and was impressed by his smooth delivery of his lines. He was not aware at the time that Jones's performance was enhanced by another actor dubbing his dialogue.

Lean did know that Jones had played Jesse James in a series on television. The pale, sad-looking actor was being touted as the next James Dean, someone who could play the kind of loser whose heroism only the camera could detect—a description that fit Randolph Doryan. Rounding out the cast was Leo McKern, who had played Oliver Cromwell in Fred Zinnemann's film of Bolt's play *A Man for All Seasons* (1966). McKern was tapped to play the barkeep Tom Ryan, Rosy's father.

With John Box unavailable, Lean turned to the Irish-born Stephen Grimes for his production designer. Grimes had earned his spurs by assisting Box as an art director on *Lawrence*. But old-timers like the cinematographer Freddie Young and the composer Maurice Jarre, each of whom had copped Oscars for both *Lawrence* and *Zhivago*, were back in harness. So was the editor Norman Savage, who had cut *Zhivago*, not to mention Eddie Fowlie, officially the prop man, unofficially Lean's factotum all the way back to *Kwai*.

Roy Stevens had moved up from being an assistant director on *Lawrence* and *Zhivago* to being the associate producer of *Ryan's Daughter*. Stevens was doubling as a second-unit director; another second-unit director was Harold French, who had codirected *Major Barbara* with Lean for the ostensible director, Gabriel Pascal (see chapter 2). French, like Lean, had gone on to become a director himself with films like *Rob Roy* (1953). Still another second-unit director was Charles Frend, who had coedited *Major Barbara* with Lean. Frend too had become a director in his own right, with films like the John Mills vehicle *Scott of the Antarctic* (1948). Both French and Frend came out of retirement to work for Lean on *Ryan's Daughter* for old times' sake. Having endured the volatile Gabriel Pascal while working on *Major Barbara* together, Lean, French, and Frend ever after shared the kind of camaraderie that characterized the survivors of the *Titanic*.

Lean had decided to make *Ryan's Daughter* entirely on location in Ireland. "The financial success of *Zhivago* meant that no corners needed to be cut on the period re-creation, which saw an entire village built in the west of Ireland."[31] Though *Dr. Zhivago* earned an enormous amount of money, MGM had fallen into yet another financial crisis by the time Lean began shooting *Ryan's Daughter*. Lean had already rescued Metro with *Zhivago*; now Robert O'Brien was banking on Lean to do it again.

O'Brien approved *Ryan's Daughter* being shot in seventy-millimeter Panavision, as *Lawrence* had been. Lean, as noted, had also wanted *Dr. Zhivago* to be filmed in seventy millimeter, but Metro had refused because it was expensive. "We did *Zhivago* in 35mm and MGM blew up the negative in 70mm," Young explains. "I couldn't see the difference myself. I thought 35mm was just as good as the 70mm."[32] But Lean, ever the purist, held out for seventy millimeter on *Ryan's Daughter*. So Young made a point of securing Ernest Day as his camera operator since Day had been his operator on both *Zhivago* and *Lawrence*.

Lean was criticized in the industry as extravagant, not just for insisting on seventy millimeter, but especially for erecting an entire village on location. He contended that it was cheaper in the long run to construct his own village than to attempt to use an existing one and transform it to fit the film's period, World War I. Moreover, there was the problem of tourists flocking to watch the filming and getting in the way when shooting occurred in a real location. This is just what happened when Lean was shooting *Summertime* in Venice. "If you own your own village, you see, you're in clover; you keep people out and run it like a studio."[33] (Lean, we recall, built two complete Moscow streets on the outskirts of Madrid for *Zhivago*, for the same reason.)

In a television interview that Lean gave during the making of the picture, he explained, "My fear about *Ryan's Daughter* at the outset was that it was going to fall into the class of 'little gem' films. You can't spend a lot of money doing little gems! We have a large budget because the film is set in the wild west of Ireland and we are at the mercy of the weather; that makes it an expensive film to do. We could have done it in the studio for less, but we wanted to get the real smell of the outdoors, so we filmed on the isolated, windswept Dingle peninsula."[34]

Lean dispatched Eddie Fowlie on a recce (reconnaissance) mission to spy out suitable locations in Ireland. Fowlie first found Banner Beach near Tralee, which would be ideal for one of Rosy's outings with Randolph. The great stretch of coastline would, likewise, serve for the strategic site where the IRA collects a boatload of weapons from a German ship during the Easter Rebellion. It turned out to be only a few miles from the actual location where the Irish insurgent Roger Casement "was captured, trying to land a shipment of German arms in 1916 to help the rebellion in Dublin," says Anthony Havelock-Allan.[35]

The site selected for the principal village set was near Dunquin, at the end of the Dingle peninsula in County Kerry, a four-hour drive from Dublin. It was, in fact, the first piece of land spotted by Charles Lindbergh when he made his historical solo flight across the Atlantic in 1927. Stephen Grimes, a red-bearded giant of a man, designed and built Lean's village, which was named Kirrary in the film.

"It was a whole village," writes Freddie Young, "including shops, a schoolhouse, church, pub, and a post office. Most movie sets are just facades, made of plaster and hardboards; but for this film they used real stone. Anything less substantial would never have stood up to the gales." Beginning in November 1968, two hundred workmen built the houses, using slate and twenty thousand tons of granite from a dozen local quarries. "Many had fitted interiors, with ceilings, lighting, plumbing, and working fire grates."[36] Kirrary was finished in March 1969, shortly after shooting commenced in February.

When shooting was completed a year later, says Sarah Miles, Lean asked the locals if they wanted the film unit to leave the village standing. "Take the fuckin' thing down," they responded. "We're sick of the lot of ye!" Lean and his largely English cast and crew were never really welcome in Ireland. Indeed, Stanley Kubrick told me that, when he was filming *Barry Lyndon* there five years later, he received several threats from the IRA, which wanted him to take his British film unit back to England where it belonged. Lean was offended by the locals' response. "They could have had the whole bloody village," he commented.[37]

After most of the village set had been dismantled and the land returned to the farmers in its original condition, a delegation from the Dingle town council reported to Lean that they had reconsidered his offer and wanted to keep the village after all, to attract tourists. But their request came too late. Nevertheless, the making of a Hollywood film in Dingle precipitated an influx of tourists into the area that continues to this day.

When John Mills was cast in *Ryan's Daughter*, he was informed that filming would last six months. But, given the unpredictable Irish weather and other variables, Mills did not believe it. Furthermore, he knew by experience that Lean simply would not be hurried. So he figured that six months would stretch into a year and rented a cottage for himself and his family, rather than stay in a hotel. His conjecture proved accurate; principal photography ran from February 1969 to February 1970.

Freddie Young agreed with Mills that filming on location is "always a ticklish business": "There are so many imponderables; not only the weather, but schedule changes and actors' contractual dates." The seventy-millimeter Panavision cameras needed more light than thirty-five-millimeter cameras did and, consequently, required more equipment. It got very cramped in some of the sets, such as Rosy and Charles's cottage. "The pub had been constructed with removable walls, so that brute lamps could be squeezed in, provided that they were out of shot," Young explains. The schoolhouse was built in the same manner.[38]

After principal photography commenced, the American journalist Herb Lightman made a field trip to Dingle to observe the shooting. He reported: "Lean and Young appear to jog everywhere. Up and down vast stretches of beach, selecting camera angles. Their vitality is absolutely incredible. Freddie seems to be in eight places at once, personally checking out every detail relating to the camera. The rapport between director and cinematographer is a lovely thing to behold—two highly individualized cinema craftsmen functioning as a single entity. One can finally begin to understand how *Lawrence* and *Zhivago* came into being."[39]

"Because of the erratic weather, the shooting schedule had to be flexible," says Young. Sometimes reaching the location site for the day's shooting meant that the unit traveled in a convoy of trucks like Barnum and Bailey's circus, down twenty-five miles of bumpy Irish country roads. Lean would start filming sunny scenes with a glorious blue sky overhead. By midday the area would be enveloped in a thick mist, the sky would be slate gray, and it would start to rain.

"This made continuity very difficult in the exterior scenes," Young continued, "since the weather conditions in a given sequence had to remain constant throughout the sequence, despite the fact that it was filmed over a period of several days."[40] Lean's basic rule of thumb was that, when the weather was cooperative, he filmed outdoors and that, when it was not, he moved indoors.

Filming indoors, Young often had to adjust his lighting because of the differing qualities of daylight coming in through the windows. Lightman got a graphic demonstration of this technical problem when the unit was shooting inside the pub: "This set had large windows opening into the village street. When they start the sequence there is a pea-soup mist outside that blocks out all detail. Then the weather clears suddenly and there is blazing sunlight outside. In another hour, the skies go leaden, the wind begins to howl and rain beats down on the roof. While Freddie copes with the exterior balance, the soundman supervises covering the roof with felt and rubber mats to deaden the pounding of the rain."[41] As Sarah Miles puts it, "The technical problems were endless; I thought I'd go bonkers before it was over."[42]

Two weeks into the schedule, in early March 1969, Lean was slated to film the scene in which John Mills and Trevor Howard row out to sea in a curragh, a rowboat used by Irish fishermen. This is the very scene that Guinness had questioned. The sequence was filmed at Coumeenoole Cave, "where off-shore currents flowed swiftly and dangerously between the mainland and the great Basket Islands, visible in the distance." John Mills spent the morning practicing by himself in the curragh until Lean was satisfied that his dummy runs were safe. "Right, we're ready to go," he announced. "Where's Trevor Howard?" Lean was informed that Howard was late. The wind began to rise, and storm clouds were gathering. "Go and dig him out!" Lean ordered an assistant director. "And hurry; the wind's getting up."[43]

A short time later, Howard, clad in his cassock and boots, strode down to the shore. "When I arrived on the set," he remembers, "the ruddy waves were getting frighteningly high, and the wind had become a gale. I didn't like the look of it, but one doesn't argue with David Lean." Then Lean shouted, "Get in the bloody boat! We'll just make it!" Howard continues, "So I got in the bloody boat." Six frogmen with safety ropes around their waists were swimming nearby, out of camera range, in the event that anything went awry. One of them was the associate producer Roy Stevens.

Lean waved a red flag, signaling "Action!" Mills writes in his autobiography, "A big swell came up behind us, and I rowed like mad and caught the crest of the wave." Once the wave caught up with the curragh, Mills realized that the boat was going to spill over. So he had the presence of mind to remove the false teeth that he wore in character and put them in his pocket. "I didn't want to swallow the bloody things and choke to death," he said later. Suddenly, without warning, the wind shifted. "A bloody great wave hit us," says Howard. "I was hanging on to the boat for dear life; and Johnny was rowing like crazy, when we were tossed into the air like a ruddy great pancake."[44] The boat capsized and then rammed into Mills; it struck him in the back of the neck, and he blacked out.

Howard floundered in the water, weighed down by his heavy cassock and boots. Some of the frogmen swam toward him and grabbed him. Others went after the unconscious Mills, who was being dragged, face down, out to sea by the strong current. Stevens and the other frogmen deposited the two half-drowned actors on the shore; they looked like two beached whales.

The makeup man Charles Parker had watched the whole ordeal through his binoculars. When he was told that Mills was safe, Parker replied, "Never mind Johnny; where are my fucking teeth?" Young comments that Parker's precious teeth "weren't lost, much to the make-up man's relief."[45] After a medical examination in the local hospital, Mills was found to have suffered a mild concussion. He was pronounced fit to return to the set two days later. Lean commented, "We ran some terrible risks on that film, because those Atlantic waves had tremendous force in them. Johnny did get bashed in the head, . . . but he was very game, a real professional."[46] This was the worst catastrophe to strike a Lean picture since Lili Murati had fallen under a moving train during the *Zhivago* shoot.

Ryan's Daughter was only at the beginning of the shooting schedule, which would run for a whole year. Mitchum recalls that, by the time he arrived, most of the accommodations for the actors had been taken, so the production office obtained for him nine rooms in a boardinghouse as a kind of hotel suite. In fact, the production office took over the whole boardinghouse for the duration of the shoot, with many of the crew staying there. When shooting ran overtime in the evening and the restaurants were closed, Mitchum would cook supper for up to twelve members of the cast and crew.

When tourists phoned the boardinghouse to ask about lodgings, Mitchum told them in the Irish brogue he had acquired for his role, "Oh, you wouldn't be liking it here. Americans are running it now; nudists, you know."[47] If Mitchum could not be found in the caravan the studio had provided for him near the set, he was either at the boardinghouse or joining Howard and the other revelers in their daily outing to a local pub run by an Irish cousin of Gregory Peck.

In the early days of the shoot, the cast and crew were by and large in high spirits. But, as time wore on, they realized that they were in for a long haul. As a matter of fact, after the first two weeks of shooting, Lean was already behind schedule. The members of the unit complained candidly about being marooned in an isolated location for months on end.

"It's a terrible trap, Ireland," said Anthony Havelock-Allan. The actors had long periods of not working because of the problems with the weather, he explained. But they had to remain on call for the duration of the shoot because, "if the sun shone, they were needed. . . . So there was nothing to do but drink." Christopher Jones particularly resented being stuck in the sticks. "We were in Ireland for a year, right; and David would not let us leave. I suppose he was trying to get us in the mood." (Recall that he had similarly sequestered the cast and crew of *Lawrence* in the desert.) "Have you ever spent a year in Ireland? Boy!"[48]

Mitchum complained the most. Commenting on his negative attitude, Lean said, "Bob Mitchum and I did not get on at all because he simply didn't like me." Mitchum was uncooperative from the get-go. When Lean called him to a costume fitting shortly after he arrived, he declined to show up. He told Lean that he had never done a "dress parade" before and that he was not prepared to march up and down "like a tailor's dummy."[49] And so it went.

Sarah Miles remembers that Lean's caravan was on the left of hers, Mitchum's on the right. Consequently, she was elected to play go-between for the duration of the shoot. When Mitchum was to play the scene in which Charles becomes aware of Rosy's infidelity, he was supposed to look disheveled. Lean asked Miles to tell him that he was to have his shirt hanging out of his trousers. Mitchum shot back, "Tell David I'm fucking not going to wear my shirt out!" Concludes Miles, "The whole time Mohammed would never go to the mountain." Nor would the mountain come to Mohammed. She thought they behaved like schoolboys.[50]

Things were not helped by Mitchum's substance-abuse problem, which had dogged the actor throughout his career. After he was jailed in 1948 for possession of marijuana, he made alcohol his drug of choice and developed a serious drinking problem. It was an open secret in film circles that Mitchum was a tippler, even while shooting.

The day that Lean shot the scene where Charles wanders silently along the beach after he learns of Rosy's love affair, the word around the set was that Mitchum had drunk his lunch from a bottle of vodka. But Lean, who had coped with a boozer like Robert Mitchum while making *Oliver Twist,* managed to get him through the scene. The assistant editor Tony Lawson said later that it was difficult to cut the scene together because Mitchum was in an alcoholic stupor—that he had "to look for the bits where Mitchum looked like he wasn't about to topple over."[51] Of course, Lean was provoked by the incident.

Havelock-Allan believed that Lean and Mitchum clashed because Mitchum was prone to display a cynical disregard for acting; it was apparently merely a job for which he was being paid, in this instance $870,000. Asked whether he thought he was being overpaid, Mitchum retorted with a wisecrack: "David already has spent $10 million on hay for the horses." As time wore on, Mitchum's remarks became more caustic. "It's all inefficiency," he fumed. "I could have made three pictures in this time just as good." Trevor Howard felt that Mitchum did have what appeared to be a casual attitude toward acting: "He liked to make people believe he didn't give a damn."[52]

The film historian David Thomson takes a different view of Mitchum. The actor was mocked throughout his career for "listlessness, hooded eyes, and lack of interest." But that was far from the case. Mitchum maintained a calm exterior on the screen because he saw no need to make his acting obvious on the surface. This made him appear "indifferent to the great work he was doing" and belied the fact that he was a dedicated actor. In brief, Mitchum was a character actor trapped in a leading man's body; he was very much underestimated.[53] John Mills agrees. He says that, during the wedding reception for Rosy and Charles, he got confused when he was jostled by the actors and was facing away from the camera, which was some distance away. Mitchum unobtrusively took him by the shoulder and turned him around so that Lean could move in for a close-up. Mills thought Mitchum very professional.

Mitchum did do some great acting in *Ryan's Daughter*. Sometimes he would be kidding around with the crew right up to the moment Lean called for action. Then he would overwhelm Lean by shifting gears immediately and delivering the goods on the first take. Lean would be almost tearful, says Mitchum. He would say, "Bob, that was spot on! That was simply marvelous." Mitchum, who always cavalierly waved aside compliments, would take the wind out of Lean's sails with a curious non sequitur like "You don't think it was a little too Jewish?"[54] Howard was more amused by these antics than Lean was. Still, when all was said and done, Mitchum sought to play Charles with conviction.

Lean experienced even greater difficulties with Christopher Jones than with Mitchum. Put simply, Mitchum, despite his vagaries, was an experienced professional; Jones, by comparison, was a tyro actor with only a few roles under his belt. Havelock-Allan, who was a real English gentleman, had some sympathy for Jones. He remembered him as a tortured young man who had grown up in an orphanage and run away to join the army, then gone AWOL and landed in the brig. After he left the service, he endeavored to get a new lease on life by trying his luck at acting.

Be that as it may, Jones was difficult to deal with. He was a remote individual who seemed to be in a fog most of the time. Furthermore, he was self-conscious about his short stature in a way that John Mills was not. (Sarah Miles nicknamed Jones the dwarf.) Jones kept himself aloof from the rest of the cast and spent much of his time sulking in his hotel room. Miles thought that Jones was pretty much a washout. "Christopher wouldn't let anyone help him on the set," she said. "No one could get near Christopher"—even to give him a little friendly advice on how to play a scene during rehearsals.[55]

For his part, Lean complained that Jones did not respond to his direction. Jones, in turn, claimed that Lean gave him very little input so that he was at a loss to know what he was looking for in a given scene. One day, when Lean said that Jones was underacting, Jones got miffed and replied that he was doing the scene for the camera, not to impress the crew—or the director.

Havelock-Allan observed diplomatically that Jones needed a director who would coach him with infinite patience—and that David Lean was not that director. The producer sensed that, when Lean would lose patience with Jones on the set, Jones would get scared and lapse into sullen silence. "We discovered that Christopher was practically inarticulate," says Young. In an early scene, Captain Smith, an older officer (Gerald Sim), confesses his fear to Jones's character, Major Randolph Doryan, about returning to the battlefront in France. Lean rehearsed Jones and Sim and then called for a take. "The camera started turning," says Young, "and Christopher sat there. He didn't say anything, but just stared straight ahead."[56]

Lean hollered "Cut!" Then he exclaimed, "For God's sake, Christopher, what's the matter with you?" Jones responded, "I'm not an actor." His disarming candor, however, did not improve his performance. Finally, Lean took Young aside and whispered, "Throw his face in shadow as much as you can." So Young photographed Jones immersed in shadow, and Lean shot the scene with the camera mostly concentrated on Sim. "Christopher was just sitting there trembling," concludes Young.[57] After that, Young photographed Jones in silhouette whenever he could.

Throughout the shooting period, Lean sought for tricky ways to cover up the woodenness of Jones's acting. He declared that he found Jones to be a strange young man whom he did his best to help. A genuine crisis arose while he was filming the climactic love scene between Rosy and Randolph in a forest glade in Killarney. Things went swimmingly at first. Young got some fine establishing shots of the pair on horseback, cantering through a wooded area carpeted with bluebells. (This scene originated in Flaubert's *Madame*

Bovary.) As Rosy gazes fervently at Randolph astride his stallion, she sees him as her knight-errant, the embodiment of her romantic fantasies.

Miles and Jones dismounted and began to make love. Without warning, it started to rain. Lean decided to return to the forest on another day, when the weather was more promising, to complete the sequence. But it was now autumn, and the fall weather continued to deteriorate. By late November, the leaves in the forest had fallen, and the incessant rain, which is customary in Ireland, had transformed the woods into a sea of mud. The script called for the couple to make love on the ground, which was impossible under the circumstances.

In desperation, Lean decided, at Eddie Fowlie's suggestion, to shoot the scene indoors on a forest set. Fowlie rented a dance hall in the village of Murreigh and turned it into a small studio. Stephen Grimes placed a cyclorama of blue sky all the way round the back wall of the makeshift soundstage. Eddie Fowlie and his assistants brought in truckloads of trees, moss, and turf. "We heated it with arc lamps," says Young. "We had butterflies come in and fly around the set." There were even birds twittering in the trees. "The foliage was quite luxuriant," and the atmosphere was warm as a result of the arc lamps.[58]

Bolt had written in the script that "a squadron of dandelion parachutes takes off, hovers, drifts away."[59] Accordingly, Fowlie saved some dandelion heads for use in the lovemaking scene. At the climax, he would have the seeds wafted gently, by means of a blow dryer, across the lovers.

Bolt had also indicated in the script that the lovers were naked. Lean intended to employ artistic indirection in filming the actors, showing only their heads and shoulders. But Bolt lobbied for a brief shot of Rosy's breast. Lean was not in favor of it. He maintained that love scenes should be shot with restraint. He stated in a television interview at the time that, in photographing love scenes, "You've got to be careful not to shock the audience, to the extent that they forget the characters involved; otherwise the story will go down the drain."[60] Nevertheless, he sanctioned a fleeting glimpse of Rosy's breast.

When Lean rehearsed the scene on the forest set, he instructed Miles and Jones to start out by kneeling on the grass. Miles complied, but Jones refused. "I'm not getting on my knees for you or anybody else!" he told Lean. The latter said that he was forced to scold Jones like a dyspeptic schoolteacher. Lean replied, "Now come on, you've signed for it"—reminding Jones of the nudity clause in his contract. He puffed furiously on his cigarette holder in silence until Jones said, "David, she doesn't do anything to me." Jones refused to touch her.[61]

The fact of the matter was that Jones did not like Miles and the feeling was mutual. They did not get on well, so he simply declined to do a love scene with her. "This made it difficult," Miles says, "because Rosy's first real climax was meant to be the most important of her life"—she had never reached climax with her shy husband Charles. After a day of bickering with Jones, Lean had still not gotten the scene in the can. As they wrapped for the day, one of the crew volunteered, "I'll do it with her!"[62] Lean delayed filming the scene for a couple of days.

Miles was really cross with Jones for saying that he did not find her attractive. She was determined that he was going to do the scene with her. She got together with Mitchum to discuss how Jones could be goaded into doing the scene. Mitchum was off drugs, as noted above, but he still knew of a drug that would help make Jones more susceptible to Miles's charms. By the next morning, Mitchum had somehow obtained an unspecified narcotic that he surreptitiously sprinkled into Jones's breakfast cereal. "Christopher stumbled out of his trailer in a haze," Miles says. Obviously, Mitchum had been too generous with the dosage.[63] When Lean called for a rehearsal of the love scene, Jones was too dazed and confused to undo the buttons on his shirt, so the camera crew obligingly stripped off his clothes and deposited him on the mat of artificial grass, next to Miles.

"It was like having a wet fish on top of me," Miles recalls; "I'm pretending that I'm experiencing heaven, and he can't move a muscle." Lean whispered to her to do something to make Jones react. So she poked him with her index finger in a strategic area of his body. Concludes Miles: "He moved, and we got the shot."[64]

There were many dicey moments on the set during the extended shooting schedule of *Ryan's Daughter*, and Miles was asked how she found working with Lean for a year. She answered that he was a perfectionist and very demanding when working with actors, as we have seen Julie Christie and others testify. "In order to get what you want, you have to be fairly ruthless," Miles continued. "David has a bit of a mean streak in him; I'm glad I never saw it. . . . But you have to remember that I loved and respected the man very deeply." The respect came from the fact that all he cared about was "what was good for the movie." She agreed with Katharine Hepburn's observation, cited earlier, that Lean was relentless. "People can die or drown"— a reference to the perilous boating scene with Mills and Howard—"it doesn't matter, as long as he gets what he wants," she says. "Nice men do good work, but not great work."[65]

John Mills noticed that, when he was working with him in England back in the 1940s, Lean was still willing to learn from the people he was working with, like Noël Coward and Charles Laughton. But, by the time he made *Ryan's Daughter,* he had "arrived." He was now classified as a "great director," and he had become more of an authoritarian. It was more obvious than ever that he was not "mad-keen" about working with actors. Lean much preferred cutting the film in the editing room, with no actors around. To see him at work in the cutting room, running the film footage through his fingers, is, according to Mills, "like watching a master painter at work." "I don't care if I do have to wait a year [for him to finish a picture]," Mill concluded. There would not be a single bad shot in the whole film. It did, in fact, take a whole year to shoot *Ryan's Daughter:* "But it was worth it—I got another Oscar out of it!"[66]

With a shooting schedule that seemed like an eternity, Trevor Howard got restless and would sometimes lope off on long rambles around the countryside. He was more critical of Lean's meticulous working methods than Mills. "David doesn't really like actors," Howard observed. "He's really only in love with celluloid and his Moviola." He added jokingly, "All he wants to do is get rid of the actors and start cutting them out of the picture [in the editing room]. Mind you, what he did capture on the screen looked beautiful. David has a talent for that; and I can't criticize him, because not only is he a friend of mine, but a bloody marvelous director."[67]

Robert Mitchum was likewise bored with the slow pace of the shoot, and he lost patience with Lean's methods to an extent that Mills and Howard, who had worked with Lean before, did not. Mitchum made fun of Lean's painstaking way of working, saying, "Working for David Lean is like being made to build the Taj Mahal out of toothpicks."[68] Nevertheless, in his more serious moments, he appreciated Lean as a topflight director. "I knew he was an eccentric director," he told a radio interviewer. "The rewarding part of it was that I finally met somebody who considered the medium as important as I did."[69]

The actor that one might assume would nurse an abiding grudge against Lean was Christopher Jones since Lean gave him a rough ride during shooting. But Jones said he admired Lean in retrospect. He admitted that he and Lean had gone head-to-head on occasion: "But we got along great most of the time." For example, Lean loved the compelling way Jones played the scene in which Randolph collapses in the pub. "I totally respected him; I loved him. A brilliant director; the best there was."[70]

The administration of MGM was in Lean's corner, so long as Robert O'Brien was president of the studio. But O'Brien's days were numbered. Some of Metro's expensive 1968 productions had not performed well at the box office, for example, Michael Anderson's *The Shoes of the Fisherman,* a lackluster religious epic about the papacy with Anthony Quinn as the pope. Metro was in dire straits. In fact, during the year and a half that Lean spent making *Ryan's Daughter* for the studio, he worked for three different administrations. As one wag put it, "Last one to leave, turn out the lights."

Robert O'Brien was finally deposed in January 1969 and replaced by Louis Polk, an executive who came to MGM from the breakfast food industry. Not surprisingly, Polk was ousted in October, in favor of James Aubrey, known in the industry as "the Smiling Cobra." After O'Brien, his chief supporter, departed, Lean began to feel pressure from the MGM front office to accelerate his sluggish working pace. Still there was no thought of canceling *Ryan's Daughter;* Lean's track record on *Dr. Zhivago* ensured that. As Pauline Kael said, Lean had proved to be the savior of O'Brien's regime; now Aubrey and his new regime were "hoping that Lean would rescue *them*."[71]

Nevertheless, Aubrey growled that he could finance several modestly budgeted movies for what Lean's picture was costing. Stanley Kubrick told me that Aubrey went on an economy drive, which included canceling Kubrick's film *Napoleon* at the script stage in October 1969 in the wake of the failure of some large-scale productions. "The lights had gone out in Hollywood," Kubrick laconically commented in conversation. "MGM was no longer interested in making mega-movies." Hence, Kubrick said, even if *Ryan's Daughter* had not gone over budget, his own *Napoleon* would have been aborted anyway. MGM was fending off creditors, and any project that involved a huge outlay of money had to be scuttled.

Aubrey flew to Ireland in November 1969 for a personal powwow, admonishing Lean that his excessive pursuit of perfection had sent his film spiraling way over budget. In his own defense, Lean cited the problems of shooting on location, with the cast and crew waiting for the sun or the rain, whichever the script dictated for a given scene. Moreover, he emphasized that there were other serious holdups that were likewise beyond his control. For example, Trevor Howard was hospitalized when he fell from a horse, injuring his collarbone and five ribs. Christopher Jones "demolished his brand-new Ferrari on a narrow, winding road": "His survival from the pile-up was little short of miraculous."[72] Finally, two weeks of shooting were lost when, during processing, the laboratory accidentally damaged some footage beyond repair, necessitating reshoots.

Aubrey remained adamant, insisting that Lean economize. As a parting shot, he reminded Lean ruefully, "The days of *Dr. Zhivago* are over."[73] Lean continued filming for another two months and, by the time principal photography had wrapped, would go $4 million over his original budget of $9 million.

Gossip spread in Hollywood about *Ryan's Daughter*, for example, that Lean's meticulous attention to detail was getting out of hand. He was increasingly being labeled a reckless spendthrift—a reputation that he did not entirely deserve. One widely circulated rumor had it that he had made Mitchum and Miles sit for hours in the middle of a field, waiting for the right cloud configuration, in order to get the exact shot he wanted. Lean's only response was that a journalist who had visited the set had concocted that story because it made good copy.

"An awful exaggeration," said Freddie Young of the reporter's allegation. "We might wait sometimes for an hour or two to get an effect with the clouds scudding across the sky, and the shadows of the clouds on the ground. Well, I was delighted to go along with that."[74] Young, like Lean, wanted each shot to be the best that could be achieved: "It's only by taking infinite care over details that you make memorable pictures.[75]

There was one set piece in the script that Lean intended to film with great care, regardless of pressure to make cutbacks in the shooting schedule. That was the storm sequence, in the course of which a German ship, which is supplying arms to the IRA, unloads a shipment on the beach near Kirrary. When Father Collins sees the awesome storm clouds gathering overhead, he mutters, "You'd think they were announcing the coming of Christ."[76]

Lean looked on this as a pet project. He wanted to stage a storm sequence to end all storm sequences. So he decided to direct it himself—whereas normally an action scene of this sort would be turned over to the second unit. Lean was still wary of entrusting a sequence he looked on as special to anyone but himself.

Eddie Fowlie suggested the coast of the Ennis peninsula in County Clare, about a two-hour drive from the main set in Dingle. The camera, of course, would have to be protected from the rain by a big umbrella. In addition, it was necessary to come up with an apparatus that would shield the camera lens from the rain and sleet; otherwise, the images captured on film would be blurred by the elements. Freddie Young got the brainstorm to utilize an instrument used on naval vessels, called a Clear Screen (rain deflector). Young fitted it on the camera, directly in front of the lens, as a kind of huge lens cap.

The Clear Screen, according to Young, is a Plexiglas windshield that spins at high speed, with the result that, when waves or rain hit it, the spray is shaken off by centrifugal force. "We couldn't have done the scene without the Clear Screen, because [during the storm] the rain and the waves were pouring onto the camera lens," said Young. "We were all in wet suits, and we had to chain the camera to the rocks because of the wind." Safety ropes were attached to the actors, but it was still dangerous.[77]

"The storms came in sort of gusts and only lasted an hour or two," Lean recalled. Hence, the storm sequence had to be filmed over an extended period of time. Young added, "Whenever we received advanced warning of an approaching storm, the unit would dash off to the rocky coast of the Ennis Peninsula." They would then get the full fury of the tumultuous storms, "which came straight across the Atlantic." A storm "would rage for about two hours and then die away": "Then we would have to leave until the next storm warning. We went on like this for months."[78]

In December 1969, Lean decided to take the main unit to South Africa for additional location work. So he was forced to leave the completion of the storm sequence to Roy Stevens, for whom he laid out the shots he wanted. In all, it took two months of intermittent filming, first by Lean, then by Stevens, to nail things down. But Lean achieved his goal and captured on film a terrific storm sequence.

The impetus behind the South Africa trip was Stevens pointing out to Lean that there was no hope of filming the remaining summer scenes in Ireland during the month of December, when the sun never shone and there was a constant drizzle. They had run out of sun, so these scenes would have to be shot somewhere else. Havelock-Allan was delegated by Lean to intercede with Aubrey. He explained in his customary diplomatic fashion that the money they were spending while being idle in Ireland would be better spent in taking the unit to a more benign climate like South Africa. Aubrey could hardly say no; after all, the studio had allowed Lean to make a foray to Finland for snow while he was making *Zhivago* in Spain.

At the end of December, after the Christmas holidays, the main unit flew to Capetown in a chartered plane for a five-week stay. "I'll tell you, if you showed me the film now, I'd have to think hard which beach was Ireland and which was South Africa," Lean said afterward.[79] One of the key sequences shot in South Africa was the suicide of Randolph Doryan. Lean filmed the sequence on a beach at twilight; ever the perfectionist, he wanted Randolph to blow himself to kingdom come just as the sun was sinking into the sea. The crew got very impatient waiting around for the sun to set, and Lean said, "Just wait a few minutes, and the sun will be ideal for the scene."[80] Admittedly, it is a stunning shot.

Not long before the troupe decamped to return to Ireland, Freddie Young received word that he had been awarded the OBE (Order of the British Empire) by Queen Elizabeth II for his contribution to British cinema. Lean had received the CBE (commander of the British Empire) in 1953.

Principal photography was finished on February 24, 1970, almost one year to the day after it began. Lean then moved his headquarters to the Great Southern Hotel in Killarney, where he established a state-of-the-art editing facility. He had to pare down the huge accumulation of footage into a feature film of reasonable proportions in time for the premiere on November 9, 1970, in New York. In doing so, he worked carefully with Norman Savage in cutting the film. (There is a photo in Silver and Ursini's book on Lean of Lean and Savage examining footage at the editing table; inexplicably, Savage is misidentified in the caption as Robert Bolt!)[81]

Lean became increasingly convinced during editing that Christopher Jones's delivery of his lines was unsatisfactory; he too often spoke in a flat tone of voice. So Lean took the drastic measure of having Jones's lines redubbed by Julian Holloway, the son of the actor Stanley Holloway (*Brief Encounter*). This was the same fate that Jones had endured on *The Looking Glass War*. He simply lacked the range that his role in *Ryan's Daughter* required; nor did he have a strong enough screen presence to hold his own opposite old pros like Trevor Howard and John Mills. In fact, he was so discouraged by the poor notices he subsequently received for *Ryan's Daughter* that he dropped out of films altogether.

After viewing the material that Stevens shot for the storm sequence, Lean summoned him to the editing room. Stevens found him looking depressed. "I don't know how the fuck you did it," stormed Lean. "All I know is I wish I'd done it. Now fuck off!"[82] Stevens deeply resented Lean's jealous tantrum, which was prompted by Stevens allegedly attempting to steal his thunder. He thought Lean was overreacting since Lean's footage certainly was a match for his.

The rift between Lean and Stevens lasted for two years. Then the two met for drinks at the Hotel Principe in Rome, where Lean often stayed. It was a known fact that Lean tended to drink more when he was not filming; at times he would get a bit tiddly, as the British expression goes. "David—who couldn't hold his drink by the way—had two whiskies," Steven remembers. That was enough to encourage him to apologize. Lean reminded him that he had tried to make amends for his ill-tempered behavior by giving Stevens a special screen credit on the film, as second-unit director of the storm sequence. Nevertheless, Stevens vowed never to work with Lean again.

Maurice Jarre contributed a finely tuned background score for the movie, one redolent of traditional Irish folk music. His background music is built on subdued, elusive melodies; hints of wistful, aching themes thread their way through it. There is little of the sweeping grandeur of the scores for *Lawrence* or *Zhivago*. "The subject dictates the scope of the sound," he explains. "Obviously it would be wrong to have big orchestrations [for a touching love story]."[83] Lean very much agreed with Jarre that *Ryan's Daughter* was first and foremost a love story when they discussed it during postproduction. Indeed, Lean had crafted a poignant romantic tale, carefully developed and sustained.

Ryan's Daughter takes place in 1916, during the Troubles, in the coastal village of Kirrary. Rosy Ryan, a brash, immature girl, nurtures a crush on Charles Shaughnessy, a former teacher of hers; she charms him into marrying her. After a typically boisterous Irish wedding reception, Rosy and Charles retire to the nuptial bedchamber. Tom Ryan, Rosy's father, kisses her good night and calls her his "princess," his nickname for her.

"Upstairs in the bedroom, we're treated to a scene not dissimilar to the wedding night scene in *Hobson's Choice*," Maxford writes. Like Willie Mossop, Charles Shaughnessy fumbles about uncertainly as he undresses before joining his bride under the covers. "The act of lovemaking proves a disappointment to Rosy; she and Charles fall asleep back-to-back." Jerry Roberts is of the opinion that Charles is impotent.[84] But there is no evidence of this in the movie. Suffice it to say that Charles's lovemaking disappoints Rosy because he does not measure up to her adolescent fantasies.

Rosy and Charles settle into an uneventful life of routine domesticity, and Rosy sheepishly confesses to Father Collins that she does not find married life with Charles fulfilling. Like Emma Bovary, she was led by the romantic fiction that she devoured to expect a more intense love relationship with her husband. In fact, Charles seems more like a father figure than a husband.

Father Collins responds to Rosy's complaints by giving her the back of his hand, as if she were still a naughty schoolgirl, because she does not appreciate her good, upstanding husband. Rosy says she wants more out of life, implying that her middle-aged husband cannot satisfy her sexual wants. "Don't nurse your wishes," Collins admonishes her, "or, sure to God, you'll get what you're wishing."

At that very moment, Lean cuts to the arrival of Major Randolph Doryan on the bus from Derry. It is readily apparent that Randolph walks with a limp, the result of a war injury. His affliction symbolizes that his personality is likewise impaired. That is, the shell-shocked officer is crippled both psychologically and physically.

Not long after, Rosy witnesses the war-shattered Randolph's seizure in her father's pub. After everyone leaves, Rosy soothes Randolph, who lies shuddering on the floor, with a kiss, and their love affair is under way. Rosy and Randolph share a tryst in a secluded wood; Rosy achieves her first genuine orgasm as they make love in the grass.

When Rosy returns home, Charles inquires why her skirt is soiled with mud. She replies that she was out riding her horse Princess and that "Princess took a fall." Rosy, whose nickname is Princess, has also taken a fall, as her soiled garment implies metaphorically. "Rosy, you'd never be unfaithful to me, would you?" Charles asks her apprehensively. She responds that she surely would not. But Charles is not really reassured, and he soon learns that the village is buzzing about Rosy's "fancy man." As the first part of the film comes to a close, he continues to suspect her of infidelity, but he is, apparently, going to wait it out with almost paternal patience.

As the second part of the movie gets rolling, Tim O'Leary (Barry Foster), an IRA activist, enlists Tom Ryan's assistance in rounding up villagers to help him and his cohort with a crucial operation. It seems that a German ship is delivering a shipment of guns and ammunition for the IRA. The villagers, led by Father Collins, are to help in salvaging the cargo as it floats ashore on rafts.

Ryan, a turncoat, phones the British garrison to warn them about what O'Leary is up to. As luck would have it, a raging storm erupts; the villagers, including Rosy and Charles, turn out to aid in the IRA retrieval operation. Lean provides a superb montage of howling winds, relentless rain, and enormous waves crashing against the rocky shore. This sequence represents Maurice Jarre's one opportunity in the movie to pull out all the stops with his underscore. His implacable motif for this scene is all pounding percussion, bellowing brass, and shrieking woodwinds.

All in all, the storm sequence is the high point of the entire film. What is more, it is among the greatest set pieces of Lean's—or anyone else's—career. Lean subsequently stated that he had favorite bits in several of his movies: "But for one moment in a picture, I would say I was rather pleased with the storm sequence in *Ryan's Daughter*."[85]

After the cargo is loaded on a waiting truck, O'Leary and his comrades start down the road, but Randolph and his soldiers block their path. O'Leary makes a run for it, and Randolph draws a bead on him with his rifle and brings him down with a single bullet. As the wounded rebel is taken into custody, he shouts defiantly at Randolph, "Get out of my country!" Lean felt that O'Leary should be allowed to make this honest, straightforward declaration, in order to indicate that he sees himself as a patriot, not a terrorist—

someone who is just as dedicated to his cause as Randolph and the British are to theirs.

The thunderclap of the rifle shot that Randolph fired off causes him to suffer another seizure. He begins to tremble uncontrollably and collapses on the road. Without thinking of the consequences, Rosy rushes to comfort him, much to the shock and dismay of the onlookers. Charles takes her home amid the derisive jeers of the crowd.

Charles sullenly meanders along the beach alone during the night, pondering whether to leave his unfaithful wife. When he returns home, an angry mob is gathering outside the house. The townspeople assume that, because of her liaison with Randolph, Rosy—not her father—betrayed O'Leary to the British. Charles loyally stands by her side, but he cannot prevent the villagers from dragging her out of the house to avenge O'Leary's capture. Lean employs artistic indirection in staging the ensuing riot. As Rosy is engulfed by the mob, Lean implies that her clothes are being ripped from her body by having remnants of her garments tossed into the air. Indeed, the handling of the scene is more discreet than the director's critics are prepared to concede.

Finally, as Rosy's hair is snipped off with shears, Tom Ryan, her father, unwilling to admit his treachery even to save his daughter from further humiliation, runs away frantically from the scene. He becomes a tiny figure, disappearing into the distance, thereby suggesting how he has been diminished as a human being because of his cowardice.

Collins finally puts a stop to Rosy's humiliating ordeal by marching up to McArdle, the ringleader, and slapping him across the face; then he orders the mob to disperse. McArdle shouts, "You're taking advantage of your cloth, Father Hugh!" The priest roars back, "That's what it's for!" Charles then takes Rosy back inside the house.

Randolph knows without being told that his affair with Rosy is over. His response is one of total despair. He proceeds to the shore, where he plans to destroy himself with one of the sticks of dynamite he confiscated from O'Leary. When Lean was shooting this scene on a beach in South Africa, he came across the hulk of an abandoned ship. "David decided to incorporate it into the scene, in which the major blows himself into oblivion," says Young. "The action was meant to coincide with the sinking of the sun."[86] Silver and Ursini comment, "Among the skeletal ribs of a bleached ship, in the red glow of the setting sun, Doryan ultimately perishes in his own inferno."[87]

Though Rosy has been publicly ostracized, Charles is determined to stick by her. Rosy and Charles decide to leave Kirrary together, with the hope of getting a fresh start in Dublin. Father Collins and Michael are the only two townspeople who come to see them off as they wait for the bus to Dublin. Because Lean insisted that Bolt write an ending implying that Rosy and Charles will go on together, Bolt has the priest say to them, "I doubt very much that you two will separate. That's my parting gift to you—that doubt."

Charles takes Rosy's arm, and they climb aboard the bus. Collins and Michael watch it disappear over the hill, taking Rosy and Charles to a new life. Lean sees their trip to Dublin as a metaphor for their journey down the road of life. Their lives will continue to be arduous, with no rest as yet in sight. Sarah Miles said in a recent television interview, "I think it's an optimistic ending; I think Rosy and Charles would go on together. Charles never stopped loving her."[88]

Rosy Ryan is a Lean heroine of the same stamp as most of his other heroes and heroines. She rises above all her misfortunes and resolutely looks to the future. Once again, it is clear that Lean has been drawn to a person who refuses to face defeat and disappointment.

In October 1970, the Museum of Modern Art in New York honored Lean with a retrospective of his work, in anticipation of the premiere of *Ryan's Daughter*. In the event, the film's critical reception was quite a letdown for those who had great expectations of a new Lean film. In retrospect, *Ryan's Daughter* had been an ill-starred project from the start, marked with every possible harbinger of doom—casting woes, script rethinks, reshoots, and budget overruns. The crack of doom finally came when the film was generally disparaged by the critical establishment when it opened in New York on November 8, 1970.

Pauline Kael's review in the *New Yorker* was absolutely merciless. "Lean probably enjoys working in his characteristic . . . gargantuan style," Kael pontificated, "but his movies have a way of falling apart on him." *Ryan's Daughter* may be an "expensive movie," but it is still "a cheap romance—gush made respectable by millions of dollars 'tastefully' wasted." Lean hopes to repeat the financial success of *Dr. Zhivago* "with twinkling orgasms and cosmetic craftsmanship": "Yet the emptiness of *Ryan's Daughter* shows in practically every frame."[89] In a similar vein, *Variety* stated that the film's excessive length tends "to dissipate the impact of performances and to overwhelm outstanding photography and production."[90]

"The reviews were appalling," moaned Lean. "There wasn't a single good notice in America; the English notices were worse."[91] Alexander Walker wrote in the London *Evening Standard*, "Three hours is a bit long for a trifling little love story, . . . which stubbornly resists being pressed in the epic mould." Lean had lavished "excruciating care" on a trite narrative.[92]

After the picture had opened, Lean was invited to attend an informal discussion of the movie with the National Society of Film Critics at the Algonquin Hotel in New York. The critics had a cocktail party beforehand, to which the guest of honor curiously was not invited. The "informal discussion" soon degenerated into a free-for-all. "I think they were tight," Lean observed afterward.[93]

The critics present were violently against the film. Richard Schickel, who had praised *Dr. Zhivago,* was no longer on the Lean bandwagon. He endeavored to summarize their discussion toward the end by asking, "Mr. Lean, could you please tell us how the man who directed *Brief Encounter* could come up with a load of bullshit like *Ryan's Daughter?*"[94] Lean took umbrage at Schickel's brusque remark and refused to answer.

"They just took me to bits," Lean remembered. When they assaulted him for inflating a small-scale love story into a sprawling epic, he sensed that big historical romances were decidedly out of fashion. He confronted Pauline Kael, who had, he felt, come across as the Dragon Lady, before he headed for the nearest exit: "You won't be content until you have reduced me to making a film in black-and-white on 16mm!" Kael retorted, "No, we'll let you use color."[95] As a matter of fact, *Ryan's Daughter* was the last movie to be filmed in seventy millimeter for almost twenty years. So Lean was reduced to using thirty-five millimeter in the future, if not sixteen millimeter.

One night after we had appeared on a talk show together, I asked Richard Schickel about the debacle at the Algonquin Hotel. "The critics, myself included, failed to take into consideration that a director is at his most vulnerable right after he has finished a film," he explained. "So he was easily offended by what we said." As a matter of fact, Lean had made the same point in more than one interview. "The power of the printed word is tremendous," he said. "The critics can become a pack"—badgering a director about his work. "One is easily shaken, you know?"[96] Elsewhere, he noted that the critics fundamentally resented the scope of the picture. He conceded that perhaps they had a valid point: "But they didn't have to *hammer* me about it."[97]

Freddie Young was convinced that the critics "gave *Ryan's Daughter* a slating" because it was a big-budget picture, as Lean suggested. What is more, there was a lot of resentment toward the picture in the industry for the same reason. The film industry was in a slump, owing to declining movie attendance, Young continues. "Many of the soundstages at MGM were idle, and there was a general atmosphere of dejection and uncertainty."[98] As James Aubrey grumbled when he met with Lean on location, he could have made several moderately budgeted films for what Lean was spending on one movie.

"Poor David Lean," commented Sarah Miles wryly. *Dr. Zhivago* came out: "And the critics wee-wee'd all over it and said, 'Oh, what a shame! *Dr. Zhivago* isn't as good as *Lawrence of Arabia*. David Lean has lost his touch.' Then he did *Ryan's Daughter*, and they wee-wee'd all over it and said, 'He'll never do another *Zhivago!*'"[99]

The original version of *Ryan's Daughter* shown at the New York premiere was 206 minutes. Given the chorus of complaints in the press that the movie was slow and—at nearly three and a half hours—exhausting, Lean advised the MGM front office that he would shave away some footage, in order to improve the film's pacing. He thought it imperative to do so immediately, before the picture opened in its initial road-show engagements. He went ahead and edited 14 minutes from the picture's running time, bringing it down to 194 minutes. I am bound to say that, because of Lean's adroit editing, it is virtually impossible to detect precisely where he made his trims in the original version of the movie.

By the time the film was set to go into general release in the United States, Lean had long since returned to Europe. Then Metro decided to further shorten it. This would allow for an additional daily showing, thereby increasing the movie's revenue. Metro officials wired Lean, "Please can we make some cuts?" Havelock-Allan remembers, "David began to weaken." Lean replied that they could proceed, but he declined to suggest where the additional cuts should be made.[100] He was wise to refuse to be involved; that way, he could not be blamed for the resulting lapses in narrative continuity and character development. In the end, MGM whittled *Ryan's Daughter* down to a drastically shortened 165 minutes, cutting nearly half an hour of footage. Lean, of course, disowned this truncated version of the movie.

Lean had to wait until *Ryan's Daughter* was released on home video in 1989 to amend the situation by insisting that his 194-minute cut be released on videocassette. Then, in 1997, when the film was released on videocassette in a spiffed-up digital package—and in wide-screen format for the first time—it was restored to its original running time of 206 minutes. And it is the original version of the movie that became available on DVD in 2006.

After the picture was launched in 1970, Anthony Havelock-Allan retired from the picture business. It was appropriate that someone associated with several of Lean's early British films should have worked on a David Lean film as his last production. But it was a pity that he could not have bowed out with a movie that was better received.

That *Ryan's Daughter* falls below the exacting standard set by Lean in his previous epic films is due in the last analysis to Robert Bolt's script, which failed to create a dramatic line strong enough to support the weight of a film over three hours in length. *Ryan's Daughter* really has two subjects: Rosy Ryan's love affair and the Irish Troubles. Unfortunately, the two subjects are barely on speaking terms with one another in the movie. Whereas the Russian Revolution is a constant presence in *Dr. Zhivago,* the Easter Rebellion hardly ever intrudes on the story of Rosy, beyond provoking the horror of the townsfolk when they discover that she is two-timing her husband with an officer of the British occupation forces.

The film has some virtues that are frequently overlooked. "Lean has applied epic values to a fragile and delicate love story," says Ivan Butler in one of the film's few positive assessments. "The picture entrances the eye with huge vistas of cliffs and sand, sea and sky."[101] Some film historians have called *Ryan's Daughter* epic cinema's last gasp. Be that as it may, it is a gasp that sings and howls like a grand tenor at an Irish wake, for the story is ultimately compelling and quite moving and very well cast.

Sarah Miles is bright and restive as Rosy; Robert Mitchum has never been better than as a ruggedly handsome man who can convey a sense of old-fashioned decency; John Mills artfully inhabits the character of the village half-wit; and Trevor Howard gives an immaculate performance as the forthright, blustering Father Collins. Furthermore, Maurice Jarre once again demonstrates his ability to evoke ethnic musical styles; the score is run through with Irish tunes and jigs. The film is superbly acted, and it is photographed with accomplished professionalism by Freddie Young. In brief, *Ryan's Daughter* is not a great movie, but it is big enough to carry its flaws. "No doubt," writes Robert Murphy, "the cinema would be a poorer place without such grandiloquent epics."[102] Indeed it would.

Ryan's Daughter was nominated for four Academy Awards. Sarah Miles was nominated as best actress and John Mills as best supporting actor; Freddie Young was nominated for his cinematography and Gordon McCullum and John Bramall for their sound design. At the Oscar ceremonies on April 15, 1971, Freddie Young was awarded his third Oscar for a Lean film, following his wins for *Lawrence of Arabia* and *Dr. Zhivago*. John Mills also received an Oscar for playing the mute Michael. In his acceptance speech, Mills said that he had been speechless in front of the camera for a year in Ireland and was again speechless in accepting the award. Significantly, when Mills died in 2005, the obituaries highlighted his films with David Lean—"his definitive Pip in *Great Expectations,* his own favorite role," "that other upwardly mobile hero, the bootmaker Willie Mossop in *Hobson's Choice,*" and his Oscar-winning turn in *Ryan's Daughter.*[103]

Lean later said that his own personal favorite performance in *Ryan's Daughter* was Trevor Howard's as Father Collins. Similarly, Sarah Miles states, "The one who went by almost unnoticed in the film was Trevor Howard. If you look at the film again you will see that he is giving a truly remarkable performance."[104]

Ryan's Daughter is frequently referred to as an infamous financial failure; that was not really the case. The film's budget finally amounted to $13 million, and it grossed $14.7 million domestically during its first year of release, 1971. Consequently, not only did it recoup its cost, but it also turned a modest profit. In fact, the movie attracted fairly large audiences, becoming the fourth-highest-grossing film of 1971. Lean was quick to point out that it ran at the Empire Cinema in London for over a year. The film really came into its own when it was released on DVD in 2006. The transfer from the original seventy-millimeter material was hailed as one of the most spectacular video presentations ever produced, a marvelous restoration. "Critics who assailed its excesses and ignored its virtues did so mainly because of the era in which it was released," says *Premiere*. By the early 1970s, a highly polished studio attraction was considered dated. "Today *Ryan's Daughter*'s picture-perfect style of filmmaking is a pleasure to revisit."[105]

Still, after the drubbing that Lean took from the critics for the picture, he said to himself, "What the hell am I doing, if my work is as bad as all this?" He continued, "It shakes one's confidence terribly; you don't have faith in yourself." He thought, "Why am I making movies? I don't have to."[106] So he decided not to make another movie for the foreseeable future: "I thought that I'd do something else. So I went traveling around the world. I thought, 'What's the point?'"[107] After all, he was wealthy and could afford to travel. He and his companion, Sandy Hotz, chose ports of call in Egypt, India, Africa, and Italy.

In retrospect, Lean thought that he had taken the critics too seriously and let them get him down. Still, he explained that a director has to heed reviewers: "You can't meet the general public; and if your mother tells you the movie is great, you say, 'Yes, very sweet of you, but you would.' The only people who really don't give a damn, who are out there giving their opinion, are the critics. They are the only people, as it were, you can believe."[108]

One reason Lean was disinclined to make another film was that it was difficult to find a subject that was up to his level—filmmakers are always out to top the films they have already made. But the assumption that he was merely coasting throughout the 1970s is not accurate. As a matter of fact, he did become involved with various projects that did not reach fruition. During a time when economic pressures were making it less and less feasible to produce the sort of large-scale epic films he had become accustomed to making, he found it difficult to come up with a viable project. Nor was he in a hurry to do so. He had often said, "I would rather make one good picture in three years than four others in the same time."[109] As a matter of fact, from *Kwai* on, there had usually been a span of roughly five years from one Lean picture to the next. This time, however, it was to be a decade before he launched another production.

Lean was accorded some solace for the disastrous critical reception of *Ryan's Daughter* when the Directors Guild of America presented him with a Lifetime Achievement Award in October 1973. (He had, after all, been working in the American film industry for nearly two decades.) The award was bestowed at a ceremony in Hollywood by George Stevens, for whom Lean had served as an uncredited second-unit director on *The Greatest Story Ever Told*. Coupled with that accolade was another; in March 1974, Lean was awarded a Lifetime Fellowship in the British Film Academy. He joined a roll of honor that numbered filmmakers of the likes of Billy Wilder and John Schlesinger in its ranks.

A couple of months earlier, on December 9, 1973, Lean's father, Frank, expired in a nursing home. Frank's demise was followed on October 28, 1974, by the death of David Lean's younger brother, Edward, an executive at the BBC. Lean had seen little of his family over the years; after all, he had not resided in England since the mid-1950s. So he did not experience an overwhelming sense of loss at the deaths of his father and brother. Never a family man, Lean spent little time with his son, Peter, and his family.

Lean's itinerary of world travel also included the South Pacific. After a tour of the South Sea Islands, Lean became caught up with the idea of making a film about the British explorers who had voyaged to the South Pacific in the eighteenth century. In researching the period, he came across Richard Hough's 1972 book *Captain Bligh and Mr. Christian*, a revisionist account of the mutiny on the HMS *Bounty*. Consequently, he decided to make a new film version of *Mutiny on the Bounty*.

The Bounty (1984)

Richard Hough's historical novel portrayed Captain William Bligh more benignly than either of the two previous Hollywood films on the *Bounty* incident. Frank Lloyd's *Mutiny on the Bounty* (1935) features Charles Laughton as Captain Bligh and Clark Gable as First Officer Fletcher Christian, who foments the mutiny against Bligh. The film, which was a big hit for Metro, was based on Charles Nordhoff and James Hall's 1932 novel of the same title. Lean contended, "Bligh was a much-maligned man."[110] Nordhoff and Hall depicted Bligh as a petty tyrant, whereas Hough shows him to be a decent, tenacious commander, saddled with an insubordinate first officer.

Lean had been asked by MGM to direct the 1962 remake with Marlon Brando as Christian and Trevor Howard as Captain Bligh, who was once again portrayed as a martinet. But, at the time, Lean preferred to make *Lawrence* instead. Now he was entranced by the subject. Following Hough, he was convinced that Bligh was not a sadistic bully who flogged hapless sailors at the least provocation but a "gifted seaman whose long friendship with Fletcher Christian was destroyed during the five-month sojourn of the *Bounty* in Tahiti."[111]

After months at sea, Christian surrenders to the lure of the hedonism of this primeval paradise. Viewing the natives as noble savages, he goes native and lives a life of indolence with a Tahitian girl. "Christian was knocked out by the exotic South Sea Island," Lean affirmed. "Bligh couldn't help but disapprove. I was raised a Quaker, so I know about these things."[112] Consequently, when Bligh endeavors to reinforce naval discipline aboard the *Bounty* on the ship's return to England, Christian stirs up a rebellion. Christian casts Bligh, and the sailors who remain loyal to him, adrift in an open boat. Then he steers the *Bounty* to Pitcairn Island, where he attempts to set up a colony made up of his sailors and the natives, in order to escape the long arm of the law.

Lean and Sandy Hotz took up residence in a hotel in Bora Bora, an island recommended to Lean by Noël Coward that was 160 miles from Tahiti. Robert Bolt soon was on hand to start work on the screenplay. He and Sarah Miles having by this time split, Bolt was free to travel. "When I got there," he says, "David said he now wanted to make two films, which would tell the story of the *Bounty*." Lean aimed to make the best and the fullest account of the *Bounty* saga. "I agreed to write two scripts," he recalled, scripts entitled *The Lawbreakers* and *The Long Arm*.[113]

Lean and Bolt set to work on the script on October 10, 1977; their plan was to write screenplays for two interrelated, feature-length films. *The Lawbreakers* would begin with the *Bounty's* departure from Portsmouth and encompass the period in Tahiti. The climax would, of course, be the mutiny on April 28, 1789, en route back to England, followed by Bligh's being cast adrift in an open boat manned by the crewmen still loyal to him. The second film, *The Long Arm,* would cover the mutineers' life on Pitcairn Island, Bligh's eventual return to Britain, the search for the mutineers, and the naval tribunal that inquires into Bligh's conduct aboard the *Bounty* leading up to the mutiny.

The other members of Lean's team with him at this point, besides Bolt, were John Box, the production designer of *Lawrence of Arabia* and *Dr. Zhivago,* who was back after a stint at producing, and Eddie Fowlie, Lean's ever-faithful factotum. Warner Bros. had initially agreed to finance one film about the *Bounty.* But, when Lean upped the ante to two interrelated movies to be shot back-to-back, the studio bailed out on the project as too expensive and too risky. Lean remained determined to find a production company that would commit to both pictures.

Faced with the daunting task of constructing full-scale sets for two elaborate historical films, including a replica of the *Bounty,* Box informed Lean that he might withdraw from the production. He was getting too old, he said, for such mammoth undertakings. Lean pressed Box to make up his mind: "Are you with me on this film or not?" Box responded that, if Lean demanded an immediate answer, it must be no. Box left within hours by motorboat. "It was horrible," he recalls. Lean was on the pier when the boat pulled out: "And he pretended not to be looking." His figure was fading into the distance: "It was like the ending of a David Lean film."[114]

Back in Hollywood, Box was asked by a Warners executive what had gone wrong with the project. Box snapped irritably that Lean "had gone mad." He explained that Lean had gotten a bit grandiose: "If you can't be God, be a film director!" Box immediately regretted his acrid remarks, but a rumor spread quickly through the film colony that Lean had turned into a megalomaniac, that the great director had become the great dictator. A Hollywood wag dubbed Lean's *Bounty* project "the Old Man and the Sea."[115] At any rate, the breach between Lean and Box was not healed until Box consented to design Lean's *Passage to India* some four years later.

At the beginning of 1978, Lean had left Bora Bora, preferring to base his production headquarters in Papeete, the capital of the island of Tahiti. Once there, Lean learned that Captain James Cook, the eighteenth-century British explorer, had lost an anchor in 1777 when his ship nearly foundered off the coast. (Captain Bligh had sailed with Captain Cook before assuming command of the *Bounty.*) Lean had a hunch that the discovery of Cook's anchor would make an interesting documentary, and that is how he came to make *Lost and Found: The Story of an Anchor.*

The redoubtable Eddie Fowlie got in touch with the shipwreck expert Kelly Tarlton, who assured him that the anchor lay off the northeast coast of Tahiti. Fowlie assembled a team of divers and exhumed the anchor from its watery grave.

Lean, who had not been behind a movie camera for nearly a decade, contacted George Andrews, a producer for South Pacific TV in New Zealand.

He advised Andrews that he was prepared to bankroll a documentary, to be shot in sixteen millimeter, about the retrieval of Cook's two-hundred-year-old anchor, at a cost of $10,000. The screenplay would be written by Robert Bolt, who continued as part of Lean's small contingent in Tahiti. Andrews showed up ten days later with a crew, including the documentary filmmaker Wayne Tourell, who was willing to act as Lean's assistant director for the chance to work with an old pro. Andrews asked Lean to narrate the film. "I'd be delighted," he responded, pointing out that he had "narrated *British Movietone News* in the 1930s," when he was a film editor.[116]

Lean reenacted the recovery of the anchor for the camera by having Fowlie sink it in shallow water offshore and then filming the divers hauling it to the surface. He firmly believed that it was cricket to cheat a bit while making a documentary—in order to reproduce an incident that was not filmed when it happened in real life—and made no apologies for doing so. Similarly, James Hawes restaged Lawrence's fatal motorcycle crash for his documentary *Lawrence of Arabia: The Battle for the Arab World.*

Lean and Bolt participated onscreen in the sequence in *Lost and Found* depicting the celebration that followed the recovery of this hallowed relic of Captain Cook's adventures. The documentary ends with Lean saying to Bolt, "Come on, we've got a film to make."

Lost and Found was shot in sixteen millimeter in the summer of 1978. (Lean had chided Pauline Kael that the critics would not be satisfied until he had been reduced to making a sixteen-millimeter movie; he had, in fact, done just that!) *Variety* reviewed the forty-minute film when it was eventually shown on New Zealand television in May 1979. The critic expected a more polished piece of work from an eminent filmmaker like David Lean. The documentry, he wrote, "lacks magic and shows no sign that it is the work of a major cinematic talent."[117] For his part, Lean felt that the film had turned out all right, considering that it was shot off-the-cuff and on a shoestring. It was shown at the London Film Festival in 1980 and in other distinguished venues since, including a screening at the Cinémath que Français in Paris in 2004.

That "we've got a film to make" was, of course, easier said than done. After the defection of Warner Bros. from the *Bounty* project, the Italian producer Dino De Laurentiis, a former partner of Carlo Ponti's, had stepped into the breach. De Laurentiis, like Sam Spiegel, maintained his own independent production company, which had produced pictures like the spy thriller *Three Days of the Condor* (Sydney Pollack, 1975). By early 1978, De Laurentiis reached an agreement with Lean whereby he would produce the two *Bounty* pictures and obtain studio backing for them, with an estimated $25 million budget for each picture. De Laurentiis would himself act as executive producer for the two movies.

De Laurentiis turned out to be a domineering movie mogul, a driven man whose wheels were always spinning. "Spiegel was bad," Lean commented later, "but I have to say that Dino was worse." De Laurentiis, said Lean, would "piss in your pocket and tell you it was raining."[118] By September 1978, it was painfully evident that he had overextended himself. He was in financial straits because of huge budget overruns on his production of *Hurricane* (Jan Troell, 1979), a spectacle set in the tropics. He confessed to Lean that he could no longer be personally involved in the *Bounty* project and had been unable to interest a major studio in funding it. Besides, he declared ruefully, he already knew that the draft of the first script was overlength because he could hardly lift it!

De Laurentiis then reminded Lean that he had been loaning him seed money for several months for script development, an expenditure that he could ill afford. Now that he was withdrawing from the project, he maintained that, according to their contract, Lean must reimburse him in full. Failure to do so meant that the scripts would automatically become De Laurentiis's property.

There followed a great deal of financial and contractual wrangling about the reimbursement clause. Lean had not worried about it when he signed the contract because he assumed it a safe bet that De Laurentiis was going to produce the two *Bounty* films. But that was no longer the case. Lean attempted to cajole De Laurentiis into reconsidering his demand, contending that there was simply no precedent in the movie industry for a producer who has pulled out of a project being reimbursed for seed money. De Laurentiis responded characteristically that no precedent was necessary—a deal was a deal.

In effect, De Laurentiis was forcing Lean to buy back his own screenplays. As one Hollywood insider put it, "Dino not only pulled the rug out from under David; he tried to sell it back to him!" She added, "Dino and David—a marriage made in hell."[119] Lean realized that, if he wanted to retain the rights to the screenplays, he would have to pay up. So he did. It cost him well over $1 million.

To make matters worse, Lean and Bolt were not making much headway on the second screenplay, *The Long Arm;* they seemed to be at loggerheads much of the time over rewrites. The drudgery of composing two interrelated scripts was beginning to take its toll on Bolt; he was smoking and drinking too much and was overweight. Finally, he suffered a heart attack on April 9, 1979, followed by a massive stroke two days later.

Fred Zinnemann told me that there was a jungle telegraph in Hollywood, by which gossip was circulated. The telegraph spread a rumor that Bolt blamed Lean for driving him too hard and causing his physical breakdown. Bolt's friends, including Zinnemann, testified that they never heard him say anything of the kind during his convalescence. Nevertheless, Bolt made no effort to scotch the rumors, and Lean was hurt when the gossip persisted. As a result, Lean and Bolt gradually drifted apart.[120]

With Bolt benched indefinitely, Lean continued to work on the script solo throughout the summer of 1979, even though he had failed to find a producer willing to take on the project. He finally became reconciled to the fact that he would have to conflate the two screenplays into one.

Out of sheer desperation, Lean turned to the only producer he thought capable of saving his project: Sam Spiegel, his former "sparring partner." Lean flew to New York for a conference with Spiegel in June 1979. Spiegel agreed to endeavor to make a deal with a major studio to finance Lean's *Bounty*, with the understanding that Lean would condense the two scripts into one, to make a film about the same length as *Lawrence*. Lean accomplished this task and delivered the condensed screenplay to Spiegel in December 1979.

But their story conferences inevitably degenerated into a tug-of-war, as in the past. Spiegel contended that Fletcher Christian was a villain, while Lean saw him as a nautical version of Lawrence—an idealistic but rash individual. "There were terrible quarrels over the script." Spiegel reprised his old tactic of pretending to have a heart attack whenever Lean disagreed vehemently with him, but Lean was no longer taken in by such melodramatics. Spiegel finally threw up his hands and bellowed, "It's too late to bring me in on this. You always bring me in as an afterthought!"[121] Spiegel pulled out of the project, and Lean was left once again without a producer. Lean and Spiegel never crossed paths (or swords) again.

The colossal failure of Michael Cimino's supersized western *Heaven's Gate* (1980) had bankrupted United Artists, and producers shied away from making historical spectacles for some time to come. After a yearlong odyssey of slamming doors and "Don't call us, we'll call you," Lean at long last gave up hope of ever making his *Bounty* film.

In November 1981, De Laurentiis finally brokered a deal with Orion Pictures, an independent distributor, to make a movie entitled *The Bounty* for $25 million, the projected budget for each of Lean's two *Bounty* movies.

The screenplay was actually an abridgement of the first Lean-Bolt script, *The Lawbreakers*, which climaxes with the mutiny. Lean declined to consider making the picture because De Laurentiis absolutely refused to grant him full artistic control. Though Lean had collaborated on the screenplay, Bolt received sole screen credit. But then Lean had really not insisted on a shared screen credit for any screenplay that he had worked on since *Summertime*.

The Bounty was directed by Roger Donaldson, an Australian filmmaker who would go on to become a major director but who at this point in his career was still inexperienced in handling a complex production of this sort. The picture, by the way, was edited by Tony Lawson, who had been one of Lean's assistant editors on *Ryan's Daughter*. Mel Gibson was featured as Fletcher Christian and Anthony Hopkins as Captain Bligh.

The *Bounty* was released in 1984 to mixed reviews and tanked. The critics found the story misshapen, probably because De Laurentiis had commissioned Bolt to considerably abridge the screenplay of *The Lawbreakers*—on which it was based—from three hours to two.[122] The critical consensus was that *The Bounty* was only a passable action film, lacking the scope or emotional surge of an epic tale. The British critic Nick Roddick said it all when he deemed the picture "a long voyage to nowhere."[123] Seeing the film today, one is inclined to agree.

Some reviewers mistakenly assumed that Donaldson's movie was derived from Lean's condensed version of the two scripts. Lean, for his part, was disappointed that his condensation was never filmed. He thought it "the best script I ever had." He looked back on the whole *Bounty* episode as the worst experience of his career.[124]

Notified by his accountant that he no longer needed to live abroad, Lean, accompanied by Sandy, left Tahiti for London in July 1981, moving temporarily into a suite at the Berkeley Hotel. "I just thought it was time to come home," Lean observed.[125] Lean having divorced his fourth wife, Leila, in 1978, the couple were at long last free to make wedding plans. They tied the knot on October 28, 1981. It proved to be the longest relationship Lean ever had with a woman, nearly two decades (beginning in 1966).

After their marriage, Lean purchased a derelict warehouse on the Thames in the gentrified section of the Limehouse district in East London (most of East London is a slum). He and Sandy converted it into the first permanent residence in London in which he had lived. For the first time in a quarter century, David Lean was not living out of a suitcase.

Having given up the ghost on the *Bounty* project, Lean began searching for another property. As luck would have it, the producer John Brabourne phoned him, asking whether he would consider filming E. M. Forster's 1924 novel *A Passage to India*. Lean had, in fact, endeavored to obtain the screen rights to the novel from Forster himself as early as 1960, without success. But Brabourne had managed to purchase the rights from the late novelist's estate. The story is set during the period when India was still under British rule. It deals with cultural conflicts between East and West: a headstrong young Englishwoman goes to India to visit her fiancé, a British officer, and eventually precipitates an international scandal. Lean hoped to fashion Forster's classic novel into a colorful historical epic.

It is ironic that Lean divorced his Indian wife, Leila, before setting out to make a film in India. But Sandy, his present wife, was born in India, though she was of English descent. So it was that Lean returned to India with Sandy, not Leila, to make his first feature film in more than a decade. So many of his projects had foundered that he had joined the ranks of such hard-luck masters as Orson Welles. Indeed, he was becoming as famous for the movies he had not made as for those he had. Now the man that some predicted would never make another picture was going to make a megamovie in India.

Chapter Sixteen

DARKNESS AT NOON

A PASSAGE TO INDIA

The world is a globe of men who are trying to reach one another and can best do so by the help of good will plus intelligence.
> —*Cyril Fielding, a British educator in E. M. Forster's* Passage to India

The coin that buys the truth has not yet been minted.
> —*E. M. Forster*

In his world travels, David Lean developed a predilection for India. He eventually set his sights on adapting for film E. M. Forster's *Passage to India*, a novel that had become an instant classic when it was published in 1924. But he encountered a firm wall of resistance from Forster, who did not consider motion pictures a serious art form.

Edward Morgan Forster, who had written the six novels that constitute his main claim to fame by the age of forty-five, was born in London on January 1, 1879. While he was still an infant, his father died, and he was brought up in a household dominated by women—his mother, his grandmother, and a great-aunt. Forster said that he spent his youth "in a household of elderly ladies."[1] He never confided to the females in his home that he grew up homosexual. His sexual orientation is relevant to the study of *Passage to India* because some critics have found a hint of homosexuality in the book.

Forster attended King's College, Cambridge, from 1897 to 1901, where he had his first full-blown homosexual affair. On graduating, he accepted a position as an instructor in adult education at the Working Men's College in London, and he taught there part-time for two decades. In 1906, he was engaged to tutor a young Indian, Syed Ross Masood, in Latin. They had an intimate relationship, but one that never became sexual.

After publishing *Howard's End,* his most acclaimed novel up to that time, Forster made his first trip to India from the fall of 1912 to the spring of 1913. He of course visited Masood, who had returned to India and become a barrister, in Bankipore, which would serve as the model of Forster's fictional Chandrapore in *Passage.* He began gathering material for *Passage;* in fact, he would partly base Dr. Aziz in the novel on Masood, though Aziz is a physician and Masood was a lawyer. He ultimately dedicated the novel to Masood.[2]

The incident that forms the spine of the novel centers on an Englishwoman who, while visiting her British fiancé in India, accuses an Indian of attacking her during a tour of some caves. Forster very likely found the germ of the attempted assault in an actual incident that occurred in the spring of 1913, just before he left India. A Miss Wildman, an English nurse, charged that she was drugged and robbed while traveling on an Indian railway train. "The documents in the case made their way to the British Viceroy, by which time she had withdrawn the charge."[3] Forster employed a similar but far more serious situation involving an Englishwoman in India to fuel the plot of his book.

During World War I, Forster worked as a volunteer for the Red Cross in Alexandria, Egypt, where he pursued a torrid love affair with Mohammed el Adl, a young trolley car conductor. Forster believed that their liaison implicitly demonstrated how he had "broken through the barriers of class and color"—a theme that permeates *Passage.*[4]

Forster returned home after the war in 1919 and continued writing and teaching. He was shocked to learn of the Amritsar massacre in India on April 13, 1919, when General Reginald Dyer ordered English troops to slaughter an unarmed crowd of peaceful demonstrators. The British killed 379 Indian citizens and wounded over 1,000. The massacre is graphically portrayed in Richard Attenborough's film *Gandhi* (1982).

Tripthi Pilai, a native of India living in Chicago, has told me in conversation that, when Forster made his second visit to India in 1921, he noted the festering resentments between the Indians and the British, which were the result primarily of the Amritsar massacre. He realized that *Passage* was going to have to be a darker novel than he had originally intended. Forster renewed his friendship with Masood while in India and asked Masood to check the trial scenes in his manuscript for the accuracy of the courtroom procedures that he depicted. Forster went back to England with his book still unfinished.

It was around this time that Forster met T. E. Lawrence—whom he described as a short, fair-haired boy—through a mutual friend in London, and they became friends. Lawrence was toiling on *Seven Pillars of Wisdom*. He duly allowed Forster to borrow an early draft of the text in December 1923, and Forster was astonished by it. He wrote Lawrence on February 20, 1924, praising the vigor and largeness of vision of Lawrence's magnum opus: "You will never show your book to anyone who will like it more than I do."[5]

Forster was so taken with Lawrence's book that he was inspired to finish off the final chapters of *Passage* with renewed energy. Soon after, he visited Lawrence, who was nine years his junior, at Clouds Hill. The two formed a platonic relationship, and their friendship continued to prosper over the years. In fact, Forster was preparing to pay another visit to Lawrence at Clouds Hill when he received word of his death.

A Passage to India was published on June 6, 1924, to critical acclamation and huge sales on both sides of the Atlantic. The novel's title comes from Walt Whitman's optimistic "Passage to India," which was published for the first time in the 1872 edition of *Leaves of Grass*. Whitman hailed the building of the Suez Canal because it made possible a new trade route to India. He thus saw the canal as a symbol of the unity between peoples that would, he believed, characterize the modern world:

I see . . . the Suez Canal initiated, open'd.
. . . .
Nature and Man shall be disjoin'd and diffused no more.
. . . .
Year of the marriage of continents, climates and oceans![6]

To be specific, Whitman believed that advanced methods of travel were making the world shrink. Hence, he was convinced that, in the modern age, it would be easier to unify all the nations of the earth into a single global family. Forster's novel is obviously an ironic comment on Whitman's poem because the book implies that the unification of mankind is a goal that will not be easily attained.

Forster's novel is set during the era of the British Raj (or rule) of India. Mrs. Moore, an elderly British matron, accompanies Adela Quested, the young woman who plans to marry Mrs. Moore's son Ronny, on a trip to India, where Ronny serves as a British magistrate in Chandrapore. During their sojourn in India, the pair become acquainted with Cyril Fielding, the principal of the local government school. Forster modeled Fielding on himself; like Fielding, Forster was a British teacher who tried to relate to the people of India when he was there. Fielding introduces Adela Quested and Mrs. Moore to Dr. Aziz. Aziz invites the two Englishwomen on a tour of the famous Marabar Caves. The situation turns tragic when Adela hysterically accuses the young doctor of attempting to assault her in the dark recesses of one of the caves. The sensational trial of Aziz so galvanizes India against Englishmen that, regardless of the verdict, Anglo-Indian relations have been severely damaged for some time to come.

In the course of the novel, Fielding and Aziz endeavor to reach a common ground of understanding between themselves, but their efforts meet with little success. The breakdown of communication between nations, Forster suggests, begins and ends with the lack of communication among individuals. The novel reflects Forster's pervasive theme, which he expressed succinctly in the epigraph to *Howard's End:* "Only connect."[7] In *Passage,* Forster suggests that the separate worlds of East and West must continue to strive to connect. East is East, and West is West—and *maybe* the twain shall meet.

At the beginning of the novel Dr. Aziz discusses with his comrades "whether or not it is possible to be friends with an Englishman."[8] At the end, writes Norman Page, Fielding and Aziz "recognize that the time for real friendship between races has not yet come."[9] They are riding horseback, and they take off in opposite directions.

Charu Malik suggests that the friendship between Aziz and Fielding has a "homoerotic" tinge. She points to the disapproval of the British colony for their relationship as evidence for her assertion.[10] On the contrary, the rejection of Fielding's affiliation with Aziz by the colonials reflects the judgment of the English community on any personal relationship between the races. The British, after all, maintain that they are superior to the Indians.

Still, Malik contends that the camaraderie of Fielding and Aziz is grounded in "homoerotic desires" because Forster himself was party to homosexual relationships.[11] She seems to be drifting into overinterpretation of the novel by invoking Forster's personal life to prove her point—never a sound path for a critic to follow.

In his authoritative biography, F. N. Furbank maintains that Forster did not intend the Aziz-Fielding friendship to be homosexual in character. Furbank, who had access to all Forster's private papers at Cambridge, states that the relationship is modeled on that of Forster and Masood. In fact, Furbank found ample evidence in Forster's correspondence with Masood to demonstrate that their relationship "was never fulfilled physically."[12] So Lean, strictly following Forster in this matter, does not indicate any homosexual attraction between Aziz and Fielding.

Passage answers the question posed at the outset of the novel, about the possibility of friendship between an Englishman and an Indian, in the negative. "Why can't we be friends now?" Fielding asks Aziz in a last effort to rekindle their relationship.[13] This question, Forster later commented, is "ill-suited to Chandrapore," so long as the British Raj holds sway in India.[14] The two friends are not able to "connect," so they regretfully part, never to see each other again.

If Forster desired to write a novel about a homosexual liaison, he could do so without beating around the bush. Such a novel is *Maurice,* in which a middle-class Englishman becomes sexually involved with a working-class lad (a relationship that in some ways parallels Forster's own liaison with an Egyptian trolley car conductor). For the record, Forster arranged to have *Maurice* published posthumously since there was no possibility of its being published when he finished it in 1914. Had he done so, he and his publisher would have wound up in the police court, homosexuality being a taboo subject for literature in England at the time.

In 1956, the Indian writer Santha Rama Rau approached Forster for permission to adapt *Passage* for the London stage. Forster, who esteemed the theater, if not the cinema, granted her the stage rights to the novel. The play, which is built around the courtroom scene, premiered at the Comedy Theater in London on April 20, 1960, with Zia Mohyeddin as Aziz. The drama garnered respectable notices, and Forster was likewise pleased with the production. The play opened at the Ambassador Theater on Broadway on January 31, 1961.

After seeing the play in London, Lean was so impressed that he petitioned Forster for the movie rights. Forster responded that he would not authorize any film version of his book. The movie producer John Brabourne had likewise contacted Forster around this time regarding the screen rights of the book, and he received a polite but firm handwritten reply, refusing to consider the idea. Forster, it seems, nurtured an abiding distrust of high-powered movie producers and had no intention of "selling a work of art to barbarians."[15]

"A whole lot of movie makers wanted to film *Passage,* but Forster wouldn't let it be filmed," Lean says in a television interview he gave at the time of the film's London premiere. Forster wanted a filmmaker to be true to the spirit of the book, Lean continues, "and he didn't trust any director to do that."[16] In fact, Forster suspected that, even if he found someone conscientious, control would be wrested away from the director by studio executives of lesser integrity.

Brabourne and his partner, Richard Goodwin, had coproduced Franco Zeffirelli's *Romeo and Juliet* in association with Anthony Havelock-Allan. The producing team had also brought *Murder on the Orient Express* (Sidney Lumet, 1974) and other Agatha Christie novels to the screen. Forster had bequeathed the rights to his literary works to King's College, Cambridge, his alma mater, and it is there that Brabourne went to solicit the film rights to *Passage*.

John Brabourne was actually Lord Brabourne; his father had been the viceroy of India, and he was married to the daughter of Lord Mountbatten, who had been the last viceroy and, as we know, supported the Lean-Coward film *In Which We Serve*. Brabourne went to see Bernard Williams, the master of King's College, Forster's literary executor, in the spring of 1981. Williams was impressed by Brabourne's aristocratic breeding and distinguished credentials. "He was a great movie fan," adds Brabourne. "He agreed to let us make a film based on Forster's work."[17]

Brabourne and Goodwin figured that, with several period pictures to his credit, David Lean was the director most likely to make a successful film of the novel. "He had already heard on the grapevine that I'd got the rights," said Brabourne. Lean had also admitted that he had wanted to make the movie ever since he had seen the play.[18]

Lean in due course met with the Cambridge dons at King's College, in order to reassure them about his intention to make a film worthy of the book. He notes, "I pointed out to these erudite gentlemen that I'd like to make a film that is true to the spirit of the novel." Nevertheless, he stated, it would be necessary for him to make cuts in the text: "It's a huge book." He emphasized: "I'm to make a *motion picture* of the novel. It will have to differ from the book, because books differ from films." Those who prefer to read the book do not have to see the movie, he continued. "Moreover, I can't damage the book; if my movie fails, it will quickly be forgotten." The book was here before the movie, he concluded, "and it will still be here when the film is gone."[19]

A Passage to India (1984)

Lean approached his adaptation of Forster the same way he approached his film adaptations of Dickens. He went through his copy of the novel, picking out those episodes that were indispensable and passing over those that did not advance the plot.

Meanwhile, Brabourne and Goodwin made a foray to Hollywood to raise financing for the film. They met their living expenses by surviving as long as they could on their credit cards. As they made the rounds of the studios, they were met largely with indifference to the project. The pair frankly reported to Lean that the young turks who had replaced the old guard, like Harry Cohn at Columbia and Robert O'Brien at MGM, were wary of entrusting an aging director, who admittedly had not made a picture in several years, with a substantial budget for a costume drama. It did not seem to matter to them that Lean's films had grossed millions of dollars over the years.

"In Hollywood, a director is as good as his last picture," John Schlesinger told me, "and David's last picture, *Ryan's Daughter,* was a failure." Moreover, the studio chiefs, whom Schlesinger called "the kids with the beards," were convinced that the vogue of the big-movie spectacle had passed. Lean, they informed Brabourne and Goodwin, had once been King of the Road (roadshow picture)—but not for some years. As Lean recalled, "Everybody said, 'This is a good art house film,'" meaning that it would not appeal to the mass audience. "So they turned it down."[20]

Lean observed with disdain that the movie executives were "money-obsessed." He remembered: "One studio chief said that he'd do it if we put in an explicit rape scene. That would ruin the story, of course," the point at issue being whether the alleged assault actually took place. Still another mogul sent Lean a memo stating flatly, "Our audiences are young people; young people are bored by old people. Cut the old dame." He meant Mrs. Moore. As a matter of fact, Peggy Ashcroft would win an Academy Award for playing "the old dame." This same executive suggested, "Adela, rather than the elderly Mrs. Moore, could encounter the handsome Dr. Aziz in the moonlight at the mosque."[21]

Lean heard through the movie industry's jungle telegraph that the Hollywood rumormongers talked "a lot of cock" about him, gossiping about his tendency to fall way behind schedule on location while waiting for "the right cloud configuration."[22] Lean had occasionally heard some of this gossip firsthand. Robert Mitchum, for one, had perpetuated tales about Lean's excessive perfectionism on *Ryan's Daughter.*

Some years after the release of that film, Lean was having lunch in a posh restaurant while Mitchum, who was in his cups, was regaling some friends at another table with anecdotes about Lean. Mitchum recounted how Lean kept everyone waiting endlessly for "the perfect cloud formation" before he would shoot a scene. "Rubbish," Lean muttered to himself. Mitchum was blithely unaware of Lean's presence. Lean kept mum until Mitchum and his party rose to leave, at which point he said, "Hello, Bob; made any good movies lately?" Mitchum was abashed; he waved at Lean nervously and hurried out. As a matter of fact, Mitchum had just starred in Michael Winner's thriller *The Big Sleep* (1978), along with Sarah Miles and John Mills, two of his costars in *Ryan's Daughter.* The critics had savaged the picture, terming it "the big snooze" and dismissing it as "private-eye wash." So Lean's "greeting" was really quite waspish.[23]

Lean continued mapping out a detailed outline of the *Passage* scenario while Brabourne and Goodwin soldiered on, looking for backers. Whenever he was tempted to think that the picture would be stalled indefinitely, he would say to himself, "To hell with this! They'll find the money somehow."[24] Somehow they did.

In the end, *Passage* was funded for $17.5 million by three principal investors. Columbia Pictures bought the American distribution rights to the movie. Columbia had recently entered into a partnership with Home Box Office (HBO), the cable television network; HBO bought the television rights. And Thorn-EMI, an English conglomerate active in film production, bought the British distribution rights. "The money," said Lean, "was on the table."[25] Curiously, the New York Film Critics Circle would later vote *A Passage to India* the best foreign film of the year—when, in fact, the picture was a Hollywood film, backed principally by two American production companies, one of which released it throughout the United States.

Verity Lambert, a Thorn-EMI executive, who was aware of Lean's reputation for extravagance, warned him in no uncertain terms not to go over budget. Lean flippantly told her to "stop squawking"; he explained that he had no intention of making *Passage* an expensive historical spectacle on the grand scale of *Lawrence*. Brabourne suggested that Lean make a promise in writing that would reassure Lambert and the other investors to this effect. Lean did so, committing himself not to surreptitiously add "an elephant charge" to the script or anything else that would significantly inflate the budget.[26]

Forster had stipulated in his will that, should his literary executor permit a film version of *Passage*, Santha Rama Rau, who had done the stage play, should write the screenplay. She accordingly submitted a draft of the screenplay to Brabourne, who, in turn, passed it on to Lean. Initially, Lean had hoped to make some use of her version of the script, but, ultimately, he found that much of it was simply unworkable. As he explained to Brabourne, it stuck too close to her play, with most of the scenes taking place indoors, in offices. But Lean wanted to make *Passage* an outdoor film as much as possible, to take advantage of the vast Indian landscapes. With *India* in the title of the film, he reasoned, audiences would expect a picture with some location scenes filmed in India.

Lean finally gave up trying to rework Rau's draft, deciding that it was much too wordy, filled as it was with long-winded dialogue scenes taken from her play. He finally wrote Rau a tactful letter on February 18, 1982, attempting to "let her down easy" by implying that some of her script was a trifle "too literary" and, thus, not quite suited for film.[27] He did not tell her that he had jettisoned her draft; nor did he contact her again for some months.

Lean discussed the whole matter with Brabourne, and the producer encouraged him to have a go at the script himself. Lean did not call on Robert Bolt, with whom he had not been on good terms since the *Bounty* debacle, for help. He was determined to tackle the screenplay alone. What is more, he insisted on receiving sole screen credit for his script, with a view toward possibly snagging an Oscar nomination for his efforts. He explained to Brabourne that he had collaborated on the screenplay for every film he had made but that he had not taken a writer's credit since *Summertime* in 1955: "So why shouldn't I get a credit for this one?"[28]

While writing the script, Lean spent six months at the Maurya Sheraton Hotel in New Delhi, in case he needed advice from the locals about Indian customs and traditions. Then he moved on for another three months to the Dolder Grand Hotel in Zurich, where he finished. Lean typed out the whole screenplay himself with two fingers, using his customary hunt-and-peck system. He believed that typing so slowly gave him a chance to reexamine what he was writing as he went along and make further revisions in the bargain. As Robert Bolt used to say, scripts are not written; they are rewritten.

Lean mailed a copy of the screenplay to Rau in September 1982. She found it very disappointing, further noting that she was not listed as coauthor. Rau was especially dismayed that Lean had departed from Forster at certain points; to her his novel was gospel. She told Lean as much in her letter of September 27, a copy of which she mailed to Brabourne.

Lean refused to reply to her directly, for he did not want to set up a bickering match by mail. He asked Brabourne to serve as a referee. Lean bluntly told Brabourne that Rau fancied herself "keeper of the flame"; that is, she wanted the film to have infinite fidelity to Forster's novel. "She is a complete amateur as far as writing for the screen is concerned," Lean said. He thought this quite evident in her script draft, which was heavy on stage dialogue. Elsewhere he noted, "I want to write a script and make a movie which is true to the book, but which will also appeal to the man in the street."[29]

In the end, Lean did, in fact, crib some material from Rau's draft so that very probably she was as eligible for a shared screen credit for the *Passage* screenplay as Carl Foreman was for a shared credit on *Kwai*. In view of the liberties that Lean had taken with the book, however, Rau ultimately informed Brabourne that she did not wish to be listed as coauthor and let it go at that. She was not inclined to submit the matter to arbitration.[30] Lean did, however, list her play in the screen credits, along with Forster's novel, as a source for the screenplay.

Rau was especially distressed with one scene in Lean's script, which he had admittedly wholly invented. That scene involved Adela bicycling in the country and happening on erotic sculptures depicting ancient fertility rites in the ruins of the Khajuraho temple. Rau dismissed this scene out of hand as vulgar. "The temple was discovered by a couple of men who were tiger shooting," Lean remembered, "and they got into some thickets and realized that there were some erotic statues there. These were all overgrown with vines."[31]

Lean in due course arranged for the production designer John Box to build plaster replicas of the erotic carvings, guided by photographs that Lean himself had taken at the temple site. In the shooting script, Lean directed that the scene should begin with a couple of long shots of the actual temple, as seen through the trees, and then cut to close-ups of the erotic figures created by John Box in the studio. In the script, the temple is guarded by a swarm of aggressive, jabbering monkeys; they charge at Adela, causing her to flee the scene.

In this sequence, Lean wished to depict some sexual stirrings, that is, the awakening of desire in Adela. In the book and in the film, he said, "she's a bit of a 'stick.'" Invoking Noël Coward's old dictum that the director has to know more about a character than is actually portrayed on the screen, Lean explained: "Although we don't show it in the movie, I always imagined that Adela was brought up in a vicarage, very protective and in proper surroundings. Then she leaves England for the first time and goes off to India, and she is fascinated by this exotic country. She begins to realize the sexuality within herself—remember this is the mid-1920s."[32]

"I wanted to have a scene where a rather prudish, very repressed girl becomes aware of her own sexuality," he explained. "And then there was this question of an assault in the cave. I wanted to prepare the way for it being possible."[33] He meant the temple scene to be sexually frightening for Adela, he concluded, given her slowly surfacing sexual desires and the monkeys menacing her. The scene thus foreshadows her romantic interest in Aziz, which likewise frightens her. In short, Lean wanted to show how Adela's dormant sexuality had been aroused by the graphic detail of the primitive erotic art.

Lean provides a pointed reminder of Adela's traumatizing experience at the temple when she must drive to the courthouse through the streets teeming with unruly mobs. One of the demonstrators, "a man in a monkey costume, leaps on the running board of her car, pressing his face menacingly against the window."[34]

Because Lean interpolated this material into the film, Norman Page finds him "apparently distrustful of the unexplained."[35] But Lean did not apologize for clarifying some enigmatic passages in the novel. "I like a fairly strong narrative in a film," he said, "and Forster, I don't think he's as concerned with narrative as a lot of people claim." As a matter of fact, Lean found it frustrating to cope with Forster's plot ambiguities and half-defined characters: "He's got a narrative thread, but sometimes it's awfully hard to find."[36]

Lean sent Alec Guinness a copy of the screenplay for feedback in September 1982. Guinness complimented Lean for clarifying the story line with scenes like that in the temple. He also noticed that Lean's strong visual sense had not deserted him. Guinness told me that British directors who adapted literary works to the screen too often had an overabundance of literary dialogue in their scripts. "David Lean and Carol Reed," he said, "wanted to tell a story visually, rather than to make films that were too talky." That many filmgoers thought the temple scene came from the book was a compliment to Lean, Francis Ford Coppola told me: "The art of adaptation is when you can do something that wasn't in the literary source but is so much like the source that it could have been."

When Forster's book appeared, he was criticized in the British press for harboring anti-English sentiments. The Forster expert Mary Lago attests, though, that Forster's portrayal of the "master race" mentality of most British officials, which made them "unkind and scornful" toward their Indian subjects, was not too far from the truth.[37] Lean, however, believed that Forster was somewhat biased against his countrymen, that he was a bit anti–British Raj, and that that was why Forster came down hard on the English colonials.

Lean sought to redress the balance, in order to be fair to both sides. "[Forster] was queer, and you can imagine how the British disapproved of that," Lean explained. "The dislike was mutual, and I've toned that down a bit."[38]

In the screenplay, Lean comments rather benignly on Harry Turton, the collector (actually the governor—since government officials collected taxes, the governor was known as the collector). As Lean described Turton in the screenplay, though his attitude toward the subject people "may be questioned today, he is one of the administrators who held the Empire together."[39] One wonders why Lean felt the need to defend the manner in which the British treated the Indians when he made no effort in *Lawrence* to defend the way they treated the Arabs. In that film, Lawrence speaks out against British officialdom, which always maintains the upper hand over the Arabs, who are never accepted as equals.

At any rate, some commentators on *Passage*—especially Indian writers and intellectuals—contend that, for most of the British officers in India, the empire's purpose had much more to do with the preservation of British power than with the improvement of India and that Lean soft-pedals that fact in his film. Be that as it may, *Passage* does not "straightforwardly endorse the empire," according to John Hill. The English community remains "brutal and stupid" in the movie, with few exceptions, and "we are invited to share the novel's verbal criticism of the Raj."[40] In fact, Lean rightly implies that white paternalism is really the basis of the English officials' dealings with the subject people—an attitude that Mrs. Moore openly deplores in the British colonials.

Once Lean finished his screenplay in September 1982, he turned in earnest to preproduction. The first order of business was casting. Alec Guinness told me of his having dinner with Lean in London in 1983, when he inquired about what actors Lean had in mind for *Passage*. Lean replied that he wanted Peggy Ashcroft to play Mrs. Moore. Ashcroft had seen Rau's play in London; afterward, she met with Forster, who said to her, "I hope one day you will play Mrs. Moore."[41] Nevertheless, she was inclined to pass up the part when Lean offered it to her. She had just returned from India, where she had spent several months filming *The Jewel in the Crown,* a fifteen-hour miniseries for British television set during the time of the British Raj, and she was worn out.

Ashcroft endeavored to beg off by pleading her advanced age of seventy-six, but Lean countered that he too was seventy-six. Ashcroft had been born in Croydon, Lean's birthplace, only a few months before Lean. "Peggy is a dear friend of mine," Guinness told me, "so I later interceded with her for David, and she finally gave in." It is true that Lean simply would not take no for an answer—because he esteemed Ashcroft as a very accomplished and experienced actress.

When, during the same dinner conversation, Guinness asked Lean who would play Professor Godbole, the Hindu teacher and a Brahmin of the highest caste, he met with one of Lean's proverbial moments of silence. Then Lean replied, "I thought perhaps you would." Guinness told me that he initially thought it absurd casting, that Godbole must be played by a genuine Hindu. Lean reminded Guinness that he had wanted him to play the title role in the film *Gandhi,* which Lean had hoped to make in the early 1960s, and that Guinness had agreed. Guinness himself chimed in that he had enacted the role of Prince Feisal in *Lawrence* with dark makeup and pulled it off. Guinness told me that he was intrigued by the inscrutable guru Godbole, whom he jokingly called "Professor Gobbledigook." He was instinctively drawn to challenging roles that he thought were nearly impossible for him to play. "Don't ask me why."

After thinking things over, Guinness contacted Lean and accepted the role of Godbole—in the event that Lean could not find an Indian to play it. In short, he said that he loved the role, the novel, and Lean's script and wanted to be part of another David Lean enterprise. Lean said that the role was his.

Asked later on by Brabourne and Goodwin why he cast Guinness as a Hindu teacher, Lean answered that Guinness had started his film career with him in *Great Expectations* and had played a total of five roles in his movies up to that point. He and Guinness had, therefore, developed a good working relationship. Furthermore, Lean frankly admitted that he needed to have some old friends around him since he had not made a picture in several years. So he simply must have Guinness in the picture. "I like Alec, and I think he has the most difficult role in this film," Lean explained. "Godbole is part mumbo-jumbo, part highly intelligent. It's a real bag of tricks to contain in one character; it requires a tremendously good character actor to bring it off."[42]

When it came to filling the part of Aziz, the male lead, there was no question in Lean's mind that the actor must be a real Indian. Zia Mohyeddin had created the role of Dr. Aziz on the London stage in Rau's play, and Lean had cast him as Lawrence's guide in *Lawrence*. He considered Mohyeddin for Aziz, but, by 1983, the actor was simply too old. Lean said it broke the actor's heart because he so wanted to be in the film.

On March 15, 1983, while holding casting sessions in a hotel suite in New Delhi, Lean interviewed an Indian actor, Victor Bannerjee, who was popular in Indian films like *The Chess Players* (Satyajit Ray, 1977). When Lean opened the door of his hotel suite, Bannerjee immediately noticed his piercing blue eyes, which were fixed on him—"eyes like the sea on a cold day." (Lean's eyes, we remember, were the first thing that Omar Sharif noticed about him.) At the conclusion of their desultory conversation over lunch, Bannerjee blurted out, "David, am I playing Dr. Aziz?" Lean responded, "Of course, you are." The impetuous Bannerjee then confessed to Lean with much relief that the director was not at all the stern, forbidding person he had been led to expect. "What bloody nonsense," said Lean. "They're always making up stories about me."[43]

Judy Davis (*My Brilliant Career* [Gillian Armstrong, 1979]), the Australian actress chosen to play Adela, and Lean did not initially get along well. "I don't think he trusted me because I was new and young," she explained; "it was a matter of winning his respect."[44] Davis, as we shall see, certainly didn't trust him.

James Fox (*The Servant*), who had built a career by playing upper-crust Englishmen, actually campaigned for the role of Fielding, the sophisticated headmaster of the local school. Lean had his eye on Peter O'Toole for the part. "But it didn't work out," Fox remembers. Having spent several months wilting in the desert heat with Lean while making *Lawrence,* O'Toole found the prospect of spending several months sweating out a summer in India too daunting. "I was hanging on his door almost, because I'd read the book," Fox says. "I managed to get David at the right moment."[45] Lean would later recruit his own wife, Sandy Hotz Lean, to play Fielding's wife, Stella, who appears late in the picture.

While putting together a production crew, Brabourne and Goodwin contacted John Box to act as production designer. Box replied that his bitter breakup with Lean over the *Bounty* project precluded his returning to the fold. The producers informed Box that Lean was prepared to let bygones be bygones, in the same fashion that he had buried the hatchet with Freddie Young years before.

Box accordingly wrote Lean a conciliatory letter: "I ask for your forgiveness for my wretched behavior in Bora Bora, and after." (Recall that Box had gossiped about Lean back in Hollywood.) When Lean invited Box to come to India in June 1982, his friends told him that he was mad to have someone who had betrayed him before. Lean replied that he was willing to forgive and forget because Box was very capable: "We'd better have him again."[46] With that, John Box was reinstated among Lean's dedicated maniacs.

Freddie Young, another of the dedicated maniacs, was now over eighty; understandably, he was not amenable to a long shoot in the rugged Indian subcontinent. Ernest Day, who had been Young's camera operator on Lean's last three pictures, became director of photography on *Passage*. Years before, Lean had promoted Guy Green, Ronald Neame's camera operator on Lean's early British films, to cinematographer on *Great Expectations* when Neame moved on to become a producer. After *Ryan's Daughter,* Day had been lighting cameraman on the Peter Sellers vehicle *Revenge of the Pink Panther* (Blake Edwards, 1978) and some other films.

Day was finishing a picture in Hollywood when he got a phone call from London, offering him the post of director of photography on *Passage*. "An invitation to photograph a film for David Lean is, in my opinion, the highest accolade a cinematographer could receive," says Day.[47] Since Day was Young's former assistant, Lean had great expectations for him (too great, as things turned out).

The sound technician John Mitchell had known Lean during their early days in the film industry at Elstree Studios in 1934, when Lean was an assistant editor and Mitchell was a tyro technician. Now, half a century later, Mitchell was a respected sound designer (sound recordist and sound mixer). He had recently served in that capacity on Roger Donaldson's *The Bounty*, which Lean, we recall, had wanted to make. The supervising sound editor on *Passage* was once again Winston Ryder, who had been with Lean since his days with Korda in the 1950s.

New to Lean's entourage was the costume designer Judy Moorcroft. Eddie Fowlie, of course, was an old hand. Fowlie, the official property master and unofficial general assistant, helped Lean scout locations in India. Lean had to dip into his own pocket to finance a preliminary trip to search out appropriate locations, as there was no allocation in the stringent budget for such an expedition. "I went out on a limb," he said later, "and hoped for the best."[48]

Lean and Fowlie looked for locations in Bangalore, where they came across the derelict palace of a maharaja. Lean reasoned that on its extensive grounds Box could erect a large section of Forster's fictional city of Chandrapore, just as he had built some Moscow streets in Spain for *Dr. Zhivago*. Lean set up his production office in Bangalore in the West End Hotel; there he also allocated space for the wardrobe and production design facilities, and the cast and crew were ensconced in the hotel as well. The West End Hotel, which had been the officers' headquarters under the British Raj, was still clinging to its past glories. It was quintessentially colonial and redolent of period elegance. Consequently, Lean could easily photograph some scenes there.

Box's principal Chandrapore set covered six acres of the palace grounds and included an entire street, complete with a bazaar that looked like the real thing. Now that Box and Lean were reconciled, the crew thought that Box had become too patronizing in dealings with "the great director." Guinness noted that some of the crew snidely referred to Box and Lean as "Arse-lick and Old Lace."[49]

A journalist from the London *Times*, Ian Jack, who visited the elaborate Chandrapore set, criticized Lean's extravagance in building his own "India-within-India."[50] Lean erected the exteriors of the town, instead of using real city streets, for the same reason he had built the exteriors of the village of Kirrary for *Ryan's Daughter*: to avoid the hassle of having to cope with milling crowds of onlookers during shooting. Working on sets allowed for "almost 100% crowd control," Day adds. This was especially important "in a country renowned for inquisitive citizens appearing in thousands," who just get in the way.[51]

Most of the interiors, including the courtroom, would be built at Shepperton Studios back in England. However, as Day explains, "One of the bungalows on the palace grounds would be used for interiors as well." It would be redecorated and furniture rearranged so that the rooms could be used for different interior sets. Day found shooting in the bungalow "like shooting in a real Indian house": "The fact that the furnishings in an Indian house tend to be sparse made it more difficult to conceal lamps within the set." Freddie Young had encountered precisely this problem when employing an actual house for interiors in Seville on *Lawrence*.[52]

For one sequence, the unit traveled to the town of Ootcamund, which is on a plateau 7,220 feet above sea level; it was a six-hour drive from Bangalore. The town is approached from the plain below by a mountain railway, which has fifteen miles of steep track through stunning scenery. Brabourne and Goodwin obtained the use of this ancient train, with its steam engine and wooden carriages, for the journey of Aziz and the two English-women to the Marabar Caves. En route, Victor Bannerjee executed his own stunt work—hanging on to the outside of the train, hollering exuberantly, "I am Douglas Fairbanks!" as the train went chuffing and hooting over a gorge.

Lean had envisioned Forster's fictional Marabar Caves as located in the side of a cliff at Savandurga, about an hour out of Bangalore. It was there that Fowlie found the granite cliff face that Lean wanted. It was "a prehistoric outcrop of rock," striped with varied colors in the granite rock, "rising upward out of the flat plain," according to the sound man John Mitchell.[53] But there were no caves in the area; the interiors of the caves were to be shot on sets at Shepperton Studios back in England. So on the location site Lean needed to construct only entrances that appeared to lead to the inner caves. That led Pauline Kael to state later on, "Lean has an appetite for grandeur. That explains why, the caves in India not being imposing enough, he dynamited and made his own."[54]

When rumors spread throughout India that Lean was blasting gaping holes in the venerable cliffs at Savandurga, there was a public outcry in the press. The Archaeological Heritage Society in New Delhi accused him of desecrating a cliff that had been untouched by nature for centuries. Lean says that he had the producers respond by explaining that the film unit had employed skilled Indian craftsmen only to drill holes in the face of the solid rock cliffs to serve as the entrances to the caves. They did not desecrate the Indian landscape with dynamite explosions, in order to create all-new caves.[55]

The movie's final sequence was filmed in Kashmir in the north of India, high in the Himalayas. "Dr. Aziz's office was built overlooking the wooden bridge of Fateh Kadez, spanning the Jhelum River at Srinagar in Kashmir," Day reports. "It was an extremely picturesque location."[56]

It is customary in the Indian film industry to have the cast and crew participate in a traditional religious ceremony called Mahurat at the start of production. Now that all the sets were built and the locations ready, the producers obtained a high-caste Brahmin, very much like Godbole, to preside over the service with the full unit present. It was held in front of the maharaja's palace. Lean dutifully donned a golden turban while the Brahmin solemnly blessed the production and prayed over the director for what seemed an eternity. Still, Lean was totally cooperative, realizing that participating in the interminable ceremony represented a gracious gesture of goodwill.

Principal photography commenced officially on December 13, 1983, in Bangalore on the sprawling grounds of the maharaja's palace. Because HBO-TV was providing a substantial amount of the up-front funding, Lean was compelled to abandon the wide-screen format and shoot the picture in a ratio that would easily be reduced for the TV screen. Hence, while composing each shot, he and Day had to keep in mind how it would look both on the big theater screen and on the small television screen. Day was employing a Panaflex camera. "We marked the glass of the Panaflex lens with two vertical side lines to indicate TV cut-off," says Day. This would ensure that the frame composition would include every significant detail of the shot for the television screen. "Sometimes there were moments of indecision about what to include in the composition, to keep both theater and TV audiences happy."[57]

Lean and Day agreed that the film should have the heat-soaked, stifling atmosphere that characterizes high summer in India. This mood symbolized how the action heats up as the lurid events of the plot unfold. As a result, Lean was prepared to wait, on a hazy day, until the sun came out and scorched the land below. But, once the sun appeared, says Day, Lean made up for lost time by shooting at a brisk pace. Furthermore: "Because of his experience as an editor, he is able to shoot only what is really needed; and so filming proceeds like clockwork."[58]

Lean found that he felt rather rusty on the first few days of shooting. "I was like an engine that needed running again," he remarked. "But my producers were very good to me; they let me kick off with some simple shots."[59] The first scene to be filmed on the first day of shooting has Adela Quested and Mrs. Moore visiting Ronny Heaslop (Nigel Havers), the city magistrate, in his bungalow. Ronny also happens to be Mrs. Moore's son by her first marriage as well as Adela's fiancé. Lean arrived on the set at precisely 8:30 A.M. and rehearsed the scene with Peggy Ashcroft, Judy Davis, and Havers. He had an incredible eye for detail, according to John Mitchell; he took more time arranging the silverware and dishes on the dining room table than rehearsing the actors. Mitchell suspected that Lean preferred that part of his job to working with the actors.[60]

When Ernest Day was satisfied with the lighting, Lean called for his first take on a film set in more than a decade. No one responded. It had been so long since Lean had been on a movie set that, on this momentous occasion, he forgot to call "Action"! Flustered, he said, "Oh—begin." At the end of the first take, Lean did remember to say "Cut." Then he added, "I don't think we can do better than that—print it!"[61] Having heard of Lean's reputation for doing innumerable takes, the cast and crew were nonplussed. But Lean knew he had what he needed to edit the scene, so he moved on.

Always a demanding director, Lean had become more cantankerous with age. "David committed the crime of getting old," Day noted stoically. Pressure is harder to bear as one ages, and Lean was under a good deal of pressure. Nevertheless, he did not think that, on this picture, his disagreements with cast and crew—which were manifold—had anything to do with age. After all, he had quarreled vociferously with cast and crew as far back as *Kwai* in 1957: "Shooting *Passage,* I didn't feel I was getting old; I didn't feel more tired than I used to."[62] And, after the first few days, he did not even feel rusty anymore; once he commenced shooting, he was as energetic as he had ever been. Columbia had a representative with the film unit on location, which had also been the case on Lean's earlier Columbia pictures. Progress reports were regularly dispatched to the studio in Hollywood. But, this time around, Lean resented being checked up on by the front office more than he had in the past, and it made him testy to receive admonitions to stay on schedule.

"The mood on the set was very tense," said Day. "David had changed a lot. He had terrible budget problems and was forced into compromises." One such compromise was having to relinquish the wide-screen format. "He thought everyone was against him."[63] When the shooting of a particular scene was slow going, Lean more and more took his frustration out on Day and his camera crew, all of whom were experienced professionals. In addition, when viewing rushes, he tended to complain that Day's cinematography was not up to the standard he had come to expect from Freddie Young.

Yet the coproducer Richard Goodwin and the camera operator Roy Ford, as well as Day himself, consistently judged the rushes to be quite acceptable. When they disagreed with Lean, he was nettled. According to one of the camera crew, who spoke on condition of anonymity, "Lean was looking for yes-men who would always agree with him; and we didn't." Despite the rancor that inevitably characterized the relationship between Lean and Day, they developed an uneasy truce and continued to collaborate satisfactorily.

Lean afterward claimed that he rescued Day's mediocre cinematography by the way he carefully refined the footage in the editing room. He said he had to adjust the color balance in some scenes by tweaking the tones and shadows. But, as the technician just cited maintained, "You can do a million things in the editing room, but you can't do what you don't have on film." Pace David Lean, Day's atmospheric lighting was a hallmark of the movie's technical excellence. Every dog has his day, and Ernest Day had his when he received an Academy Award nomination for photographing *Passage*.

John Mitchell concedes that, during shooting, Lean was very cranky at times: "There were moments of tension when he became exasperated by things not being ready on time or by a query which so often prompted him to comment impatiently, 'It's in the script; read the script!'" His disciplined shooting script was "a masterpiece of information, giving precise details of requirements for camera, sound, wardrobe, props, or any other facet of the film."[64]

Mitchell points to an early scene in which the collector, Harry Turton, and his wife are driven through the marketplace. Lean interrupted the first rehearsal of the scene to call for the wardrobe mistress, Rosemary Burrows. He inquired why Mrs. Turton was not wearing a silk scarf. The bemused costumer was at a loss for words. "Why don't you read the script?" Lean asked pointedly. "There it says, 'The car passes, disclosing a glimpse of Mrs. Turton's flying scarf fluttering in the breeze behind her.'"[65] After a slight delay, Burrows duly reappeared with a gossamer scarf that would flutter properly in the breeze. Comments Mitchell: "Some people find these precise instructions and requirements excessive. I love them, for they are the result of much deliberation during the script-writing process."[66]

As sound technician on the picture, Mitchell was deputized by Lean to hire an Indian band to play at the collector's garden party, to be filmed on the palace grounds at Bangalore. Mitchell imported a military band from nearby Mysore that had once been the palace band of the maharaja on whose estate Lean was filming. Mitchell notes wryly that their attempting to play unfamiliar Western popular tunes like "Tea for Two" was "just discordant enough to be credible." They played at the garden party decked out in re-splendent green uniforms, topped off by splendid red headgear. Kael writes, "Lean's appetite for grandeur accounts for such memorable images [as the green uniforms and red turbans on] the Indian band mangling Western music in the brilliant sunshine at the whites-only club."[67]

During the production Lean had an uphill battle not only with some of the crew but also with some of the actors. As Mitchell noticed, "Judy Davis and David Lean never built up any kind of affinity." All too often they reached an impasse "with daggers drawn."[68] As we have seen, Julie Christie thought Lean controlling but tried to do his bidding just the same. By contrast, Davis found the experience of working with such a paternalistic director much more galling. "He made me feel inadequate initially and, I thought, unfairly," said Davis. "He was very nervous about making that film; he hadn't made one for so long." Indeed, at one point Davis reminded Lean of this fact in front of the entire unit, snapping, "You can't fucking direct any more."[69]

Guinness may have had his differences with Lean, but he was appalled at the tactless way Davis spoke to Lean. "I am highly suspicious of Miss Judy Davis," he wrote a friend on February 14, 1984. He considered her "very chippy-on-the-shoulder. . . . But she acts remarkably well."[70] Lean sensed that, because of the megamovies he had made, Davis thought him a commercial hack rather than a serious filmmaker and that that was why she was rude to him. She said that *Kwai* was the only one of his movies that she had seen and that it had virtually an all-male cast. Consequently, she seriously doubted that he could direct women. "Well, every now and again I can, I suppose," Lean replied. He was too civilized to answer her in kind. He suggested that she check out Celia Johnson's performance in *Brief Encounter*, but she never did.[71]

One of Davis's tiffs with Lean occurred when, as Adela, she climbed onto an elephant for the last leg of the journey to the Marabar Caves. She sat in a seat atop the elephant with her legs apart in a relaxed position, and Lean hollered imperiously at her, "Do sit with your legs together. You don't want to look unbecoming!"[72] Lean learned through the grapevine that Davis thought that he talked down to her on that occasion because she was a colonial from Australia, not an English lady, and that did not help their relationship.

On another occasion, Lean decided that a dress that Davis and the costume designer Judy Moorcroft had agreed on was too dowdy and made her change into a more attractive outfit. Davis believed that Forster had written Adela as a rather frumpy spinster, whereas Lean saw her as an elegantly dressed young lady. Whenever she felt that Lean was departing from the book, as in this instance, she would chide him that he should follow the novel because his script was not nearly as good. Lean would respond that they had to stick to his script if they were ever to finish filming.

Asked once about his working relationship with actors, Lean answered, "Actors who have a deep sense of insecurity are difficult." (He certainly thought Davis was insecure, though he did not mention her name here.) "They try to bluff you. One of my biggest jobs is to relieve the pressures on an actor. After a bit they get confident, and they're all right."[73] Davis later cavalierly dismissed Lean's remark when she heard of it. David Lean, she said, would like to be approachable, but "there is a touch of the bully about him."[74]

Lean himself said that he did not get along with Davis until the courtroom sequence, which was shot at Shepperton Studios after the unit returned to Britain. She actually listened to his direction, Lean realized, and she followed his suggestions. So they stopped quarreling. When they finished the trial sequence, Davis even told Lean that she had learned more from him than she thought she would ever learn from any director—an admission he had never hoped to hear from her. Summing up Judy Davis as an actress, Leslie Felperin writes, "Judy Davis never seems to have been afraid of an argument. She butted heads with David Lean on the set of *A Passage to India*, though her performance as the sexually repressed Adela Quested earned her an Oscar nomination."[75] For the record, when word got back to Hollywood that Davis had told off the likes of David Lean on the set more than once, directors were wary of hiring her. So she returned to Australia.

Lean, we recall, had battles royal with Alec Guinness on most of the films they made together, and *Passage* was no exception. "I have a great fondness for David," says Guinness, "but the atmosphere on the *Passage* was overly tense."[76] As we have seen, Ernest Day was of the same opinion.

During one of his disagreements with Lean, Guinness complained acerbically that his Indian makeup made him look like "an old turkey for sale."[77] After this altercation with Guinness, Lean reportedly muttered in the hearing of Judy Davis, "Fuck Alec Guinness."[78] Apparently, word got back to Guinness about Lean's expletive. At any rate, he informed Richard Goodwin that he was fed up with bickering with Lean. As an actor, he had to trust his own instincts, and too often they ran contrary to Lean's. Guinness stated that he was prepared to walk off the picture, provided that Goodwin paid his plane fare back to England. Not surprisingly, Goodwin would not hear of Guinness throwing in the towel. (Guinness had likewise offered to quit *Kwai* under similar circumstances and was turned down that time too.)

Another one of Guinness's squabbles with Lean occurred during a rehearsal for the scene in which Guinness as Professor Godbole shows up at the train station to see off Mrs. Moore, who is too unwell to remain in India any longer. Guinness became irritated when Lean moved him around the set like a pawn. Lean told him at one point to move "two feet to your left." Guinness exclaimed that he hated being "fixed like a specimen" in a laboratory. He wrote his wife, Merula, on February 5, 1984: "It would be nice to give a performance without the director saying every half minute, 'Could you move half an inch to your left? And now could you lean back a fraction?'"[79]

Lean subsequently remarked, "I don't think actors like me very much. I've got to make them measure up to my imagination." That is, he had to get them to envision a scene the way he did. He had trouble getting Guinness to do this, he said. Indeed, he confessed that working with Guinness on the film was an unhappy experience for him: "Alec really rattled me on *Passage*."[80] "The shooting script," O'Connor writes, "came to wield an almost inflexible authority, like the Bible." Some members of the unit, like John Mitchell, "accepted such authority without complaint." Others, like Alec Guinness, would sometimes rebel. Guinness afterward referred to the "deadly" atmosphere on the set.[81]

Be that as it may, there were times when Lean and Guinness were in harmony. One such instance occurred during the station scene, already mentioned. Lean and Guinness agreed that Guinness should play Godbole as "obscure and fatalistic, a character who represents the inscrutability of the East."[82] So, because the guru is a shadowy figure, Godbole is appropriately immersed in shadow as he bids an unspoken farewell to Mrs. Moore. Guinness as Godbole makes a slight reverential bow to Mrs. Moore while pressing his palms together in benediction. He thus wordlessly acknowledges that he believes that they are kindred souls. Guinness's silent gesture was so touching that Lean murmured, "Clever old bugger."[83] After he called "Cut," Lean came from behind the camera to congratulate Guinness for nailing the scene perfectly—a rare compliment coming from the taciturn director. But there was more trouble ahead.

The screenplay called for Guinness to execute an intricate Hindu temple dance during the closing credits of the movie. He was to take tiny steps around the perimeter of a giant cartwheel lying on the ground, clashing finger cymbals together all the while. The cartwheel represented life as a wheel with many spokes. Guinness had carefully rehearsed the dance with the help of a Hindu teacher, and, when he finished filming the dance, the Indian bystanders burst into applause. Nevertheless, the Hindu dance was a bone of contention between Lean and Guinness.

"We did have a dust-up concerning the small dancing scene I had,"

Guinness remembers. "I had rehearsed quite a bit for it, and then David didn't even come around the day I did it; he said he never liked Indian dancing anyway."[84] When Lean did view Guinness's dance on film, it hit the cutting room floor.

Looking back on the episode, Guinness writes in his autobiography, "The fact that my bizarre Hindu dance was cut from *A Passage to India* was probably good judgment on his part, even if it left me presenting Prof. Godbole . . . without the necessary Oriental mystery." He goes on to reflect that, admittedly, "David is a man of genius cocooned with outrageous charm." Nevertheless, he had grown somewhat mistrustful of Lean in his later years, fearing that he depended too much on sycophants. Similarly, the member of the camera crew cited above referred to Lean's predilection for yes-men. Withal, Guinness concludes loyally, "Any skill in front of the camera that is still left me is entirely due to his early guidance."[85]

Victor Bannerjee, who played Aziz, wrangled with Lean at the outset of the shoot when Lean complained that his voice was too English—Bannerjee had attended a school in Calcutta modeled on the English public schools. Bannerjee argued that Lean wanted him to speak like Peter Sellers. He was referring to a picture called *The Millionairess* (Anthony Asquith, 1960), in which Sellers played a bumbling Indian doctor. For the role, Sellers affected a stereotypical singsong Indian accent.

Bannerjee's point was that, as one Indian writer put it, Indians in Hollywood films like *Gunga Din* (George Stevens, 1939) always spoke in an obsequious chi-chi accent to the British colonials, "to please the Western audience." In short, Bannerjee flatly refused "to imitate Peter Sellers imitating an Indian."[86] Lean and Bannerjee locked horns for four days, and Bannerjee's speech preference finally prevailed. He and Lean then shook hands on their agreement.

Peggy Ashcroft summarized Lean's squabbling with cast members this way: "I never had any problem with him myself." But she was convinced that Lean was too impatient, especially with young actors like Victor Bannerjee and Judy Davis. "He was autocratic," she thought. And he "bulldozed Judy" in particular when she had a conception of a scene different from his.[87] "I don't think David liked actors," was the verdict of James Fox, who played Fielding. "He was intolerant of actors in a way; they just served his purposes and his grand design." Yet: "To my mind he was the greatest film director this country has produced."[88]

Lean was reaching the end of the schedule for location shooting in India. He needed an actress to appear as Fielding's wife, Stella, at the end of the picture, and Priscilla John, the casting director, suggested Lean's wife, Sandy. Sandy had some misgivings about doing the part, but Lean reassured her by pointing out that she had no dialogue.

By the time location filming was over in India, Lean had achieved a remarkable sense of place in the film that he had shot so far—a vivid evocation of the Indian landscape and cityscape. The unit moved on to Shepperton Studios to shoot interiors, most especially the trial sequence. Principal photography wrapped in June 1984, bringing to an end a six-month shoot. *Kwai* had been the last picture that Lean had shot on what was for him a short schedule.

As soon as shooting was finished at Shepperton, Lean moved to an editing suite at Pinewood Studios, where he had not worked since filming *Madeleine* three decades before. The pressure was on him once again to complete postproduction in time for the picture to qualify for the Academy Awards, a deadline that he had had to meet on every picture all the way back to *Kwai*.

Lean said that someone had asked him after he finished filming *Passage* what the movie was like. He answered, "I won't know until I see it all put together, with all of the fourteen hundred shots in place. Then I'll get the dramatic flavor of the movie." Shooting a picture is a holy circus, Lean continued, so he much preferred working steadily in the quiet of an editing room, with just a couple of other people around. An actress (Judy Davis) was not around to tell him he was goofy, he added.[89]

Before editing a scene Lean would visualize it in his mind's eye. Then he would endeavor to make the edited scene approximate what he had pictured in his imagination. Some filmmakers give the film editor a list of instructions on how to edit each scene and then disappear into their office. Not David Lean; he always supervised the cutting of each of his films on a daily basis. John Mitchell remembers Lean summoning him to the cutting room one day and inquiring, "Did you record the train whistle as the train came into the station at Ootacamund?" Mitchell consulted his log book and shortly presented Lean with a roll of tape marked FX104, which Lean had been unable to find. Lean took the roll, "ran it on his Moviola, marked off three feet of film, and tore it off between his teeth"—a habit he had formed when he was editing newsreels back in 1930 and sometimes still fell into. He spliced the train whistle into the footage that he was editing, saying, "I knew you would have recorded it."[90]

Eunice Mountjoy, who had been an assistant editor on *Lawrence*, had since become a full-fledged film editor. John Brabourne engaged her to edit *Passage* under Lean's supervision. Lean would sit behind her at the editor's bench and hand her the footage he wanted cut. He would himself mark on the strip of film with a soft Chinagraph grease pencil exactly where he wanted it cut; then she would make the physical cut with the editor's shears. Lean never permitted her to edit a single scene on her own, as he had allowed his previous editors, Norman Savage and Anne Coates, to do.

One day, Lean casually mentioned to Brabourne that he planned to take the editing credit on the movie for himself: "Directed and edited by me!" After Brabourne communicated the bad news to Mountjoy, she confronted Lean. She explained that she would never have taken on the film for an assistant editor's credit, which would be, in effect, a demotion for her. Lean reminded Mountjoy that she had not chosen a single cut on her own; all she had done was follow his instructions.

Lean attempted to mollify her by saying that she had many more years of editing films ahead of her but that *Passage* just might be his last picture. He had always wanted the editing credit on his pictures, he went on, and this might be his last chance to have it. Anyway, he promised to give her what he considered "a jolly nice credit": associate editor, rather than assistant editor. Brabourne thought it was pathetic that Lean, approaching the end of a distinguished career, was greedy for screen credits.[91] Lean had likewise refused to acknowledge Rau with a cowriter's credit on the screenplay. He probably hoped that multiple screen credits would yield him multiple Oscar nominations, which in the end proved to be the case.

The composer Maurice Jarre enjoyed conferring with Lean; he had scored every Lean movie since *Lawrence*. After the collapse of the *Bounty* project, Jarre observed that Lean looked as if "something inside of him had died." But *Passage* seemed to have revitalized him. Lean seemed younger and more dynamic. Jarre said that, as usual, Lean made his task easier for him "by writing into the script where the music should start and stop": "But he was always very demanding."[92]

Jarre had employed appropriate ethnic sounds and instruments in his previous Lean scores. Similarly, his score for *Passage* was inspired by Indian music and included exotic instruments like the sitar and the theremin. The background score itself is rather sparse. Jarre did not think that music always had to be present on the sound track to comment on the action or to create filler, just so that the audience did not get restless.

Jarre recalls discussing Adela's traumatic encounter with the erotic statuary with Lean, who told him, "Don't be afraid about making the score a little romantic. When she's going through that grass, it isn't a girl going on a nice country bicycle ride; there's something in the air that she doesn't know." Jarre continues, "The girl was brought up with Victorian values, very inhibited. So David told me: 'You have to tell the audience what the girl is feeling when she sees the pornographic statues.' David realized that the music must sometimes convey what the images don't say. So I wrote in my notes for this scene: 'The music starts lightly for the bicycle ride, becoming mysterious and sensual in the garden of statues.'" Jarre composed a languid, sultry theme, featuring the ondes martenot, while Adela gazed at the statues. "When the monkeys frightened her, I wrote scary music."[93] Jarre accordingly accompanies the shots of the monkeys driving Adela away from the derelict shrine with heavy percussion and brass on the sound track, to signal her turbulent state of mind.

Still, Jarre's overall musical score of *Passage* is a lot less melodramatic than were his earlier scores for Lean. In general, the themes are built from simple ideas, repeated with slight modification, thereby creating a mosaic of music. Jarre conducted the Royal Philharmonic at the recording sessions, and, once his score was added to the sound track, the picture was finished.

The opening credits are played over a series of Indian murals, accompanied by Jarre's main title music, which starts out with the twanging of a sitar to establish the Indian flavor of the score. Mrs. Moore and Adela Quested travel five thousand miles to Chandrapore to visit Ronny Heaslop. They are soon distressed by the straitlaced, officious manner with which Ronny, the city magistrate, and the other snobbish Brits treat the Indians. Mrs. Moore winces when Ronny refers to the difficulties in governing "this benighted country." Adela is disappointed that she has not had the chance to see the "real India," which she will never find if she stays within the confines of the British compound. The colonials are cocooned in their own insulated world. "My dear, life rarely gives us what we want at the moment we consider appropriate," chides Mr. Moore. "Adventures do occur, but not punctually."

In due course, Adela has an adventure of sorts while she is on a bicycle excursion in the country, as already discussed. She comes on a ruined temple with blatantly erotic statuary. The sexually repressed young woman is deeply disturbed by what she sees. The experience subtly suggests her fear of sexuality.

Mrs. Moore, bored with the British colony, wanders into a moonlit mosque one evening and encounters the winsome Dr. Aziz. He is impressed with the respect that she displays for the mosque, and the eager young man sizes her up as a worldly, wise, compassionate woman. He is also quite taken by the kindness of Richard Fielding, the headmaster of the government school. (Fielding is named Richard, rather than Cyril, as in the novel.) Fielding is the only Englishman to welcome Aziz into his home. "In a symbolic act expressing his trust and desire for brotherhood, Aziz shows the

Darkness at Noon

other man a photograph of his dead wife, declaring, 'You are the first Englishman she has ever come before.'" Aziz believes that "kindness is needed between the races that live together—yet apart—in India" if they are to overcome social and cultural barriers.[94]

In depicting the development of the friendship between Aziz and Fielding, Lean follows Forster in not implying that their relationship is homosexual, as stated earlier. Forster "proves the possibilities and limits of male friendship between colonial unequals in a cross-cultural encounter."[95] One commentator on the film pointed to the scene in which Aziz chats with Fielding while the latter is showering as having homoerotic implications. Aziz sits on Fielding's bed and talks with him while Fielding's naked body is visible in silhouette in the pebbled glass of the shower stall. To suggest that this scene is fraught with homosexual innuendo is really stretching a point. Forster could not create true equality between the races where none exists, but he could examine the possibility of genuine friendship between Fielding and Aziz. And Lean follows suit.

In any event, the impetuous Aziz is so grateful because the two Englishwomen do not treat him with the condescension he has learned to expect from the British that he invites them to make a sightseeing expedition with him to the famed Marabar Caves, accompanied by a tour guide. After they arrive at the cave site, Mrs. Moore, who is overcome by heat and fatigue, has a dizzy spell, leaving Adela and Aziz to proceed on the tour unchaperoned.

Adela is preoccupied with her upcoming marriage to Ronny and asks Aziz about his wife. Then she shows some sexual interest in Aziz by inquiring if he practices polygamy as allowed by Islamic law. Aziz shrugs off her offensive remark and leaves her temporarily, to sit outside and smoke a cigarette. Adela goes off to explore another cave alone.

Adela's questions about marriage indicate that she has begun to be conscious of her budding sexuality. Moreover, she has not been able to shake off the memory of the sexually explicit temple carvings. Lean explains, "She comes on this excursion with Aziz, a young Indian whom she finds very attractive; subconsciously she wants him."[96] All this colors her tormented state of mind when she enters a cave alone; she becomes hysterical in the semidarkness and imagines that Aziz has attempted to rape her. Lean thus develops the notion, Brown writes, that the alleged rape was, in fact, "a figment of a sexually repressed woman's imagination."[97] Adds Levine: "It is not difficult to believe that the meagre Adela could project onto Aziz her need to be found physically attractive and turn her need into a full-blown hallucination."[98]

Forster leaves open the possibility that Adela may in fact have been attacked by the Indian tour guide. When questioned in later years about what really happened to Adela in the cave, he invariably replied, "*I don't know.*"[99] The crucial point for him was that Aziz was innocent. As for what really occurred, readers are free to draw their own conclusions.

For Lean there is no question of Aziz's innocence. He is merely "a red herring"—and second-rate Agatha Christie at that.[100] Lean leaves the film-goer to infer that Adela's fancied rape was most likely the product of her own sexual fantasies, subconsciously stoked by her suppressed attraction to the handsome Aziz.

But what of Mrs. Moore? On entering the cave, she suffers an attack of claustrophobia and is further unsettled by a strange echo that reverberates throughout the tunnel. Lean writes of the echo in the screenplay, "There is the sound of an undulating rumble; the resonance increases in volume: 'Boum!' The resounding echo pours back down the walls."[101] Aziz calls out to Mrs. Moore, but she does not know who is shouting at her and does not reply. She walks unsteadily out of the cave into the sunlight. The Marabar Caves provide the central metaphor of both the novel and the film: individuals call out to each other and receive nothing but an echo in reply, suggesting the failure of human beings to communicate with each other in a meaningful way.

After her baffling experience in the cave, along with the ensuing arrest of Aziz, Mrs. Moore sinks gradually into spiritual apathy and cynicism; she finds Christianity less comforting than ever before. "When she goes to the caves Mrs. Moore's faith is badly shaken," Lean explained. So he has her express her disenchantment this way: "Like most old people, I wonder if we are passing figures in a godless universe." Lean concluded, "That was the best effort I could make at saying that her faith was shaken."[102] Asked whether he agreed with such sentiments, Lean answered, "I don't think, as Mrs. Moore says, that it is a godless universe. But I wouldn't know what God is."[103]

Except for Fielding, who staunchly stands by Aziz during the ordeal of his trial, the British colony closes ranks. When Mrs. Moore is asked to testify on Aziz's behalf, she stoically refuses to appear in court as a witness, explaining, "Nothing I say or do will make the slightest difference." She becomes more distressed and finally books passage home. She "retreats from the social scene and from life itself, so her death on the voyage home seems inevitable."[104]

At the trial, the prosecutor, Police Superintendent McBride, leads Adela back to relive her traumatic experience in the cave. Lean adroitly intercuts her testimony with flashbacks to the cave sequence. For example, Adela says, "I lit a match." Lean recalls, "Then I cut back to her in the cave, lighting a match; Aziz comes looking for her. You see Aziz at the entrance of the cave; he calls her name, but she doesn't respond." When Adela envisions the cave scene in the course of her testimony, she is unable to picture Aziz following her into the cave. She has the gumption to admit her confusion about what happened and to withdraw her charges.

It is worth noting that the trial in the film is remarkably close to the trial in the novel. Though Lean necessarily had to compress Forster's narrative, in general he captures a significant portion of the book in his movie.

The British colonials are livid when Adela recants. In fact, one English matron, Mrs. Callendar, hisses at her in the courtroom, "Bitch!"—a line of dialogue not in the novel, where the collector's wife protests to the judge that Adela's recantation should be disregarded.[105] In any case, the novel and the film both make it clear that Adela has been ostracized by the British community. It goes without saying that her marriage to the haughty and rigid Ronny is out of the question and that she will pack up and go home.

In the chaos following the verdict of innocent, Adela is left aimlessly wandering the streets in the rain. Fielding rescues her and takes her temporarily to his campus quarters. The distraught Aziz views this action as consorting with his enemy and, hence, as the ultimate betrayal by his British friend. He vows never to communicate with Fielding again.

Aziz starts life anew as court physician to a potentate in Srinagar, a town in Kashmir near the snowcapped Himalayas that is outside the jurisdiction of the British Raj. In the epilogue that rounds off the film, Fielding pays a visit to Aziz and introduces him to his wife, Stella, Mrs. Moore's daughter by her second husband. Aziz and Fielding, who championed Aziz's innocence all along, confirm their comradeship.

Indeed, Aziz makes good his promise to Fielding to write Adela back in England, telling her of his meeting with Fielding, who reminded him that Adela had gotten the worst of both worlds—despised by the Indians for accusing Aziz and by the British for withdrawing her charge. He says that he can now acknowledge that it took considerable courage for her to recant. Back home in Hampstead, Adela reads Aziz's letter; it is raining outside, and she stares through the rain-speckled windowpane at the final fade-out. This open-ended accommodation between two adults is true to life and enduringly affecting. The final image recalls the film's opening scene, in which Adela stands on a wet London street and peers through the rain-streaked window of a tourist agent's office, as she prepares to book her passage to India. So the film is bookended by these two similar shots of Adela, as the picture comes full circle.

The rapprochement between Aziz and Fielding that Lean depicts in the epilogue drew strenuous objections from reviewers familiar with the book. In the novel, Forster expresses a deep pessimism about the possibility for Aziz and Fielding to "only connect" (a favorite phrase of Forster's) because they represent different cultures. As Hill notes, "The men are unable to regain their original relationship, and their horses symbolically swerve apart."[106] They both acknowledge that the time of genuine friendship between the races has not yet come.

But, in the movie, Aziz and Fielding are reconciled and embrace warmly, as a sign that they have become friends on an equal footing. Lean was criticized in some quarters for having manufactured a traditional Hollywood-style ending, thereby undermining Forster's. For his part, Lean firmly believed that he could not portray the novel's downbeat ending convincingly on film: "I thought that bit was rather tacked on."[107] Elsewhere, he elaborated on that remark: "I think the end of the novel is a lot of hogwash, as far as the movie is concerned." It was evident to the filmgoer that "these two men liked each other very much," he maintained, and, therefore, their restored friendship was essential in order to meet the audience's expectations. In fact, their mutual gesture of friendship at film's end suggests that understanding between different races and nations must begin with communication between individuals.[108]

When *A Passage to India* had its world premiere in Los Angeles on December 13, 1984, it was celebrated as "a triumphant comeback film, a splendid visual spectacle," Lean's best work since *Lawrence of Arabia*.[109] Pauline Kael and Richard Schickel, who had led the opposition to *Ryan's Daughter*, had decidedly changed their tune. Lean's picture is "an admirable piece of work," wrote Kael in the *New Yorker*, "intelligent and enjoyable."[110] According to Schickel, Forster's novel was "a David Lean film waiting to be made; and now we have it." Schickel concluded: "That Lean has brought this notoriously elusive novel to the screen "with such sureness, elegance, and hypnotic power is akin to a miracle."[111] Once *Passage* had passed muster with Kael and Schickel, Lean felt that he was nearly home free.

David Denby in *New York* magazine hailed the picture as "a rather startling revival of the large-scale Anglo-American prestige epic that many of us had taken for dead." In fact, Lean himself said that he made *Passage* to remind filmgoers of how movies used to be. "The movie is built the old way," Denby went on; "the narrative is solid, the characters pleasingly complex." Best of all, he said, Lean had not lost the knack of making a spectacle that never loses its human focus. "For all its pachyderms and mountains and crowds, *A Passage to India* attends to the hearts of its troubled characters;

and that is something of which even the fanatically private Forster might have approved."[112] Similarly, David Ansen stated in *Newsweek*, "At 76, Lean has not lost his touch." In this slapdash era, he still knows how to put together a competently made, beautifully wrought picture. His polished craftsmanship is a marvel, Ansen concluded; "Relish it."[113]

Several of the notices singled out the superb contingent of actors whom Lean had marshaled for the movie: Peggy Ashcroft is incandescent as the venerable dowager Mrs. Moore. Judy Davis delivers a harrowing performance as the tormented Adela Quested. Victor Bannerjee is compelling as the mercurial Dr. Aziz. James Fox is top-notch as the humane Richard Fielding. And Alec Guinness is excellent as the eccentric Godbole, slyly stealing every scene he is in.

Guinness personally judged his own performance wide of the mark. After he attended an advance screening of the movie, he rang up Peggy Ashcroft in the middle of the night to tell her that his performance was meaningless and irritating—in short, a disaster. Though most of the critics did not agree with him, he did single out J. Hoberman's notice in the *Village Voice* as particularly dismaying. Hoberman wrote that Guinness "gives the juiciest portrayal of an Indian by a European since Peter Sellers" in movies like *The Millionairess,* mentioned above.[114]

Only a few critics questioned the propriety of Guinness playing a character of an Eastern race. One reviewer did snipe at his portrayal of Godbole as "Alec Guinness in blackface."[115] Still, other critics believed that Guinness had brought Forster's "mystical Brahman" convincingly to life. Besides, Guinness's long-standing professional association with Lean as the director's "standby" actor amply explained why Lean cast him.[116]

Lean attended the Los Angeles premiere on December 13 but skipped the New York opening the next day; he had not forgotten how the New York critics had trashed *Ryan's Daughter* as an overinflated period piece. He was, of course, on hand for the royal premiere in London in February 1985, attended by Queen Elizabeth, the Queen Mother, and Prince Charles, the Prince of Wales. The British critics lavishly praised *Passage* as the capstone of Lean's long and distinguished career. The film went on to become an enormous commercial success both in America and in Europe. Some exhibitors initially underestimated its commercial potential in the United States. In Chicago, for example, it was booked into a small art house but soon had to be transferred to a big, mainstream cinema because of the overflow crowds.

Guinness blamed himself, not Lean, for what he considered to be his disappointing performance in the movie. He wrote Lean on December 16, 1984, that he found the movie "expansive, handsome, gripping, and yet somehow intimate." At two hours and forty-three minutes "it did not seem a minute too long."[117] Lean received another congratulatory letter from Peggy Ashcroft. He reflected that he was like William Wyler, in that actors "always use to say about Willie, 'I'll never work with him again.' Until they saw the film."[118]

So the old lion roared back to life with a sublime work and reclaimed his place as the movies' lion king. Lean gave *A Passage to India* enough vigor and rigor to shame younger directors. The picture is patently an attempt to revive old-fashioned pomp, sweep, and grandeur. It shows that large-scale big-budget filmmaking had regained some of its traditional energy and ambition. Lean's editing is immensely stylish and assured, with gorgeous use of color. Then there is the fluid camerawork—the long takes, the gliding camera movements, the complexly layered deep-focus compositions. In brief, the movie has an epic sweep that blends beautifully with the subtle shadings of character. Yet it is gritty and frank in depicting the racial tensions of the era.

The picture received no fewer than eleven Academy Award nominations. Lean himself was personally nominated in three categories, as director, screenwriter, and editor. The other nominations were Judy Davis (actress), Peggy Ashcroft (supporting actress), Maurice Jarre (composer), Ernest Day (cinematographer), John Box (production designer), John Mitchell (sound technician), and Judy Moorcroft (costume designer). Oscars went to Peggy Ashcroft and Maurice Jarre—his third Oscar for a Lean film. As an emblem of the continued popularity of Jarre's music for Lean's films, a DVD was released in 2005, *Lean by Jarre,* which is a filmed record of Jarre's 1992 London concert "A Musical Tribute to Sir David Lean." Clips from the four films that Jarre scored are intercut in the course of the film with the concert footage of Jarre conducting the Royal Philharmonic in a suite from each of the films. The DVD also includes an extended interview with Jarre.

"I was terribly pleased," said Lean, when the film got eleven nominations. "It was terribly encouraging. That gave me a new lease on life."[119] If his own three nominations did not yield him an Oscar, he nevertheless received some other tributes that served to cap his entire career. In October 1983, the British Film Institute bestowed on him a Lifetime Fellowship, in recognition of his achievements as a film artist. He thereby joined a roll of honor that included Orson Welles, Ingmar Bergman, and John Schlesinger. Because he was still in India at the time, the award was accepted from Prince Charles on Lean's behalf by Alec Guinness at London's Guildhall.

The most prestigious award that Lean had yet received came to him on October 30, 1984, when he was knighted by Queen Elizabeth II. An orchestra accompanied his investiture with a medley of themes from his movies. Afterward, he reflected that the ceremony made him think that perhaps he was an artist of sorts after all.

After Lean finished *Passage,* his marriage to his fifth wife, Sandy, began to unravel. When Sandy discovered that Lean had surreptitiously taken up with a London art dealer named Sandra Cooke, she had no qualms about walking out on him. Besides, there was another man waiting in the wings for her. The Leans were divorced on November 12, 1985. Sandra Cooke, who was thirty years Lean's junior, became his sixth wife on December 14, 1990. As his widow, she wrote a biography of him that is based on her extended conversations with him about his career.[120]

Whenever Lean was asked whether, after the phenomenal success of *Passage,* he was going to rest on his laurels and let *Passage* be his last movie, he invariably replied laconically, "I didn't feel that movie would be my last."[121] As a follow-up to *Passage,* he chose yet another classic British novel, Joseph Conrad's *Nostromo,* a complicated tale of a South American revolution. Adapting Conrad's sprawling novel to the screen would prove quite a challenge indeed.

EPILOGUE

THE CRAFTSMAN AS ARTIST

The fabulous is never anything more than the commonplace touched by the hand of genius.

—*Boris Pasternak*

David Lean to my mind is the greatest film director our country has produced.
—*James Fox*

It is somewhat ironic that David Lean set his sights on filming Joseph Conrad's 1904 novel *Nostromo* as his last project since Conrad never thought of motion pictures as a suitable medium for the adaptation of literature. Indeed, he was even more acerbic in his attitude toward movies than E. M. Forster. If Forster said that the movie studios were run by barbarians, Conrad called films "just a silly stunt for silly people."[1] Conrad, who died in 1924, considered most of the silent pictures of his day to be crude and shallow; he believed that the cinema had yet to develop into an art form.

Moreover, he wrote his friend Richard Curle, in a letter dated October 9, 1920, that he thought the whole business of translating a literary work to the screen seemed "as futile and insecure as walking a tightrope—and at bottom much less dignified."[2] Given his condescending attitude toward cinematic adaptations of literature, it is not surprising that Conrad mistrusted any attempt to translate his own work for the screen. Indeed, he sold the screen rights to his novels only when he was desperate for cash.

Despite Conrad's misgivings about film versions of his fiction, however, his work has found its way onto the screen, especially in the years since his death. For example, in 1952, Carol Reed filmed *Outcast of the Islands*, starring Trevor Howard, and Peter O'Toole played the title role in Richard Brooks's *Lord Jim* in 1965.

As a filmmaker gifted with an epic touch, David Lean seemed to be the right director to bring *Nostromo* to the screen. *Nostromo* is "the most panoramic of all great novels, *War and Peace* alone excepted," writes Harlan Kennedy.[3] It is an immense, complex work, one that Conrad himself termed his largest canvas.

Nostromo takes place during a military revolution in the fictitious Latin American republic of Costiguana, a land that has endured fifty years of misrule. The title character, an Italian sailor, is assigned by the supporters of the regime still in power to hide a cargo of silver from the San Tomé mine, to keep it out of the hands of the rebel army. But Nostromo covertly steals the horde in order to enrich himself. Conrad wished to portray the crisis of conscience that someone who has been honest all his life experiences when he succumbs to the temptation of greed. Indeed, in the end Nostromo despises himself and his secret enslavement to the treasure, the ill-gotten plunder he has stolen.

It was none other than Robert Bolt who interested Lean in adapting *Nostromo* for film. "I was the first person who suggested *Nostromo* to him," Bolt remembers. When Lean gave a lecture to the Cambridge University Film Society in 1985, some of the students said, "Why don't you do *Nostromo?*" Bolt concludes, "And he went and bought a copy."[4]

Nostromo

Lean said that he started to read the novel principally because he had "enormous respect for Robert's taste," but he found it a difficult read. Not until his third attempt did he get beyond the first hundred pages. "Round about page 170 it really takes off," said Lean. He went on to explain that the novel portrays how not only Nostromo but a whole host of characters living in Costiguana are corrupted by their lust for the silver. The central image of Conrad's story, then, is the silver of the San Tomé mine, about which the plot turns. Lean added that he considered *Nostromo* to be "very modern, in that it is about greed," for the silver of the mine symbolizes human greed throughout the story.[5]

Because Bolt and Lean had been somewhat estranged since they split over the *Bounty* project, Lean enlisted the playwright-screenwriter Christopher Hampton, who had earlier composed a scenario for a television adaptation of *Nostromo* that had gone unproduced. Lean contacted Hampton in

1986 to collaborate with him on a script for *Nostromo,* and they labored on the screenplay for a full year.

With the first draft of the screenplay completed, Lean asked Steven Spielberg to produce the movie. Lean had first met Spielberg on a transatlantic flight, when Spielberg told him how impressed he was with his work. Spielberg also offered to help Lean with a future project. "As far as I'm concerned," Spielberg declared, "you could direct the yellow pages of the phone book."[6]

Lean in good time made a deal whereby Spielberg would produce *Nostromo* for Warner Bros. for $30 million. Lean gratuitously assumed that Spielberg's casual remark on the plane meant that, if Spielberg produced a film for him, Lean would have carte blanche, with no interference from the producer. Consequently, when Spielberg called Lean to Hollywood for a preliminary story conference on February 13, 1987, Lean was startled to be presented with an itemized list of revisions to be made in the script.

Essentially, Spielberg felt that the script required clarification. He confessed that he got confused in his effort to keep track of the huge cast of characters. For example, the character of Charles Gould, the British owner of the San Tomé silver mine, the individual from whom Nostromo pilfers the silver, was not well defined. "We need to know more about him," said Spielberg. He concluded diplomatically, "*Nostromo* is written so well that it is somewhat embarrassing for me to make any suggestions about how to improve it."[7]

But Spielberg's diplomacy was wasted on Lean, who had become more of a curmudgeon with the years. On his return to London, Lean angrily waved Spielberg's list of revisions in Hampton's face and said, "Who does he think he is?" Hampton answered, "He thinks he's the producer, and he is."[8] But not for long. Spielberg did not want to wage a war with a director he admired over a common project, so he withdrew. Warners accordingly pulled the plug on the whole project. With that, Hampton decamped as well and moved on to write his Oscar-winning screenplay for *Dangerous Liaisons* (Stephen Frears, 1988), based on his own play.

Lean then turned to Robert Bolt, with whom he had not been in touch for some time, to carry on the work of adapting *Nostromo* for film. Bolt agreed to attend Lean's eightieth birthday party on March 25, 1988, along with his wife, Sarah Miles, whom he had remarried, at Lean's London home. Lean and Bolt ironed out their differences on the spot. Lean characteristically saw Hampton's leaving the project as a kind of desertion. The next time Hampton phoned Lean, he got a chilly response. "Robert is here," said Lean, and that was that.[9]

Bolt found working on the screenplay of *Nostromo* a monumental task. After all, the bursts of action in the novel take place within a densely layered plot and moral climate, and, as Bolt points out, a theatrical film can encompass "only one-tenth of the book." The work went slowly because Bolt never fully regained his strength after his combination heart attack and stroke. He and Lean had "occasional flare-ups," but they eventually hewed out a screenplay with which they were both "reasonably satisfied."[10]

On May 20, 1988, the British Academy of Film and Television Arts hosted a gala testimonial dinner at the Cannes Film Festival in honor of David Lean, on the occasion of his eightieth birthday. Lean took the opportunity to exhort his fellow filmmakers not to lose their passion for making big movies—like his planned film of *Nostromo*.

Lean was having a tough time finding a producer to replace Spielberg since "people in the industry were convinced that *Nostromo* was a European art house movie" and that a screen version of Conrad's dark, labyrinthine tale was "likely to find mass-market appeal elusive."[11] While in Cannes, Lean heard of an enterprising French producer named Serge Silberman who had produced Luis Buñuel's *The Discreet Charm of the Bourgeoisie* (1972) and Akira Kurosawa's *Ran* (1985). He subsequently met with Silberman in London to negotiate a deal for *Nostromo*, and it was Silberman who found the financing. By the fall of 1989, Silberman had brokered a deal with Columbia Pictures, which had released *Kwai* and *Lawrence*, to finance and distribute *Nostromo* with a budget of $44 million.

Silberman had managed to coax Lean into making a significant concession to the backers, in order to secure financing. It seemed that the customarily healthy Lean had been plagued by a series of illnesses. He accordingly agreed to name a standby director. "If I keeled over, as they delicately put it," said Lean, "this director would take over."[12] Lean, at the advanced age of eighty-one, was willing to accept this stipulation. He chose Guy Hamilton (*Goldfinger* [1964]). Lean trusted Hamilton because he had begun his film career as an assistant to Lean's old friend and colleague Carol Reed.

Lean and Silberman had some bitter arguments about casting and other issues. Silberman was given to towering rages, after the manner of Sam Spiegel; at such times, he really showed his fangs. Still, Lean could not afford to alienate him permanently since he could not risk losing another producer, so they got along.

Despite his failing health, Lean flew to Hollywood to receive from the American Film Institute (AFI) its Life Achievement Award on March 8, 1990, at a celebration that was televised the following week. Lean made his entrance to the strains of "The Colonel Bogey March." He insisted on walking with a cane despite the fact that a recent illness had left him using a wheelchair back home. He had no intention of appearing to be an invalid on this exalted occasion.

Several of his fellow directors paid tribute to him. Steven Spielberg, who was anxious to wipe away his falling-out with Lean over *Nostromo,* affirmed that Lean's films were the equivalent of great novels. He went on to say that *Kwai* and *Lawrence* had inspired him to become a filmmaker. Billy Wilder (*Sunset Boulevard*) took the occasion to ask the AFI, "What took you so long?" Lean was now eighty-two.

Lean's acceptance speech ended with a plea to the film community: Recalling previous winners of the AFI award like Alfred Hitchcock, William Wyler, and Billy Wilder, Lean observed, "Nearly all of them are innovators; this business lives on pathfinders. Give young directors a chance; take risks and put some money their way. It's a very nervous job, making a film; one needs luck. Anyway, I wish them luck."

After the AFI tribute, Lean set his sights in earnest on preproduction for *Nostromo.* Shooting was scheduled to begin in May 1991 in Almeria, the Spanish port where Lean had filmed some scenes for *Lawrence.* John Box was busy designing the sets. Lean was in good spirits and proposed to Sandra Cooke; they were wed, as mentioned, on December 15, 1990.

But Lean fell seriously ill in January 1991. His physician, Peter Wheeler, diagnosed a tumor in his throat. Though Lean had long since quit smoking, his years of chain-smoking had finally taken their toll. He underwent radiation therapy, declaring, "I don't want to die; maybe I can still do the film if I get better."[13]

Maurice Jarre says that he chatted with Lean on the phone around this time: "He had finished the screenplay of *Nostromo,* and he was asking me about the musical score. He was already into the film enough to be discussing the music!"[14] Soon after, the filmmaker John Boorman visited Lean, who said to him, "Haven't we been lucky? They let us make films." Boorman replied, "They did everything to stop us." To this Lean responded, "But we fought them!"[15]

Lean soon developed a severe case of pneumonia along with cancer of the throat, and it became evident that this was to be his last illness. John Box, who had been told by the studio to cease work on the sets, broke the news to Lean that he had been notified that *Nostromo* had been canceled. When his hopes of making one last film were dashed, Lean equivalently gave up the ghost, expiring on Thursday, April 11, 1991, in his Thames-side home in London. His funeral took place at Putney Vale Crematorium in London on April 22. Alec Guinness and John Mills, among others, were in attendance.

After Lean's death, Christopher Hampton composed a version of the screenplay of *Nostromo* that was totally his own and did not draw on any of Bolt's contributions. It was his hope that another director would make a theatrical feature of *Nostromo*. Hampton published his screenplay in 1996, but, as he himself admits, he has small hope that it will ever go before the cameras.[16]

After Lean's film of *Nostromo* ran aground, BBC-TV announced that it would produce a miniseries derived from the Conrad novel. But Hampton inexplicably was not asked to do the teleplay. The five-hour miniseries was filmed in Colombia at a cost of $20 million, with a cast largely composed of unknowns. It was broadcast in Britain in 1996 and, cut to four hours, in the United States the following year. Critical response in both England and America was lukewarm, and the miniseries has been all but forgotten.

In the wake of Lean's death, encomiums poured in from all over the world. On October 3, 1991, a memorial service was held in St. Paul's Cathedral, echoing T. E. Lawrence's. Maurice Jarre conducted the Royal Philharmonic in a medley of his music for Lean's films. In addition, a solo pianist played passages from Rachmaninoff's Piano Concerto no. 2, which had provided the score for *Brief Encounter*, and a military band played "Colonel Bogey" on the cathedral steps.

Alec Guinness told me that he slipped into the cathedral unobserved to attend what he termed "the big show." While listening to the eulogies from Peter O'Toole, Omar Sharif, Robert Bolt, and Ernest Day, Guinness said, "I had to push aside my recollections of David's unpleasantness in later years and remember the rapport which we shared on the earlier films." He remembered that one of the last times he and Lean had been together was at a reception at 10 Downing Street. The prime minister, Margaret Thatcher, hosted a cocktail party for "a great flurry of show business and media folk": "David and I fell over backward to be affectionate to each other. I was always fond of him; he had a strong personality, but then so do I."

John Box recalled working with Lean on *Lawrence* when his turn came to speak at the memorial service. Surveying the desert, Box remembered, "I found myself saying to David, 'I think we're face-to-face with eternity.' David said, 'You're right, John. And by the grace of God, and if we keep our heads, we will make a good movie.'"[17] That anecdote reminded Kevin Brownlow of Lean's saying, "Practically every day I thank God I am doing what I'm doing."[18]

John Mitchell hazarded that, when Lean looked down from heaven at the twenty-five hundred people assembled to pay him their respects, he would have said, "Jolly good show!" He added that *A Passage to India* had marked a summit in Lean's career. He even went so far as to say that it might have been providential that Lean did not live to make another film after *Passage*. After all, he would have found it increasingly difficult to work with the "whiz kids" now running Hollywood, who thought Lean was an "old-timer." So maybe the fact that Lean did not live to direct *Nostromo* was, to use Alec Guinness's phrase, "a blessing in disguise."[19]

The Craftsman as Artist

Michael Sragow observes that Lean's films were "too mammoth in scope and Olympian in style" for moviegoers to get an impression of the man behind the camera. "Yet Lean's greatest actor, Peter O'Toole, has honored his mentor with the most complete impression of a (then) living director ever committed to celluloid." In Richard Rush's film *The Stunt Man* (1980), O'Toole plays Eli Cross, "a driven, hawk-eyed visionary filmmaker." His model for the character was none other than David Lean.[20]

As a matter of fact, in reviewing *The Stunt Man*, Pauline Kael made reference to O'Toole's playing a legendary movie director very much like David Lean. Eli Cross is, she writes, like Lean, "completely aware of his craggy magnificence": "He mesmerizes whomever he's talking to." Cross makes his first entrance in *The Stunt Man* riding with the cameraman in a helicopter just before landing—as if he were some god descending from the heavens to mingle with the mere mortals below. "He's always hovering overhead, dangling from his helicopter or on the camera crane. He is on top of everything." To the cast and crew the irascible director is "God the Father as a son-of-a-bitch."[21]

Kael's reference to God the Father reminds one that Lean's associates compared him to a god-like figure on the set. John Box, as already noted, commented on Lean's grandiose manner by saying, "If you can't be God, be a film director!" At one point Cross upbraids the assistant director for calling "Cut" without his permission: "How dare you call 'Cut' on my set! I seem to be unable to keep you from fucking up my film!" One remembers Lean storming at André de Toth and Roy Stevens, both of whom vowed never to work for him again. Like David Lean, Sragow concludes, Eli Cross "is not the warmest or most accessible of men": "But he's how most of us imagine God."[22]

Lean was a god-like figure on the set; those who worked for him on a picture found that he taxed them to the limit at times and pushed them to new heights. "He expected high standards," said Sandra Lean, "only because he had already set himself ones that were even higher."[23]

Lean's reluctance to give interviews in later life played a part in his being underrated by some film critics. After all, the subtlety of his visual style and his unobtrusive approach to direction meant that his contribution to his films was not always overt or obvious. Nevertheless, in his best work, there is a supreme visual mastery and a real enthusiasm for the potential of the movie medium that make it obvious that Lean was a genuine auteur.

Lean approached his work like an artist, not just a craftsman. He was aware of an obvious but troubling truth. Mass entertainment, if it is any good, cannot be mass-produced. Instead, it must be improvised anew each time, just like art—because it *is* art. Every film poses a unique struggle. Lean's superior technique is evident throughout his films, and his complicated tracking shots through crowded rooms and his careful blending of color and sound sometimes transcend his subject matter.

Still, Lean was a showman as well as an artist; he knew how to grab the audience's attention and hold on to it. The rise of letterboxed DVDs and the popularity of ever-bigger television sets has made it possible to watch wide-screen pictures without losing the integrity of the image. Wide-screen movies, especially those made by masters of the form like Lean, are not so much viewed as inhabited.

Be that as it may, Lean did not pander to the mass audience in his spectacles. He made movies for filmgoers who do not get antsy if there is not an explosion every few minutes, viewers who appreciate films as landscape paintings, with strong heroes who are not dwarfed by the big sky, as it were. Thus, he took a prisoner-of-war story and turned it into Shakespearean tragedy in *Kwai*. He took a story about scientific research and made it into a tense suspense film about mankind conquering nature in *The Sound Barrier*. Spielberg, as noted, believed that Lean's films were the equivalent of great novels. Lean showed that films could be literature—movies as high art.

In short, Lean combined narrative sweep and psychological detail as few directors have, before or since. He thus created what Martin Scorsese calls "the intelligent epic," giving epic filmmaking a sophistication and scope rarely seen before.[24] For example, winners and losers are frequently too clearly defined in contemporary cinema, whereas Lean's best films always found thoughtful shades of gray in key characters like Colonel Nicholson and T. E. Lawrence. Such characters twisted the image of what it meant to be noble while at the same time displaying courage in the fight.

Moreover, Lean, a pitchman for movie humanism, showed in a character like Dr. Zhivago how a strong man would also be a gentle man, revealing a hint of pacifism at the heart of heroism. Maurice Jarre says, "David Lean was a master of cinema, a model of rigor and professionalism in the service of cinema."[25]

At the time that *Passage* was released, critics celebrated Lean's return to form, and he was once again one of the world's most highly regarded directors. When he began *Passage* after a long hiatus, Lean feared that, as James Thurber once put it, an artist's talent "could be lost like his watch or mislaid like his hat or slowly depleted like his bank account."[26] But Lean's talent stayed with him right to the end, perhaps more mature than it had ever been.

Not all film historians would place Lean among the great auteur directors. In the current flood of film books "there is rarely an extended discussion of Lean and his work."[27] Such a phenomenon is all too common in an America that Thurber describes as "a country of fickle and restless tastes that goes in for the Book of the Month Club, the Man of the Year, and the Song of the Week."[28]

So an examination of Lean's films raises again the old problem of the director's auteur status. David Lean was by no means an anonymous studio technician. On the contrary, he was the single "controlling force" who shaped and guided each of his films, working closely with the writer, the cinematographer, and the editor.[29] To many filmgoers, as David Ehrenstein wrote in endorsing Lean's AFI Life Achievement Award, "Lean is the man behind four decades of first-class entertainment. The Lean label marks the contributions of many, but orchestrated by one man alone."[30]

Lean accordingly managed to make movies that coalesced into a single, coherent body of work. Despite the factory atmosphere of the studio system, his vision transcended each story he was telling, no matter who wrote it—Dickens, Pasternak, or Forster. Lean himself certainly had the mind-set of an auteur, long before the term came into common parlance. As early as his 1947 essay on directing, he wrote that, to be a film director, "you must be a pretty big ego. How can you be anything else, if you are to make everyone see the film your way? The best films are generally those that have the stamp of one man's personality."[31] In other words, Lean recognized the concept of the auteur long before it was officially promulgated by Andrew Sarris and others.

The very popularity of his movies, however, is reason enough for some film historians to write him off as a mere crowd-pleaser. That a director can be both a crowd-pleaser and an authentic artist is suggested by the fact that Lean's finest films, for example, *Great Expectations* and *Lawrence of Arabia*, are also among his most popular. Nevertheless, Lean was not unduly bothered by the fact that his artistry was frequently overlooked by critics since, for him, the mark of good technique is that it goes unnoticed.

Commenting on the popularity of his films, Lean said that he always followed the rule given him years ago by Noël Coward: "'Do what pleases you, and if that doesn't please the public, leave the entertainment business.' If what I have done in the past has happened to please a lot of people, I suppose that makes me a common denominator." He continued, "I personally often worry about being old-fashioned." Like the average filmgoer, Lean explained, "I like a good strong story. I like a beginning, a middle, and an end." He went on to say, "I like to be excited when I go to the movies; I like to be touched. And I like a good yarn, I suppose."[32]

Lean is in good company. Ron Meyer, the president of Universal Studios, was asked recently whether audiences are becoming jaded by special effects films that depend on computer-generated imagery. Meyer replied that "it is still the basics" that count: "Movies made by directors starring actors with the right screenplay will be exactly what we'll be seeing succeed for the next decade."[33]

The official recognition that Lean's work has received brings into relief how this British-born filmmaker unquestionably left his unmistakable mark on American cinema. It is significant that the Library of Congress claimed the films of this native Englishman as part of the American film heritage when it bestowed a singular honor on Lean in 1997. *Kwai* and *Lawrence* were selected as two of the American motion pictures to be preserved in the permanent collection of the National Film Registry of the Library of Congress as culturally, historically, and aesthetically important.

Moreover, the AFI honored the hundred best American films made during the first century of cinema with a television special aired in 1998. The films, chosen by a panel of film professionals and critics, include *The Bridge on the River Kwai*, *Lawrence of Arabia*, and *Dr. Zhivago*, all high on the list. In addition, when *Time* magazine honored the hundred greatest films of all time in 2005, *Lawrence of Arabia* was among the selections.

But not all such recognition has come from the United States. Lean has received laurels from other sectors of the film world, particularly Great Britain, as when he was knighted in 1984. When in 1999 the British Film Institute chose the hundred best British films of cinema's first century, *Brief Encounter* and *Great Expectations* were among the top ten. What is more, an international poll of filmmakers and film critics conducted in 2002 by *Sight and Sound*, the venerable London film journal, voted Lean one of the top ten directors of all time and listed *Lawrence* among the ten greatest motion pictures ever made. Lean received yet another singular honor posthumously when in 1995 a building at Shepperton Studios outside London, where he filmed part of *Passage*, was dedicated to his memory. A few years later, the

FILMOGRAPHY

Lean served as film editor on several routine, low-budget pictures (quota quickies) before becoming a director as well as on some quality productions. Only the key films that he edited for major directors are listed below, and they are highlighted in the text accordingly.

Films Edited by David Lean

Nell Gwyn (British Dominion, 1934)

Director: Herbert Wilcox
Screenplay: Miles Malleson
Cinematographer: Freddie Young
Editors: Merrill White, and David Lean (uncredited)
Cast: Anna Neagle and Cedric Hardwicke
Running Time: 85 minutes

Escape Me Never (British Dominion, 1935)

Director: Paul Czinner
Screenplay: Carl Zuckerman and Robert Cullen, from the play by Margaret Kennedy
Cinematographer: Georges Perinal
Music: William Walton
Editor: David Lean
Cast: Elizabeth Bergner, Penelope Dudley Ward, and Griffith Jones
Running Time: 95 minutes

The 49th Parallel (U.S. title: *The Invaders*)
(General Film Distributors, 1941)

Director: Michael Powell
Screenplay: Emeric Pressburger
Cinematographer: Freddie Young
Music: Ralph Vaughan Williams
Editor: David Lean
Cast: Laurence Olivier, Eric Portman, Leslie Howard, and Raymond Massey
Running Time: 123 minutes; 107 minutes (U.S. release)

Films on Which David Lean Did Uncredited Directorial Work

Pygmalion (Pascal Film Productions, 1938)

Producer: Gabriel Pascal
Directors: Anthony Asquith, Leslie Howard, and David Lean (uncredited)
Screenplay: George Bernard Shaw, based on his play
Adaptation: Cecil Lewis, W. P. Lipscomb, and Ian Dalrymple
Cinematographer: Harry Stradling
Production Designers: Lawrence Irving and John Bryan
Music: Arthur Hoenneger
Sound: Alex Fisher
Editor: David Lean
Cast: Leslie Howard (Henry Higgins), Wendy Hiller (Eliza Doolittle), Wilfred Lawson (Alfred P. Doolittle), Scott Sunderland (Colonel Pickering), Jean Cadell (Mrs. Pearce), and David Tree (Freddy Eynsford-Hill)
Running Time: 96 minutes; 90 minutes (U.S. release)
Premiere: October 6, 1938

Major Barbara (Pascal Film Productions, 1941)

Producer: Gabriel Pascal
Directors: Gabriel Pascal and David Lean (uncredited)
Screenplay: George Bernard Shaw, based on his play
Scenario: Gabriel Pascal and Anatole de Grunwald
Cinematographers: Ronald Neame, and Freddie Young (uncredited)
Assistants to the Director: David Lean and Harold French
Production Designer: Vincent Korda and John Bryan

Music: William Walton
Sound: Martin Paggi
Editors: Charles Frend and David Lean
Cast: Wendy Hiller (Major Barbara), Rex Harrison (Adolphus Cusins), Robert Morley (Undershaft), Robert Newton (Bill Walker), Sybil Thorndyke (the General), Deborah Kerr (Jenny Hill), Felix Aylmer (James), Stanley Holloway (Policeman)
Running Time: 131 minutes; 121 minutes (U.S. release)
Premiere: April 26, 1941

Film for Which David Lean Was an Uncredited Screenplay Coauthor

The Bounty (Dino De Laurentiis, 1984)

Producer: Bernard Williams
Director: Roger Donaldson
Screenplay: Robert Bolt, and David Lean (uncredited), from the novel *Captain Bligh and Mr. Christian,* by Richard Hough
Cinematographer: Arthur Ibbetson
Production Designer: John Graysmark
Music: Vangelis
Sound: John Mitchell
Editor: Tony Lawson
Cast: Anthony Hopkins (Captain Bligh), Mel Gibson (Fletcher Christian), Laurence Olivier (Admiral Hood), Edward Fox (Captain Greetham), Daniel Day-Lewis (John Fryer), and Liam Neeson (Churchill)
Running Time: 130 minutes
Premiere: June 1984

Film Codirected by David Lean

In Which We Serve
(Two Cities/British Lion/United Artists, 1942)

Producer: Noël Coward
Associate Producer: Anthony Havelock-Allan
Directors: Noël Coward and David Lean
Screenplay: Noël Coward

Adaptation: David Lean (uncredited), Anthony Havelock-Allan (uncredited), and Ronald Neame (uncredited)

Cinematographer: Ronald Neame

Production Designers: David Rawnsley and Gladys Calthrop

Music: Noël Coward

Sound: C. C. Stevens

Editors: Thelma Myers, and David Lean (uncredited)

Cast: Noël Coward (Captain Edward Kinross), Bernard Miles (Chief Petty Officer Walter Hardy), John Mills (Ordinary Seaman Shorty Blake), Celia Johnson (Mrs. Kinross), Kay Walsh (Freda Lewis), Joyce Carey (Mrs. Hardy), Derek Elphinstone (Number One), Robert Sansom ("Guns"), Philip Friend ("Torps"), Michael Wilding ("Flags"), Hubert Gregg (Pilot), Ballard Berkeley (Engineer Commander), James Donald (Doctor), Kathleen Harrison (Mrs. Blake), George Carney (Mr. Blake), Richard Attenborough (Young Sailor, uncredited), Daniel Massey (Bobby), and Leslie Howard (Narrator, uncredited)

Running Time: 114 minutes

Premiere: October 1942

Films Directed by David Lean

This Happy Breed
(Cineguild/General Film Distributors/Universal, 1944)

Producer: Noël Coward

Associate Producer: Anthony Havelock-Allan

Assistant Director: George Pollock

Screenplay: Noël Coward, from his play

Adaptation: David Lean, Ronald Neame, and Anthony Havelock-Allan

Cinematographer: Ronald Neame (Technicolor)

Special Effects: Percy Day

Production Designers: C. P. Norman and Gladys Calthrop

Music: Noël Coward

Dress Supervisor: Hilda Collins

Sound: C. C. Stevens, John Cooke, and Desmond Drew

Editor: Jack Harris

Cast: Robert Newton (Frank Gibbons), Celia Johnson (Ethel Gibbons), Amy Veness (Mrs. Flint), Alison Leggatt (Aunt Sylvia), Stanley Holloway (Bob Mitchell), John Mills (Billy Mitchell), Kay Walsh (Queenie Gibbons),

Eileen Erskine (Vi Gibbons), John Blythe (Reg Gibbons), Guy Verney (Sam Leadbitter), Betty Fleetwood (Phyllis Blake), Merle Tottenham (Edie), and Laurence Olivier (Narrator, uncredited)
Running Time: 110 minutes; 101 minutes (U.S. release)
Premiere: June 1944 (Great Britain); April 1947 (United States)

Failure of a Strategy (L'echec d'une strategie) (Cineguild, 1944)

(Documentary short for the British Ministry of Information)
Producer: Arthur Calder-Marshall
Director: David Lean (uncredited)
Editor: Peter Tanner
Running Time: 20 minutes
Premiere: June 1944

Blithe Spirit (Cineguild/General Film Distributors/ United Artists, 1945)

Producer: Noël Coward
Associate Producer: Anthony Havelock-Allan
Assistant Director: George Pollock
Screenplay: Noël Coward, from his play
Adaptation: David Lean, Ronald Neame, and Anthony Havelock-Allan
Cinematographer: Ronald Neame
Special Effects: Tom Howard
Production Designers: C. P. Norman and Gladys Calthrop
Costumes: Rahvia
Music: Richard Addinsell
Sound: John Cooke and Desmond Drew
Editor: Jack Harris
Cast: Rex Harrison (Charles Condomine), Constance Cummings (Ruth), Kay Hammond (Elvira), Margaret Rutherford (Madame Arcati), Joyce Carey (Mrs. Bradman), Hugh Wakefield (Doctor Bradman), Jacqueline Clark (Edith), and Noël Coward (Narrator, uncredited)
Running time: 96 minutes
Premiere: April 1945 (Great Britain); September 1945 (United States)

Brief Encounter (Cineguild/General Film Distributors/ Universal, 1945)

Producer: Noël Coward
Associate Producers: Anthony Havelock-Allan and Ronald Neame
Assistant Director: George Pollock
Adaptation: Noël Coward, from his play *Still Life* from *Tonight at 8:30*
Screenplay: David Lean, Ronald Neame, and Anthony Havelock-Allan
Cinematographer: Robert Krasker
Production Designers: L. P. Williams and Gladys Calthrop
Music: Rachmaninoff's Piano Concerto no. 2 played by Eileen Joyce, with the National Symphony Orchestra conducted by Muir Mathieson
Sound: Stanley Lambourne and Desmond Drew
Editor: Jack Harris
Associate Editor: Marjorie Saunders
Cast: Celia Johnson (Laura Jesson), Trevor Howard (Dr. Alec Harvey), Cyril Raymond (Fred Jesson), Stanley Holloway (Albert Godby), Joyce Carey (Myrtle Bagot), Margaret Barton (Beryl Waters), Valentine Dyall (Stephen Lynn), Everley Gregg (Dolly Messiter), Marjorie Mars (Mary Norton), and Jack May (Boatman)
Running Time: 86 minutes
Premiere: November 1945 (Great Britain); August 1946 (United States)

Great Expectations (Cineguild/General Film Distributors/ Universal, 1946)

Producer: Ronald Neame
Executive Producer: Anthony Havelock-Allan
Assistant Director: George Pollock
Screenplay: David Lean, Ronald Neame, and Anthony Havelock-Allan, with Kay Walsh and Cecil McGivern, adapted from the book by Charles Dickens
Cinematographers: Guy Green, and Robert Krasker (uncredited)
Production Designer: John Bryan
Art Director: Wilfred Shingleton
Costumes: Sophia Harris (of Motley) assisted by Margaret Furse
Music: Walter Goehr, Kenneth Pakeman (uncredited), and G. Linley (uncredited)

Sound: Stanley Lambourne, Gordon K. McCullum, and Desmond Drew (uncredited)
Sound Editor: Winston Ryder
Editor: Jack Harris
Cast: John Mills (Pip, grown up), Valerie Hobson (Estella, grown up), Bernard Miles (Joe Gargery), Francis L. Sullivan (Jaggers), Finlay Currie (Magwitch), Martita Hunt (Miss Havisham), Anthony Wager (Pip, as a boy), Jean Simmons (Estella, as a girl), Alec Guinness (Herbert Pocket), John Forrest (Pale Young Gentleman), Ivor Barnard (Wemmick), Freda Jackson (Mrs. Joe Gargery), Torin Thatcher (Bentley Drummle), Eileen Erskine (Biddy), Hay Petrie (Uncle Pumblechook), George Hayes (Compeyson, the other convict), Richard George (the Sergeant), Everly Gregg (Sarah Pocket), O. B. Clarence (the Aged Parent), John Burch (Mr. Wopsle), and Valerie Hobson (Molly, uncredited)
Running Time: 118 minutes
Premiere: December 1946 (Great Britain); April 1947 (United States)

Oliver Twist (Cineguild/General Film Distributors/ Eagle-Lion, 1948)

Producers: Ronald Neame, and Anthony Havelock-Allan (uncredited)
Assistant Director: George Pollock
Screenplay: David Lean and Stanley Haynes, adapted from the book by Charles Dickens
Cinematographer: Guy Green
Special Effects: Joan Suttie and Stanley Grant
Production Designer: John Bryan
Costumes: Margaret Furse
Makeup: Stuart Freeborn
Music: Sir Arnold Bax, played by Harriet Cohen, solo pianist, with the London Philharmonic Orchestra conducted by Muir Mathieson
Sound: Stanley Lambourne and Gordon K. McCullum
Sound Editor: Winston Ryder
Editor: Jack Harris
Cast: Robert Newton (Bill Sikes), Alec Guinness (Fagin), Kay Walsh (Nancy), Francis L. Sullivan (Mr. Bumble), Henry Stephenson (Mr. Brownlow), Mary Clare (Mrs. Corney), John Howard Davies (Oliver Twist), Josephine Stuart (Oliver's Mother), Henry Edwards (Police Official), Ralph Truman (Monks), Anthony Newly (Artful Dodger), Kenneth Downey (Workhouse

Master), Gibb McLaughlin (Mr. Sowerberry), Kathleen Harrison (Mrs. Sowerberry), Amy Veness (Mrs. Bedwin), W. G. Fay (Bookseller), Maurice Denham (Chief of Police), Frederick Lloyd (Mr. Grimwig), Ivor Barnard (Chairman of the Board), Deirdre Doyle (Mrs. Thingummy), Diana Dors (Charlotte), Michael Dear (Noah Claypole), and Peter Bull (Landlord of the Three Cripples)

Running Time: 116 minutes; 104 minutes (U.S. release); 116 minutes (2004 restored version)

Premiere: June 1948 (Great Britain); July 1951 (United States)

The Passionate Friends (U.S. title: *One Woman's Story*) (Cineguild/General Film Distributors/Universal, 1949)

Producer: Ronald Neame
Associate Producer: Norman Spencer
Assistant Director: George Pollock
Screenplay: Eric Ambler, based on the novel by H. G. Wells
Adaptation: David Lean and Stanley Haynes
Cinematographer: Guy Green
Production Designer: John Bryan
Assistant Art Director: Tim Hopwell-Ashe
Set Decorator: Claude Manusey
Costumes: Margaret Furse
Music: Richard Addinsell
Sound: Stanley Lambourne and Gordon K. McCullum
Sound Editor: Winston Ryder
Editors: Jack Harris (supervisor) and Geoffrey Foot
Cast: Ann Todd (Mary Justin), Claude Rains (Howard Justin), Trevor Howard (Steven Stratton), Isabel Dean (Pat), Betty Ann Davies (Miss Layton), Arthur Howard (Servant), Guide Lorraine (Hotel Manager), Natasha Sikolova (Chambermaid), and Helen Burls (Flower Woman)
Running Time: 91 minutes; 89 minutes (U.S. release)
Premiere: January 1949 (Great Britain); June 1949 (United States)

Madeleine (Cineguild/General Film Distributors/Universal, 1950)

Producer: Stanley Haynes
Assistant Director: George Pollock

Screenplay: Stanley Haynes and Nicholas Phipps, based on the case of Madeleine Hamilton Smith
Cinematographer: Guy Green
Production Designer: John Bryan
Costumes: Margaret Furse
Music: William Alwyn
Editor: Geoffrey Foot
Cast: Ann Todd (Madeleine Smith), Ivan Desny (Emile L'Angelier), Norman Wooland (William Minnoch), Leslie Banks (Mr. Smith), Barbara Everest (Mrs. Smith), Susan Stranks (Janet Smith), Patricia Raine (Bessie Smith), Elizabeth Sellars (Christina), Edward Chapman (Dr. Thompson), Jean Cadell (Mrs. Jenkins), Eugene Deckers (Monsieur Thuau), Ivor Barnard (Mr. Murdoch), Harry Jones (Lord Advocate), David Horne (Lord Justice), Andre Morell (Dean of Faculty), Amy Veness (Miss Aiken), John Laurie (Scots Divine), and James McKechine (Narrator)
Running time: 114 minutes
Premiere: February 1950 (Great Britain); September 1950 (United States)

The Sound Barrier (U.S. title: *Breaking the Sound Barrier*) (London Films/British Lion/Lopert Films, 1950)

Producer: David Lean
Associate Producer: Norman Spencer
Aerial-Unit Director: Anthony Squire
Screenplay: Terence Rattigan
Cinematography: Jack Hildyard
Aerial-Unit Cinematography: John Wilcox, Jo Jago, and Peter Newbrook
Production Designer: Vincent Korda
Art Director: Joseph Bato and John Hawkesworth
Music: Malcolm Arnold
Editor: Geoffrey Foot
Cast: Ralph Richardson (Sir John Ridgefield), Ann Todd (Susan Ridgefield Garthwaite), Nigel Patrick (Tony Garthwaite), John Justin (Philip Peel), Dinah Sheridan (Jess Peel), Joseph Tomelty (Will Sparks), Denholm Elliot (Christopher Ridgefield), Jack Allen (Windy Williams), and Ralph Michael (Fletcher)
Running Time: 118 minutes; 109 minutes (U.S. release)
Premiere: July 1952 (Great Britain); November 1952 (United States)

Hobson's Choice (London Films/British Lion/ Lopert Films, 1954)

Producer: David Lean
Associate Producer: Norman Spencer
Assistant Director: Adrian Pryce-Jones
Screenplay: David Lean, Norman Spencer, and Wynyard Browne, from the play by Harold Brighouse
Cinematographer: Jack Hildyard
Production Designer: Wilfred Shingleton
Costumes: John Armstrong, Julia Squire
Music: Malcolm Arnold
Sound: John Cox
Sound Recording: Buster Ambler and Red Law
Editor: Peter Taylor
Cast: Charles Laughton (Henry Hobson), John Mills (William Mossop), Brenda de Banzie (Maggie Hobson), Daphne Anderson (Alice Hobson), Prunella Scales (Vicky Hobson), Richard Wattis (Albert Prosser), Derek Blomfield (Freddy Beenstock), Helen Haye (Mrs. Hepworth), Joseph Tomelty (Jim Heeler), Julian Mitchell (Sam Minns), Gibb McLaughlin (Tudsbury), and John Laurie (Dr. McFarlane)
Running Time: 107 minutes
Premiere: February 1954 (Great Britain); June 1954 (United States)

Summertime (British title: *Summer Madness*) (London Films/Independent Film Distributors/ Lopert Films, 1955)

Producer: Ilya Lopert
Associate Producer: Norman Spencer
Assistant Directors: Adrian Pryce-Jones and Alberto Cardone
Screenplay: H. E. Bates and David Lean, from the play *The Time of the Cuckoo* by Arthur Laurents
Cinematographer: Jack Hildyard (Technicolor)
Production Designer: Vincent Korda
Art Directors: Bill Hutchinson and Ferdinand Bellan
Music: Alessandro Cicognini; Rossini's "La Gazza Ladra"

Sound: Peter Hanford and John Cox

Editor: Peter Taylor

Cast: Katharine Hepburn (Jane Hudson), Rossano Brazzi (Renato de Rossi), Isa Miranda (Signora Fiorini), Darren McGavin (Eddie Jaeger), Mari Aldon (Phyllis Jaeger), Jane Rose (Mrs. Edith McIlhenny), MacDonald Parke (Lloyd McIlhenny), Gaetano Autiero (Mauro), Andre Morell (Englishman on Train), Jeremy Spenser (Vito), and Virginia Simeon (Giovanna)

Running time: 100 minutes

Premiere: May 1955 (Great Britain); June 1955 (United States)

The Bridge on the River Kwai
(Horizon/Columbia Pictures, 1957)

Producer: Sam Spiegel

Assistant Directors: Gus Agosti and Ted Sturgis

Screenplay: Pierre Boulle, Carl Foreman (uncredited), Michael Wilson (uncredited), and David Lean (uncredited), from Boulle's novel

Cinematographer: Jack Hildyard (Technicolor, CinemaScope)

Production Designer: Donald M. Ashton

Costumes: John Apperson

Technical Adviser: Major-General L. E. M. Perowne

Music: Malcolm Arnold; Kenneth Alford's "Colonel Bogey March"

Sound: John Cox and John Mitchell

Chief Sound Editor: Winston Ryder

Editor: Peter Taylor

Cast: William Holden (Shears), Alec Guinness (Colonel Nicholson), Jack Hawkins (Major Warden), Sessue Hayakawa (Colonel Saito), James Donald (Major Clipton), Geoffrey Horne (Lieutenant Joyce), Andre Morell (Colonel Green), Peter Williams (Captain Reeves), John Boxer (Major Hughes), Percy Herbert (Grogan), Harold Goodwin (Baker), Ann Sears (Nurse), Henry Okawa (Captain Kanematsu), Keiichiro Katsumoto (Lieutenant Miura), M. R. B. Chakrabandhu (Yai), and Vilaiwan Seeboonreaung, Ngamta Suphaphongs, Javanart Punynchoti, and Kannikar Dowklee (Siamese Girls)

Running time: 161 minutes

Premiere: November 1957

Lawrence of Arabia (Horizon/Columbia Pictures, 1962)

Producer: Sam Spiegel

Assistant Director: Roy Stevens

Second-Unit Directors: Andre Smagghe, Noel Howard, and André de Toth (uncredited)

Screenplay: Robert Bolt, and Michael Wilson (uncredited)

Cinematographer: Freddie Young (70mm Panavision, Technicolor)

Second-Unit Photography: Skeets Kelly, Nicholas Roeg, and Peter Newbrook

Special Effects: Cliff Richardson

Production Designer: John Box

Art Director: John Stoll

Set Director: Dario Simoni

Costumes: Phyllis Dalton

Music: Maurice Jarre

Sound: Paddy Cunningham

Sound Editor: Winston Ryder

Editor: Ann V. Coates

Cast: Peter O'Toole (T. E. Lawrence), Alec Guinness (Prince Feisal), Anthony Quinn (Auda Abu Tayi), Jack Hawkins (General Allenby), Omar Sharif (Sherif Ali), Jose Ferrer (Turkish Bey), Anthony Quayle (Colonel Brighton), Claude Rains (Mr. Dryden), Arthur Kennedy (Jackson Bentley), Donald Wolfit (General Murray), I. S. Johan (Gasim), Gamil Ratib (Majid), Michael Ray (Ferraji), Zia Mohyeddin (Tafas), John Dimech (Daud), Howard Marion Crawford (Medical Officer), Jack Gwillim (Club Secretary), Hugh Miller (RAMC Colonel)

Running time: 222 minutes (premiere); 200 minutes (general release); 187 minutes (1971 U.S. rerelease); 217 minutes (1989 restored version)

Premiere: December 9, 1962

Dr. Zhivago (Carlo Ponti/Metro-Goldwyn-Mayer, 1965)

Producer: Carlo Ponti

Executive Producer: Arvid L. Griffin

Assistant Directors: Roy Stevens and Pedro Vidal

Second-Unit Director: Roy Rossotti

Screenplay: Robert Bolt, from the novel by Boris Pasternak

Photography: Freddie Young (70mm Panavision, color)

Second-Unit Photography: Manuel Berenguer
Special Effects: Eddie Fowlie
Production Designer: John Box
Art Director: Terence Marsh
Assistant Art Directors: Ernest Archer, Bill Hutchinson, and Roy Walker
Set Decorator: Dario Simoni
Costumes: Phyllis Dalton
Music: Maurice Jarre
Sound: Paddy Cunningham
Sound Editor: Winston Ryder
Editor: Norman Savage
Cast: Omar Sharif (Yuri Zhivago), Julie Christie (Lara), Geraldine Chaplin (Tonya Gromeko Zhivago), Tom Courtenay (Pasha/Strelnikov), Alec Guinness (General Yevgraf Zhivago), Siobhan McKenna (Anna Gromeko), Ralph Richardson (Alexander Gromeko), Rod Steiger (Komarovsky), Rita Tushingham (Tonya, as a girl), Adrienne Corri (Lara's Mother), Geoffrey Keen (Professor Kurt), Jeffrey Rockland (Sasha Zhivago), Lucy Wetmore (Katya), Noel William (Razin), Gerard Tichy (Liberius), Klaus Kinski (Kostoyed), Jack MacGowran (Petya), Maria Martin (Gentlewoman), Tarek Sharif (Yuri, at age eight), Mercedes Ruiz (Tonya, at age seven), Roger Maxwell (Colonel in Charge of Replacements), Inigo Jackson (Major), Virgilio Texeira (Captain), Bernard Kay (Bolshevik Deserter), Erik Chitty (Old Soldier), Jose Nieto (Priest), and Mark Eden (Young Engineer)
Running Time: 197 minutes (premiere); 180 minutes (general release); 200 minutes (1995 restored version)
Premiere: December 1965 (United States); April 1966 (Great Britain)

Ryan's Daughter (Faraway Productions/A.G. Film/ Metro-Goldwyn-Mayer, 1970)

Producer: Anthony Havelock-Allan
Associate Producer: Roy Stevens
Assistant Directors: Pedro Vidal and Michael Stevenson
Second-Unit Directors: Roy Stevens (storm sequence), Charles Frend, and Harold French (uncredited)
Screenplay: Robert Bolt, suggested by *Madame Bovary* by Gustave Flaubert (uncredited)
Cinematographer: Freddie Young (70mm Panavision, Technicolor)

Second-Unit Photography: Denys Coop and Bob Huke
Special Effects: Robert MacDonald
Production Designer: Stephen Grimes
Art Director: Roy Walker
Set Decorator: Josie MacAvin
Costumes: Jocelyn Richards
Music: Maurice Jarre
Sound: John Bramall
Sound Editors: Ernie Grimsdale and Winston Ryder
Editor: Norman Savage
Cast: Sarah Miles (Rosy Ryan), Robert Mitchum (Charles Shaughnessy), Trevor Howard (Father Hugh Collins), Christopher Jones (Major Randolph Doryan), John Mills (Michael), Leo McKern (Tom Ryan), Barry Foster (Tim O'Leary), Arthur O'Sullivan (McCardle), Evin Crowley (Moureen), Marie Keen (Mrs. McCardle), Barry Jackson (Corporal), Douglas Sheldon (Driver), Philip O'Flynn (Paddy), Gerald Sim (Captain), Des Keogh (Lanky Private), Niall Toibin (O'Keefe), Donald Neligan (Moureen's boyfriend), Brian O'Higgins (Constable O'Connor), Niall O'Brien (Bernard)
Running Time: 206 minutes (premiere); 194 minutes (premiere engagements); 165 minutes (U.S. general release); 206 minutes (1997 restored version)
Premiere: November 9, 1970 (United States); December 9, 1970 (Great Britain)

Lost and Found: The Story of an Anchor (South Pacific TV, 1979)

(Television documentary for New Zealand television)
Producer: George Andrews
Directors: David Lean and Wayne Tourell
Writers: Wayne Tourell, David Lean (uncredited), and Robert Bolt (uncredited)
Cinematographers: Ken Dorman and Lynton Diggle
Editor: David Reed
Narrator: Kelly Tarlton
Running Time: 40 minutes
Premiere: May 1979

A Passage to India (A John Brabourne and Richard Goodwin Production of a David Lean Film for Home Box Office, Thorn-EMI, and Columbia, 1984)

Producers: John Brabourne and Richard Goodwin
Executive Producers: John Heyman and Edward Sands
Screenplay: David Lean, based on the novel by E. M. Forster and the play by Santha Rama Rau
Director of Photography: Ernest Day (Technicolor)
Production Designer: John Box
Music: Maurice Jarre (Royal Philharmonic Orchestra conducted by the composer); "Freely Maisie" tune composed by John Dalby
Casting: Priscilla John
Editor: David Lean
Associate Editor: Eunice Mountjoy
Sound Design: John Mitchell
Supervising Sound Editor: Winston Ryder
Music Editor: Robin Clarke
Second-Unit Photography: Robin Browne
Art Directors: Leslie Tomkins, Clifford Robinson, Ram Yedekar, and Herbert Westbrook
Set Decoration: Hugh Scaife
Production Supervisor: Barrie Melrose
Production Managers: Jim Brennan and Shama Habibullah
Assistant Directors: Patrick Caddell, Christopher Figg, Nick Laws, Arundhati Rao, and Ajit Kumar
Costume Designer: Judy Moorcroft
Cast: Judy Davis (Adela Quested), Victor Bannerjee (Dr. Aziz), Peggy Ashcroft (Mrs. Moore), James Fox (Fielding), Alec Guinness (Godbole), Nigel Havers (Ronny Heaslop), Richard Wilson (Turton), Michael Culver (McBryde), Art Malik (Mahmoud Ali), Saeed Jaffrey (Hamidullah), Clive Swift (Major Callendar), Ann Firbank (Mrs. Callendar), Roshen Seth (Amritrao), Sandra Hotz (Stella), Rashid Karapiet (Das), H. S. Krishnamurthy (Hassan), Ishaq Bux (Selim), Moti Makam (Guide), Mohammed Ashiq (Haq), Phyllis Bose (Mrs. Leslie), Sally Kinghorne (Ingenue), Paul Anin (Court Clerk), Z. H. Khan (Dr. Panna Lai), Ashok Mandanna (Anthony), Dina Pathek (Begum

Hamidullah), Adam Blackwood (Mr. Hadley), Mellan Mitchell (Businessman), and Peter Hughes (P&O Manager)
Running Time: 163 minutes
Premiere: December 1984 (United States); February 1985 (Great Britain)

NOTES

In the summer of 1989, David Lean provided comments in response to a detailed précis that I had developed for this book. All quotations of Lean not specifically attributed to another source are from those comments.

PROLOGUE

1. Gerald Pratley, "Interview with David Lean," in *Interviews with Film Directors,* ed. Andrew Sarris (New York: Avon, 1967), 319.

2. Andrew Sarris, *Confessions of a Cultist: On the Cinema, 1955–1969* (New York: Simon & Schuster, 1971), 363.

3. Ibid., 361.

4. Alfred Hitchcock, "Film Production," in *Hitchcock on Hitchcock: Selected Writings and Interviews,* ed. Sidney Gottlieb (Berkeley and Los Angeles: University of California Press, 1997), 210.

5. Gerald Pratley, *The Cinema of David Lean* (New York: Barnes, 1974), 12.

6. Sarris, *Confessions of a Cultist,* 361.

7. Ben Hecht, "Enter the Movies," in *Film: An Anthology,* ed. Daniel Talbot (Berkeley and Los Angeles: University of California Press, 1966), 258.

8. Gerald Mast and Bruce Kawin, *A Short History of the Movies* (1971), rev ed. (New York: Longman, 2006), 444.

9. Undated transcript in the files of the British Film Institute Library.

10. Pratley, *The Cinema of David Lean,* 21.

11. Kevin Brownlow, *David Lean: A Biography* (New York: St. Martin's, 1997). Stephen Silverman, *David Lean* (New York: Abrams, 1989). Sandra Lean, with Barry Chattington, *David Lean: An Intimate Portrait* (New York: Universe, 2001). Howard Maxford, *David Lean* (London: Batsford, 2000).

12. Robert Morris and Lawrence Raskin, *Lawrence of Arabia: The Pictorial History* (New York: Doubleday, 1992). Adrian Turner, *The Making of Lawrence of Arabia* (London: Dragon's World, 1994).

13. Pratley, *The Cinema of David Lean*. Michael Anderegg, *David Lean* (Boston: Twayne, 1984). Alain Silver and James Ursini, *David Lean and His Films* (Los Angeles: Silman-James, 1992).

14. "Introduction" in Robert Murphy, ed., *The British Cinema Book* (1997), rev. ed. (London: British Film Institute, 2001), 2.

15. David Lean, "The Filmmaker and the Audience," in *Filmmakers on Filmmaking*, ed. Harry Geduld (Bloomington: Indiana University Press, 1969), 282.

1. FROM SILENTS TO SOUND

1. Brownlow, *David Lean*, 13.

2. Jay Cocks, "David Lean," *Time*, December 31, 1984, 60.

3. S. Lean, *David Lean*, 12.

4. Sandra Lean's remarks are taken from the audio commentary track included on the DVD of *Dr. Zhivago* (released by Turner Entertainment in 2001).

5. Cocks, "David Lean," 60.

6. Chris Steinbrunner and Norman Michaels, *The Films of Sherlock Holmes* (Secaucus, NJ: Citadel, 1978), 13.

7. Cocks, "David Lean," 60.

8. "Dialogue on Film: David Lean," *American Film* 15, no. 6 (March 1990): 24.

9. S. Lean, *David Lean*, 12.

10. Liam O'Leary, "*The Four Horsemen of the Apocalypse*," in *International Dictionary of Films and Filmmakers* (1997), ed. Nicolet Elert, Andrew Sarris, and Grace Jeromski, rev. ed., 4 vols. (New York: St. James, 2000), 1:367.

11. Brownlow, *David Lean*, 43. See also David Thomson, *The New Biographical Dictionary of Film*, rev. ed. (New York: Knopf, 2004), 429–30.

12. Silverman, *David Lean*, 27, 24.

13. "Dialogue on Film: David Lean," 24.

14. Brian McFarlane, *An Autobiography of British Cinema by Filmmakers and Actors* (London: Methuen, 1997), 329.

15. Brownlow, *David Lean*, 49.

16. David Lean, "The Film Director," in *Working for the Films*, ed. Oswell Blakeston (London: Focal, 1947), 27–37.

17. Rachael Low, *The History of British Film: The Films of the 1930s* (London: Allen & Unwin, 1979), 186.

18. Ronald Neame, with Barbara Cooper, *Straight from the Horse's Mouth: An Autobiography* (Lanham, MD: Scarecrow, 2003), 35.

19. Stephen Shafer, *British Popular Films, 1929–39* (New York: Routledge, 1997), 2. See also Sarah Street, *British Cinema in Documents* (New York: Routledge, 2000), 12–13.

20. Mark Glancey, "Hollywood and Britain: The British Quota," in *The Unknown 1930s: An Alternative History of the British Cinema, 1929–39,* ed. Jeffrey Richards (London: Tauris, 1998), 72. See also David Cook, *A History of Narrative Film* (New York: Norton, 2004), 290.

21. Richard Corliss, "Now Hear This!" *Time,* March 31, 2003, A9.

22. Hitchcock, "Film Production," 214.

23. Harlan Kennedy, "A Modest Magician," in *Michael Powell: Interviews,* ed. David Lazar (Jackson: University Press of Mississippi, 2003), 174.

24. Cocks, "David Lean," 60.

25. Neame, *Straight from the Horse's Mouth,* 46–47. S. Lean, *David Lean,* 187.

26. Cocks, "David Lean," 12. See also Silver and Ursini, *David Lean and His Films,* 232.

27. Philip Horne, "Martin Scorsese on Thorold Dickinson," *Sight and Sound,* n.s., 13, no. 11 (November 2003): 25.

28. Ken Russell, *The Lion Roars: Ken Russell on Film* (Boston: Faber & Faber, 1994), 9–10.

29. Lean, "The Filmmaker and the Audience," 283.

30. Ivan Butler, *Cinema in Britain* (New York: Barnes, 1973), 105.

31. Jay Nash and Stanley Ross, eds., *The Motion Picture Guide,* 12 vols. (Chicago: Cinebooks, 1985), 6:2118.

32. Freddie Young, with Peter Busby, *Seventy Light Years* (New York: Faber & Faber, 1999), 32.

33. Philip Kemp, "Book Roundup," *Sight and Sound,* n.s., 13, no. 9 (September 2003): 30.

34. Herbert Wilcox, *Twenty-five Thousand Sunsets: The Autobiography of Herbert Wilcox* (London: Bodley Head, 1967), 93.

35. The 1935 *Escape Me Never* is not to be confused with the inferior Hollywood remake in 1947, directed by Peter Godfrey, with Ida Lupino and Errol Flynn both miscast in the leads.

2. A TOUCH OF CLASS

1. Neame, *Straight from the Horse's Mouth,* 34.

2. John Tibbetts, "*Major Barbara,*" in James Tibbetts and John Welsh, eds., *The Encyclopedia of Stage Plays into Film* (New York: Facts on File, 2001), 193.

3. Valerie Pascal, *The Disciple and His Devil: Gabriel Pascal* (New York: McGraw-Hill, 1970), 82 (see also 77–78).

4. Ibid., 1.

5. Bert Cardullo, "On Shaw's *Pygmalion;* Play and Film: Stanley Kauffmann Interview," *Literature/Film Quarterly* 31, no. 4 (fall 2003): 247.

6. Donald Costello, *The Serpent's Eye: Shaw and the Cinema* (Notre Dame, IN: University of Notre Dame Press, 1965), 54.

7. See George Bernard Shaw, *Pygmalion: A Screenplay* (Baltimore: Penguin, 1941).

8. Michael Holroyd, *Bernard Shaw*, 3 vols. (London: Chatto & Windus, 1997), 3:392.

9. Pascal, *The Disciple and His Devil*, 85. See also Ben Brantley, "Celebrating Shaw," *New York Times*, September 16, 2005, B31.

10. McFarlane, *Autobiography of British Cinema*, 295.

11. Brownlow, *David Lean*, 123.

12. Cocks, "David Lean," 60.

13. Silverman, *David Lean*, 30.

14. Costello, *The Serpent's Eye*, 63–64.

15. Silverman, *David Lean*, 30.

16. Holroyd, *Bernard Shaw*, 3:392.

17. Butler, *Cinema in Britain*, 125.

18. Costello, *The Serpent's Eye*, 83.

19. McFarlane, *Autobiography of British Cinema*, 212.

20. Silver and Ursini, *David Lean and His Films*, 233. See also Young, *Seventy Light Years*, 57.

21. Pascal, *The Disciple and His Devil*, 97.

22. Costello, *The Serpent's Eye*, 80.

23. Ibid.

24. Pascal, *The Disciple and His Devil*, 97.

25. Ibid., 100. See also Neame, *Straight from the Horse's Mouth*, 50.

26. Holroyd, *Bernard Shaw*, 3:435–36. See also McFarlane, *Autobiography of British Cinema*, 296.

27. McFarlane, *Autobiography of British Cinema*, 295–96.

28. Rex Harrison, *Rex: An Autobiography* (New York: Morrow, 1975), 71.

29. Neame, *Straight from the Horse's Mouth*, 48.

30. Costello, *The Serpent's Eye*, 84. See also Neame, *Straight from the Horse's Mouth*, 48.

31. Neame, *Straight from the Horse's Mouth*, 49.

32. Brian McFarlane, "Wendy Hiller," *Sight and Sound*, n.s., 14, no. 3 (March 2004): 31.

33. Ian Christie, "Powell and Pressburger," in Lazar, ed., *Michael Powell*, 107.

34. Michael Powell, *A Life in the Movies* (New York: Knopf, 1987), 379.

35. Kevin Macdonald, *Emeric Pressburger: The Life and Death of a Screenwriter* (Boston: Faber & Faber, 1994), 180.

36. Silverman, *David Lean*, 32.

37. Ian Christie, "Michael Powell," *Sight and Sound*, n.s., 15, no. 9 (September 2005): 31.

38. McFarlane, *Autobiography of British Cinema*, 455.

39. Leslie Halliwell, *Who's Who in the Movies* (1965), ed. John Walker (New York: HarperCollins, 2003), 377.

40. W. Speakman, "What's Happening to the Movies?" in Lazar, ed., *Michael Powell*, 13. See also Powell, *A Life in the Movies*, 379.

41. Nash and Ross, eds., *The Motion Picture Guide*, 5:1399.

42. Pratley, *The Cinema of David Lean*, 28.

3. HOPE AND GLORY

1. Noël Coward, *Autobiography* (London: Methuen, 1986), 421–22. See also John Walker, "Great Britain," in Halliwell, *Who's Who in the Movies*, 581.

2. Coward, *Autobiography*, 423.

3. Sheridan Morley, *A Talent to Amuse: A Biography of Noël Coward* (London: Pavilion, 1985), 230. See also Coward, *Autobiography*, 422–23.

4. S. Lean, *Dr. Zhivago* DVD audio commentary track.

5. Coward, *Autobiography*, 423.

6. Undated transcript in the files of the British Film Institute Library.

7. Silverman, *David Lean*, 38.

8. Brownlow, *David Lean*, 152. Compare Silverman, *David Lean*, 43.

9. Silverman, *David Lean*, 38.

10. Brownlow, *David Lean*, 135–36. See also Silverman, *David Lean*, 40–41.

11. Neame, *Straight from the Horse's Mouth*, 10.

12. A typescript copy of this excerpt from Havelock-Allan's unpublished memoir was supplied by Kevin Brownlow. See also Neame, *Straight from the Horse's Mouth*, 59, 62.

13. Neame, *Straight from the Horse's Mouth*, 64. Havelock-Allan (unpublished memoir) notes that he was "very cross" that his involvement in the second unit was not mentioned by Neame in his writings about this picture.

14. McFarlane, *Autobiography of British Cinema*, 414.

15. Silverman, *David Lean*, 44.

16. Geoffrey Macnab, "Eager Beaver: Richard Attenborough," *Sight and Sound*, n.s., 13, no. 9 (September 2003): 22.

17. Coward, *Autobiography*, 424.

18. Silverman, *David Lean*, 46.

19. Coward, *Autobiography*, 425.

20. Ibid., 425.

21. Ibid., 432.

22. Ibid. Neame, *Straight from the Horse's Mouth*, 69.

23. Coward, *Autobiography*, 432.

24. Ibid., 433.

25. Bosley Crowther, *The Great Films* (New York: Putnam, 1967), 262.

26. Harlan Kennedy, "British Cinema in World War II," *Film Comment* 32, no. 5 (September–October 1996): 28.

27. Russell, *The Lion Roars*, 21–23.

28. James Agee, *Film Writing and Selected Journalism*, ed. Michael Sragow (New York: Library of America, 2005), 36.

29. Coward, *Autobiography*, 435. See also "Anthony Havelock-Allan: Obituary," *Times* (London), January 14, 2003, 35.

30. Lean, "The Film Director," 28.

31. Philip Hoare, *Noel Coward: A Biography* (New York: Simon & Schuster, 1995), 336.

32. Ibid.

33. Coward, *Autobiography*, 440.

34. Sue Harper and Vincent Porter, *British Cinema of the 1950s: The Decline of Deference* (New York: Oxford University Press, 2003), 35. Raymond Durgnat, "J. Arthur Rank," in Elert, Sarris, and Jeromski, eds., *International Dictionary of Films and Filmmakers*, 4:693.

35. Neame, *Straight from the Horse's Mouth*, 76.

36. Brownlow, *David Lean*, 171.

37. Noël Coward, *This Happy Breed*, in *To-Night at 8:30; Present Laughter; This Happy Breed*, vol. 4 of *The Collected Plays of Noel Coward* (London: Heinemann, 1962), 554.

38. Tony Williams, "*This Happy Breed*," in Tibbetts and Welsh, eds., *The Encyclopedia of Stage Plays into Film*, 300.

39. Noël Coward, introduction to *To-Night at 8:30; Present Laughter; This Happy Breed*, xiv.

40. Coward, *Autobiography*, 440.

41. See Williams, "*This Happy Breed*," 300. Compare Maxford, *David Lean*, 43.

42. Neame, *Straight from the Horse's Mouth*, 77.

43. Silver and Ursini, *David Lean and His Films*, 21.

44. Brownlow, *David Lean*, 177.

45. Neame, *Straight from the Horse's Mouth*, 79–80. See also John Mills, *Up in the Clouds, Gentlemen, Please* (London: Ticknor & Fields, 1981), 189–90.

46. Andrew Higson, "Reconstructing the Nation: *This Happy Breed*," in *Re-Viewing British Cinema*, ed. Wheeler Dixon (Albany: State University of New York Press, 1994), 71. "Reconstructing the Nation" is adapted from Andrew Higson, *Waving the Flag: Constructing a National Cinema in Britain* (Oxford: Clarendon, 1994), 243–71.

47. Nash and Ross, eds., *The Motion Picture Guide*, 8:3389.

48. Neame, *Straight from the Horse's Mouth*, 77–78.

49. Williams, "*This Happy Breed*," 302.

4. ENCHANTMENT

1. Leslie Halliwell, "World Movies," in Halliwell, *Who's Who in the Movies*, 581.

2. Percy Bysshe Shelley, "To a Skylark," in *History of English Literature*, ed. Martin Day, 3 vols. (Garden City, NY: Doubleday, 1963), 2:429.

3. Morley, *A Talent to Amuse*, 227.

4. Silverman, *David Lean*, 55.

5. Neame, *Straight from the Horse's Mouth*, 80.

6. Hoare, *Noel Coward*, 354.

7. Neame, *Straight from the Horse's Mouth*, 80.

8. Hoare, *Noel Coward*, 354.

9. Undated transcript in the files of the British Film Institute Library.

10. Lionel Godfrey, "It Wasn't Like That in the Play," *Films and Filming*, August 1967, 8.

11. Powell, *A Life in Movies*, 417.

12. Pratley, *The Cinema of David Lean*, 491.

13. Neame, *Straight from the Horse's Mouth*, 81.

14. Ibid.

15. Ibid.

16. Dawn Langley Simmons, *Margaret Rutherford: A Blithe Spirit* (New York: McGraw-Hill, 1983).

17. Brownlow, *David Lean*, 185. It is worth noting that Hoare (*Noel Coward*, 354) gets the anecdote wrong by writing that the electrician admired Hammond's looks more than Cummings's. Brownlow has the incident from Havelock-Allan, who was present on the set at the time. Similarly, Pratley (*The Cinema of David Lean*, 49–50) consistently misidentifies Constance Cummings as playing Elvira and Kay Hammond as playing Ruth.

18. Harrison, *Rex*, 81.

19. Brownlow, *David Lean*, 186.

20. Ibid., 187.

21. "Super Tramp," *Sight and Sound*, n.s., 13, no. 10 (October 2003): 28. See also Hoare, *Noel Coward*, 354.

22. McFarlane, *Autobiography of British Cinema*, 289.

23. Pauline Kael, *5001 Nights at the Movies* (New York: Holt, 1991), 81.

24. Anderegg, *David Lean*, 21. Silver and Ursini (*David Lean and His Films*, 25) endorse Anderegg's faulty description of the scene.

25. Neame, *Straight from the Horse's Mouth*, 82.

26. Coward, *Autobiography*, 444.

27. Ibid., 445.

28. Morley, *A Talent to Amuse*, 255.

29. Brownlow, *David Lean*, 759. Brownlow's mistake is repeated in Tony

Williams, "*Still Life*," in Tibbetts and Welsh, eds., *The Encyclopedia of Stage Plays into Film*, 282.

30. Coward, introduction to *To-Night at 8:30; Present Laughter; This Happy Breed*, x, xiii.

31. Silverman, *David Lean*, 57.

32. Neame, *Straight from the Horse's Mouth*, 94. A. R. Fulton, *Motion Pictures: The Development of an Art* (1960), rev. ed. (Norman: University of Oklahoma Press, 1980), 174.

33. David Lean, "*Brief Encounter*," in *Penguin Film Review*, no. 4 (Harmondsworth: Penguin, 1947), 32.

34. Because *Brief Encounter* was released in 1945, the majority of filmgoers assumed (and still do assume) that it is set in the mid-1940s, despite the fact that the screenplay was not updated with, e.g., war references. Nevertheless, the film is, in fact, set in the same time period as the play, the mid-1930s. Also, because it was released several months after the end of World War II, the film qualifies as a postwar movie, even though it was made near the end of the war.

35. Lean, "*Brief Encounter*," 32.

36. Neame, *Straight from the Horse's Mouth*, 95. Compare Noël Coward, *Still Life*, in *To-Night at 8:30; Present Laughter; This Happy Breed*, 237–83.

37. John Russell Taylor, introduction to *Brief Encounter: A Screenplay* by Noël Coward, with David Lean, Ronald Neame, and Anthony Havelock-Allan, in *Masterworks of the British Cinema* (Boston: Faber & Faber, 1990), 112.

38. Bruce Eder's remarks are taken from the audio commentary track included on the DVD of *Brief Encounter* (released by Criterion in 2000).

39. Hoare, *Noel Coward*, 361. See also Morley, *A Talent to Amuse*, 214–15.

40. Eder, *Brief Encounter*, DVD audio commentary track.

41. Hoare, *Noel Coward*, 360.

42. Neame, *Straight from the Horse's Mouth*, 96. See also Brownlow, *David Lean*, 195.

43. Neame, *Straight from the Horse's Mouth*, 94.

44. Kate Fleming, *Celia Johnson: A Biography* (London: Weidenfeld & Nicolson, 1991), 25.

45. See Maxford's *David Lean*.

46. Pratley, *The Cinema of David Lean*, 52, 53.

47. Ibid., 57.

48. Silverman, *David Lean*, 63.

49. Fleming, *Celia Johnson*, 142. See also Brownlow, *David Lean*, 199.

50. Thomas Erskine, "Robert Krasker," in Elert, Sarris, and Jeromski, eds., *International Dictionary of Films and Filmmakers*, 4:459.

51. Russell, *The Lion Roars*, 30.

52. Ibid.

53. Eder, *Brief Encounter*, DVD audio commentary track.

54. Brownlow, *David Lean*, 759.

55. Roger Manvell, "*Brief Encounter,*" in *Masterworks of the British Cinema,* 116.

56. Stephen Bourne, *Brief Encounters: Lesbians and Gays in British Cinema, 1930–1971* (New York: Cassell, 1996), 77.

57. Russell, *The Lion Roars,* 31.

58. Eder, *Brief Encounter,* DVD audio commentary track.

59. Richard Dyer, *Brief Encounter* (London: British Film Institute, 1993), 11.

60. The sailor was Michael Redgrave, who would become a prominent actor after the war. Redgrave was bisexual, and his wife complained to Coward about the time her husband was spending in Coward's cottage near Denham Studios during the shoot of *In Which We Serve.* See Hoare, *Noel Coward,* 324, and Leslie Gaus, "The Redgraves," *New York Times,* May 4, 2003, sec. 2, p. 7.

61. Bourne, *Brief Encounters,* 77.

62. Ibid., 222.

63. Coward, introduction to *To-Night at 8:30; Present Laughter; This Happy Breed,* x, xiii.

64. Steven Caton, *Lawrence of Arabia: A Film's Anthropology* (Berkeley and Los Angeles: University of California Press, 1999), 49.

65. Laura Miller, "The Last Word," *New York Times Book Review,* January 25, 2004, 27.

66. Gene Phillips, *Major Film Directors of the American and British Cinema* (1990), rev. ed. (Cranbury, NJ: Associated University Presses, 1999), 181.

67. Raymond Durgnat, *A Mirror for England: British Movies from Austerity to Affluence* (New York: Praeger, 1971), 180.

68. Harlan Kennedy, "'I'm a Picture Chap': David Lean," *Film Comment* 21, no. 1 (January–February 1985): 29. See also Bourne, *Brief Encounters,* 78.

69. Neame, *Straight from the Horse's Mouth,* 102.

70. The British director Alfred Hitchcock had already been nominated for three films he made after going Hollywood—*Rebecca* (1940), *Lifeboat* (1943), and *Spellbound* (1944). But these were American, not British, productions.

71. Geoffrey Macnab, "Howard's Way: Trevor Howard," *Sight and Sound,* n.s., 10, no. 5 (May–June 2000): 27.

72. Michael Munn, *Trevor Howard: The Man and His Films* (London: Robson, 1990), 34.

73. Lean, "*Brief Encounter,*" 27–31.

74. Cited in Adrian Turner, "David Lean's *Brief Encounter,*" an essay accompanying the DVD (released by Criterion in 2000).

75. Ronald Bowers, "Noel Coward," in Elert, Sarris, and Jeromski, eds., *International Dictionary of Films and Filmmakers,* 4:175. For a recent reappraisal of the film, see Jurgen Muller, ed., *Movies of the Forties* (Los Angeles: Taschen/BFI, 2005), 298–301.

76. Glenn Kenny, "The 100 Greatest Movies, Part II," *Premiere* 16, no. 10 (June 2003): 3.

77. Silverman, *David Lean*, 65.

78. Neame, *Straight from the Horse's Mouth*, 102.

79. Leslie Halliwell, *Film Guide* (1977), ed. John Walker (New York: HarperCollins, 2005), 46.

80. Coward, introduction to *To-Night at 8:30; Present Laughter; This Happy Breed*, xi.

81. Brian McFarlane, "Outrage: *No Orchids for Miss Blandish*," in *British Crime Cinema*, ed. Steve Chibnall and Robert Murphy (New York: Routledge, 1999), 41–42.

5. LONG DAY'S JOURNEY

1. Penelope Houston, *Contemporary Cinema* (Baltimore: Penguin, 1969), 39–40. See also Phillips, *Major Film Directors*, 179.

2. Sergei Eisenstein, "Dickens, Griffith, and the Film Today," in *Film Form*, trans. Jay Leyda (New York: Harcourt Brace, 1949), 232–33. See also Garrett Stewart, "Dickens, Eisenstein, Film," in *Dickens on Screen*, ed. John Glavin (New York: Cambridge University Press, 2003), 122.

3. Robert Geddings, Keith Selby, and Chris Wensley, *Screening the Novel: The Theory and Practice of Literary Adaptations* (New York: St. Martin's, 1996), 1.

4. Rick Altman, "Dickens, Griffith, and Film Theory Today," in *Classical Hollywood Narrative*, ed. Jane Gaines (Durham, NC: Duke University Press, 1992), 11. Dickens's use of crosscutting in *Oliver Twist* will be taken up in the next chapter.

5. Joy Gould Boyum, *Double Exposures: Fiction into Film* (New York: New American Library, 1985), 4.

6. Charles Dickens, *Great Expectations* (New York: Oxford University Press, 1993), 482. For the original ending in full, see ibid., 481–82.

7. John Forster, *The Life of Charles Dickens* (New York: Doubleday, 1928), 737.

8. Dickens, *Great Expectations*, 480.

9. Margaret Cardwell, afterword to Dickens, *Great Expectations*, 482.

10. Stuart Walker made the first sound film of Dickens's book in 1934 for Universal. The sole claim to fame of this mediocre film is the standout performance of Francis L. Sullivan as the solicitor Jaggers—a role that he would recreate in Lean's film. Valerie Hobson had a bit part in the 1934 film.

11. Alec Guinness, *Blessings in Disguise* (New York: Penguin, 1996), 58. Brownlow, *David Lean*, 207.

12. Neame, *Straight from the Horse's Mouth*, 94.

13. Lean, "The Film Director," 30–35. See also Andrew Higson, *English Her-*

itage, English Cinema: Costume Dramas (London: Oxford University Press, 2003), 20.

14. "Dialogue on Film: David Lean," 26.

15. Ibid.

16. Ibid.

17. Brian McFarlane, *Novel to Film: The Theory of Adaptation* (New York: Oxford University Press, 1996), 119–20.

18. Garry O'Connor, *Alec Guinness: Masks of Disguise* (London: Hodder & Storighton, 1994), 97. Compare Neame, *Straight from the Horse's Mouth*, 96.

19. Geddings, Selby, and Wensley, *Screening the Novel*, xiv.

20. Dickens, *Great Expectations*, 84.

21. Neame, *Straight from the Horse's Mouth*, 104.

22. Butler, *Cinema in Britain*, 103.

23. Kenneth Von Gunden, *Alec Guinness: The Films* (1987), rev. ed. (Jefferson, NC: McFarland, 2001), 17.

24. Neame, *Straight from the Horse's Mouth*, 97.

25. Neame, *Straight from the Horse's Mouth*, 97. Von Gunden, *Alec Guinness*, 17.

26. "Dialogue on Film: David Lean," 52.

27. Maxford, *David Lean*, 55. Compare John Tibbetts, with Kenneth Pellow, "*Great Expectations*," in *The Encyclopedia of Novels into Film* (1998), by John C. Tibbetts and James M. Welsh, 2nd ed. (New York: Facts on File, 2005), 157.

28. Karel Reisz, with Gavin Miller, *The Technique of Film Editing* (1960), rev. ed. (New York: Communication Arts, 1968), 237–40.

29. Pratley, *The Cinema of David Lean*, 62.

30. David Lean, Ronald Neame, and Anthony Havelock-Allan, with Kay Walsh and Cecil McGivern, *Great Expectations: Unpublished Screenplay* (Universal, 1945), 1. The final shooting script is preserved in the Theater Arts Library of the University of California, Los Angeles.

31. Reisz, *The Technique of Film Editing*, 240.

32. Neame, *Straight from the Horse's Mouth*, 99–100.

33. Silver and Ursini, *David Lean and His Films*, 46.

34. Roger Manvell and R. K. Neilson-Baxter, *The Cinema* (London: Pelican, 1952), 20.

35. Julian Moynahan, "*Great Expectations*: Seeing the Book, Reading the Movie," in *The English Novel and the Movies*, ed. Michael Klein and Gillian Parker (New York: Unger, 1981), 144–45.

36. Neil Sinyard, *Filming Literature: The Art of Screen Adaptation* (New York: St. Martin's, 1986), 125.

37. Dickens, *Great Expectations*, 218.

38. Regina Barreca, "David Lean's *Great Expectations*," in Glavin, ed., *Dickens on Screen*, 40.

39. Neame, *Straight from the Horse's Mouth,* 101, 103.

40. Stewart, "Dickens, Eisenstein, Film," 133.

41. McFarlane, *Novel to Film,* 125.

42. Guerric DeBona, "Plot Mutations in Lean's *Great Expectations,*" *Literature/Film Quarterly* 20, no. 4 (winter 1997): 83.

43. Lean, Neame, and Havelock-Allan, *Great Expectations: Unpublished Screenplay,* 150.

44. Sinyard, *Filming Literature,* 121.

45. Dickens, *Great Expectations,* 232.

46. Barreca, "David Lean's *Great Expectations,*" 39.

47. Moynahan, "*Great Expectations,*" 151.

48. Von Gunden, *Alec Guinness,* 18. See also Carol MacKay, "The Case of *Great Expectations,*" *Literature/Film Quarterly* 13, no. 2 (spring 1985): 131–32.

49. Lean, "The Filmmaker and the Audience," 283.

50. Houston, *Contemporary Cinema,* 39.

51. Agee, *Film Writing and Selected Journalism,* 309–10.

52. Robert Murphy, "*Great Expectations,*" in Elert, Sarris, and Jeromski, eds., *International Dictionary of Films and Filmmakers,* 1:411.

53. Neame, *Straight from the Horse's Mouth,* 100.

54. Ibid., 103.

55. Brownlow, *David Lean,* 217.

6. CHILD'S PLAY

1. Michael Sragow, "David Lean's Right of *Passage,*" *Film Comment* 21, no. 1 (January–February 1985): 21.

2. Pratley, *The Cinema of David Lean,* 76.

3. Charles Dickens, *Oliver Twist* (New York: Oxford University Press, 1966), lxx–lxxi.

4. Pauline Kael, *Going Steady* (New York: Boyars, 1994), 204.

5. Anderegg, *David Lean,* 52.

6. Eisenstein, "Dickens, Griffith, and the Film Today," 217.

7. Ibid., 218.

8. For the passage that Eisenstein examines, see Dickens, *Oliver Twist,* 91–95.

9. Neame, *Straight from the Horse's Mouth,* 108.

10. Silverman, *David Lean,* 75.

11. Roy Armes, *A Critical History of British Cinema* (London: Secker & Warburg, 1978), 210.

12. Lean, "The Filmmaker and the Audience," 285.

13. David Lean and Stanley Haynes, *Oliver Twist: Unpublished Screenplay* (Eagle-Lion, 1947), 3. The screenplay is preserved in the British Film Institute Library.

14. Pratley, *The Cinema of David Lean,* 80.

15. Neame, *Straight from the Horse's Mouth*, 112.

16. O'Connor, *Alec Guinness*, 98.

17. Al McKee, "Art or Outrage? *Oliver Twist* and Fagin," *Film Comment* 36, no. 1 (January–February 2000): 43.

18. Piers Paul Read, *Alec Guinness: The Authorized Biography* (New York: Simon & Schuster, 2005), 217. Read relies heavily on Von Gunden's and O'Connor's critical studies of Guinness; hence, I tend to quote those sources directly, rather than by way of Read's citations of them.

19. O'Connor, *Alec Guinness*, 98.

20. Nash and Ross, eds., *The Motion Picture Guide*, 6:2241.

21. Neame, *Straight from the Horse's Mouth*, 112.

22. McKee, "Art or Outrage?" 41.

23. Stewart, "Dickens, Eisenstein, Film," 135.

24. Anderegg, *David Lean*, 47.

25. McFarlane, *Autobiography of British Cinema*, 234.

26. Neame, *Straight from the Horse's Mouth*, 112–13.

27. Ibid., 113.

28. Maxford, *David Lean*, 69.

29. Brownlow, *David Lean*, 235.

30. Silver and Ursini, *David Lean and His Films*, 70.

31. Lean, "The Filmmaker and the Audience," 285.

32. John Huntley and Roger Manvell, *Techniques of Film Music* (London: Focal, 1957), 74–75.

33. Dickens, *Oliver Twist*, 50.

34. "The Production Code: Formulated by the Association of Motion Picture Producers," in Gregory Black, *Hollywood Censored: Morality, Codes, and the Movies* (New York: Cambridge University Press, 1994), 308. This is the original industry production code of 1930, implemented in 1934.

35. Harper and Porter, *British Cinema of the 1950s*, 43. See also Geoffrey Macnab, "Unknown Pleasures: British Cinema of the 1950s," *Sight and Sound*, n.s., 14, no. 4 (April 2004): 38.

36. Sarah Street, *Transatlantic Crossings: British Feature Films in the United States* (New York: Continuum, 2002), 132. The letter is on file in the office of the Production Code Administration in Hollywood.

37. Ibid.

38. Silverman, *David Lean*, 78. According to Pauline Kael (*5001 Nights at the Movies*, 543) and other commentators on the film, the cuts amounted to seven minutes. But, if one compares an American release print of the movie with a British print, eleven minutes is correct.

39. Lean, "The Filmmaker and the Audience," 283.

40. Street, *Transatlantic Crossings*, 133. The cable is on file in the office of the Production Code Administration.

41. See Black, *Hollywood Censored*, 129–30.

42. Lean, "The Filmmaker and the Audience," 285.

43. Neame, *Straight from the Horse's Mouth,* 113.

44. Robert Tanitch, *Guinness* (New York: Applause, 1984), 54.

45. Gerhard Joseph, "Dickens, Psychoanalysis, and Film," in Glavin, ed., *Dickens on Screen,* 19. See also Guinness, *Blessings in Disguise,* 59.

46. "Cinema: *Oliver Twist,*" in *Time Capsule: 1951* (New York: Time-Life, 2001), 53.

47. Silverman, *David Lean,* 78.

48. Roger Ebert, *The Great Movies II* (New York: Broadway, 2005), 184.

49. William Honan, "David Lean Plans to Film a Conrad Story," *New York Times,* October 17, 1989, 13.

50. Michael Gross, "A Face Lift for Withered Old Fagin," *New York Times,* August 21, 2005, sec. 2, pp. 13, 27.

7. THE BEAUTIFUL AND THE DAMNED

1. H. G. Wells, *Experiment in Autobiography* (New York: Lippincott, 1962), 465–66.

2. Michael Foot, *H.G.: The History of Mr. Wells* (Washington, DC: Counterpoint, 1995), 129.

3. J. R. Hammond, *H. G. Wells and Rebecca West* (New York: St. Martin's, 1991), 72.

4. H. G. Wells, *The Passionate Friends* (New York: Harper Bros., 1913), 289.

5. Hammond, *H. G. Wells and Rebecca West,* 75.

6. Neame, *Straight from the Horse's Mouth,* 118.

7. Ibid.

8. Ibid., 119 (see also 121–22).

9. Brownlow, *David Lean,* 252.

10. Silverman, *David Lean,* 83.

11. Brownlow, *David Lean,* 255.

12. Neame, *Straight from the Horse's Mouth,* 120.

13. Brownlow, *David Lean,* 226, 252.

14. Neame, *Straight from the Horse's Mouth,* 124.

15. Brownlow, *David Lean,* 251. See also Silverman, *David Lean,* 83.

16. Brownlow, *David Lean,* 251.

17. Neame, *Straight from the Horse's Mouth,* 121.

18. Brownlow, *David Lean,* 251.

19. Silverman, *David Lean,* 85.

20. Ibid.

21. Brownlow, *David Lean,* 262.

22. Anderegg, *David Lean,* 67.

23. See Reisz, *The Technique of Film Editing*, 91–95.

24. Ibid., 95.

25. Eric Ambler, with David Lean and Stanley Haynes, *The Passionate Friends: Unpublished Screenplay* (Rank, 1948), 45–46. The shooting script is preserved in the British Film Institute Library.

26. Silver and Ursini, *David Lean and His Films*, 122.

27. Ibid., 126.

28. "*The Passionate Friends*," in *Variety Film Reviews: 1907–1996*, 24 vols. (New Providence, NJ: Bowker, 1997), vol. 8, n.p.

29. Silverman, *David Lean*, 55.

30. Neame, *Straight from the Horse's Mouth*, 122.

31. Ann Todd, *The Eighth Veil* (New York: Putnam's, 1981), 95. The title of Todd's autobiography is a reference to her first big hit, *The Seventh Veil* (Compton Bennett, 1945).

32. I acknowledge the aid of T. J. Martinez, S.J., counselor at law, in dealing with the British divorce law.

33. Tony Williams, *Structures of Desire: British Cinema, 1939–55* (Albany: State University of New York Press, 2000), 181.

34. Silver and Ursini, *David Lean and His Films*, 80.

35. Ibid., 80–81.

36. Tony Thomas, "William Alwyn," in Elert, Sarris, and Jeromski, eds., *International Dictionary of Films and Filmmakers*, 4:26.

37. Todd, *The Eighth Veil*, 97.

38. Steven Ross, "In Defense of David Lean," *Take One*, July–August 1972, 14.

39. McFarlane, *Autobiography of British Cinema*, 561.

40. Robert Murphy, *Realism and Tinsel: Cinema and Society in Britain* (New York: Routledge, 1998), 145.

41. Anderegg, *David Lean*, 70.

42. Williams, *Structures of Desire*, 182.

43. Sragow, "David Lean's Right of *Passage*," 22.

44. Murphy, *Realism and Tinsel*, 145.

45. Silverman, *David Lean*, 83.

46. Pratley, *The Cinema of David Lean*, 95.

47. "*Madeleine*," in *Variety Film Reviews*, vol. 8, n.p.

48. Harper and Porter, *British Cinema of the 1950s*, 40.

49. Neame, *Straight from the Horse's Mouth*, 122.

50. Harper and Porter, *British Cinema of the 1950s*, 37.

51. McFarlane, *Autobiography of British Cinema*, 432.

52. Silverman, *David Lean*, 89.

53. Neame, *Straight from the Horse's Mouth*, 123.

8. THE WILD BLUE YONDER

1. Greene, *The Graham Greene Reader*, 424, 102.

2. Ephraim Katz, *The Film Encyclopedia*, 4th ed., rev. Fred Klein and Ronald Dean Nolen (New York: HarperResource, 2001), 761.

3. Harper and Porter, *British Cinema of the 1950s*, 96, 153.

4. Thelma Schoonmaker, Peter Von Bagh, and Raymond Durgnat, "Midnight Sun Film Festival," in Lazar, ed., *Michael Powell*, 138–39.

5. Sylvia Hardy, "H. G. Wells: His Cinematic Legacy," *Sight and Sound*, n.s., 15, no. 7 (July 2005): 29.

6. John Tibbetts, "Alexander Korda," in *The Encyclopedia of Filmmakers*, by John C. Tibbetts and James M. Welsh, 2 vols. (New York: Facts on File, 2002), 1:333. See also Halliwell, *Who's Who in the Movies*, 268.

7. Tibbetts, "Alexander Korda," 333.

8. Philip Kemp, "Alexander Korda," in Elert, Sarris, and Jeromski, eds., *International Dictionary of Films and Filmmakers*, 4:449.

9. Brownlow, *David Lean*, 281.

10. S. Lean, *David Lean*, 28.

11. Silverman, *David Lean*, 90.

12. S. Lean, *David Lean*, 29.

13. Ibid.

14. Silverman, *David Lean*, 91. Compare S. Lean, *David Lean*, 29.

15. Gene Phillips, *Creatures of Darkness: Raymond Chandler, Detective Films, and Film Noir* (Lexington: University Press of Kentucky, 2000), 199.

16. Brownlow, *David Lean*, 289.

17. Sylvia Paskin, "Terence Rattigan," in Elert, Sarris, and Jeromski, eds., *International Dictionary of Films and Filmmakers*, 4:688.

18. Roger Manvell, "Malcolm Arnold," in Elert, Sarris, and Jeromski, eds., *International Dictionary of Films and Filmmakers*, 4:31.

19. Brownlow, *David Lean*, 289.

20. McFarlane, *Autobiography of British Cinema*, 338.

21. Phillips, *Major Film Directors*, 174.

22. Pratley, *The Cinema of David Lean*, 100.

23. "*The Sound Barrier,*" unpublished program notes, National Film Theater, London, May 1990, 2.

24. Manvell, "Malcolm Arnold," 21.

25. Robert Browning, "Andrea Del Sarto," in *The Complete Poetical Works of Robert Browning* (1907), new ed. (New York: Macmillan, 1915), 452.

26. Silver and Ursini, *David Lean and His Films*, 103.

27. Pratley, *The Cinema of David Lean*, 106.

28. Anderegg, *David Lean*, 78.

29. McFarlane, *Autobiography of British Cinema*, 338.

30. Chuck Yeager, with Leo Janos, *Yeager: An Autobiography* (London: Century Hutchinson, 1986), 220.

31. Silverman, *David Lean,* 92.

32. Yeager, *Yeager,* 220–21.

33. "*The Sound Barrier,*" 2.

34. Pratley, *The Cinema of David Lean,* 196.

35. McFarlane, *Autobiography of British Cinema,* 362.

36. Cocks, "David Lean," 58.

37. S. Lean, *David Lean,* 188.

38. Ibid.

39. Ibid.

40. Michael Balcon, "Ten Years of British Films," in *Films of 1951: The Festival of Britain* (London: British Film Institute, 1951), 37.

41. Armes, *A Critical History of British Cinema,* 211.

9. THE STAG AT EVE

I wish to acknowledge the input of Micael Clarke, associate professor of English, Loyola University of Chicago, and an expert on feminist literature, for discussing with me the rise of the feminist movement in England, which comes up in my treatment of *Hobson's Choice.* On the movement for women's rights in the Victorian period in England, see Ray Strachey, *The Cause: A Short History of the Women's Movement in Great Britain,* rev. ed. (London: Virago, 1979), 272–85.

1. Rebecca West reviewed books by suffragettes like Olive Schreiner for the *New Freewoman.* On West and the campaign for women's rights, see "Rebecca West," in Sandra M. Gilbert and Susan Gubar, eds., *The Norton Anthology of Literature by Women* (1985), 2nd ed. (New York: Norton, 1996), 1335–36. (Gilbert and Gubar mistakenly refer to the *Freewoman,* instead of the *New Freewoman.*)

2. Hitchcock, "Film Production," 214.

3. "*Hobson's Choice,*" in *Variety Film Reviews,* vol. 9, n.p.

4. Thomas Erskine, "*Hobson's Choice,*" in *Video Versions: Film Adaptations of Plays,* ed. Thomas Erskine and James Welsh (Westport, CT: Greenwood, 2000), 134.

5. Simon Callow, *Charles Laughton: A Difficult Actor* (New York: Grove, 1987), 222. Compare Katz, *The Film Encyclopedia,* 797.

6. Callow, *Charles Laughton,* 224.

7. Brownlow, *David Lean,* 301.

8. Mills, *Up in the Clouds, Gentlemen, Please,* 224.

9. Ibid.

10. McFarlane, *Autobiography of British Cinema,* 416.

11. Pratley, *The Cinema of David Lean,* 115–16.

12. Silverman, *David Lean,* 99.

13. McFarlane, *Autobiography of British Cinema,* 416.

14. Callow, *Charles Laughton,* 130.

15. Anderegg, *David Lean,* 84.

16. "Film Crew in Salford," *Guardian* (Manchester), September 9, 1953, 1.

17. Manvell, "Malcolm Arnold," 31.

18. Ibid. See also Maxford, *David Lean,* 83.

19. Silver and Ursini, *David Lean and His Films,* 114.

20. Durgnat, *A Mirror for England,* 207.

21. Callow, *Charles Laughton,* 224.

22. Maxford, *David Lean,* 85.

23. Hugo Cole, *Malcolm Arnold: An Introduction to His Music* (London: Faber, 1989), 61.

24. Maxford, *David Lean,* 85.

25. "*Hobson's Choice,*" in *Variety Film Reviews,* vol. 9, n.p.

26. Nash and Ross, eds., *The Motion Picture Guide,* 4:1247.

27. Harper and Porter, *British Cinema of the 1950s,* 102.

28. Ibid., 103.

29. Tibbetts, "Alexander Korda," 335.

10. LOVE IN THE AFTERNOON

1. Harper and Porter, *British Cinema of the 1950s,* 169.

2. Robert Murphy, *Sixties British Cinema* (London: British Film Institute, 1992), 10.

3. McFarlane, *Autobiography of British Cinema,* 346, 614.

4. Harper and Porter, *British Cinema of the 1950s,* 97.

5. John Tibbetts, "*The Time of the Cuckoo,*" in Tibbetts and Welsh, eds., *The Encyclopedia of Stage Plays into Film,* 306–7.

6. Silver and Ursini, *David Lean and His Films,* 126.

7. Arthur Laurents, *The Time of the Cuckoo* (New York: Random House, 1953), i.

8. Silverman, *David Lean,* 85.

9. Caton, *Lawrence of Arabia,* 50.

10. Brownlow, *David Lean,* 329.

11. Tibbetts, "*The Time of the Cuckoo,*" 307. See also Thomas Erskine, "*The Time of the Cuckoo,*" in Erskine and Welsh, eds., *Video Versions,* 357–58.

12. Silverman, *David Lean,* 14, 101.

13. Katharine Hepburn, "Get a Tough Director," *Panorama,* March 1981, 60.

14. Cocks, "David Lean," 58.

15. Katharine Hepburn, "So Just Keep a-Goin'—You Can Win," *TV Guide,* January 27, 1979, 5.

16. Michael Korda, *Charmed Lives* (New York: Random House, 1979), 387–88.

17. Anne Edwards, *A Remarkable Woman: A Biography of Katharine Hepburn* (New York: Morrow, 1985), 291.

18. Silverman, *David Lean*, 14.

19. Brownlow, *David Lean*, 321.

20. From a taped dialogue between George Cukor and Katharine Hepburn in Cukor's personal archive, dated summer 1969. Unless specified otherwise, subsequent quotations of Katharine Hepburn in this chapter are from this source.

21. Edwards, *A Remarkable Woman*, 292. Korda, *Charmed Lives*, 390.

22. Brownlow, *David Lean*, 319–20.

23. Edwards, *A Remarkable Woman*, 292.

24. Silverman, *David Lean*, 108.

25. S. Lean, *David Lean*, 38.

26. Ibid.

27. Ibid.

28. Hepburn, "Get a Tough Director," 60.

29. Anderegg, *David Lean*, 87.

30. Edwards, *A Remarkable Woman*, 292.

31. Silver and Ursini, *David Lean and His Films*, 133.

32. Anderegg, *David Lean*, 86.

33. Maxford, *David Lean*, 92.

34. Pratley, *The Cinema of David Lean*, 128.

35. Pauline Kael, *Kiss Kiss Bang Bang* (New York: Bantam, 1969), 445.

36. Nash and Ross, eds., *The Motion Picture Guide*, 7:3205.

37. Tibbetts, "*The Time of the Cuckoo*," 307.

38. S. Lean, *David Lean*, 137.

39. Lean, "The Filmmaker and the Audience," 282.

40. Brownlow, *David Lean*, 326.

41. S. Lean, *David Lean*, 132.

42. Harper and Porter, *British Cinema of the 1950s*, 134.

11. THE UNDEFEATED

1. Turner, *The Making of Lawrence of Arabia*, 19. See also James Harvey, "Sam Spiegel," *New York Times Book Review*, April 13, 2003, 29.

2. Andrew Sinclair, *Spiegel: The Man behind the Pictures* (Boston: Little, Brown, 1987), 74. Compare *The Bridge on the River Kwai*, souvenir program (Columbia Pictures, 1957), 2.

3. Harper and Porter, *British Cinema of the 1950s*, 134–35.

4. Thomson, *New Biographical Dictionary*, 170. It is interesting to observe that Spiegel and Cohn were both portly, outspoken types and, hence, sometimes mistaken for one another. In fact, there is a full-page photograph of Sam Spiegel in the *International Dictionary of Films and Filmmakers* that is misidentified as

a picture of Harry Cohn. See Richard Dyer MacCann, "Sam Spiegel," in Elert, Sarris, and Jeromski, eds., *International Dictionary of Films and Filmmakers*, 4:161.

5. Murphy, *Sixties British Cinema*, 257.

6. Lucille Becker, *Pierre Boulle* (New York: Twayne, 1996), 56.

7. Pierre Boulle, *My Own River Kwai*, trans. Xan Fielding (New York: Vanguard, 1967), 214.

8. Becker, *Pierre Boulle*, 47.

9. Ian Watt, "Bridges over the Kwai," *Partisan Review* 26, no. 1 (winter 1959): 94. See also Benjamin Schwarz, "The Fall of British Asia: 1941–45," *New York Times Book Review*, April 17, 2005, 30.

10. Becker, *Pierre Boulle*, 24.

11. See Ian Watt, "The Myth of the River Kwai," *Observer Magazine*, September 1, 1968, 18.

12. Pierre Boulle, *The Bridge on the River Kwai*, trans. Xan Fielding (New York: Time, 1964), 28–29.

13. Becker, *Pierre Boulle*, 48.

14. Boulle, *The Bridge on the River Kwai*, ix.

15. Becker, *Pierre Boulle*, 53.

16. Boulle, *The Bridge on the River Kwai*, 227–28.

17. Brownlow, *David Lean*, 76.

18. Ibid., 348.

19. Memo from Lean to Spiegel, January 31, 1956, cited in Natasha Fraser-Cavassoni, *Sam Spiegel* (New York: Simon & Schuster, 2003), 181.

20. Ibid.

21. Pierre Boulle, with Michael Wilson (uncredited) and Carl Foreman (uncredited), *The Bridge on the River Kwai: Unpublished Screenplay* (Columbia Pictures, 1956), 31. Foreman's draft of the *Kwai* screenplay, long thought lost, turned up in the mid-1990s at the David Lean Archive, which is now in the Netherlands. The final shooting script is in the Research Library at the University of California, Los Angeles.

22. Fraser-Cavassoni, *Sam Spiegel*, 181.

23. *The Making of "The Bridge on the River Kwai"* (Laurent Bouzereau, 2000, television documentary). Bouzereau's documentary includes interviews with cast and crew members. Unless specifically noted otherwise, all quotations from the cast and crew in this chapter are from this source.

A reviewer of one of my previous books opined that a television documentary is not a recognized research tool for a critical study. On the contrary, the present documentary features firsthand information, provided by participants in the making of this movie, that is available nowhere else.

24. Fraser-Cavassoni, *Sam Spiegel*, 183.

25. Silverman, *David Lean*, 118. See also Boulle, *The Bridge on the River Kwai: Unpublished Screenplay*, 4.

26. Fraser-Cavassoni, *Sam Spiegel*, 183.

27. Silverman, *David Lean*, 118.

28. Boulle, *The Bridge on the River Kwai: Unpublished Screenplay*, 131.

29. Fraser-Cavassoni, *Sam Spiegel*, 183.

30. Ibid., 184.

31. Ibid., 184–85.

32. Sinclair, *Spiegel*, 83.

33. Fraser-Cavassoni, *Sam Spiegel*, 182.

34. Silverman, *David Lean*, 80.

35. Jay Boyer, "Michael Wilson," in Elert, Sarris, and Jeromski, eds., *International Dictionary of Films and Filmmakers*, 4:901.

36. Sarah Holmes, "*The Bridge on the River Kwai*," in Tibbetts and Welsh, *The Encyclopedia of Novels into Film*, 43.

37. Fraser-Cavassoni, *Sam Spiegel*, 184.

38. "New York Sound Track," *Variety*, April 25, 1956, 4.

39. Fraser-Cavassoni, *Sam Spiegel*, 184.

40. Silverman, *David Lean*, 121.

41. Guinness, *Blessings in Disguise*, 216.

42. Fraser-Cavassoni, *Sam Spiegel*, 186.

43. Sinclair, *Spiegel*, 79.

44. *The Bridge on the River Kwai*, souvenir program, 8.

45. Fraser-Cavassoni, *Sam Spiegel*, 185.

46. *The Bridge on the River Kwai*, souvenir program, 7.

47. Silverman, *David Lean*, 8.

48. Larry Timm, *The Soul of Cinema: Film Music* (Upper Saddle River, NJ: Prentice-Hall, 2003), 169.

49. Gene Phillips and Rodney Hill, *The Stanley Kubrick Encyclopedia* (New York: Facts on File, 2002), 245.

50. Sessue Hayakawa, "Zen Showed Me the Way," *Films and Filming*, February 1967, 21–22.

51. Guinness, *Blessings in Disguise*, 225.

52. Ibid., 220.

53. S. Lean, *David Lean*, 75.

54. Silverman, *David Lean*, 121.

55. Fraser-Cavassoni, *Sam Spiegel*, 191, 192.

56. The prime minister of Japan reiterated this apology at a Pan-Asian summit in Jakarta in April 2005. Raymond Bonner and Norimitsu Onishi, "Japan Apologizes for War Misdeeds," *New York Times*, April 23, 2005, A5.

57. For the record, the information about Percival's refusal to allow the participation of British soldiers in the film is available only in *The Making of "The Bridge on the River Kwai."* All other accounts of the incident blame Spiegel.

58. Fraser-Cavassoni, *Sam Spiegel*, 189.

59. Ibid., 190.

60. Sinclair, *Spiegel*, 81.

61. Hayakawa, "Zen Showed Me the Way," 21.

62. Kenneth Tynan, *Alec Guinness* (London: Rockliff, 1953), 17.

63. O'Connor, *Alec Guinness*, 161. See also Read, *Alec Guinness*, 293.

64. Silverman, *David Lean*, 124. See also Read, *Alec Guinness*, 293.

65. Guinness, *Blessings in Disguise*, 216.

66. "Dialogue on Film: David Lean," 26.

67. Becker, *Pierre Boulle*, 56.

68. O'Connor, *Alec Guinness*, 160.

69. Brownlow, *David Lean*, 347.

70. Obviously, the camera operator Peter Newbrook's eyewitness account (in *The Making of "The Bridge on the River Kwai"*) of the actual blowing up of the bridge during filming is the most reliable. See also *The Bridge on the River Kwai*, souvenir program, 9–10.

71. *The Bridge on the River Kwai*, souvenir program, 9.

72. Fraser-Cavassoni, *Sam Spiegel*, 194.

73. Silver and Ursini, *David Lean and His Films*, 143.

74. Ibid., 97.

75. Lean, "The Filmmaker and the Audience," 282.

76. Fraser-Cavassoni, *Sam Spiegel*, 195.

77. Sinclair, *Spiegel*, 83.

78. S. Lean, *David Lean*, 112.

79. Becker, *Pierre Boulle*, 54.

80. Guinness, *Blessings in Disguise*, 219.

81. Phillips, *Major Film Directors*, 185.

82. Anderegg, *David Lean*, 94.

83. Michael Sragow, "David Lean's Magnificent *Kwai*," *Atlantic Monthly*, February 1994, 109. See also Read, *Alec Guinness*, 294, 299.

84. Interview included on the DVD of *Kind Hearts and Coronets* (Robert Hamer, 1949), released 2006.

85. Boulle, *The Bridge on the River Kwai*, 3.

86. *Reflections of David Lean*, a documentary included on the DVD of *A Passage to India* (released by Columbia Pictures in 2000).

87. Silver and Ursini, *David Lean and His Films*, 150.

88. Sragow, "David Lean's Magnificent *Kwai*," 109.

89. "David Lean," in *Conversations with the Great Moviemakers of Hollywood's Golden Age at the American Film Institute*, ed. George Stevens Jr. (New York: Knopf, 2006), 443. This is a reprinted version of "Dialogue on Film: David Lean," which originally appeared in *American Film* (see chapter 1, n. 8). Inexplicably, the present quotation is not included in the transcript published in *American Film*. In general, I have cited the original published version, except when, as here, there are differences.

90. Phillips, *Major Film Directors*, 185.

91. Cocks, "David Lean," 58.

92. Frank Brewer, ed., *100 Years of American Film* (New York: Macmillan, 2000), 69.

93. Lawrence Quirk, *The Great War Films* (New York: Carol, 1994), 159.

94. Fraser-Cavassoni, *Sam Spiegel*, 3.

95. S. Lean, *David Lean*, 29, 32.

96. Harper and Porter, *British Cinema of the 1950s*, 134.

97. Brownlow, *David Lean*, 381.

98. Fraser-Cavassoni, *Sam Spiegel*, 196.

99. Ibid., 198.

100. Becker, *Pierre Boulle*, 133. See also Brownlow, *David Lean*, 767.

101. S. Lean, *David Lean*, 32.

102. Jason Clark et al., "100 Best Action Movies on DVD," *Premiere* 16, no. 6 (February 2003): xi.

103. Glenn Kenny, "The 75 Most Influential Movies on DVD," *Premiere* 17, no. 4 (January 2004): 5.

104. "Jewels of Thailand," illustrated brochure (Thailand Tours, 2004), 1. See also Jurgen Muller, ed., *Movies of the Fifties* (Los Angeles: Taschen/BFI, 2005), 346–51.

105. *The Making of Indiana Jones and the Temple of Doom,* a documentary included on the DVD of *Indiana Jones and the Temple of Doom* (released by Paramount in 2003).

106. Phillips, *Major Film Directors,* 185.

107. See Sinclair, *Spiegel,* 94.

12. PILLAR OF FIRE

1. John Kifner, "In Lawrence of Arabia's Time Iraq Was No Picnic," *New York Times,* July 20, 2003, sec. 4, p. 1.

2. S. Lean, *David Lean,* 20.

3. Turner, *The Making of Lawrence of Arabia,* 23.

4. Morris and Raskin, *Lawrence of Arabia,* 6.

5. Renée Guillaume and André Guillaume, *An Introduction and Notes: T. E. Lawrence's Seven Pillars of Wisdom,* trans. Hilary Mandelberg (Otley: Tabard, 1998), 7.

6. Kifner, "Iraq Was No Picnic," 4.

7. John Kifner, "A Tide of Islamic Fury," *New York Times,* January 30, 2005, sec. 4, p. 4.

8. Turner, *The Making of Lawrence of Arabia,* 8.

9. [Robert Bolt], "Lawrence of Arabia," in *Lawrence of Arabia,* souvenir program (Columbia Pictures, 1962), 5.

10. Lowell Thomas, *With Lawrence in Arabia* (New York: Century, 1924), vii.

11. Excerpts from the footage that Thomas employed in his show are included in the feature-length documentary *Lawrence of Arabia: The Battle for the Arab World* (James Hawes, 2003).

12. Turner, *The Making of Lawrence of Arabia*, 8.

13. Anthony Nutting, *Lawrence of Arabia* (London: Hollis & Carter, 1961), 211.

14. [Bolt], "Lawrence of Arabia," 1.

15. *Lawrence of Arabia: The Battle for the Arab World*.

16. Nutting, *Lawrence of Arabia*, 211, 214.

17. [Bolt], "Lawrence of Arabia," 2.

18. Nutting, *Lawrence of Arabia*, 214.

19. Guillaume and Guillaume, *An Introduction and Notes*, 11.

20. Philip Knightly and Colin Simpson, *The Secret Lives of Lawrence of Arabia* (New York: McGraw-Hill, 1969), 226.

21. A. W. Lawrence, preface to *Seven Pillars of Wisdom: A Triumph*, by T.E. Lawrence (New York: Anchor, 1991), 18.

22. Nutting, *Lawrence of Arabia*, 216.

23. A. W. Lawrence, preface, 19. Doubleday reprinted *Revolt in the Desert* in 1986 with the approval of A. W. Lawrence.

24. T. E. Lawrence, preface to *Seven Pillars of Wisdom*, 1.

25. T. E. Lawrence to W. E. Stirling, October 15, 1924, in *The Letters of T. E. Lawrence*, ed. Malcolm Brown (New York: Oxford University Press, 1991), 275.

26. Lawrence, *Seven Pillars of Wisdom*, 23.

27. Nutting, *Lawrence of Arabia*, 218.

28. [Bolt], "Lawrence of Arabia," 1.

29. Knightly and Simpson, *The Secret Lives of Lawrence of Arabia*, 309.

30. Winston Churchill, "The War and After," in *T. E. Lawrence and His Friends*, ed. A. W. Lawrence (London: Jonathan Cape, 1937), 202.

31. Coward, *Autobiography*, 452.

32. Morris and Raskin, *Lawrence of Arabia*, 28.

33. *Lawrence of Arabia: The Battle for the Arab World*.

34. Stephen Tabachnick, *Lawrence of Arabia: An Encyclopedia* (Westport, CT: Greenwood, 2004), 42.

35. T. E. Lawrence, *Seven Pillars of Wisdom*, i.

36. Michael Asher, *Lawrence: The Uncrowned King of Arabia* (Woodstock, NY: Overlook, 1995), 295.

37. Tabachnick, *Lawrence of Arabia*, 27.

38. *Lawrence after Arabia* (Julia Cave, 1986).

39. Brownlow, *David Lean*, 405.

40. Turner, *The Making of Lawrence of Arabia*, 26.

41. Ibid.

42. Morris and Raskin, *Lawrence of Arabia*, 14.

43. Ibid.

44. Ibid., 15.

45. Morris and Raskin, *Lawrence of Arabia*, 119.

46. Guinness, *Blessings in Disguise*, 98.

47. Read, *Alec Guinness*, 332, 333. See also Tanitch, *Guinness*, 104.

48. Morris and Raskin, *Lawrence of Arabia*, 39.

49. Wilcox, *Twenty-five Thousand Sunsets*, 205.

50. Caton, *Lawrence of Arabia*, 110. See also Lawrence, *Seven Pillars of Wisdom*, 563.

51. Michael Wilson to David Lean, January 17, 1960, in Turner, *The Making of Lawrence of Arabia*, 65.

52. Morris and Raskin, *Lawrence of Arabia*, 34–35.

53. Brownlow, *David Lean*, 409.

54. Sinclair, *Spiegel*, 98.

55. Turner, *The Making of Lawrence of Arabia*, 21.

56. Pratley, *The Cinema of David Lean*, 151–52.

57. Turner, *The Making of Lawrence of Arabia*, 71, 17, 73.

58. Fraser-Cavassoni, *Sam Spiegel*, 226. See also Tabachnick, *Lawrence of Arabia*, 173.

59. Turner, *The Making of Lawrence of Arabia*, 77.

60. Fraser-Cavassoni, *Sam Spiegel*, 227, 228.

61. Brownlow, *David Lean*, 425.

62. Turner, *The Making of Lawrence of Arabia*, 82.

63. Ivan Butler, *The Making of Feature Films: A Guide* (Baltimore: Penguin, 1971), 40–41.

64. Morris and Raskin, *Lawrence of Arabia*, 138.

65. "Interview with Robert Bolt," *Evening Standard* (London), May 11, 1989, 28–29.

66. Fraser-Cavassoni, *Sam Spiegel*, 134.

67. Turner, *The Making of Lawrence of Arabia*, 87.

68. Sinclair, *Spiegel*, 98.

69. Phillips, *Creatures of Darkness*, 36.

70. Roger Ebert, *The Great Movies* (New York: Broadway, 2003), 266.

71. Bourne, *Brief Encounters*, 169.

72. Jonathan Vankin and John Whalen, *Based on a True Story: Fact and Fantasy in 100 Favorite Movies* (Chicago: A Cappella, 2005), 372.

73. Caton, *Lawrence of Arabia*, 216.

74. Lawrence, *Seven Pillars of Wisdom*, 444–45.

75. Asher, *Lawrence*, 294.

76. Lawrence, *Seven Pillars of Wisdom*, 447, 445. See also Asher, *Lawrence*, 292.

77. Tabachnick, *Lawrence of Arabia*, 46. See also Knightly and Simpson, *The Secret Lives of Lawrence of Arabia*, 246.

78. Vito Russo, *The Celluloid Closet: Homosexuality in the Movies* (1981), rev. ed. (New York: Harper & Row, 1987), 133–34.

79. Tabachnick, *Lawrence of Arabia*, 108.

80. Brownlow, *David Lean*, 476.

81. Vankin and Whalen, *Based on a True Story*, 373.

82. Turner, *The Making of Lawrence of Arabia*, 89. Turner dates this letter November 7, 1962, while Fraser-Cavassoni (*Sam Spiegel*, 251) dates it November 11. Because Fraser-Cavassoni was a personal friend of Spiegel and his family, she had unlimited access to Spiegel's private papers. Her dating is, therefore, to be preferred when scholarly disagreements arise.

83. Compare Michael Wilson, *Seven Pillars of Wisdom: A Screenplay* (Columbia Pictures, 1961), 1–4, and Robert Bolt, with Michael Wilson (uncredited), *Lawrence of Arabia: Unpublished Screenplay* (Columbia Pictures, 1961), pt. 1, pp. 1–4. Wilson's draft of the script is preserved in the Research Library at the University of California, Los Angeles. Bolt's shooting script is preserved in the script repository at Columbia Pictures.

84. Turner, *The Making of Lawrence of Arabia*, 90. See Wilson, *Seven Pillars of Wisdom: Unpublished Screenplay*, 68–71, 79–81, and Bolt, *Lawrence of Arabia: Unpublished Screenplay*, pt. 1, pp. 72–76, 96–98.

85. Compare Wilson, *Seven Pillars of Wisdom: Unpublished Screenplay*, 184–87, and Bolt, *Lawrence of Arabia: Unpublished Screenplay*, pt. 2, pp. 45–51.

86. Turner, *The Making of Lawrence of Arabia*, 91–92. Wilson's letter is preserved in the Research Library at the University of Texas, Austin.

87. Ibid., 93.

88. Silverman, *David Lean*, 181.

89. Caton, "*Lawrence of Arabia*," *New York Times*, September 14, 1995, D7.

90. For example, the detailed analysis of the Wilson and the Bolt scripts in Turner's *The Making of Lawrence of Arabia*.

91. David Robb, "Credit, at Last, for *Lawrence of Arabia*," *New York Times*, September 14, 1995, D7.

92. Sinclair, *Spiegel*, 99.

93. Morris and Raskin, *Lawrence of Arabia*, 40.

94. Sinclair, *Spiegel*, 99. See also Morris and Raskin, *Lawrence of Arabia*, 40.

95. Morris and Raskin, *Lawrence of Arabia*, 67. See also S. Lean, *David Lean*, 71.

96. See, e.g., the newsreel footage incorporated in *Lawrence of Arabia: The Battle for the Arab World*.

97. Sinclair, *Spiegel*, 99.

98. Von Gunden, *Alec Guinness*, 147.

99. Brownlow, *David Lean*, 418.

100. Guinness, *Blessings in Disguise*, 98. See also Read, *Alec Guinness*, 329–32.

101. O'Connor, *Alec Guinness*, 183.

102. Brownlow, *David Lean*, 425–26.

103. *The Making of "Lawrence of Arabia"* (Laurent Bouzereau, 2000, television documentary).

104. Turner, *The Making of Lawrence of Arabia*, 125.

105. Fraser-Cavassoni, *Sam Spiegel*, 232.

106. *The Making of "Lawrence of Arabia"* (Bouzereau).

107. Fraser-Cavassoni, *Sam Spiegel*, 233.

108. Tabachnick, *Lawrence of Arabia*, 7.

109. Morris and Raskin, *Lawrence of Arabia*, 128.

110. Young, *Seventy Light Years*, 93.

111. Frank Mannion, "An Interest in Photography: Freddie Young," in *Projections 6: Film-makers on Film-making*, ed. John Boorman and Walter Donohue (London: Faber & Faber, 1996), 216. See also Young, *Seventy Light Years*, 99.

112. Lawrence, *Seven Pillars of Wisdom*, 419.

113. *The Making of "Lawrence of Arabia"* (Bouzereau).

114. Ibid.

115. Gariella Oldham, *First Cut: Conversations with Film Editors* (Berkeley and Los Angeles: University of California Press, 1995), 158.

116. S. Lean, *David Lean*, 92.

117. Fraser-Cavassoni, *Sam Spiegel*, 228.

118. Ibid., 228–29.

119. Silverman, *David Lean*, 131.

13. IN SEARCH OF A HERO

1. *The Making of Troy*, a documentary included on the DVD of *Troy* (released by Warner Bros. in 2004).

2. Morris and Raskin, *Lawrence of Arabia*, 86.

3. Ibid., 77.

4. Fraser-Cavassoni, *Sam Spiegel*, 229.

5. Young, *Seventy Light Years*, 99.

6. Morris and Raskin, *Lawrence of Arabia*, 113.

7. Undated transcript in the files of the British Film Institute Library.

8. Mannion, "An Interest in Photography," 216, 216–17. See also Young, *Seventy Light Years*, 93.

9. Young, *Seventy Light Years*, 93, 93–94.

10. Fraser-Cavassoni, *Sam Spiegel*, 234.

11. Morris and Raskin, *Lawrence of Arabia*, 94.

12. Turner, *The Making of Lawrence of Arabia*, 152. See also Fraser-Cavassoni, *Sam Spiegel*, 224.

13. Turner, *The Making of Lawrence of Arabia*, 129.

14. *The Making of "Lawrence of Arabia"* (Bouzereau).

15. Brownlow, *David Lean,* 453.

16. Morris and Raskin, *Lawrence of Arabia,* 132.

17. Read, *Alec Guinness,* 355.

18. David Lean, "Out of the Wilderness: *Lawrence of Arabia," Films and Filming,* January 1963, 12.

19. Morris and Raskin, *Lawrence of Arabia,* 104.

20. Ibid.

21. Ibid., 141.

22. Young, *Seventy Light Years,* 100–101.

23. *The Making of "Lawrence of Arabia"* (Bouzereau).

24. Ibid.

25. Turner, *The Making of Lawrence of Arabia,* 143.

26. Fraser-Cavassoni, *Sam Spiegel,* 243.

27. Vincent LoBrutto, ed., *By Design: Interviews with Film Production Designers* (Westport, CT: Praeger, 1992), 133–34. See also Fraser-Cavassoni, *Sam Spiegel,* 243–44.

28. Brownlow, *David Lean,* 462.

29. *The Making of "Lawrence of Arabia"* (Bouzereau).

30. Turner, *The Making of Lawrence of Arabia,* 142.

31. Fraser-Cavassoni, *Sam Spiegel,* 245.

32. Lean, "Out of the Wilderness," 13.

33. Fraser-Cavassoni, *Sam Spiegel,* 245.

34. Ibid., 245.

35. Turner, *The Making of Lawrence of Arabia,* 143.

36. Ibid., 149.

37. Fraser-Cavassoni, *Sam Spiegel,* 245.

38. Nicholas Wapshott, *Peter O'Toole* (New York: Beaufort, 1983), 90.

39. *The Making of "Lawrence of Arabia"* (Bouzereau).

40. Fraser-Cavassoni, *Sam Spiegel,* 243.

41. Sinclair, *Spiegel,* 103.

42. Morris and Raskin, *Lawrence of Arabia,* 140.

43. Pratley, "Interview with David Lean," 319.

44. Oldham, *First Cut,* 159. See also Brownlow, *David Lean,* 470.

45. Turner, *The Making of Lawrence of Arabia,* 153. See also Vincent LoBrutto, *Selected Takes: Film Editors on Editing* (New York: Praeger, 1991), 67.

46. Morris and Raskin, *Lawrence of Arabia,* 141.

47. *The Making of "Lawrence of Arabia"* (Bouzereau).

48. LoBrutto, *Selected Takes,* 46. See also Oldham, *First Cut,* 161.

49. Timm, *The Soul of Cinema,* 201.

50. Ibid. See also Morris and Raskin, *Lawrence of Arabia,* 144.

51. Timm, *The Soul of Cinema,* 201.

52. *Lean by Jarre* (DVD, 2005, Milan Records). This is a rerelease, with added commentary, of a live 1992 recording.

53. Ibid.

54. Timm, *The Soul of Cinema*, 199.

55. Anderegg, *David Lean*, 117.

56. Russell, *The Lion Roars*, 122.

57. Lawrence, *Seven Pillars of Wisdom*, 30.

58. Turner, *The Making of Lawrence of Arabia*, 84.

59. *The Making of "Lawrence of Arabia"* (Bouzereau).

60. Joseph Roquemore, *History Goes to the Movies: Historical Films* (New York: Doubleday, 1999), 348.

61. *The Making of "Lawrence of Arabia"* (Bouzereau).

62. Roquemore, *History Goes to the Movies*, 107.

63. Anderegg, *David Lean*, 112.

64. Sragow, "David Lean's Right of *Passage*," 25.

65. Brownlow, *David Lean*, 480, 481.

66. Kael, *5001 Nights at the Movies*, 415.

67. Martin Scorsese, foreword to Morris and Raskin, *Lawrence of Arabia*, xiv–xv.

68. Sinclair, *Spiegel*, 104.

69. Morris and Raskin, *Lawrence of Arabia*, 183.

70. Sinclair, *Spiegel*, 104.

71. A. W. Lawrence, "The Fiction and the Fact," *Observer* (London), December 16, 1962, 1.

72. Murray Schumack, "*Lawrence of Arabia* Producer Defends Film Story of Hero," *New York Times*, January 26, 1963, 5.

73. Peter Worthington, "That's the Way It Was," *Toronto Telegram*, January 31, 1963, 1.

74. Morris and Raskin, *Lawrence of Arabia*, 153.

75. *Lean by Jarre.*

76. Morris and Raskin, *Lawrence of Arabia*, 185, 187.

77. Ibid., 177.

78. Silverman, *David Lean*, 149.

79. *The Making of "Lawrence of Arabia"* (Bouzereau).

80. Maxford, *David Lean*, 100.

81. *The Making of "Lawrence of Arabia"* (Bouzereau).

82. Ibid.

83. Morris and Raskin, *Lawrence of Arabia*, 203.

84. Oldham, *First Cut*, 159–60.

85. *The Making of "Lawrence of Arabia"* (Bouzereau).

86. Janet Maslin, "*Lawrence* Seen Whole," *New York Times*, January 29, 1989, sec. 2, p. 13. See also Mast and Kawin, *A Short History of the Movies*, 717.

87. Maslin, "*Lawrence* Seen Whole," 13. See also Caton, *Lawrence of Arabia,* 228.

88. Alan Barra, "At Long Last the Real *Lawrence*," *American Film* 14, no. 6 (March 1989): 44.

89. Roy Frumkes, "The Restoration of *Lawrence of Arabia*," *Films in Review* 40 (May 1989): 287.

90. Clark et al., "The Best Action Movies," vi.

91. Glenn Kenny, "The 100 Greatest Movies, Part I," *Premiere* 16, no. 7 (March 2003): 71.

92. John Cape, "Movie Music," *Film Comment* 39, no. 1 (November–December 2003): 40.

93. Richard Corliss, "Movies on a Grand Scale," *Time,* September 3, 2005, 88.

94. "T. E. Lawrence," *New York Times,* May 20, 2005, B4.

95. Fraser-Cavassoni, *Sam Spiegel,* 252–53.

96. Silverman, *David Lean,* 117.

97. Turner, *The Making of Lawrence of Arabia,* 168.

98. Ibid., 174.

99. "Oscar Bound," *Time,* December 24, 1965, 44.

14. KNIGHT WITHOUT ARMOR

1. Silverman, *David Lean,* 152.

2. Roquemore, *History Goes to the Movies,* 331.

3. Ibid., 336.

4. J. W. Dyck, *Boris Pasternak* (Boston: Twayne, 1972), 107.

5. Boris Pasternak, *Dr. Zhivago,* trans. Max Hayward and Manya Harari (New York: Pantheon, 1958), 146.

6. Larissa Rudova, *Understanding Boris Pasternak* (Columbia: University of South Carolina Press, 1997), 163.

7. Pasternak, *Dr. Zhivago,* 223.

8. *Dr. Zhivago: The Making of a Russian Epic* (Scott Benson, 1995, documentary).

9. Dyck, *Boris Pasternak,* 108.

10. *Dr. Zhivago: The Making of a Russian Epic.*

11. Boris Pasternak, *I Remember: Sketch for an Autobiography,* trans. David Magarshack (New York: Pantheon, 1959), 121–22.

12. "The Making of the Film," in Robert Bolt, *Dr. Zhivago: The Screenplay* (New York: Random House, 1965), xvii.

13. Edmund Wilson, *The Bit between My Teeth* (New York: Farrar Strauss Giroux, 1965), 446.

14. Brownlow, *David Lean,* 509.

15. S. Lean, *David Lean,* 28.

16. McFarland, *Autobiography of British Cinema*, 359.

17. "*Dr. Zhivago*," *Catholic Film Newsletter*, February 24, 1966, 4.

18. S. Lean, *David Lean*, 24.

19. Silverman, *David Lean*, 154.

20. Robert Bolt, introduction to *Dr. Zhivago: The Screenplay*, xi.

21. Ibid., xii.

22. S. Lean, *David Lean*, 26.

23. Phillips, *Major Film Directors*, 187. See also Pratley, "Interview with David Lean," 318.

24. *Dr. Zhivago: The Making of a Russian Epic.*

25. Betty Jeffries Demby, "An Interview with Robert Bolt," *Filmmakers Newsletter*, October 1973, 30. See also Bolt, introduction to *Dr. Zhivago: The Screenplay*, xv–xvi, ix.

26. Pratley, *The Cinema of David Lean*, 196.

27. Anderegg, *David Lean*, 123.

28. Brownlow, *David Lean*, 107.

29. *Dr. Zhivago: The Making of a Russian Epic.*

30. Ibid.

31. "Tom Courtenay," *Films in Review* 35, no. 2 (February 1984): 125.

32. *Dr. Zhivago: The Making of a Russian Epic.*

33. Brownlow, *David Lean*, 313.

34. Silverman, *David Lean*, 164.

35. S. Lean, *David Lean*, 123.

36. Read, *Alec Guinness*, 382–85.

37. Brownlow, *David Lean*, 514.

38. Pratley, "Interview with David Lean," 319.

39. Ibid.

40. Brownlow, *David Lean*, 516.

41. *Dr. Zhivago: The Making of a Russian Epic.*

42. Young, *Seventy Light Years*, 100.

43. Ibid.

44. Pratley, *The Cinema of David Lean*, 180. See also S. Lean, *David Lean*, 157.

45. Vincent LoBrutto, *The Filmmaker's Guide to Production Design* (New York: Allworth, 2002), 173. See also Floyd Martin, "John Box," in Elert, Sarris, and Jeromski, eds., *International Dictionary of Films and Filmmakers*, 4:97.

46. *Dr. Zhivago: The Making of a Russian Epic.*

47. Jonathan Hacker and David Price, *Take 10: Contemporary British Film Directors* (New York: Oxford University Press, 1992), 356.

48. Brownlow, *David Lean*, 522.

49. Pratley, *The Cinema of David Lean*, 189.

50. *Dr. Zhivago: The Making of a Russian Epic.*

51. S. Lean, *David Lean*, 123.

52. *Dr. Zhivago: The Making of a Russian Epic*.

53. Caton, *Lawrence of Arabia*, 235–36.

54. Pratley, *The Cinema of David Lean*, 168.

55. *Dr. Zhivago: The Making of a Russian Epic*.

56. Read, *Alec Guinness*, 383–84.

57. S. Lean, *David Lean*, 173.

58. R. S. Stewart, "*Dr. Zhivago:* The Making of a Movie," *Atlantic Monthly*, August 1965, 60.

59. Brownlow, *David Lean*, 520.

60. Omar Sharif's remarks are taken from the audio commentary track included on the 2001 DVD of *Dr. Zhivago*.

61. Ibid.

62. Ibid.

63. Young, *Seventy Light Years*, 100.

64. Ibid., 119.

65. "Freddie Young: Obituary," *Times* (London), December 3, 1998, 25.

66. Pratley, *The Cinema of David Lean*, 192.

67. Young, *Seventy Light Years*, 106.

68. Brownlow, *David Lean*, 528.

69. John McInerney, "Lean's *Zhivago:* A Reappraisal," *Literature/Film Quarterly* 15, no. 1 (winter 1987): 47.

70. Young, *Seventy Light Years*, 107.

71. "Dialogue on Film: David Lean," 52.

72. Pratley, *The Cinema of David Lean*, 199. See also Pratley, "Interview with David Lean," 312.

73. Mannion, "An Interest in Photography," 222.

74. Brownlow, *David Lean*, 520, 528.

75. Pratley, *The Cinema of David Lean*, 181.

76. Ibid., 192.

77. Silverman, *David Lean*, 159.

78. Brownlow, *David Lean*, 536.

79. Pratley, *The Cinema of David Lean*, 189–90.

80. Brownlow, *David Lean*, 536.

81. Geoffrey Macnab, "Sensitive to Nature: Maurice Jarre," *Sight and Sound*, n.s., 12, no. 2 (February 2000): 70.

82. Pratley, *The Cinema of David Lean*, 187.

83. Macnab, "Sensitive to Nature," 70.

84. Timm, *The Soul of Cinema*, 202.

85. *Lean by Jarre*.

86. Alan Leigh, "Maurice Jarre," *Hollywood Reporter*, September 6, 1999, 6.

87. Maxford, *David Lean*, 128.

88. Sragow, "David Lean's Right of *Passage*," 26.

89. Maxford, *David Lean*, 128.

90. Bolt, *Dr. Zhivago: The Screenplay*, 13.

91. Frank Beaver, *One Hundred Years of American Film* (New York: Macmillan, 2000), 152.

92. Anderegg, *David Lean*, 124.

93. McInerney, "Lean's *Zhivago*," 46.

94. Pratley, *The Cinema of David Lean*, 196.

95. Rod Steiger's remarks are taken from the audio commentary track included on the 2001 DVD of *Dr. Zhivago*.

96. McInerney, "Lean's *Zhivago*," 46.

97. Pasternak, *Dr. Zhivago*, 464.

98. Sarris, *Confessions of a Cultist*, 228.

99. Richard Schickel, "Lean's *Dr. Zhivago*," *Life*, January 21, 1966, 62A.

100. Bolt, *Dr. Zhivago: The Screenplay*, 224.

101. Brownlow, *David Lean*, 538.

102. Maxford, *David Lean*, 131. See also Douglas Brode, *The Films of the Sixties* (New York: Carol, 1993), 159.

103. Judith Crist, *The Private Eye, the Cowboy, and the Very Naked Girl: Movies from Cleo to Clyde* (New York: Popular Library, 1970), 156.

104. Fraser-Cavassoni, *Sam Spiegel*, 274.

105. Schickel, "Lean's *Dr. Zhivago*," 62A.

106. Pauline Kael, *For Keeps* (New York: Dutton, 1996), 92.

107. Pratley, "Interview with David Lean," 321.

108. Morris and Raskin, *Lawrence of Arabia*, 197.

109. Silverman, *David Lean*, 167.

110. Pratley, *The Cinema of David Lean*, 196.

111. Brownlow, *David Lean*, 541.

112. S. Lean, *David Lean*, 40. The quote from Tynan that serves as the epigraph to Alec Guinness's foreword to this book indicates that Tynan could be quite generous at times.

113. Sragow, "David Lean's Magnificent *Kwai*," 109.

114. Morris and Raskin, *Lawrence of Arabia*, 197.

115. Halliwell, *Who's Who in the Movies*, 281.

116. Turner, *The Making of Lawrence of Arabia*, 175.

117. Brownlow, *David Lean*, 547–48.

118. Ibid., 549.

119. Halliwell, *Who's Who in the Movies*, 281.

120. Silverman, *David Lean*, 167.

121. Brownlow, *David Lean*, 544.

122. For a reevaluation of the film, see Jurgen Muller, ed., *Movies of the Sixties* (Los Angeles: Taschen/BFI, 2005), 308–13.

15. THE LOWER DEPTHS

1. William Berg and Laurey Martin, *Gustave Flaubert* (New York: Twayne, 1997), xxi.

2. Wendy Everett, "*Madame Bovary,*" in Tibbetts and Welsh, *The Encyclopedia of Novels into Film,* 274.

3. Malcolm Bowie, introduction to *Madame Bovary: Provincial Manners,* by Gustave Flaubert, trans. Margaret Mauldon (New York: Oxford University Press, 2004), vii.

4. Flaubert, *Madame Bovary,* 150.

5. Ibid., 350.

6. Bowie, introduction to *Madame Bovary,* xx. See also James Wood, "The Man behind Bovary," *New York Times Book Review,* April 16, 2006, 10.

7. Pauline Kael, *Deeper into Movies* (New York: Bantam, 1974), 241.

8. Pratley, *The Cinema of David Lean,* 204.

9. Brownlow, *David Lean,* 535.

10. Silverman, *David Lean,* 171.

11. Robert Stam, *Literature through Film: Realism, Magic, and the Art of Adaptation* (Malden, MA: Blackwell, 2005), 168.

12. Demby, "An Interview with Robert Bolt," 31.

13. "Anthony Havelock-Allan: Obituary," 35.

14. Morris and Raskin, *Lawrence of Arabia,* 230. See also S. Lean, *David Lean,* 88.

15. Pratley, *The Cinema of David Lean,* 204.

16. Ross, "In Defense of David Lean," 14.

17. Brownlow, *David Lean,* 564.

18. Ibid., 564–65.

19. See Robert Bolt, *Ryan's Daughter: Unpublished Screenplay* (Metro-Goldwyn-Mayer, 1970), 178–82.

20. Brownlow, *David Lean,* 563.

21. Ibid., 563–64.

22. See also Silverman, *David Lean,* 169.

23. Mills, *Up in the Clouds, Gentlemen, Please,* 261.

24. Ibid.

25. *The Making of "Lawrence of Arabia"* (Bouzereau).

26. I owe this clarification to Donal Godfrey, S.J., the Irish-born chaplain at Loyola University of Chicago.

27. "Dialogue on Film: David Lean," 26.

28. Munn, *Trevor Howard,* 131.

29. Jerry Roberts, *Robert Mitchum: A Bio-Bibliography* (Westport, CT: Greenwood, 1992), 4.

30. Ibid., 20.

31. Silver and Ursini, *David Lean and His Films,* 238.

32. Mannion, "An Interest in Photography," 284.

33. Silverman, *David Lean,* 172.

34. The TV interview is included on the DVD of *Ryan's Daughter,* released by MGM in 2006.

35. Paul Rowan, interview with Anthony Havelock-Allan, November 2000, typescript, 2. I thank Paul Rowan for providing me with a copy of the typescript.

36. Young, *Seventy Light Years,* 117.

37. McFarlane, *Autobiography of British Cinema,* 406.

38. Young, *Seventy Light Years,* 118.

39. Herb Lightman, "Creative Techniques for *Ryan's Daughter,*" *American Cinematographer,* August 1969, 788.

40. Young, *Seventy Light Years,* 117.

41. Lightman, "Creative Techniques for *Ryan's Daughter,*" 778.

42. "An Interview with Sarah Miles," *Los Angeles Times,* November 15, 1970, Calendar, 28.

43. Munn, *Trevor Howard,* 128–29.

44. Ibid., 129. See also Mills, *Up in the Clouds, Gentlemen, Please,* 263.

45. Young, *Seventy Light Years,* 120.

46. Brownlow, *David Lean,* 568.

47. Munn, *Trevor Howard,* 128. See also Roberts, *Robert Mitchum,* 20, 21.

48. Brownlow, *David Lean,* 568, 574.

49. Roberts, *Robert Mitchum,* 276. See also Brownlow, *David Lean,* 557.

50. Silverman, *David Lean,* 172.

51. Brownlow, *David Lean,* 558.

52. Nick James, "The Big Stealer: Robert Mitchum," *Sight and Sound,* n.s., 15, no. 8 (August 2005): 41. See also Roberts, *Robert Mitchum,* 309.

53. Thomson, *New Biographical Dictionary,* 619–20.

54. Roberts, *Robert Mitchum,* 6.

55. "An Interview with Sarah Miles," 28. See also Silverman, *David Lean,* 174.

56. Young, *Seventy Light Years,* 121, 122.

57. Ibid., 122.

58. Mannion, "An Interest in Photography," 223.

59. Bolt, *Ryan's Daughter: Unpublished Screenplay,* 104.

60. *The Making of "Lawrence of Arabia"* (Bouzereau).

61. Silverman, *David Lean,* 176.

62. Sarah Miles, *Serves Me Right* (London: Phoenix, 1996), 180. See also Silverman, *David Lean,* 176.

63. Miles, *Serves Me Right,* 180.

64. Silverman, *David Lean,* 177.

65. McFarlane, *Autobiography of British Cinema,* 407.

66. Ibid., 414.

67. Munn, *Trevor Howard*, 130. See also Pratley, *The Cinema of David Lean*, 15.

68. Nigel Andrews, "Robert Mitchum Interviewed," *International Express*, April 24, 1991, 46.

69. Roberts, *Robert Mitchum*, 139.

70. Brownlow, *David Lean*, 574.

71. Kael, *Deeper into Movies*, 238.

72. Munn, *Trevor Howard*, 128.

73. Peter Bart, *Fade Out* (New York: Simon & Schuster, 1990), 40.

74. Mannion, "An Interest in Photography," 223–24.

75. Young, *Seventy Years of Light*, 122, 126.

76. Ibid., 120.

77. Mannion, "An Interest in Photography," 222–23.

78. Young, *Seventy Light Years*, 120. See also Mannion, "An Interest in Photography," 227.

79. Brownlow, *David Lean*, 579.

80. S. Lean, *David Lean*, 106.

81. Silver and Ursini, *David Lean and His Films*, 201.

82. Brownlow, *David Lean*, 582.

83. Macnab, "Sensitive to Nature," 70.

84. Maxford, *David Lean*, 136. Roberts, *Robert Mitchum*, 138.

85. Silver and Ursini, *David Lean and His Films*, 238.

86. Young, *Seventy Light Years*, 185.

87. Silver and Ursini, *David Lean and His Films*, 202.

88. Undated transcript in the files of the British Film Institute Library.

89. Kael, *Deeper into Movies*, 237–38, 241, 243.

90. Roberts, *Robert Mitchum*, 139. Roberts cites several of the American reviews of the movie.

91. Silverman, *David Lean*, 177.

92. Alexander Walker, *Double Takes: Notes and Afterthoughts on the Movies, 1956–76* (London: Elm Tree, 1977), 60–61.

93. Maxford, *David Lean*, 141.

94. Morris and Raskin, *Lawrence of Arabia*, 198.

95. Ibid.

96. Pratley, *The Cinema of David Lean*, 197. See also Pratley, "Interview with David Lean," 321.

97. Morris and Raskin, *Lawrence of Arabia*, 197–98.

98. Young, *Seventy Light Years*, 126.

99. Miles, *Serves Me Right*, 186.

100. Rowan, interview with Havelock-Allan, 3.

101. Butler, *Cinema in Britain*, 288.

102. Murphy, *Sixties British Cinema*, 91.

103. Brian McFarlane, "Obituary: Sir John Mills," *Sight and Sound,* n.s., 15, no. 6 (June 2005): 3.

104. McFarlane, *Autobiography of British Cinema,* 407.

105. "*Ryan's Daughter,*" *Premiere* 19, no. 7 (April 2006): 102. See also Dave Kehr, "New DVDs: *Ryan's Daughter,*" *New York Times,* February 7, 2006, 14.

106. Honan, "David Lean Plans to Film a Conrad Story," 13.

107. S. Lean, *David Lean,* 52.

108. Cocks, "David Lean," 59.

109. Kennedy, "'I'm a Picture Chap,'" 28.

110. Cocks, "David Lean," 61.

111. Turner, *The Making of Lawrence of Arabia,* 178.

112. Tony Williams, "*Mutiny on the Bounty,*" in Tibbetts and Welsh, *The Encyclopedia of Novels into Film,* 307. See also Pauline Kael, *State of the Art* (New York: Dutton, 1985), 185.

113. Turner, *The Making of Lawrence of Arabia,* 179.

114. Cocks, "David Lean," 62. See also S. Lean, *David Lean,* 165.

115. Turner, *The Making of Lawrence of Arabia,* 181. See also S. Lean, *David Lean,* 163–65.

116. George Andrews, "*Lost and Found,*" *American Cinematographer,* March 1979, 300.

117. "*Lost and Found: The Story of an Anchor,*" *Variety,* May 9, 1979, 35.

118. Silverman, *David Lean,* 181. See also Fraser-Cavassoni, *Sam Spiegel,* 328–29.

119. Brownlow, *David Lean,* 612. See also Steven Bach, *Final Cut: Art, Money, and Ego in the Making of Heaven's Gate, the Film that Sank United Artists* (1985), rev. ed. (New York: Newmarket, 1999), 126.

120. See Brownlow, *David Lean,* 634.

121. Sinclair, *Spiegel,* 193. See also Fraser-Cavassoni, *Sam Spiegel,* 329.

122. See Turner, *The Making of Lawrence of Arabia,* 181. See also Kael, *State of the Art,* 184–85.

123. Halliwell, *Film Guide,* 111.

124. Silverman, *David Lean,* 112.

125. Ibid., 190.

16. DARKNESS AT NOON

1. P. N. Furbank, *E. M. Forster: A Life,* 2 vols. in 1 (New York: Harcourt, Brace, Jovanovich, 1978), 1:28. Furbank is still considered to have written the most authoritative life of Forster, having enjoyed Forster's cooperation.

2. Mary Lago, *E. M. Forster: A Literary Life* (New York: St. Martin's, 1995), 65–66.

3. Ibid., 79.

4. Furbank, *E. M. Forster,* 2:40.

5. Ibid., 120.

6. Walt Whitman, "Passage to India," in *Walt Whitman: Complete Poetry and Collected Prose,* ed. Justin Kaplan (New York: Library of America, 1982), 532, 535. See also Maureen McLane, "An American Epic: *Leaves of Grass,*" *Chicago Tribune,* July 31, 2005, sec. 14, p. 5.

7. E. M. Forster, *Howard's End* (Boston: Bedford, 1997), iii.

8. E. M. Forster, *A Passage to India* (New York: Harcourt, Brace, Jovanovich, 1984), 6–7.

9. Norman Page, *E. M. Forster* (London: Macmillan, 1989), 116.

10. Charu Malik, "The Subject of Friendship in *A Passage to India,*" in *Queer Forster: Homosexuality in the Fiction of E. M. Forster,* ed. Robert K. Martin and George Piggford (Chicago: University of Chicago Press, 1997), 230–31.

11. Ibid., 230.

12. Furbank, *E. M. Forster,* 1:146.

13. Forster, *A Passage to India,* 361.

14. Abraham Lass, *Fifty British Novels* (New York: Simon & Schuster, 1966), 291.

15. Lago, *E. M. Forster,* 128–29.

16. *Reflections of David Lean.* The interview is priceless because it is the only filmed interview of Lean discussing *Passage* that remains available.

17. McFarlane, *Autobiography of British Cinema,* 95.

18. Ibid.

19. *Reflections of David Lean.*

20. Aljean Harmetz, "David Lean Interviewed," *New York Times,* December 9, 1984, sec. 2, p. 1.

21. "Dialogue on Film: David Lean," 52. See also Von Gunden, *Alec Guinness,* 271.

22. Silverman, *David Lean,* 187.

23. S. Lean, *David Lean,* 187.

24. Brownlow, *David Lean,* 267.

25. Honan, "David Lean Plans to Film a Conrad Story," 15.

26. Brownlow, *David Lean,* 657.

27. S. Lean, *David Lean,* 204.

28. Ibid.

29. Ibid. Brownlow, *David Lean,* 655.

30. See Brownlow, *David Lean,* 651–52, 688.

31. "Dialogue on Film: David Lean," 27.

32. *Reflections of David Lean.*

33. Ibid.

34. Richard Schickel, "A Superb *Passage to India,*" *Time,* December 31, 1984, 57.

35. Page, *E. M. Forster,* 71, 90.

36. June Levine, "Too Lean: *A Passage to India,*" *Literature/Film Quarterly* 14, no. 3 (fall 1986): 140.

37. Lago, *E. M. Forster,* 71, 90.

38. *Reflections of David Lean.*

39. David Lean, *A Passage to India: Unpublished Screenplay* (Columbia Pictures, 1982), 5. The screenplay is preserved in the script repository at Columbia Pictures, dated September 4, 1982.

40. Arthur Lindley, "Lean's and Forster's *Passage to India,*" *Literature/Film Quarterly* 20, no. 1 (winter 1992): 61–62.

41. Brownlow, *David Lean,* 679.

42. Kennedy, "'I'm a Picture Chap,'" 32. See also Read, *Alec Guinness,* 528.

43. Cocks, "David Lean," 58.

44. Ibid., 62.

45. McFarlane, *Autobiography of British Cinema,* 205.

46. Brownlow, *David Lean,* 663–64.

47. Ernest Day, "*A Passage to India,*" *American Cinematographer,* February 1985, 59.

48. Harmetz, "David Lean Interviewed," 1.

49. Read, *Alec Guinness,* 526.

50. Ian Jack, "Lean's *Passage to India,*" *Times* (London), April 8, 1984, 33.

51. Day, "*A Passage to India,*" 59.

52. Ibid.

53. John Mitchell, *Flickering Shadows: A Lifetime in Film* (London: Martin & Redman, 1997), 289.

54. Kael, *For Keeps,* 1045. See also John Hill, *British Cinema in the 1980s* (Oxford: Clarendon, 1999), 100.

55. *Reflections of David Lean.*

56. Day, "*A Passage to India,*" 60.

57. Ibid., 62.

58. Ibid., 51.

59. "David Lean and *A Passage to India,*" *Daily Express* (London), April 2, 1984, 9.

60. Mitchell, *Flickering Shadows,* 294.

61. Ibid.

62. Brownlow, *David Lean,* 566, 569.

63. Turner, *The Making of Lawrence of Arabia,* 181.

64. Mitchell, *Flickering Shadows,* 294.

65. Ibid., 295. See also Lean, *A Passage to India: Unpublished Screenplay,* 10.

66. Mitchell, *Flickering Shadows,* 295.

67. Kael, *For Keeps,* 1045.

68. Mitchell, *Flickering Shadows,* 305.

69. Gavin Smith, "Judy Davis Interview," *Film Comment* 21, no. 6 (November–December 1992): 47.

70. Read, *Alec Guinness,* 527.

71. Brownlow, *David Lean,* 673.

72. Silverman, *David Lean,* 189.

73. *Reflections of David Lean.*

74. Halliwell, *Who's Who in the Movies,* 281.

75. Leslie Felperin, "Ms. Tough: Judy Davis," *Sight and Sound,* n.s., 9, no. 6 (June 1999): 12.

76. Cocks, "David Lean," 62.

77. Read, *Alec Guinness,* 527.

78. Smith, "Judy Davis Interview," 49.

79. Read, *Alec Guinness,* 528.

80. Silver and Ursini, *David Lean and His Films,* 224–25. See also Read, *Alec Guinness,* 528.

81. O'Connor, *Alec Guinness,* 245–46.

82. Von Gunden, *Alec Guinness,* 273.

83. Mitchell, *Flickering Shadows,* 303.

84. Cocks, "David Lean," 62.

85. Guinness, *Blessings in Disguise,* 216. See also Read, *Alec Guinness,* 294.

86. Prem Chowdhry, *Colonial India and the Making of Empire Cinema* (New York: Manchester University Press, 2000), 267–68. See also Cocks, "David Lean," 62.

87. Brownlow, *David Lean,* 479–80.

88. McFarlane, *Autobiography of British Cinema,* 265.

89. *Reflections of David Lean.*

90. Mitchell, *Flickering Shadows,* 297.

91. Brownlow, *David Lean,* 687–88.

92. Leigh, "Maurice Jarre," 6. See also Cocks, "David Lean," 62.

93. The Jarre interview is included on the DVD of *A Passage to India* released in 2000.

94. Page, *E. M. Forster,* 102.

95. Caton, *Lawrence of Arabia,* 237. See also Lago, *E. M. Forster,* 67.

96. *Reflections of David Lean.*

97. Brown, "*A Passage to India,*" 339.

98. Levine, "Too Lean," 143.

99. Lago, *E. M. Forster,* 79.

100. Brownlow, *David Lean,* 647.

101. Lean, *A Passage to India: Unpublished Screenplay,* 66–67.

102. "Dialogue on Film: David Lean," 27.

103. Cocks, "David Lean," 62.

104. Page, *E. M. Forster,* 107.

105. Forster, *A Passage to India,* 256.

106. Hill, *British Cinema in the 1980s,* 109.

107. Lindley, "Lean's and Forster's *Passage to India,*" 61.

108. "David Lean," *Guardian* (Manchester), April 17, 1991, 37.

109. Louis Giannetti and Scott Eyman, *Flashback: A Brief History of Film*, 5th ed. (Upper Saddle River, NJ: Prentice-Hall, 2006), 218.

110. Kael, *For Keeps*, 1042–43.

111. Schickel, "A Superb *Passage to India*," 57, 55.

112. Jerome Ozer, ed., *Film Review Annual* (Englewood, NJ: Film Review Publications, 1985), 1042–43. For reprints of several periodical reviews of the film, see ibid., 1041–53.

113. Ibid., 1046.

114. Ibid., 1043.

115. Read, *Alec Guinness*, 531.

116. Von Gunden, *Alec Guinness*, 267.

117. Read, *Alec Guinness*, 530.

118. Brownlow, *David Lean*, 683.

119. Honan, "David Lean Plans to Film a Conrad Story," 13.

120. See S. Lean, *David Lean*.

121. Brownlow, *David Lean*, 669.

EPILOGUE

1. Daniel Rosenthal, "The Grim Tales of Joseph Conrad," *Times* (London), May 18, 1995, 35.

2. Joseph Conrad, *Letters to a Friend*, ed. Richard Curle (New York: Doubleday, Doran, 1928), 90.

3. Harlan Kennedy, "*Nostromo*," *American Film* 15, no. 6 (March 1990): 28.

4. Ibid., 31.

5. Honan, "David Lean Plans to Film a Conrad Story," 18.

6. S. Lean, *David Lean*, 220.

7. Brownlow, *David Lean*, 717.

8. Ibid., 718.

9. Kennedy, "*Nostromo*," 54. See Brownlow, *David Lean*, 719.

10. Kennedy, "*Nostromo*," 56.

11. Rosenthal, "The Grim Tales of Joseph Conrad," 35.

12. Turner, *The Making of Lawrence of Arabia*, 183.

13. Brownlow, *David Lean*, 731.

14. Jarre, *A Passage to India* DVD interview.

15. The interview is included on the DVD of *Ryan's Daughter*.

16. Christopher Hampton, *The Secret Agent and Nostromo: Two Screenplays* (Boston: Faber & Faber, 1996), xvii.

17. Morris and Raskin, *Lawrence of Arabia*, 272.

18. Brownlow, *David Lean*, 274.

19. Mitchell, *Flickering Shadows*, 312.

20. Sragow, "David Lean's Right of *Passage*," 27.

21. Kael, *For Keeps*, 843–44.

22. Sragow, "David Lean's Right of *Passage*," 27.

23. Morris and Raskin, *Lawrence of Arabia*, 233.

24. Scorsese, foreword to Morris and Raskin, *Lawrence of Arabia*, xiv.

25. Jarre, *A Passage to India* DVD interview.

26. James Thurber, *Credos and Curios* (New York: Harper & Row, 1963), 162.

27. Sragow, "David Lean's Magnificent *Kwai*," 109.

28. Thurber, *Credos and Curios*, 163.

29. Robert Kolker, *Film, Form, and Culture* (2000), rev. ed. (Boston: McGraw-Hill, 2006), 135.

30. David Ehrenstein, "David Lean: AFI Life Achievement Award," *American Film* 15, no. 6 (March 1990): 20–22.

31. Lean, "The Film Director," 36.

32. Pratley, "Interview with David Lean," 321. See also Gene Phillips, *The Movie Makers* (Chicago: Nelson-Hall, 1973), 162–63.

33. Jeffrey Ressner, "Ten Questions for Ron Meyer," *Time*, September 5, 2005, 6.

34. Kennedy, "'I'm a Picture Chap,'" 36.

SELECT BIBLIOGRAPHY

Agee, James. *Film Writing and Selected Journalism*. Edited by Michael Sragow. New York: Library of America, 2005.

Altman, Rick. "Dickens, Griffith, and Film Theory Today." In *Classical Hollywood Narrative*, edited by Jane Gaines, 11–32. Durham, NC: Duke University Press, 1992.

Ambler, Eric, with David Lean and Stanley Haynes. *The Passionate Friends: Unpublished Screenplay*. Rank, 1948.

American Film Institute. *A Special Gala in Honor of David Lean*. Washington, DC: American Film Institute, 1990. Souvenir program for the tribute to Lean on March 8, 1990.

Anderegg, Michael. *David Lean*. Boston: Twayne, 1984.

Andrews, George. "*Lost and Found*." *American Cinematographer*, March 1979, 295–308. Concerns a documentary by Lean.

Ansen, David. "Saved from the Sands of Time: *Lawrence of Arabia*," *Newsweek*, February 6, 1989, 75.

"Anthony Havelock-Allan: Obituary." *Times* (London), January 14, 2003, 35.

Armes, Roy. *A Critical History of the British Cinema*. London: Secker & Warburg, 1978.

Asher, Michael. *Lawrence: The Uncrowned King of Arabia*. Woodstock, NY: Overlook, 1995.

Baillieu, Bill, and John Goodchild. *The British Film Business*. New York: Wiley, 2002.

Barra, Alan. "At Long Last, the Real *Lawrence*." *American Film* 14, no. 6 (March 1989): 44.

Baston, Jane. "Word and Image: *Great Expectations.*" *Literature/Film Quarterly* 24, no. 3 (spring 1996): 322–31.

Bayer, William. *The Great Movies.* New York: Grossett & Dunlap, 1973.

Beaver, Frank. *One Hundred Years of American Film.* New York: Macmillan, 2000.

Becker, Lucille. *Pierre Boulle.* New York: Twayne, 1996.

Bluestone, George. *Novels into Film.* Berkeley: University of California Press, 1968.

Bolt, Robert. *Dr. Zhivago: The Screenplay.* New York: Random House, 1965.

———. *Ryan's Daughter: Unpublished Screenplay.* Metro-Goldwyn-Mayer, 1970.

Bolt, Robert, with Michael Wilson (uncredited). *Lawrence of Arabia: Unpublished Screenplay.* Columbia Pictures, 1961. Parts 1 and 2 are paginated separately.

Boulle, Pierre. *The Bridge on the River Kwai.* Translated by Xan Fielding. New York: Time, 1964. A translation of Boulle's 1952 novel *Le pont de la rivière Kwai.*

———. *My Own River Kwai.* Translated by Xan Fielding. New York: Vanguard, 1967.

Boulle, Pierre, with Michael Wilson (uncredited) and Carl Foreman (uncredited). *The Bridge on the River Kwai: Unpublished Screenplay.* Columbia Pictures, 1956.

Bourne, Stephen. *Brief Encounters: Lesbians and Gays in British Cinema 1930–1971.* New York: Cassell, 1996.

The Bridge on the River Kwai. Souvenir program. Columbia Pictures, 1957.

Brighouse, Harold. *Hobson's Choice.* New York: Samuel French, 1916.

Brode, Douglas. *The Films of the Fifties.* New York: Carol, 1993.

———. *The Films of the Sixties.* New York: Carol, 1993.

———. *Lost Films of the Fifties.* New York: Carol, 1991.

Brown, Malcolm, ed. *The Letters of T. E. Lawrence.* New York: Oxford University Press, 1991.

Brownlow, Kevin. *David Lean: A Biography.* New York: St. Martin's, 1997.

Butler, Ivan. *Cinema in Britain.* New York: Barnes, 1973.

Callow, Simon. *Charles Laughton: A Difficult Actor.* New York: Grove, 1987.

Cardullo, Bert. "On Shaw's *Pygmalion;* Play and Film: Stanley Kauffmann Interview." *Literature/Film Quarterly* 31, no. 4 (fall 2003): 242–47.

Castelli, Louis, and Caryn Cleeland. *David Lean: A Guide to References and Resources.* Boston: G. K. Hall, 1980.

Caton, Steven. *Lawrence of Arabia: A Film's Anthropology.* Berkeley and Los Angeles: University of California Press, 1999.

Chibnall, Steve, and Robert Murphy, eds. *British Crime Cinema.* New York: Routledge, 1999.

Chowdhry, Prem. *Colonial India and the Making of Empire Cinema.* New York: Manchester University Press, 2000.

Christie, Ian. "Michael Powell." *Sight and Sound,* n.s., 15, no. 9 (September 2005): 30–31.

"Cinema: *Oliver Twist.*" In *Time Capsule: 1951,* 53. New York: Time-Life, 2001.

Clark, Jason, et al. "100 Best Action Movies on DVD." *Premiere* 16, no. 6 (February 2003): i–xi. Includes *Bridge on the River Kwai* and *Lawrence of Arabia.*

Cocks, Jay. "David Lean." *Time,* December 31, 1984, 58–62.

Cole, Hugo. *Malcolm Arnold: An Introduction to His Music.* London: Faber, 1989.

Collins, Ray. "Rising Damp: *Great Expectations.*" *Sight and Sound,* n.s., 9, no. 3 (March 1999): 33.

Corliss, Richard. "Blessings in Disguise: Alec Guinness." *Time,* August 21, 2000, 21.

———. "A Masterpiece Restored: *Lawrence of Arabia.*" *Time,* February 6, 1989, 62.

———. "Movies on a Grand Scale." *Time,* September 3, 2005, 88.

Costello, Donald. *The Serpent's Eye: Shaw and the Cinema.* Notre Dame, IN: University of Notre Dame Press, 1965.

Coward, Noël. *Autobiography: Consisting of Present Indicative, Future Indefinite and the Uncompleted Past Conditional.* London: Methuen, 1986. The three-part autobiography that Coward published over the years collected into a single volume.

———. *Blithe Spirit.* 1941. In *Three Plays,* 9–127. New York: Grove, 1979.

———. *This Happy Breed.* 1942. In *The Collected Plays of Noel Coward,* vol. 4, *To-Night at 8:30; Present Laughter; This Happy Breed,* 429–554. London: Heinemann, 1962.

———. *Tonight at 8:30.* 1936. In *The Collected Plays of Noel Coward,* vol. 4, *To-Night at 8:30; Present Laughter; This Happy Breed,* 237–83. London: Heinemann, 1962.

Coward, Noël, with David Lean, Ronald Neame, and Anthony Havelock-Allan. *Brief Encounter: A Screenplay.* In *Masterworks of the British Cinema,* 9–126. Boston: Faber & Faber, 1990.

Crowther, Bosley. *The Great Films.* New York: Putnam, 1967.

———. *Reruns: Fifty Memorable Films.* New York: Putnam, 1978.

———. *Vintage Films.* New York: Putnam, 1977.

"David Lean Talks to Roger Manvell." In *The Cinema,* ed. Roger Manvell and R. K. Nelson-Baxter, 19–24. London: Penguin, 1952.

Day, Ernest. "*A Passage to India.*" *American Cinematographer,* February 1985, 56–62.

DeBona, Guerric. "Plot Mutations in Lean's *Great Expectations.*" *Literature/ Film Quarterly* 20, no. 4 (winter 1992): 77–100.

Demby, Betty Jeffries. "An Interview with Robert Bolt." *Filmmakers Newsletter,* October 1973, 30–34.

Desowitz, Bill. "Revisiting Film's Biggest Stories." *New York Times,* June 17, 2001, sec. 2, p. 20.

"Dialogue on Film: David Lean." *American Film* 15, no. 6 (March 1990): 22–27, 52–53. Edited transcript of a seminar that Lean gave for the students at the American Film Institute.

Dickens, Charles. *Great Expectations.* New York: Oxford University Press, 1993.

———. *Oliver Twist.* New York: Oxford University Press, 1966.

Dixon, Wheeler, ed. *Re-Viewing British Cinema.* Albany: State University of New York Press, 1994.

Durgnat, Raymond. *A Mirror for England: British Movies from Austerity to Affluence.* New York: Praeger, 1971.

Dyck, J. W. *Boris Pasternak.* Boston: Twayne, 1972.

Dyer, Richard. *Brief Encounter.* London: British Film Institute, 1993.

Ebert, Roger. *The Great Movies.* New York: Broadway, 2003.

———. *The Great Movies II.* New York: Broadway, 2005.

Edwards, Anne. *A Remarkable Woman: A Biography of Katharine Hepburn.* New York: Morrow, 1985.

Ehrenstein, David. "David Lean: AFI Lifetime Achievement Award." *American Film* 15, no. 6 (March 1990): 20–22.

Eisenstein, Sergei. "Dickens, Griffith, and Film Today." In *Film Form,* translated by Jay Leyda, 195–255. New York: Harcourt Brace, 1949.

Elert, Nicolet, Andrew Sarris, and Grace Jeromski, eds. *International Dictionary of Films and Filmmakers.* 1997. Rev. ed. 4 vols. New York: St. James, 2000.

"Film Crew in Salford: *Hobson's Choice.*" *Guardian* (Manchester), September 9, 1953, 1.

Flaubert, Gustave. *Madame Bovary: Provincial Manners.* Translated by Margaret Mauldon. New York: Oxford University Press, 2004. The source of *Ryan's Daughter.*

Fleming, Kate. *Celia Johnson: A Biography.* London: Weidenfeld & Nicolson, 1991.

Foot, Michael. *H.G.: The History of Mr. Wells.* Washington, DC: Counterpoint, 1995.

Forster, E. M. *A Passage to India.* New York: Harcourt, Brace, Jovanovich, 1984.

Fraser-Cavassoni, Natasha. *Sam Spiegel.* New York: Simon & Schuster, 2003.

Frumkes, Roy. "The Restoration of *Lawrence of Arabia.*" *Films in Review* 40, no. 4 (April 1989): 204–10; 40, no. 5 (May 1989): 285–91.

Fulton, A. R. *Motion Pictures: The Development of an Art.* 1960. Rev. ed. Norman: University of Oklahoma Press, 1980.

Furbank, P. N. *E. M. Forster: A Life.* 2 vols. in 1. New York: Harcourt, Brace, Jovanovich, 1978. Each volume is separately paginated.

Geduld, Harry, ed. *Filmmakers on Filmmaking*. Bloomington: Indiana University Press, 1969.

Giannetti, Louis, and Scott Eyman. *Flashback: A Brief History of Film*. 5th ed. Upper Saddle River, NJ: Prentice-Hall, 2006.

Glavin, John, ed. *Dickens on Screen*. New York: Cambridge University Press, 2003.

"*Great Expectations.*" *Life*, June 2, 1947, 61–62.

Greene, Graham. *The Graham Greene Film Reader: Reviews, Essays, and Interviews*. Edited by David Parkinson. New York: Applause, 1995.

Guinness, Alec. *Blessings in Disguise*. New York: Penguin, 1996.

Halliwell, Leslie. *Film Guide*. 1977. Edited by John Walker. Revised edition. New York: HarperCollins, 2005.

———. *Who's Who in the Movies*. 1965. Edited by John Walker. Revised edition. New York: HarperCollins, 2003.

Hammond, J. R. *H. G. Wells and Rebecca West*. New York: St. Martin's, 1991.

Harmetz, Aljean. "David Lean Interviewed." *New York Times,* December 9, 1984, sec. 2, p. 1.

Harper, Sue. *Picturing the Past: The Rise and Fall of the British Costume Film*. London: British Film Institute, 1994.

Harper, Sue, and Vincent Porter. *British Cinema of the 1950s: The Decline of Deference*. New York: Oxford University Press, 2003.

Harrison, Rex. *Rex: An Autobiography*. New York: Morrow, 1975.

Harvey, James. "Sam Spiegel." *New York Times Book Review,* April 13, 2003, 29.

Hawkins, Jack. *Anything for a Quiet Life*. London: Elm Tree, 1973.

Hayakawa, Sessue. "Zen Showed Me the Way." *Films and Filming,* February 1967, 21–24.

Hepburn, Katharine. "Get a Tough Director." *Panorama,* March 1981, 58–61, 77.

———. "So Just Keep a-Goin'—You Can Win." *TV Guide,* January 27, 1979, 5.

Higson, Andrew. *English Heritage, English Cinema: Costume Dramas*. London: Oxford University Press, 2003.

Hill, John. *British Cinema in the 1980s*. Oxford: Clarendon, 1999.

Hoare, Philip. *Noel Coward: A Biography*. New York: Simon & Schuster, 1995.

"*Hobson's Choice.*" *Sight and Sound,* n.s., 10, no. 8 (August 2000): 64.

Holroyd, Michael. *Bernard Shaw*. 3 vols. London: Chatto & Windus, 1997.

Honan, William. "David Lean Plans to Film a Conrad Story." *New York Times,* October 17, 1989, 13.

"Interview with Robert Bolt." *Evening Standard* (London), May 11, 1989, 28–29.

Kael, Pauline. *Deeper into Movies*. New York: Bantam, 1974.

———. *5001 Nights at the Movies*. New York: Holt, 1991.

———. *For Keeps*. New York: Dutton, 1996.

———. *Kiss Kiss Bang Bang*. New York: Bantam, 1969.

Kehr, Dave. "Epic *Lawrence of Arabia* Returns in All Its Irony." *Chicago Tribune*, March 17, 1989, 7A.

Kennedy, Harlan. "British Cinema in World War II." *Film Comment* 32, no. 5 (September–October 1996): 25–34.

———. "'I'm a Picture Chap': David Lean." *Film Comment* 21, no. 1 (January–February 1985): 28–32.

———. "*Nostromo*." *American Film* 15, no. 6 (March 1990): 27–31, 53–55.

Kenny, Glenn. "The 100 Greatest Movies, Part I." *Premiere* 16, no. 7 (March 2003): 54–78.

———. "The 100 Greatest Movies, Part II." *Premiere* 16, no. 10 (June 2003): 1–12.

———. "The 75 Most Influential Movies on DVD." *Premiere* 17, no. 4 (January 2004): 1–10.

Kifner, John. "In Lawrence of Arabia's Time Iraq Was No Picnic." *New York Times*, July 20, 2003, sec. 4, pp. 1, 4.

———. "A Tide of Islamic Fury." *New York Times*, January 30, 2005, sec. 4, p. 4.

Klein, Michael, and Gillian Parker, eds. *The English Novel and the Movies*. New York: Ungar, 1981.

Knightly, Philip, and Colin Simpson. *The Secret Lives of Lawrence of Arabia*. New York: McGraw-Hill, 1969.

Kolker, Robert. *Film, Form, and Culture*. 2000. Rev. ed. Boston: McGraw-Hill, 2006.

Korda, Michael. *Charmed Lives*. New York: Random House, 1979.

Lago, Mary. *E. M. Forster: A Literary Life*. New York: St. Martin's, 1995.

Laurents, Arthur. *The Time of the Cuckoo*. New York: Random House, 1953. The source of *Summertime*.

Lawrence, A. W., ed. *T. E. Lawrence and His Friends*. London: Jonathan Cape, 1937.

Lawrence, T. E. *Seven Pillars of Wisdom: A Triumph*. New York: Anchor, 1991.

Lawrence of Arabia. Souvenir program. Columbia Pictures, 1962.

Lazar, David, ed. *Michael Powell: Interviews*. Jackson: University Press of Mississippi, 2003.

Lean, David. "*Brief Encounter*." In *Penguin Film Review* (no. 4), 27–35. Harmondsworth: Penguin, 1947.

———. "The Film Director." In *Working for the Films*, ed. Oswell Blakeston, 27–37. London: Focal, 1947.

———. "Out of the Wilderness: *Lawrence of Arabia*." *Films and Filming*, January 1963, 12–15.

———. *A Passage to India: Unpublished Screenplay*. Columbia Pictures, 1982.

Lean, David, and Stanley Haynes. *Oliver Twist: Unpublished Screenplay*. Eagle-Lion, 1947.

Lean, David, Ronald Neame, and Anthony Havelock-Allan, with Kay Walsh and Cecil McGivern. *Great Expectations: Unpublished Screenplay.* Universal, 1945.

Lean, Sandra, with Barry Chattington. *David Lean: An Intimate Portrait.* New York: Universe, 2001.

Leigh, Alan. "Maurice Jarre." *Hollywood Reporter,* September 6, 1999, 6.

Levine, June. "Too Lean: *A Passage to India.*" *Literature/Film Quarterly* 14, no. 3 (fall 1986): 138–50.

Lightman, Herb. "Creative Techniques for *Ryan's Daughter.*" *American Cinematographer,* August 1969, 788.

Lindley, Arthur. "Lean's and Forster's *Passage to India.*" *Literature/Film Quarterly* 20, no. 1 (winter 1992): 61–67.

LoBrutto, Vincent, ed. *By Design: Interviews with Film Production Designers.* Westport, CT: Praeger, 1992.

———. *Selected Takes: Film Editors on Editing.* New York: Praeger, 1991.

Low, Rachael. *The History of the British Film: The Films of the 1930s.* London: Allen & Unwin, 1979.

Macdonald, Kevin. *Emeric Pressburger: The Life and Death of a Screenwriter.* Boston: Faber & Faber, 1994.

MacKay, Carol. "The Case of *Great Expectations.*" *Literature/Film Quarterly* 13, no. 2 (spring 1985): 127–34.

Macnab, Geoffrey. "Howard's Way: Trevor Howard." *Sight and Sound,* n.s., 10, no. 5 (May 2000): 26–29.

———. *Searching for Stars: Stardom and Screen Acting in British Cinema.* New York: Cassell, 2000.

———. "Sensitive to Nature: Maurice Jarre." *Sight and Sound,* n.s., 12, no. 2 (February 2000): 70.

———. "Unknown Pleasures: British Cinema of the 1950s." *Sight and Sound,* n.s., 14, no. 4 (April 2004): 38.

Maltin, Leonard, Cathleen Anderson, and Luke Sader, eds. *Movie Guide.* 1969. Rev. ed. New York: Penguin, 2005.

Mannion, Frank. "An Interest in Photography: Freddie Young." In *Projections Six: Filmmakers on Filmmaking,* ed. John Boorman and Walter Donohue, 208–27. London: Faber & Faber, 1996.

Marill, Alvin. *The Films of Anthony Quinn.* Secaucus, NJ: Citadel, 1977.

Martin, Robert K., and George Piggford, eds. *Queer Forster: Homosexuality in the Fiction of E. M. Forster.* Chicago: University of Chicago Press, 1997.

Maslin, Janet. "*Lawrence* Seen Whole." *New York Times,* January 29, 1989, sec. 2, pp. 1, 13.

Mast, Gerald, and Bruce Kawin. *A Short History of the Movies.* 1971. Rev. ed. New York: Longman, 2006.

Maxford, Howard. *David Lean.* London: Batsford, 2000.

Mayer, Geoff. *Guide to British Cinema.* Westport, CT: Praeger, 2003.

McFarlane, Brian. *An Autobiography of British Cinema by Filmmakers and Actors.* London: Methuen, 1997.

———. *Novel to Film: The Theory of Adaptation.* New York: Oxford University Press, 1996.

———. "Obituary: Sir John Mills." *Sight and Sound,* n.s., 15, no. 6 (June 2005): 3.

McInerney, John. "Lean's *Zhivago:* A Reappraisal." *Literature/Film Quarterly* 15, no. 1 (winter 1987): 43–48.

McKee, Al. "Art or Outrage? *Oliver Twist* and Fagin." *Film Comment* 36, no. 1 (January–February 2000): 40–45.

Miles, Sarah. *Serves Me Right: A Memoir.* London: Phoenix, 1996.

Mills, John. *Up in the Clouds, Gentlemen, Please.* London: Ticknor & Fields, 1981.

Mitchell, John. *Flickering Shadows: A Lifetime in Film.* London: Martin & Redman, 1997.

Morley, Sheridan. *A Talent to Amuse: A Biography of Noël Coward.* London: Pavilion, 1985.

Morris, Robert, and Lawrence Raskin. *Lawrence of Arabia: The Pictorial History.* New York: Doubleday, 1992.

Muller, Jurgen, ed. *Movies of the Fifties.* Los Angeles: Taschen/BFI, 2005. Includes a discussion of *The Bridge on the River Kwai.*

———, ed. *Movies of the Forties.* Los Angeles: Taschen/BFI, 2005. Includes a discussion of *Brief Encounter.*

———, ed. *Movies of the Sixties.* Los Angeles: Taschen/BFI, 2005. Includes a discussion of *Lawrence of Arabia* and *Dr. Zhivago.*

Munn, Michael. *Trevor Howard: The Man and His Films.* London: Robson, 1989.

Murphy, Robert, ed. *The British Cinema Book.* 1997. Rev. ed. London: British Film Institute, 2001.

———. *Realism and Tinsel: Cinema and Society in Britain.* New York: Routledge, 1998.

———. *Sixties British Cinema.* London: British Film Institute, 1992.

Nash, Jay, and Stanley Ross, eds. *The Motion Picture Guide.* 12 vols. Chicago: Cinebooks, 1985. Pagination is consecutive throughout all 12 vols.

Neame, Ronald, with Barbara Cooper. *Straight from the Horse's Mouth: An Autobiography.* Lanham, MD: Scarecrow, 2003.

Nutting, Anthony. *Lawrence of Arabia.* London: Hollis & Carter, 1961.

O'Connor, Garry. *Alec Guinness: Master of Disguise.* London: Hodder & Storighton, 1994.

Oldham, Gabriella. "Touching the Heart: Anne V. Coates." In *First Cut: Conversations with Film Editors,* 151–69. Berkeley and Los Angeles: University of California Press, 1995.

Orlans, Harold. *T. E. Lawrence: Biography of a Broken Hero.* Jefferson, NC: Mc-Farland, 2002.

O'Toole, Peter. *Loitering with Intent.* New York: Hyperion, 1992.

Ozer, Jerome, ed. *Film Review Annual.* Englewood, NJ: Film Review Publications, 1985.

Pascal, Valerie. *The Disciple and His Devil: Gabriel Pascal.* New York: McGraw-Hill, 1970.

Pasternak, Boris. *Dr. Zhivago.* Translated by Max Hayward and Manya Harari. New York: Pantheon, 1958.

———. *I Remember; Sketch for an Autobiography.* Translated by David Magarshack. New York: Pantheon, 1959.

Plain, Gill. *John Mills and British Cinema.* Edinburgh: Edinburgh University Press, 2006.

Powell, Michael. *A Life in the Movies.* New York: Knopf, 1987.

Pratley, Gerald. *The Cinema of David Lean.* New York: Barnes, 1974.

Quirk, Lawrence. *The Great War Films.* New York: Carol, 1994.

Raw, Lawrence. "T. E. Lawrence, the Turks, and the Arab Revolt in the Cinema." *Literature/Film Quarterly* 33, no. 4 (fall 2005): 252–61.

Read, Piers Paul. *Alec Guinness: The Authorized Biography.* New York: Simon & Schuster, 2005.

Reisz, Karel, with Gavin Millar. *The Technique of Film Editing.* 1960. Rev. ed. New York: Communication Arts, 1968.

Rich, Frank. "*Lawrence of Arabia* Redux." *New York Times,* April 18, 2004, sec. 2, pp. 1, 17.

Richards, Jeffrey, ed. *The Unknown 1930s: An Alternative History of the British Cinema, 1929–39.* London: Tauris, 1998.

Roberts, Jerry. *Robert Mitchum: A Bio-Bibliography.* Westport, CT: Greenwood, 1992.

"Rod Steiger." *Times* (London), July 2, 2002, 3.

Roquemore, Joseph. *History Goes to the Movies: Historical Films.* New York: Doubleday, 1999.

Ross, Steven. "In Defense of David Lean." *Take One,* July–August 1972, 14–15.

Rudova, Larissa. *Understanding Boris Pasternak.* Columbia: University of South Carolina Press, 1997.

Russell, Ken. *The Lion Roars: Ken Russell on Film.* Boston: Faber & Faber, 1994.

Sarris, Andrew. *Confessions of a Cultist: On the Cinema, 1955–69.* New York: Simon & Schuster, 1971.

———, ed. *Film Directors Encyclopedia.* New York: St. James, 2000.

———, ed. *Interviews with Film Directors.* New York: Avon, 1967.

Schickel, Richard. "A Superb *Passage to India.*" *Time,* December 31, 1984, 54–57.

Shafer, Stephen. *British Popular Films, 1929–39.* New York: Routledge, 1997.

Sharif, Omar, with Marie Thérèse Guinchard. *The Eternal Male.* Translated by Martin Sokolinsky. Garden City, NY: Doubleday, 1977.

Shaw, George Bernard. *Major Barbara: A Screenplay.* Baltimore: Penguin, 1951.

————. *Pygmalion: A Screenplay.* Baltimore: Penguin, 1941.

Silver, Alain, and James Ursini. *David Lean and His Films.* Los Angeles: Silman-James, 1992.

Silverman, Stephen. *David Lean.* New York: Abrams, 1989.

Sinclair, Andrew. *Spiegel: The Man behind the Pictures.* Boston: Little, Brown, 1987.

Sinyard, Neil. *Filming Literature: The Art of Screen Adaptation.* New York: St. Martin's, 1986.

Sragow, Michael. "David Lean's Magnificent *Kwai.*" *Atlantic Monthly,* February 1994, 104–9.

————. "David Lean's Right of *Passage.*" *Film Comment* 21, no. 1 (January–February 1985): 20–27.

Stam, Robert. *Literature through Films: Realism, Magic, and the Art of Adaptation.* Malden, MA: Blackwell, 2005.

Stevens, George, Jr., ed. *Conversations with the Great Moviemakers of Hollywood's Golden Age at the American Film Institute.* New York: Knopf, 2006. Includes the interview listed above as "Dialogue on Film: David Lean."

Stewart, R. S. "*Doctor Zhivago:* The Making of a Movie." *Atlantic Monthly,* August 1965, 58–64.

Street, Sarah. *Transatlantic Crossings: British Feature Films in the United States.* New York: Continuum, 2002.

"*Summertime.*" *Film Center Notes* (Chicago Art Institute), August 2003, 6.

Tabachnick, Stephen. *Lawrence of Arabia: An Encyclopedia.* Westport, CT: Greenwood, 2004.

Tanitch, Robert. *Guinness.* New York: Applause, 1984.

Thomas, Cathy. "Flying Faster Than Sound." *Time,* March 31, 2003, A27.

Thomas, Lowell. *With Lawrence in Arabia.* New York: Century, 1924.

Thompson, Kristin, and David Bordwell. *Film History: An Introduction.* 1986. Rev. ed. New York: McGraw-Hill, 2003.

Tibbetts, John C., and James M. Welsh. *The Encyclopedia of Filmmakers.* 2 vols. New York: Facts on File, 2002.

Tibbetts, John C., and James M. Welsh, eds. *The Encyclopedia of Novels into Film.* 1998. 2nd ed. New York: Facts on File, 2005.

————. *The Encyclopedia of Stage Plays into Film.* New York: Facts on File, 2001.

Timm, Larry. *The Soul of Cinema: Film Music.* Upper Saddle River, NJ: Prentice-Hall, 2003.

Todd, Ann. *The Eighth Veil.* New York: Putnam's, 1981.

Turner, Adrian. *The Making of Lawrence of Arabia*. London: Dragon's World, 1994.

Vankin, Jonathan, and John Whalen. *Based on a True Story: Fact and Fantasy in 100 Favorite Movies*. Chicago: A Cappella, 2005.

Variety Film Reviews: 1907–1996. 24 vols. New Providence, NJ: Bowker, 1997. This collection of reviews is unpaginated.

Vineberg, Steve. "A Modest Creator of Quiet Dreamers: Alec Guinness." *New York Times*, August 13, 2000, sec. 2, p. 24.

Von Gunden, Kenneth. *Alec Guinness: The Films*. 1987. Rev. ed. Jefferson, NC: McFarland, 2001.

Wagner, Geoffrey. *The Novel and the Cinema*. Teaneck, NJ: Fairleigh Dickinson University Press, 1975.

Walker, Alexander. *Double Takes: Notes and Afterthoughts on the Movies, 1956–76*. London: Elm Tree, 1977.

Wapshott, Nicholas. *Peter O'Toole*. New York: Beaufort, 1983.

Watt, Ian. "Bridges over the Kwai." *Partisan Review* 26, no. 1 (winter 1959): 83–94.

Wells, H. G. *Experiment in Autobiography*. New York: Lippincott, 1962.

———. *The Passionate Friends*. New York: Harper Bros., 1913.

Williams, Tony. *Structures of Desire: British Cinema, 1939–55*. Albany: State University of New York Press, 2000.

Wilson, Michael. *Seven Pillars of Wisdom: A Screenplay*. Third Draft. Columbia Pictures, 1961. Based on T. E. Lawrence's memoir.

Young, Freddie, with Peter Busby. *Seventy Light Years*. New York: Faber & Faber, 1999.

INDEX

39, 40, 41, 43, 451; in *Pygmalion,* 31, 33–34, 35, 43, 450

historical epics, 8, 24, 101, 168. *See also* epics

Hitchcock, Alfred, 4, 6, 19, 149, 189; advent of sound film and, 20; *To Catch a Thief,* 214; departure for United States, 29; Elstree Studios and, 22; *Man Who Knew Too Much, The,* 161; *Paradine Case, The,* 147, 194; *Rope,* 206; *Stage Fright,* 159; *39 Steps, The,* 192

Hitler, Adolf, 26, 223, 236

Hives, Lord, 174

Hoberman, J., 433

Hobson, Valerie, 109, 121, 455

Hobson's Choice (Brighouse play), 187–89, 204

Hobson's Choice (film, 1920), 188

Hobson's Choice (film, 1931), 188

Hobson's Choice (Lean film), 85, 180, 189–200, 202, 253, 393, 458; camerawork, 195, 197; cast, 191–93, 198, 200; commercial success of, 201; comparison with other Lean films, 387; plot, 195–99; popularity in Britain *versus* America, 226

Hogarth, David, 275

Holden, William, 234, 237–38, 249, 276, 285, 326, 459

Holloway, Julian, 386

Holloway, Stanley, 90, 386, 451, 452, 454

Hollywood film industry, 3, 5, 8; blockbuster films, 224; *Bridge on the River Kwai* and, 251–52; British cinema and, 6, 19, 29; censorship in, 62; distribution and, 218; gossip in, 252, 400, 409, 416; independent producers in, 223–24; sound pictures, advent of, 20; stars, 204, 205, 234; studios and studio bosses, 22, 223, 226; women's pictures, 99. *See also* blacklist, Hollywood

Home Box Office (HBO), 410, 419

Home of the Brave (film), 204

homosexuality/homoeroticism, 18, 96; Asquith and, 68; *Brief Encounter* and, 95–96; Coward and, 51, 68,

95, 96, 193; Forster and, 403; Guinness and, 269; Laughton and, 191, 192–93; in *Lawrence of Arabia,* 96, 309, 310; Lawrence (T. E.) and, 266–67, 269, 286; in *Passage to India,* 406, 429; rumors about Lean spread by third wife, 185

Honegger, Arthur, 31, 35, 450

Hopkins, Anthony, 401, 451

Hopper, Hedda, 252

Hopwell-Ashe, Tim, 456

Horizon Pictures, 223, 224, 225, 232; *Bridge on the River Kwai* and, 239; *Lawrence of Arabia* and, 271, 289, 296, 301, 305

Horne, Geoffrey, 234, 459

Horse's Mouth, The (film), 288–89

Hotz, Sandy (fifth wife), 358–59, 361, 394, 396; born in India, 302; divorce from Lean, 435; marriage to Lean, 401; in *Passage to India,* 416, 426, 463

Hough, Richard, 395, 396, 451

Hound of the Baskervilles, The (film), 14, 17, 18

House of Bamboo (film), 234

Howard, Arthur, 456

Howard, Leslie: in *49th Parallel,* 44, 46, 47, 450; in *Pygmalion,* 31, 33, 34, 35, 36, 450; *Revolt in the Desert* and, 268; *In Which We Serve* and, 60, 452

Howard, Noel, 298, 460

Howard, Tom, 79, 80, 453

Howard, Trevor, 158, 438; in *Brief Encounter,* 89, 91, 98, 161, 370, 454; in *Mutiny on the Bounty,* 396; in *Passionate Friends,* 148, 370, 456; in *Ryan's Daughter,* 369–70, 375–76, 378, 382, 383, 386, 393, 394, 462

Howard's End (Forster novel), 406

Hughes, Howard, 319

Hughes, Peter, 464

Huke, Bob, 462

Hungary, 171

Hunt, Martita, 104, 108, 121, 122

Huntley, Raymond, 200